Lecture Notes in Computer Science

Commenced Publication in 1973
Founding and Former Series Editors:
Gerhard Goos, Juris Hartmanis, and Jan van Leeuwen

Kan Zhang   Yuliang Zheng (Eds.)

Information Security

7th International Conference, ISC 2004
Palo Alto, CA, USA, September 27-29, 2004
Proceedings

 Springer

Volume Editors

Kan Zhang
Hewlett-Packard Laboratories
3353 Alma Street, #233, Palo Alto, CA 94306, USA
E-mail: zhangkan@sbcglobal.net

Yuliang Zheng
University of Noth Carolina at Charlotte
Department of Software and Information Systems
9201 University City Blvd, Charlotte, NC 28223, USA
E-mail: yzheng@uncc.edu

Library of Congress Control Number: 2004112165

CR Subject Classification (1998): E.3, D.4.6, F.2.1, C.2, J.1, C.3, K.4.4, K.6.5

ISSN 0302-9743
ISBN 3-540-23208-7 Springer Berlin Heidelberg New York

Springer is a part of Springer Science+Business Media

springeronline.com

© Springer-Verlag Berlin Heidelberg 2004
Printed in Germany

Typesetting: Camera-ready by author, data conversion by PTP-Berlin, Protago-TeX-Production GmbH
Printed on acid-free paper   SPIN: 11325864   06/3142   5 4 3 2 1 0

Preface

The 2004 Information Security Conference was the seventh in a series that started with the Information Security Workshop in 1997. A distinct feature of this series is the wide coverage of topics with the aim of encouraging interaction between researchers in different aspects of information security. This trend continued in the program of this year's conference. The program committee received 106 submissions, from which 36 were selected for presentation. Each submission was reviewed by at least three experts in the relevant research area. We would like to thank all the authors for taking their time to prepare the submissions, and we hope that those whose papers were declined will be able to find an alternative forum for their work.

We were fortunate to have an energetic team of experts who took on the task of the program committee. Their names may be found overleaf, and we thank them warmly for their time and efforts. This team was helped by an even larger number of external reviewers who reviewed papers in their particular areas of expertise. A list of these names is also provided, which we hope is complete.

We would also like to thank the advisory committee for their advice and support. The excellent local arrangements were handled by Dirk Balfanz and Jessica Staddon. We made use of the electronic submission and reviewing software supplied by COSIC at the Katholieke Universiteit Leuven. Both the software and the ISC 2004 website were run on a server at UNC Charlotte, and were perfectly maintained by Seung-Hyun Im. We also appreciate assistance from Lawrence Teo in editing the proceedings.

September 2004

Kan Zhang
Yuliang Zheng

Information Security Conference 2004

September 27–29, 2004, Palo Alto, CA, USA

General Chair

Yuliang Zheng, University of North Carolina at Charlotte, USA

Advisory Committee

Tom Berson, Anagram Lab, USA
Li Gong, Sun Microsystems, China
Wenbo Mao, Hewlett-Packard Laboratories, UK
Eiji Okamoto, University of Tsukuba, Japan

Program Co-chairs

Kan Zhang, Hewlett-Packard Laboratories, USA
Yuliang Zheng, University of North Carolina at Charlotte, USA

Program Committee

Martin Abadi .... UC Santa Cruz, USA
Carlisle Adams .... University of Ottawa, Canada
Gail-Joon Ahn .... UNC Charlotte, USA
N. Asokan .... Nokia, Finland
Tuomas Aura .... Microsoft Research, UK
Jean Bacon .... Cambridge University, UK
Dirk Balfanz .... PARC, USA
Feng Bao .... i2r, Singapore
Elisa Bertino .... University of Milan, Italy
Colin Boyd .... QUT, Australia
Yvo Desmedt .... University College London, UK
Warwick Ford .... Verisign, USA
Craig Gentry .... NTT DoCoMo Labs, USA
Stuart Haber .... HP Labs, USA
Markus Jakobsson .... RSA Labs, USA
Marc Joye .... Gemplus, France
Michiharu Kudoh .... IBM Tokyo, Japan
Javier Lopez .... University of Malaga, Spain
Tsutomu Matsumoto .... Yokohama National University, Japan
Kanta Matsuura .... University of Tokyo, Japan
Catherine Meadows .... Naval Research Lab, USA
Jonathan Millen .... SRI International, USA
John Mitchell .... Stanford University, USA
Peng Ning .... North Carolina State University, USA
Joe Pato .... HP Labs, USA
Josef Pieprzyk .... Macquarie University, Australia
Jean-Jacques Quisquater .... UCL, Belgium

Michael Reiter . . . . CMU, USA
Scarlet Schwiderski-Grosche . . . . Royal Holloway, University of London, UK
Hovav Shacham . . . . Stanford University, USA
Dawn Song . . . . CMU, USA
Jessica Staddon . . . . PARC, USA
Clark Thomborson . . . . University of Auckland, New Zealand
Serge Vaudenay . . . . EPFL, Switzerland
Michael Waidner . . . . IBM Research, Switzerland
Yumin Wang . . . . Xidian University, China
Moti Yung . . . . Columbia University, USA
Kan Zhang . . . . HP Labs, USA
Yuliang Zheng . . . . UNC Charlotte, USA
Jianying Zhou . . . . i2r, Singapore

External Reviewers

Giuseppe Ateniese	Zhenjie Huang	Diana Smetters
Joonsang Baek	Zhengtao Jiang	Mike Stay
Thomas Baigneres	Pascal Junod	Ron Steinfeld
Julien Brouchier	Jonathan Katz	Paul Syverson
Julien Cathalo	Yongdae Kim	Anat Talmy
Mathieu Ciet	Mei Kobayashi	Lawrence Teo
Scott Contini	Tieyan Li	Haibo Tian
Nora Dabbous	Yi Lu	Gene Tsudik
Chen Dan	Benjamin Lynn	Chenxi Wang
Tanmoy Das	Greg Maitland	Guilin Wang
Alex Deacon	Krystian Matusiewicz	Huaxiong Wang
Anand Desai	Keith Mayes	Bogdan Warinschi
Glenn Durfee	Bruce Mills	Claire Whelan
Dan DuVarney	Jean Monnerat	Nathan Whitehead
Tim Ebringer	Jose A. Montenegro	Hao Chi Wong
Hiroaki Etoh	Sara Miner More	Yongdong Wu
Serge Fehr	Ram Moskovitz	Dingbang Xu
Dan Forsberg	Zhihua Niu	Mariemma I. Yague
Michael J. Freedman	Juan J. Ortega	Adam Young
Steven Galbraith	Olivier Pereira	Ting Yu
Vaibhav Gowadia	Gilles Piret	John Zachary
Phillip Hallam-Baker	Zulfikar Ramzan	Jianhong Zhang
Thomas Hardjono	Louis Salvail	

Table of Contents

Intrusion Detection

Access Control

Human Authentication

Certificate Management

Mobile and Ad Hoc Security

Web Security

Digital Rights Management

Software Security

Practical Authenticated Key Agreement Using Passwords

Taekyoung Kwon

School of Computer Engineering, Sejong University, Seoul 143-747, Korea
tkwon@sejong.ac.kr

Abstract. Due to the low entropy of human-memorable passwords, it is not easy to conduct password authenticated key agreement in a secure manner. Though there are many protocols achieving this goal, they may require a large amount of computation specifically in the augmented model which was contrived to resist server compromise. Our contribution in this paper is two fold. First, we propose *a new practical password authenticated key agreement protocol* that is efficient and generic in the augmented model. Our scheme is considered from the practical perspective (in terms of efficiency) and is provably secure under the Diffie-Hellman intractability assumptions in the random-oracle model. Our second contribution is more realistic and generic; *a conceptually simple but novel password guessing attack* which can be mounted on every three-pass password-based protocol unless care is taken in both the design and implementation phases. This is due to the server's failure to synchronize multiple simultaneous requests. Experimental results and possible prevention methods are also discussed.

1 Introduction

User authentication is necessary for the typical case that a human being resides as a client and tries to log on to a remote server machine. The server must be able to determine the user's identity reliably over a public or private channel. Password authentication is one of such methods, in which simply the user memorizes a (short) password while the server maintains a user profile that associates the user name and the password verifying information. The intrinsic problem with this method is the memorable password, associated with each user, has low entropy, so that it is not easy to protect the password information against the notorious password guessing attacks by which attackers could search the relatively small space of human-memorable passwords.

Since a pioneering method that resists the password guessing attacks was introduced to cryptographic protocol developers [24], there has been a great deal of work for password authenticated key agreement, preceded by EKE [5], on the framework of Diffie-Hellman [10]. Readers are referred to [15] for complete references. Compared to the typical authenticated key agreement, the password-based schemes are more expensive due to the low entropy of passwords, specifically in the augmented model which was contrived to resist server compromise. Provable

K. Zhang and Y. Zheng (Eds.): ISC 2004, LNCS 3225, pp. 1–12, 2004.

security is important but tends to make the schemes harder to be practical in some cases. From the theoretical perspective, several methods that are much more expensive but provably secure in the standard model, were presented [12, 18,19]. From the practical perspective, the practice-oriented security models are applied for examining the security of protocols [1,2,3,7]. For example, EKE2 and AuthA are provably secure in both the random oracle and ideal cipher models [3, 4,8], while PAK and PAK-Z (that improves the efficiency of PAK-X impressively by specifying a generic digital signature) are in the random oracle model [7,25, 26]. However, it is (arguably) still expensive to assume ideal ciphers or digital signatures along with many costly operations on them, while PAK-Y is reasonably efficient with Schnorr signature in terms of computational costs [4,26,30].

At present, SPEKE [16], SRP [32], PAK [26], and AMP [21] are being discussed by the IEEE P1363 Standard Working Group and more recently by the ISO/IEC JTC 1/SC 27 group as practical protocols for standardization on password-based public key cryptographic techniques [13,14]. Among them, PAK and SPEKE are 'three-pass' protocols, while AMP and SRP are 'four-pass' protocols. The standardization work is valuable in many aspects; for instance, a new attack called the 'two-for-one' guessing attack[1] against the four-pass protocols was found and resolved in the process [13,31]. Any preference between three-pass and four-pass is still open for password-based protocols while typical authenticated key agreement such as STS and SIGMA is three-pass [11,20].

In this paper, our contribution is two fold from the practical perspective.

1) An efficient three-pass password-based protocol in the augmented model
2) A generic password-guessing attack against three-pass protocols

A password-based protocol designed in the augmented model can resist server compromise. In other words, an adversary who compromised a password profile from a server cannot impersonate a user without launching dictionary attacks. For this additional property, the related protocols (for example, A-EKE, AMP, AuthA, B-SPEKE, PAK-Z, and SRP) are more expensive than those are not (for instance, EKE, EKE-2, SPEKE, and PAK) in the augmented model [6,21,4,17, 26,32]. We observe that the existing provably-secure schemes are still expensive in the augmented model in terms of the amount of computation, and that it is desirable to minimize the number of message passes and the size of message blocks for practice on expensive communication channels. So we design a new three-pass password-based protocol in the augmented model with both security and efficiency in mind. We achieve this goal interestingly by a composition under the careful observation of the existing schemes discussed by the IEEE P1363 Standard Working Group, say without losing the presumed level of security. We call the protocol TP-AMP and prove its security in the random oracle model.

On developing the new three-pass password-based protocol, we find a conceptually simple but novel password guessing attack which can be mounted on every

---

[1] An active attacker can validate two password guesses in one impersonation attempt. The first attack against SRP was discovered by D. Bleichenbacher in 2000, while the similar attack on AMP was by M. Scott [31]. However, both protocols were fixed to resist respective attacks by each original author [13].

three-pass password-based protocol by exploiting a small window of vulnerability resulting from a standard technique to resist on-line guessing attacks, say from counting the number of failed requests. Our attack is due to the server's failure to synchronize multiple simultaneous requests, and is unavoidable in three-pass protocols unless special care is taken in both the design and implementation phases. We call this attack a *many-to-many* (or *parallel*) guessing attack[2] because an active attacker can validate as many password guesses as (s)he makes server instances invoked concurrently, regardless of its upper limit of on-line guessing. A prototype of the proposed protocol is implemented to show how our attack works and is prevented. We first consider this attack and possible resolution in the literature.

This paper is organized as follows. In the following section, the so-called TP-AMP protocol (our first contribution) is presented. In Section 3, the many-to-many guessing attack (our second contribution) is described in more detail. In Section 4, security and efficiency of TP-AMP are discussed. Finally this paper is concluded in Section 5.

2   A Practical Protocol

2.1   Preliminaries

Our principal motivation comes from the fact that password-based protocols designed in the augmented model are much less efficient than those are not in that model, in terms of either computation or communication costs. When we regard PAK as a fundamental structure for three-pass protocols due to its simplicity and clarity, we can easily observe that its augmentation such as PAK-X, PAK-Y, and PAK-Z are far from its intrinsic nature and get much more complicated in the augmented model [7,25,26]. AMP and SRP show better performance in that model but in four passes [21,32]. So, our basic idea is to make AMP squeezed into PAK or PAK augmented by AMP, since AMP is another protocol that can be computed very efficiently over various numerical groups [21]. However, a simple composition is not sufficient, and consequently we obtain a new practical protocol by more careful consideration on them.

The reason for choosing PAK rather than EKE2 is obviously that the former can formally be proved by postulating the random oracles only, while the latter requires the additional assumption of ideal cipher [7,26,3]. However, EKE2 or similar schemes that are proved sufficiently secure, can also be applied to constructing the practical augmented protocol in the way of our composition. In that sense, our construction is quite generic.

In Table 1, we enumerate the notation, in part, to be used in the remaining of this paper. Additional ones will be self-contained in each part of this paper. Let κ be a general security parameter (say 160 bits) and ℓ be a special security parameter for public keys (1024 or 2048 bits). A client C and a server S should

---

[2] We first introduced this attack at IEEE P1363.2 meeting and also discussed a few names for it.

Table 1. Basic Notation

C	Client (User)	S	Server
π	Password	τ_C	Transformed password for C
$\leftarrow$	Derivation	$\overset{R}{\leftarrow}$	Random selection
κ, ℓ	Security parameters	q	Prime of size κ
r	Integer co-prime to q	p	Prime of size ℓ such that $p = rq + 1$
$\mathbb{Z}_p^*$	Multiplicative group of p	$\mathbb{G}_q$	q-order subgroup of $\mathbb{Z}_p^*$
g	Generator of $\mathbb{G}_q$	h_i, H_i	Random oracles
α, β	Agreed values	sk_i	Session key

agree on algebraic parameters[3] related to Diffie-Hellman key agreement such as p, q, and g. Define $\bar{\mathbb{G}}_q = \{g^x \bmod p | x \in \mathbb{Z}_q^*\}$ where $|\bar{\mathbb{G}}_q| = q - 1$. Let us often omit 'mod p' from the expressions that are obvious in $\mathbb{Z}_p^*$. Let $\{0,1\}^*$ denote the set of finite binary strings and $\{0,1\}^n$ the set of binary strings of length n. We then define random oracles such that $h_i: \{0,1\}^* \to \{0,1\}^\kappa$ and $H_i: \{0,1\}^* \to \{0,1\}^\ell$. Their instances are also defined as $h_i(\cdot) = h(i, \cdot, i)$ and $H_i(\cdot) = (h(i, \cdot, i))^{\frac{p-1}{q}}$ mod p where $h(\cdot)$ is a strong one-way hash function. Let ACCEPTABLE($\cdot$) denote an acceptable function which may return true if its pre-image satisfies the given security properties, as defined in Section 2.3. Readers who are not familiar with the legacy protocols, are referred to the previous work of [7,13,21,25,26].

2.2   Proposed Protocol – TP-AMP

TP-AMP stands for the Three-Pass Authenticated key agreement via Memorable Passwords and is depicted in Figure 1. Let us borrow the name AMP from [21] for our basic motivation.

Protocol Setup On the registration phase, a user chooses a name C and a password π while the server S saves user's profile $\langle C, \tau_C \rangle$ in its stable storage where $\gamma = H_0(C, \pi)$, $\gamma' = \gamma^{-1} \bmod p$, $u = h_1(C, \pi)$, $\nu = g^u$, and $\tau_C = \langle \gamma', \nu \rangle$. For convenience, S is assumed as an IP address of the server machine.

Protocol Run A user may type C and π into the client machine. The client (C on behalf of the user from now on) then chooses x at random from $\mathbb{Z}_q^*$ (not $\mathbb{Z}_p^*$), and computes γ in order to obtain $m = g^x \gamma$. The client sends ($\to$) a commitment message $\langle C, m \rangle$ to the server.

$$1.\ C \to S : C, g^x \gamma$$

---

[3] In spite that PAK, in general, does not require gcd(r, q)=1 and only PAK-R requires it for further randomization, we recommend to use a *secure prime* such that each factor of r except 2 is of size at least κ or a *safe prime* such that $r = 2$ for $p = rq + 1$ as discussed in [21,23,32,29]. They satisfy gcd(r, q)=1. Specifically, we observe that TP-AMP shows the best performance with a secure prime, while PAK-Y does with a safe prime and arbitrarily smaller exponents [28].

client$[C, \pi]$ $\qquad\qquad\qquad\qquad$ server$[C, \tau_C(\gamma', \nu)]$ on S

$\qquad\qquad\qquad\qquad\qquad\qquad\qquad\qquad$ $\langle \gamma' = \gamma^{-1} \bmod p, \nu = g^u \bmod p \rangle$

$x \xleftarrow{\text{R}} \mathbb{Z}_q^*$

$\gamma \leftarrow H_0(C, \pi)$

$m \leftarrow g^x \gamma \bmod p$

$\qquad\qquad\qquad\qquad \xrightarrow{\quad C, m \quad}$

$\qquad\qquad\qquad\qquad\qquad\qquad$ abort if $\neg\textsc{acceptable}(C, m)$

$\qquad\qquad\qquad\qquad\qquad\qquad$ $y \xleftarrow{\text{R}} \mathbb{Z}_q^*$

$\gamma' \leftarrow \gamma^{-1} \bmod p$ $\qquad\qquad\quad$ $\mu \leftarrow \nu^y \bmod p$

$u \leftarrow h_1(C, \pi)$ $\qquad\qquad\qquad$ $\beta \leftarrow (m\gamma' g^m)^y \bmod p$

$w \leftarrow u^{-1}(x + m) \bmod q$ $\qquad\quad$ $k_1 \leftarrow h_2(C, S, m, \mu, \beta, \gamma')$

$\qquad\qquad\qquad\qquad \xleftarrow{\quad \mu, k_1 \quad}$

$\alpha \leftarrow \mu^w \bmod p$

$k_1' \leftarrow h_2(C, S, m, \mu, \alpha, \gamma')$

abort if $k_1 \neq k_1'$

$k_2 \leftarrow h_3(C, S, m, \mu, \alpha, \gamma')$ $\qquad\quad$ $k_2' \leftarrow h_3(C, S, m, \mu, \beta, \gamma')$

$\qquad\qquad\qquad\qquad \xrightarrow{\quad k_2 \quad}$

$\qquad\qquad\qquad\qquad\qquad\qquad$ abort if $k_2 \neq k_2'$ or time is out

$sk_C \leftarrow h_4(C, S, m, \mu, \alpha, \gamma')$ $\qquad\quad$ $sk_S \leftarrow h_4(C, S, m, \mu, \beta, \gamma')$

Fig. 1. TP-AMP (Three-Pass AMP Protocol)

After or before sending message 1, the client could compute γ' and the user's *amplified password* such that $w = u^{-1}(x + m) \bmod q$ by obtaining $u = h_1(C, \pi)$, and keeps them while waiting for message 2. In practice, we can hash m so that we have $q|h(m)$ with negligible probability.

Upon receiving message 1, the server should abort it if $\textsc{acceptable}\ (C, m)$ returns false. Otherwise, the server fetches $\langle C, \tau_C \rangle$ from its storage and chooses y at random from $\mathbb{Z}_q^*$ so as to obtain $\mu = \nu^y$. The server then computes $\beta \equiv (m\gamma' g^m)^y \equiv g^{(x+m)y}(\bmod\ p)$ and $k_1 = h_2(C, S, m, \mu, \beta, \gamma')$, and sends a challenge message $\langle \mu, k_1 \rangle$ to the client.

$$2.\ S \to C : \nu^y, h_2(C, S, m, \mu, \beta, \gamma')$$

After or before sending message 2, the server could compute $k_2' \leftarrow h_3\ (C, S, m, \mu, \beta, \gamma')$ and keeps it while waiting for message 3. The server should abort if time is run out.

Upon receiving message 2, the client raises μ to the amplified password so that $\alpha \equiv \mu^w \equiv g^{y(x+m)}\ (\bmod\ p)$, and computes $k_1' = h_2(C, S, m, \mu, \alpha, \gamma')$. If k_1 is not equal to k_1', the client should abort this session. Otherwise, the client computes $k_2 = h_3(C, S, m, \mu, \alpha, \gamma')$ and sends a response message k_2 to the server.

$$3.\ C \to S : h_3(C, S, m, \mu, \alpha, \gamma')$$

After or before sending message 3, the client could compute a session key such that $sk_C = h_4(C, S, m, \mu, \alpha, \gamma')$ and deletes any other ephemeral values.

Upon receiving message 3, the server should abort this session if k_2 is not equal to k_2'. Otherwise, the server should compute a session key such that $sk_S = h_4(C, S, m, \mu, \beta, \gamma')$ and deletes any other ephemeral values.

As a result, the client and the server could authenticate each other using the passwords and agree on the same session key $sk_C(= sk_S)$ because $\alpha \equiv \beta \equiv g^{(x+m)y}(\mathrm{mod}\, p)$.

2.3   Small Discussion

One can easily see that message 1 is extracted from PAK while message 2 and session key are motivated by AMP. This protocol performs simple computation in three passes and works in the augmented model where τ_C is defined as $\langle \gamma', \nu \rangle$. For efficiency, it would be better to hash m when we compute β and w, say $\beta = (m\gamma' g^{h(m)})^y$ and $w = u^{-1}(x + h(m)) \bmod q$ for a strong one-way hash function $h(\cdot)$. For more efficiency, we recommend to use a secure prime for TP-AMP. Security and efficiency of the proposed protocol will be discussed in Section 4.

In the legitimate protocol run, g^x and ν^y are assumed not to be trivial values such as 0 and 1 as in the Diffie-Hellman relatives. We need to define a *failure count* that must be manipulated by the server and increased by one when $k_2 \neq k_2'$. The server should abort further requests of the client if the (subsequent) failure count exceeds its pre-defined limit, δ. This is a standard technique for resisting on-line guessing attacks. We also need to define the special function called ACCEPTABLE$(\cdot)$ since the server should abort when it returns false upon receiving $\langle C, m \rangle$. An example of the function follows:

ACCEPTABLE$(\cdot)$

INPUT: $\langle C, m \rangle$
OUTPUT:
Return *false*
   if C is being served by another instance; /* See Section 3 */
   else if the failure count of C is greater than or equal to its limit δ;
   else if $q|m$; /* Check if $m \notin Z_p^*$ only when hashing m before raising g */
Return *true* otherwise;

Note that the first condition (for resisting the many-to-many guessing attacks in the next section) can be considered in very flexible ways, for example, an IP address instead of C, and can be substituted by a more effective way in the future. This function is valid for authentication sessions only. Note also that $q|m$ means q divides m, but it might be enough to assure $m \in Z_p^*$ only when we hash m for β and w in the protocol.

3   Many-to-Many Guessing

3.1   A Real World Attack

It is widely recognized that three-pass (say, smaller-pass) protocols are favorable to the channel efficiency for authenticated key agreement. However, care must be taken for password authenticated key agreement in a practical sense.

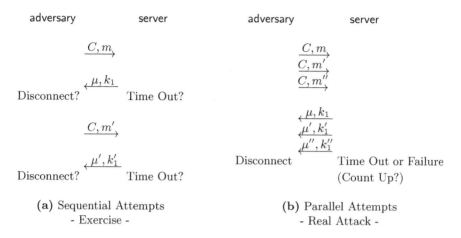

Fig. 2. Basic Concept of Many-to-Many Guessing Attacks

Let us glance over Theorem 1, in advance, that is introduced in Section 4 and proved in [22]. There exists an adversarial advantage that is bounded by $\frac{q_{se}}{N}$. The similar results can be found from the closely related work [3,8,26]. These advantages imply that the adversary is reduced to a simple online guessing attacker that can easily be detected and prevented from exceeding the pre-defined limit, δ, on the number of sequential on-line trials allowed by the server's policy. For example, an adversary posing as a user C sends an arbitrary message $\langle C, m \rangle$ to the server, based on her guessed password. The server may respond with $\langle \mu, k_1 \rangle$ in the three-pass protocols while only μ in the four-pass protocols. Then, the adversary is assumed to check her guess with probability bounded by $\frac{q_{se}}{N}$ under the limit δ in three-pass protocols. Is this standard assumption really true?

Unfortunately, the answer is No! This classical prevention method can be fooled out of making the adversarial advantage much larger and in some cases disclosing a password, in a surprisingly simple way. Figure 2 depicts the possible bad events. Our attack is motivated from the fact that the server is typically implemented as a multi-threaded or multi-process application for handling many user requests simultaneously, and that the three-pass password-based protocol is not an exception. As summarized in Figure 2-(a), the adversary is able to exercise the real attack (that is described in Figure 2-(b)), for example, in order to approximate the maximum amount of time the server may wait for the third message k_2. The adversary then starts simultaneous authentication sessions, which the server processes independently in separate threads, and in that amount of time, is able to drive many different initiating messages based on different password guesses concurrently to the server. The adversary may get as many replies as allowed in that time boundary, by exceeding δ obviously. Figure 2-(b) abbreviates this idea. It could be a real world attack from the automated (and multi-threaded) adversary. The server instances must respond to each request and wait for the replies k_2 from the adversary who can even disconnect without answering, for example, by manually unplugging the network cable or automatically manipulating the transport layer.

As a result, the adversary is able to gather many triples, $\langle m, \mu, k_1 \rangle$, and mount the further guessing attacks off-line. The adversary is able to check *many* password guesses over δ while the server may notice *many* guessing attempts bounded by δ afterwards. So we call this simple attack the *many-to-many guessing attack*[4]. The window of vulnerability can be thought of as

$$O(T) = t_S + t_C + 2t_{CS} + \varepsilon + (\delta - 1)\epsilon$$

where 1) t_S is the time between receiving $\langle C, m \rangle$ and sending out $\langle \mu, k_1 \rangle$ in the server, 2) t_C is the time between receiving $\langle \mu, k_1 \rangle$ and sending out k_2 in the client, 3) t_{CS} is the time delay for exchanging messages over a communication channel, 4) ε is the (most influential) additional waiting time defined by the server considering T_C and T_{CS}, and 5) ϵ is the (most negligible) amount of time that defines the average time difference between one request and another subsequent one (so, $(\delta - 1)\varepsilon$ must be the time between the first notice of a failed attempt and the last one under δ). We address that this window of vulnerability is not negligible and is sufficient to allow the adversary to gather as many triples as she can fool the protocol out of being over δ and disclosing the password in the worst case.

3.2   Possible Prevention

We designed the ACCEPTABLE$(\cdot)$ function in Section 2.3 so as to return false if C (or a corresponding IP address) is being served already by another server instance upon receiving a new message $\langle C, m \rangle$. Note that the 'serving' corresponds to the authentication session only. This was actually contrived for resisting the many-to-many guessing attack. For the purpose, a small hash table may be maintained by the server to track the currently served or blocked clients. The blocking policy should be considered carefully but flexibly. This resolution method may reduce the window of vulnerability notably but still leaves an issue about DoS (Denial of Service). Note that there is a recent literature considering DoS attacks on password-based protocols [9]. Aside from the danger of DoS attacks, a race condition and some bottleneck to the hash table are now only concerns while they could be negligible by careful consideration. The possible prevention methods might be considered both in the design and implementation phases.

In order to examine the reality of our attack, we implement a prototype of TP-AMP and launch the many-to-many guessing attack on it. We implement both client and server using `CreateThread(·)` functions and `WinSock` in Pentium IV 1.8GHz, 512MB, MS-Windows platforms. Simply a single run takes

---

[4] This attack is negligible in the four-pass protocols since the server does not give sufficient information to the adversary forward and the client is usually not capable of listening to so many concurrent requests in the opposite case. Also, the best-known predecessors, EKE [5] and A-EKE [6], avoid this attack very *impressively* by not optimizing the protocol steps.

297 milliseconds. We then drive multi-threaded clients to starts many simultaneous authentication sessions. We summarize the results. Let $\delta = 5$ (times) and $\varepsilon = 3$ (seconds), without correct ACCEPTABLE$(\cdot)$ function. Until we increase the number of adversarial client threads to 100, we could observe all requests are stably served and the same number of triples, $\langle m, \mu, k_1 \rangle$, are gathered. When 150 threads are driven, about 20 requests are only declined, and about 130 triples are gathered. However, about 145 threads are blocked with correct ACCEPTABLE$(\cdot)$ function.

4 Security and Efficiency Analysis

In this section, we discuss security and efficiency of TP-AMP.

4.1 Security of TP-AMP

For formal security, we adapt the improved models of [26] and [8]. Our refreshed security model is described in [22]. Readers are referred to it due to the page restriction of this paper. We prove that the TP-AMP protocol is secure, in the sense that an adversary attacking the system cannot determine session keys of fresh instances with greater advantage than that of an online dictionary attack, and cannot determine session keys of semi-fresh instances with greater advantage than that of an off-line dictionary attack. We define q_{se}, q_{ex}, q_{re}, q_{co} queries as those of type Send, Execute, Reveal, Corrupt, respectively, and q_{ro} queries to be made to the random oracles. Also we define some events related to the adversary making a password guess. Note that $[\alpha, \beta]$ means one of α and β is drawn. Also recall that the order of $\bar{\mathbb{G}}_q$ is $q - 1$. Security arguments for the following theorems are described in [22].

Theorem 1. *Let $\mathcal{P}$ be the TP-AMP protocol with a password dictionary of size N. Fix an adversary $\mathcal{A}$ that runs in time t, and makes q_{se}, q_{ex}, q_{re}, q_{co} queries and q_{ro} queries. Then for $t' = O(t + (q_{ro} + q_{se} + q_{ex})t_{exp})$ with t_{exp} denoting the computational time for exponentiation in $\mathbb{G}_q$:*

$$\mathsf{Adv}_{\mathcal{P}}^{\mathrm{ake-fs}}(\mathcal{A}) \leq \frac{q_{se}}{N} + O((q_{se} + q_{ex})q_{ro}\mathsf{Adv}_{\mathbb{G}_q}^{\mathrm{CDH}}(t', q_{ro}))$$

$$+ \frac{O((q_{se} + q_{ex})^2)}{q - 1} + \frac{O(q_{se} + q_{ro}^2)}{2^\kappa}$$

and

$$\mathsf{Adv}_{\mathcal{P}}^{\mathrm{ake-fs.s}}(\mathcal{A}) = \frac{q_{ro}}{N} + \mathsf{Adv}_{\mathcal{P}}^{\mathrm{ake-fs}}(\mathcal{A}).$$

Proof sketch: Our proof will proceed by defining a sequence of games starting at the real game $\mathbf{G}_0$ and ending up at $\mathbf{G}_7$. In the beginning we simulate all protocol queries, and remove possible collisions and lucky events. We then reduce our protocol from solving CDH in a stringent way, for respective Execute and Send queries. So $\mathbf{G}_5$ models passive adversaries, while $\mathbf{G}_6$ does active adversaries. Finally, server compromise is manipulated in $\mathbf{G}_7$. $\square$

Theorem 2. *Let $\mathcal{P}$ be the TP-AMP protocol with a password dictionary of size N. Fix an adversary $\mathcal{A}$ that runs in time t, and makes q_{se}, q_{ex}, q_{re}, q_{co} queries and q_{ro} queries. Then for $t' = O(t + (q_{ro} + q_{se} + q_{ex})t_{exp})$ with t_{exp} denoting the computational time for exponentiation in $\mathbb{G}_q$:*

$$\mathsf{Adv}_{\mathcal{P}}^{\mathsf{ma}}(\mathcal{A}) \leq \frac{q_{se}}{N} + O((q_{se} + q_{ex})q_{ro}\mathsf{Adv}_{\mathbb{G}_q}^{\mathrm{CDH}}(t', q_{ro}))$$

$$+ \frac{O((q_{se} + q_{ex})^2)}{q - 1} + \frac{O(q_{se} + q_{ro}^2)}{2^\kappa}$$

and

$$\mathsf{Adv}_{\mathcal{P}}^{\mathsf{c2s.s}}(\mathcal{A}) = \frac{q_{ro}}{N} + \mathsf{Adv}_{\mathcal{P}}^{\mathsf{ake-fs}}(\mathcal{A}).$$

We believe the given security argument in the random oracle model in [22] is sufficient to ensure that TP-AMP is a secure password authenticated key agreement protocol in the augmented model, though a full proof might be more intricate. A resistance to our real world attack can be observed by manipulating the ACCEPTABLE$(\cdot)$ function. Since TP-AMP is simple in its structure, it might also be easy and obvious to examine its security heuristically but we do not manipulate any heuristic analysis in this paper.

4.2   Efficiency of TP-AMP

We may consider the number of expensive operations, for example, multiple precision multiplications (MPM) in $\mathbb{Z}_p^*$, in order to analyze the performance of TP-AMP. We approximate the number of multiplications on average, by assuming the use of a left-to-right binary exponentiation method or a simultaneous exponentiation method (denoted by sim) [27]. A slight computational difference between squaring and multiplication can be ignored for convenience.

Let $\kappa' = \kappa'' = \kappa''' = \kappa$ for secure prime p while $\kappa' = \kappa'' = \kappa''' = \ell - 2/3$ for safe prime p for simple analysis. Practically we can set $\kappa'' = 2\kappa$ with intentionally smaller exponents, for example, $x \xleftarrow{\mathrm{R}} \{0,1\}^{\kappa''}$ and not $\xleftarrow{\mathrm{R}} \mathbb{Z}_q^*$ for safe prime p though it is not general for security argument. For the client, γ may take $1.5(\ell - \kappa')$ while m may need $1.5\kappa'' + 1$ MPM. For the server, β may take $1.5(\kappa + \kappa'') + 2$ or $2\kappa'' + 1$(sim) MPM. Finally the client may need $1.5\kappa'''$ for α. As a result, the client may need $1.5(\ell - \kappa' + \kappa'' + \kappa''') + 1$ while the server may require $1.5(\kappa + 2\kappa'') + 2$ MPM totally. Also if we assume an ideal cipher for γ as like EKE2 and AuthA [3,4], the client may need $1.5(\kappa'' + \kappa''')$ MPM only. One can easily see that the TP-AMP protocol is efficient when we use a secure prime, p, since $\kappa' = \kappa'' = \kappa''' = \kappa$.

TP-AMP is comparable to the most closely related protocol PAK-Z (with an efficient instance Y using Schnorr's signature [30]) [25,26] and AuthA [4,8] in terms of efficiency. In general, TP-AMP is more efficient than those related schemes under the same assumption, for example, on a safe or secure prime with group size exponents, or an ideal cipher. However, when we use a safe prime with intentionally smaller exponents, PAK-Y shows better in the client, while TP-AMP does still better in the server. Though TP-AMP is not a direct instance of PAK-Z, we can say it provides efficiency on the framework of PAK in the augmented model. As we mentioned already, TP-AMP can be instantiated on EKE2 [3,4,8] and provide efficiency on that framework. Thus, we would like to address that TP-AMP is a practical password authenticated key agreement protocol with sufficient security and generic features in the augmented model.

5 Conclusion

Though three-pass protocols may reduce one-round from four-pass protocols and are easier to apply provable security, we show that they are vulnerable to the novel many-to-many password guessing attacks for password authenticated key agreement. From the practical perspective we design and analyze a new three-pass protocol, TP-AMP, in the augmented model and show several interesting features. In the future study, we will conduct more intensive work on three-pass and four-pass protocols for password authenticated key agreement.

Acknowledgement. This work was supported in part by Korea Research Foundation Grant (KRF-2003-003-D00434). The author thanks anonymous referees for kind comments.

References

1. M. Bellare and P. Rogaway, "Entity authentication and key distribution," In *Crypto 1993*, LNCS 773, pp.232-249, 1993.
2. M. Bellare and P. Rogaway, "Provably secure session key distribution-the three party case," In *ACM Symposium on the Theory of Computing*, pp.232-249, 1993.
3. M. Bellare, D. Pointcheval and P. Rogaway, "Authenticated key exchange secure against dictionary attack," In *Eurocrypt 2000*, LNCS 1807, pp.139-155, 2000.
4. M. Bellare and P. Rogaway, "The AuthA protocol for password-based authenticated key exchange," Submission to the IEEE P1363.2 study group, available from http://www.cs.ucdavis.edu/~rogaway /papers/autha.ps
5. S. Bellovin and M. Merritt, "Encrypted key exchange : password-based protocols secure against dictionary attacks," In *IEEE Symposium on Research in Security and Privacy*, pp. 72-84, 1992.
6. S. Bellovin and M. Merritt, "Augmented encrypted key exchange: a password-based protocol secure against dictionary attacks and password-file compromise," In *ACM Conference on Computer and Communications Security*, pp. 244-250, 1993.
7. V. Boyko, P. MacKenzie and S. Patel, "Provably secure password authenticated key exchange using Diffie-Hellman," In *Eurocrypt 2000*, LNCS 1807, pp.156-171, 2000.
8. E. Bresson, O. Chevassut, and D. Pointcheval, "Security proofs for an efficient password-based key exchange," In *ACM Conference on Computer Communications Security*, 2003.
9. E. Bresson, O. Chevassut, and D. Pointcheval, "New security results on Encrypted Key Exchange," In *International Workshop on Theory and Practice in Public Key Cryptography*, LNCS 2947, pp. 145-158, 2004.

10. W. Diffie and M. Hellman, "New directions in cryptography," *IEEE Transactions on Information Theory*, vol.22, no.6, pp.644-654, November 1976.
11. W. Diffie, P. van Oorschot, and M. Wiener, "Authentication and authenticated key exchanges," Designs, Codes and Cryptography, 2, pp. 107-125, 1992.
12. O. Goldreich and Y. Lindell, "Session-Key Generation Using Human Passwords Only," In *Cypto 2001*, LNCS 2139, pp.408-432, 2001.
13. IEEE P1363.2, *Standard specifications for password-based public key cryptographic techniques*, available from `http://grouper.ieee.org/groups/1363/`, December 2002.
14. ISO/IEC WD 11770-4, *Information technology - Security techniques - Key management - Part 4: Mechanisms based on weak secrets*, ISO/IEC JTC 1/SC 27, November 2003.
15. Phoenix Technologies, Inc., "Research Papers on Strong Password Authentication," available from `http://www.integritysciences.com/links.html`, 2002.
16. D. Jablon, "Strong password-only authenticated key exchange," *ACM Computer Communications Review*, vol.26, no.5, pp.5-26, 1996.
17. D. Jablon, "Extended password key exchange protocols," In *WETICE Workshop on Enterprise Security*, pp.248-255, 1997.
18. J. Katz, R. Ostrovsky, and M. Yung, "Efficient Password-Authenticated Key Exchange Using Human-Memorable Passwords ," In *Eurocrypt 2001*, LNCS 2045, pp.475-494, 2001.
19. K. Kobara and H. Imai, "Pretty-simple password-authenticated key-exchange protocol proven to be secure in the standard model," IEICE Trans., E85-A(10), pp.2229-2237, 2002.
20. H. Krawczyk, "SIGMA: The 'SINGn-and-MAc' approach to authenticated Diffie-Hellman and its use in the IKE protocols," *Advances in Cryptology - CRYPTO 2003*, Lecture Notes in Computer Science, Vol. 2729, Springer-Verlag, pp. 400-425, 2003.
21. T. Kwon, "Authentication and key agreement via memorable password," In *ISOC Network and Distributed System Security Symposium*, February 2001.
22. T. Kwon, "Practical authenticated key agreement using passwords," Full version of this paper, available from `http://dasan.sejong.ac.kr/~tkwon/amp.html`.
23. C. Lim and P. Lee, "A key recovery attack on discrete log-based schemes using a prime order subgroup," In *CRYPTO 97*, pp.249-263, 1997.
24. M. Lomas, L. Gong, J. Saltzer, and R. Needham, "Reducing risks from poorly chosen keys," In *ACM Symposium on Operating System Principles*, pp.14-18, 1989.
25. P. MacKenzie, "More efficient password-authenticated key exchange," In *RSA Conference*, Cryptographers Track, LNCS 2020, pp.361-377, 2001.
26. P. MacKenzie, "The PAK suite: Protocols for Password-Authenticated Key Exchange," Submission to IEEE P1363.2, April 2002.
27. A. Menezes, P. van Oorschot and S. Vanstone, *Handbook of applied cryptography*, CRC Press,Inc., pp.517-518, 1997.
28. P. van Oorschot and M. Wiener, "On Diffie-Hellman key agreement with short exponents," In *Eurocrypt 96*, pp. 332-343, 1996.
29. R. Perlman and C. Kaufman, "PDM: A new strong password-based protocol," In *USENIX Security Symposium*, pp.313-321, 2001.
30. C. Schnorr, "Efficient identification and signatures for smart cards," In *Crypto 89*, pp.239-251, 1989.
31. M. Scott, *Personal communication*, July 2001.
32. T. Wu, "Secure remote password protocol," In *ISOC Network and Distributed System Security Symposium*, 1998.

Further Analysis of Password Authenticated Key Exchange Protocol Based on RSA for Imbalanced Wireless Networks

Muxiang Zhang

Verizon Communications Inc.
40 Sylvan Road, Waltham, MA 02451, USA
muxiang.zhang@verizon.com

Abstract. Password-authenticated key exchange protocols allow two entities who only share a human-memorable password to authenticate each other and agree on a large session key. Such protocols are attractive for their simplicity and convenience and have received much interest in the research community. In *ISC'02*, Zhu et al. [18] proposed an efficient password-authenticated key exchange protocol which is suitable to the imbalanced wireless network environment where a low-power client communicates with a powerful server. In *ISC'03*, Bao [1] pointed out that the password protocol of Zhu et al. is subject to off-line dictionary attack if entity's identity is too short. Bao presented two kinds of dictionary attacks which can exclude two possible passwords in each protocol run. In this paper, we present a more efficient attack on the password protocol of Zhu et al.. In our attack, an adversary can exclude multiple possible passwords in each protocol run, regardless of whether entity's identity is short or long. To thwart the attack, we provide further improvement on Zhu et al.'s password-authenticated key exchange protocol.

1 Introduction

Password-authenticated key exchange protocols allow two entities who share a small password to authenticate each other and agree on a large session key between them. Such protocols are attractive for their simplicity and convenience and have received much interest in the research community. A major challenge in designing password-authenticated key exchange protocols is to deal with the so-called exhaustive guessing or off-line dictionary attack, as passwords are generally drawn from a small space enumerable, *off-line*, by an adversary. In 1992, Bellovin and Merritt [2] presented a family of protocols, known as *Encrypted Key exchange* (EKE), which was shown to be secure against off-line dictionary attack. Using a combination of symmetric and asymmetric (i.e. public key) cryptographic techniques, EKE provides insufficient information for an adversary to verify a guessed password and thus defeats off-line dictionary attack. Following EKE, a number of protocols for password-based authentication and key exchange have been proposed, e.g., [3-8, 10-12, 17]. A comprehensive list of such protocols can be found in Jablon's research link [9].

K. Zhang and Y. Zheng (Eds.): ISC 2004, LNCS 3225, pp. 13–24, 2004.

Unlike other public-key based key exchange protocols such as SSL, the EKE-like protocols do not rely on the existence of a public key infrastructure (PKI). This is appealing in many environments where the deployment of a public key infrastructure is either not possible or would be overly complex. Over the last decade, many researchers have investigated the feasibility of implementing EKE using different types of public-key cryptosystems such as RSA, ElGamal, and Diffie-Hellman key exchange. Nonetheless, most of the well-known and secure variants of EKE are based on Diffie-Hellman key exchange. It seems that EKE works well with Diffie-Hellman key exchange, but presents subtleties one way or the other when implemented with RSA and other public-key cryptographic systems. In their original paper [2], Bellovin and Merritt pointed out that the RSA-based EKE variant is subject to a special type of dictionary attack, called *e-residue attack*. In 1997, Lucks [13] proposed an RSA-based password-authenticated key exchange protocol (called OKE) which was claimed to be secure against the e-residue attack. Later, Mackenzie et al. [14] found that the OKE protocol is still subject to the e-residue attack. In [14], Mackenzie et al. proposed an RSA-based EKE variant (called SNAPI) and provided a formal security proof in the random oracle model. Unfortunately, the SNAPI protocol has to use a prime public exponent e which is larger than the RSA modulus n. This renders the SNAPI protocol impractical in resource-limited platforms, such as mobile phones and personal digital assistants.

To avoid using large public exponents, Zhu et al. [18] proposed an "interactive" protocol which is revised from an idea of [2]. In their protocol, one of the entities (the client) validates the public key of the other entity (the server) by sending a number of messages encrypted using the public key. If the server can successfully decrypt the encrypted messages, then the client is ensured that the encryption based on the server's public key is a permutation. Simulation [18] shows that this protocol is suitable to the imbalanced wireless network environment where a low-power client communicates with a powerful server. Recently, Bao [1] pointed out a weakness of the imbalanced password-authenticated key exchange protocol of Zhu et al.. Bao's analysis shows that the security of the protocol is dependent on the length of the client's identity. If the client's identity is too short, then an attacker can exclude two passwords in each run of the protocol. Bao [1] also suggested countermeasures to deal with the impact of identity length.

In this paper, we provide further security analysis of Zhu et al.'s password authenticated key exchange protocol. We present a more efficient attack, which is a variant of the e-residue attack as described in [2]. Using our attack, an adversary can exclude multiple possible passwords in each run of the password protocol of Zhu et al., regardless of whether the client's identity is short or long. To thwart the e-residue attack, we provide further improvement on the password-authenticated key exchange protocol described in [18].

The rest of the paper is organized as follows. In Section 2, we provide an overview of security against off-line dictionary attack, including e-residue attack against password-authenticated key exchange protocols based on RSA. In

Section 3, we describe Bao's attacks as well as his countermeasures for Zhu et al.'s password-authenticated key exchange protocol. In Section 4, we present an off-line dictionary attack on Zhu et al.'s password-authenticated key exchange protocol and provides ideas for further improvement. Section 5 concludes the paper.

2   Security Against Offline Dictionary Attack

We consider two-party protocols for authenticated key-exchange using human-memorable passwords. In its simplest form, such a protocol involves two entities, say *Alice* and *Bob* (denoted by A and B), both possessing a secret password drawn from a password space $\mathcal{D}$. Based on the password, Alice and Bob can authenticate each other and upon a successful authentication, establish a session key which is known to nobody but the two of them. There is present an adversary who intends to defeat the goal for the protocol. The adversary has full control of the communications between Alice and Bob. She can deliver messages out of order and to unintended recipients, concoct messages of her own choosing, and create multiple instances of entities and communicate with these instances in parallel sessions. She may also enumerate, either on-line or off-line, all the passwords in the password space $\mathcal{D}$. She can even acquire session keys of accepted entity instances.

Due to the small size of the password space $\mathcal{D}$, e.g., $|\mathcal{D}| = 10^6$, the goal of a password-authenticated key exchange protocol might be easily defeated by a powerful adversary as described above. For example, after observing the messages sent or received by Alice and Bob, the adversary randomly selects passwords from $\mathcal{D}$ and tests the selected passwords against the observed messages. This way, the adversary might be able to exclude many candidate passwords from the password space and eventually recovers the correct password. This type of attack is known as *off-line dictionary attack*. Of course, the adversary can always test a guessed password, *on-line*, by impersonating as Alice (or Bob) in a protocol run. As long as the adversary can not get more information about the right password than a random guess, the on-line dictionary attack can be thwarted by simply placing a limit on the number of unsuccessful protocol runs. In recent years, the formal definition of security against off-line dictionary attack has been studied in several papers, e.g., [3, 4, 7]. Informally, we say that a password-authenticated key exchange protocol is secure against off-line dictionary attack if no efficient adversary can defeat the goal of the protocol with a probability higher than $\frac{t}{|\mathcal{D}|} + \varepsilon$, using only t impersonation attempts, where ε is a negligible function of the security parameters.

As public key certificates are not involved, one of the difficulties in designing secure password protocols is to validate entities' public keys. Otherwise, an adversary could obtain password information by using invalid public keys. To see this, let's consider the RSA-based password-authenticated key exchange protocol as described in Fig. 1. Alice starts the protocol by sending her RSA public key (n, e) and a random number $r_A \in \{0, 1\}^l$ to Bob. Bob selects an integer a at

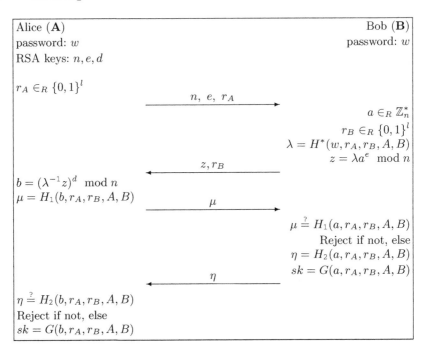

Fig. 1. An insecure password-authenticated key exchange protocol based on RSA

random from $\mathbb{Z}_n^*$, that is, a is a positive integer less than n and also relatively prime to n. Bob selects another random number r_B from $\{0,1\}^l$ and computes

$$z = H^*(w, r_A, r_B, A, B) \cdot a^e \mod n,$$

where w is the password of Bob and $H^* : \{0,1\}^* \to \mathbb{Z}_n^*$ is a hash function. Then Bob sends z and r_B back to Alice. Subsequently, Alice recovers a from z and performs authentication and key exchange with Bob based on the established number a. An adversary, say Eva, cannot recover the number a after observing the messages sent and received by Alice and Bob. Hence, Eva can not test a guessed password by passively observing the protocol run. However, Eva can impersonate as Alice and performs the following attack:

Step 1. Eva selects two positive integers n and e such that $\gcd(e, \phi(n)) > 1$. Eva then sends (n, e) and a random number $r_E \in \{0,1\}^l$ to Bob.

step 2. After receiving z and r_B from Bob, Eva terminates the communication session and performs off-line dictionary attack by repeating the following two steps.

Step 3. Eva select a password α at random from the password space $\mathcal{D}$.

Step 4. Eva computes $\lambda = H^*(\alpha, r_E, r_B, A, B)$ and checks if the following congruence

$$x^e = \lambda^{-1} z \mod n \tag{1}$$

has a solution in $\mathbb{Z}_n^*$. If the congruence has a solution, Eva returns to Step 3. If the congruence has no solution in $\mathbb{Z}_n^*$, then Eva knows that α is not the password of Bob. Next, Eva removes α from $\mathcal{D}$ and returns to Step 3.

Since $\gcd(e, \phi(n)) \neq 1$, the function $f(x) = x^e \bmod n$ is not a permutation on $\mathbb{Z}_n^*$, which means that congruence (1) may not have a solution for some $\lambda \in \mathbb{Z}_n^*$. On the other hand, Eva knows the factorization of n, she can test whether congruence (1) has a solution or not. If congruence (1) has no solution, then α is not equal to w; otherwise $\lambda^{-1}z = a^e \bmod n$, which leads to a contradiction. With the above attack, Eva could exclude many possible passwords from $\mathcal{D}$ in a single run of the protocol. This attack is called e-residue attack in [2] and has been studied further in [15].

3 Weakness of the Password Authenticated Key Exchange Protocol of Zhu et al.

Let A and B denote the identities of Alice and Bob, respectively. Also let $w \in \mathcal{D}$ denote the password shared between Alice and Bob. The password-authenticated key exchange protocol given in [18] is shown in Fig. 2 and described as follows. We take the same notations as in [18].

- Alice generates a pair of RSA keys n, e and d, $ed \equiv 1 \pmod{n}$, and sends the public key (n, e) and a random number $r_A \in_R \{0, 1\}^l$ to Bob.
- Bob encrypts a number of integers, $m_i \in \mathbb{Z}_n, 1 \leq i \leq N$, using the received public key and sends back $c_i = m_i^e \bmod n, 1 \leq i \leq N$.
- Alice decrypts the received number and sends back $H(m_i'), 1 \leq i \leq N$, where $m_i' = c_i^d \bmod n$ and $H : \{0, 1\}^* \to \{0, 1\}^{Q'(l)}$ is a hash function, $Q'(l)$ is a polynomial function of l.
- Bob checks if $H(m_i') = H(m_i)$ for all i's. If not, Bob rejects the connection. Else, Bob selects $r_B \in_R \{0, 1\}^l$ and $s_B \in \mathbb{Z}_n$ and computes $\pi = T(w, A, B, r_A, r_B)$, where $T : \{0, 1\}^* \to \mathbb{Z}_n$ is a hash function independent of H. Then Bob sends r_B and $z = (s_B)^e + \pi \bmod n$ to Alice and destroys π from his memory.
- Alice recovers s_B from z, that is, $s_B = (z - T(w, A, B, r_A, r_B))^d \bmod n$. Then she selects a random number $c_A \in_R \{0, 1\}^l$ and generates a temporary symmetric key $K = G_1(s_B)$, where G_1 is a hash function from $\{0, 1\}^*$ to $\{0, 1\}^l$. Next, Alice encrypts c_A, B using a symmetric cipher E and sends $E_K(c_A, B)$ back to Bob.
- Bob computes $K = G_1(s_B)$ and $c_B = G_2(S_B)$, where $G_2 : \{0, 1\}^* \to \{0, 1\}^l$ is a hash function independent of G_1. Then Bob decrypts $E_K(c_A, B)$ and checks if the decrypted message is a concatenation of B and some l-bit binary string. If not, Bob terminates the protocol run with failure. Else, Bob accepts and the established session key is $\sigma' = G_3(c_A', c_B, A, B)$, where c_A' is the l-bit binary string derived from the decryption of $E_K(c_A, B)$. Bob sends $h(\sigma')$ back to Alice.

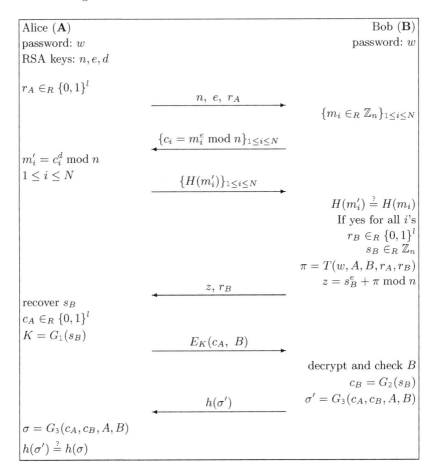

Fig. 2. The password-authenticated key exchange protocol of Zhu et al. [18]

- Alice computes $\sigma = G_3(c_A, c_B, A, B)$ and checks if the incoming message $h(\sigma')$ is equal to $h(\sigma)$. If yes, Alice accepts and uses σ as the session key for subsequent communications. Else, Alice terminates the protocol run with failure.

In Fig. 2, z is computed as an encrypted random number of $\mathbb{Z}_n$ followed by a modulo addition of another random number π. The authors of [18] suggested two alternative methods to generate z from and s_B and π:

Method 1. The RSA encryption is performed over the multiplicative group $\mathbb{Z}_n^*$, that is, $s_B \in \mathbb{Z}_n^*$ and $z = s_B^e \cdot \pi \mod n$.

Method 2. Let $T : \{0,1\}^* \to \{0,1\}^{|n|-1}$ and $z = y \oplus \pi$ for all $y \in \{0,1\}^{|n|-1}$. Since more than half of the elements in $\mathbb{Z}_n$ is smaller than $2^{|n|-1}$, the expected number of times the RSA encryption needs to perform before picking an $s_B \in_R \mathbb{Z}_n$ such that $y = s_B^e \mod n$ is only $|n| - 1$ bits long is less than 2.

Bao [1] analyzed the protocol in Fig. 2 and pointed out that, if the identity B is too short, e.g., $|B| = 20$, then the protocol in Fig. 2 is susceptible to two kinds of dictionary attacks. In the first attack, an adversary, say Eva, generates a pair of RSA keys and impersonates as Alice. After receiving z and r_B in the forth flow, Eva computes all the possible K's corresponding to all the passwords in the password space. Then Eva randomly selects a number $C \in \{0,1\}^{l+|B|}$ and decrypts C using all the possible K's. If there exists K_1 and K_2 such that the decryption of C under K_1 and K_2 is equal to $x\|B$, where x is an l-bit string, then Eva sends C to Bob in the fifth flow. It is clear that Bob will accept after receiving C. Assume that K_1 and K_2 are derived from two passwords α_1 and α_2, respectively. After Eva receives the last message $h(\sigma')$ from Bob, Eva checks if $h(\sigma') = h(x, G_2(s_B), A, B)$. If they are not equal, then Eva knows that α_1 and α_2 are not the passwords of Alice. In this way, Eva can exclude two passwords in each impersonation attempt. The second attack applies if $|B|$ is smaller than the length (number of bits) of the password. In such a circumstance, Bao [1] shows that Eva can recover the password with a probability of $2^{-|B|}$, which is larger than $1/|\mathcal{D}|$.

To thwart the two attacks as described above, Bao suggested that the protocol in Fig. 2 be improved as follows. Instead of sending $E_K(c_A, B)$ to Bob, Alice sends $g = G_2(s_B, c_A)$ and c_A in the fifth flow. Bob applies G_2 to the received number c_A and the random number s_B he picked preciously, and then decides to reject or not.

4   More Efficient Attack and Further Improvement

In this section, we present a more efficient attack on the password-authenticated key exchange protocol as described in Fig. 2. Our attack is a variant of the e-residue attack as described in [2]. With our attack, an adversary can exclude multiple possible passwords in each run of the protocol, regardless of whether $|B|$ is large or small. To thwart the e-residue attack, we provide further improvement on the password protocol described in Fig. 2.

4.1   Description of the Attack

Our attack is based on the following observation: given positive integers n and e such that $\gcd(e, \phi(n)) = 1$, the function $f(x) = x^e \bmod n$ is a permutation on $\mathbb{Z}_n^*$, but $f(x)$ may not be a permutation on $\mathbb{Z}_n$. It is well known that, if n is the product of two *distinct* prime numbers p and q and e is relatively prime to $\phi(n)$, then the function $f(x) = x^e \bmod n$ is not only a permutation on $\mathbb{Z}_n^*$ but also a permutation on $\mathbb{Z}_n$. This, however, may not be the case if n is not the product of two distinct prime numbers. To see this, let $n = p^a q$, where $a > 1$ and p and q are distinct prime numbers. Also let e, $e \geq a$, be an integer relatively prime to $\phi(n)$. For any integer $x \in \mathbb{Z}_n$, if x is a multiple of p, then we have

$$x^e = 0 \bmod p^a,$$

which means that $x^e \bmod p^a$ is not a permutation on $\mathbb{Z}_n$. For any integer $y \in \mathbb{Z}_n$, by the Chinese Remainder Theorem, the congruence

$$x^e = y \bmod n$$

has solutions in $\mathbb{Z}_n$ if and only if the following system of congruence has simultaneous solutions in $\mathbb{Z}_n$,

$$x^e = y \bmod p^a$$
$$x^e = y \bmod q$$

Assume that $y \in \mathbb{Z}_n$ is a multiple of p but not a multiple of p^a. If the congruence $x^e = y \bmod p^a$ has a solution $b \in \mathbb{Z}_n$, then b must be a multiple of p. Since $e \geq a$, we have $b^e = 0 \bmod p^a$. On the other hand, y is not a multiple of p^a, $y \neq 0 \bmod p^a$. Hence the congruence $x^e = y \bmod p^a$ has no solution in $\mathbb{Z}_n$. Therefore, for any such y, one can not find an integer $x \in \mathbb{Z}_n$ such that $x^e = y \bmod n$.

Based on the above observation, an adversary, say, Eva again, can launch the following attack.

Step 1. Eva selects a large integer $n = p^a q$, where $a > 1$, p and q are distinct prime numbers, and N/p is small, e.g., $N/p \leq 0.1$. Eva selects another integer $e \geq a$ such that e is relatively prime to $\phi(n)$. Eva then impersonates as Alice and sends n, e, and $r_E \in_R \{0, 1\}^l$ to Bob.

Step 2. After receiving integers $c_1, c_2, \ldots, c_N$ from Bob, Eva checks if the integers $c_1, c_2, \ldots, c_N$ are relatively prime to n. If not, Eva aborts. If $c_1, c_2, \ldots, c_N$ are relatively prime to n, Eva computes $m'_i = c_i^d \bmod n$ for $1 \leq i \leq N$, where d is a positive integer such that $ed = 1 \bmod \phi(n)$. Then Eva sends, $H(m'_i), 1 \leq i \leq N$, back to Bob.

Step 3. After receiving z and r_B from Bob, Eva terminates the communication session. Eva then performs off-line dictionary attack by repeating the following three steps.

Step 4. Eva selects a password α at random from the password space $\mathcal{D}$.

Step 5. Eva computes $\pi = T(\alpha, A, B, r_E, r_B)$ and $\gamma = z - \pi \bmod n$.

Step 6. Eva checks if $p \mid \gamma$ and $p^a \nmid \gamma$. If not, Eva returns to Step 4. Otherwise, Eva excludes α from $\mathcal{D}$ and returns to Step 4.

In Step 6 of the attack, if Eva detects that $\gamma = z - \pi \bmod n$ is a multiple of p but not a multiple of p^a, then the following congruence

$$x^e = z - \pi \bmod p^a$$

has no solution in $\mathbb{Z}_n$. By the Chinese Remainder Theorem, the following congruence

$$x^e = z - \pi \bmod n$$

has no solution in $\mathbb{Z}_n$. In such an occurrence, Eva knows that α is not the password of Bob; otherwise,

$$z - \pi = s_B^e \bmod n,$$

which leads to a contradiction. So Eva excludes α from the password space whenever she detects that $p \mid \gamma$, but $p^a \nmid \gamma$.

Now, we show that Eva could exclude multiple passwords in each run of the attack. Note that Eva aborts in Step 2 if $c_1, c_2, \ldots, c_N$ are not relatively prime to n. Assume that Bob selects $m_1, m_2, \ldots, m_N$ at random from $\mathbb{Z}_n$. Then the probability that $c_i = m_i^e \bmod n$ is relatively prime to n is equal to $\phi(n)/n$. Since $n = p^a q$, $\phi(n) = p^{a-1}(p-1)(q-1)$. When q is large, e.g., $q > 2^{512}$, we have

$$Pr(\gcd(c_i, n) = 1) \approx 1 - \frac{1}{p}$$

Hence, that probability that $c_1, c_2, \ldots, c_N$ are relatively prime to n is equal to

$$Pr(\gcd(c_i, n) = 1, 1 \le i \le N) = (1 - \frac{1}{p})^N$$

Also since $N/p \le 0.1$, we have

$$Pr(\gcd(c_i, n) = 1, 1 \le i \le N) \approx (1 - \frac{N}{p}) \ge 90\%.$$

Hence, the probability that $c_1, c_2, \ldots, c_N$ are relatively prime to n is pretty high.

Assume that the hashed value of T has uniform distribution on $\mathbb{Z}_n$. Then for each integer $z \in \mathbb{Z}_n$, $\gamma = z - T(\alpha, A, B, r_A, r_B) \bmod n$ also has uniform distribution on $\mathbb{Z}_n$. On the other hand, the number of integers in $\mathbb{Z}_n$ which are divisible by p is equal to n/p and the number of integers divisible by p^a is equal to n/p^a. Thus, the probability that γ is divisible by p but not divisible by p^a is equal to

$$Pr(p \mid \gamma, \ p^a \nmid \gamma) = p^{-1} - p^{-a},$$

which means that for each password α selected in Step 4, the probability for Eva to exclude α from $\mathcal{D}$ is equal to $p^{-1} - p^{-a}$. If $p \ll |D|$, then Eva could exclude many candidate passwords in each run of the attack. For example, $p = 127$, $a = 5$, $e = 5$, $N = 10$ and $|D| = 10^4$, then Eva could exclude approximately 78 passwords in each run of the attack.

In the attack described above, Eva and Bob only carry out the first three flows in Fig. 2. The attack is still applicable if the modulo addition for the computation of z is replaced by the modulo multiplication as suggested in Method 1 or by the bit-wise exclusive-or operation as suggested in Method 2.

4.2   Further Improvement

In the attack described in Section 4.1, Eva makes use of the fact: for some passwords, $z - T(w, A, B, r_A, r_A)$ is not an element of $\mathbb{Z}_n^*$ and thus the following congruence

$$z = x^e + T(w, A, B, r_A, r_A) \bmod n$$

has no solution in $\mathbb{Z}_n$, although $f(x) = x^e \bmod n$ is a permutation on $\mathbb{Z}_n^*$. To thwart the attack, Bob can compute z as follows

$$z = s_B^e \cdot T(w, A, B, r_A, r_A)/\gcd(n, T(w, A, B, r_A, r_A)) \quad \bmod n,$$

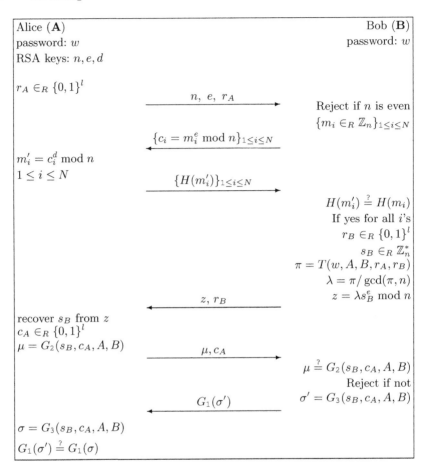

Fig. 3. Further improvement on the password protocol of Zhu et al.

where s_B is an integer randomly selected from $\mathbb{Z}_n^*$. Note that the following integer

$$\lambda = T(w, A, B, r_A, r_A) / \gcd(n, T(w, A, B, r_A, r_A))$$

is relatively prime to n. Thus, z is always an integer of $\mathbb{Z}_n^*$. If $f(x) = x^e \bmod n$ is a permutation on $\mathbb{Z}_n^*$, then for any password $\alpha \in \mathcal{D}$, the following congruence

$$z = x^e \cdot T(\alpha, A, B, r_A, r_A) / \gcd(n, T(w, A, B, r_A, r_A)) \quad \bmod n,$$

always has a solution in $\mathbb{Z}_n^*$. In this way, Eva can only test a single password in each impersonation attempt. Following this idea, Fig. 3 describes further improvement on the password-authenticated key exchange protocol described in Fig. 2. In Fig. 3, Bob first tests if the received integer n is odd. If the integer n is odd, but the integer e, $e > 2$, is not relatively prime to $\phi(n)$, then we can prove that the probability for Bob (most likely, Eva) to correctly recover $m_i, 1 \leq i \leq N$ from $c_i, 1 \leq i \leq N$ is less than or equal to 2^{-N}, i.e.,

$$Pr(H(m_i') = H(m_i), 1 \leq i \leq N) \leq 2^{-N},$$

which is not rigorously proved in [2, 18].

5   Conclusion

In this paper, we provide further security analysis of Zhu et al.'s password-authenticated key exchange protocol. We present an e-residue attack to show the weakness of this protocol. With the e-residue attack, an adversary could exclude multiple candidate passwords in each run of the protocol, regardless of whether the client's identity is short or long. To thwart the e-residue attack, we provide further improvement on Zhu et al.'s password-authenticated key exchange protocol.

References

1. F. Bao, Security analysis of a password authenticated key exchange protocol, *Proc. of the 6th Information Security Conference*, Lecture Notes in Computer Science, vol. 2851, Springer-Verlag, 2003, pp. 208-217.
2. S. M. Bellovin and M. Merritt, Augmented encrypted key exchange: A password-based protocol secure against dictionary attacks and password file compromise, *Proc. of the 1st ACM Conference on Computer and Communications Security*, ACM, November 1993, pp. 244-250.
3. V. Boyko, P. MacKenzie, and S. Patel, Provably secure password authenticated key exchange using Diffie-Hellman, *Advances in Cryptology - EUROCRYPT 2000 Proceedings*, Lecture Notes in Computer Science, vol. 1807, Springer-Verlag, 2000, pp. 156-171.
4. M. Bellare, D. Pointcheval, and P. Rogaway, Authenticated key exchange secure against dictionary attack, *Advances in Cryptology - EUROCRYPT 2000 Proceedings*, Lecture Notes in Computer Science, vol. 1807, Springer-Verlag, 2000, pp. 139-155.
5. O. Goldreich and Y. Lindell, Session-key generation using human passwords only, *Advances in Cryptology - Crypto 2001 Proceedings*, Lecture Notes in Computer Science Vol. 2139, Springer-Verlag, 2001, pp.408-432.
6. L. Gong, Optimal authentication protocols resistant to password guessing attacks, *Proc. IEEE Computer Security Foundation Workshop*, June 1995, pp. 24-29
7. S. Halevi and H. Krawczyk, Public-key cryptography and password protocols, *Proc. of the Fifth ACM Conference on Computer and Communications Security*, 1998, pp. 122-131.
8. D. Jablon, Strong password-only authenticated key exchange, *Computer Communication Review, ACM SIGCOMM*, vol. 26, no. 5, 1996, pp. 5-26.
9. D. Jablon, http://www.integritysciences.com.
10. J. Katz, R. Ostrovsky, and M. Yung, Efficient password-authenticated key exchange using human-memorable passwords, *Advances in Cryptology – Eurocrypt'2001 Proceedings*, Lecture Notes in Computer Science, Vol. 2045, Springer-Verlag, 2001.

11. K. Kobara and H. Imai, Pretty-simple password-authenticated key-exchange under standard assumptions, *IEICE Trans.*, vol. E85-A, no. 10, 2002, pp. 2229-2237.

12. T. Kwon, Authentication and key agreement via memorable passwords, *Proc. Network and Distributed System Security Symposium*, February 7-9, 2001.

13. S. Lucks, Open key exchange: How to defeat dictionary attacks without encrypting public keys, *Proc. Security Protocol Workshop*, Lecture Notes in Computer Science, Vol. 1361, Springer-Verlag, 1997, pp. 79-90.

14. P. MacKenzie, S. Patel, and R. Swaminathan, Password-authenticated key exchange based on RSA, *Advances in Cryptology—ASIACRYPT 2000 Proceedings*, Lecture Notes in Computer Science, vol. 1976, Springer-Verlag, 2000, pp. 599–613.

15. S. Patel, Number theoretic attacks on secure password schemes, *Proc. IEEE Symposium on Security and Privacy*, Oakland, California, May 5-7, 1997.

16. K. H. Rosen, *Elementary Number Theory and Its Applications*, 4th ed., Addison Wesley Longman, 2000.

17. T. Wu, The secure remote password protocol , *Proc. Network and Distributed System Security Symposium*, San Diego, March 1998, pp. 97-111.

18. F. Zhu, D. Wong, A. Chan, and R. Ye, RSA-based password authenticated key exchange for imbalanced wireless networks, *Proc. Information Security Conference 2003 (ISC'02)*, Lecture Notes in Computer Science, vol. 2433, Springer-Verlag, 2002, pp.150-161.

Storage-Efficient Stateless Group Key Revocation*

Pan Wang, Peng Ning, and Douglas S. Reeves

Cyber Defense Lab
North Carolina State University
Raleigh NC 27695, USA
{pwang3, pning, reeves}@ncsu.edu

Abstract. Secure group communication relies on secure and robust distribution of group keys. A *stateless* group key distribution scheme is an ideal candidate when the communication channel is unreliable. Several stateless group key distribution schemes have been proposed. However, these schemes require all users store a certain number of auxiliary keys. The number of such keys increases as the group size grows. As a result, it is quite challenging to use these schemes when the users in a relatively large group have memory constraints. Thus, it is desirable to develop new schemes that can reduce the memory requirement. This paper introduces two novel stateless group key revocation schemes named key-chain tree (KCT) and layered key-chain tree (LKCT), which combine one-way key chains with a logical key tree. These schemes reduce the user storage requirements by trading off it with communication and computation costs. Specifically, these schemes can revoke any R users from a user group of size N by sending a key update message with at most $4R$ keys, while only requiring each user to store $2\log N$ keys.

1 Introduction

A multicast group can be efficiently protected by using a single symmetric key known only to the group members. However, group privacy requires that only the legitimate users have access to the group communication. Thus, the group key must change each time when new users join or old users leave the group. In particular, past users must be revoked from the group so that they cannot derive the future group keys, even if they are able to derive previous group keys with previously-distributed keying information.

Based on the interdependency of key update messages, group key revocation schemes can be classified into either *stateful* ones or *stateless* ones. In a stateful scheme, a legitimate user's state (fail/success) in the current round of group key update will affect its ability to decrypt future group keys. Example schemes in this class include LKH [25, 24] and its variations. In contrast, the group key

---

* This work is partially supported by NCSU Center for Advanced Computing & Communcation (CACC)

K. Zhang and Y. Zheng (Eds.): ISC 2004, LNCS 3225, pp. 25–38, 2004.
© Springer-Verlag Berlin Heidelberg 2004

update in a stateless scheme is only based on the current group key update message and the user's initial configuration [12]. A non-revoked user can decrypt the updated group key independently from the previous key update messages without contacting the Group Key Manager (GKM), even if the user is off-line for a while. This property makes stateless group key distribution very useful in situations where some users are not constantly on-line, or experience burst packet losses.

Stateless group key revocation schemes provide the above flexibility by having users store a number of auxiliary keys [15], and the number of such keys increases as the group size grows. Several recent schemes have managed to reduce the storage requirements for users by taking advantage of techniques such as pseudo random number generators [20, 12]. Though these advances make stateless group key revocation schemes practical in most typical applications, there are still some applications in which it is either necessary or desirable to further reduce the storage requirements. For example, when a tamper-resistant smart card is used (e.g., in a satellite TV system) to decrypt the group key, the more tamper-resistant memory required to store the keying materials, the higher each smart card will cost. Given a typical smart card with 1K bytes tamper-resistant memory and 128-bit keys, the SD scheme [20] can only support a group with about 1000 users. Thus, it is desirable to develop new schemes that can further reduce the memory requirement in stateless group key distribution.

In this paper, we propose two storage-efficient stateless group key revocation schemes. We assume each user is uniquely identified by an ID. Our schemes are based on a *Dual Directional Key Chains (DDKC)* structure, which employs two one-way key chains to facilitate revocation of a set of users with consecutive IDs. By combining DDKCs with a logical key tree, we introduce a storage-efficient stateless group key revocation scheme named *Key-Chain Tree (KCT)*. Given a group of total N users, the KCT scheme only requires $O(\log N)$ storage at each user, and requires at most $2R$ keys in a key update message in order to revoke R users. However, the KCT scheme may require up to N hash operations in the worst case. To further reduce the computation overhead, we extend the KCT scheme to a *Layered Key-Chain Tree (LKCT)* scheme, which maintains the same storage overhead, slightly increases the communication overhead to at most $4R$ keys, but reduces the computation overhead in deriving a group key to $\sqrt{N}$ hash operations.

These two schemes provide another trade-off between communication, computation, and storage. In particular, they significantly reduce the storage requirements per user with slightly more computation and communication overheads, compared with the previous stateless group key distribution schemes such as SD [20] and LSD [12]. For instance, considering a group with 2^{20} users and 128-bit keys, each user needs to store 211 keys (3,376 bytes) in the SD scheme [20], 90 keys (1,140 bytes) in the LSD scheme [12], but only 40 keys (640 bytes) in the proposed schemes.

The rest of this paper is organized as follows. Section 2 discusses related work. Section 3 presents the DDKC structure and the two proposed group key revocation schemes. Section 4 compares the various overheads and performance of proposed schemes with the existing ones. Finally, section 5 concludes this paper and points out some future research directions.

2   Related Work

Securing group communication, which is also called as *broadcast encryption*, has received attention from both the network and cryptography communities. A number of approaches [7, 16, 21, 20, 25, 24, 18] have been proposed. Early surveys are available in [10, 14], and a recent one can be found in [6]. In the following, we give a brief outline of the existing approaches.

Fiat and Naor [11] first formally studied the broadcast encryption problem in 1994. With $O(tn^2\log(t))$ user stored keys and $O(t^2n\log^2(t))$ messages, their proposed schemes allow a GKM to revoke any number of users where at most t of them collude. Blundo *et al.* [1, 3] and Stinson *et al.* [23] studied broadcast encryption in the unconditionally secure model and gave the lower and the upper bounds on the communication cost and a user's storage overhead. Luby and Staddon [19] showed the tradeoff between the storage overhead and the communication cost.

Wallner *et al.* [25] and Wong *et al.* [24] independently discovered the Logical Key Hierarchy (LKH) (or Key Graph) scheme. LKH is an efficient stateful group key revocation method. It requires each user store $\log(n)$ keys and the GKM broadcast $2\log(n)$ messages for a key update operation, where n is the number of legitimate users.

Naor *et al.* [20] first proposed two stateless revocation schemes, termed CS and SD. Given the maximum total number of users N and each user has $\log(N)$ keys, the CS scheme can revoke any R users with $O(R\log(N/R))$ messages. The SD scheme reduces the message number to $O(R)$ while it increases the user storage overhead to $O(\log^2(N))$ and requires $O(\log(N))$ cryptographic operations.

Halevy and Shamir [12] proposed a variant scheme of SD, the Layered Subset Difference (LSD). LSD reduces the storage overhead from $O(\log^2(N))$ to $O(\log^{1+\epsilon}(N))$ with increased communication overhead. Their experiments show that the average communication overhead is close to $2R$, which is 1.6 times larger than that in SD.

In addition to the property of statelessness, some recent works address the *self-healing* property that a group member could recover the missed session keys from the latest key update message on its own. Staddon *et al.* [22] first proposed a self-healing group key distribution approach, which is based on two dimensional t-degree polynomials. Their scheme is improved by Liu and Ning [18]. Blundo *et al.* [2] further presented a new mechanism for implementing the self-healing approach.

3   Storage-Efficient Stateless Group Key Revocation

Let $\mathcal{N}$ be the set of all potential users, where $|\mathcal{N}| = N$, and let $\mathcal{R}$ be the set of revoked users, where $\mathcal{R} \subset \mathcal{N}$ and $|\mathcal{R}| = R$. The goal of group key revocation is to have the GKM transmit a key update message efficiently over a broadcast channel shared by all users so that any user $u \in \mathcal{N} \setminus \mathcal{R}$ can decrypt this message, but any users in $\mathcal{R}$ cannot decrypt this message properly, even if they collude with each other in an arbitrary manner. We are interested in stateless group key revocation schemes, in which a legitimate user can always derive a group key from a key update message even if it has not received some previous key update messages.

In this section, we present two group key revocation schemes that are both stateless and storage-efficient. In the following, we first introduce the Dual Directional Key Chains (DDKC) scheme, which itself is not a complete group key revocation scheme, but the foundation of the proposed schemes. We then present in detail the proposed schemes. Notation used throughout this paper is summarized in Table 1.

Table 1. Notations

$\mathcal{N}$	the set of all potential users
N	the number of potential users, $N = |\mathcal{N}|$
$\mathcal{R}$	the set of revoked users
R	the number of revoked users, $R = |\mathcal{R}|$
$K_{i,j}^F$	the forward key assigned to user j in subset $\mathcal{N}_i$
$K_{i,j}^B$	the backward key assigned to user j in subset $\mathcal{N}_i$
u_i	user i
$\mathcal{T}$	an arbitrary set of users

3.1   Dual Directional Key Chains

A DDKC is composed of two one-way key chains with equal length, a *forward key chain* (K^F) and a *backward key chain* (K^B). Each one-way key chain [17] is a chain of cryptographic keys generated by repeatedly applying a one-way hash function $\mathcal{H}$ to a random number (key seed). For example, to construct a key chain of size N, the GKM first randomly chooses a key seed K_0, and then computes $K_1 = \mathcal{H}(K_0)$, ..., until $K_N = \mathcal{H}(K_{N-1})$. Because of the one-way property of the hash function $\mathcal{H}$, given K_i, it is computationally infeasible for a user to compute K_j for $j < i$. However, a user can compute any K_j for $j > i$ efficiently (by calculating $K_j = \mathcal{H}^{j-i}(K_i)$).

We may use a DDKC to facilitate revocation of a set of users that have consecutive IDs. Specifically, we construct a DDKC and assign a key in each key chain to each user. For example, Figure 1 shows a DDKC with 8 keys in each key chain and 8 users. We may assign each user the key below it in both key chains.

Fig. 1. An example of dual directional key chains

For instance, we may assign K_5^F and K_4^B to u_5. In general, each user u_i gets K_i^F in the forward key chain and K_{N+1-i}^B in the backward key chain. Obviously, u_i can then compute all the keys K_j^F for $j > i$ in the forward key chain and K_j^B for $j > N + 1 - i$ in the backward key chain. This property can be used to facilitate revoking a user. For example, if u_6 in Figure 1 denotes a revoked user, the non-revoked users then can be divided into two subsets $\mathcal{T}_1 = \{u_1, ..., u_5\}$ and $\mathcal{T}_2 = \{u_7, u_8\}$. We notice that K_5^F is only known by the users in subset $\mathcal{T}_1$ and K_2^B is only known by users in subset $\mathcal{T}_2$. So, we say K_5^F *covers* subset $\mathcal{T}_1$ and K_2^B *covers* subset $\mathcal{T}_2$. In general, if an encryption key k_i is only known by the users in subset T_i, we say that subset T_i is covered by k_i and k_i is the subset cover key for T_i. Thus, if we use these two subset cover keys, K_5^F and K_2^B, to encrypt the new group key separately and broadcast the cipher-texts to the group. All the users except for u_6 will be able to derive at least one of K_5^F and K_2^B and then decrypt the new group key.

This observation leads to the following DDKC revocation scheme. Clearly, this scheme is a subset-cover algorithm [20]. Note that this scheme is only intended to revoke one or a set of users with consecutive IDs. We will discuss how to revoke arbitrary sets of users in the later schemes.

System Setup Construct a DDKC as follows:

1: For a given potential group size N and a set of users $\mathcal{T} = \{u_1, ..., u_n\}$, $n < N$, the GKM randomly chooses two initial key seeds, *the forward key seed* S^F and *the backward key seed* S^B.
2: The GKM repeatedly applies a one-way hash function $\mathcal{H}$ to these initial key seeds, respectively, and gets two *one-way key chains* of equal length N, *the forward key chain* $K_i^F = \mathcal{H}[K_{i-1}^F] = \mathcal{H}^{i-1}[S^F]$ and *the backward key chain* $K_i^B = \mathcal{H}[K_{i-1}^B] = \mathcal{H}^{i-1}[S^B]$.
3: The GKM assigns the secret keys, K_i^F and K_{N+1-i}^B to user u_i via a secure channel.

User Revocation. In order to revoke a set of consecutive users $\{u_i, u_{i+1}, ..., u_j\}$ $\subset \mathcal{T}$, the GKM first locates two encryption keys, K_{i-1}^F and K_{N-j}^B, if they exist. The GKM then uses these two encryption keys to encrypt the new group key and broadcasts both cipher-texts in the key update message. Thus, only the remaining users can get the new group key by calculating one of the encryption keys (either K_{i-1}^F or K_{N-j}^B) and then decrypting the new group key.

Security Analysis. Naor et al. [20] proved that any subset-cover algorithm is secure if it satisfies the key-indistinguishability property. Informally, a key is indistinguishable if it is not possible to say whether this key, or a randomly generated key, was used to encrypt a message. Since the DDKC scheme is a subset-cover method, to prove it is secure we only need to show that the encryption keys which are used to encrypt the new group key are indistinguishable for the non-legitimate users.

Theorem 1. *The encryption (subset cover) keys produced by the DDKC scheme are key-indistinguishable for the non-legitimate users, if $\mathcal{H}$ is a perfect cryptographic hash function.*

Proof. The random oracle methodology [4,5] shows that given a random oracle and a query x, if the oracle has not been given the query x before it generates a random response which has uniform probability of being chosen from anywhere in the output domain. Therefore, if the one-way hash function $\mathcal{H}$ is a perfect cryptographic hash function, without knowing the initial key seed S^F or S^B, it is computationally infeasible for an attacker to figure out the encryption keys, K_{i-1}^F and K_{N-i}^B. Even given the personal secrets, K_i^F and K_{N-i+1}^B, it is also computationally infeasible for a revoked user $u_i \in \mathcal{R}$ to calculate the encryption keys K_{i-1}^F and K_{N-i}^B. Thus, the encryption keys in the DDKC scheme are indistinguishable from random keys for any user $u_i \notin \mathcal{N} \setminus \mathcal{R}$.

The properties related to the performance of the DDKC scheme is summarized as follows:

Theorem 2. *In the DDKC scheme, (i) the user storage overhead is 2 keys; (ii) the length of the broadcast key update message is at most 2 keys; and (iii) the average computation overhead is less than $(N - R - 1)/2$.*

Proof. (i) Clearly, the storage overhead for each user is the initially assigned two personal keys. (ii) According to the scheme, the GKM needs at most two encryption keys to exclude a single user or a continuous block of users. The new group key is encrypted with these two encryption keys separately. Thus, the length of the key update message is at most 2 keys. (iii) A user's computation cost depends on both its and the revoked users' positions. Suppose the new group key is encrypted with K_{i-1}^F and K_{N-j}^B separately. A legitimate user u_p $(p < i)$ needs $i - p - 1$ hash operations to get K_{i-1}^F. Similarly, u_q $(q > j)$ needs $q - j - 1$ hash operations to get K_{N-j}^B. The average computation overhead

$$\theta = \frac{\sum_{p=1}^{i-1}(i-p-1) + \sum_{q=j+1}^{N}(q-j-1)}{N-j+i-1}$$ where $R = j - i + 1$. When $i = 1$ or $j = N$, θ

reaches its maximum value $\frac{N-R-1}{2}$.

3.2   Key-Chain Tree Revocation Scheme

Generally, the GKM needs to revoke multiple users which might not be adjacent to each other. The proposed DDKC method unfortunately cannot handle such situations. Inspired by the logical key trees in the SD scheme [20], we propose to use a tree structure along with (multiple) DDKCs to address this problem. The resulting scheme is named the *key-chain tree (KCT)* scheme. This KCT scheme allows the GKM to revoke any number of users regardless of their positions, and works very well even when the excluded users collude with each other in an arbitrary way.

System Setup. Given the maximum group size N, the KCT scheme maps the users to the leaves of a binary tree. (For simplicity, we assume $N = 2^d$, where d is an integer.) A subgroup G_i is defined as the collection of users in the subtree rooted at an internal node i. Each subgroup G_i is associated with a DDKC. Therefore, there are totaly $N-1$ DDKCs corresponding to the $N-1$ subgroups. Figure 2 shows an example of a key-chain tree. Moreover, each user u_i is associated with $\log(N)$ DDKCs along the path from the root to leaf i. The corresponding backward/forward keys are assigned to u_i as its personal secrets. For instance, in Figure 2, the personal secrets of u_3 are $\{K_{0,3}^F, K_{0,6}^B, K_{1,3}^F, K_{1,2}^B, K_{4,1}^F, K_{4,2}^B\}$. We use $K_{i,j}^F$ denote the key at position j in the forward key chain associated with subgroup G_i. $K_{i,j}^B$ is defined similarly.

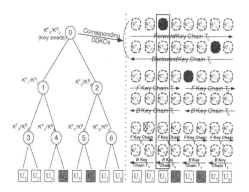

Fig. 2. An example key-chain tree

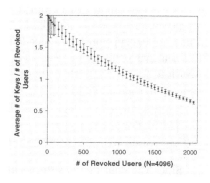

Fig. 3. Simulated communication cost

User Revocation. Clearly, the R revoked users partition the remaining set of users into at most $R + 1$ contiguous blocks. We call each block of non-revoked users a *contiguous subset (of users)*. Formally, there exists a contiguous subset $S_{m\_n} = \{u_i \mid m < i < n, \ m = 0 \text{ or } u_m \in \mathcal{R}, \ n = N+1 \text{ or } u_n \in \mathcal{R}, \ u_i \notin \mathcal{R} \text{ for all } i\}$. Similar to the DDKC scheme, the GKM needs to find a set of encryption keys to cover every $u_i \in \mathcal{N} \setminus \mathcal{R}$. For instance, the set of cover keys in Figure 2 is $\{K_{0,3}^F, K_{0,2}^B, K_{2,5}^F\}$. The *cover key discovery* algorithm is given below:

1: Sort the revoked users by their IDs. Assume the resulting IDs are $r_1, r_2, ...,$ r_R.
2: Find K_{0,r_1-1}^F and K_{0,r_R+1}^B, if they exist.
3: Let $i = 1$.
4: In the logical key tree, find the least common ancestor V of users u_{r_i} and $u_{r_{i+1}}$. Let V_l and V_r be the two children of V such that u_{r_i} is a descendant of V_l and $u_{r_{i+1}}$ is a descendant of V_r. Let p_l denote the relative position of

user u_{r_i+1} in subtree V_l and p_r denote the relative position of user u_{r_i+1-1} in the subtree V_r. Find the cover keys, $K^B_{V_l,p_l}$ and $K^F_{V_r,p_r}$, if they exist[1]. For briefly, we do not distinguish the node and the ID associated with this node in this paper.

5: Repeat step 4 with $i = i + 1$, until $i = R - 1$.

Security Analysis. Before proving KCT is secure, we first show a contiguous subset in KCT satisfies the key-indistinguishability property.

Lemma 1. *The encryption keys for a contiguous subset in KCT is key-indistinguishable for users not in this subset.*

Proof. Given a contiguous subset S_{m_n}, if $m = 0$, the subset S_{0_n} is covered by the encryption key $K^F_{0,n-1}$, since this encryption key is only known by user u_j, $0 < j < n$. Thus, $K^F_{0,n-1}$ is key-indistinguishable to any user $u_i \notin S_{0\_n}$. Similarly, if $n = N+1$, $K^B_{0,N-m}$ is key-indistinguishable to any user $u_i \notin S_{m\_N+1}$.

If $m \neq 0$ and $n \neq N + 1$, find the least common ancestor V of u_m and u_n. Let V_l and V_r be the left child and the right child of V, respectively. Therefore, u_m is the descendant of V_l and u_n is the descendant of V_r. Consider all possible scenarios: (1) $V_l = u_m$ and $V_r = u_n$ i.e.,$n = m + 1$. This means S_{m_n} is empty. Thus, no encryption key is needed. (2) $V_l \neq u_m$ and $V_r \neq u_n$. Let p_{m+1} denote the relative position of leaf u_{m+1} in subtree V_l and p_{n-1} denote the relative position of leaf u_{n-1} in subtree V_r. If $K^B_{V_l,p_{m+1}}$ exists, it is only known by a legitimate user u_i where $\{u_i \mid u_i \in G_{V_l}, m < i < n\}$. Similarly, if $K^F_{V_r,p_{n-1}}$ exists, it is only known by a legitimate user $u_j \in \{u_j \mid u_i \in G_{V_r}, m < i < n\}$. Clearly, $\{u_i \mid u_i \in G_{V_l}, m < i < n\} \cap \{u_j \mid u_i \in G_{V_r}, m < i < n\} = S_{m\_n}$. Therefore, $K^B_{V_l,p_{m+1}}$ and $K^F_{V_r,p_{n-1}}$ are key-indistinguishable to any user $u_i \notin S_{m\_n}$.

Since the contiguous subsets in KCT are disjoint with each other, it is clear that they satisfy the key-indistinguishability. Therefore, based on Theorem 12 in [20], the KCT scheme does provide a secure encryption of the messages even if the revoked users collude with each other.

Theorem 3 summarizes the properties related to the performance of the KCT scheme.

Theorem 3. *The KCT scheme requires (i) message length of at most $2R$ keys, (ii) $2 \log N$ keys stored at each receiver, and (iii) a single decryption operation and at most $N - 1$ one-way hash function operations to decrypt a key update message.*

Proof. (i) For a contiguous subset S_{m_n}, where $m \neq 0$ and $n \neq N+1$, it requires at most 2 encryption keys to cover this subset, while there are at most $R - 1$ such subsets. For subset S_{m_n}, where $m = 0$ or $n = N + 1$, 1 encryption key is enough. Therefore, the length of the key update message is no greater than

---

[1] Non-existing means either u_{r_i} is the rightmost node in subtree V_l or u_{r_i+1} is the leftmost node in subtree V_r. For example, u_4 is the rightmost node of subtree 1 in Figure 2.

$1 + 2(R - 1) + 1 = 2R$ keys. (ii) Each user is associated with $\log N$ DDKCs along the path from the leaf to the root, and keeps 2 keys for each DDKC. Thus, the total number of keys that a user needs to store is $2 \log N$. (iii) It is clear that the computation overhead of a legitimate user varies. It not only depends on the set of the revoked users and their positions in the logical tree, but also on the position of this legitimate user. The upper bound is decided by the size of the contiguous subset of which this non-revoked user is a member. Since the maximum contiguous subset size is N in the case of no revoked user at all, the computation overhead in the KCT scheme is bounded to $N - 1$ one-way function operations, and one decryption operation.

Theorem 3 shows the worst case of communication overhead in KCT scheme. As we stated, the real cost depends on $\mathcal{N}$, $\mathcal{R}$ and the positions of the revoked users. We performed simulation experiments to further examine the average cost for randomly revoked users, which show that the average cost is lower than the upper bound $2R$. Figure 3 shows the communication overhead obtained in the simulations, in which R users are randomly selected to be revoked from a group of 4,096 users. For each data point, the average, the minimum, and the maximum values measured for the indicated number of revoked users are shown.

3.3 Layered Key-Chain Tree Scheme

The main disadvantage of the KCT scheme is its high computation overhead, which involves $N - 1$ one-way hash function operations in the worst case. In this subsection we further reduce the computation overhead by introducing layers into the KCT scheme. We call the resulting scheme the *layered key-chain tree (LKCT)* scheme.

The basic idea of the LKCT scheme is to divide a large group into a collection of smaller subgroups as illustrated in Figure 4. The upper-layer KCT is used to cover the subgroups, and the lower-layer KCTs are used to cover the real group members.

System Setup. Given the maximum group size N, the GKM first constructs a KCT (upper-layer KCT) of size $\sqrt{N}$. Each leaf node in the upper-layer KCT corresponds to a subgroup of $\sqrt{N}$ users. The GKM then constructs another $\sqrt{N}$ lower-layer KCTs, each of which has $\sqrt{N}$ leaves. Each leaf of a lower-layer KCT corresponds to a user. A subgroup is defined as the users in a lower-layer KCT.

When a new user joins the group, the GKM puts it in a subgroup that has less than $\sqrt{N}$ users, and maps it to an unused leaf node in the corresponding lower-lay KCT. The GKM then assigns the keys in both KCTs to the new user following the KCT scheme.

User Revocation. To revoke a set of users, the GKM uses the KCT scheme to revoke the subgroup which contains some revoked users from the upper-layer KCT, and then for each lower-layer KCT including revoked users, the GKM revokes these users with the lower-layer KCTs corresponding to their subgroups

For instance, in order to revoke u_i in Figure 4, the GKM first finds a set of encryption keys to cover all the subgroups except for subgroup 1 in the upper-layer KCT. This step requires determining at most 2 encryption keys. After that, the GKM needs to find another set of encryption keys to cover the remaining users in subgroup 1. It is clear this revocation also requires determining at most 2 keys. Finally, the GKM uses the resulting keys to encrypt the new group key separately and broadcasts all the cipher-texts in the key update message. All the users except u_i can decrypt the new group key from the key update message.

Security Analysis. LKCT is an extension to KCT. We can easily prove the subsets in LKCT also satisfy the key-indistinguishability property as in KCT. (We omit the details to avoid repetition.) Therefore, the key update messages in LKCT are inaccessible to the revoked users even they collude with each other.

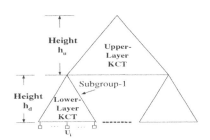 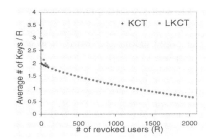

Fig. 4. An illustration of a LKCT   **Fig. 5.** Average communication cost (N=4096)

The performance properties of LKCT scheme is summarized as follows.

Theorem 4. *The LKCT method requires (i) message length of at most $4r$ keys, (ii) $2\log N$ keys stored at each receiver, and (iii) at most $\sqrt{N}-1$ one-way function operations and a single decryption to decrypt a key update message.*

Proof. (i) Assume the revoked R users are distributed in w low-layer KCTs, denoted as $g_1, ..., g_w$. Further assume in the low-layer KCT g_i, there are x_i revoked users, where $i = 1, ..., w$. Thus, we have $x_1 + x_2 + ... + x_w = R$. According to Theorem 3, we need at most $2w$ keys to revoke the w lower-layer KCTs. Moreover, for each low-layer KCT g_i, where $i = 1, ..., w$, we need at most $2x_i$ keys to revoke the x_i users in g_i. Thus, totally we need $2w + 2x_1 + ... + 2x_w = 2w + 2R \leq 4R$ keys to generate the key update message. (ii) Each user needs to store keys in the upper-layer KCT and the lower-layer KCT in which it resides. The total number of keys each user keeps is $2\log\sqrt{N} + 2\log\sqrt{N} = 2\log N$. (iii) To compute the group key, a legitimate user needs to use either the upper-layer KCT if no user in its subgroup is revoked, or the lower-layer KCT otherwise. Thus, according to Theorem 3, it needs at most $\sqrt{N}-1$ hash operations to compute the encryption key, and one decryption to get the group key.

By introducing the layers into the original KCT scheme, we gain a significant reduction in computation overhead, from at most $N-1$ to at most $\sqrt{N}-1$, but at the expense of a slightly increased communication overhead. Figure 5 compares the communication overhead between LKCT and KCT on a group of 4,096 users. It shows that the communication overhead in LKCT scheme is still low for the average case.

4   Performance Comparison and Discussion

In this section, we compare the performance of our proposed schemes with some existing stateless group key revocation approaches. Table 2 shows the storage, the communication, and the computation complexities of these schemes. From Table 2, we can see that the SC scheme and our proposed schemes have a lower storage overhead than SD and LSD. However, the SC scheme has a much higher communication overhead than the others. The SC scheme has the lowest computation overhead, while our proposed schemes have the highest computation overhead. Our proposed schemes trade off the storage and communication overhead with the computation overhead.

Table 2. Performance Comparison on Major Features

	Storage Overhead	Communication Overhead	Computation Overhead
SC [20]	$O(\log(N))$	$O(r\log(N/R))$	$O(\log(\log(N)))$
SD [20]	$O(\log^2(N))$	$O(R)$ worst case $(2R)$	$O(\log(N))$
LSD [12]	$O(\log^{1+\epsilon}(N))$	$O(R)$ worst case $(4R)$	$O(\log(N))$
KCT	$O(\log(N))$	$O(R)$ worst case $(2R)$	$O(N)$
LKCT	$O(\log(N))$	$O(R)$ worst case $(4R)$	$O(\sqrt{N})$

Table 2 only compares the worst case performance of the methods. The real performance (especially the communication cost) of a stateless group key revocation scheme not only depends on the number of revoked users R, but also on the revoked users' positions in the logical tree. To further compare the average communication cost of these schemes, we performed simulation. In our simulation, we randomly selected R revoked users and calculated the number of key update messages for each scheme. For each number R, we repeated our experiments 10,000 times. We then calculated the average number of keys in a key update message for each scheme. Figure 6 shows the result.

As shown in Figure 6, (1) the SC scheme has the highest average communication overhead (which is much higher than the others), (2) the SD scheme has the lowest average communication overhead, (3) the KCT scheme has a slightly higher average communication overhead than SD, but lower than LSD, and (4) if R is large enough, the LKCT scheme has a similar average communication overhead to LSD.

Figure 7 shows the storage overhead of each scheme. Clearly, the SD scheme has the highest storage overhead. Our proposed schemes have a lower storage overhead than SD and LSD, but higher than SC.

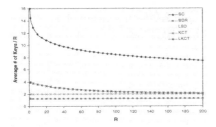
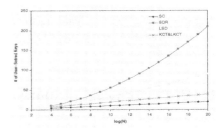

Fig. 6.   Communication   Overhead   **Fig. 7.** User Storage With Different
($N=2^{16}$)   Group Sizes

Based on the above analysis, we can see that the SC scheme is a better
solution for scenarios in which a user has a high communication bandwidth but
very limited memory and computation power. The LKCT and KCT schemes are
suitable for scenarios in which a user's memory and communication bandwidth
are critically limited. If a user has enough memory to store all the keys, both
SD and LSD are more suitable than the other schemes, and SD is better than
LSD on communication overhead.

We notice that our proposed schemes perform better when the revoked users
are clustered rather than randomly distributed. Since group members may be
ordered based on specific organizational requirements, e.g., geographic location,
the scenario of excluding a cluster of users from a group may be common in real
life.

The higher computation overhead of our proposed schemes is not a major
obstacle in real implementation. [9] shows the speed of computing a MD5 hash
function on a Pentium 4 2.1Ghz processor is 204.55 Megabytes/second. Thus,
it takes about $40\mu s$ for 1024 hash operations with 64 bit key lengths, which is
the maximum computation overhead for the LKCT scheme with 1 million users.
The real processing time may be longer, since the cost of hashing many short
messages is different from that of hashing large quantities of data.

Jakobsson [13] as well as Coppersmith and Jakobsson [8] proposed schemes
to improve the performance of the one-way key chain, which requires only
$O(log(N))$ storage and $O(log(N))$ computation to access an element. By adopt-
ing their schemes, the proposed KCT and LKCT can achieve the same theoretic
complexity as the SD [20] scheme on the performances. That is, the computation overhead is further reduced to $O(log(N))$, while the storage overhead is
increased to $O(log^2(N))$.

5   Conclusion and Future Work

In this paper, we presented two storage-efficient stateless group key revocation schemes, which reduce the user storage requirement by trading-off with
the communication and computation cost. Given a group of N users, the proposed schemes only require each user store $O(\log N)$ symmetric keys, and allow

a group manager to revoke R users with at most $2R$ or $4R$ keys in a key update message. The proposed schemes are especially suitable for scenarios in which the memory and the bandwidth are critically limited. Several issues are worth further research, including applying the proposed schemes in storage-constrained applications, and further reducing the computation entailed by the proposed schemes.

References

1. C. Blundo and A. Cresti, *Space Requirements for Broadcast Encryption*, Advances in Cryptology-EUROCRYPTO'94, LNCS 950, 287-298. 1994.
2. C. Blundo and P. D'Arco and et al., *Design of Self-Healing Key Distribution Schemes*, Design, Codes, and Cryptography, N. 32, 2004.
3. C. Blundo and L. A. Frota Mattos and D. R. Stinson, *Trade-offs Between Communication and Storage in Unconditionally Secure Schemes for Broadcast Encryption and Interactive Key Distribution*, CRYPTO'96, 1996, 387-400.
4. R. Canetti and O. Goldreich and S. Halevi, *The Random Oracle Methodology, Revisited*, Proceedings of 30th Annual ACM Symposium on the Theory of Computing, 1998.
5. R. Canetti and D. Micciancio and O. Reingold, *Perfectly One-Way Probabilistic Hash Functions*, Proceedings of 30th Annual ACM Symposium on the Theory of Computing, 1998.
6. K. Chan and S. Chan, *Key Management Approaches to Offer Data Confidentiality for Secure Multicast*, IEEE Network, **17**, Sept-Oct 2003, 30-39.
7. I. Chang and R. Engel and et.al, *Key Management for Secure Internet Multicast Using Boolean Function Minimisation Technique*, Proceedings of INFOCOM'99, New York, NY, 1999.
8. D. Coppersmith and M. Jakobsson, *Almost Optimal Hash Sequence Traversal*, the Sixth International Conference on Financial Cryptography 2002, 2002.
9. W. Dai, http://www.eskimo.com/~weidai/benchmarks.html
10. L. R. Dondeti and S. Mukherjee and A. Samal, *Survey and Comparison of Secure Group Communication Protocols*, University of Nebraska-Lincoln, June 1999.
11. A. Fiat and M. Naor, *Broadcast Encryption*, Advances in Cryptology – CRYPTO'93.
12. D. Halevy and A. Shamir, *The LSD Broadcast Encryption Scheme*, Advances in Cryptology-CRYPTO'02, 2002.
13. M. Jakobsson, *Fractal Hash Sequence Representation and Traversal*, the IEEE International Symposium on Information Theory 2002 (ISIT'02), July 2002.
14. P.S. Kumar, *A survey of Multicast Security Issues and Architectures*, Proceedings of 21st National Information Systems Security Conferences, Arlington, VA, 1999.
15. R. Kumar and R. Rajagopalan and A. Sahai, *Coding Constructions for Blacklisting Problems without Computational Assumptions*, Advances in Cryptology-CRYPTO'99, LNCS 1666.
16. H. Kurnio and L. McAven and R. Safavi-Naini and H. Wang, *A Dynamic Group Key Distribution Scheme with Flexible User Join*, ICISC 2002, 2003, LNCS 435, 478-496.
17. L. Lamport, *Password Authentication with Insecure Communication*, Communications of the ACM, November 1981, **24**, number 11, 770-772.

18. D. Liu and P. Ning, *Efficient Self-Healing Group Key Distribution with Revocation Capability*, Proceedings of CCS 2003, Washington D.C., October 2003.
19. M. Luby and J. Staddon, *Combinatorial Bounds for Broadcast Encryption*, Advances in Cryptology-EUROCRYPTO'98, 1998.
20. D. Naor and M. Naor and J. Lotspiech, *Revocation and Tracing Schemes for Stateless Receivers*, Advances in Cryptology-CRYPTO'01, LNCS 2139.
21. R. Safavi-Naini and H. Wang, *New Constructions of Secure Multicast Re-keying Schemes using Perfect Hash Families*, Proceedings of CCS'2000, Athens, Greece, 2000.
22. J. Staddon and S. Miner and et.al., *Self-Healing Key Distribution with Revocation*, Proceedings of 2002 IEEE Symposium on Security and Privacy, Berkeley, California, USA, 2002.
23. D. R. Stinson and T. van Trung, *Some New Results on Key Distribution Patterns and Broadcast Encryption*, Designs, Codes and Cryptography, **14**, 1998, 261-279.
24. C. Wong and M. Gouda and S. Lam, *Secure Group Communications Using Key Graphs*, Proceedings of the ACM SIGCOMM '98, Vancouver, B.C, 1998.
25. D. Wallner and E. Harder and R. Agee, *Key Management for Multicast: Issues and Architectures*, IETF Request For Comments, RFC2627, 1999.

Low-Level Ideal Signatures and General Integrity Idealization

Michael Backes, Birgit Pfitzmann, and Michael Waidner

IBM Zurich Research Lab
{mbc,bpf,wmi}@zurich.ibm.com

Abstract. Recently we showed how to justify a Dolev-Yao type model of cryptography as used in virtually all automated protocol provers under active attacks and in arbitrary protocol environments. The justification was done by defining an ideal system handling Dolev-Yao-style terms and a cryptographic realization with the same user interface, and by showing that the realization is as secure as the ideal system in the sense of reactive simulatability. This holds the standard model of cryptography and under standard assumptions of adaptively secure primitives. While treating a term algebra is the point of that paper, a natural question is whether the proof could be more modular, e.g., by using a low-level idealization of signature schemes similar to the treatment of encryption. We present a low-level ideal signature system that we tried to use as a lower layer in prior versions of the library proof. It may be of independent interest for cryptography because idealizing signature schemes has proved surprisingly error-prone. However, we also explain why using it makes the overall proof of the justification of the Dolev-Yao type model more complicated instead of simpler.

We further present a technique, integrity idealization, for mechanically constructing composable low-level ideal systems for other cryptographic primitives that have "normal" cryptographic integrity definitions.

1 Introduction

Automated proofs of security protocols with model checkers or theorem provers typically abstract from cryptography by deterministic operations on abstract terms and by simple cancellation rules. An example term is $E_{pke_w}(E_{pke_v}(\mathsf{sign}_{sks_u}(m, N_1), N_2))$, where m denotes an arbitrary message and N_1, N_2 two nonces. A typical cancellation rule is $D_{ske}(E_{pke}(m)) = m$ for corresponding keys. The proof tools handle these terms symbolically, i.e., they never evaluate them to bitstrings. In other words, they perform abstract algebraic manipulations on trees consisting of operators and base messages, using the cancellation rules, the transition rules of a particular protocol, and abstract models of networks and adversaries. Such abstractions, although different in details, are called the Dolev-Yao model after the first authors [17].

For many years there was no cryptographic justification for such abstractions. The problem lies in the assumption, implicit in the adversary model, that

K. Zhang and Y. Zheng (Eds.): ISC 2004, LNCS 3225, pp. 39–51, 2004.
© Springer-Verlag Berlin Heidelberg 2004

actions that cannot be expressed with the abstract operations are impossible, and that no relations hold between terms unless derivable by the cancellation rules. It is not hard to make artificial counterexamples to these assumptions. Nevertheless, no counterexamples against the method for protocols proved in the literature were found so far. Further, the overall approach of abstracting from cryptographic primitives once with rigorous hand-proofs, and then using tools for proving protocols using such primitives, is highly attractive: Besides the cryptographic aspects, protocol proofs have many distributed-systems aspects, which make proofs tedious and error-prone even if they weren't interlinked with the cryptographic aspects. To use existing efficient automated proof tools for security protocols, cryptography must indeed be abstracted into simple, deterministic ideal systems. The closer one can stay to the Dolev-Yao model, the easier the adaptation of the proof tools will be.[1]

Cryptographic underpinnings of a Dolev-Yao model were first addressed by Abadi and Rogaway in [2]. However, they only handled passive adversaries and symmetric encryption. The protocol language and security properties handled where extended in [1,23], but still only for passive adversaries. This excludes most of the typical ways of attacking protocols, e.g., man-in-the-middle attacks and attacks by reusing a message part in a different place or concurrent protocol run. A full cryptographic justification for a Dolev-Yao model, i.e., for arbitrary active attacks and within the context of arbitrary surrounding interactive protocols, was first given recently in [5]. Based on the specific Dolev-Yao model whose soundness was proven in [5] and called the *cryptographic library* there, the well-known Needham-Schroeder-Lowe protocol was proved in [3]. This shows that in spite of adding certain operators and rules compared with simpler Dolev-Yao models (in order to be able to use arbitrary cryptographically secure primitives without too many changes in the cryptographic realization), such a proof is possible in the style already used in automated tools, only now with a sound cryptographic basis. It was also shown how the cryptographic library, in other words the term algebra and rules, can be modularly extended by additional cryptographic primitives, using the example of symmetric authentication [8] and symmetric encryption [4]. Subsequent to the work of [5], several papers presented cryptographic underpinnings of Dolev-Yao models under active attacks for specific primitives, e.g., [24] for symmetric encryption and [20,21,27] for public-key encryption.

The full version of [5] with its rigorous proofs is of considerable length. This is not too surprising compared with, e.g., the length of [2]. Nevertheless, it seems an interesting question whether the cryptographic library, in other words the precise Dolev-Yao model used, as well as its proof could not be presented in a

---

[1] Efforts are also under way to formulate syntactic calculi for dealing with probabilism and polynomial-time considerations, in particular [28,25,29,22] and, as a second step, to encode them into proof tools. However, this approach can not yet handle protocols with any degree of automation. Generally this approach should be seen as complementary to the approach of getting simple deterministic abstractions of cryptography and working with those wherever cryptography is only used in a blackbox way.

more modular way. There are several aspects to this question. We will discuss easy ones first and then come to the question of a more modular proof, which is the main motivation for this paper.

The trivial answer is that we could have left out some operators and then added them again in a separate paper as in [8]. Clearly the text would be much shorter if only encryption, application data, and lists would be retained as a minimum repertoire for building nested encryption terms of the Dolev-Yao style, or similarly for signatures. This would be a simple textual deletion of the subsections dealing with the other operators in the ideal system, the real system, the simulator, and the proof. However, the scientific credibility of the overall framework is indeed much clearer if at least two really different cryptographic systems are present. The reason is that the main point of such term algebras is to define the grammar of correct nested terms and cancellation rules, and to guarantee that terms that cannot be transformed into each other by cancellation rules are always unequal in reality. The facts that terms are type-safe across different cryptographic systems and that no unwanted cancellation can occur must be established by the overall framework, e.g., by defining how the simulator parses received nested abstract messages from the ideal system and received nested concrete terms received from the adversary (including that it cannot always parse them completely). One could also define and name sublibraries of [5], in other terminologies sub-algebras or sub-functionalities, corresponding to textual subsets as described in the previous paragraph. However, this is not much use, because a protocol designer needing only a subset of the operators is not bothered by the presence of additional operators.

However, another version of the modularization question is of more interest. This question is why the proof would not become simpler by using a low-level ideal signature system similar to the low-level ideal encryption system that is used. In the following, we show the functionality that we used in prior versions of the proof and why we removed it again, although it was correct in itself. By "low-level" we mean that the interface of the ideal system is not yet abstract in the sense needed for current automatic tools, and as in Dolev-Yao models. For encryption, such low-level ideal functionalities were introduced in [33, Section 5.3.1] and [10]. For signatures, formalizing and proving an ideal version is actually easier because their security property is an integrity property. Their established cryptographic definition is from [19]. It was known since [30,31] that such properties can be formulated abstractly, e.g., in temporal logic. A similar formulation for authentication is known from [35], but without cryptographic proofs with respect to it. In essence, a low-level ideal system for signatures combines the real signature functionality with a system-internal verification whether the desired integrity property is still fulfilled. We will call this the integrity idealization paradigm. Such an idealization was first made in [26] for symmetric authentication. A somewhat similar ideal signature system was presented in [10], with variations in [13,14]. However, the precise approach taken there cannot be used to construct nested Dolev-Yao style terms, because while a term $\mathsf{E}_{pke}(\mathsf{sign}_{sks}(m))$ in reality keeps m secret from the adversary even if sent over an insecure connection, its mere construction by an honest participant would give m to the adversary in these ideal functionalities.

In the following, we present an ideal low-level signature system that could be used as a submodule in the cryptographic implementation of the library from [5]. However, we also show that using it would make the overall proof of that library (or of the addition of signature schemes to that library if one first restricted it to encryption) more complicated instead of simpler. While this argument necessarily depends on the proof technique used in [5], an important aspect depends solely on the simulator, and not on the details of the cryptographic bisimulation, so that it does not seem easy to circumvent. A low-level signature system similar to the one presented here was also developed in [11] based on initial joint discussions.

2   A Low-Level Ideal Signature System and Its Realization

In this section, we present an ideal system which, at a low level of abstraction, offers the functionality of a secure signature scheme in a reactive and composable fashion. Essentially, it stores which keys belong to honest users and which messages the users signed with these keys, and it never accepts signatures that are supposedly made with one of these keys on different messages, i.e., forgeries.

2.1   Underlying Cryptographic Definition

As cryptographic primitive, we use a signature system secure against adaptive chosen-message attacks [19]. Further, we assume that it uses memory about previously signed messages only in the form of a counter. Besides memoryless signature schemes, this class comprises important provably secure signature schemes such as [19,34,18,15,16]. While efficient implementations of such signature schemes also store a path in a tree at any time, in theory such a path or any other function of random values chosen during earlier applications of sign_{sk} is equivalent to just a counter, because the random values can be regarded as part of the secret key sk and thus as chosen during key generation. At the same time, this class of signature schemes excludes pathologic cases that could not be used safely in a normal Dolev-Yao style library, e.g., if every signature divulges the history of all previous signatures with the same key. A proof that secure signature systems with this pathologic property exist and that they can make applications insecure is given in [7]. We summarize the GMR definition for this subclass in the following two definitions.

Definition 1. *(Signature Schemes) A signature scheme is a triple* ($\mathsf{gen}, \mathsf{sign}, \mathsf{test}$) *of polynomial-time algorithms, where* gen *and* sign *are probabilistic.* gen *takes an input* $(1^k, 1^s)$ *with* $k, s \in \mathbb{N}$, *where* k *denotes a security parameter and* s *the desired maximum number of signatures, and outputs a pair* (sk, pk) *of a secret signing key and a public test key in* $\{0,1\}^+$. sign *takes such a secret key, a counter* $c \in \{1, \dots, s\}$, *and a message* $m \in \{0,1\}^+$ *as inputs and produces* *a signature in* $\{0,1\}^+$. *We write this* sig $\leftarrow$ sign$_{sk,c}(m)$. *Similarly, we write verification as* $b := $ test$_{pk}(m, sig)$ *with* $b \in \{$true, false$\}$. *If the result is* true, *we say that the signature is* valid *for* m. *For a correctly generated key pair, a correctly generated signature for a message* m *must always be valid for* m. $\diamond$

Security of a signature scheme is defined against existential forgery under adaptive chosen-message attacks:

Definition 2. *(Signature Security) Given a signature scheme* (gen, sign, test) *and a polynomial* $s \in \mathbb{N}[x]$, *a signature oracle* O_s *is defined as follows: It has variables* sk, pk *and a counter* c *initialized with* 0, *and the following transition rules:*

- *First generate a key pair* $(sk, pk) \leftarrow$ gen$(1^k, 1^{s(k)})$ *and output* pk.
- *On input* (sign, m) *with* $m \in \{0,1\}^+$, *and if* $c < s(k)$, *set* $c := c + 1$ *and return sig* $\leftarrow$ sign$_{sk,c}(m)$.

The signature scheme is called existentially unforgeable under adaptive chosen-message attack *if for every polynomial* s *and every probabilistic polynomial-time machine* A$_{\text{sig}}$ *that interacts with* O_s *the following holds: The probability is negligible (in* k*) that* A$_{\text{sig}}$ *finally outputs two values* m *and sig (meant as a forged signature for the message* m*) with* test$_{pk}(m, sig) = $ true *and where* m *is not among the messages previously signed by the signature oracle.* $\diamond$

2.2   The Low-Level Ideal System

We now present an ideal signature system that, at a low level of abstraction, summarizes the functionality guaranteed by the cryptographic definition. It uses a list *keys* of key tuples belonging to honest users and a list *signed* of message tuples honestly signed with these keys. Using lookup in these lists, it never accepts forgeries, i.e., signatures on other messages that are supposedly made with one of these keys.

We define this by an ideal machine whose honest users are, without loss of generality, numbered $\{1, ..., n\}$. Its ports from and to user u are in$_{\text{sig},u}$? and out$_{\text{sig},u}$!.[2]

Definition 3 (Low-level Ideal Signature Machine). *Let a signature scheme* (gen, sign, test) *and parameters* $n \in \mathbb{N}$ *and* $s \in \mathbb{N}[x]$ *be given. A corresponding ideal signature machine* Sig$_{\text{bw\_id},n,s}$ *is defined as follows:*

It maintains two initially empty lists keys and signed. The transition function is given by the following rules. Let u *be the index of the port* in$_{\text{sig},u}$? *where the current input occurs; the resulting output goes to* out$_{\text{sig},u}$!.

---

[2] The representation of the Dolev-Yao-style library in [5] is based on the system model from [33], containing details of the state-transition model used for abstract functionalities and its realization by interacting Turing machines. Ports correspond to individual input or output tapes in the Turing machine realization. We use the same model here, but omit some notation although it would allow a more compact presentation.

- On input (generate): Set $(sk, pk) \leftarrow \text{gen}(1^k, 1^{s(k)})$, add the tuple $(u, sk, pk, 0)$ to the list keys, and output pk.
- On input (sign, pk, m): Retrieve a tuple $(u, sk, pk, c) \in$ keys with the given u and pk. If none or more than one exist or if $c = s(k)$, return the error symbol $\downarrow$. Else set $c := c + 1$, i.e., increase the signature counter for this key in keys. Then set $sig \leftarrow \text{sign}_{sk,c}(m)$, add the pair (pk, m) to the list signed, and output sig.
- On input (test, pk, m, sig): Retrieve a tuple $(v, sk, pk, c) \in$ keys with the given pk. If none or more than one exist, output $\text{test}_{pk}(m, sig)$. Else if the pair (pk, m) exists in signed, then output $\text{test}_{pk}(m, sig)$, else false.

Other inputs are ignored. We omit the indices n, s of $\text{Sig}_{\text{low\_id}, n, s}$ where they are irrelevant. $\diamond$

The low-level ideal machine never outputs secret keys. For signing, user u inputs the public key to designate the desired private key, and the machine verifies internally that the key tuple belongs to u. The test function is a normal signature test for unknown public keys (typically keys generated by the adversary). For known public keys, the low-level ideal machine first verifies that the message was indeed signed with this key, and then it additionally verifies that the signature presented is valid. In the long version of this paper [6], we consider several variants of the low-level ideal machine for capturing, e.g., memory-less signature schemes, schemes with fixed-length keys, schemes containing explicit polynomial bounds, or scheduling variants to model local sub-routine behavior.

The main difference to the signature functionality in [10] is that the adversary learns nothing about what honest users sign. In the notation from [33] used here, this would show up as outputs at an adversary port $\text{out}_{\text{sig},a}!$ during individual transitions, e.g., an output (m, sig) during signing.

The low-level ideal machine formally depends on the real system, like the first instantiation of this paradigm in [26]. This could be alleviated by the technique from [12] of letting the adversary choose the algorithms, so that the overall low-level ideal functionality comprises all possible instantiations. However, in all use cases known to us it is not necessary: One can either assume given algorithms because the low-level idealization is only used to prove a larger system, e.g., like the algorithm-dependent low-level encryption idealization is used to prove the algorithm-independent cryptographic library in [5]. Or a really abstract idealization fits better because arguing about the evaluation of an arbitrary algorithm input by an adversary is far beyond the kind of theories implemented in current automated proof tools. In particular, cryptographic objects that would be output by such arbitrary algorithms can be addressed by handles (names, pointers) in such an abstraction, as in [5].

2.3   Cryptographic Realization and Security

The claimed cryptographic realization of the low-level ideal signature functionality is the natural use of digital signatures in a distributed system, i.e., it consists of a separate machine Sig_u for each user u, and each machine signs and tests in the normal way. Together, these machines offer the same ports and accept the same inputs as the ideal machine.

Definition 4 (Real Signature Machines). *Let a signature scheme* (gen, sign, test) *and parameters $u \leq n \in \mathbb{N}$ and $s \in \mathbb{N}[x]$ be given. Then the low-level ideal signature machine* $\mathsf{Sig}_{u,s}$ *is defined as follows. It has ports* $\mathsf{in}_{\mathsf{sig},u}?$ *and* $\mathsf{out}_{\mathsf{sig},u}!$ *and maintains an initially empty list* keys_u. *The transition function is given by the following rules.*

- *On input* (generate): *Set* $(sk, pk) \leftarrow \mathsf{gen}(1^k, 1^{s(k)})$, *add the tuple* $(sk, pk, 0)$ *to* keys_u, *and output* pk.
- *On input* (sign, pk, m): *Retrieve a tuple* $(sk, pk, c) \in \mathsf{keys}_u$ *with the given* pk. *If none or more than one exist or if* $c = s(k)$, *return* $\downarrow$. *Else set* $c := c + 1$ *and output* $sig \leftarrow \mathsf{sign}_{sk,c}(m)$.
- *On input* (test, pk, m, sig): *output* $\mathsf{test}_{pk}(m, sig)$.

Other inputs are ignored. We denote the set of these machines by $\mathsf{Sig}_{\mathsf{real},n,s}$, *and omit the indices* n, s *(also for* $\mathsf{Sig}_{u,s}$*) where they are irrelevant.* ◇

We now claim that the real signature system is as secure as the low-level ideal system. In slight abuse of notation of [33], we can write this as follows.

Theorem 1. *Given a secure signature system according to Definitions 1 and 2, we have*

$$\forall n \in \mathbb{N} \forall s \in \mathbb{N}[x] : \mathsf{Sig}_{\mathsf{real},n,s} \geq^{\mathsf{poly}} \mathsf{Sig}_{\mathsf{lw\_id},n,s}.$$

This holds with blackbox simulatability; actually no simulator is necessary which corresponds to the notion of observational equivalence as introduced in [25]. □

We omit the proof due to space constraints and refer to the long version of this paper [6].

3 Using the Low-Level Ideal Signature System in a Dolev-Yao-Style Cryptographic Library

We now discuss why the use of low-level idealized signature machines in the proof of the Dolev-Yao style cryptographic library in [9] does not work quite as expected and actually makes the proof more complicated.

The proof of the Dolev-Yao-style library is based on a simulator. For all polynomial-time honest users and adversaries on the real system, the simulator achieves essentially the same effect in the ideal system. More precisely, it achieves that the views of the honest users in both systems are indistinguishable. This is the standard blackbox technique for showing that a system is as secure as another one in a sense that guarantees composability, as first formalized in detail for reactive, i.e., multi-step systems in [32].

A possible use of low-level ideal signature machines in the overall proof is shown in Figure 1. First the real cryptographic library is rewritten to use the real signature machines Sig_u (Step 1 in Figure 1). This happens after the step of rewriting with encryption machines from [9], which we omit in Figure 1.[3]

---

[3] Both these steps are obsolete if one defines the real library directly with these functionalities, but we first presented an entirely real version in [5] for concreteness.

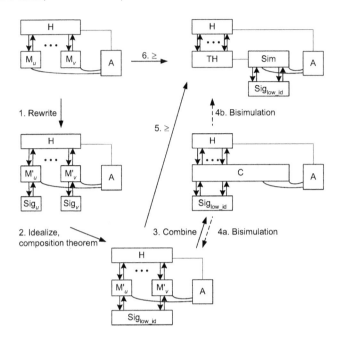

Fig. 1. Overview of a potential proof of the Dolev-Yao-style library with signature machines

Next, the real signature machines Sig_u can jointly be replaced by their low-level ideal counterpart $\mathsf{Sig}_{\text{low\_id}}$ according to a composition theorem, in this case of [33] (Step 2 in Figure 1). The simulator can immediately be defined with the signature machine $\mathsf{Sig}_{\text{low\_id}}$ (upper right system in Figure 1).

The major part of the proof shows that the simulator is correct, both in general aspects like parsing, type determination, and handling of unparsable terms, and in handling the individual cryptographic operations. For this, we first define a combined system C that essentially has the combined ideal and real state space (Step 3 in Figure 1). Now it would also get the signature submachine. Then so-called cryptographic bisimulations are shown between the combined system and the real system with the signature and encryption machines, and with the ideal system with the simulator (Steps 4a and 4b in Figure 1). These bisimulations include a definition of error sets, containing runs where the simulation does not work. They also include an embedded information-flow analysis whose necessity will become clear in Section 3.2. Finally, cryptographic reduction proofs show that the error sets are negligible, based on the information-flow analysis. This yields that the rewritten real system is as secure as the ideal system (Step 5 in Figure 1), and by transitivity of "as secure as" this also holds for the original real system (Step 6 in Figure 1).

3.1   More Complicated Bisimulation by Diverging States

Our main argument for deciding to delete the signature machines again was that, surprisingly to us grown up with the idea that modularization simplifies things, they make the bisimulation more complicated. A long part of the proof in [5] is the standard aspects of the bisimulations. This comprises the definition of mappings from combined states to real and ideal states, respectively, as well as invariants of all three systems (combined, real and ideal). It is then shown that, given mapped states fulfilling the invariants, every input from the adversary or honest users leads to equal outputs and to mapped next states with equal probability distributions, and that the invariants are retained (except for the error sets).

Usually, the more machines one has in a bisimulation, the more complicated the state spaces and invariants get, i.e., modularization is typically not useful. Nevertheless, one might hope that introducing low-level ideal signature machines is useful because their states would simply be mapped identically, and their state transitions would trivially retain this mapping.[4] However, this is not so. The individual signatures are not made in the same order in the simulator as in the real system. For instance, honest user u might make a signature sig on a message m, encrypt it as $\mathsf{E}_{pk}(sig)$ with a key pk of another honest user, and send it over an insecure channel. Now the signature exists in $\mathsf{Sig}_{\mathrm{bw\_id}}$ in the real system, i.e., a counter has been updated and the message m is stored in $signed$. However, the simulator only gets an abstract ciphertext from the ideal system and simulates it by $\mathsf{E}_{pk}(m_{sim})$ for a fixed message m_{sim} (using its low-level ideal encryption system). There is no way for the simulator to know at this point that it should simulate a signature. The signature will only be simulated if it is ever sent in a form readable for the adversary.

Hence although the signature subsystems in the overall systems to be compared are functionally equal, they are usually in different states. Hence they are just an additional burden on the bisimulation.[5]

3.2   Other Error Sets and Information-Flow Analysis Remain

The low-level idealization of signatures certainly avoids the error set corresponding to signature forgeries in the bisimulations, and the reduction proof showing that this set is negligible. However, this is a short and simple part of the overall proof.

Avoiding error sets would mainly be useful if one could get rid of all of them, and thus have "classical" probabilistic bisimulations. Towards this goal, one could introduce a low-level ideal nonce system that excludes nonce collisions, while still outputting real nonces. This system falls under the integrity-

---

[4] However, even in this case one would need invariants about the consistency between the state of the overall "term machines" and the signature machines.

[5] Comparing Figure 1 with the corresponding figure in [5], one sees that encryption machines were not used in the simulator and the combined system. This is for the same reason of diverging states.

idealization paradigm: Equip a real nonce system with a virtual, global non-repetition test over the nonces of all honest parties.

However, one also has to demonstrate that the adversary cannot guess certain values. Here the low-level ideal systems do not help. For instance, with both real nonces and the low-level ideal nonce system, it is trivial that the adversary cannot guess a nonce of an honest participant if he obtained no information about it (except with exponentially small probability). But whether or not he obtained such information depends on all potential nested terms that were sent containing this nonce, i.e., this belongs to the overall proof and not to the proof of the subsystem. Concretely, this proof aspect is the static information-flow analysis embedded in the cryptographic bisimulation, a novel proof technique in [9].

In other words, idealizing signatures and nonces only eliminates the easier parts of the final reduction proofs and of the non-standard aspects of the bisimulations.

3.3   Simulator Needs Reordered Signatures

The example in Section 3.1 also shows that the simple low-level ideal system from Section 2.2, derived from the GMR definition by integrity idealization, is not quite the functionality we need in a reactive scenario.

If one only considers the real system, the following additional property is needed: If the adversary only sees a subset (adaptively chosen) of the signatures made by a signer, this divulges nothing about other signatures. This is already discussed in [7]. It is shown there that this property follows from the GMR definition as restricted in our Definition 1, but that the concrete security can be improved by additional randomization. In the cryptographic library of [5], such an additional randomization is present in the real system anyway.

For proceeding as in Section 3, one also has to consider the simulator. The example in Section 3.1 shows that the simulator has to make signatures with an arbitrary non-repeating sequence of counter values. Thus, to define the simulator with a low-level ideal signature system, that system must take the counter value as an input, instead of incrementing it internally as done in reality (this problem disappears for memory-less underlying signature systems). Hence for the overall proof technique with signature submachines, we must prove that the underlying signature schemes are secure for this behavior. (The proof in [5] does not need this aspect of a signature scheme.) We are not aware that this follows from Definition 2, although we believe that it holds for all known systems (because the tree constructions are essentially symmetric if one considers all randomness as chosen in advance, e.g., the third leaf does not depend on the first leaf any more than vice versa). Nevertheless, this is not easy to point out in, say, the proof in [19].

4   Outlook on Integrity Idealization Paradigm

We have repeatedly mentioned integrity idealization as a common concept for defining certain low-level ideal functionalities. In the long version of this paper, we show that this concept can be formalized and used to mechanically construct many simple ideal systems and the corresponding proofs. Due to space constraints, we only give the basic ideas of this formulation here: Typically, a cryptographic primitive is defined as a tuple of algorithms $(A_1, \ldots, A_t)$, such as $(\mathsf{gen}, \mathsf{sign}, \mathsf{test})$ for signatures, with certain parameter domains. The security definition is typically given by an "oracle" (such as the signature oracle O_s) interacting with an adversary, where an oracle call corresponds to an algorithm invocation. A typical integrity property can be (re-)written as a property of the trace of in- and outputs of the oracle, where the first violation can only occur by an output of the oracle. This makes sense particularly for cases like signatures where the adversary only wins if he can successfully cheat an honest participant with a forgery. Other examples of such integrity properties are all other authentication properties, the collision-freeness of a nonce system, and the correctness properties of a payment system. For a system defined by such integrity requirements, we define the corresponding ideal system by one joint machine, corresponding closely to the oracle, that interacts with the honest users and the adversary and that, before every output, verifies that the output does not violate the integrity properties. Thus it fulfills the integrity properties perfectly by definition. This gives a general underpinning for using integrity properties in proofs that otherwise use a composition theorem, since an arbitrary real system fulfilling an arbitrary integrity property is automatically as secure as a mechanically derivable low-level idealization.

5   Conclusion

We have presented a low-level ideal signature functionality that can be realized by every secure signature scheme that uses memory only for a counter and random values, without additional techniques like padding or randomization.

However, we also showed multiple pitfalls when using such a low-level idealization for proving a larger protocol. While we showed this for the specific example of our cryptographic library, we believe that the problems are of a general nature. For instance, every protocol where some signatures are only sent in encrypted form has the problem from Section 3.1, and if such signatures become known to the adversary later in a different order than they were made, the problems from Section 3.3 are added. (Recall that prior low-level ideal signature systems cannot handle this case at all.) In many cases, it will be simpler to work either with a real abstraction, such as the cryptographic library from [5], or directly with the integrity properties.

References

1. M. Abadi and J. Jürjens. Formal eavesdropping and its computational interpretation. In *Proc. 4th International Symposium on Theoretical Aspects of Computer Software (TACS)*, pages 82–94, 2001.

2. M. Abadi and P. Rogaway. Reconciling two views of cryptography: The computational soundness of formal encryption. In *Proc. 1st IFIP International Conference on Theoretical Computer Science*, vol. 1872 of *LNCS*, pages 3–22. Springer, 2000.
3. M. Backes and B. Pfitzmann. A cryptographically sound security proof of the Needham-Schroeder-Lowe public-key protocol. In *Proc. 23rd Conference on Foundations of Software Technology and Theoretical Computer Science (FSTTCS)*, pages 1–12, 2003.
4. M. Backes and B. Pfitzmann. Symmetric encryption in a simulatable Dolev-Yao style cryptographic library. In *Proc. 17th IEEE Computer Security Foundations Workshop (CSFW)*, 2004.
5. M. Backes, B. Pfitzmann, and M. Waidner. A composable cryptographic library with nested operations (extended abstract). In *Proc. 10th ACM Conference on Computer and Communications Security*, pages 220–230, 2003. Full version in IACR Cryptology ePrint Archive 2003/015, Jan. 2003.
6. M. Backes, B. Pfitzmann, and M. Waidner. Low-level ideal signatures and general integrity idealization. Research Report RZ 3511, IBM Research, Nov. 2003.
7. M. Backes, B. Pfitzmann, and M. Waidner. Reactively secure signature schemes. In *Proc. 6th Information Security Conference (ISC)*, pages 84–95, 2003.
8. M. Backes, B. Pfitzmann, and M. Waidner. Symmetric authentication within a simulatable cryptographic library. In *Proc. 8th European Symposium on Research in Computer Security (ESORICS)*, *LNCS* 2808, pages 271–290. Springer, 2003.
9. M. Backes, B. Pfitzmann, and M. Waidner. A universally composable cryptographic library. IACR Cryptology ePrint Archive 2003/015, Jan. 2003.
10. R. Canetti. Universally composable security: A new paradigm for cryptographic protocols. In *Proc. 42nd IEEE Symposium on Foundations of Computer Science*, pages 136–145, 2001.
11. R. Canetti. On universally composable notions of security for signature, certification and authorization. In *Proc. 17th IEEE Computer Security Foundations Workshop (CSFW)*, 2004.
12. R. Canetti and S. Goldwasser. An efficient threshold public key cryptosystem secure against adaptive chosen ciphertext attack. In *Advances in Cryptology: EUROCRYPT '99*, volume 1592 of *LNCS*, pages 90–106. Springer, 1999.
13. R. Canetti and H. Krawczyk. Universally composable notions of key exchange and secure channels (extended abstract). In *Advances in Cryptology: EUROCRYPT 2002*, volume 2332 of *LNCS*, pages 337–351. Springer, 2002.
14. R. Canetti and T. Rabin. Universal composition with joint state. In *Advances in Cryptology: CRYPTO 2003*, volume 2729 of *LNCS*, pages 265–281. Springer, 2003.
15. R. Cramer and I. Damgård. Secure signature schemes based on interactive protocols. In *Advances in Cryptology: CRYPTO '95*, volume 963 of *LNCS*, pages 297–310. Springer, 1995.
16. R. Cramer and I. Damgård. New generation of secure and practical RSA-based signatures. In *Advances in Cryptology: CRYPTO '96*, volume 1109 of *LNCS*, pages 173–185. Springer, 1996.
17. D. Dolev and A. C. Yao. On the security of public key protocols. *IEEE Transactions on Information Theory*, 29(2):198–208, 1983.
18. C. Dwork and M. Naor. An efficient existentially unforgeable signature scheme and its applications. *Journal of Cryptology*, 11(3):187–208, 1998.
19. S. Goldwasser, S. Micali, and R. L. Rivest. A digital signature scheme secure against adaptive chosen-message attacks. *SIAM Journal on Computing*, 17(2):281–308, 1988.

20. J. Herzog. Computational soundness of formal adversaries. Master Thesis, MIT, 2002.
21. J. Herzog, M. Liskov, and S. Micali. Plaintext awareness via key registration. In *Advances in Cryptology: CRYPTO 2003*, volume 2729 of *LNCS*, pages 548–564. Springer, 2003.
22. R. Impagliazzo and B. M. Kapron. Logics for reasoning about cryptographic constructions. In *Proc. 44th IEEE Symposium on Foundations of Computer Science*, pages 372–381, 2003.
23. P. Laud. Semantics and program analysis of computationally secure information flow. In *Proc. 10th European Symposium on Programming (ESOP)*, pages 77–91, 2001.
24. P. Laud. Symmetric encryption in automatic analyses for confidentiality against active adversaries. In *Proc. 25th IEEE Symposium on Security & Privacy*, pages 71–85, 2004.
25. P. Lincoln, J. Mitchell, M. Mitchell, and A. Scedrov. A probabilistic poly-time framework for protocol analysis. In *Proc. 5th ACM Conference on Computer and Communications Security*, pages 112–121, 1998.
26. P. Lincoln, J. Mitchell, M. Mitchell, and A. Scedrov. Probabilistic polynomial-time equivalence and security analysis. In *Proc. 8th Symposium on Formal Methods Europe (FME 1999)*, volume 1708 of *LNCS*, pages 776–793. Springer, 1999.
27. D. Micciancio and B. Warinschi. Soundness of formal encryption in the presence of active adversaries. In *Proc. 1st Theory of Cryptography Conference (TCC)*, volume 2951 of *LNCS*, pages 133–151. Springer, 2004.
28. J. Mitchell, M. Mitchell, and A. Scedrov. A linguistic characterization of bounded oracle computation and probabilistic polynomial time. In *Proc. 39th IEEE Symposium on Foundations of Computer Science*, pages 725–733, 1998.
29. J. Mitchell, M. Mitchell, A. Scedrov, and V. Teague. A probabilistic polynominal-time process calculus for analysis of cryptographic protocols (preliminary report). *Electronic Notes in Theoretical Computer Science*, 47:1–31, 2001.
30. B. Pfitzmann. Sorting out signature schemes. In *Proc. 1st ACM Conference on Computer and Communications Security*, pages 74–85, 1993.
31. B. Pfitzmann. *Digital Signature Schemes – General Framework and Fail-Stop Signatures*, volume 1100 of *LNCS*. Springer, 1996.
32. B. Pfitzmann and M. Waidner. Composition and integrity preservation of secure reactive systems. In *Proc. 7th ACM Conference on Computer and Communications Security*, pages 245–254, 2000.
33. B. Pfitzmann and M. Waidner. A model for asynchronous reactive systems and its application to secure message transmission. In *Proc. 22nd IEEE Symposium on Security & Privacy*, pages 184–200, 2001.
34. J. Rompel. One-way functions are necessary and sufficient for secure signatures. In *Proc. 22nd Annual ACM Symposium on Theory of Computing (STOC)*, pages 387–394, 1990.
35. P. Syverson and C. Meadows. A logical language for specifying cryptographic protocol requirements. In *Proc. 14th IEEE Symposium on Security & Privacy*, pages 165–177, 2003.

Cryptanalysis of a Verifiably Committed Signature Scheme Based on GPS and RSA

Julien Cathalo*, Benoît Libert**, and Jean-Jacques Quisquater

Université catholique de Louvain
Place du Levant 3
1348 Louvain-la-Neuve, Belgium
{cathalo,libert,jjq}@dice.ucl.ac.be

Abstract. This paper describes a powerful attack on a verifiably committed signature scheme based on GPS and RSA proposed in Financial Cryptography 2001. Given any partial signature, the attacker can extract the corresponding full signature. The attack works provided the attacker previously obtained a full signature of a special form, which can be done simply by eavesdropping a very small number of full signatures. For example, with the originally recommended parameters choice, 66% of the signatures are of this form. As a consequence, two "fair" protocols using this primitive do not satisfy the fairness property. Of independent interest, our attack shows that special attention should be paid when building cryptographic protocols from GPS and RSA.

Keywords: Verifiably Committed Signatures, Optimistic Fair Exchange, GPS Signature, Cryptanalysis

1 Introduction

Consider the following situation. Alice wants to buy a CD on Bob's web site, but Alice and Bob do not trust each other. Alice does not want to sign the payment unless she is sure that she will get the CD, and Bob does not want to send the CD unless he is sure that Alice is going to pay him. This is an example of an important issue in electronic commerce and digital rights management: the problem of exchanging items and information in a fair way, which is known as fair exchange. For such situations, a trusted third party, Charlie, is always required. A trivial fair exchange protocol would involve Charlie in any step of the exchange, but it is clear that this solution is not practical. It is thus natural to try and minimize the intervention of Charlie, by designing protocols where Charlie only intervenes in case of problem. Such protocols are called *optimistic* fair exchange protocols.

Several solutions have been proposed to achieve this [1,2,3,4,5,6,13]. They all rely on some cryptographic primitive allowing the commitment to a signature. This notion was generalized by Dodis and Reyzin in [7], who proposed a

---

* Supported partly by *Communauté francaise de Belgique - Actions de Recherche Concertées* and partly by *Walloon Region / WIST-MAIS project*
** Supported by *DGTRE / First Europe project*

K. Zhang and Y. Zheng (Eds.): ISC 2004, LNCS 3225, pp. 52–60, 2004.

model for non-interactive fair exchange protocols. The model relies on a kind of cryptographic primitives called *verifiably committed signatures* that generalize verifiably encrypted signatures and two-signatures.

The principle of verifiably committed signatures can be summarized as follows. The participants in the protocol are Alice the signer, Bob the verifier, and Charlie the semi-trusted arbitrator. The signer Alice wants to give Bob a signature on a message m, but only if Bob fulfills some obligation I in exchange. Bob does not want to fulfill I until he is sure that he will eventually get Alice's signature on m. In order to do this, Alice first computes a partial signature σ' on m. Bob can check that this partial signature corresponds to Alice's valid signature on m, but cannot extract the valid signature from the partial one. Then Bob fulfills I. Alice then sends the final signature σ on m back to Bob. In case Alice aborts the protocol, Bob can call the arbitrator Charlie, and if Bob can prove that he fulfilled I, Charlie extracts the full signature from the partial one. Thus Charlie is only needed in case of problem.

We recall that a verifiably committed signature scheme should satisfy the following (informal) security requirements [7]:

- *Security against Alice:* Alice should not be able to produce a valid partial signature σ' which Charlie cannot convert into a valid full signature σ.
- *Security against Bob:* Bob should not be able to produce a valid partial signature σ' which he did not get from Alice, and Bob should not be able to produce a valid full signature σ which he did not get from Alice or Charlie.
- *Security against Charlie:* Charlie should not be able to produce a valid full signature σ without seeing a valid partial signature σ' computed by Alice.

In [12], Markowitch and Saeednia proposed an optimistic fair exchange scheme. The scheme relies on a verifiably committed signature scheme that they introduce[1]. The verifiably committed signature scheme is constructed from the basic RSA encryption scheme [15] and the GPS signature scheme [9,14], and was also used later in the context of a non-repudiation protocol [11].

In this paper, we show that the security against Bob is not satisfied in the verifiably committed signature from [12]. We describe an attack allowing to extract the full signature σ from a partial signature σ'. Our attack is extremely efficient (it only requires that the attacker previously obtained a very small number of full signatures, and has a computational cost of a few exponentiations), and breaks the fairness property of two protocols [12,11].

Of independent interest, we show how the combination of GPS and RSA can be very sensitive to attacks. Informally, the problem of extracting a RSA root of a GPS commitment has some poor security properties: there is a (non-negligible) subset of the instances of this problem for which the knowledge of a solution allows the computation of the solution for *any* instance.

The remaining of the paper is organized as follows: section 2 briefly describes the basic GPS signature scheme, section 3 describes the verifiably committed

---

[1] The committed signature scheme was not presented separately but appeared as an element of the optimistic fair exchange protocol; nevertheless, from the claimed security properties, it is clear that it is a verifiably committed signature scheme.

signature scheme based on GPS and RSA, section 4 explains the attack and discusses its efficiency, section 5 describes some attempts at repairing the scheme, and section 6 concludes.

2   The GPS Signature Scheme

In this section we briefly describe the GPS signature scheme. It is derived from the GPS identification scheme [9,14] using the standard method from Fiat and Shamir [8]. It works as follows.

Setup. The TTP generates an RSA modulus $n = pq$ where $p = 2p'+1, q = 2q'+$
1 and p, p', q, q' are primes. It chooses three integers A, B and S such that $A >> BS$, and a hash function h such that the outputs of h are uniformly distributed over $[0, B[$. The TTP chooses an integer α of large order modulo n. It publishes n, α, h.
To generate her key pair, the signer chooses a random integer $x \in [0, S[$ as her secret key and computes $y = \alpha^x \bmod n$ as her public key.

Sig. To compute a signature on a message m, the signer takes a random integer $r \in [0, A[$ and computes $t = \alpha^r \bmod n$, and $z = r + h(t, m)x$. The signature is (t, z).

Ver. To verify a signature (t, z) on m, the verifier checks that $h(t, m) \in [0, B[$, that $z \in [0, A + (B - 1)(S - 1)[$ and that $\alpha^z \equiv ty^{h(t,m)} \pmod{n}$.

The security of the scheme against existential forgeries under adaptive chosen message attacks was proven (in the random oracle model) in [14] under the hypothesis that computing discrete logarithms with short exponents modulo n is hard.

3   Description of the Committed Signature Scheme

This section describes the verifiably committed signature scheme of [12]. In this scheme, the idea is to use GPS signatures combined with the RSA encryption primitive, a valid signature being a GPS signature along with the RSA decryption of the corresponding commitment. As a consequence, the hardness of extracting a full signature from a partial signature implicitly relies on the problem of computing the RSA decryption of a GPS commitment given the corresponding challenge and answer, but without knowing nor the GPS private key or the RSA private key.

We now describe the committed signature scheme according to the formal model of [7].

Setup. Charlie generates an RSA modulus $n = pq$ where $p = 2p'+1, q = 2q'+1$
and p, p', q, q' are primes. He chooses a hash function h. Charlie chooses an integer α of order $p'q'$. He also chooses an integer c coprime to $p'q'$, and computes $d = c^{-1} \bmod p'q'$. Charlie publishes n, α, h and c. Charlie's secret arbitration key is d.
To generate her key pair, Alice chooses a random integer x as her secret key and computes $y = \alpha^x \bmod n$ as her public key.

PSig. To compute a partial signature on a message m, Alice takes a random integer r and computes $t = \alpha^{cr} \bmod n$, and $z = cr + h(t, m)x$. The partial signature is (t, z).

PVer. To verify a partial signature (t, z) on m, Bob - or any verifier - checks if $\alpha^z \equiv t y^{h(t,m)} \pmod{n}$.

Sig. To compute a full signature on m corresponding to her partial signature (t, z), Alice computes $t' = \alpha^r \bmod n$, with the value of r used in the partial signature process. The full signature is (t', z) with the same z than in the partial signature.

Ver. To verify a full signature, (t', z) on m, Bob - or any verifier - checks if $\alpha^z \equiv t'^c y^{h(t'^c \bmod n, m)} \pmod{n}$.

Res. In case Alice refuses to open her signature to Bob, Charlie uses the partial signature (t, z) and his secret arbitration key d to compute the corresponding final signature (t', z) where $t' = t^d \bmod n$.

The signature protocol is as follows: Alice computes a partial signature (t, z), where $t = \alpha^{cr} \bmod n$, sends this partial signature to Bob, and stores the value $t' = \alpha^r \bmod n$. Bob checks that $\alpha^z \equiv t y^{h(t,m)} \pmod{n}$, then fulfills his obligation I. Alice sends t' to Bob, and Bob checks that $t'^c \equiv t \pmod{n}$.

Remarks:

1. Notice that this verifiably committed signature scheme does not exactly fit the model of [7], since both the Sig and Ver algorithm depend on the public arbitration key c.
2. Since $z \bmod c = h(t, m)x \bmod c$, where $z, h(t, m)$ and c are public, it is clear that some information on $x \bmod c$ leaks. For this reason, the authors of [12] recommend to take $c = 3$ to minimize the amount of information leaked on the secret x.

4   Extracting Full Signatures from Partial Signatures

In this section we describe an attack that allows an attacker to extract the full signature (t', z) on m from the partial signature (t, z). The main idea of the attack is that computing t', the c-th root of $t = \alpha^z y^{-e} \bmod n$, is simple when one knows the c-th root of $\alpha^{ez \bmod c} y^{-e \bmod c} \bmod n$ thanks to the euclidian division. We now explain this more in the detail.

4.1   Preliminary: The F Function

Let F be the application from $[0, c[$ to $[0, n[$ defined by:

$$F(\overline{e}) = \left(\alpha^{\overline{e}x \bmod c} y^{-\overline{e}}\right)^d \bmod n$$

We are going to show how the properties of this function allow attacking the scheme. In fact the two first properties already show the insecurity of the scheme for small values of c; thus the third property may be viewed as an enhancement of the attack.

A first remark is that $F(0) = 1$..

Property 1 *Knowing a full signature* (t', z) *allows computing* $F(e \bmod c)$, *where* $e = h(t'^c \bmod n, m)$.

Proof: Since $t'^c \equiv \alpha^z y^{-e} \bmod n$, we have:

$$(t'\alpha^{-(z \text{ div } c)} y^{e \text{ div } c})^c \equiv \alpha^{z \bmod c} y^{-(e \bmod c)} \pmod{n}$$
$$\equiv \alpha^{ex \bmod c} y^{-(e \bmod c)} \pmod{n} \tag{1}$$

Thus $F(e \bmod c) = t'\alpha^{-(z \text{ div } c)} y^{e \text{ div } c} \bmod n$. $\square$

Property 2 *Given a partial signature* (t, z), *the knowledge of* $F(e \bmod c)$ *where* $e = h(t \bmod n, m)$ *allows computing the corresponding full signature* (t', z).

Proof: From equation (1), we have

$$t' = \alpha^{z \text{ div } c} y^{-(e \text{ div } c)} F(e \bmod c) \bmod n$$

$\square$

Property 3 *Knowing* $F(e_0 \bmod c)$ *where* $e_0 = h(t_0'^c \bmod n, m)$ *is coprime to* c *for some full signature* (t_0', z_0) *allows computing* $F(e)$ *for any* $e \in [0, c[$.

Proof: We can compute $k = e_0^{-1} e \bmod c$, and we have:

$$F(e_0 \bmod c)^{ck} = \left(\alpha^{e_0 x \bmod c} y^{-e_0}\right)^k \bmod n$$
$$= \left(\alpha^{k(e_0 x \bmod c) \text{ div } c} y^{-(ke_0 \text{ div } c)}\right)^c \alpha^{ke_0 x \bmod c} y^{-(ke_0 \bmod c)} \bmod n$$
$$= \left(\alpha^{k(z_0 \bmod c) \text{ div } c} y^{-(ke_0 \text{ div } c)}\right)^c (F(ke_0 \bmod c))^c \bmod n$$

Thus

$$F(e) = F(ke_0 \bmod c) = F(e_0 \bmod c)^k \alpha^{-(k(z_0 \bmod c) \text{ div } c)} y^{ke_0 \text{ div } c} \bmod n \tag{2}$$

$\square$

4.2   Attack Strategy

The attack proceeds in two steps. In the first step, the attacker eavesdrops a small number of full signatures from the signer. In the second step, he asks the signer any number of committed signatures and extracts the corresponding full signature.

1. In this step, the attacker eavesdrops a number of full signatures until he finds a signature (t_0', z_0) (on a message m_0) such that $e_0 \bmod c$ is coprime with c, where $e_0 = h(t_0'^c \bmod n, m_0)$. Once he has obtained such a signature, he computes $F(e_0 \bmod c)$ and stores the triple $(e_0 \bmod c, z_0 \bmod c, F(e_0 \bmod c))$.

2. In this step, the attacker plays the role of the verifier. Once he gets a committed signature (t, z), he computes $F(e \mod c)$ where $e = h(t \mod n, m)$, using the stored triple $(e_0 \mod c, z_0 \mod c, F(e_0 \mod c))$ and equation (2). He then uses this value of $F(e \mod c)$ to extract the full signature from the committed one, according to property 2. The attacker thus obtains the full signature without fulfilling his obligation. This step obviously succeeds with probability 1, and can be done with any number of committed signatures.

4.3 An Example with Artificially Small Parameters

We take $c = 3$, and very small values for the other parameters. Alice, whose private key is $x = 110$, takes a random $r = 213$, and computes $t = \alpha^{3 \times 213} \mod n$. She computes $h(t, m) = 16$, and $z = cr + h(t, m)x = 3 \times 213 + 16 \times 110 = 2399$. The full signature is t' such that $t'^3 \equiv \alpha^{2339} y^{-16} \mod n$. Since $2339 = 799 \times 3 + 2$ and $16 = 5 \times 3 + 1$, the attacker computes $\tau = t'\alpha^{-799} y^5 \mod n$. This τ is such that $\tau^3 \equiv \alpha^2 y^{-1} \pmod{n}$.

Now, given a partial signature $(\widetilde{t}, \widetilde{z} = 1933)$ such that $h(\widetilde{t}, \widetilde{m}) = 14$, he has $\widetilde{t} = \alpha^{1933} y^{-14} \mod n = \alpha^{3 \times 644 + 1} y^{-3 \times 4 - 2} \mod n$, thus he needs to find a c-th root of $\alpha y^{-2} \mod n$. This root is $\tau^2 \alpha^{-1}$ thanks to equation (2).

Thus the attacker can compute $\widetilde{t}' = \alpha^{644} y^{-4} \tau^2 \alpha^{-1} \mod n$, where $\widetilde{t}'^c \mod n = \widetilde{t}$, that is, $\widetilde{t}'$ is the full signature corresponding to the committed one.

4.4 Efficiency: Discussion on the c Parameter

Since the second step always succeeds once the first step ended successfully, the efficiency of the attack only depends on the number of full signatures the attacker has to obtain in the first step. For each signature (t', z), the probability that $e \mod c$ is coprime with c is $\varphi(c)/c$. Thus the first step succeeds after at most l tries with probability

$$P_l = 1 - \left(1 - \frac{\varphi(c)}{c}\right)^l$$

This formula allows us to evaluate the efficiency of the attack depending on the value of the c parameter.

The $c = 3$ case. It is natural to study this single case since it is the value suggested by the authors. We have $\varphi(3) = 2$, thus the attack succeeds after at most l tries with probability

$$P_l = 1 - \frac{1}{3^l}$$

Thus eavesdropping one signature allows a success probability of 66%, while 5 signatures allow a probability of success of more than 99%.

The $c \le 2^{10}$ case. In [12], it is specified that c must be a very small integer. Thus we can assume that $c < 2^{10}$. To compute a lower bound of $\varphi(c)/c$ for values of c between 2 and 2^{10}, we simply compute all the possible values of $\varphi(c)/c$. The lower bound is reached for $c = 210$. Thus we have that

$$\forall c \in [1, 2^{10}], \quad \frac{\varphi(c)}{c} \ge \frac{\varphi(210)}{210} = \frac{8}{35} \approx 0.22857$$

While with a single signature, the lower bound on the probability of success is already 22%, we can see that, with 10 signatures, we have a probability of success of at least 92%.

5   Attempts to Repair the Scheme

5.1   Increasing the Value of c

A natural idea to repair the scheme, since the efficiency of our attack depends on $\varphi(c)/c$, is to minimize this value by taking a larger and specific value for c. Of course, since $x \bmod c$ leaks during any execution of the protocol, we have to take a larger value for x. More precisely, we have to ensure that x div c is large enough (160 bits) because $y\alpha^{-x\bmod c} = (\alpha^c)^{x \text{ div } c} \pmod{n}$ thus finding x is equivalent to solve the discrete logarithm of $y\alpha^{-x\bmod c} \bmod n$ in basis $\alpha^c \bmod n$. This implies a performance decrease since the size of the commitments must be such that $r >> 2^{|h|}c$.

But we have the following well-known bound: when c is any number such that $c \ge 5$,

$$\varphi(c) \ge \frac{c}{6 \ln \ln c} \tag{3}$$

Thus even if c is 4000 bit long, then 2.1% of the full signatures are such that e is coprime with c. Thus with 33 full signatures the attacker will succeed with probability $1/2$.

In short, taking a larger value for c does not prevent the attack, but just makes it a little less efficient. We conclude that the scheme is insecure for *any* value of c.

5.2   Other Attempts

One might also try to remove some multiplicative properties to prevent the attack, but these multiplicative properties seem necessary to ensure the verifiability of partial signatures.

Another attempt to repair the scheme makes use of non-interactive proofs-of-knowledge. The idea is that the attack is possible because t', the c-th root of t, is revealed by Alice. Thus we keep the same protocol except for the full signature process. Alice proves that she knows t', but this time she does not reveal it. This can be done with a non-interactive zero-knowledge proof-of-knowledge of c-th root of t, such as a non-interactive version of the Guillou-Quisquater [10] protocol, for example. However, this does not lead to an efficient verifiably committed signature scheme.

6 Conclusion

We showed that the security against the verifier was not verified in the committed signature scheme from [12] (also used in [11]) by describing a very simple and fast method to extract a full signature from a partial signature.

This attack is a new example of a well-known fact: constructing a new cryptographic primitive from two secure primitives can lead to a totally insecure result. But, interestingly, we notice that GPS and RSA can be securely combined; in fact, the RSA primitive was already used in the initial design of GPS, with self-certified public keys [9].

We conclude that the security of a cryptographic protocol should not rely on the hardness of computing the RSA decryption of a GPS commitment.

References

1. N. Asokan, V. Shoup, and M. Waidner. Optimistic Fair Exchange of Digital Signatures. In K. Nyberg, editor, *Advances in Cryptology - Eurocrypt 98*, volume 1403 of *Lecture Notes in Computer Science*, pages 591–606. Springer-Verlag, 1998.
2. N. Asokan, V. Shoup, and M. Waidner. Optimistic Fair Exchange of Digital Signatures. *IEEE Journal on Selected Areas in Communication*, 18(4):593–610, 2000.
3. G. Ateniese. Efficient Verifiable Encryption (and Fair Exchange) of Digital Signatures. In G. Tsudik, editor, *Sixth ACM Conference on Computer and Communication Security and Privacy*, pages 138–146. ACM, November 1999.
4. F. Bao, R. Deng, and W. Mao. Efficient and Practical Fair Exchange Protocols with Off-line TTP. In *Proceedings of the IEEE Symposium on Security and Privacy*, pages 77–85, 1998.
5. D. Boneh, C. Gentry, B. Lynn, and H. Shacham. Aggregate and Verifiably Encrypted Signatures from Bilinear Maps. In E. Biham, editor, *Advances in Cryptology - Eurocrypt 2003*, volume 2656 of *Lecture Notes in Computer Science*, pages 416–432. Springer-Verlag, 2003.
6. J. Camenisch and I.B. Damgård. Verifiable Encryption, Group Encryption, and their Application to Group Signatures and Signature Sharing Schemes. In T. Okamoto, editor, *Advances in Cryptology - Asiacrypt 2000*, volume 1976 of *Lecture Notes in Computer Science*, pages 331–345. Springer-Verlag, 2000.
7. Y. Dodis and L. Reyzin. Breaking and Repairing Optimistic Fair Exchange from PODC 2003. In M. Yung, editor, *ACM Workshop on Digital Rights Management (DRM)*, 2003. available at http://eprint.iacr.org/2003/146/.
8. A. Fiat and A. Shamir. How to prove yourself : practical solutions of identification and signature problems. In G. Brassard, editor, *Advances in Cryptology - Proceedings of CRYPTO '86*, volume 263 of *Lecture Notes in Computer Science*, pages 186–194. Springer-Verlag, 1987.
9. M. Girault. Self-Certified Public Keys. In D.W. Davies, editor, *Advances in Cryptology - Proceedings of EUROCRYPT 1991*, volume 0547 of *Lecture Notes in Computer Science*, pages 490–497. Springer, 1991.
10. L. Guillou and J.-J. Quisquater. A "Paradoxical" Identity-Based Signature Scheme Resulting from Zero-Knowledge Minimizing Both Transmission and Memory. In C.G. Günther, editor, *Advances in Cryptology - Proceedings of CRYPTO 1988*, pages 216–231. Springer, 1988.

11. O. Markowitch and S. Kremer. An Optimistic Non-Repudiation Protocol with Transparent Trusted Third Party. In G.I. Davida and Y. Frankel, editors, *Proceedings of the 4th International Conference on Information Security (ISC 2001)*, volume 2200 of *Lecture Notes in Computer Science*, pages 363–378. Springer, 2001.
12. O. Markowitch and S. Saeednia. Optimistic Fair Exchange with Transparent Signature Recovery. In P.F. Syverson, editor, *Proceedings of Financial Cryptography 2001*, volume 2339 of *Lecture Notes in Computer Science*, pages 339–350. Springer, 2002.
13. J.M. Park, E. Chong, H. Siegel, and I. Ray. Constructing Fair Exchange Protocols for E-Commerce via Distributed Computation of RSA Signatures. In *Proceedings of the 22th Annual ACM Symposium on Principles of Distributed Computing (PODC 2003)*, pages 172–181, July 2003.
14. G. Poupard and J. Stern. Security Analysis of a Practical *on the fly* Authentification and Signature Generation. In K. Nyberg, editor, *Advances in Cryptology - Proceedings of EUROCRYPT 1998*, volume 1403 of *Lecture Notes in Computer Science*, pages 422–436. Springer, 1998.
15. R.L. Rivest, A. Shamir, and L. Adleman. A method for obtaining digital signatures and public-key cryptosystems. LCS TM82, MIT Laboratory for Computer Science, Cambridge, Massachusetts, 1977.

How to Break and Repair a Universally Composable Signature Functionality

Michael Backes[1] and Dennis Hofheinz[2]

[1] IBM Zurich Research Lab
mbc@zurich.ibm.com
[2] IAKS, Arbeitsgruppe Systemsicherheit, Prof. Dr. Th. Beth,
Fakultät für Informatik, Universität Karlsruhe
hofheinz@ira.uka.de

Abstract. Canetti and Rabin recently proposed a universally composable ideal functionality $\mathcal{F}_{\mathrm{SIG}}$ for digital signatures. We show that this functionality cannot be securely realized by *any* signature scheme, thereby disproving their result that any signature scheme that is existentially unforgeable under adaptive chosen-message attack is a secure realization.

Next, an improved signature functionality is presented. We show that our improved functionality can be securely realized by precisely those signature schemes that are secure against existential forgery under adaptive chosen-message attacks.

Keywords: Digital signature schemes, universal composability, adaptive chosen-message attack.

1   Introduction

In this contribution, we investigate the idealization $\mathcal{F}_{\mathrm{SIG}}$ of digital signatures, as defined in [6] for the framework of universal composability [2]. This framework enjoys a composition theorem which states that specifically, larger protocols may be formulated and investigated by means of an idealization of, e.g., digital signatures, while later a concrete digital signature scheme may be plugged in for the idealization while preserving the security of the large protocol. Certainly, this does not work for any signature scheme, but the scheme must—in a specified sense—*securely realize* the considered idealization, which makes the notion of secure realization (often also called *emulation*) the central notion of the framework.

We show that the idealization $\mathcal{F}_{\mathrm{SIG}}$ cannot be securely realized by *any* real signature scheme. This in particular invalidates the results of [6, Claim 2] and [2, Claim 14 of full version].[1,2]

---

[1] Our proof applies to the $\mathcal{F}_{\mathrm{SIG}}$-formulation from [6] as well as to the slightly older formulation in [2].

[2] After we had completed and published this manuscript as an IBM research report [1], the paper [6] was updated. In the updated version [7], the functionality $\mathcal{F}_{\mathrm{SIG}}$ was re-

Next, we propose an improvement of $\mathcal{F}_{\mathrm{SIG}}$ and we show that it can be securely realized by suitable real signature schemes, i.e., by precisely those ones that are secure against existential forgery under adaptive chosen-message attack as defined in [11].

The proof of unrealizability reveals a general problem with detached idealizations of digital signatures: In case of a corrupted signer, signatures for arbitrary messages may be generated *locally* by anyone who has knowledge of the signing key, hence it cannot be guaranteed that the ideal functionality, i.e., the idealization of digital signatures is notified upon every single signature generation. (Consider a larger protocol that honestly generates digital signatures using the publicly distributed signing key of a corrupted signer.) Thus, considering signatures as invalid which are not explicitly "registered" at the ideal functionality causes problems and indeed leads to our attack on $\mathcal{F}_{\mathrm{SIG}}$ discussed below. On the other hand, all signatures not obtained via explicit signing queries to the ideal functionality should intuitively be rejected when they are verified. Our modification of $\mathcal{F}_{\mathrm{SIG}}$ does not have this intuitive rejection property.

1.1   Overview of This Paper

We first briefly review the universal composability framework in Section 2 to prepare the ground for our subsequent results.

In Section 3, we review the ideal signature functionality proposed by Canetti and Rabin and show that it is not securely realizable at all.

In Section 4, we propose an improved functionality for digital signatures, and we show that it can be securely realized precisely by those signature schemes that are existentially unforgeable under adaptive-chosen message attack.

The paper ends with a conclusion (Section 5).

2   Preliminaries

To start, we shortly outline the framework for multi-party protocols as defined in [2]. First of all, *parties*, denoted by P_1 through P_n, are modeled as *interactive Turing machines (ITMs)* and are supposed to run some fixed protocol π. There also is an *adversary*, denoted $\mathcal{A}$ and modeled as an ITM as well, which carries out attacks on protocol π. $\mathcal{A}$ may corrupt parties in which case it learns their current and all past states as well as the contents of all their tapes; furthermore, it controls their future actions. $\mathcal{A}$ may further intercept or, when assuming unauthenticated message transfer (which is called the "bare" model in [2]), also fake messages sent between parties. If $\mathcal{A}$ corrupts parties only *before* the actual protocol run of π takes place, $\mathcal{A}$ is called *non-adaptive*, otherwise $\mathcal{A}$ is said to be *adaptive*. The respective local inputs for protocol π are supplied by an *environment machine*, which is also modeled as an ITM and denoted $\mathcal{Z}$, that

---

placed by a functionality $\mathcal{F}_{\mathrm{CERT}}$. Furthermore, a modification of $\mathcal{F}_{\mathrm{SIG}}$—independent of the one described here—was put forward in [3]. The generic attack discussed in this paper does not apply to the modified $\mathcal{F}_{\mathrm{SIG}}$ functionality in [3].

may read all outputs locally made by the parties and communicate with the adversary. Here we only consider environments that guarantee a polynomial (in the security parameter) number of total steps of all participating ITMs. Further discussions on this issue will be given later on, cf. Remark 3.

The model we have just described is called the *real* model of computation. In contrast to this, the *ideal* model of computation is defined just like the real model with the following exceptions. First, we have an additional ITM called the *ideal functionality* $\mathcal{F}$ that is allowed to send messages to and receive messages from the parties privately, i.e., the adversary can neither eavesdrop nor intercept these messages. The ideal functionality cannot be corrupted by the adversary, yet may send messages to and receive messages from it. Secondly, the parties $P_1, \dots, P_n$ are replaced by *dummy parties* $\tilde{P}_1, \dots, \tilde{P}_n$ that simply forward their respective inputs to $\mathcal{F}$ and take messages received from $\mathcal{F}$ as output. Finally, the adversary in the ideal model is denoted $\mathcal{S}$ and often called a *simulator*. The attack capabilities of the simulator are restricted to corrupting parties, delaying or even suppressing messages sent from $\mathcal{F}$ to a party, and all actions that are explicitly specified in $\mathcal{F}$. In particular, $\mathcal{S}$ does not have access to the contents of the messages sent from $\mathcal{F}$ to the dummy parties unless the receiving party is corrupted, nor are there any messages actually sent between uncorrupted parties that $\mathcal{S}$ could intercept. Intuitively, the ideal model of computation or, more precisely, the ideal functionality $\mathcal{F}$ itself should represent what we ideally expect a protocol to do. In fact, for a number of standard tasks, there are formulations as such ideal functionalities, e.g., in [2].

To decide whether a given protocol π is a secure realization of some ideal functionality $\mathcal{F}$, the framework of [2] uses a *simulatability*-based approach: At a time of its choice, $\mathcal{Z}$ may enter its halt state and leave output on its output tape. The probability for $\mathcal{Z}$'s first output bit to be 1 in the real model, when running on security parameter $k \in \mathbb{N}$ and with adversary $\mathcal{A}$ and protocol π is denoted $\mathbf{P}(\mathcal{Z} \to 1 \mid \pi, \mathcal{A})(k)$. The corresponding probability in the ideal model, running with simulator $\mathcal{S}$ and ideal functionality $\mathcal{F}$, is denoted $\mathbf{P}(\mathcal{Z} \to 1 \mid \mathcal{F}, \mathcal{S})(k)$. Now the protocol π is said to *securely realize* the functionality $\mathcal{F}$ if for any adversary $\mathcal{A}$ in the real model, there exists a simulator $\mathcal{S}$ in the ideal model such that for every environment $\mathcal{Z}$, we have that

$$|\mathbf{P}(\mathcal{Z} \to 1 \mid \pi, \mathcal{A})(k) - \mathbf{P}(\mathcal{Z} \to 1 \mid \mathcal{F}, \mathcal{S})(k)| \tag{1}$$

is a negligible[3] function in k.[4] Intuitively, this means that any attack carried out by an adversary in the real model can also be carried out in the idealized modeling with an ideal functionality by a simulator such that no environment is able to tell the difference. In the framework of [2], the above definition of security is equivalent to the seemingly weaker requirement that there is a simulator $\mathcal{S}$

---

[3] A function $f \colon \mathbb{N} \to \mathbb{R}$ is called *negligible* if for any $c \in \mathbb{N}$ there exists $k_0 \in \mathbb{N}$ such that $|f(k)| < k^{-c}$ for all $k > k_0$.

[4] The formulation in [2] is slightly different but equivalent to the one chosen here which allows to simplify our presentation.

so that (1) is a negligible function in k for any environment $\mathcal{Z}$ and the special real-model *dummy adversary* $\tilde{\mathcal{A}}$ which follows explicit instructions from $\mathcal{Z}$.

Both the original functionalities $\mathcal{F}_{\mathrm{SIG}}$ of [2,6] and our variation are *immediate* functionalities. This means that only those simulators are allowed in the ideal model which respect commands from the ideal functionality to deliver a message to a party immediately. This models that only "local" and non-interactive protocols are desired for realizing some functionality. In the case of $\mathcal{F}_{\mathrm{SIG}}$, this intuitively captures that signatures and signature verifications are to be made locally and instantly. Finally and analogously to [2], we restrict to *terminating* protocols, i.e., those ones that generate output if all messages are delivered and no party gets corrupted.

Remark 1. In [2], the environment machine is modeled as a non-uniform ITM, i.e., as an ITM whose initial input $z = z(k)$ depends on the security parameter k. However, it has been shown in [12] that the composition theorem of [2] remains valid if one restricts to uniform environment machines, i.e., those ones whose initial inputs do not depend on k. Hence it makes sense to alternatively consider only uniform environments where appropriate. In particular, all proofs given below hold for both uniform and non-uniform environments. Of course, then also the respective assumption (security of a signature scheme) has to be considered with respect to uniform, resp. non-uniform attackers.

Remark 2. The modeling of [2] does not involve explicit notifications of the ideal functionality upon corruptions of parties. However, a change of model causing ideal functionalities to be informed upon party corruptions was taken in [4,5]. As it is very helpful in our situation and allows for catching adaptively secure realizations of signature schemes, we assume that ideal functionalities are notified upon party corruptions. For our unrealizability result, this makes no difference; see also the remark in the original description of $\mathcal{F}_{\mathrm{SIG}}$ in [6].

3   The Attack on the Signature Functionality

In this section, we prove the ideal functionality $\mathcal{F}_{\mathrm{SIG}}$ from [6], as depicted in Figure 1, to be unrealizable even with respect to non-adaptive adversaries. In particular, this disproves Claim 2 of [6] which asserts any existentially unforgeable signature scheme to be securely realizing $\mathcal{F}_{\mathrm{SIG}}$. Although there is also a formulation of $\mathcal{F}_{\mathrm{SIG}}$ in the full version of [2] that slightly differs from the newer formulation in [6], we remark that our proof applies without changes also to this former version of $\mathcal{F}_{\mathrm{SIG}}$.

Before we show that $\mathcal{F}_{\mathrm{SIG}}$ cannot be securely realized in general, we point out where the proof of [6, Claim 2] goes wrong. The proof is conducted by reduction to the security of the considered signature scheme. It is shown that if an environment $\mathcal{Z}$ existed that distinguished whether it is run with an adversary $\mathcal{A}$ and the signature scheme or with a special simulator $\mathcal{S} = \mathcal{S}(\mathcal{A})$, which is explicitly constructed in [6] for any given $\mathcal{A}$, and $\mathcal{F}_{\mathrm{SIG}}$, one could define an

---

Functionality $\mathcal{F}_{\mathrm{SIG}}$

$\mathcal{F}_{\mathrm{SIG}}$ proceeds as follows, running with parties $P_1, \ldots, P_n$ and an adversary $\mathcal{S}$.

Set-up: In the first activation, expect to receive a value (signer, sid) from some party P_i. Then, send (signer, sid, P_i) to the adversary. From now on, ignore all (signer, sid) values.

Signature Generation: Upon receiving a value (sign, sid, m) from P_i, hand (sign, sid, m) to the adversary. Upon receiving (signature, sid, m, σ) from the adversary, set $s_m = \sigma$, send (signature, sid, m, σ) to P_i, and request the adversary to deliver this message immediately. Save the pair (m, s_m) in memory.

Signature Verification: Upon receiving a value (verify, sid, $P_{i'}$, m, σ) from P_j, do:

1. If $i = i'$ (i.e., the sender identity in the verification request agrees with the identity of the actual signer) then do: If m was never signed then let $f = 0$. If m was signed before (i.e., s_m is defined) and $s_m = \sigma$ then let $f = 1$. If m was signed but $s_m \neq \sigma$ then let the adversary decide on the value of f. (That is, hand (verify, sid, P_j, $P_{i'}$, m, σ) to the adversary. Upon receiving $\phi \in \{0, 1\}$ from the adversary, let $f = \phi$.)
2. If $i \neq i'$ then do: If $P_{i'}$ is uncorrupted then set $f = 0$. If $P_{i'}$ is corrupted then let the adversary decide on the value of f, as in Step 1.
3. Once the value of f is set, send (verified, sid, m, f) to P_j, and request the adversary to deliver this message immediately.

Fig. 1. The signature functionality $\mathcal{F}_{\mathrm{SIG}}$ reproduced from [6]

attacker G that is able to forge signatures under an adaptive chosen-message attack. In the reasoning that G successfully forges signatures, it is argued that "[...] as long as event B does not occur, $\mathcal{Z}$'s view of an interaction with $\mathcal{A}$ and parties running the protocol is distributed identically to its view of an interaction with $\mathcal{S}$[5] and $\mathcal{F}_{\mathrm{SIG}}$ in the ideal process." Here, B denotes the event that during a protocol run in the real model, "[...] $ver(v, m, \sigma) = 1$ for some message m and signature σ, but the signer is uncorrupted and never signed m during the execution of the protocol," where ver denotes the signature verification algorithm and v the verification key. This statement is wrong. In case of a corrupted signer, $\mathcal{S}$ takes no actions to signal signatures of messages to $\mathcal{F}_{\mathrm{SIG}}$—however, messages may be signed "legitimately" in case of, e.g., a passively corrupted signer. We will even show below that there is no way to circumvent this problem for the given functionality, since intuitively, there can be no way for $\mathcal{S}$ to determine *which* messages have been signed by an environment taking the role of a corrupted signer. As a consequence, verification requests of such signatures are answered differently in the real model and the ideal one.

In our proof, we use the fact that $\mathcal{F}_{\mathrm{SIG}}$ answers verification requests in the positive only if the corresponding message was already signed *by $\mathcal{F}_{\mathrm{SIG}}$ itself*. In Section 4, we will introduce an improved idealization of digital signatures

---

[5] Here we have corrected what seems to be a typo in [6].

which drops this requirement if the signing party gets corrupted: In case of a corrupted signer, we have to expect even the environment to be able to produce valid signatures for arbitrary messages.

Theorem 1. *The functionality $\mathcal{F}_{\mathrm{SIG}}$, as specified in [6] and depicted in Figure 1, cannot be securely realized by any terminating n-party-protocol π $(n \geq 2)$, even when assuming authenticated message transfer and only non-adaptive adversaries.*

Proof. Suppose that a protocol π that has the mentioned termination property securely realizes $\mathcal{F}_{\mathrm{SIG}}$. Fix two different parties P_i and P_j, and also a simulator S which in the ideal model mimics attacks carried out by the dummy adversary $\tilde{A}$ on the protocol π. Consider the following environment $\mathcal{Z}_1$, expecting to be run with $\tilde{A}$ in the real model; of course, in the ideal model, the simulator S is not bound to these instructions:

1. Activate P_i with input (`signer`, *sid*) and ask the adversary to deliver all messages possibly sent between parties.
2. In the following steps, do *not* request the adversary to deliver any more messages sent between parties.
3. Randomly pick a message r and activate P_i with (`sign`, *sid*, r); extract the signature σ from P_i's answer (`signature`, *sid*, r, σ).
4. Activate P_j with input (`verify`, *sid*, P_i, r, σ); output whatever P_j outputs.

Since π is terminating, we may assume that $\mathcal{Z}_1$ finishes the first of these steps in polynomial time in the real model, and thus in the ideal model. Moreover, the remaining party queries of $\mathcal{Z}_1$ are answered instantly in the ideal model by definition of $\mathcal{F}_{\mathrm{SIG}}$, and thus this also has to hold in the real model. By definition of $\mathcal{F}_{\mathrm{SIG}}$, it follows that $\mathcal{Z}_1$ always outputs 1 if it is run in the ideal model, regardless of the simulator. If it does not do so also in the real model except with negligible probability, $\mathcal{Z}_1$ successfully distinguishes π and $\mathcal{F}_{\mathrm{SIG}}$, which finishes the proof.

Hence assume that $\mathcal{Z}_1$ outputs 1 in the real model with overwhelming probability. Consider the following environment $\mathcal{Z}_2$ that we expect to run with the dummy adversary $\tilde{A}$ in the real model as well:

1. Tell the adversary to corrupt P_i. Run a local simulation $P_i^{(s)}$ of P_i.
2. Activate $P_i^{(s)}$ with input (`signer`, *sid*) and ask the adversary to deliver—in the name of the corrupted "relay" P_i—all messages sent by the simulated $P_i^{(s)}$ and vice versa.
3. Randomly pick a message r and activate $P_i^{(s)}$ with input (`sign`, *sid*, r), but *suppress* messages sent to or from $P_i^{(s)}$. Wait for $P_i^{(s)}$ to produce output (`signature`, *sid*, r, σ).
4. Invoke P_j with input (`verify`, *sid*, P_i, r, σ); output whatever P_j outputs.

Note that the corruption of P_i is completely passive until step 3. So also $\mathcal{Z}_2$ runs in polynomial time by the termination property of π in the real model, and thus we may assume that, except with negligible probability, it does so also in the ideal model.[6] We analyze the behavior of $\mathcal{Z}_2$ when it is run in the real model. From P_j's point of view, a "regular" run of protocol π exactly as with environment $\mathcal{Z}_1$ takes place. Particularly, since we know that $\mathcal{Z}_1$ outputs 1 with overwhelming probability, we can conclude that σ is accepted by P_j as a valid signature of r in step 4 with overwhelming probability. Consequently, $\mathcal{Z}_2$ will output 1 with overwhelming probability if it is run in the real model.

On the other hand, suppose $\mathcal{Z}_2$ is run in the ideal model with simulator $\mathcal{S}$. Since $\mathcal{S}$ is asked in step 1 to corrupt the signing party P_i, it has the ability to sign message of its choice, i.e., send the corresponding (sign, sid, m) message to $\mathcal{F}_{\mathrm{SIG}}$. However, the randomly chosen message r for which $\mathcal{Z}_2$ locally generates a signature in step 3 cannot be known to $\mathcal{S}$ before step 4. Hence r is registered in $\mathcal{F}_{\mathrm{SIG}}$ as signed (i.e., there is an entry (r, σ) in $\mathcal{F}_{\mathrm{SIG}}$'s list of messages and signatures) in step 4 only with negligible probability. By definition of $\mathcal{F}_{\mathrm{SIG}}$, this means that the uncorrupted party P_j replies in step 4 with 1 only with negligible probability.[7] So in the ideal model, $\mathcal{Z}_2$ outputs 0 with overwhelming probability and therefore distinguishes protocol π and $\mathcal{F}_{\mathrm{SIG}}$.   □

4   The Repaired Signature Functionality

We now present a modification of $\mathcal{F}_{\mathrm{SIG}}$, which is realizable even in the bare model by any signature scheme that is existentially unforgeable under adaptive chosen-message attacks. Such schemes exist under reasonable assumptions, e.g., [11,13, 8,9,10].

Consider the family of functionalities $\{\mathcal{F}_{\mathrm{SIG}}^{(i)}\}_{P_i}$, where functionality $\mathcal{F}_{\mathrm{SIG}}^{(i)}$ is described in Figure 2. Note that we parameterized the ideal functionality with the identity of the signer. This seems to be necessary since a trivial distinguisher could otherwise activate two parties with input (signer, sid) and then simply check which of these parties is able to actually sign messages. In the ideal model, this is the party that was activated first by definition of $\mathcal{F}_{\mathrm{SIG}}$, yet in the real model this order of activations cannot even be decided by any protocol. We refer to [12] for a similar problem that arises with the public-key encryption functionality $\mathcal{F}_{\mathrm{PKE}}$. Furthermore, our functionality ensures that signatures never change their validity status which is not always guaranteed in the original formulations of $\mathcal{F}_{\mathrm{SIG}}$. Finally, just like these original formulations, our functionalities $\mathcal{F}_{\mathrm{SIG}}^{(i)}$ are immediate.

---

[6] In fact, to be strictly polynomial, $\mathcal{Z}_2$ has to be modified to abort when running longer than a hardcoded polynomial bound—however, this is guaranteed to happen only with negligible probability.

[7] There is a subtlety here: The functionality $\mathcal{F}_{\mathrm{SIG}}$ is not completely specified in [6], and it is not clear what happens when signature or verification requests take place without prior "(signer, $\cdot$, $\cdot$)" initialization, which $\mathcal{S}$ is not forced to send to $\mathcal{F}_{\mathrm{SIG}}$ in the name of an initially corrupted P_i. We find it reasonable to assume that such requests are then ignored; however, our proof applies also to other completions of the specification.

Functionality $\mathcal{F}_{\mathrm{SIG}}^{(i)}$

$\mathcal{F}_{\mathrm{SIG}}^{(i)}$ proceeds as follows, running with parties $P_1, \dots, P_n$ and an adversary $\mathcal{S}$. (All messages not covered here are simply ignored.)

- Upon receiving (signer, sid) from P_i (and P_i alone) *for the first time*, send a message (key, sid) to $\mathcal{S}$; then, upon receiving an answer (key, sid, v) from $\mathcal{S}$, forward this answer to P_i and store v. Ignore further (signer, sid) requests. *The following rules apply* only *after this initial* (signer, sid) *message.*
- Upon receiving (sign, sid, m) from P_i (and only P_i), forward this message to $\mathcal{S}$; upon receiving an answer (signature, sid, m, σ) from $\mathcal{S}$, forward this answer to P_i. Also store the pair $(m, \sigma, 1)$.
- Upon receiving (verify, sid, m, σ, v') from any party P_j, where $v \neq v'$ or v is not determined yet, send this entire tuple to $\mathcal{S}$; upon receiving an answer (verified, sid, m, f) from $\mathcal{S}$, forward this answer to P_j.
- Upon receiving (verify, sid, m, σ', v') from any party P_j, where $v = v'$, answer with (verified, sid, m, f), where f is determined as follows:
  - If there is a pair (m, σ, g) with $\sigma = \sigma'$ stored, let $f = g$.
  - If P_i is uncorrupted and there is no pair (m, σ, g) for any σ and g stored, let $f = 0$.
  - In all other cases, send this entire tuple to $\mathcal{S}$; upon receiving an answer (verified, sid, m, f) from $\mathcal{S}$, extract f from this answer and store the pair (m, σ', f).

Fig. 2. The modified signature functionality $\mathcal{F}_{\mathrm{SIG}}^{(i)}$

Now analogously to the construction in [6], we regard a signature scheme $S = (\mathsf{K}, \mathsf{S}, \mathsf{V})$ consisting of probabilistic polynomial-time algorithms for key generation, signing and verifying signatures as a protocol aimed at securely realizing $\mathcal{F}_{\mathrm{SIG}}$. Moreover, if we restrict the execution of K and S to a fixed party P_i and to return the verification key upon (signer, sid) requests instead of distributing it, we obtain a protocol called $\pi_S^{(i)}$ that is tailored towards realizing $\mathcal{F}_{\mathrm{SIG}}^{(i)}$. Note that in contrast to the construction in [6], the distribution of the verification key does not have to be covered here, since it is simply a parameter of signature verification requests.

Theorem 2. *For a fixed party P_i, protocol $\pi_S^{(i)}$ securely realizes $\mathcal{F}_{\mathrm{SIG}}^{(i)}$ if and only if the signature scheme S is existentially unforgeable under adaptive chosen-message attacks.*

Proof. For proving the "only if" direction, consider an attacker G that takes part in the following experiment $\mathbf{Exp}_{G,S}^{\mathrm{ef\text{-}cma}}(k)$ which is used to define security of digital signature schemes against existential forgery under adaptive chosen-message attack., cf. [11]. Here, $S = (\mathsf{K}, \mathsf{S}, \mathsf{V})$ denotes a signature scheme and $G_k^{\mathsf{S}_s(\cdot)}$ means that G interacts with the corresponding signature oracle with respect to a signing key s.

1. $(s, v) \leftarrow \mathsf{K}(k)$
2. $(m, \sigma) \leftarrow G_k^{\mathsf{S}_s(\cdot)}(v)$
3. **Return** $(\mathsf{V}_v(m, \sigma) \rightarrow \texttt{accept}) \wedge$ "$\mathsf{S}_s(\cdot)$ was never queried on m in step 2".

Let $\mathcal{Z}$ be the environment that performs the above experiment with a simulated G: $\mathcal{Z}$ triggers G with the public key v gathered through an initial request for key generation to P_i and carries out G's signing requests by redirecting them to P_i in an $\mathcal{F}_{\mathrm{SIG}}^{(i)}$-compatible form. Moreover, the verification request in step 3 is also redirected to P_i. Finally, $\mathcal{Z}$ outputs 1 exactly if the experiment returns $\texttt{true}$. Now in the real model, since all requests to P_i are answered "authentically" as it would happen in $\mathbf{Exp}_{G,S}^{\mathrm{ef\text{-}cma}}(k)$, the probability that $\mathcal{Z}$ returns 1 is precisely $\mathbf{P}(\mathbf{Exp}_{G,S}^{\mathrm{ef\text{-}cma}}(k) \rightarrow \texttt{true})$. On the other hand, $\mathcal{Z}$'s output in the ideal model cannot be 1 at any time regardless of the simulator $\mathcal{S}$ since the condition in step 3 is never fulfilled by definition of $\mathcal{F}_{\mathrm{SIG}}^{(i)}$. So for any simulator $\mathcal{S}$ we have:

$$\left| \mathbf{P}(\mathcal{Z} \rightarrow 1 \mid \pi_S^{(i)}, \tilde{\mathcal{A}})(k) - \mathbf{P}(\mathcal{Z}_k \rightarrow 1 \mid \mathcal{F}_{\mathrm{SIG}}^{(i)}, \mathcal{S})(k) \right| = \mathbf{P}(\mathbf{Exp}_{A,S}^{\mathrm{ef\text{-}cma}}(k) \rightarrow \texttt{true}).$$

That means that if G is able to forge signatures under an adaptive chosen-message attack with non-negligible probability, then we can construct an environment $\mathcal{Z}$ that successfully distinguishes $\mathcal{F}_{\mathrm{SIG}}^{(i)}$ and $\pi_S^{(i)}$.

Now for the "if" direction, consider the simulator $\mathcal{S}_{\mathrm{SIG}}^{(i)}$ as described in Figure 3 that mimics attacks carried out by the dummy adversary $\tilde{\mathcal{A}}$ on π. Fix an environment $\mathcal{Z}$. From $\mathcal{Z}$'s point of view, there is no difference between communicating with $\mathcal{S}_{\mathrm{SIG}}^{(i)}$ in the ideal model and talking to $\tilde{\mathcal{A}}$ in the real model by construction of the simulator $\mathcal{S}_{\mathrm{SIG}}^{(i)}$. The only way for $\mathcal{Z}$ to detect a difference between real and ideal model is consequently through requests to parties—note here that the protocol $\pi_S^{(i)}$ does not involve any communication which could possibly be eavesdropped or altered by $\tilde{\mathcal{A}}$.

The following event is defined in analogy to the notation in [6]. Let B denote the event that at some point in time at which the signing party P_i is not corrupted, $\mathcal{Z}$ requests any party to verify a valid signature σ of a message m (valid in the sense that $\mathsf{V}(m, \sigma) \rightarrow \texttt{accept}$), where m has not been signed before by an explicit request to P_i. Let $\bar{B}$ denote the event that B does not occur.

We show that by construction of $\mathcal{F}_{\mathrm{SIG}}^{(i)}$ and $\pi_S^{(i)}$, $\mathcal{Z}$'s views in the real and the ideal model do not differ until the event B occurs. If P_i is corrupted, all verification requests of signatures that are not explicitly generated or evaluated by $\mathcal{S}_{\mathrm{SIG}}^{(i)}$ are relayed to it, hence requests are answered exactly as in the real model. On the other hand, if P_i is not corrupted, then the ideal functionality $\mathcal{F}_{\mathrm{SIG}}^{(i)}$ answers on its own only verification requests for signatures that either have been formerly generated or checked by $\mathcal{S}_{\mathrm{SIG}}^{(i)}$, or signatures for messages that have never been signed before. In that case, an answer may only be different to the corresponding answer in the real model if $\mathcal{F}_{\mathrm{SIG}}^{(i)}$ is requested to verify a valid signature of a message that has never been signed before. This is exactly what the event B captures.

The simulator $\mathcal{S}_{\mathrm{SIG}}^{(i)}$

– **Communication with $\mathcal{F}_{\mathrm{SIG}}^{(i)}$:**
  - Upon receiving a message $(\texttt{key}, sid)$ from $\mathcal{F}_{\mathrm{SIG}}^{(i)}$, run algorithm K to receive a keypair (s, v); keep s in memory and send $(\texttt{key}, sid, v)$ back to $\mathcal{F}_{\mathrm{SIG}}^{(i)}$.
  - Upon receiving $(\texttt{sign}, sid, m)$ from $\mathcal{F}_{\mathrm{SIG}}^{(i)}$, let $\sigma \leftarrow \mathsf{S}_s(m)$ and send $(\texttt{signature}, sid, m, \sigma)$ back to $\mathcal{F}_{\mathrm{SIG}}^{(i)}$; if s has not yet been initialized (i.e., if there was no former request for key generation), then hand back an error message just as $\pi_S^{(i)}$ would do.
  - Upon receiving $(\texttt{verify}, sid, m, \sigma, v')$ from $\mathcal{F}_{\mathrm{SIG}}^{(i)}$, let $f \leftarrow \mathsf{V}_{v'}(m, \sigma)$ and send $(\texttt{verified}, sid, m, f)$ back to $\mathcal{F}_{\mathrm{SIG}}^{(i)}$.
  - Deliver all messages sent from $\mathcal{F}_{\mathrm{SIG}}^{(i)}$ to the parties immediately.
– **Communication with $\mathcal{Z}$:**
  - When being requested by $\mathcal{Z}$ to check for messages sent by parties, reply that no messages were sent.
  - When being asked by $\mathcal{Z}$ to deliver a message m to some party P_j, store this request for future use.
  - When being told by $\mathcal{Z}$ to corrupt some party P_j, first corrupt the dummy party $\tilde{P}_j$ to gather information about $\mathcal{Z}$'s communication with $\tilde{P}_j$; then prepare state information for P_j taking into account all of $\tilde{P}_j$'s communication with $\mathcal{Z}$, all messages $\mathcal{S}_{\mathrm{SIG}}^{(i)}$ was asked to deliver to $\tilde{P}_j$ and, if $i = j$, add to this information the signing key s if there was a key generation request and prepare a random tape consistent with the one used by $\mathcal{F}_{\mathrm{SIG}}^{(i)}$ during a possible key generation.

Fig. 3. The simulator $\mathcal{S}_{\mathrm{SIG}}^{(i)}$

It follows that for any fixed security parameter k, we have

$$
\begin{aligned}
\textbf{(a)} \quad & \mathbf{P}(B \mid \mathcal{F}_{\mathrm{SIG}}^{(i)}, \mathcal{S}_{\mathrm{SIG}}^{(i)}) = \mathbf{P}(B \mid \pi_S^{(i)}, \tilde{\mathcal{A}}) \\
\textbf{(b)} \quad & \mathbf{P}(\mathcal{Z} \to 1 \mid \bar{B}, \mathcal{F}_{\mathrm{SIG}}^{(i)}, \mathcal{S}_{\mathrm{SIG}}^{(i)}) = \mathbf{P}(\mathcal{Z} \to 1 \mid \bar{B}, \pi_S^{(i)}, \tilde{\mathcal{A}}).
\end{aligned}
$$

Let G be an attacker on the signature scheme S built from $\mathcal{Z}$ in the following way:

1. Run a simulation of $\mathcal{Z}$.
2. When $\mathcal{Z}$ requests a key generation from party P_i, deliver $\mathcal{Z}$ with the challenge public key v.
3. When $\mathcal{Z}$ asks P_i to sign a message m, redirect this request to the signing oracle $\mathsf{S}_s(\cdot)$.
4. When $\mathcal{Z}$ lets a party P_j verify a signature σ of some message m, compute $f \leftarrow \mathsf{V}_v(m, \sigma)$. If $f = \texttt{accept}$ and m was not requested to be signed before by the simulated $\mathcal{Z}$, quit the simulation and exit with (m, σ); else answer $\mathcal{Z}$'s request with f.

5. When $\mathcal{Z}$ asks the adversary to report messages sent between parties, reply that no messages were sent; when $\mathcal{Z}$ asks the adversary to deliver a message to a party, ignore this request.
6. When $\mathcal{Z}$ halts or asks the adversary to corrupt P_i, exit with `failed`.

Taking into consideration **(a)** and **(b)** from above, we obtain for a fixed security parameter k:

$$\left| \mathbf{P}(\mathcal{Z} \to 1 \mid \pi_S^{(i)}, \tilde{\mathcal{A}}) - \mathbf{P}(\mathcal{Z} \to 1 \mid \mathcal{F}_{\mathrm{SIG}}^{(i)}, \mathcal{S}_{\mathrm{SIG}}^{(i)}) \right|$$
$$= \left| \mathbf{P}(B) \cdot \left(\mathbf{P}(\mathcal{Z} \to 1 \mid B, \pi_S^{(i)}, \tilde{\mathcal{A}}) - \mathbf{P}(\mathcal{Z} \to 1 \mid B, \mathcal{F}_{\mathrm{SIG}}^{(i)}, \mathcal{S}_{\mathrm{SIG}}^{(i)}) \right) \right|$$
$$\leq \mathbf{P}(B) = \mathbf{P}(\mathbf{Exp}_{G,S}^{\mathrm{ef\text{-}cma}} \to \mathtt{true}).$$

Therefore, if $\mathcal{Z}$ successfully distinguishes $\pi_S^{(i)}$ and $\mathcal{F}_{\mathrm{SIG}}^{(i)}$, then G successfully forges signatures. $\qquad\square$

Remark 3. In this exposition, certain timing issues have been neglected: For the validity of the composition theorem of [2], it is essential that all machines, in particular environment machines and adversaries, underlie computational restrictions. For example it is mandated in [2] that all machines only perform a polynomial number of *total* steps. However, to avoid a "trivial" distinction of real and ideal model, it may make more sense to require machines which are polynomially bounded only *per activation*, and to consider only environments explicitly bounded in their total running time, cf. the approach in [12]. For the environments $\mathcal{Z}_1$ and $\mathcal{Z}_2$ from the proof of our Theorem 1, this is clear by assumption about the protocols π inspected there. Yet, it remains to ensure a polynomial number of steps per activation for our proposed functionalities $\mathcal{F}_{\mathrm{SIG}}^{(i)}$ and the corresponding simulators. One way might be to bound these machines explicitly by a polynomial, thus yielding a *family* of functionalities and simulators. (Note that also the "original" dummy adversary $\tilde{\mathcal{A}}$ from [2] is not computationally bounded in any way—so when bounding the simulator, we may assume a bounded real-model adversary, too.)

Remark 4. Our functionalities $\mathcal{F}_{\mathrm{SIG}}^{(i)}$ allow the adversary to determine the validity of unseen signatures in case of a corrupted signer. This drawback can be mildened by a method used in [3]: at the start of the protocol, the ideal functionality can ask the simulator for a deterministic algorithm to determine the validity of unseen signatures. Then, the adversary may no longer determine the validity of unseen signatures dynamically.

5   Conclusion

We have shown the idealization of signature schemes $\mathcal{F}_{\mathrm{SIG}}$ from [6] to be unrealizable, thus invalidating the results of [6, Claim 2] and [2, Claim 14 of full version]. We have proposed a variant of this digital signature functionality, and we have proven it to be securely realizable by precisely those digital signature schemes that are existentially unforgeable under adaptive chosen-message attacks.

Acknowledgements. We would like to thank Jörn Müller-Quade and Rainer Steinwandt for interesting and valuable discussions.

References

1. Michael Backes and Dennis Hofheinz. How to break and repair a universally composable signature functionality. Technical Report RZ 3512, IBM Research Division, November 2003. Online available at
   http://www.research.ibm.com/resources/paper_search.shtml.
2. Ran Canetti. Universally composable security: A new paradigm for cryptographic protocols. In *Proc. 42nd IEEE Symposium on Foundations of Computer Science (FOCS)*, pages 136–145. IEEE Computer Society, 2001. Full version at
   http://eprint.iacr.org/2000/067.
3. Ran Canetti. On universally composable notions of security for signature, certification and authentication. Cryptology ePrint archive, November 2003.
4. Ran Canetti and Hugo Krawczyk. Universally composable notions of key exchange and secure channels. In *Advances in Cryptology: EUROCRYPT 2002*, volume 2332 of *Lecture Notes in Computer Science*. Springer, 2002. Full version at
   http://eprint.iacr.org/2002/059.
5. Ran Canetti, Yehuda Lindell, Rafail Ostrovsky, and Amit Sahai. Universally composable two-party and multi-party secure computation. In *Proc. 34th Annual ACM Symposium on Theory of Computing (STOC)*, pages 494–503, 2002. Full version at http://eprint.iacr.org/2002/140.
6. Ran Canetti and Tal Rabin. Universal composition with joint state. Cryptology ePrint archive, April 2002. Short version appeared in *Advances in Cryptology: CRYPTO 2003*.
7. Ran Canetti and Tal Rabin. Universal composition with joint state. Cryptology ePrint archive, November 2003.
8. Ronald Cramer and Ivan Damgård. Secure signature schemes based on interactive protocols. In *Advances in Cryptology: CRYPTO '95*, volume 963 of *Lecture Notes in Computer Science*, pages 297–310. Springer, 1995.
9. Ronald Cramer and Ivan Damgård. New generation of secure and practical RSA-based signatures. In *Advances in Cryptology: CRYPTO '96*, volume 1109 of *Lecture Notes in Computer Science*, pages 173–185. Springer, 1996.
10. Cynthia Dwork and Moni Naor. An efficient existentially unforgeable signature scheme and its applications. *Journal of Cryptology*, 11(3):187–208, 1998.
11. Shafi Goldwasser, Silvio Micali, and Ronald L. Rivest. A digital signature scheme secure against adaptive chosen-message attacks. *SIAM Journal on Computing*, 17(2):281–308, 1988.
12. Dennis Hofheinz, Jörn Müller-Quade, and Rainer Steinwandt. On modeling IND-CCA security in cryptographic protocols. Cryptology ePrint Archive, Report 2003/024, February 2003. http://eprint.iacr.org/2003/024.
13. John Rompel. One-way functions are necessary and sufficient for secure signatures. In *Proc. 22nd Annual ACM Symposium on Theory of Computing (STOC)*, pages 387–394, 1990.

RSA Accumulator Based Broadcast Encryption

Craig Gentry and Zulfikar Ramzan

DoCoMo Communications Laboratories USA, Inc.
181 Metro Drive, Suite 300,
San Jose, CA 95110
{cgentry, ramzan}@docomolabs-usa.com

Abstract. Broadcast encryption schemes allow a center to transmit encrypted data over a broadcast channel to a large number of users such that only a select subset of privileged users can decrypt it. In this paper, we analyze how RSA accumulators can be used as a tool in this area. First, we describe a technique for achieving full key derivability given any broadcast encryption scheme in the general subset-cover framework [16]. Second, we show that Asano's Broadcast Encryption scheme [5], can be viewed as a special-case instantiation of our general technique. Third, we use our technique to develop a new stateless-receiver broadcast encryption scheme that is a direct improvement on Asano's scheme with respect to communication complexity, amount of tamper-resistant storage needed, and key derivation costs. Fourth, we derive a new lower bound that characterizes the tradeoffs inherent in broadcast encryption schemes which use our key derivability technique.

1 Introduction

Broadcast encryption (BE) schemes allow a center to transmit encrypted data over a broadcast channel to a large number of users such that only a select subset $\mathcal{P}$ of *privileged users* can decrypt it. Traditional applications include Pay TV, content protection on CD or DVD, secure Internet multicast of privileged content such as video or music. BE schemes can, however, be used in any setting that might require selective disclosure of potentially lucrative content.

BE schemes typically involve a series of pre-broadcast transmissions at the end of which only users in $\mathcal{P}$ can compute a session key bk. The broadcast data is encrypted using bk. There are several variations on the general problem:

- **Revocation:** $\mathcal{P}$ may be determined arbitrarily, have fixed size, or contain some type of hierarchical structure. They can be static across all broadcasts or be dynamic.
- **Coalition Resistance:** The scheme may be secure against any coalition of revoked users, or there may be some bound on the size of the coalition the scheme can tolerate.
- **Key Management:** User keys may be fixed at the onset, be updated each time period, or be a function of previous transmissions.
- **Free Riders:** The center may be willing to tolerate some number of "free riders" outside of $\mathcal{P}$ who can still decrypt the broadcast.

K. Zhang and Y. Zheng (Eds.): ISC 2004, LNCS 3225, pp. 73–86, 2004.

This paper considers the most robust setting: $\mathcal{P}$ is determined dynamically, security is provided against arbitrary coalitions, and the user keys can be fixed at initialization without requiring any updates; in fact, in our schemes, each user only needs a single key from which it can derive only those keys to which it is allowed access. Our schemes can also incorporate the notion of free riders. In addition, we are also interested in the following performance-related metrics:

- The number of pre-broadcast transmissions t made by the center.
- The amount of keying material k the receivers must persistently store.
- The amount of time c the receiver must spend when deriving the broadcast session key bk from the pre-broadcast transmissions.

Simple Approaches. In a system of n users, r of which are to be revoked, a BE scheme must find a favorable balance among t, k, and c. At one inefficient extreme, we can achieve $k = 1$ by giving a unique key $\mathcal{K}_u$ to each user $u \in \mathcal{P}$. However, in the absence of computational assumptions, the center must make $t = n - r$ pre-broadcast transmissions, one for each privileged user. This scheme does not scale well when it is often the case that most users are privileged.

At another extreme, we can achieve $t = 1$ by assigning a unique key $\mathcal{K}_S$ to each subset $\mathcal{S} \subseteq \mathcal{U}$. Then, to broadcast to $\mathcal{P}$, the center only has to encrypt the broadcast session key bk under the key $\mathcal{K}_{\mathcal{P}}$. Unfortunately, the user must store 2^{n-1} keys – one for each subset it belongs to, which is clearly impractical especially given that keying material is highly sensitive and needs to be placed in some form of tamper-resistant non-volatile storage.

One can even achieve $k = 1$ and $t = 1$ simultaneously by having the center establish a single global key $\mathcal{K}_{\mathcal{G}}$ given to all users in $\mathcal{P}$. Broadcasts would then be encrypted with this global key. Of course this scheme is inflexible since it can tolerate neither any form of collusion nor any change to the privileged sets.

As a simple example of a more sophisticated approach, consider the "Complete Subtree Method" [16], which achieves a more favorable tradeoff between k and t. The center constructs a binary tree and associates each node v with a distinct key k_v, and each user u with a distinct leaf v_u. During set-up, the center provides u with the keys corresponding to the vertices on the path from v_u to the root. To broadcast, the center uses a method described in [16] to find a set of $r \log(n/r)$ vertices – called a *cover* – such that the leaves of the subtrees rooted at vertices in the cover correspond exactly to $\mathcal{P}$. The center then encrypts the session key with the keys corresponding to the vertices in the cover, and encrypts the broadcast with the session key. In this scheme, $(k, t) = (\log n, r \log(n/r))$.

All schemes except the third one mentioned above are examples of the subset-cover framework which was first formalized by [16]. In this framework, cryptographic keys are assigned to specific user subsets; furthermore any arbitrary user subset can be formed by taking the union of some number of the specific subsets. All such schemes have the highly desirable property that receiver's keys may be fixed at the onset of the scheme and do not need to be changed thereafter. This situation is often termed the *stateless receiver case*.

Stateless Receivers. This paper focuses on the case of *stateless receivers* which is preferable since it accurately captures the real-world constraints associated with the motivating applications. Here, users are provided with some initial key or set of keys (which may be hardwired during the manufacture of the receiving device), and can use only this keying material when decrypting future broadcasts. This model accurately captures off-line devices such as CD or DVD players which may be offline and therefore incapable of accommodating key updates. The detailed requirements of the stateless model were articulated in [13] (see also [14], [16]). We reiterate them here for completeness.

1. Each user in the privileged set $\mathcal{P}$ can decrypt the broadcast by himself.
2. No coalition of users outside the privileged set $\mathcal{P}$ can decrypt the broadcast.
3. Consecutive broadcasts may address unrelated privileged sets.
4. A user need not update its keys if other users leave or join the privileged set.
5. A user's keys are unaffected by its viewing history.

Other Related Work. The BE literature is extensive and goes beyond the stateless case we consider in this paper. A full survey is beyond our scope so we limit our discussion to more germane work. To begin with, Berkovits [7] first identified the concept of BE. Later, Fiat and Naor [12] carefully formalized the basic problem. One paradigm employed in these two schemes is the use of secret sharing or error-correcting codes. Such schemes, while elegant, suffer from the limitation that the number of revoked users r the system can tolerate must be pre-specified. For example, $O(n)$ overhead is required to tolerate up to $O(n)$ revoked users, even if the *actual* number of revoked users is small.

A second paradigm in BE involves the use of tree-based schemes (e.g., [16], [13]), like the Complete Subtree Method, described above. These schemes have the advantage that r need not be bounded in advance. Instead, t can increase as r increases. The state of the art in tree-based BE schemes is the "Subset Difference" (SD) method [16] and the subsequent improvement called the "Layered Subset Difference" (LSD) technique [13]. With SD, the number of pre-broadcast transmissions is reduced to $t = O(r)$, a user must store $k = O(log^2(n))$ keys, and the receiver must perform $c = O(\log(n))$ computation to compute the broadcast key bk. The LSD techique improves upon this construction; for any $\epsilon > 0$, they achieve $k = O(\log^{1+\epsilon}(n))$ without substantially increasing t. Both SD and LSD fall into the subset cover framework formalized by [16]. Such schemes aim to come up with a subset cover construction that permits storage-efficient key derivability. However, an important problem left open by [16] and [13] is to come up with a generic key derivability mechanism that works for *any* cover and requires *minimal* storage. In this paper, we resolve this issue.

Asano [5] suggested an approach based on a connection between BE and hierarchical access control. Using techniques from the latter ([9], [2], [3]), he constructed efficient BE schemes. Most impressively, his "Method 1" only requires each user to store a single "master key." Letting a denote the branching factor in the tree-like constructions he proposes, this scheme has a transmission requirement of $t = O(r \log_a(n/r))$. However, the receiver may require considerable computation to decrypt the broadcast session key; specifically, the receiver must perform $c = O((2^a - 1) \log_a n)$ exponentiations by reasonably "small" prime exponents. (Alternatively, the receiver could multiply these "small" exponents together and perform one "large" exponentiation by an exponent with bit-length proportional to c, but the computation involved is the same asymptotically.) Asano's result [5] is our starting point. Independently of our work, Attrapadung et al. [4] used Asano's techniques to achieve a BE scheme in which t is a constant independent of n and r. However, their scheme is practical only for small broadcast groups, since the scheme can be made resilient against size k coalitions only by making c exponential in k. We remark that both Asano's scheme and the cited work on access control (initiated by [2]) involve the use of one-way RSA-based accumulators (first formally introduced by [6]).

Our Results. Our first contribution is a technique for enabling full key derivability given any BE scheme in the general subset-cover framework of [16]. Using this technique, the receiver only needs to store a single cryptographic key at the onset, and all subset keys can be securely derived from it regardless of how complex the key hierarchies are. Our technique can be used to separate the key derivability problem (which is computational in nature) from the subset-cover set-up problem (which is combinatorial in nature). We then look at Asano's BE scheme [5], which turns out to be just a special case of our general technique. When we separate Asano's set-up of key hierarchies from the key derivability it becomes clear that Asano's key-hierarchy set-up is somewhat ad-hoc; specifically, for a given value of k and t – e.g., $k = 1$ and $t = O(r \log_a(n/r))$ – the value of $c = O((2^a - 1) \log_a n)$ not optimal. We construct an alternate key hierarchy and apply our key derivability technique to it to achieve a direct improvement over Asano's scheme. Specifically, for $k = 1$ and $t = O(r \log_a(n/r))$, we get a much lower computational cost for the receiver: $c = O(a \log_a n)$. In other words, with respect to the "configurability parameter" a, a receiver in our scheme needs exponentially less computation to decrypt. (As mentioned previously, the receiver's computational cost in Attrapadung et al.'s scheme [4] also quickly becomes prohibitive, growing exponentially in the largest permitted coalition size.) Finally, we derive a new lower bound that characterize the tradeoffs inherent in BE schemes that use our key derivability technique. Table 1 summarizes our results.

Table 1. Comparison among Complete Subtree [16], Subset Difference [16], Asano Method 1 [5], and our scheme. Note that the key derivation cost in our scheme is smaller (by an exponential factor in a) than Asano's scheme.

	CS [16]	SD [16]	LSD [13]	Asano-1 [5]	Us
# Ciphertexts	$r \log \frac{n}{r}$	$2r - 1$	$4r - 2$	$r(\log_a \frac{n}{r} + 1)$	$r(\log_a \frac{n}{r} + 1)$
Keys @ Receiver	$\log n$	$\frac{1}{2} \log^2 n$	$O(\log^{1+\epsilon} n)$	1	1
PRG cost	-	$O(\log n)$	$O(\log n)$	-	-
"Small" Exps.	-	-	-	$(2^a - 1) \log_a n$	$(2a - \log a - 1) \log_a n$

2   Notation and Preliminaries

For a given broadcast, we denote the set of users by $\mathcal{U}$, the set of privileged users by $\mathcal{P}$, and the set of revoked users by $\mathcal{R}$. Let $n = |\mathcal{U}|$ and $r = |\mathcal{R}|$. The schemes we describe can be characterized in the *Subset-Cover* framework of [16]. Here, we have a number of subsets $S_1, \ldots, S_w \subseteq \mathcal{U}$ such that any subset of $\mathcal{U}$ (and in particular $\mathcal{P}$) can be formed as a union of a collection of the S_i's. Each subset S_i is assigned a distinct cryptographic key. If a user is in a given subset, then it will be provided with the key assigned to that subset.

Let $\mathcal{K}_{\mathcal{U}}$ denote the set of all such establishment keys, and let $\mathcal{K}_u$ denote the subset of these keys stored on user u's receiver. When broadcasting to $\mathcal{P}$, the center chooses a random string bk as its broadcast session key, finds a set of keys $\mathcal{K}_{\mathcal{P}} \subset \mathcal{K}_{\mathcal{U}}$ such that a user can compute a key in $\mathcal{K}_{\mathcal{P}}$ if and only if it is privileged, and encrypts bk under each key in $\mathcal{K}_{\mathcal{P}}$. The number of transmissions in the pre-broadcast is $t = |\mathcal{K}_{\mathcal{P}}|$. The broadcast itself, which may be bandwidth intensive (e.g., a multimedia stream), is encrypted once under the key bk.

In most of the schemes we discuss, a privileged user u typically will not use a key in $\mathcal{K}_u$ directly to decrypt one of the pre-broadcast transmissions; rather, it will use a key in $\mathcal{K}_u$ to *derive* a key in $\mathcal{K}_{\mathcal{P}}$, and use this secondary key to decrypt. Let $\mathcal{K}'_u \subset \mathcal{K}_{\mathcal{P}}$ denote the set of secondary keys that u can derive from its primary keys $\mathcal{K}_u$, and let $\mathcal{U}_i = \{u \in \mathcal{U} : k_i \in \mathcal{K}'_u\}$ – i.e., the subset of users that can derive key k_i. Before broadcasting to $\mathcal{P}$, the center finds a set $\mathcal{K}_{\mathcal{P}} \subseteq \mathcal{K}_{\mathcal{U}}$ of minimal cardinality such that $\mathcal{P} = \cup_{k_i \in \mathcal{K}_{\mathcal{P}}} \mathcal{U}_i$. Finding optimal tradeoffs for this problem in terms of $|\mathcal{U}|$, $|\mathcal{P}|$, $\max_u |\mathcal{K}'_u|$ and $|\mathcal{K}_{\mathcal{P}}|$ is a purely combinatorial problem. We write $k_i \to k_j$ if key k_j can be derived from key k_i (including the case $k_i = k_j$). More generally, we write $\mathcal{K} \to k_j$ if k_j can be derived from the keys in set $\mathcal{K}$. Deriving keys has a computational cost for the user. To be efficient, a BE scheme must find a favorable balance among the pre-broadcast bandwidth t, the maximum number of keys $k = \max_u |\mathcal{K}_u|$ stored on a user's receiver, and the maximum computation c a privileged user must perform to recover bk.

We say that a BE scheme is *collusion-resistant* if $\mathcal{K}_{u_1} \cup \cdots \cup \mathcal{K}_{u_z} \to k_j$ if and only if $\mathcal{K}_{u_y} \to k_j$ for some $1 \leq y \leq z$. In a collusion-resistant BE scheme, a group of users that pools its keys cannot compute any keys to which one of its individual members was not already entitled. We also define the (stronger) notion of *key immiscibility*: $\{k_{i_1}, \ldots, k_{i_z}\} \to k_j$ if and only if $k_{i_y} \to k_j$ for some $1 \leq y \leq z$. If a scheme is key immiscible, then we can model key derivability as a directed acyclic graph (DAG) $\mathcal{G} = (\mathcal{V}, \mathcal{E})$, where each vertex $v_i \in \mathcal{V}$ corresponds to a key $k_i \in \mathcal{K}_{\mathcal{U}}$, and edge e_{ij} is in $\mathcal{E}$ when $k_i \to k_j$. (We abuse the term "acyclic" slightly by allowing edges from a vertex to itself: $v_i \to v_i$.) We may write $v_i \to v_j$ to indicate that $e_{ij} \in \mathcal{E}$. We may also characterize a set of immiscible keys as a poset, in that there is a bijection between key $k_i \in \mathcal{K}_{\mathcal{U}}$ and user subset $\mathcal{U}_i$.

3   RSA-Based Access Control

Akl and Taylor [2], [3] described an access control scheme based on RSA [17]. In their scheme, each user is a member of one or more security groups. These groups form a partially-ordered set (poset) under the inclusion relation. For example, all members of a top-secret security group $\mathcal{U}_i$ may be included as members of a lower security class $\mathcal{U}_j$; in this case, $\mathcal{U}_i \leq \mathcal{U}_j$. Akl-Taylor uses RSA to generate a set of immiscible keys tailored for a given poset. Here, we describe Akl-Taylor, and make some observations that will be useful when we adapt their scheme to the BE problem. First, in Akl-Taylor, a key k_i is created for each security group $\mathcal{U}_i$ as follows. First, one generates a graph $\mathcal{G} = (\mathcal{V}, \mathcal{E})$ with a vertex v_i for each security group $\mathcal{U}_i$. If $\mathcal{U}_i \subseteq \mathcal{U}_j$, then one inserts a directed edge $v_i \rightarrow v_j$. From this DAG $\mathcal{G}$, one generates a set of immiscible keys using RSA accumulators as follows. The center generates an RSA modulus $n = pq$ and fixes some $m \in (\mathbb{Z}/n\mathbb{Z})^*$. Keys have the form $k_i = m^{1/e_i} \pmod{n}$ for publicly known e_i. Clearly, $k_i \rightarrow k_j$ if e_j divides e_i. More generally,

$$\{k_{i_1}, \ldots, k_{i_z}\} \rightarrow k_j \text{ if and only if } e_j \text{ divides } \mathsf{LCM}(e_{i_1}, \ldots, e_{i_z}). \tag{1}$$

Thus, key derivability is completely dictated by the factorization of the e_i's. In Akl-Taylor, each vertex v_i in the DAG is associated with a distinct prime p_i, and $e_i = \prod_{v_i \rightarrow v_j} p_j$. It is clear that the keys are immiscible (as shown in, e.g., [2] and [4]), since the LCM in Equation 1 will be divisible by p_j only if one of the e_{i_y}'s is, in which case $v_{i_y} \rightarrow v_j$ and thus $k_{i_y} \rightarrow k_j$. Since the keys are immiscible, nonmembers of a security class (which in the BE setting consist of revoked users) cannot collude to gain access.

Now, consider the computational cost of deriving one key from another. Let $|k_i|$ denote $|\{k_j \in \mathcal{K}_\mathcal{U} \mid k_i \rightarrow k_j\}|$ – i.e., the number of keys in $\mathcal{K}_\mathcal{U}$ derivable from k_i. In Akl-Taylor, if $|k_i|$ is large, then e_i is also large – in particular, e_i has $|k_i|$ prime factors. In the worst case, computing k_j from k_i may involve exponentiation by $|k_i| - 1$ of these factors, which may be computationally expensive if $|k_i|$ is large.[1] By the following theorem, this situation is unavoidable. (Some more notation: Let $\|e_i\|$ denote $\alpha_1 + \cdots + \alpha_\ell$ where $e_i = p_1^{\alpha_1} \cdots p_\ell^{\alpha_\ell}$ is the prime factorization of e_i. Also, let c denote a user's key derivation cost $\max_{k_i \rightarrow k_j}^{k_i \in \mathcal{K}_\mathcal{U}}(\|e_i/e_j\|)$ – i.e., the maximum number of "small exponentiations" a user must make to derive a key.[2]) Theorem 1 below states that c rises (more or less) in proportion to the number of keys that can be derived from a single key.

Theorem 1. *Let $\mathcal{K}_\mathcal{U} = \{k_i = m^{1/e_i} \pmod{n}\}$ be a set of immiscible keys. Then, for any i' there exists a j' such that $k_{i'} \rightarrow k_{j'}$ and $\|e_{i'}/e_{j'}\| \geq |k_{i'}| - 1$.*

Proof. Associate $\mathcal{K}_\mathcal{U}$ with DAG $\mathcal{G} = (\mathcal{V}, \mathcal{E})$ where vertex v_i corresponds to key k_i and $v_i \rightarrow v_j$ when $k_i \rightarrow k_j$. Let $\mathcal{G}_{i'} = (\mathcal{V}_{i'}, \mathcal{E}_{i'}) \subseteq \mathcal{G}$ be the subgraph formed by the vertices $\{v_j : v_{i'} \rightarrow v_j\}$. Then, $|k_{i'}| = |\mathcal{V}_{i'}|$. Any subgraph of a DAG is a DAG, and any DAG must have a vertex with out-degree 0. Renumber the vertices in

---

[1] Note that in the implementation, one could first calculate the exponent by performing a series of (less expensive) *integer* multiplications and then perform a single modular exponentiation, but, since a user cannot reduce this exponent modulo (the unknown) $\phi(n)$, this does not significantly reduce the user's computation.

[2] We ignore the fact that the size of the primes involved in these "small exponentiations" by "small" prime exponents depends on $|\mathcal{K}_\mathcal{U}|$.

$\mathcal{G}_{i'}$ (and the associated keys) so that v_j has out-degree 0 in subgraph $\mathcal{G}_{i',j} \subseteq \mathcal{G}_{i'}$ formed by $\{v_1, \ldots, v_j\}$. By key immiscibility, and since $v_i \to v_j$ only if $i \leq j$, e_j must not divide $\mathrm{LCM}(e_{j+1}, \ldots, e_{|\mathcal{V}_{i'}|})$, implying that $\mathrm{LCM}(e_{j+1}, \ldots, e_{|\mathcal{V}_{i'}|})$ is a proper divisor of $\mathrm{LCM}(e_j, \ldots, e_{|\mathcal{V}_{i'}|})$. Since j was arbitrary, we get a chain of proper divisors, and $\|\mathrm{LCM}(e_1, \ldots, e_{|\mathcal{V}_{i'}|})/e_{|\mathcal{V}_{i'}|}\| \geq |\mathcal{V}_{i'}| - 1$. Since $v_1 \to v_j$ for all $1 \leq j \leq |\mathcal{V}_{i'}|$, $e_1 = \mathrm{LCM}(e_1, \ldots, e_{|\mathcal{V}_{i'}|})$, and the claimed inequality follows.

Remark 1. Theorem 1 is a simpler but weaker version of Theorem 2 in [15].

Thus, in applying Akl-Taylor (and any close variant) to a fixed DAG access structure, the key derivation cost c and key storage cost $k = |\mathcal{K}_u|$ have an inverse relationship. Using Theorem 1, we can relate the tradeoffs in Akl-Taylor:

$$\max_u |\mathcal{K}'_u| \leq \max_u (|\mathcal{K}_u||c_u|) , \tag{2}$$

where $|\mathcal{K}_u|$ is user u's key storage requirement and c_u is user u's worst-case key derivation cost. This tradeoff makes Akl-Taylor more configurable than a trivial access control scheme in which there is no derivability among keys and the user's key storage cost is simply $|\mathcal{K}'_u|$.

Remark 2. The Akl-Taylor technique involves the use of a one-way RSA-based accumulator [6]. Within the context of our framework, it may be possible to replace it with an alternative accumulator construction.

4   Asano's Broadcast Encryption Scheme

Asano[5] proposed a BE scheme where each terminal needs only a single key. His scheme can now be viewed as an instantiation of our above technique to a specific DAG. When looked at this way, it becomes clear, as we will later show, that the DAG which Asano chose leads to poor performance.

The Construction. In Asano's "Method 1", users are positioned as leaves in a hierarchical tree such that each node in the tree (other than the root) has $a - 1$ siblings. As a concrete example, a might be 5 or 6. Each user u can derive $|\mathcal{K}'_u| = (2^{a-1} - 1) \log_a n + 1$ subset keys, where each subset corresponds to an ancestor of the user's leaf, together with some number (but not all) of the ancestor's siblings. These subsets form a poset under inclusion, and key derivability can be modeled by a DAG. The subset keys are computed as in [2], [3]. Each user is given a single "master key" that can be used to derive the subset key for any subset to which he belongs.

To encrypt a broadcast to $\mathcal{P}$, the center must find a set of keys $\mathcal{K}_\mathcal{P}$ such that all users in $\mathcal{P}$ can derive a key in $\mathcal{K}_\mathcal{P}$, but no user in $\mathcal{R}$ can. This step is straightforward given the hierarchical arrangement of users and subsets. The center then chooses a random broadcast session key bk, encrypts bk under each key in $\mathcal{K}_\mathcal{P}$, and encrypts the broadcast under bk. The center transmits $\mathcal{R}$ and the encrypted broadcast. To decrypt, a user uses $\mathcal{R}$ to determine which key in $\mathcal{K}_\mathcal{P}$ it should derive, and uses this key to recover bk and the broadcast.

Method 1 is very efficient in terms of key storage on a user's receiver; each user stores only one key: its master key.[3] The number of pre-broadcast transmissions is $t = |\mathcal{K}_\mathcal{P}| = r(1 + \log_a(n/r))$. Notice that the parameter a can be adjusted to calibrate the value of t.

Receiver Key Derivation Cost. Unfortunately, a can be calibrated only within a very narrow range before the receiver's computational cost to decrypt bk becomes prohibitive. By Theorem 1, deriving a key in $\mathcal{K}_\mathcal{P}$ from a master key requires up to $c = (2^{a-1} - 1)\log_a n$ exponentiations (by small prime exponents). Since a user's key derivation cost grows *exponentially* with a, a must be rather small in practice. Asano's "Method 2" does not solve this problem; it simply increases the user's key storage cost and decreases its key derivation cost by a factor of $\log_a n$ compared to Method 1, which one can obviously do as a corollary of Theorem 1. Asano's constructions, while interesting, are somewhat *ad hoc* when viewed in our framework. We would prefer constructions that are, at least arguably, a nearly *optimal* application of Akl-Taylor to the BE problem. In the next two sections, we consider what is possible, and arguably impossible, for Akl-Taylor-based BE.

5   Our Improved Construction

Here we make a fundamental observation; namely, we can take *any* BE scheme in the subset-cover framework of [16] (given by some poset of user subsets) and convert it to a stateless receiver BE scheme where the terminal only needs to store a single key, and which achieves good (or possibly better) tradeoff between transmission bandwidth and key derivation cost. This allows us to separate accumulator-based BE into two, largely orthogonal, subproblems: 1) generate an optimal set of accumulator-based keys for a given poset (solved by Akl-Taylor [2] [3]), and 2) generate a combinatorially optimal poset for the BE problem. Asano never makes this observation, which may explain the ad hoc nature of his construction. Independently, Attrapadung et al. [4] allude to this fact, but their goal is to make $t = 1$; thus, to get reasonable coalition-resilience in their scheme, the receiver's key derivation cost must be huge. The combinatorial problem has been considered in connection with information-theoretically secure one-time BE schemes (e.g., [14]), where the goal is to minimize $\max_u |\mathcal{K}'_u|$ for given (n, r, t). Notice that, by Theorem 1, minimizing $\max_u |\mathcal{K}'_u|$ has the effect of minimizing $\max_i c_u$ (the maximum receiver key derivation cost) if we set $|\mathcal{K}_u|$ to be constant (e.g., 1) for all users. We could, in theory, therefore take advantage of these combinatorial results. However, to our knowledge, these combinatorial results all require that r be specificied in advance, rather than allowing t to increase or decrease with the *actual* value of r.

Here, we describe a construction that adapts the poset induced by the Subset Difference Method [16] to get an RSA-based BE scheme in which $k = 1$, $t = O(r \log_a(n/r))$, and $c = O(a \log_a n)$. Notice that, for a given k and t, a receiver

---

[3] A user's *total* storage, as opposed to its (e.g., nonvolatile) key storage, depends on whether it stores the p_i's or generates them on the fly. See [5] for details.

in our scheme uses exponentially less computation to decrypt than in Asano's scheme, with respect to the configurability parameter a. At a high level, our approach is similar to LSD [13]. In LSD, each SD key k_{n_i,n_j} is decomposed into several LSD keys $k_{n_i,N_1}, k_{N_1,N_2}, \ldots, k_{N_z,n_j}$; a user in LSD who would have received k_{n_i,n_j} in SD instead receives one of the keys in the decomposition. The SD keys are decomposed by "cutting" the user tree at several "special" levels. Our scheme also decomposes SD keys according to "special" levels, but the considerations are different. In LSD there is no need to minimize $\mathcal{K}'_u$, since the receiver's key derivation cost is not proportional to the total number of keys u can derive, but is instead proportional to the length of the path in the hash tree. We now describe our construction in more detail.

Set Up. We construct a binary tree of depth $\lceil \log n \rceil$ (where logarithms are base 2) and associate each user to a leaf of this tree. Let n_i and n_j be nodes in this tree (interior or leaf). Node n_i is defined to be an ancestor of node n_j if $n_i \neq n_j$ and n_i is on the path from n_j to the root of the tree. Define $l(n_i)$ and $l(n_j)$ to be the depth in the tree of these nodes from the root in terms of levels. An integer b is chosen such that $1 \leq b \leq \log n$, and integer a is set to 2^b. (The variable a does not necessarily need to be an exact power of 2; in this case, the b-level subtrees with a leaves will not be full.) A key k_{n_i,n_j} is generated for all node pairs (n_i, n_j) such that n_i is an ancestor of n_j and $\lfloor l(n_i)/b \rfloor = \lfloor (l(n_j) - 1)/b \rfloor$; i.e., n_i and n_j are in the same "block" when the tree is stratified into b-levels blocks. Define K to be the set of all such keys. A user u associated with leaf node n_u is given the keys k_{n_i,n_j} in K for which n_i is an ancestor of n_u, but n_j is not an ancestor of n_u. In other words, a user u is given the keys k_{n_i,n_j} for which its leaf n_u is in the subtree rooted at n_i *minus* the subtree rooted at n_j. In [16] this notion is termed the "subset difference." In total, each user receives at most $(2a - b - 2)\frac{\log n}{b} = (2a - \log a - 2) \log_a n$ keys. (See figure 1 for a graphical depiction of the construction when $n = 16$ and $b = 2$.) The set of users corresponding to the leaves defined by U (as exemplified in figure 1) will be given key k_{n_i,n_j}.

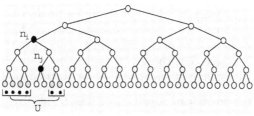

Fig. 1. Our improved construction tree construction for $n = 32$ and $b = 2$. The set of users corresponding to the leaves defined by U will be given key k_{n_i,n_j}.

Pre-Broadcast Transmission. To restrict its encrypted broadcast to a set of privileged users $\mathcal{P}$, the broadcast source must find a set of keys $K_{\mathcal{P}} \subseteq K$, preferably of minimal size, such that each user in $\mathcal{P}$ knows at least one key in $K_{\mathcal{P}}$, but no revoked user does. Computing $K_{\mathcal{P}}$ consists of two steps. In the first step, the broadcast source generates a node-pair set $\{(n_i, n_j) : n_i$ is an ancestor of $n_j\}$ – again, preferably of minimal size – such that each privileged user u (but no revoked user) has a node pair in the set such that n_i is an ancestor of n_u, but n_j is not an ancestor of n_u. In the second step, each node pair is decomposed into a node-pair key-set $k_{n_i, N_1}, k_{N_1, N_2}, \ldots, k_{N_z, n_j} \in K$, where n_i is an ancestor of N_1 such that $\lfloor l(n_i)/b \rfloor = \lfloor (l(N_1) - 1)/b \rfloor$, and so on. If n_i is an ancestor of n_u while n_j is not, then user u will know exactly one of these keys. The broadcast source sets $K_{\mathcal{P}}$ to be the union of the node-pair key-sets over all node pairs in the node-pair set.

As in [16], let $T = ST(\mathcal{R})$ be the Steiner tree formed by the root of the tree and the leaves $\{n_{\mathcal{R}_1}, \ldots, n_{\mathcal{R}_r}\}$ of the revoked users $\mathcal{R}$. The node-pair set is generated iteratively by repeating the following sequence of steps:

1. Find two leaves $n_k, n_l \in T$ such that their least common ancestor n_{kl} does not contain another leaf of T in its subtree.
2. Let n_i be the child of n_{kl} that is an ancestor of n_k, and let n_j be the child of n_{kl} that is an ancestor of n_l. Add (n_i, n_k) to the node-pair set if $n_i \neq n_k$, and add (n_j, n_l) to the node-pair set if $n_j \neq n_l$.
3. Remove all descendants of n_{kl} from T so that it becomes a leaf.

In the special case where only one leaf n_k remains, and where $n_k \neq n_0$ (the root node), the node pair (n_0, n_k) and the descendants of n_0 are removed from T. After each iteration, all privileged leaves that are descendants of a leaf in T are covered by some node pair. The process above terminates after at most r iterations, since each iteration (except in the special case) reduces the number of leaves in T by one. This process will generate a node-pair set consisting of at most $2r - 1$ node pairs.

Once the node-pair set has been generated, the broadcast source decomposes each node pair into a node-pair key-set, preferably of minimal size. For example, node pair (n_i, n_j) can be decomposed into $\lceil (l(n_j) - l(n_i))/b \rceil$ keys by letting N_1 be n_j's ancestor at level $\lceil (l(n_i) + 1)/b \rceil b$ and letting N_{y+1} be n_j's ancestor at level $l(N_y) + b$ for all y until $l(n_j) - l(N_z) \leq b$. Once the broadcast source has generated $K_{\mathcal{P}}$, it encrypts bk under each key in $K_{\mathcal{P}}$ to generate a set of ciphertexts $C_{\mathcal{P}}$. The broadcast source transmits $C_{\mathcal{P}}$, together with information sufficient for members of $\mathcal{P}$ to determine which ciphertext to decrypt. If $|\mathcal{R}|$ is much less than $|\mathcal{P}|$, where $\mathcal{R}$ is the set of revoked users, the information sent is $\mathcal{R}$. Alternatively, the broadcast could send $\mathcal{P}$, or the node-pair set.

Decrypting a Transmission. A privileged user U must first determine which ciphertext it should decrypt. It can do so by determining the node-pair set, using the same technique as the broadcast source. U then finds a node pair (n_i, n_j) in the node pair set such that n_i is an ancestor of n_u, the user's leaf, but n_j is not an ancestor of n_u. The privileged user then determines which key k_{n_k, n_l} in the decomposition of (n_i, n_j), as computed above, has n_k as an ancestor of n_u while n_l is not an ancestor of n_u. U uses k_{n_k, n_l} to decrypt the appropriate ciphertext in $C_{\mathcal{P}}$ to recover the bk and then the broadcast.

Application of Key Derivability Technique. The number of derivable keys $\mathcal{K}'_u$ per user is at most $(2a - b - 2)\lceil \frac{\log n}{b} \rceil \approx (2a - \log a - 2) \log_a n$. The number of transmissions is $t = K_{\mathcal{P}}$. Let $N_{\mathcal{P}}$ be the number of node pairs computed in the procedure above. Then, since each node pair decomposes into an average of at most $\log(n/N_{\mathcal{P}})/b$ node-pair keys, t is at most $N_{\mathcal{P}} \log_a(n/N_{\mathcal{P}})$, which assumes its maximum at $N_{\mathcal{P}} = 2r - 1$, the maximum number of node-pairs. Thus, t is at most $(2r - 1) \log_a(n/(2r - 1))$.[4] In total, each user can derive at most $(2a - b - 1)\lceil \frac{\log n}{b} \rceil \approx (2a - \log a - 1) \log_a n$ keys, and this is approximately the user's worst-case key derivation cost. The number of transmissions is increased by a factor of at most $\lceil \frac{\log n/r}{b} \rceil \approx \log_a(n/r)$ over SD, due to expansion caused by the decomposition of SD keys, so that the number of transmissions is about $2r \log_a(n/r)$. So, for roughly equivalent transmission efficiency as Asano's Method 1, we obtain a much lower key derivation cost: $(2a - \log a - 1) \log_a n$ integer multiplications (and one exponentiation) versus $(2^{a-1} - 1) \log_a n$. The improvement achieved by our proposed construction is exponential (in a) and provides about a factor of 3 improvement for even modest values such as $a = 6$.

We have thus provided one construction which improves upon Asano's method 1 construction. However, we believe that the true potential of our key derivability technique is in separating the computational key derivation problem from the combinatorial subset-cover construction problem. It is important now to consider the question of how good a construction we can develop using our key derivability technique. Thus, we turn our attention to lower bounds.

6   Combinatorial Bounds for Broadcast Encryption

On the negative side, Luby and Staddon [14] prove lower bounds on unconditionally secure one-time BE schemes (OTBESs). In this model, each user u is given some number $|\mathcal{K}_u|$ of independent keys off-line. As usual, the center finds a set of keys $\mathcal{K}_{\mathcal{P}}$ that precisely covers the privileged set $\mathcal{P}$. It then encrypts the broadcast under each key in $\mathcal{K}_{\mathcal{P}}$. The keys are not used for subsequent broadcasts – multiple-use keys, as well as the notion of deriving keys from other keys, is incompatible with information-theoretic security. Though their model is different from ours, they proved a lower bound that we find useful.

Theorem 2. (Luby-Staddon) *In any BE system with OR protocols,* $\max_u |\mathcal{K}_u|$ $\geq (\frac{\binom{n}{r}^{1/t}}{t} - 1)/r.$

Remark 3. In an "OR" protocol, a user needs one key in $\mathcal{K}_{\mathcal{P}}$ to decrypt (as opposed to "AND" protocols, where a user needs all keys in $\mathcal{K}_{\mathcal{P}}$).

Luby and Staddon only consider the information-theoretic case; however, their bound is purely combinatorial in nature and its relevance is not necessarily

---

[4] In the appendix we prove that t is at most $r(\log_a(n/r) + x)$ when $2ra^{2-x} \leq n$ using more sophisticated techniques. In particular, this implies t is at most $r(\log_a(n/r)+1)$, when $2ra \leq n$.

limited to the information-theoretic context. For example, the total number of keys that a user can *derive* in Akl-Taylor corresponds to the number k of keys stored in the Luby-Staddon framework. This number must satisfy the Luby-Staddon lower bound, even in the computational setting, under the (reasonable) assumption that a user must be able to derive one of the establishment keys to recover the broadcast, which gives us:

$$\max_u |K'_u| \geq (\frac{\binom{n}{r}^{1/t}}{t} - 1)/r \tag{3}$$

$$\max_u (|\mathcal{K}_u||c_u|) \geq (\frac{\binom{n}{r}^{1/t}}{t} - 1)/r, \tag{4}$$

where the latter equation, which follows from Equation 2, completely characterizes the BE tradeoffs for our key derivability technique.

7   Conclusions

We proposed a technique that achieves storage-efficient key derivability for any BE scheme in the generic subset-cover model. Our technique can be used in designing BE schemes with favorable trade-offs among the relevant performance parameters t, k, c. Using this technique, we developed a specific construction that directly improves upon Asano's construction [5]. Moreover, we derived lower bounds for schemes that use our technique. We consider some extensions in the appendix, and move on to discussing open issues.

One natural open issue that immediately suggests itself is the design of an alternate key derviability technique that either is more efficient with respect to one of the relevant performance parameters or whose security is based on a hardness assumption other than RSA. Also, previous works [16,13] have had to address the computational key derivability aspect together with the combinatorial subset-cover design aspect hand-in-hand since one might have affected the other. However, the key derivability technique we presented works for *any* subset cover. Therefore, one can focus on the combinatorial aspects of the subset-cover design and know that key derivability has essentially been "taken care of." Since our lower bounds do not match our upper bounds exactly, perhaps one can develop either a combinatorially better scheme or tighten the lower bounds.

References

1. M. Abdalla, Y. Shavitt, and A. Wool. Key Management for Restricted Multicast Using Broadcast Encryption. In *ACM Trans. on Networking*, vol. 8, no. 4, pages 443–454. 2000.
2. S.G. Akl and P.D. Taylor. Cryptographic Solution to a Multilevel Security Problem. In *Proc. of Crypto 1982*, pages 237–250. Plenum Press, 1982.
3. S.G. Akl and P.D. Taylor. Cryptographic Solution to a Problem of Access Control in a Hierarchy. In *ACM Trans. on Comp. Sys.*, vol. 1, no. 3, pages 239–248. 1983.

4. N. Attrapadung, K. Kobara, H. Imai. Broadcast Encryption with Short Keys and Transmissions. In *Proc. of DRM 2003*, LNCS 2770, Springer-Verlag, 2003.
5. T. Asano. A Revocation Scheme with Minimal Storage at Receivers. In *Proc. Of Asiacrypt 2002*, LNCS 2501, pages 433–450. Springer-Verlag, 2002.
6. J. Benaloh and M. de Mare. One-Way Accumulators: A Decentralized Alternative to Digital Signatures. In *Proc. of Eurocrypt 1993*, LNCS 765, pages 274–285.
7. S. Berkovits. How to Broadcast a Secret. In *Proc. of Eurocrypt 1991*, LNCS 547, pages 535–541. Springer-Verlag, 1991.
8. R. Canetti, T. Malkin and K. Nissim. Efficient Communication-Storage Tradeoffs for Multicast Encryption. In *Proc. of Eurocrypt 1999*, pages 459–474.
9. G.C. Chick and S.E. Tavares. Flexible Access Control with Master Keys. In *Proc. of Crypto 1989*, LNCS 435, pages 316–322. Springer-Verlag, 1990.
10. B. Chor, A. Fiat and M. Naor. Tracing Traitors. In *Proc. of Crypto 1994*, LNCS 839, pages 257–270. Springer-Verlag, 1994.
11. *Content Protection for Pre-recorded Media Specification* and *Content Protection for Recordable Media Specification*, available from http://www.4centity.com/tech/cprm.
12. A. Fiat and M. Naor. Broadcast Encryption. In *Proc. of Crypto 1993*, LNCS 773, pages 480–491. Springer-Verlag, 1994.
13. D. Halevy and A. Shamir. The LSD Broadcast Encryption Scheme. In *Proc. of Crypto 2002*, LNCS 2442, pages 47–60. Springer-Verlag, 2002.
14. M. Luby and J. Staddon. Combinatorial Bounds for Broadcast Encryption. In *Proc. of Eurocrypt 1998*, LNCS 1403, pages 512–526. Springer-Verlag, 1998.
15. S.J. MacKinnon, P.D. Taylor, H. Meijer, and S.G. Akl. An Optimal Algorithm for Assigning Cryptographic Keys to Access Control in a Hierarchy. In *IEEE Trans. on Comp.*, vol. C-34, no. 9, pages 797–802. 1985.
16. D. Naor, M. Naor and J. Lotspiech. Revocation and Tracing Schemes for Stateless Receivers. In *Proc. of Crypto 2001*, LNCS 2139, pages 41–62. Full version available as Electronic Colloquium on Computational Complexity Report No. 43, 2002.
17. R.L. Rivest, A. Shamir and L. Adleman. A Method for Obtaining Digital Signatures and Public-Key Cryptosystems. In *Comm. of the ACM*, 21. 1978.

A   Upper Bound on the Number of Transmissions

We prove a bound on the number of transmissions t for the construction given in section 5.

Theorem 3. *The number of tranmissions t is at most $r(\log_a(n/r) + x)$ when $2ra^{2-x} \leq n$. In particular t is at most $r(\log_a(n/r) + 1)$, when $2ra \leq n$.*

Proof. A sketch of the proof is as follows. Consider the user tree T_n with n leaves, r of which are revoked. Now, consider the tree $T_{n/a}$ with the bottom b levels removed, which has n/a leaves. Suppose that SD is applied to T_n, and consider how it affects $T_{n/a}$. Basically, its effect is similar to what would happen if SD were applied directly to $T_{n/a}$, where $r' \leq r$ revocations are occurring in $T_{n/a}$ corresponding to the $r' \leq r$ ancestors of the r revoked leaves that are at the bottom of $T_{n/a}$. So, let's assume that, for $T_{n/a}$, the number of transmissions (the number of subset-difference keys) is less than or equal to $r' \log_a(n/ar')$. How many keys are added to this when the bottom b levels are added back in?

First, again based on how SD works, up to $2(r - r')$ new SD keys can be added. Second, new keys may be necessary due to the fact that, in our method, the n_i and n_j in our keys need to be in the same b-block. Thus, a line at each level divisible by b slices though any SD keys that bridge over that level. At most r' keys can run "in parallel" from $T_{n/a}$, and so at most r' keys are sliced though by a b-line. So, the number of keys for T_n is at most:

$$r' \log_a(n/ar') + 2(r - r') + r' = \frac{r' \log(n/ar') + 2r \log a - r' \log a}{\log a} \tag{5}$$

$$= \frac{r' \log(n/a^2 r') + r \log a^2}{\log a} \tag{6}$$

$$\leq \frac{r \log(n/a^2 r) + r \log a^2}{\log a} = \frac{r \log(n/r)}{\log a}. \tag{7}$$

The above inequality works as long as $a^2 r \leq n/2$. This proof can be adapted to nonzero values of x.

B   Extensions

Relaxing Revocation. Abdalla, Shavitt and Wool [1] describe how, in the information-theoretic context, pre-broadcast transmission bandwidth and/or key storage cost can be reduced if the center is willing to tolerate some members of $\mathcal{R}$ receiving the broadcast (in addition to all members in $\mathcal{P}$). Specifically, they define a key allocation to be f-*redundant* if, for all privileged sets $\mathcal{P}$, $|r(\mathcal{P})|/|\mathcal{P}| \leq f$, where $r(\mathcal{P})$ is the set of users that can decrypt the broadcast intended for $\mathcal{P}$, and they obtain a less restrictive lower bound:

$$\max_u |K_u| \geq \max_{1 \leq k \leq n/f} \left(\frac{1}{t} \left[\binom{n}{k} / \binom{kf}{k} \right]^{1/t} - 1 \right) / (n - k). \tag{8}$$

They also provide constructions, and a greedy algorithm for finding a good key cover. Extending this approach to use constructions resulting from our key derviability technique is straightforward, where we obtain similar tradeoffs.

Traitor Tracing. Traitor tracing – as introduced in [10] – is desirable in a broadcast encryption scheme, and indeed many schemes (for example SD [16]) can be modified to include such a capability. Any traitor tracing scheme based in the subset-cover framework can be combined with our key derivability techniques.

Inclusion-Exclusion. Halevy and Shamir [13] introduce the notion of an IE-tree which allows nesting of multiple inclusion and exclusion conditions to succinctly capture seemingly complex privileged sets. They propose minor variations on the SD and LSD schemes to efficiently deal with the privileged sets defined by IE-trees. We can easily apply our key derivability techniques to these schemes to achieve comparable results.

Chameleon Hashing Without Key Exposure*

Xiaofeng Chen[1], Fangguo Zhang[1] and Kwangjo Kim[2]

[1] School of Information Science and Technology,
Sun Yat-sen University, Guangzhou 510275, P.R.China
{isschxf,isdzhfg}@zsu.edu.cn
[2] International Research center for Information Security (IRIS)
Information and Communications University(ICU),
103-6 Munji-dong, Yusong-ku, Taejon, 305-714 KOREA
kkj@icu.ac.kr

Abstract. Chameleon signatures are based on well established hash-and-sign paradigm, where a *chameleon hash function* is used to compute the cryptographic message digest. Chameleon signatures simultaneously provide the properties of non-repudiation and non-transferability for the signed message, *i.e.*, the designated recipient is capable of verifying the validity of the signature, but cannot disclose the contents of the signed information to convince any third party without the signer's consent.
One disadvantage of the initial chameleon signatures is that signature forgery results in the signer recovering the recipient's trapdoor information, *i.e.*, private key. Therefore, the signer can use this information to deny *other* signatures given to the recipient. This creates a strong disincentive for the recipient to forge signatures, partially undermining the concept of non-transferability. In this paper, we first propose a novel chameleon hashing scheme in the gap Diffie-Hellman group to solve the problem of key exposure. We can prove that the recipient's trapdoor information will never be compromised under the assumption of Computation Diffie-Hellman Problem (CDHP) is intractable. Moreover, we use the proposed chameleon hashing scheme to design a chameleon signature scheme.

Keywords: Chameleon hashing, Gap Diffie-Hellman group, Key exposure.

1   Introduction

The ordinary digital signature provides the functions of integration, authentication, and non-repudiation for the signed message. Anyone can verify the signature with the signer's public key. However, it may be undesirable in many business situations that a signature can be verified universally. For example, disclosing a signed contract to a competitor can benefit one party but jeopardize the interests of the other. This is the conflict between authenticity (non-repudiation)

---

* This work was supported by a grant No.R12-2003-004-01004-0 from the Ministry of Science and Technology, Korea.

K. Zhang and Y. Zheng (Eds.): ISC 2004, LNCS 3225, pp. 87–98, 2004.

and privacy (controlled verifiability) in the digital signatures. Chaum and van Antwerpen [9] first introduced the notion of undeniable signatures to solve this conflict. The distinct property of undeniable signatures is that verification of a signature requires the collaboration of the signer. So the signer can control to whom the signed document is being disclosed. After the initial work of Chaum and van Antwerpen, plenty of undeniable signature schemes were proposed [4,8, 16,14,15,21].

Chameleon signatures, introduced by Krawczyk and Rabin [20], are based on well established hash-and-sign paradigm, where a *chameleon hash function* is used to compute the cryptographic message digest. A chameleon hash function is a trapdoor one-way hash function, which prevents everyone except the holder of the trapdoor information from computing the collisions for a randomly given input. Chameleon signatures simultaneously provide non-repudiation and non-transferability for the signed message as undeniable signatures do, but the former allows for simpler and more efficient realization than the latter.[1] More precisely, chameleon signatures are non-interactive and do not involve the design and complexity of zero-knowledge proofs on which traditional undeniable signatures are based. Though there exist non-interactive versions of undeniable signatures [19], chameleon signatures are less complicated, at the sacrifice of not conferring the signer the ability to engage in non-transferable secondary proofs of signature (non-)validity [1].

One limitation of the initial chameleon signature scheme is that signature forgery results in the signer recovering the recipient's trapdoor information, *i.e.*, private key. Such feature has some advantages in certain applications. For example, the user can deny the forged message without revealing the original message. However, the signer can use this information to deny *other* signatures given to the recipient. In the worst case, the signer can sign any document or decrypt any message on behalf of the recipient. In fact, exposure of secret keys is perhaps the most important devastating attack on a cryptosystem [11]. This potential damage will create a strong disincentive for the recipient to forge signatures and thus weakens the property of non-transferability.

Ateniese and de Mederious [1] argue that non-transferability is more convincing if the scheme is such that collision forgery does not compromise the secret key of the recipient.[2] They firstly introduced the idea of identity-based chameleon hashing to solve this problem. Due to the distinguishing characteristic of identity-based system, the signer can sign a message to an intended recipi-

---

[1] There are some difference on non-transferability between undeniable signatures and chameleon signatures. In undeniable signatures, the verification of the signature needs the cooperation of the signer, which ensures the non-transferability. In chameleon signatures, the recipient is fully capable of providing any indistinguishable chameleon hashing inputs to satisfy the signature, thus the third party can not trust the recipient's claim.

[2] This problem can be solved in any chameleon signature scheme if the signer changes his key pair frequently, however, it is only meaningful in theoretical sense because the key distribution problem arises simultaneously.

ent, without having to first retrieve the recipient's certificate.[3] Furthermore, the signer uses a different public key (corresponding a different private key) for each transaction with a recipient, so that signature forgery only results in the signer recovering the trapdoor information associated to a single transaction. Therefore, if the recipient produces a hash collision, the signer can recover the corresponding trapdoor information to deny the forged signature by providing a different collision. However, she will not be capable of denying signatures on any message in other transactions. We argue that their scheme does not solve the problem of key exposure essentially. The basic idea is still that the recipient's public keys are changed often.[4] To the best of our knowledge, there seems no efficient chameleon hashing scheme which enjoys the message hiding property without exposing the private key.

In this paper, we propose a novel chameleon hashing scheme without key exposure under certificate-based systems, which covers all the properties of traditional chameleon hashing schemes, but the trapdoor information cannot be compromised even if the recipient forges a hash collision. Thus, the non-transferability is strengthened. Moreover, we use the proposed chameleon hashing scheme to design a chameleon signature scheme.

1.1 Related Work

There are plenty of researches on the conflict between authenticity (non-repudiation) and privacy (controlled verifiability) in the digital signatures. Undeniable signatures enable the signer to decide *when* her signature can be verified. An extended notion is "designated confirmer signatures" [7], where a designated confirmer, instead of the signer, can be involved in the verification of the signature when the signer is inconvenient to cooperate. In some applications, it is important for the signer to decide not only *when* but also *by whom* her signature can be verified due to the attacks of blackmailing [13,18] and mafia [12]. For example, the voting center presents a proof to convince a certain voter that his vote was counted without letting him to convince others (*e.g.*, a coercer) of his vote, which is important to design a receipt-free electronic voting scheme preventing vote buying and coercion. This is the motivation of the concept of "designated verifier signatures" [19]. The designated verifier will trust the signer indeed signed a message with a proof of the signer. However, he cannot present the proof to convince any third party because he is fully capable of generating the same proof by himself. Recently, Steinfeld *et al.* [24] introduced the conception of "universal designated verifier signatures", which can be viewed as an extended notion of designated verifier signatures. Universal designated verifier signatures

---

[3] It is easily to see that any key-insulated system with a physically secure device can substitute the identity-based system.

[4] In identity-based system, the identity information acts as the public key of the user. Identity-based chameleon hash can be computed under a *customized* identity $J = \mathcal{C}(ID_{Recipient}\|ID_{Signer}\|ID_{Transaction})$. The signer uses a different public key J for each transaction with different $ID_{Transaction}$.

allow any holder of the signature (not necessarily the signer) to designate the signature to any desired designated verifier. The verifier can be convinced that the signer indeed generated the signature, but cannot transfer the proof to convince any third party. In some applications, it is also important for the recipient to decide *when* and *whom* the signer's signature should be verified. This facilitates the concept of "limited verifier signatures" [2,10].

The rest of the paper is organized as follows: Some preliminary works are given in Section 2. Our novel chameleon hashing scheme is given in Section 3. The proposed chameleon signature scheme is given in Section 4. Finally, conclusions will be made in Section 5.

2   Preliminary Works

In this Section, we will briefly describe the basic definition and properties of gap Diffie-Hellman group. We also introduce the formal definition and properties of chameleon hashing scheme.

2.1   Gap Diffie-Hellman Group

Let G be a cyclic multiplicative group generated by g with the prime order q. Assume that the inversion and multiplication in G can be computed efficiently. We introduce the following problems in G.

1. Discrete Logarithm Problem (DLP): Given two elements g and h, to find an integer $a \in Z_q^*$, such that $h = g^a$ whenever such an integer exists.
2. Computation Diffie-Hellman Problem (CDHP): Given (g, g^a, g^b) for $a, b \in Z_q^*$, to compute g^{ab}.
3. Decision Diffie-Hellman Problem (DDHP): Given (g, g^a, g^b, g^c) for $a, b, c \in Z_q^*$, to decide whether $c \equiv ab \bmod q$.

We call G a gap Diffie-Hellman group if DDHP can be solved in polynomial time but there is no polynomial time algorithm to solve CDHP with non-negligible probability. Such group can be found in supersingular elliptic curve or hyperelliptic curve over finite field. For more details, see [5,6,17,23]. We call $< g, g^a, g^b, g^c >$ a valid Diffie-Hellman tuple if $c \equiv ab \bmod q$.

2.2   Chameleon Hashing

A chameleon hashing function is a trapdoor collision resistant hash function, which is associated with a key pair (sk, pk). Anyone who knows the public key pk can efficiently compute the hash value for each input. However, there exists no efficient algorithm for anyone except the holder of the secret key sk, called a trapdoor, to find collisions for every given input. Formally, a chameleon hashing scheme consists of the following efficient algorithms:

- **System Parameters Generation** $\mathcal{PG}$: An efficient probabilistic algorithm that, on input a security parameter k, outputs the system parameters SP.
- **Key Generation** $\mathcal{KG}$: An efficient algorithm that, on input the system parameters SP, outputs a secret/public key pair (sk, pk) for each user.
- **Hashing Computation** $\mathcal{H}$: An efficient probabilistic algorithm that, on input the public key pair pk of a certain user, a message m, and a random integer $r \in Z_q^*$, outputs the hashed value $h = \mathrm{Hash}(m, r)$.
- **Collision Computation** $\mathcal{F}$: An efficient algorithm that, on input the secret key sk of the user, a message m, a random integer r, and another message m', outputs an integer $r' \in Z_q^*$ that satisfies

$$\mathrm{Hash}(m', r') = \mathrm{Hash}(m, r)$$

A secure chameleon hashing scheme satisfies the following properties:

- **Collision resistance:** Without the knowledge of trapdoor information sk, there exists no efficient algorithm that, on input a message m, a random integer r, and another message m', outputs a random integer r' that satisfy $\mathrm{Hash}(m', r') = \mathrm{Hash}(m, r)$, with non-negligible probability.
- **Semantic security:** For all pairs of messages m and m', the probability distribution of the random value $\mathrm{Hash}(m', r)$ and $\mathrm{Hash}(m, r)$ are computationally indistinguishable.

3   The Proposed Chameleon Hashing Scheme

We describe our scheme in two stages. First we present a basic chameleon hashing scheme without key exposure which enjoys the properties of message hiding and semantic security. However, it is not secure against collision forgery if a signer tries to re-use the hashing scheme for a same recipient. The only reason for describing the basic scheme is to make the presentation easier to follow. We then propose our full chameleon hashing scheme without key exposure in Section 3.3.

3.1   The Basic Chameleon Hashing Scheme

- **System Parameters Generation** $\mathcal{PG}$: Let G be a gap Diffie-Hellman group generated by g, whose order is a prime q. The system parameters are $SP = \{G, q, g\}$.
- **Key Generation** $\mathcal{KG}$: Each user randomly chooses an integer $x \in Z_q^*$ as his private key, and publishes his public key $y = g^x \bmod q$. The validity of y can be ensured by a certificate issued by a trusted third party. Note that all the modular operations throughout the paper are to be interpreted as modulo q. In the following, we omit mod q for the sake of simplicity.
- **Hashing Computation** $\mathcal{H}$: On input the public key y of a certain user. Randomly chooses an integer $a \in Z_q^*$, and computes (g^a, y^a). Our novel hash function is defined as

$$h = \mathrm{Hash}(m, g^a, y^a) = g^m y^a$$

- **Collision Computation $\mathcal{F}$:** For any valid hash value h, the algorithm $\mathcal{F}$ can be used to compute a hash collision with the trapdoor information x

$$\mathcal{F}(x, h, m, g^a, y^a, m') = (g^{a'}, y^{a'}),$$

where $g^{a'} = g^a g^{x^{-1}(m-m')}$ and $y^{a'} = y^a g^{m-m'}$.

Note that

$$\text{Hash}(m', g^{a'}, y^{a'}) = g^{m'} y^{a'} = g^{m'} y^a g^{m-m'} = g^m y^a = \text{Hash}(m, g^a, y^a)$$

and $< g, y, g^{a'}, y^{a'} >$ is a valid Diffie-Hellman tuple. Therefore, the forgery is successful.

3.2   Security Analysis

We firstly introduce two variants of CDHP in G:

1. Square Computation Diffie-Hellman Problem (Squ-CDHP): Given (g, g^a) for $a \in Z_q^*$, to compute g^{a^2}.
2. Inverse Computation Diffie-Hellman Problem (Inv-CDHP): Given (g, g^a) for $a \in Z_q^*$, to compute $g^{a^{-1}}$.

Lemma 1. *Squ-CDHP, Inv-CDHP and CDHP are polynomial-time equivalent to each other in G [3,22,25].*

Theorem 1. *The basic chameleon hashing scheme is resistant to forgery provided that the CDHP in G is intractable.*

Proof. (sketch) Given two collisions (m, g^a, y^a) and $(m', g^{a'}, y^{a'})$ which satisfy $\text{Hash}(m', g^{a'}, y^{a'}) = \text{Hash}(m, g^a, y^a)$, *i.e.*, $g^{m'} y^{a'} = g^m y^a$, we can easily deduce $g^{x^{-1}} = (g^a/g^{a'})^{(m'-m)^{-1}}$. From Lemma 1, we know it is equivalent to solve the CDHP in G. $\square$

Theorem 2. *The basic chameleon hashing scheme is semantically secure.*

Proof. The proof is similar to [1]. Given a hash value h, and any message m, there exists exactly one pair (g^a, y^a) such that $h = \text{Hash}(m, g^a, y^a)$. $\square$

3.3   The Full Chameleon Hashing Scheme

In the basic scheme, collision forgery will result in the signer recovering the information $g^{x^{-1}}$. Though the secret key x cannot be recovered from this information, it enables the signer to compute the hash collisions if he re-uses the hash function for other transactions with the same recipient. Therefore, the signer should use different public key for each transaction with the recipient, *i.e.*, the recipient should change his private key often. Identity-based chameleon hashing scheme also has this disadvantage: Though the signer does not need to retrieve the certificate of the intended recipient, the recipient should apply for his private key whenever he wants to compute a collision.

We propose our full chameleon hashing scheme without key exposure by using the idea of "Customized Identities" [1]. Let $H : \{0,1\}^* \to G^*$ is a secure cryptographic hash function, define $I = H(ID_S||ID_R||ID_T)$, where ID_S, ID_R, and ID_T denote the identity of signer, recipient, and transaction, respectively.

3.3.1 The Scheme

- **System Parameters Generation** $\mathcal{PG}$: Let G be a gap Diffie-Hellman group generated by g, whose order is a prime q. Define a secure cryptographic hash function $H : \{0,1\}^* \to G^*$. The system parameters are $SP = \{G, q, g, H\}$.
- **Key Generation** $\mathcal{KG}$: Each user randomly chooses an integer $x \in Z_q^*$ as his private key, and publishes his public key $y = g^x$. The validity of y can be ensured by a certificate issued by a trusted third party.
- **Hashing Computation** $\mathcal{H}$: On input the public key y of a certain user. Randomly chooses an integer $a \in Z_q^*$, and computes (g^a, y^a). Our novel hash function is defined as

$$h = \text{Hash}(m, I, g^a, y^a) = (g * I)^m y^a,$$

  where I is a customized identity.
- **Collision Computation** $\mathcal{F}$: For any valid hash value h, the algorithm $\mathcal{F}$ can be used to compute a hash collision

$$\mathcal{F}(x, h, m, g^a, y^a, m', I) = (g^{a'}, y^{a'}),$$

where $g^{a'} = g^a(g * I)^{x^{-1}(m-m')}$ and $y^{a'} = y^a(g * I)^{m-m'}$.

Note that

$$\begin{aligned}
\text{Hash}(m', I, g^{a'}, y^{a'}) &= (g * I)^{m'} y^{a'} \\
&= (g * I)^{m'} y^a (g * I)^{m-m'} \\
&= (g * I)^m y^a \\
&= \text{Hash}(m, I, g^a, y^a)
\end{aligned}$$

and $< g, y, g^{a'}, y^{a'} >$ is a valid Diffie-Hellman tuple. Therefore, the forgery is successful.

3.3.2 Security Analysis

Theorem 3. *The full chameleon hashing scheme is resistant to forgery under the assumption of CDHP in G is intractable.*

Proof. Given (g', g'^x), let $g = g'/I$, where I is the customized identity. Define the chameleon hash function $h = \text{Hash}(m, I, g^a, y^a) = (g * I)^m y^a$. Given two collisions (m, g^a, y^a) and $(m', g^{a'}, y^{a'})$ that satisfy $\text{Hash}(m', I, g^{a'}, y^{a'}) = \text{Hash}(m, I, g^a, y^a)$, i.e., $(g * I)^{m'} y^{a'} = (g * I)^m y^a$, we can deduce $g'^{x^{-1}} = (g * I)^{x^{-1}} = (g^a/g^{a'})^{(m'-m)^{-1}}$. From Lemma 1, we know it is equivalent to solve the CDHP in G.

Note that the signer uses a different customized identity for each transaction. We remark that collision forgery in a transaction I will result in the signer recovering the information $(g * I)^{x^{-1}}$, however, the signer cannot use it to compute the information of $(g * I')^{x^{-1}}$ for a different transaction I'. Otherwise, he can compute $(I' I^{-1})^{x^{-1}}$, which is equivalent to solve CDHP in G. Therefore, the recipient does not require to change his key pair even if the hash function is reused by the same signer. □

Similar to the proof of Theorem 2, we have

Theorem 4. *The full chameleon hashing scheme is semantically secure.*

4   The Proposed Chameleon Signature Scheme

4.1   Precise Definition

A chameleon signature is generated by digitally signing a chameleon hash value of the message. The signer cannot repudiate his signature, but he can deny an invalid signature if he can provide a collision of the chameleon hash function. A good chameleon signature should satisfy the properties of *unforgeability, non-transferability, non-repudiation, deniability,* and *message hiding* [1,20]. Besides, we add the property of *key exposure freeness, i.e.,* collision forgery does not result in the signer recovering the recipient's trapdoor information. Formally, a chameleon hashing scheme consists of the following efficient algorithms and a specific denial protocol:

- **System Parameters Generation** $\mathcal{PG}$: An efficient probabilistic algorithm that, on input a security parameter k, outputs the system parameters SP.
- **Key Generation** $\mathcal{KG}$: An efficient algorithm that, on input the system parameters SP, outputs a secret/public key pair (sk, pk) for each user.
- **Signature Generation** $\mathcal{SG}$: An efficient probabilistic algorithm that, on input the public key pair pk_R of the recipient, the secret key sk_S of the signer, a message m, a customized identity I, and a random integer $a \in Z_q^*$, outputs a signature σ on the chameleon hash value $h = \text{Hash}(m, I, g^a, y^a)$.
- **Signature Verification** $\mathcal{SV}$: An efficient deterministic algorithm that, on input the public key pk_R of the recipient, the public key pk_S of the signer, a message m, a customized identity I, g^a, y^a, and a chameleon signature σ, outputs a verification decision $b \in \{0, 1\}$.
- **Denial Protocol** $\mathcal{DP}$: A non-interactive protocol between the signer and the judge. Given a signature σ on the message m, the signer computes a different collision $(m', g^{a'}, y^{a'})$. If and only if $m \neq m'$ and $< g, y, g^{a'}, y^{a'} >$ is a valid Diffie-Hellman tuple, the judge claims that the signature is a forgery.

4.2   Our Scheme

There are two users, a signer S and a recipient R, in our scheme. When dispute occurs, a judge J is involved in the scheme.

- **System Parameters Generation** $\mathcal{PG}$: Let G be a gap Diffie-Hellman group generated by g, whose order is a prime q. Define a secure cryptographic hash function $H : \{0,1\}^* \rightarrow G^*$. The system parameters are $SP = \{G, q, g, H\}$.
- **Key Generation** $\mathcal{KG}$: Each user U randomly chooses an integer $x_U \in Z_q^*$ as his private key, and publishes his public key $y_U = g^{x_U}$. The validity of y_U can be ensured by a certificate issued by a trusted certification authority.
- **Signature Generation** $\mathcal{SG}$: Suppose the signed message is m. The signer S randomly chooses an integer $a \in Z_q^*$, and computes the chameleon hash function value $h = (g*I)^m y_R^a$, here y_R denotes the public key of the recipient R. Assume SIGN is any secure signature scheme based on the assumption that CDHP in G is intractable. The signature σ for message m consists of

$$(m, I, g^a, y_R^a, \mathrm{SIGN}_{x_S}(h)).$$

Where x_S denotes the private key of the signer S.
- **Signature Verification** $\mathcal{SV}$: Given a signature σ, the recipient first verifies whether $< g, y_R, g^a, y_R^a >$ is a valid Diffie-Hellman tuple. If tuple is invalid, he rejects the signature; else, he then computes the chameleon hash value $h = (g * I)^m y_R^a$ and verifies the validity of $\mathrm{SIGN}_{x_S}(h)$ with the public key y_S of the signer.
- **Denial Protocol** $\mathcal{DP}$: When dispute occurs, *i.e.*, the recipient provides a signature of the signer $\sigma = (m^*, I, g^{a^*}, y_R^{a^*}, \mathrm{SIGN}_{x_S}(h))$ to the judge J. The judge asks the signer to provide a collision $(m', g^{a'}, y_R^{a'})$ for the chameleon hash. If the signer can provide such a collision which satisfies that $m^* \neq m'$ and $< g, y_R, g^{a'}, y_R^{a'} >$ is a valid Diffie-Hellman tuple, the judge can be convinced that the recipient forged the signature. If the signer cannot provide such a collision, the judge can be convinced that the signer indeed generated the signature.

  The signer can simply provide (m, g^a, y^a) as the hash collision. However, it will reveal the information of the original message m, which is undesirable in some applications. In section 4.3, we will show in detail how the signer can provide a different collision to ensure the property of message hiding.

4.3   Security Analysis

Theorem 5. *The proposed chameleon signature scheme satisfies the properties of unforgeability, non-transferability, non-repudiation, deniability, message hiding, and key exposure freeness.*

Proof. We prove the proposed chameleon signature scheme satisfies the above properties one by one.

- *Unforgeability*: It is trivial because we assume SIGN is a secure signature scheme based on the assumption that CDHP is intractable. Though the recipient can generate random collisions for the chameleon hash function, it is meaningless since the judge can detect this forgery after the signer provides a different collision.
- *Non-transferability*: Note that the semantic security of a chameleon hashing scheme implies the non-transferability of the corresponding chameleon signature scheme [1]. Therefore, the recipient cannot transfer a signature of the signer to convince any third party.
- *Non-repudiation*: Given a valid signature $\sigma = (m, g^a, y_R^a, \mathrm{SIGN}_{x_S}(h))$, the signer cannot generate a valid hash collision $(m', g^{a'}, y_R^{a'})$ which satisfies $h = \mathrm{Hash}(m', g^{a'}, y_R^{a'})$ and $m \neq m'$ because it is equivalent to computing the CDHP in G.
- *Deniability*: It is ensured by the denial protocol.
- *Message hiding*: Given a forgery $\sigma' = (m', g^{a'}, y_R^{a'}, \mathrm{SIGN}_{x_S}(h))$ of the recipient, the signer can provide (m, g^a, y_R^a) as the collision in the denial protocol. However, this will reveal the information of the original message m. Note that $T = (g * I)^{x_R^{-1}} = (g^a/g^{a'})^{(m-m')^{-1}}$, the signer can provide any other collision $(m^*, g^{a^*}, y_R^{a^*})$ to ensure the confidentiality of the original message m even against the judge, where $g^{a^*} = g^a T^{m-m^*}, y_R^{a^*} = y_R^a(g * I)^{m-m^*}$.
- *key exposure freeness*: Given a collision (m, g^a, y^a) and $(m', g^{a'}, y^{a'})$, the information of $(g * I)^{x_R^{-1}}$ can be recovered. However, it is impossible for anyone to compute x_R from $(g * I)^{x_R^{-1}}$. Therefore, collision forgery cannot result in the signer recovering the recipient's trapdoor information x_R, which strengthens the property of non-transferability.   □

4.4   Convertibility

In our chameleon signature scheme, it is impossible for the signer to prove which message was the original one, which is similar to the previous schemes [1,20]. In some applications, it is more desirable that the signer can confirm the original message if required. Our scheme can be converted into a universally verifiable instance as [1]. The signer encrypts the message using a semantically secure probabilistic encryption algorithm ENC and includes the ciphertext in the signature.[5] That is, the signature σ for the message m becomes:

$$\sigma = (m, I, g^a, y^a, \mathrm{SIGN}_{x_S}(h, \mathrm{ENC}(m))).$$

Our scheme can also achieve selective convertibility by having the signer expose the random bits used for the specific probabilistic encryption algorithm, and complete convertibility by exposing the decryption key.

---

[5] As [1] stated, the signer can just include the hash of the ciphertext in the signature.

4.5 Comparison with Two Previous Schemes

The proposed chameleon hashing scheme is almost as efficient as the two previous schemes. Our scheme needs one more modular exponentiation computation in G. Besides, our scheme needs a (very) little more communication cost than the previous schemes. However, we argue that it is worthy to add a (very) little computation and communication expense to overcome the limitation of key exposure. In Table 1, we present the comparison between our scheme and two previous schemes.

Table 1. Comparison with two previous schemes

Properties	Assumption	System	Key exposure	Message hiding
Krawczyk et al.'s scheme	DLP	CA-based	Yes	Yes
Ateniese et al.'s scheme	RSA	ID-based	Yes	Yes
Our scheme	CDHP	CA-based	No	Yes

5 Conclusions

Chameleon signatures simultaneously provide the properties both non-repudiation and non-transferability for the signed message, thus can be used to solve the conflict between authenticity and privacy in the digital signatures. One limitation of the initial chameleon signature scheme is that signature forgery results in the signer recovering the recipient's trapdoor information, *i.e.*, private key. Therefore, the signer can use this information to deny *other* signatures given to the recipient. This creates a strong disincentive for the recipient to forge signatures, partially undermining the concept of non-transferability.

In this paper, we first propose a chameleon hashing scheme in the gap Diffie-Hellman group to solve the problem of key exposure. We can prove that the recipient's trapdoor information will never be compromised under the assumption of CDHP in the group is intractable. Moreover, we use the proposed chameleon hashing scheme to design a chameleon signature scheme, which enjoys all advantages of the previous schemes.

References

1. G. Ateniese and B. de Medeiros, *Identity-based chameleon hash and applications*, FC 2004, to appear. Cryptology ePrint Archive, http://eprint.iacr.org/2003/167.
2. S. Araki, S. Uehara, and K. Imamura, *The limited verifier signature and its application*, IEICE Trans. Fundamentals, vol.E82-A, No.1, pp.63-68, 1999.
3. F. Bao, R. Deng, and H. Zhu, *Variations of Diffie-Hellman problem*, ICICS 2003, LNCS 2836, pp.301-312, Springer-Verlag, 2003.
4. D. Boyar, D. Chaum, and D. Damgård, *Convertible undeniable signatures*, Advances in Cryptology-Crypto 1990, LNCS 537, pp.183-195, Springer-Verlag, 1991.

5. D. Boneh, B. Lynn, and H. Shacham, *Short signatures from the Weil pairings*, Advances in Cryptology-Asiacrypt 2001, LNCS 2248, pp.514-532, Springer-Verlag, 2001.

6. J.C. Cha and J.H. Cheon, *An identity-based signature from gap Diffie-Hellman groups*, PKC 2003, LNCS 2567, pp.18-30, Springer-Verlag, 2003.

7. D. Chaum, *Designated confirmer signatures*, Advances in Cryptology-Eurocrypt 1994, LNCS 950, pp.86-91, Springer-Verlag, 1994.

8. D. Chaum, *Zero-knowledge undeniable signatures*, Advances in Cryptology-Eurocrypt 1990, LNCS 473, pp.458-464, Springer-Verlag, 1991.

9. D. Chaum and H. van Antwerpen, *Undeniable signatures*, Advances in Cryptology-Crypto 1989, LNCS 435, pp.212-216, Springer-Verlag, 1989.

10. X. Chen, F. Zhang and K. Kim, *Limited verifier signature from bilinear pairings*, ACNS 2004, LNCS 3089, pp.135-148, Springer-Verlag, 2004.

11. Y. Dodis, J. Katz, S. Xu, and M. Yung, *Key-insulated public-key cryptosystems*, Advances in Cryptology-Eurocrypt 2002, LNCS 2332, pp.65-82, Springer-Verlag, 2002.

12. Y. Desmedt, C. Goutier, and S. Bengio, *Special uses and abuses of the Fiat-Shamir passport protocol*, Advances in Cryptology-Crypto 1987, LNCS 293, pp.21-39, Springer-Verlag, 1988.

13. Y. Desmedt and M. Yung, *Weaknesses of undeniable signature schemes*, Advances in Cryptology-Eurocrypt 1991, LNCS 547, pp.205-220, Springer-Verlag, 1992.

14. S. Galbraith, W. Mao, and K. G. Paterson, *RSA-based undeniable signatures for general moduli*, CT-RSA 2002, LNCS 2271, pp.200-217, Springer-Verlag, 2002.

15. S. Galbraith and W. Mao, *Invisibility and anonymity of undeniable and confirmer signatures*, CT-RSA 2003, LNCS 2612, pp.80-97, Springer-Verlag, 2003.

16. S. Gennaro, H. Krawczyk, and T. Rabin, *RSA-based undeniable signatures*, Advances in Cryptology-Crypto 1997, LNCS 1294, pp.132-149, Springer-Verlag, 1997.

17. F. Hess, *Efficient identity based signature schemes based on pairingss*, SAC 2002, LNCS 2595, pp.310-324, Springer-Verlag, 2002.

18. M. Jakobsson, *Blackmailing using undeniable signatures*, Advances in Cryptology-Eurocrypt 1994, LNCS 950, pp.425-427, Springer-Verlag, 1994.

19. M. Jakobsson, K. Sako, and R. Impagliazzo, *Designated verifier proofs and their applications*, Advances in Cryptology-Eurocrypt 1996, LNCS 1070, pp.143-154, Springer-Verlag, 1996.

20. H. Krawczyk and T. Rabin, *Chameleon hashing and signatures*, Proc. of NDSS 2000, pp.143-154, 2000.

21. B. Libert and J. Quisquater, *ID-based undeniable signatures*, CT-RSA 2004, LNCS 2694, pp.112-125, Springer-Verlag, 2004.

22. U. Maurer, *Towards the equivalence of breaking the Diffie-Hellman protocol and computing discrete logatithms*, Advances in Cryptology-Crypto 1994, LNCS 839, pp.271-281, Springer-Verlag, 1994.

23. T. Okamoto and D. Pointcheval, *The gap-problems: a new class of problems for the security of cryptographic Schemes*, PKC 2001, LNCS 1992, pp.104-118, Springer-Verlag, 2001.

24. R. Steinfeld, L. Bull, H. Wang, and J. Pieprzyk, *Universal designated-verifier signatures*, Advances in Cryptology-Asiacrypt 2003, LNCS 2894, pp.523-542, Springer-Verlag, 2003.

25. A. Sadeghi and M. Steiner, *Assumptions related to discrete logarithms: why subtleties make a real difference*, Advances in Cryptology-Eurocrypt 2001, LNCS 2045, pp.243-260, Springer-Verlag, 2001.

Radix-r Non-adjacent Form

Tsuyoshi Takagi[1], Sung-Ming Yen[2], and Bo-Ching Wu[2]

[1] Technische Universität Darmstadt, Fachbereich Informatik,
Hochschulstr.10, D-64283 Darmstadt, Germany
`takagi@informatik.tu-darmstadt.de`
[2] Laboratory of Cryptography and Information Security (LCIS),
Dept of Computer Science and Information Engineering,
National Central University, Chung-Li, Taiwan 320, R.O.C.
{yensm,wubq}@csie.ncu.edu.tw

Abstract. Recently, the radix-3 representation of integers is used for the efficient implementation of pairing based cryptosystems. In this paper, we propose non-adjacent form of radix-r representation (rNAF) and efficient algorithms for generating rNAF. The number of non-trivial digits is $(r-2)(r+1)/2$ and its average density of non-zero digit is asymptotically $(r-1)/(2r-1)$. For $r = 3$, the non-trivial digits are $\{\pm2, \pm4\}$ and the non-zero density is 0.4. We then investigate the width-w version of rNAF for the general radix-r representation, which is a natural extension of the width-w NAF. Finally we compare the proposed algorithms with the generalized NAF (gNAF) discussed by Joye and Yen. The proposed scheme requires a larger table but its non-zero density is smaller even for large radix. We explain that gNAF is a simple degeneration of rNAF — we can consider that rNAF is a canonical form for the radix-r representation. Therefore, rNAF is a good alternative to gNAF.

Keywords: *non-adjacent form, radix-r representation, signed window method, elliptic curve cryptosystem, pairing based cryptosystem*

1 Introduction

Pairing based cryptosystems [Jou02] are able to construct very attractive applications in cryptography, e.g., tripartite Diffie-Hellmann scheme, ID-based cryptosystems, short digital signature [BLS01], etc. Barreto et al. and Galbraith et al. showed efficient algorithms for pairing based cryptosystems over supersingular elliptic curves [BKL+02,GHS02]. Several efficient arithmetic for elliptic curve with characteristic three have been investigated [BGK+03,HPS02,PS02,SW02]. Particularly, the radix-3 representation of integers can be used for efficient implementation of these algorithms with characteristic three. Recently, Duursam and Lee proposed an efficient implementation of Tate pairing for hyper-elliptic curves constructed over general characteristic r [DL03]. In this case, the radix-r representation is utilized for the efficient implementation of the pairing based cryptosystems.

In order to achieve faster scalar multiplication, we have to exploit an efficient class of the radix-r representation, i.e., the number of non-zero digits is smaller.

K. Zhang and Y. Zheng (Eds.): ISC 2004, LNCS 3225, pp. 99–110, 2004.
© Springer-Verlag Berlin Heidelberg 2004

The generalized non-adjacent form (gNAF) is known as an efficient class of radix-r representation [CL73,JY02]. The average density of non-zero digits (non-zero density) of the gNAF is asymptotically $\frac{r-1}{r+1}$ with $(r-1)$ pre-computed points among which $(r-2)$ points are non-trivial. For example, $r=3$ attains 0.5 non-zero density with 1 non-trivial pre-computed point. On the other hand, the non-zero density of the standard radix-r representation is $\frac{r-1}{r}$ with the same non-trivial pre-computed point, which is 0.67 for $r=3$. Therefore, the gNAF is able to improve the efficiency of computing the paring based cryptosystem, especially scalar multiplication. On the other hand, we can achieve lower non-zero density, if we have a larger digit set. Recently, Phillips and Burgess presented a generalized sliding window method for the radix-r representation [PB04]. The canonical form using a larger digit set for the binary representation is the width-w non-adjacent form (wNAF) [BSS99,MOC97,Sol00]. However, there is no literature that reports a variation of wNAF for the radix-r representation.

In this paper, we present an efficient class of radix-r representation, called radix-r non-adjacent form (rNAF). The proposed algorithm is a natural extension of the classical non-adjacent form (NAF) for binary representation [BSS99, IEEE], namely the adjacent bits are not simultaneously non-zero. In order to construct rNAF, we define the digit set D_r, whose elements are smaller than $\frac{r^2-1}{2}$ and are not divisible by the radix r. We prove that each integer can be uniquely represented by rNAF and the Hamming weight of rNAF representation is minimal among all signed radix-r representations using digit set D_r. We also prove that the average density of non-zero digits for rNAF is asymptotically $\frac{r-1}{2r-1}$ with $\frac{(r-2)(r+1)}{2}$ non-trivial digits. For $r=3$, we have 0.4 non-zero density with 2 non-trivial pre-computed points, which is faster than the radix-3 gNAF but requires 1 more point. Moreover, we extended this result to the width-w case. Our construction is similar to wNAF proposed by Solinas [Sol00]. We prove that the proposed width-w rNAF has asymptotically $\frac{r-1}{w(r-1)+1}$ non-zero density with $\frac{r^w-r^{w-1}-2}{2}$ non-trivial digits. Finally, we investigate the relationship between the radix-r gNAF and rNAF. Interestingly, we show that gNAF is a degenerate form of rNAF, namely if some conversions for rNAF are ignored, then we can generate gNAF. Based on this observation we present a simple generation algorithm and a simple proof of the non-zero density for gNAF.

2   Generalized Non-adjacent Form (gNAF)

In this section we discuss some known properties related to the radix-r representation.

An integer d is uniquely represented using the radix-r representation, namely

$$d = \sum_{j=0}^{n-1} d_j r^j, \quad d_j \in \{0, 1, ..., r-1\}. \tag{1}$$

We denote by $d = (d_{n-1}, ..., d_1, d_0)$ the radix-r representation of d. Here d_j and n are called the j-th digit and the digit length of the radix-r representation for d. The number of non-zero digits is called the Hamming weight of the radix-r representation of d. The average density of non-zero digits of the radix-r representation is obviously $\frac{r-1}{r}$.

If digit d_j is allowed to take a negative value (i.e., $d_j \in \{0, \pm 1, ..., \pm(r-1)\}$), it is called signed radix-r representation. In general the signed radix-r representation is not unique. However, the generalized non-adjacent form (gNAF) can uniquely represent each integer and is an optimal class for the signed radix-r representation [CL73]. gNAF is the signed radix-r representation which satisfied the following two conditions.

(1) $|d_i + d_{i+1}| < r$ for all i,   (2) $|d_i| < |d_{i+1}|$ if $d_i d_{i+1} < 0$.

If we choose $r = 2$, then the definition is equal to the classical NAF for binary representation. It is known that gNAF has the minimal Hamming weight among all signed radix-r representation with digit set $\{0, \pm 1, ..., \pm(r-1)\}$. The average density of the non-zero digits (non-zero density) is asymptotically $\frac{r-1}{r+1}$. For $r = 3$, the non-zero density is 0.5.

For a given radix-r representation of integer d, gNAF is generated by computing $(r + 1)d \overset{.}{-} d$, where the minus $\overset{.}{-}$ is a digit-wise subtraction of $(r + 1)d$ by d. This construction is a generalization of Reitwiesner algorithm for generating NAF [IEEE]. There is a carry for computing the radix-r representation of $(r + 1)d$, and thus this algorithm is not computed in the left-to-right approach. Joye and Yen proposed a left-to-right based algorithm for generating a signed radix-r representation with same non-zero density and digit set as those of gNAF [JY02].

3   Radix-r Non-adjacent Form (rNAF)

In this section, we define the radix-r non-adjacent form (rNAF) representation and prove some properties of rNAF.

We define the rNAF in the following.

Definition 1. *A signed radix-r representation $d = (d_{n-1}, ..., d_1, d_0)$ is called radix-r non-adjacent form (rNAF) if it satisfies the following conditions.*
(1) $d_j d_{j-1} = 0$ for all $j = 0, 1, ..., n$, where we define $d_n = d_{-1} = 0$.
(2) $d_j \in D_r = \{0, \pm 1, \pm 2, ..., \pm \lfloor \frac{r^2-1}{2} \rfloor \} \setminus \{\pm 1 r, \pm 2 r, ..., \pm \lfloor \frac{r-1}{2} \rfloor r \}$.
(3) The leftmost non-zero digit is positive.

This definition is a natural extension of non-adjacent form for binary string to the radix-r representation. D_r is called the digit set of the rNAF. The set D_r is generated by right-to-left conversion of two consecutive unsigned digits (e_j, e_{j-1}) (for $e_{j-1} \neq 0$):

if $e_j r + e_{j-1} < \frac{r^2}{2}$, then $(0, e_j r + e_{j-1})$, else $(1, 0, (e_j r + e_{j-1}) - r^2)$.

Therefore, all possible digits (except "0") are $(e_j r + e_{j-1})$ and $((e_j r + e_{j-1}) - r^2)$ for $e_j \in \{0, 1, ..., r-1\}$ and $e_{j-1} \in \{1, ..., r-1\}$, which are equal to $D_r \setminus \{0\}$. If r is an odd integer, then there are r^2 elements in $\{0, \pm 1, \pm 2, ..., \pm \lfloor \frac{r^2-1}{2} \rfloor \}$

and $r-1$ elements in $\{\pm 1r, \pm 2r, ..., \pm \lfloor \frac{r-1}{2} \rfloor r\}$, respectively. So, there are totally $r^2 - (r-1) = r^2 - r + 1$ elements in the set D_r. On the other hand, if r is an even integer, then there are $r^2 - 1$ elements in $\{0, \pm 1, \pm 2, ..., \pm \lfloor \frac{r^2-1}{2} \rfloor \}$ and $r-2$ elements in $\{\pm 1r, \pm 2r, ..., \pm \lfloor \frac{r-1}{2} \rfloor r\}$, respectively. So, there are totally $(r^2 - 1) - (r-2) = r^2 - r + 1$ elements in D_r.

Note that if we choose $r = 2$, then D_r is just the digits of NAF for binary string, namely $\{0, \pm 1\}$. We can prove the following theorem:

Theorem 1. (1) *Every positive integer d has a unique rNAF representation.* (2) *The rNAF representation of d has the smallest Hamming weight among all signed representations of d with digit set D_r.*

Proof. We start with the proof for (1). Assume that r is odd (the even case can be similarly proven).

We prove it by induction of digit length n for the unique unsigned radix-r representation $d = (e_{n-1}, ..., e_1, e_0)$. For $n = 2$, d is uniquely represented by

$$0 = (0,0), \quad 1 = (0,1), \quad 2 = (0,2), \quad ..., \quad r-1 = (0, r-1),$$
$$r = (1,0), \quad r+1 = (0, r+1), \quad ..., \quad r + (r-1) = (0, 2r-1),$$
$$...$$
$$k_r r = (k_r, 0), \quad k_r r + 1 = (0, k_r r + 1), \quad ..., \quad k_r r + k_r = (0, \lfloor \frac{r^2-1}{2} \rfloor),$$
$$k_r r + (k_r + 1) = (1, 0, -\lfloor \frac{r^2-1}{2} \rfloor), \quad ..., \quad k_r r + (r-1) = (1, 0, k_r r + r - 1 - r^2),$$
$$...$$
$$(r-1)r = (r-1, 0), \quad (r-1)r + 1 = (1, 0, -r+1), \quad ..., \quad (r-1)r + (r-1) = (1, 0, -1),$$

where $k_r = \lfloor \frac{r-1}{2} \rfloor$ and we have $k_r r + k_r = \lfloor \frac{r^2-1}{2} \rfloor$. Note that the radix-$r$ representation of 2-digit integers can be uniquely represented by 3-digit rNAF (the leftmost digit is $\{0, 1\}$).

We assume that the radix-r representation of n-digit integers can be uniquely represented by $(n+1)$-digit rNAF (the most significant digit is $\{0, 1\}$). Then we try to prove that it is also true for $(n+1)$-digit integers. Let $d = (e_n, e_{n-1}, ..., e_0)$ be the unique unsigned radix-r representation of $(n+1)$-digit integer d. From the assumption, the first n-digit $(e_{n-1}, ..., e_0)$ has the unique rNAF representation $(b_n, b_{n-1}, ..., b_1, b_0)$. Assume that $b_{n-1} = 0$ holds, then the rNAF representation of d is $(a_{n+1}, a_n, a_{n-1}, b_{n-2}, ..., b_1, b_0)$, where $a_{n+1} = 1, a_n = 0, a_{n-1} = 0$ if $e_n + b_n = r$, otherwise $a_{n+1} = 0, a_n = e_n + b_n, a_{n-1} = 0$. Assume that $b_{n-1} \neq 0$ holds, then the rNAF representation of d is $(a_{n+1}, a_n, a_{n-1}, b_{n-2}, ..., b_1, b_0)$, where $a_{n+1} = a_n = 0, a_{n-1} = re_n + b_{n-1}$ if $re_n + b_{n-1} < \frac{r^2}{2}$, otherwise $a_{n+1} = 1, a_n = 0, a_{n-1} = re_n + b_{n-1} - r^2$. The representation of last three digits (a_{n+1}, a_n, a_{n-1}) is obviously unique due to the definition of rNAF. Thus the rNAF representation of d for $(n+1)$-digit integers is unique. Consequently, all positive integers can be uniquely represented by rNAF representation.

Next we prove assertion (2). For a give integer d, we assume that there is a radix-r representation $R(d)$ of d with digit set D_r, whose Hamming weight is smaller than that of rNAF representation of d. Then there is a non-zero digit a_i of rNAF representation of d, which should be converted to zero in representation $R(d)$, namely there are some non-zero digits c_j such that $a_i r^i = \sum_j c_j r^j$, where

$i \neq j$ and $c_j \in D_r$. However, there is no solution c_j for $a_i r^i = \sum_j c_j r^j$, because $\sum_j c_j r^j \bmod r^i \neq 0$ and $a_i \neq 0 \bmod r$. Consequently, the rNAF representation has minimal Hamming weight among all radix-r representations with digit set D_r. □

3.1 Proposed Generation Algorithm for rNAF

In this section, we explain the proposed algorithm that generates the rNAF from an integer or a usual radix-r representation.

Proposed Algorithm (Integer to rNAF) ——————————————————
Input: integer d.
Output: the rNAF of d: $cd = (..., cd_1, cd_0)$.
    1. $i \leftarrow 0$
    2. While $d > 0$ do the following
        2.1. If $d \bmod r = 0$, then $cd_i \leftarrow 0$,
        2.2.   else $cd_i \leftarrow d \bmod s r^2$, $d \leftarrow d - cd_i$
        2.3. $d \leftarrow d/r, i \leftarrow i + 1$
    3. Return $(..., cd_1, cd_0)$.

The notation 'mods' stands for the signed modulo, namely d mods r is equal to $(d \bmod r) - r$ if $(d \bmod r) \geq r/2$, otherwise $(d \bmod r)$. Note that the set of all possible digits in Step 2.2 is exactly equal to D_r, because we eliminate the integers divisible by r at Step 2.1. The computation of $d \leftarrow d - cd_i$ causes a carry $+1$ if cd_i is a negative digit. At Step 2.3, we lift to the next digit of the rNAF representation of d.

Next we investigate the average density of non-zero digits (non-zero density) appeared in rNAF representation for $n \to \infty$. It is obvious that the non-zero density of rNAF is smaller than that of the usual radix-r representation, i.e., $\frac{r-1}{r}$. Indeed, we prove the following theorem.

Theorem 2. *The average non-zero density of the rNAF is asymptotically $\frac{r-1}{2r-1}$. The number of non-trivial digits (except $\{0, \pm 1\}$ and ignoring their sign) is $\frac{(r-2)(r+1)}{2}$.*

Proof. We investigate the distribution of each digit after the conversion $d_{i+1} r + d_i$ mods r. If non-zero digit d_i appears, the next digit d_{i+1} is always zero. Then there are two cases $(d_i) = (0)$ and $(d_{i+1}, d_i) = (0, x)$ with non-zero digit x. If case $(0, x)$ with a negative digit x appears, then there is a carry $+1$ to the next bits. The carry propagates to the higher bits. However, we can assume that each digit of radix-r representation d is randomly distributed in $\{0, 1, ..., r - 1\}$, namely each digit of d appear with probability $1/r$. We can also assume that each digit of $d + 1$ appears with probability $1/r$, because we deal with the asymptotical estimation. Therefore, the zero digit with probability $1/r$ and non-zero digit appears with $(r-1)/r$ after both cases (0) and $(0,x)$. Thus, the Markov chain of the two case $(0),(0,x)$ is as follows:

$$\begin{pmatrix} (0) & : 1/r \ (r-1)/r \\ (0,x) & : 1/r \ (r-1)/r \end{pmatrix}.$$

This Markov chain is aperiodic and irreducible, and thus there is the stationary distribution: $((0),(0,x)) = (1/r,(r-1)/r)$. Thus non-zero digit asymptotically appears $r-1$ out of $1+2(r-1)$. Consequently, we prove the assertion about the non-zero density. Next, D_r has $(r^2-1)-(r-2) = r^2-r+1$ elements and the non-zero digits always have their opposite sign. Therefore second assertion is true.   □

Note that if we choose the classical binary case $r=2$, then we obtain the famous non-zero density of NAF, namely $1/3$.

3.2   Extension to Higher Width

We define the width-w radix-r non-adjacent form (wrNAF) in the following.

Definition 2. *A signed radix-r representation $d = (d_{n-1}, ..., d_1, d_0)$ is called the width-w radix-r non-adjacent form (wr NAF) if it satisfies the following conditions.*
(1) there is at most 1 non-zero digit among any w adjacent digits
(2) $d_j \in D_{w,r} = \{0, \pm1, \pm2, ..., \pm\lfloor \frac{r^w-1}{2} \rfloor\} \setminus \{\pm1r, \pm2r, ..., \pm\lfloor \frac{r^{w-1}-1}{2} \rfloor r\}.$
(3) the leftmost non-zero digit is positive.

This definition is a natural extension of width-w non-adjacent form for binary string to the radix-r representation. The set $D_{w,r}$ is generated by right-to-left conversion of w consecutive unsigned digits $(e_{j+w-1}, ..., e_{j+1}, e_j)$ (for $e_j \neq 0$):

let $e_w = e_{j+w-1}r^{w-1} + ... + e_{j+1}r + e_j$,
if $e_w < \frac{r^w}{2}$, then $(\underbrace{0, ..., 0}_{w-1}, e_w)$, else $(1, \underbrace{0, ..., 0}_{w-1}, e_w - r^w)$.

Therefore all possible digits (except "0") are (e_w) and $(e_w - r^w)$ for $e_j \in \{1, ..., r-1\}$ and $e_{j+1}, ..., e_{j+w-1} \in \{0, 1, ..., r-1\}$, which are equal to $D_{w,r} \setminus \{0\}$. The number of elements in $D_{w,r}$ is $r^w - r^{w-1} + 1$. Note that if we choose $r = 2$, then $D_{w,r}$ is just the digits of NAF for binary string, namely $\{0, \pm1, \pm3, ..., \pm(2^{w-1} - 1)\}$.
We can prove the following theorem:

Theorem 3. *(1) Every positive integer d has a unique wr NAF representation.*
(2) The wr NAF representation of d has the smallest Hamming weight among all signed representations for d with digit set $D_{w,r}$.

In the following, we explain the proposed algorithm that generates the width-w rNAF (i.e., wrNAF) from an integer or from a usual radix-r representation.

Proposed Algorithm (Integer to wrNAF) _____

Input: integer d and width w.

Output: the wrNAF of d: $wcd = (..., wcd_1, wcd_0)$.

    1. $i \leftarrow 0$

    2. While $d > 0$ do the following

      2.1. If $d \bmod r = 0$, then $wcd_i \leftarrow 0$,

      2.2.   else $wcd_i \leftarrow d \bmod s\ r^w$, $d \leftarrow d - wcd_i$

      2.3. $d \leftarrow d/r, i \leftarrow i + 1$

    3. Return $(..., wcd_1, wcd_0)$.

This is a simple generalization of rNAF to the width-w approach. The difference from the width-2 case is the signed modulus r^w operation at Step 2.2. This algorithm is also a natural extension of the wNAF generation algorithm proposed by Solinas [Sol00].

We can prove the following theorem about the non-zero density of the wrNAF.

Theorem 4. *The non-zero density of the wrNAF is asymptotically $\frac{r-1}{w(r-1)+1}$. The number of non-trivial digits (except $\{0, \pm 1\}$ and ignoring their sign) is $\frac{r^w - r^{w-1} - 2}{2}$.*

4   Comparisons

Arithmetic weight (or non-zero density) of the representation of secret key usually reflects performance of an implementation for cryptographic operation, e.g., scalar multiplication over elliptic curve or exponentiation over finite group. Performance comparisons of the proposed rNAF and wrNAF with gNAF and the well known sliding window technique will be given.

4.1   Comparison with gNAF

The gNAF representation is an approach to reduce the arithmetic weight in order to enhance the performance of computing scalar multiplication. In the following comparison, we consider only the case of width-2 rNAF since existing gNAF does not consider a width larger than two.

The gNAF achieves $\frac{r-1}{r+1}$ non-zero density recoding and needs to store $r - 2$ non-trivial precomputed values within a table. On the other hand, the proposed rNAF has $\frac{r-1}{2r-1}$ asymptotical non-zero density and needs to store $\frac{(r-2)(r+1)}{2}$ non-trivial precomputed values. Numerical enumeration of the above comparisons are provided in Table 1. The result is that the proposed rNAF has better performance for implementing scalar multiplication with the cost of additional storage space. For practical applications, a noticeable computational speedup with only one additional precomputed value is possible by selecting $r = 3$. In this case, non-trivial digits $\{\pm 2, \pm 4\}$ are selected and a 0.4 non-zero density recoding is achieved. By using gNAF, a 0.5 non-zero density recoding is obtained with non-trivial digit $\{\pm 2\}$. Note that we count the number of non-trivial digits ignoring their sign.

Table 1. Comparisons of gNAF and the proposed rNAF.

	gNAF		rNAF	
radix	non-zero density	number of non-trivial digits	non-zero density	number of non-trivial digits
2	$\frac{1}{3} \approx 0.3333$	0	$\frac{1}{3} = 0.3333$	0
3	$\frac{1}{2} = 0.5$	1	$\frac{2}{5} = 0.4$	2
4	$\frac{3}{5} = 0.6$	2	$\frac{3}{7} = 0.4286$	5
5	$\frac{2}{3} \approx 0.6667$	3	$\frac{4}{9} \approx 0.4444$	9
6	$\frac{5}{7} \approx 0.7143$	4	$\frac{5}{11} \approx 0.4545$	14

4.2 Comparison with Sliding Window Technique

Sliding window technique [Gor98,PB04,Thu73] is an enhanced windowing technique by exploiting space-time trade-off in order to speedup scalar multiplication or exponentiation computations. With the same characteristic that a larger table with appropriate precomputed values can lead to a reduction of computational load. The conventional sliding window technique for binary representation can lead to a generalized form for any radix r larger than 2, and we called this the generalized sliding window form (gSWF). In appendix, a generation algorithm of gSWF is described. In the proposed wrNAF, larger width w may reduce the non-zero density. Similarly, in the gSWF, a larger windowing width (usually denoted as w) will also reduce the computational load by reducing the non-zero density. However, storage space for both the wrNAF and the gSWF increase for larger width w. It is therefore interesting to compare both the wrNAF and the gSWF.

Table 2. Comparisons of sliding window technique and the proposed wrNAF.

	Sliding window (gSWF)		wrNAF	
(radix, width)	non-zero density	number of non-trivial table elements	non-zero density	number of non-trivial digits
(2,2)	0.3333	1	0.3333	0
(2,3)	0.25	3	0.25	1
(2,4)	0.2	7	0.2	3
(2,5)	0.1667	15	0.1667	7
(2,6)	0.1429	31	0.1429	15
(3,2)	0.4	5	0.4	2
(3,3)	0.2857	17	0.2857	8
(4,2)	0.4286	11	0.4286	5
(5,2)	0.4444	19	0.4444	9

Consider the case of $r = 3$ and $w = 2$, the elements stored within the gSWF precomputed table are $\{2, 4, 5, 7, 8\}$ and the elements of the wrNAF digit set are $\{\pm 2, \pm 4\}$ (or $\{2, 4\}$ is sufficient for scalar multiplication over elliptic curve), respectively. An interesting fact is that both wrNAF and gSWF remove elements divisible by the radix r from their tables. Evidently, storage space requirement for the proposed wrNAF is much smaller. It will be clear from the following paragraph that the non-zero densities of both wrNAF and gSWF are the same.

The number of non-trivial elements in the gSWF table is $r^w - r^{w-1} - 1$ (excluding $\{1\}$) and the non-zero density of gSWF is $\frac{r-1}{(r-1)w+1}$. Recall that there are $\frac{r^w - r^{w-1} - 2}{2}$ non-trivial elements (excluding $\{\pm 1\}$) in the wrNAF digit set (or a corresponding precomputed table) and the non-zero density of wrNAF is $\frac{r-1}{w(r-1)+1}$. With the above results, numerical enumeration of comparisons between gSWF and wrNAF are listed in Table 2. The result is that both gSWF and wrNAF have identical non-zero density and thus have equivalent computational performance. However, wrNAF is superior to gSWF due to much less storage space requirement. The wrNAF based approach needs less than half memory space as gSWF.

4.3   Relationship Between gNAF and rNAF

We explain that gNAF is a simple degeneration of rNAF. Recall that rNAF is generated by the conversion table of two consecutive digits described in Section 3.1. We show that the conversion table for gNAF can be obtained by degenerating that of rNAF. For example, the degenerated conversion table for $r = 3$ is as follows: $(0,1) \leftarrow (0,1)$, $(0,2) \leftarrow (0,2)$, $(1,0,\bar{2}) \leftarrow (2,1)$, $(1,0,\bar{1}) \leftarrow (2,2)$. The difference from the rNAF generation algorithm is to eliminate the tables $(0,\bar{4}) \leftarrow (1,2)$ and $(0,4) \leftarrow (1,1)$. In other words, if the consecutive digits $(1,2)$ or $(1,1)$ appear, we do not convert it, but slide 1 bit to the left.

Indeed the gNAF can be generated by the following algorithm, which is a simple modification of the generation algorithm for rNAF. For the sake of simplicity, we use the radix-r representation for input d.

Proposed Algorithm (Radix-r to gNAF) ――――――――――――――――
Input: radix-r representation $d = (d_{n-1}, ..., d_1, d_0)$.
Output: the radix-r gNAF of d: $cd = (cd_n, ..., cd_1, cd_0)$.
   1. $i \leftarrow 0$, $d_n \leftarrow 0$,
   2. While $i < n$ do the following
     2.1. If $d_i \bmod r = 0$,
           then $cd_i \leftarrow 0$, $d_{i+1} \leftarrow d_{i+1} + d_i/r$, $i \leftarrow i + 1$,
     2.2.   else if $d_{i+1} + d_i/r \bmod r = 0$ or $r - 1$,
           then $cd_{i+1} \leftarrow 0$, $cd_i \leftarrow d_{i+1}r + d_i$ mods r,
           $d_{i+2} \leftarrow d_{i+2} + (1 - sign(cd_i))/2$, $i \leftarrow i + 2$,
     2.3.   else $d_{i+1} \leftarrow d_{i+1} + d_i/r$,
           if $(d_i \bmod r + d_{i+1} \bmod r) > r$,
           then $cd_i \leftarrow d_i \bmod r - r$, $d_{i+1} \leftarrow d_{i+1} + 1$, $i \leftarrow i + 1$,
           else $cd_i \leftarrow d_i \bmod r$, $i \leftarrow i + 1$
   3. Return $(cd_n, ..., cd_1, cd_0)$.

―――

The only difference from the rNAF generation algorithm is the if-condition "if $d_{i+1} + d_i/r \bmod r = 0$ or $r - 1$" appeared at Step 2.2 and its branch (i.e., the whole process of Step 2.3). In order to satisfy the property of gNAF, we have an additional treatment at Step 2.3, namely we perform $(d_{i+1}, d_i) \to (d_{i+1}+1, d_i-r)$ for $(d_i \bmod r + d_{i+1} \bmod r) > r$.

In the following, we prove that this algorithm correctly returns the gNAF representation of the radix-r representation of d.

Theorem 5. *The algorithm (Radix-r to gNAF) generates radix-r gNAF.*

Proof. Let $d_i' = d_i + b \bmod r$, where b is a carry in the algorithm from right hand side, namely $d_i' = d_i + d_{i-1}/r \bmod r$.

At step 2.1., we have a branch, if digit d_i' is equal to zero, then we skip to the next bit after computing carry. If digit d_i' is non-zero, we check digit d_{i+1}' with carry is 0 or $r-1$. If $d_{i+1}' = 0$, we assign $(cd_{i+1}, cd_i) = (0, d_i')$. If $d_{i+1}' = r-1$, then we perform the conversion $(cd_{i+1}, cd_i) = (1, 0, d_{i+1}'r + d_i' - r^2)$. Note that $|d_{i+1}'r + d_i' - r^2| < r$, and thus the converted digits (cd_{i+1}, cd_i) after Step 2.2. satisfy the condition of gNAF.

If d_{i+1}' is neither 0 nor $r-1$, then we assign d_i' based on the size of $|d_{i+1}' + d_i'|$ at Step 2.3. If $|d_{i+1}' + d_i'| > r$ holds, we assign $cd_i = d_i' - r$ with carry to $d_{i+1}' = d_{i+1}' + 1$. Otherwise, $cd_i = d_i'$. Therefore, after Step 2.3. the converted digits (d_{i+1}', cd_i) satisfy the condition of gNAF. Then we have to consider the case that the digit d_{i+1}' arisen from Step 2.3 is converted by the next Step 2.2 or Step 2.3. Denote by cd_{i+1} the converted digit, and we check whether two consecutive bits (cd_{i+1}, cd_i) satisfy the condition of gNAF. Note that $d_{i+1}' > 0$ and $cd_{i+1} = d_{i+1}' - r < 0$. Recall that $|d_{i+1}' + cd_i| < r$ and $|d_{i+1}'| > |cd_i|$ for $cd_i < 0$ from the above discussion. If $cd_i < 0$, then we have $|cd_{i+1} + cd_i| = r - |d_{i+1}'| + |cd_i| < r$. In the case of $cd_i > 0$, we have $|cd_{i+1} + cd_i| = |d_{i+1}' + cd_i - r| < r$ due to $d_{i+1}' + cd_i \neq 0$, and $|cd_{i+1}| - |cd_i| = r - (d_{i+1}' + cd_i) > 0$.

Consequently, any two consecutive digits (cd_{i+1}, cd_i) obtained by the algorithm satisfied the condition of gNAF. □

The proposed algorithm has the minimal non-zero density $(r-1)/(r+1)$ with digit set $\{0, \pm 1, ..., \pm(r-1)\}$ due to the uniqueness of gNAF. However, our algorithm is able to show an easier proof about the non-zero density of gNAF.

Theorem 6. *The average density of non-zero digits arisen from the algorithm (Radix-r to gNAF) is asymptotically $\frac{r-1}{r+1}$.*

Proof. The above algorithm has four statuses of digit d_i, namely digit (0), digit (i) for $i = 1, 2, .., r-2$, digit $(r-1, y)$ with carry from the right, and digit $(r-1, n)$ without carry from the right. The statuses are transited by the following Markov chain:

$$\begin{pmatrix} (0) & : 1/r & (r-2)/r & 0 & 1/r \\ (i) & : 1/r & (r-2)/r & 1/r & 0 \\ (r-1, y) & : 1/r & (r-2)/r & 0 & 1/r \\ (r-1, n) & : 1/r & (r-2)/r & 1/r & 0 \end{pmatrix}.$$

This Markov chain is aperiodic and irreducible, and thus there is the stationary distribution: $((0), (i), (r-1, y), (r-1, n)) = (\frac{1}{r}, \frac{r-2}{r}, \frac{r-1}{(r+1)r}, \frac{2}{(r+1)r})$. Thus zero digit appears at statuses (0) and $(r-1, y)$, and thus the non-zero density is $1 - \frac{1}{r} - \frac{r-1}{(r+1)r} = \frac{r-1}{r+1}$. Consequently, we prove the theorem. □

In appendix, we show a corresponding table between rNAF and gNAF for 3-digit radix-r representation with $r = 3$.

Acknowledgement. We would like to thank the anonymous referees for their useful comments and introducing the reference [PB04]. The research of S.M. Yen was supported in part by the National Science Council R.O.C. under contract NSC 92-2213-E-008-007. T. Takagi is partially supported by SicAri Project (http://www.sicari.de/).

References

[BKL+02] P. Barreto, H. Kim, B. Lynn, and M. Scott, "Efficient Algorithms for Pairing-Based Cryptosystems," *CRYPTO 2002*, LNCS 2442, pp.354-368, 2002.

[BGK+03] G. Bertoni, J. Guajardo, S. Kumar, G. Orlando, C. Paar, and T. Wollinger, "Efficient $GF(p^m)$ Arithmetic Architectures for Cryptographic Applications," *CT-RSA 2003*, LNCS 2612, pp.158-175, 2003.

[BSS99] I. Blake, G. Seroussi, and N. Smart, *Elliptic Curves in Cryptography*, Cambridge University Press, 1999.

[BLS01] D. Boneh, B. Lynn, and H. Shacham, "Short Signatures from the Weil Pairing," *ASIACRYPT 2001*, LNCS 2248, pp.514-532, 2001.

[CL73] W. Clark and J. Liang, "On Arithmetic Weight for a General Radix Representation of Integers," *IEEE Transaction on IT*, IT-19, pp.823-826, 1973.

[DL03] I. Duursma and H -S .Lee, "Tate Pairing Implementation for Hyperelliptic Curves $y^2 = x^p - x + d$," *ASIACRYPT 2003*, LNCS 2894, pp.111-123, 2003.

[GHS02] S. Galbraith, K. Harrison, and D. Soldera, "Implementing the Tate pairing," *ANTS V*, LNCS 2369, pp.324-337, Springer-Verlag, 2002.

[Gor98] D. Gordon, "A Survey of Fast Exponentiation Methods," *Journal of Algorithms*, Vol.27, pp.129-146, 1998.

[HPS02] K. Harrison, D. Page, and N. Smart, "Software Implementation of Finite Fields of Characteristic Three," *LMS Journal of Computation and Mathematics*, Vol.5, pp.181-193, 2002

[IEEE] IEEE P1363, Standard Specifications for Public-Key Cryptography, 2000.

[Jou02] A. Joux, "The Weil and Tate Pairings as Building Blocks for Public Key Cryptosystems (survey)," *ANTS V*, LNCS 2369, pp.20-32, 2002.

[JY02] M. Joye and S. -M. Yen, "New Minimal Modified Radix-r Representation with Applications to Smart Cards," *PKC 2002*, LNCS 2274, pp.375-384, 2002.

[MOC97] A. Miyaji, T. Ono, and H. Cohen, "Efficient Elliptic Curve Exponentiation," *ICICS '97*, LNCS 1334, pp.282-291, 1997.

[PS02] D. Page and N. Smart, "Hardware Implementation of Finite Fields of Characteristic Three," *CHES 2002*, LNCS 2523, pp.529-539, 2002.

[PB04] B. Phillips and N. Burgess, "Minimal Weight Digit Set Conversions," *IEEE Transactions on Computers*, Vol.53, No.6, pp.666-677, 2004.

[SW02] N. Smart, and J. Westwood, "Point Multiplication on Ordinary Elliptic Curves over Fields of Characteristic Three," *Applicable Algebra in Engineering, Communication and Computing*, Vol.13, No.6, pp.485-497, 2003.

[Sol00] J. Solinas, "Efficient Arithmetic on Koblitz Curves," *Design, Codes and Cryptography*, Vol.19 (2/3), pp.195-249, 2000.

[Thu73] E.G. Thurber, "On Addition Chains $l(mn) \leq l(n) - b$ and Lower Bounds for $c(r)$," *Duke Mathematical Journal*, Vol.40, pp.907-913, 1973.

A   Radix-r Sliding Window Method (gSWF)

We describe the width-w sliding window method for the radix-r representation (gSWF).

We scan the digits of the radix-r representation from the most significant bit, and if a non-zero digit appears, then we convert the w-consecutive digits using the following conversion table $\mathcal{T}_{SW}$:

$$
\begin{array}{lll}
(1, 0, ..., 0) \rightarrow (1, 0, .., 0), & ..., & (r-1, 0, ..., 0) \rightarrow (r-1, 0, .., 0), \\
(1, 1, 0, ..., 0) \rightarrow (0, r+1, 0, .., 0), & ..., & (r-1, r-1, 0, ..., 0) \rightarrow (0, r^2-1, 0, ..., 0), \\
\quad\quad ... & ... & \quad\quad ... \\
(r-1, ..., r-1, 1) \rightarrow (0, ..., 0, r^w - r + 1), & ..., & (r-1, ..., r-1, r-1) \rightarrow (0, ..., 0, r^w - 1).
\end{array}
$$

Then, we convert the radix-r representation to gSWF as follows:

Proposed Algorithm (Radix-r to gSWF) ————————————————————————
Input: radix-r representation $d = (d_{n-1}, ..., d_1, d_0)$ and width-w.
Output: the width-w SW chain of d: $swd = (swd_{n-1}, ..., swd_1, swd_0)$.
  1. $i \leftarrow n-1$, $d_0 \leftarrow 0$, ..., $d_{-w+1} \leftarrow 0$
  2. While $i > 0$ do the following
     2.1. If $d_i = 0$, then $swd_i \leftarrow 0$, $i \leftarrow i-1$,
     2.2.   else $(swd_i, ..., swd_{i-w+1}) \leftarrow \mathcal{T}_{SW}(d_i, ..., d_{i-w+1})$, $i \leftarrow i-w$
  3. Return $(swd_{n-1}, ..., swd_1, swd_0)$.
——

Each integer is uniquely converted to gSWF by this algorithm. We can prove that the number of non-trivial digits of gSWF is $r^w - r^{w-1} - 1$ (excluding $\{1\}$) and the average density of non-zero digits of gSWF is asymptotically $\frac{r-1}{(r-1)w+1}$.

B   Example of gNAF, rNAF and gSWF

In this appendix, we show examples of gNAF in Section 2, rNAF in Section 3, and gSWF in Section 4.2 up to 3-digit radix-r representation for $r = 3$ and width 2.

integer	radix-3	rNAF	gNAF	gSWF	integer	radix-3	rNAF	gNAF	gSWF
1	0001	0001	0001	0001	14	0112	020$\bar{4}$	02$\bar{1}\bar{1}$	0042
2	0002	0002	0002	0002	15	0120	10$\bar{4}$0	02$\bar{1}$0	0050
3	0010	0010	0010	0010	16	0121	020$\bar{2}$	020$\bar{2}$	0051
4	0011	0004	0011	0004	17	0122	020$\bar{1}$	020$\bar{1}$	0052
5	0012	010$\bar{4}$	002$\bar{1}$	0005	18	0200	0200	0200	0200
6	0020	0020	0020	0020	19	0201	0201	0201	0201
7	0021	010$\bar{2}$	010$\bar{2}$	0007	20	0202	0202	0202	0202
8	0022	010$\bar{1}$	010$\bar{1}$	0008	21	0210	10$\bar{2}$0	10$\bar{2}$0	0070
9	0100	0100	0100	0100	22	0211	0204	10$\bar{2}$1	0071
10	0101	0101	0101	0101	23	0212	100$\bar{4}$	10$\bar{1}\bar{1}$	0072
11	0102	0102	0102	0102	24	0220	10$\bar{1}$0	10$\bar{1}$0	0080
12	0110	0040	0110	0040	25	0221	100$\bar{2}$	100$\bar{2}$	0081
13	0111	0104	0111	0041	26	0222	100$\bar{1}$	100$\bar{1}$	0082

On Related-Key and Collision Attacks: The Case for the IBM 4758 Cryptoprocessor

Raphael C.-W. Phan[1] and Helena Handschuh[2]

[1] Information Security Research (iSECURES) Lab,
Swinburne University of Technology (Sarawak Campus),
93576 Kuching, Sarawak, Malaysia
rphan@swinburne.edu.my
[2] Gemplus R&D,
Security Technologies Department,
34 rue Guynemer,
92447 Issy-les-Moulineaux, France
Helena.Handschuh@gemplus.com

Abstract. We consider how related-key attacks can be mounted on the IBM 4758 cryptoprocessor, and also show that its EDEx multiple mode is far less secure than one could believe. As few as about 2^{32} known plaintexts and related-key known ciphertexts in the first case, and 2^{34} chosen ciphertexts in the second case are required to mount key-recovery attacks. These results show that seemingly academic attacks seriously need to be taken into consideration when it comes to real-life implementations.

1 Introduction

Related-key attacks are those where the cryptanalyst can obtain the encryptions of plaintexts under both the unknown secret key, K, as well as an unknown related key, K' whose relationship to K is known or can even be chosen [2].

Most cryptographers' notion of related-key attacks is that they are merely of theoretical interest since they work under a security model that is often considered too restricted and impractical. Note that this notion is in contrast to Kelsey et al.'s [19,20] works that describe several possible related-key attack scenarios.

In this paper, we show that related-key attacks are possible by considering the case of the IBM 4758 cryptoprocessor used with automatic teller machines (ATMs) [17]. We further mount attacks on the EDEx mode used in the IBM 4758 and show it does not achieve its desired security.

In Section 2, we describe the IBM 4758 cryptoprocessor. We briefly recall in Section 3 the basics of related-key attacks and then present situations where the IBM 4758 makes it possible to mount related-key attacks. We also describe in Section 4 how one could exploit one of the block cipher modes of operation used in the IBM 4758 to further mount attacks. We conclude in Section 5.

K. Zhang and Y. Zheng (Eds.): ISC 2004, LNCS 3225, pp. 111–122, 2004.
© Springer-Verlag Berlin Heidelberg 2004

2   The IBM 4758

The IBM 4758 is a cryptoprocessor [17] used with automatic teller machines (ATMs) to store personal identification numbers (PINs) and customer keys, SKs, securely in a bank's host computer. This cryptoprocessor is tamper-resistant and the way to interact with it is through a software interface called the crypto application program interface (API) which is merely a collection of pre-defined software functions (also called verbs) that can be called to perform specific tasks. The IBM 4758's API is called the Common Cryptographic Architure (CCA).

PINs and customer keys are stored in the IBM 4758 in encrypted form. In particular, they are triple-DES encrypted by a triple-length (3×56 bits = 168-bit) master key, MK. Refer to [17], page C-14 for further details. In addition, the 4758 also uses control vectors, CVs to enforce key typing so that a key of a certain type can only be used for its corresponding designated operation.

Denote $MK = MK_1|MK_2|MK_3$ and $CV = C_1|C_1'$, where C_1 and C_1' differ in only bits 41 and 42. In particular, $C_1 \oplus C_1' = \triangle_C = (0^{40}1^20^{22})$.

To use an MK to triple-DES encrypt double-length (112-bit) customer keys, SKs, prior to being stored within a bank computer's hard drive requires that MK be first used to generate keys (K_1, K_2, K_3) and (K_4, K_5, K_6) as follows:

$$K_1 = MK_1 \oplus C_1 \tag{1}$$
$$K_2 = MK_2 \oplus C_1 \tag{2}$$
$$K_3 = MK_3 \oplus C_1 \tag{3}$$
$$K_4 = MK_1 \oplus C_1' \tag{4}$$
$$K_5 = MK_2 \oplus C_1' \tag{5}$$
$$K_6 = MK_3 \oplus C_1' \tag{6}$$

Denote $SK = SK_1|SK_2$. Then triple-DES encrypt SK_1 under keys (K_1, K_2, K_3) to obtain the left half of the operational key, K_{OP1}, as follows:

$$K_{OP1} = E_{K_3}(D_{K_2}(E_{K_1}(SK_1))). \tag{7}$$

Triple-DES encrypt SK_2 under (K_4, K_5, K_6) to obtain the other half, K_{OP2}:

$$K_{OP2} = E_{K_6}(D_{K_5}(E_{K_4}(SK_2))). \tag{8}$$

Then, $K_{OP} = K_{OP1}|K_{OP2}$ is stored in the bank computer. This is the encrypted form of SK. Note that K_1 to K_3 differ from K_4 to K_6 by only 2 bits, namely bits 41 and 42. In particular, we have the following relationship between them:

$$K_1 \oplus K_4 = \triangle_C \tag{9}$$
$$K_2 \oplus K_5 = \triangle_C \tag{10}$$
$$K_3 \oplus K_6 = \triangle_C \tag{11}$$

Alternatively, when an SK is to be transported between IBM 4758's with different master keys, then it is decrypted from its triple-DES encrypted version,

K_{OP} to get back the original SK, and then encrypted with a double-length (2 × 56 bits = 112-bit) Key-Encrypting Key, KEK. In particular, the $KEK = KEK_1|KEK_2$ is used to derive the keys (K_1, K_2, K_3) and (K_4, K_5, K_6):

$$K_1 = KEK_1 \oplus C_1 \tag{12}$$
$$K_2 = KEK_2 \oplus C_1 \tag{13}$$
$$K_3 = KEK_1 \oplus C_1 \tag{14}$$
$$K_4 = KEK_1 \oplus C_1' \tag{15}$$
$$K_5 = KEK_2 \oplus C_1' \tag{16}$$
$$K_6 = KEK_1 \oplus C_1' \tag{17}$$

These keys are used to encrypt SK similar to (7) and (8) as follows:

$$K_{EX1} = E_{K_3}(D_{K_2}(E_{K_1}(SK_1))), \tag{18}$$
$$K_{EX2} = E_{K_6}(D_{K_5}(E_{K_4}(SK_2))), \tag{19}$$

and the exported key is $K_{EX} = K_{EX1}|K_{EX2}$.

3   Mounting Related-Key Attacks on the IBM 4758

Denote $C = E_K(P)$ as the encryption of a plaintext, P under the control of a secret key, K to obtain the ciphertext, C. By related-key attacks, it means that a cryptanalyst is able to access two oracles, $E_K(.)$ and $E_{K'}(.)$ where $K' = K \oplus \triangle$ is another unknown key whose relationship to K is known or can be chosen, in particular the difference between them is $\triangle$.

In this section, we demonstrate how related-key attacks can be obtained on the IBM 4758 cryptoprocessor, which is widely in use today, for example in ATMs. This serves to strengthen the arguments by Kelsey et al. [19,20] that related-key attacks are not to be disregarded as purely of theoretical interest.

There are several scenarios with the IBM 4758 that allow one to mount both *related-key differential* and *related-key slide* attacks, as follows:

Scenario 1.
Consider when $SK = SK_1|SK_1$ (the customer key, SK consists of two equal halves). This is possible since this is a customer key so one could easily request to choose what he wants to have as his SK. An attacker could be a customer since everyone has an ATM card these days! One could also make use of either the Clear-Key-Import or the Key-Part-Import verbs [17] which allow one to have a cleartext single- or double-length DES key, SK be encrypted under the local master key, MK to obtain the operational key, K_{OP}. Then we get:

$$K_{OP1} = E_{K_3}(D_{K_2}(E_{K_1}(SK_1))), \tag{20}$$
$$K_{OP2} = E_{K_6}(D_{K_5}(E_{K_4}(SK_1))). \tag{21}$$

Recall from (9) to (11) that K_1 to K_3 and K_4 to K_6 are related, namely that their difference is $\triangle_C$. So under this scenario the plaintexts for triple-DES encryption in both (20) and (21), denoted by SK_1, are the same. We can therefore obtain related-key queries of the same plaintext, SK_1, under the related keys (K_1, K_2, K_3) and $(K_4 = K_1 \oplus \triangle_C, K_5 = K_2 \oplus \triangle_C, K_6 = K_3 \oplus \triangle_C)$. This presents a real-life scenario for mounting related-key *differential* attacks [19,20].

Scenario 2.
We recall that KEKs are also used to encrypt customer keys for transporting between IBM 4758s with different master keys, and that a KEK is used to generate the keys K_1 to K_3 and K_4 to K_6 based on (12) to (17).

To mount a related-key attack here, we use KEKs to generate K_1, K_2 and K_3 the usual way as in (12) to (14). However, to obtain the other three keys K_4 to K_6, we use Bond's attack [12] to introduce a known difference into the $KEK = KEK_1 | KEK_2$, such that bits 41 and 42 of both KEK_1 and KEK_2 are complemented. In particular, we use a modified version of KEK:

$$KEK' = KEK \oplus (\triangle_C | \triangle_C) = (KEK_1 | KEK_2) \oplus (\triangle_C | \triangle_C). \qquad (22)$$

We see then that the keys K_4 to K_6 would be obtained as below:

$$K_4 = KEK_1' \oplus C_1' = KEK_1 \oplus \triangle_C \oplus C_1' = KEK_1 \oplus C_1 = K_1 \qquad (23)$$
$$K_5 = KEK_2' \oplus C_1' = KEK_2 \oplus \triangle_C \oplus C_1' = KEK_2 \oplus C_1 = K_2 \qquad (24)$$
$$K_6 = KEK_1' \oplus C_1' = KEK_1 \oplus \triangle_C \oplus C_1' = KEK_1 \oplus C_1 = K_3 \qquad (25)$$

Therefore, both halves of SK will be triple-DES encrypted under the same keys, namely (K_1, K_2, K_3) and $(K_4, K_5, K_6) = (K_1, K_2, K_3)$. Since both encryptions are done in ECB mode [17], it is then possible to swap these encrypted halves!

This scenario allows one to mount related-key *slide* attacks on 2-key triple-DES encryptions keyed by this double-length key, SK such as those described in [23]. In more detail, an attacker obtains the 2-key triple-DES encryption of plaintexts under a key $SK = SK_1 | SK_2$ and also under a related key, $SK' = SK_2 | SK_1$. He can then mount a related-key slide attack that obtains SK requiring 2^{32} known plaintexts (KP), 2^{32} related-key known ciphertexts $(RK\text{-}KC)$, $2^{89.5}$ memory and 2^{88} single DES encryptions [23].

An anonymous referee has remarked that our requirement here to swap KEK with KEK' halfway through the computation of the keys $K_1, \ldots, K_6$ might be hard. However, we can easily work around this by obtaining the encryption of the customer key, SK first under KEK, and then under KEK' as defined in (22). KEK generates the keys $K_1, \ldots, K_6$ as usual based on equations (12) to (17) while KEK' generates the keys $K_1', \ldots, K_6'$. It is trivial to show that:

$$K_1' = K_4 \qquad (26)$$
$$K_2' = K_5 \qquad (27)$$
$$K_3' = K_6 \qquad (28)$$
$$K_4' = K_1 \qquad (29)$$
$$K_5' = K_2 \qquad (30)$$

$$K_6' = K_3. \tag{31}$$

Denote the encrypted exported keys as $K_{EX} = K_{EX1}|K_{EX2}$ and $K_{EX}' = K_{EX1}'|K_{EX2}'$ respectively, where the halves of K_{EX} are as in (18) and (19), while those of K_{EX}' are:

$$K_{EX1}' = E_{K_6}(D_{K_5}(E_{K_4}(SK_1))), \tag{32}$$
$$K_{EX2}' = E_{K_3}(D_{K_2}(E_{K_1}(SK_2))). \tag{33}$$

Since the halves are encrypted in ECB mode, we can easily swap them to produce a modified $K_{EX}'' = K_{EX2}'|K_{EX1}'$, and then forwarding this to the IBM 4758. When the exported keys, K_{EX} and K_{EX}'' are both imported under KEK, then the corresponding customer keys obtained would be the two related keys, $SK = SK_1|SK_2$ and $SK' = SK_2|SK_1$ respectively, and related-key slide attacks as in [23] are then possible.

4   Attacks on IBM 4758's EDEx Mode of Operation

In this section, we present attacks on the IBM 4758's EDEx mode of operation [3], which is a type of multiple mode [4-9, 15-16, 24-25]. We describe both collision-style chosen-plaintext/ciphertext attacks as well as related-key attacks.

We first review the three modes of operations used in the IBM 4758. They consist of straightforward extensions of the standard *electronic codebook (ECB)* and *cipher block chaining (CBC)* modes, as well as an extended variant known as the $CBC|CBC^{-1}|CBC$ mode (or called EDEx as in [17]).

Modes of operation are used when encrypting plaintext messages with length longer than the block size of a block cipher. The first mode in the IBM 4758 is the *triple-ECB* mode. This is the simplest and just triple-encrypts each block, P_i of a plaintext independently of the other blocks, under control of 3 keys, (K_1, K_2, K_3):

$$C_i = E_{K_3}(E_{K_2}^{-1}(E_{K_1}(P_i))). \tag{34}$$

Meanwhile, the second mode, also known as the *outer-CBC* mode uses the previous ciphertext block, C_{i-1} as the feedback component that is XORed to the current plaintext block, P_i, before the resulting XOR is triple-encrypted to obtain the current ciphertext block, C_i:

$$C_i = E_{K_3}(E_{K_2}^{-1}(E_{K_1}(P_i \oplus C_{i-1}))) \tag{35}$$

where $C_0 = $ initialization vector (IV).

The third mode, EDEx can in fact be viewed as a multiple mode in that it is a combination of several modes, in this case the application of the modes CBC, CBC^{-1} and CBC in sequence. There are three versions of this EDEx mode, depending on whether 2, 3 or 5 keys are used, denoted as EDE2, EDE3 and EDE5 respectively. Both EDE2 and EDE3 assume 0 as the IVs. In addition, EDE2 uses K_1 to key the first and third (CBC) layers and K_2 to key the middle

(CBC^{-1}) layer, while EDE3 uses K_1, K_2 and K_3 to uniquely key the three different layers respectively. Lastly, EDE5 uses 3 keys, K_1, K_2 and K_3 in the same way as EDE3 but also uses 2 additional keys, K_4 and K_5 as the IVs for the first and third (CBC) layers respectively. Note that the IV for the middle layer is always 0 in all three versions of EDEx. See Figure 1 that illustrates EDE5.

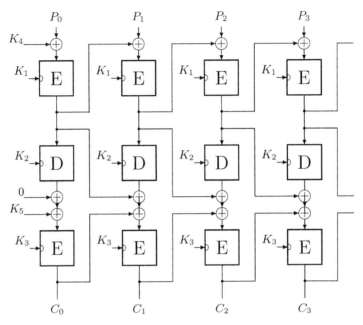

Fig. 1. The EDE5 mode

4.1   Collision Attacks on EDE2

In this section, we show that EDE2 is far from achieving the security level its key length entitles to expect, namely a 2^{112} effort for brute force key search attacks or even a 2^{68} chosen plaintexts (CPs), 2^{66} computation complexity and 2^{66} memory complexity trade-off [6,7].

A simple adaptive collision attack recovers half of the key bits in about 2^{56} operations. As the last encryption layer hides the expected collision, the birthday paradox doesn't provide any shortcut here, so we need to consider about 2^{56} times 2 plaintexts of 4 blocks each. We mount a kind of collision dictionary. Suppose we have guessed K_1. We can choose a collision to occur after the second encryption block of the first layer. Hence, for a given K_1, we can pre-compute a 4-block plaintext pair $(P_0, P_1, 0, 0)$ and $(P_0^*, P_1^*, 0, 0)$ such that (See Figure 2):

$$E_{K_1}(E_{K_1}(P_0) \oplus P_1) = E_{K_1}(E_{K_1}(P_0^*) \oplus P_1^*). \tag{36}$$

Next, we require the encryption of the 2 plaintexts, and obtain the corresponding ciphertexts (C_0, C_1, C_2, C_3) and $(C_0^*, C_1^*, C_2^*, C_3^*)$. As the collision we

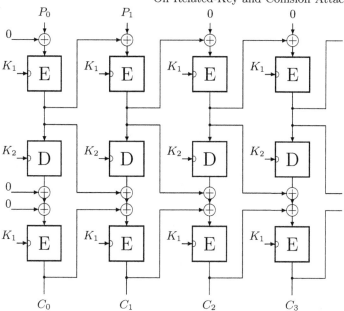

Fig. 2. Attacking the EDE2 mode

have chosen propagates to the third and last blocks of the second layer, all we need to do, is decrypt the 2 last ciphertext blocks of both ciphertexts on-the-fly, and check whether a collision occurs as predicted:

$$D_{K_1}(C_2) \oplus C_1 = D_{K_1}(C_2^*) \oplus C_1^* \tag{37}$$

and

$$D_{K_1}(C_3) \oplus C_2 = D_{K_1}(C_3^*) \oplus C_2^*. \tag{38}$$

This can be done for every pair of ciphertexts as soon as they become available (thanks to an anonymous referee for pointing this out). If both conditions hold, we can be reasonably sure that we have identified the right key K_1. All in all, we need to obtain 2^{59} ciphertext blocks corresponding to a collision pair for every choice of K_1. After identifying K_1, we can proceed to recover K_2 by exhaustive search as well. Thus the attack complexity is 2^{59} chosen plaintexts, 2^{59} computations and negligible memory, and so is much lower than expected for this multiple mode of operation.

In an even more powerful adversarial model, we can suppose the attacker can mount a chosen ciphertext (CC) attack. In this case, the complexities literally melt away. We ask for the decryption of ciphertexts of the form $(C_0,0,0,0)$ and wait for a collision as before. This should occur after about 2^{32} queries, and can be recognized by the fact that the third and fourth blocks of the plaintext pair are equal. Once the collision is identified, we check for the K_1 as follows:

$$E_{K_1}(E_{K_1}(P_0) \oplus P_1) = E_{K_1}(E_{K_1}(P_0^*) \oplus P_1^*). \tag{39}$$

After that, K_2 can be found by exhaustive search. This attack requires a total complexity of 2^{34} chosen ciphertexts, 2^{57} computations and 2^{34} memory.

Discussion. EDEx is used to encrypt RSA private key formats [17] that belong to customers who may be attackers themselves, so chosen-plaintext attacks are possible since a customer may wish to generate his own private/public key-pair and request to use that private key which would be the plaintext for EDEx. Further, when generating RSA private keys using the PKA-Key-Generate verb [17], one has the option of requesting the private key to be returned in one of 3 forms, namely in cleartext, encrypted with the local master key, MK, or encrypted with a KEK. This can be used in conjunction with the Key-Import verb [17], which either causes a cleartext private key to be encrypted under a local master key, MK, or causes a KEK-encrypted private key to be decrypted and re-encrypted with a master key, MK.

Meanwhile, chosen-ciphertext attacks could also be possible with the two verbs Key-Import and Key-Export [17] used to transport keys between IBM 4758s that use different master keys, say MK_1 and MK_2. In more detail, the Key-Export verb decrypts an operational key, K_{OP} with the master key, MK_1, and then encrypts it under a KEK to obtain an external key, K_{EX} for transport. In contrast, the Key-Import verb does the exact opposite, in that it decrypts K_{EX} under KEK and then encrypts this with MK_2.

Calling these two verbs and passing chosen K_{EX}'s for decryption hence allows for chosen-ciphertext queries. Though the complication appears to be obtaining the corresponding plaintexts and being able to check that two plaintext blocks are equal, we remark that a bank would have no reason to reject a customer's request to know his own private key (which is the plaintext in this case).

4.2 Collision Attacks on EDE3

Following the same kind of strategy, we attack EDE3 using a *double-collision*, i.e. a collision both after the second block of the first encryption layer, and in the second, third and fourth blocks, C_1, C_2 and C_3, of the ciphertext. For this phenomenon to happen, we need to query about 2^{32} chosen 4-block ciphertexts on average having their last 3 blocks equal. Once this double collision occurs, it propagates to the fourth block in such a way that we are assured to have identical input values to the third and fourth block in the first encryption layer. In other words, we can check this fact by noting that $P_2 = P_2^*$ and $P_3 = P_3^*$. Once we have identified a message pair following the right pattern, we can check for an inner collision due to K_1 by the relation

$$E_{K_1}(E_{K_1}(P_0) \oplus P_1) = E_{K_1}(E_{K_1}(P_0^*) \oplus P_1^*). \tag{40}$$

Next, we need to recover K_2 and K_3. These 2 layers can be solved by a trivial meet-in-the middle (MITM) attack on the first block requiring up to 2^{56} memory complexity, but there is a more efficient way. Since K_1 has been correctly identified, we can ask for the encryption of a collision pair as in our attack on

EDE2. For the correct value of K_1, this collision again propagates to an inner collision on the third and fourth blocks, after the second encryption layer. Thus K_3 can be recovered from the associated ciphertexts by checking the following:

$$D_{K_3}(C_2) \oplus C_1 = D_{K_3}(C_2^*) \oplus C_1^* \tag{41}$$

and also

$$D_{K_3}(C_3) \oplus C_2 = D_{K_3}(C_3^*) \oplus C_2^*. \tag{42}$$

Finally K_2 is recovered by exhaustive search. Thus the attack again requires only 2^{34} chosen ciphertexts, a pair of 4-block chosen plaintexts, 2^{58} complexity and 2^{34} memory in total.

The chosen-plaintext variant of the attack is slightly less efficient than for EDE2, requiring 2^{64} 4-block plaintexts to obtain the expected double collision in C_1. This retrieves K_1, followed by K_3 and K_2 as before. The total complexity is about 2^{66} chosen plaintexts, 2^{59} computations and 2^{66} memory.

4.3   Related-Key Differential Attack on EDE3

EDE2 and EDE3 bear some resemblance to 2-key and 3-key triple encryptions respectively. In fact, further referring to Figures 1 and 2 show that the encryption of the first block is effectively in ECB mode (recall that $K_4 = K_5 = 0$)! With this observation, we present a related-key differential attack on EDE3 as follows:

Obtain the encryption of a 1-block[1] plaintext, P under an unknown key, $K = (K_1, K_2, K_3)$, and also under an unknown related key, $K' = (K_1, K_2, K_3')$, but whose relationship to K (difference between them) is known. We then have the situation where these two encryptions have the same values up to after the second layer, and so the two ciphertexts, C and C' are related as

$$E_{K_3}^{-1}(C) = E_{K_3'}^{-1}(C') \tag{43}$$

For all 2^{56} values of K_3, verify (43) by partially decrypting C and C' by one layer and checking for a match, which immediately reveals K_3. The remaining two layers can be overcome with a basic MITM attack, or a better attack works by repeating the above attack with two further encryption queries under the related keys $K = (K_1, K_2)$ and $K' = (K_1, K_2')$ to obtain K_2. This leaves K_1 which can be determined via exhaustive search. In summary we have an attack that requires 4 related-key chosen plaintext (RK-CP) queries, $2^{58.5}$ single 1-block encryptions and no memory.

4.4   Related-Key Differential Attack on EDE5

Recall that EDE5 differs from EDE3 in that the initialization vectors for the first and third layers are keyed by unknown secret keys, K_4 and K_5. In this case, we can mount an attack as follows:

---

[1] Or it could consist of any number of blocks. But this is irrevelant since we only need the first block in our attack.

Table 1. Security of the EDEx multiple mode in IBM 4758

Mode	Type of attack	Complexity (Texts/Computations/Memory)
EDE2	Chosen Plaintext	$2^{59}CP/2^{59}/-$
EDE2	Chosen Ciphertext	$2^{34}CC/2^{57}/2^{34}$
EDE3	Chosen Plaintext	$2^{66}CP/2^{59}/2^{66}$
EDE3	Chosen Ciphertext	$2^{34}CC/2^{58}/2^{34}$
EDE3	Related-key Chosen Plaintext	2^{2} $RK\text{-}CP/2^{58.5}/-$
EDE5	Related-key Chosen Plaintext	2^{6} $RK\text{-}CP/2^{58.5}/-$
EDE5	both [6,7]	$2^{68}CP/2^{66}/2^{66}$

Obtain the encryption of a 1-block plaintext, P under an unknown key, $K = (K_1, K_2, K_3, K_4, K_5)$, and also under an unknown related key, $K' = (K_1, K_2, K_3, K_4, K_5')$, whose relationship to K is known. We would then have that these two encryptions have the same values up to after the second layer, and so the two ciphertexts, C and C' are related as

$$E_{K_3}^{-1}(C) \oplus K_5 = E_{K_3}^{-1}(C') \oplus K_5' \tag{44}$$

or

$$E_{K_3}^{-1}(C) = E_{K_3}^{-1}(C') \oplus K_5' \oplus K_5 = E_{K_3}^{-1}(C') \oplus \triangle. \tag{45}$$

Since we know the relationship, $\triangle$ between K_5 and K_5', we simply need to guess all 2^{56} values of K_3, and verify (45). Use this recovered K_3 to peel off the encryption component in the 3rd layer, and what remains is something similar to DESX [21,22] except that we have two encryption components in the middle, instead of just one in the case of DESX. Such a DESX variant can be attacked using Biryukov and Wagner's advanced sliding techniques [10], requiring $2^{32.5}$ known plaintexts, $2^{144.5}$ single encryptions and $2^{32.5}$ memory.

Or we could do better by performing a related-key differential attack as in [20] that obtains K_5 with just 64 related-key chosen plaintexts, negligible effort and no memory.

Then, use this K_5 to peel off the final XOR and so we have the initial XOR with K_4 followed by the two encryption layers keyed by K_1 and K_2 respectively. This can be attacked with a related-key differential attack similar to the previous section, with the same complexities.

In summary, we have an attack that requires $64 + 4 \approx 2^6$ related-key chosen plaintexts, $2^{58.5}$ single encryptions and no memory. Note also that other variants of this attack equally apply, for instance when the related key is $K' = (K_1, K_2, K_3', K_4, K_5)$.

4.5   Security of EDEx

We conclude that all the three EDEx modes of the IBM 4758 don't achieve their expected security level. In the most powerful adversarial model, as few as 2^{34} chosen ciphertexts or just 4 related-key chosen plaintexts are required to enable key recovery on the EDE2 and EDE3 modes. EDE5 is also insecure against a related-key attack with only 2^6 related-key chosen plaintexts.

We summarize our results in Table 1. Once again these attacks show that either outer CBC should be used, or interleaved modes such as EDEx need to initialize their individual inner mode layers and keep the associated IVs secret (for example in the form of a secret key). Ideally they should be chosen randomly for every new message and kept secret.

5   Conclusion

We have presented scenarios in the IBM 4758 where it is possible to mount related-key differential and slide attacks. This serves to further confirm that related-key attacks are not merely of theoretical interest. We have also considered the security of the IBM 4758's EDEx mode of operation against collision and related-key attacks. Therefore, extreme care has to be taken when using this mode. Instead, we suggest using the second provided mode, the outer-CBC mode which appears to be more secure against such attacks [3,4,5,6,7].

Acknowledgements. We wish to thank David Naccache for initial comments and for suggesting to consider the related-key attack scenario of commercial crypto devices such as the IBM 4758. We also wish to thank Bart Preneel for the figures and for useful comments on our attacks on multiple modes. Finally, we would like to thank the anonymous referees for pointing out a memoryless version of one of our attacks.

References

1. ANSI draft X9.52, "Triple Data Encryption Algorithm Modes of Operation", Revision 6.0, 1996.
2. E. Biham, "New Types of Cryptanalytic Attacks using Related Keys", Advances in Cryptology - Eurocrypt'93, Lecture Notes in Computer Science, Vol. 765, pp. 398-409, Springer-Verlag, 1994.
3. E. Biham, "On Modes of Operation", FSE'93, Lecture Notes in Computer Science, Vol. 809, pp. 116-120, Springer-Verlag, 1994.
4. E. Biham, "Cryptanalysis of Multiple Modes of Operation", Advances in Cryptology - Asiacrypt'94, Lecture Notes in Computer Science, Vol. 917, pp. 278-292, Springer-Verlag, 1994.
5. E. Biham, "Cryptanalysis of Multiple Modes of Operation", Journal of Cryptology, Vol. 11, No. 1, pp. 45-58, 1998.
6. E. Biham, "Cryptanalysis of Triple Modes of Operation", Technion Technical Report CS0885, 1996.
7. E. Biham, "Cryptanalysis of Triple Modes of Operation", Journal of Cryptology, Vol. 12, No. 3, pp. 161-184, 1999.
8. E. Biham and L. R. Knudsen, "Cryptanalysis of the ANSI X9.52 CBCM Mode", Advances in Cryptology - Eurocrypt'98, Lecture Notes in Computer Science, Vol. 1403, pp. 100-111, Springer-Verlag, 1998.

9. E. Biham and L. R. Knudsen, "Cryptanalysis of the ANSI X9.52 CBCM Mode", Journal of Cryptology, Vol. 15, pp. 47-59, 2002.
10. A. Biryukov and D. Wagner, "Advanced Slide Attacks", Advances in Cryptology - Eurocrypt'00, Lecture Notes in Computer Science, Vol. 1807, pp. 589–606, Springer-Verlag, 2000.
11. M. Bond, "A Chosen Key Difference Attack on Control Vectors", unpublished manuscript, November 2000.
    http://http://www.cl.cam.ac.uk/ mkb23/research/CVDif.pdf.
12. M. Bond, "Attacks on Cryptoprocessor Transactions Sets", CHES 2001, Lecture Notes in Computer Science, Vol. 2162, pp. 220-234, 2001.
13. D. Coppersmith, D. B. Johnson and S. M. Matyas, "A Proposed Mode for Triple-DES Encryption", IBM Journal of Research and Development, Vol. 40, No. 2, pp. 253-262, 1996.
14. FIPS 81, "DES Modes of Operation", US Department of Commerce, National Bureau of Standards, 1980.
15. H. Handschuh and B. Preneel, "On the Security of Double and 2-key Triple Modes of Operation", FSE'99, Lecture Notes in Computer Science, Vol. 1636, pp. 215-230, Springer-Verlag, 1999.
16. D. Hong, J. Sung, S. Hong, W. Lee, S. Lee, J. Lim and O. Yi, "Known-IV Attacks on Triple Modes of Operation of Block Ciphers", Advances in Cryptology - Asiacrypt'01, Lecture Notes in Computer Science, Vol. 2248, pp. 208-221, Springer-Verlag, 2001.
17. IBM, "CCA Basic Services for IBM 4758 Common Cryptographic Architecture (CCA)", Release 2.41, 2003.
18. IBM, "IBM Comment on 'A Chosen Key Difference Attack on Control Vectors' ", January 2001.
    http://www.cl.cam.ac.uk/ mkb23/research/CVDif-Response.pdf.
19. J. Kelsey, B. Schneier and D. Wagner, "Key-Schedule Cryptanalysis of IDEA, G-DES, GOST, SAFER and Triple-DES", Advances in Cryptology - Crypto'96, Lecture Notes in Computer Science, Vol. 1109, pp. 237-251, Springer-Verlag, 1996.
20. J. Kelsey, B. Schneier and D. Wagner, "Related-Key Cryptanalysis of 3-WAY, Biham-DES, CAST, DES-X, NewDES, RC2, and TEA", ICICS'97, Lecture Notes in Computer Science, Vol. 1334, pp. 233-246, Springer-Verlag, 1997.
21. J. Kilian and P. Rogaway, "How to Protect DES Against Exhaustive Key Search", Advances in Cryptology - Crypto'96, Lecture Notes in Computer Science, Vol. 1109, pp. 252–267, Springer-Verlag, 1996.
22. J. Kilian and P. Rogaway, "How to Protect DES Against Exhaustive Key Search (an Analysis of DESX)", Journal of Cryptology, Vol. 14, No.1, pp. 17–35, 2001.
23. R. C.–W. Phan, "Related-Key Attacks on Triple-DES and DESX Variants", CT-RSA 2004, Lecture Notes in Computer Science, Vol. 2964, pp. 15-24, 2004.
24. J. Sung, S. Lee, J. Lim, W. Lee and O. Yi, "Concrete Security Analysis of CTR-OFB and CTR-CFB Modes of Operation", ICISC'01, Lecture Notes in Computer Science, Vol. 2288, pp. 103-113, Springer-Verlag, 2001.
25. D. Wagner, "Cryptanalysis of Some Recently-proposed Multiple Modes of Operation", FSE'98, Lecture Notes in Computer Science, Vol. 1372, pp. 254-269, Springer-Verlag, 1998.

Security Analysis of Two Signcryption Schemes

Guilin Wang[1], Robert H. Deng[1], DongJin Kwak[2], and SangJae Moon[2]

[1] Institute for Infocomm Research (I²R),
21 Heng Mui Keng Terrace, Singapore 119613.
{glwang, deng}@i2r.a-star.edu.sg
[2] Mobile Network Security Technology Research Center,
Kyungpook National Univ., Korea.
neverdid@m80.knu.ac.kr, sjmoon@knu.ac.kr

Abstract. Signcryption is a new cryptographic primitive that performs signing and encryption simultaneously, at a cost significantly lower than that required by the traditional signature-then-encryption approach. In this paper, we present a security analysis of two such schemes: the Huang-Chang convertible signcryption scheme [12], and the Kwak-Moon group signcryption scheme [13]. Our results show that both schemes are insecure. Specifically, the Huang-Chang scheme fails to provide confidentiality, while the Kwak-Moon scheme does not satisfy the properties of unforgeability, coalition-resistance, and traceability.

Keywords: Signcryption, digital signature, encryption.

1 Introduction

Background. In the area of computer communications and electronic transactions, a very important concern is how to send data in a confidential and authenticated way. Usually, confidentiality of delivered data is provided by encryption algorithms, and authentication of messages is guaranteed by digital signatures. In the traditional paradigm, these two cryptographic operations are performed in the order of signature-then-encryption. Zheng [25,26] first introduced an interesting notion called *signcryption* to provide confidentiality, unforgeability, and non-repudiation for the delivered data *simultaneously*. The motivation is to achieve significantly lower overheads on both aspects of computation and communications than that of the traditional signature-then-encryption paradigm.

Following Zheng's pioneering work, a number of new schemes and improvements have been proposed [3,18,24,27,1,21,6,12,13,14], while literatures [22,4,1, 6] study the formal models and security proofs for signcryption schemes. Originally, signcryption is performed by a sender Alice for a designated receiver Bob. In [26], a variant is proposed to support multiple designated receivers. Noticed that the non-repudiation protocols in [26] are inefficient since they are based on interactive zero-knowledge proofs, Bao and Deng [3] presented schemes so that a designated receiver can efficiently convert a signcrypted message into a publicly verifiable signature. Based on the same idea, Yum and Lee [24], and

K. Zhang and Y. Zheng (Eds.): ISC 2004, LNCS 3225, pp. 123–133, 2004.

Shin et al. [21] proposed efficient schemes based on KCDSA and DSA [9]. In this paper, we call such schemes *convertible signcryptions*. In addition, Wang et al. [23] identified an interesting attack on a signcryption scheme proposed in [15]. Their attack allows a dishonest receiver Bob to forge a valid signcrypted message as if it were generated by Alice, under the assumption that Bob knows Alice's public key when he registers his public key. Furthermore, a newly convertible scheme based on the Schnorr signature scheme is presented in [23].

In [13], Kwak and Moon introduced a new notion called *group signcryption* by combining the concepts of group signature [8,7,2] and signcryption [25,26] together. In such a scheme, a member Alice from a sending group G_A can produce a signcrypted message for the receiving group G_B so that any member of G_B can unsigncrypt such a ciphertext and then know this ciphertext must be generated by some member of G_A, but cannot identify who is the actual signer. In the event of dispute, however, as in group signatures, the group manager GM_A of G_A can open a valid signcrypted message and then reveal the identity of the true signer. To construct such a concrete scheme, Kwak and Moon first modified Mu et al.'s distributed schemes [17,18] to obtain a distributed signcryption scheme supporting the confidentiality of the sender's ID. Then, based on this distributed signcryption scheme, they developed a concrete group signcryption scheme.

In the following, we introduce the security requirements for the convertible signcryption schemes and group signcryption schemes informally.

Convertible Signcryption. A convertible signcryption scheme should satisfy the following security requirements [3,12]:

- Unforgeability: Except Alice, any attacker (including Bob) cannot forge a valid signcrypted message so that the verification equation is satisfied.
- Confidentiality: Except the designated receiver Bob, any third party cannot derive the plaintext from the signcrypted message.
- Non-repudiation: Once Alice generated a valid signcryption message, she cannot deny this fact. In other words, Bob can prove (maybe inefficiently) to a third party that such a signcrypted message is indeed generated by Alice.
- Convertibility: For any signcrypted message for receiver Bob, he can efficiently convert it into a publicly verifiable signature.

Note that those security requirements are almost the same as in standard signcryption schemes [25,26], except the convertibility.

Group Signcryption. As the combination of group signatures [8,7,2] and signcryptions [25], a *secure* group signcryption scheme must satisfy the following security requirements [13]:

- Correctness: The signcrypted message produced by a group member must be accepted by the unsigncryption procedure.
- Unforgeability: Only valid group members are able to signcrypt a message on behalf of the group.
- Anonymity: With a valid decrypted message, identifying the individual who signcrypted the message is computationally hard for anyone but the group manager.

- Unlinkability: Deciding whether two valid unsigncrypted messages were generated by the same group member is computationally hard for anyone but the group manager.
- Exculpability: Neither a group member nor the group manager can signcrypt on behalf of other group members.
- Traceability: For any valid unsigncrypted message, the group manager can open it and find the true signer.
- Coalition-resistance: This means that a colluding subset of group members cannot generate a valid signcryption so that the group manager is unable to link it to one of the colluding group members.
- Confidentiality: Except the members belonging to the receiving group, any other party cannot derive the unsigncrypted message from the signcrypted message.

Our Work. In this paper, we present a security analysis of the Huang-Chang convertible signcryption scheme [12], and the Kwak-Moon group signcryption scheme [13]. Note that authenticated encryption does not necessarily provide the property of non-repudiation, so we call Huang-Chang scheme as convertible signcryption scheme, instead of convertible authenticated scheme. Our results show that both schemes do not meet all the desired security requirements. More Specifically, the Huang-Chang fails to provide confidentiality, while the Kwak-Moon scheme does not satisfy the properties of unforgeability, coalition-resistance, and traceability. In our analysis, we not only demonstrate concrete attacks to show the insecurity of those two schemes, but also discuss the reasons leading to such security flaws.

Organization. For self-contained, we first briefly review Zheng's original signcryption schemes in Section 2. Then, we review and analyze the Huang-Chang scheme and the Kwak-Moon scheme in Sections 3 and 4, respectively. Finally, Section 5 concludes the paper and proposes some future work.

2   Review of Zheng's Signcryption Schemes

In Zheng's two original signcryption schemes shown below, Alice signcrypts a message m and Bob unsigncrypts the ciphertext (c, r, s). Here, $(x_a, y_a = g^{x_a} \bmod p)$ and $(x_b, y_b = g^{x_b} \bmod p)$ denote the certified key pairs of Alice and Bob, respectively; $H(\cdot)$ is a strong one-way hash function; $H_k(\cdot)$ a keyed one-way hash function with key k; and (E_k, D_k) a pair of symmetric encryption/decryption algorithms. Note that Zheng's schemes are based on the Digital Signature Standard (DSS) [9], but with a minor modification to make his schemes more efficient. The two modified versions of DSS are referred to as SDSS1 and SDSS2, according to [25]. For more discussions on the security and efficiency of Zheng's schemes, please refer to [25,26,4].

Alice

choose $z \in_R Z_q$
compute $k = y_b^z \bmod p$
split k into k_1 and k_2
compute $r = H_{k_2}(m)$
$\qquad s = z(r + x_a)^{-1} \bmod q$ if SDSS1
$\qquad s = z(1 + x_a \cdot r)^{-1} \bmod q$ if SDSS2
$\qquad c = E_{k_1}(m)$

$\qquad\qquad \longrightarrow (c, r, s) \longrightarrow$ **Bob**

$\qquad\qquad\qquad\qquad k = (y_a \cdot g^r)^{s \cdot x_b} \bmod p$ if SDSS1
$\qquad\qquad\qquad\qquad k = (y_a^r \cdot g)^{s \cdot x_b} \bmod p$ if SDSS2
$\qquad\qquad\qquad\qquad$ split k into k_1 and k_2
$\qquad\qquad\qquad\qquad$ compute $m = D_{k_1}(c)$
$\qquad\qquad\qquad\qquad$ verify $r \equiv H_{k_2}(m)$

3   The Huang-Chang Scheme and Its Security

3.1   Review of the Huang-Chang Scheme

The Huang-Chang scheme [12] is a combination of the the ElGamal encryption system [10] and the Schnorr signature scheme [20]. There are four phases in their scheme: setup, signcryption, unsigncryption and conversion. In the setup phase, system parameters are set. At the same time, a sender Alice and a receiver Bob register their public keys with a certificate authority (CA). In the signcryption phase, the signer Alice sincrypts a message for a specified receiver Bob. Using the unsigncrption algorithm, Bob checks whether an alleged ciphertext is generated by Alice. In the event of dispute, by using the conversion algorithm, Bob converts a valid ciphertext into a publicly verifiable signature to convince a judge (or any third party) that the ciphertex is indeed generated by Alice.

(1) Setup. Initially, the system parameters (p, q, g) are set, where p and q are two large primes satisfying $q|(p-1)$, and $g \in \mathbb{Z}_p^*$ is an element of order q. It is assumed that the discrete logarithm (DL) problem and computational Diffie-Hellman (CDH) problem are difficult in the multiplicative subgroup $G_q = \langle g \rangle$. At the same time, a publicly known one-way hash function $H(\cdot)$ is selected. In addition, each user i in the system picks a random number $x_i \in_R \mathbb{Z}_q$ as its private key, and then registers the corresponding public key $y_i = g^{x_i} \bmod p$ with the CA. In the following, we use subscripts a and b to denote the sender Alice and the receiver Bob, respectively. For example, (x_a, y_a) and (x_b, y_b) are the key pairs of Alice and Bob, respectively.

(2) Signcryption. To signcrypt a message $m \in \mathbb{Z}_p$ for the receiver Bob, the sender Alice does the following using her private key x_a.

(2.1) Pick a random number $k \in_R \mathbb{Z}_p^*$, and compute $c = m \cdot y_b^{-k} \bmod p$.
(2.2) Compute $r = H(m, y_b, g^k \bmod p) \bmod q$, and $s = k - x_a r \bmod q$.
(2.3) Finally, send the ciphertext (c, r, s) to the receiver Bob.

(3) Unsigncryption. Upon receiving the ciphertext (c, r, s), the receiver Bob uses his private key x_b to recover message m and check its validity as follows.

(3.1) Recover the message m by

$$m = c \cdot (y_a^r \cdot g^s)^{x_b} \bmod p. \tag{1}$$

(3.2) Accept the ciphertext (c, r, s) iff the following equality holds:

$$r \equiv H(m, y_b, y_a^r g^s \bmod p) \bmod q. \tag{2}$$

(4) Conversion. In later potential disputes, Bob just needs to reveal the message m and the corresponding signature (r, s). Then, a judge (or any third party) can check whether the triple (m, r, s) satisfies equation (2). If the answer is positive, it is concluded that Alice indeed generated the signature (r, s) for Bob.

3.2 The Secuity of the Huang-Chang Scheme

Obviously, the Huang-Chang scheme is indeed the combination of the ElGamal encryption algorithm and the Schnorr signature scheme. At the same time, it is widely believed that the ElGamal cryptosytem is secure in practice. Furthermore, the security of the Schnorr signature scheme is proved to be equivalent to the DL problem [19]. Based on the above observations, Huang and Chang provided elaborate but informal analysis to show that their scheme is also secure. Actually, they claimed that their scheme satisfies the following three security requirements:

(1) Unforgeability: Except Alice, any attacker (including Bob) cannot forge a valid ciphertext (c, r, s) for any message m so that the verification equations (1) and (2) are satisfied.
(2) Confidentiality: Except the designated receiver Bob, any third party cannot derive the message m from the ciphertext (c, r, s).
(3) Non-repudiation: Once Bob reveals a triple (m, r, s), anybody can verify that (r, s) is Alice's signature. Therefore, a judge can settle a possible dispute between Alice and Bob.

We note that the Huang-Chang scheme indeed satisfies the unforgeability and non-repudiation requirements. The reason is that if an adaptive attacker (including Bob) can forge a valid ciphertext triple (c, r, s) for a new message m so that both equations (1) and (2) hold, this exactly means the attacker has forged a standard Schnorr signature (r, s) for the message $m||y_b$. The latter is contrary to the known result that the Schnorr signature is *existentially unforgeable* [11] in the random oracle model [5], which is proved by Pointcheval and Stern in [19].

The correctness of their conclusion on the confidentiality is another story. Firstly, let $y_{ab} = g^{x_a \cdot x_b} \bmod p$, then equation (1) can be re-written as

$$m = c \cdot y_{ab}^r \cdot y_b^s \bmod p. \tag{3}$$

This equation implies that if the value y_{ab} is known, the plaintext m can be derived from ciphertext (c, r, s) and Bob's public keys y_b directly. So, the value of y_{ab} plays a pivotal role in the Huang-Chang scheme. Any party other than Alice and Bob cannot compute the value of y_{ab} from y_a and y_b, since it is assumed that the CDH assumption hold in the subgroup $G_q = \langle g \rangle$. However, the point is that equation (3) also means the value of y_{ab} can be carried out from a valid ciphertext (c, r, s) by the following equation:

$$y_{ab} = (m \cdot c^{-1} \cdot y_b^{-s})^{r^{-1}} \bmod p. \tag{4}$$

Therefore, if an eavesdropper obtains a valid ciphertext (c, r, s) for a message m, he or she can compute the value of y_{ab} from equation (4). Then, when a new valid ciphertext (c', r', s') is received or intercepted, the eavesdropper can decrypt it easily by computing $m' = c' \cdot y_{ab}^{r'} \cdot y_b^{s'} \bmod p$. In other words, the Huang-Chang scheme is vulnerable to the known-plaintext attack. Consequently, the security requirement of confidentiality is not guaranteed.

To sincrypt a large message m, i.e., $m \geq p$, the authors of [12] also proposed a variant of the above scheme called *convertible authenticated encryption scheme with message linkage*. The above attack applies to this variant, too. Specifically, one can get the value of y_{ab} from a known message-ciphertext pair. Then, using y_{ab} any new ciphertext can be decrypted easily by first computing the hidden random number $t = c \cdot y_{ab}^r \cdot y_b^s \bmod p$, and then recovering each block of the plaintext one by one. For more details, please check Section 3.1 of [12].

4   The Kwak-Moon Scheme and Its Security

4.1   Review of the Kwak-Moon Scheme

Similar to group signatures, the Kwak-Moon group signcryption scheme consists of five procedures: setup, join, signcryption, unsigncryption, and open. In the setup procedure, system parameters are set, while the join procedure allows each system user to register with the corresponding group manager and then get his/her group membership certificate. Then, using this group membership certificate one user can generate signcrypted messages on behalf of the group according to unsigncryption procedures, and sends it to the members in the receiving group. In unsigncryption procedures, users verify signcrypted messages originated from the sending group. By using the open procedure, the sending group manager can find out the identity of the true signer who issued a valid signcrypted messages on behalf of the sending group.

(1) Setup. To setup a group, the group manager GM_A performs as follows:

(1.1) Set group manager GM_A's RSA signature public key (n_A, e_A) and private key d_A, where the RSA modulus n_A is the product of two random primes with approximately equal length, and (e_A, d_A) satisfies $e_A \cdot d_A = 1 \bmod \phi(n_A)$.

(1.2) Select a discrete logarithm triple (p, q, g), where p and q are two large primes such $q|(p-1)$, and $g \in \mathbb{Z}_p^*$ is a generator of order q, such that the DL assumption and CDH assumption hold in the multiplicative subgroup $G_q = \langle g \rangle$. In addition, select a publicly known one-way hash function $H(\cdot)$ and a random element $h \in_R \mathbb{Z}_p^*$.

(1.3) The group manager GM_A keeps d_A as his secret key, and publishes $(p, q, g, h, H(\cdot), n_A, e_A)$ as the system parameters.

(2) Join. When a user l wants to join a group, the following interactive protocols is executed.

(2.1) User l who wants to join the group G_A generates his/her own group private key ϵ_l, and computes $\tau_l = h^{\epsilon_l} \bmod p$ as *group membership key*. Then he transfers τ_l to the group manager GM_A through secure channel and proves to group manager GM_A that he knows the discrete logarithm of τ_l to the base h. ϵ_l should be kept secret by the user l.

(2.2) Then, group manager GM_A calculates $v_l = \tau_l^{d_A} \bmod n_A$ as user l's membership certificate as in [7].

(2.3) When n registration applications from n users are received, group manager GM_A computes the following polynomial $f(x)$'s coefficients α_i, $i = 1, \cdots, n$:

$$f(x) = \prod_{i=1}^{n}(x - \tau_i) = \sum_{i=0}^{n} \alpha_i x^i \in \mathbb{Z}_q[x]. \tag{5}$$

Using the set $\{\alpha_0, \alpha_1, ..., \alpha_n\}$, a new set $\{\alpha_0', \alpha_1', \cdots, \alpha_n'\}$ is defined, where $\alpha_0' = \alpha_0, \alpha_n' = \alpha_n, \alpha_1' = \cdots = \alpha_{n-1}' = \sum_{i=1}^{n-1} \alpha_i \bmod q$. Let $\beta_i = g^{\alpha_i'} \bmod p$ for each $i = 1, \cdots, n$, and $A_l = \sum_{i=1, j=1, i \neq j}^{n-1} \alpha_j \tau_l^i \bmod q$ for each $l = 1, \cdots, n$. Then, each τ_l satisfies the following property:

$$F'(\tau_l) = g^{-A_l} \prod_{i=0}^{n} \beta_i^{\tau_l^i} = g^{-A_l} g^{\sum_{i=0}^{n} \alpha_i' \tau_l^i} = g^{f(\tau_l)} = 1 \bmod p. \tag{6}$$

(2.4) In order to create a group public key, group manager GM_A picks a random number $\gamma \in_R \mathbb{Z}_q^*$, and sets $\rho_l = -\gamma \cdot A_l \bmod q$ for user l. The *group public key* is defined as $\{\beta_0, ..., \beta_{n+1}\}$, where $\beta_{n+1} = g^{\gamma^{-1}} \bmod p$.

(2.5) Finally, the pair (v_l, ρ_l) is sent to group member l, while the group manager keeps γ, and all $\{\alpha_i\}$, $\{\tau_l\}$ secret.

(3) Signcryption. Now we assume that two groups, G_A and G_B, are set up according to the above procedures, and that the sender Alice belongs to G_A and the receiver Bob belongs to G_B. In order to signcrypt a message m for group G_B, Alice with her signing key $(\epsilon_a, \tau_a, v_a)$ performs as follows.

(3.1) Choose two random numbers $z, t \in_R \mathbb{Z}_q$, and compute $k = g^z \bmod p$.

(3.2) Split k into k_1 and k_2 with appropriate lengths.

(3.3) Evaluate $r = H_{k_2}(m)$.

(3.4) Set $s = z(r + \epsilon_a \cdot t)^{-1} \bmod q$ if SDSS1, or $s = z(1 + \epsilon_a \cdot r \cdot t)^{-1} \bmod q$ if SDSS2.

(3.5) Evaluate $w = H(m)$.

(3.6) Compute $\lambda_a = (t^{e_A} \cdot \tau_a \bmod n_A) \bmod q$, $\delta_a = g^{\epsilon_a t} \bmod p$, and $\theta_a = t \cdot v_a \bmod n_A$.

(3.7) The signcrypted message (c_1, c_2) is computed by

$$c_1 \leftarrow \{a_0, ..., a_{n+2}\} \leftarrow \{k\beta_0^{w\tau_a}, \beta_1^{w\tau_a}, ..., \beta_{n+1}^{w\tau_a}, g^{\lambda_a}\},$$
$$c_2 = E_{k_1}(ID_{G_A}||m||r||s||\delta_a||\theta_a),$$

where ID_{G_A} is the identity of group G_A that includes GM_A's public key (n_A, e_A).

(4) Unsigncryption. With the secret information (τ_b, ρ_b), Bob (or any member of G_B) can unsigncrypt the signcrypted message (c_1, c_2) as follows.

(4.1) Recover the secret session key k by

$$k = a_0 \left(\prod_{i=1}^{n} a_i^{\tau_b^i}\right) a_{n+1}^{\rho_b} = g^z \prod_{i=0}^{n} g^{w\tau_a \alpha_i \tau_b^i} = g^z (g^{f(\tau_b)})^{w\tau_a} = g^z \bmod p. \qquad (7)$$

(4.2) Split k into k_1 and k_2.
(4.3) Decrypt $D_{k_1}(c_2) = ID_{G_A}||m||r||s||\delta_a||\theta_a$.
(4.4) Compute $\lambda'_a = (\theta_a^{e_A} \bmod n_A) \bmod q$.
(4.5) Accept (c_1, c_2) iff $r \equiv H_{k_2}(m)$, $k \equiv (\delta_a \cdot g^r)^s \bmod p$ if SDSS1 or $k \equiv (g \cdot \delta_a^r)^s \bmod p$ if SDSS2, and $a_{n+2} \equiv g^{\lambda'_a} \bmod p$.

(5) Open. In case of disputes, Bob forwards the (c_1, w) to group G_A's manager GM_A. Then, only the group manager GM_A can find the group member, Alice, who issued this signcryption. To do so, GM_A searches which τ_l belonging to G_A satisfying $a_i = (\beta_i^w)^{\tau_l}$, for all $i = 1, \cdots, n+1$.

4.2   The Secuity of the Kwak-Moon Scheme

The authors of [13] analyzed their scheme on both aspects of security and efficiency, and claimed that as the combination of group signatures [8,7,2] and signcryptions [25], their scheme satisfies all security requirements for group signcryption scheme listed in Section 1. However, we find this is not the fact. We now demonstrate two attacks to show that the Kwak-Moon scheme *does not* satisfy the following security requirements: coalition-resistance, traceability, and unforgeability.

Untraceability. In [13], it is argued that each v_l is the group manager's RSA signature for member l's group membership key τ_l and is sent to member l securely. So, no colluding subset can generate a valid correlated $(\epsilon_i, \tau_i, v_i)$ without the help of the right member and the group manager. This conclusion is incorrect. Firstly, after a careful checking the signcryption procedure we know that to generate a signcrypted message on behalf of the group G_A, it is sufficient that if one possesses a triple (ϵ, τ, v) such that the following equations are satisfied:

$$\tau = h^\epsilon \bmod p, \quad \text{and} \quad v = \tau^{d_A} \bmod n_A. \qquad (8)$$

Therefore, a group member, say Alice, can forge a new triple $(\epsilon'_a, \tau'_a, v'_a)$ from her old triple $(\epsilon_a, \tau_a, v_a)$ by first selecting a random number ϵ, and then computing $(\epsilon'_a, \tau'_a, v'_a)$ as

$$\epsilon'_a = \epsilon_a \cdot \epsilon \bmod q, \quad \tau'_a = \tau_a^\epsilon \bmod p, \quad \text{and} \quad v'_a = v_a^\epsilon \bmod n_A. \tag{9}$$

It is easy to know that the resulting new triple $(\epsilon'_a, \tau'_a, v'_a)$ satisfies equations in (8). Consequently, Alice can use it to generate valid but untraceable signcrypted messages. That is, any member from receiving group will accept all signcrypted messages generated by using $(\epsilon'_a, \tau'_a, v'_a)$, according to signcryption procedure. When such signcrypted messages are presented, however, the group manager GM_A cannot identify the true singer, since Alice does not use her true certificate. This attack implies that the property of coalition-resistance should be proved rigorously.

Forgeability. In the following, we show that even with out any membership certificate, an attacker can also forge signcrypted messages on behalf of the sending group G_A. In other words, the Kwak-Moon scheme is universally forgeable. The authors of [13] argued that their scheme is unforgeable, since the keyed hash function $H_k(\cdot)$ behaves as a random function, and the group member's private key ϵ_a is not revealed to anyone. However, such argument does not guarantee the unforgeability. The basic idea of the following attack is to select random values for ϵ, θ, and τ, but computing λ and δ as the desired values. To forge a sincrypted message on behalf of group G_A, an outsider without any system secret can mount the following attack.

(1) Choose random numbers $\epsilon, z, t \in_R \mathbb{Z}_q$, and compute $k = g^z \bmod p$.
(2) Split k into k_1 and k_2 with appropriate lengths.
(3) Evaluate $r = H_{k_2}(m)$.
(4) Set $s = z(r + \epsilon \cdot t)^{-1} \bmod q$ if SDSS1, or $s = z(1 + \epsilon \cdot r \cdot t)^{-1} \bmod q$ if SDSS2.
(5) Evaluate $w = H(m)$.
(6) Select random number $\theta \in_R \mathbb{Z}_{n_A}$, and compute $\lambda = (\theta^{e_A} \bmod n_A) \bmod q$, $\delta = g^{\epsilon t} \bmod p$.
(7) Pick a random number $\tau \in_R \mathbb{Z}_p$, the signcrypted message (c_1, c_2) is computed by

$$c_1 \leftarrow \{a_0, \cdots, a_{n+2}\} \leftarrow \{k\beta_0^{w\tau}, \beta_1^{w\tau}, \cdots, \beta_{n+1}^{w\tau}, g^\lambda\},$$
$$c_2 = E_{k_1}(ID_{G_A}||m||r||s||\delta||\theta).$$

We explain our attack is successful. Firstly, note that equation (7) holds for the above forged ciphertext (c_1, c_2), since this is due to the property of the values (τ_b, ρ_b). This means any member of the receiving group, say Bob, can recover the secret session key k. Then, he can decrypt c_2 and get the values of $(ID_{G_A}, m, r, s, \delta, \theta)$. By computing $\lambda' = (\theta^{e_A} \bmod n_A) \bmod q\ (= \lambda)$, Bob will find that $r \equiv H_{k_2}(m)$, $k \equiv (\delta \cdot g^r)^s \bmod p$ if SDSS1 or $k \equiv (g \cdot \delta^r)^s \bmod p$ if SDSS2, and $a_{n+2} \equiv g^{\lambda'} \bmod p$. This is, Bob will accepts such forged pair (c_1, c_2) as valid signcrypted messages. This attack results from the fact that the relationships among components of a group membership certificate are not fully used in sincryption procedure. In other words, to signcrypt a message in the Kwak-Moon scheme it is not necessarily to have a group membership certificate.

5 Conclusion

In this paper, we identified security flaws in two signcryption schemes proposed in [12] and [13]. Our results showed that the convertible signcryption scheme [12] fails to provide confidentiality, and the first group signcryption scheme [13] is insecure. About this specifical type of cryptosystems, the following problems seem interesting in future research: (a) presenting a formal model for group signcryption, and proposing provably secure schemes; (b) Designing schemes to support dynamic group member management in the sense that group member can join or leave the group efficiently and dynamically; (c) Optimizing the open procedure so that it does not linearly depend on the number of group members, so that such schemes are suitable for large groups.

References

1. J. H. An, Y. Dodis, and T. Rabin. On the security of joint signature and encryption. In: *EUROCRYPT 2002*, LNCS 2332, pages 83-107. Springer-Verlag, 2002.
2. G. Ateniese, J. Camenisch, M. Joye, and G. Tsudik. A practical and provably secure coalition-resistant group signature scheme. In: *CRYPTO 2000*, LNCS 1880, pages 255-270. Springer Verlag, 2000.
3. F. Bao and R.H. Deng. A signcryption scheme with signature directly verifiable by public key. In: *Public Key Cryptography (PKC'98)*, LNCS 1431, pages 55-59. Springer-Verlad, 1998.
4. J. Baek, R. Steinfeld, and Y. Zheng. Formal proofs for the security of signcryption. In: *Public Key Cryptography (PKC 2002)*, LNCS 2274, pages 80-98. Springer-Verlag, 2002.
5. M. Bellare and P. Rogaway. Random oracles are practical: A paradigm for designing efficient protocols. In: *Proc. of 1st ACM Conference on Computer and Communications Security (CCS'93)*, pages 62-73. ACM Press, 1993.
6. X. Boyen. Multipurpose identity-based signcryption: A swiss army knife for identity-based cryptography. In: *CRYPTO'03*, LNCS 2729, pages 383-399. Springer Verlag, 2003.
7. J. Camenisch and M. Stadler. Efficient group signature schemes for large groups. In: *CRYPTO'97*, LNCS 1294, pages 410-424. Springer Verlag, 1997.
8. D. Chaum and E. van Heyst. Group signatures. In: *EUROCRYPT'91*, LNCS 950, pages 257-265. Springer-Verlag, 1992.
9. FIPS 186. *Digital Signature Standard*. U.S. Department of Commerce/NIST, National Technical Information Service, Springfield, VA, 1994.
10. T. ElGamal. A public key cryptosystem and a signature scheme based on discrete logarithms. *IEEE Transactions on Information Theory*, July 1985, IT-31(4): 469-472.
11. S. Goldwasser, S. Micali, and R. Rivest. A digital signature scheme secure against adaptive chosen-message attacks. *SIAM Journal of Computing*, April 1988, 17(2): 281-308.
12. H.-F. Huang and C.-C. Chang. An efficient convertible authenticated encryption scheme and its variant. In: *Information and Communications Security (ICICS'03)*, LNCS 2836, pages 382-392. Springer-Verlag, 2003.

13. D. Kwak and S. Moon. Efficient distributed signcryption scheme as group sign-cryption. In: *Applied Cryptography and Network Security (ACNS'03)*, LNCS 2846, pages 403-417. Springer-Verlag, 2003.

14. B. Libert and J.-J. Quisquater. Efficient signcryption with key privacy from gap Diffie-Hellman groups. In: *Public Key Cryptography 2004*, LNCS 2947, pages 187-200. Springer-Verlag, 2004.

15. C. Ma and K. Chen. Publicly verifiable authenticated encryption. *Electronics Letters*, 39(3): 281-282, 2003.

16. J. Malone-Lee and W. Mao. Two birds one stone: signcryption using RSA. In: *CT-RSA 2003*, LNCS 2612, pages 211-225. Springer-Verlag, 2003.

17. Y. Mu, V. Varadharajan, and K. Q. Nguyen. Delegated decryption. In: *Cryptography and Coding'99*, LNCS 1746, pages 258-269. Springer Verlag, 1999.

18. Y. Mu and V. Varadharajan. Distributed signcryption. In: *INDOCRYPT 2000*, LNCS 1977, pages 155-164. Springer-Verlag, 2000.

19. D. Pointcheval and J. Stern. Security arguments for digital signatures and blind signatures. *Journal of Cryptology*, 13(3): 361-369, 2000.

20. C. Schnorr. Efficient signature generation by smart cards. *Journal of Cryptography*, 1991, 4(3): 161-174.

21. J.-B. Shin, K. Lee, and K. Shim. New DSA-verifiable signcryption schemes. In: *Information Security and Cryptology - ICISC 2002*, LNCS 2587, pages 35-47. Springer-Verlag, 2003.

22. R. Steinfeld and Y. Zheng. A signcryption scheme based on integer factorization. In: *Information Security Workshop (ISW'00)*, LNCS 1975, pages 308-322. Springer-Verlag, 2000.

23. G. Wang, F. Bao, C. Ma, and K. Chen. Efficient authenticated encryption schemes with public verifiability. In: *Proc. of the 60th IEEE Vehicular Technology Conference (VTC 2004-Fall) - Wireless Technologies for Global Security*. IEEE Computer Society, 2004.

24. D. H. Yum and P. J. Lee. New signcryption schemes based on KCDSA. In: *Information Security and Cryptology - ICISC 2001*, LNCS 2288, pages 305-317. Springer-Verlag, 2002.

25. Y. Zheng. Digital signcryption or how to achieve cost (signature & encryption) $<<$ cost (signature) + cost (encryption). In: *CRYPTO'97*, LNCS 1294, pages 165-179. Springer-Verlag, 1997.

26. Y. Zheng. Signcryption and its application in efficient public key solution. In: *Information Security Workshop (ISW'97)*, LNCS 1397, pages 291-312. Springer-Verlad, 1998.

27. Y. Zheng. Identification, signature and signcryption using high order residues modulo an RSA composite. In: *Public Key Cryptography (PKC 2001)*, LNCS 1992, pages 48-63. Springer-Verlag, 2001.

On The Security of Key Derivation Functions

Carlisle Adams[1], Guenther Kramer[2], Serge Mister[2], and Robert Zuccherato[2]

[1] University of Ottawa, Ottawa, Ontario, Canada K1N 6N5
`cadams@site.uottawa.ca`
[2] Entrust, Inc., 1000 Innovation Drive, Ottawa, Ontario, Canada K2K 3E7
{`guenther.kramer, serge.mister, robert.zuccherato`}`@entrust.com`

Abstract. Key derivation functions are commonly used within many cryptographic schemes in order to distribute the entropy contained in an uneven way in a long stream of bits into a string that can be used directly as a symmetric key or as a seed for a pseudo-random number generator, or to convert short strings such as passwords into symmetric keys. This paper examines the common key derivation function constructions and shows that most of these have some concerning properties. In some situations, the use of these key derivation functions may actually limit the security that would otherwise be obtained. A new construction is also provided which seems to have better properties and an intuitive justification for its security is given.

1 Introduction

Hash functions are used to map arbitrarily long sequences of bits into a small, fixed number of bits. They are used as a building block in many fundamental cryptographic schemes. For example, they are used for generating a message representative to be digitally signed, for distributing the entropy contained in an uneven way in a long stream of bits (e.g., a Diffie-Hellman shared secret, or the bits collected from various user and environmental inputs on a computer) into a (possibly shorter) string that can be used directly as a seed for a pseudo-random number generator or as a symmetric key, and for converting short strings such as passwords into symmetric keys.

As computers have gotten faster, the size of keys used in cryptographic applications has increased. For example, AES [8] has key sizes of 128, 192 and 256 bits, compared with DES [6], which had an effective key size of 56 bits. For most applications, 128 or 160 bits of security is almost certainly sufficient. The amount of computing power required to mount an attack on this level of security is well beyond anything currently available. However, the development of AES and the process that was used to determine Rijndael as the AES cipher, have made it acceptable to discuss "attacks" that reduce the security of ciphers, even if such "attacks" are drastically infeasible. In addition, a number of documents, including the National Institute of Standards and Technology's Key Management Guidelines document [16], provide guidance on how to obtain "equivalent" cryptographic strength between various types of algorithms that

K. Zhang and Y. Zheng (Eds.): ISC 2004, LNCS 3225, pp. 134–145, 2004.
© Springer-Verlag Berlin Heidelberg 2004

may be used in an application and recommend that applications only use algorithms with "equivalent" strength. Governments and businesses that rely upon cryptography are thus expecting and requiring advanced levels of cryptographic protection, whether or not that protection is actually needed from the point of view of a strict cryptographic risk analysis.

Therefore, many applications require 256 bits of keying material for use with a block cipher, and 256 bits (or more) of entropy to seed a random number generator that will generate the keys. Hence, a straightforward use of many current hash functions will generate fewer bits than required for the application. This has led to the development of constructions, often based on a counter (for example, [2,12,13,15]), for the last two applications above that make repeated use of a hash function to generate a larger output. This paper analyses those constructions (commonly referred to as *key derivation functions*) in light of the details of existing hash implementations. Properties of the constructions are highlighted that limit their field of use. In particular it is shown that many currently used constructions are insufficient for their intended purpose when a stipulated goal of the system is to use only algorithms of "equivalent" strength. Finally a new construction is proposed that appears to overcome the highlighted limitations.

Despite the necessity of using key derivation functions in most, if not all, cryptographic protocols, there has been surprisingly little work done on analyzing the security that they provide. Some related research was presented in [4], but the focus of that work was to construct variable-length input pseudorandom functions (VI-PRFs) from fixed-length input pseudorandom functions (FI-PRFs) such as DES [6] or the compression functions of MD5 [19] and SHA-1 [7]. The motivating applications for that work are message authentication and encryption. For the latter, the authors mention the need for a variable-length output pseudorandom function, but do not pursue the construction of such VO-PRFs. In any case, by its very definition, the cascade construction does not transfer the entropy in a large input string to a large output string (since the output is a fixed, small size), which is precisely the characteristic we desire for a good key derivation function. A different kind of construction is therefore required.

Thus, with this paper we hope that we can stimulate further research in this needed area. The results of this paper are concerning not simply because they exist, but because they have existed for so long and been incorporated into so many protocols without any serious discussion of the security properties desired and provided by the constructions used. More research is required in order to fully understand the security level provided by these key derivation functions.

2   Hash Functions and Key Derivation Functions

The results of this paper apply to the use of any of the current commonly used hash functions in a key derivation function. In particular, they apply to any hash function construction that uses a compression function to mix the current block of data with a chaining variable that is the output of the application of the compression function on the previous block. We will use SHA-1 [7] as a concrete example in the remainder of this paper. It takes as input any bit string of length up to 2^{64} bits, and outputs a fixed-length 160 bit output. However, we note that the techniques described in this paper apply to all hash functions that take the same general form as SHA-1. The important point is that the hash function takes blocks of size B and combines each successive block with an internal chaining variable, H, of size $hashlen$, to produce a hash value also of size $hashlen$.

2.1   Overview of Key Derivation Functions

Let us assume that we have a string S, of length L, which is produced from a source with e bits of entropy, $e \leq L$. The string S has some property such that we do not want to use it directly as a symmetric key or as a seed for a random number generator. Perhaps S is a master key from which other keys must be derived, or perhaps it has some structure that does not make it suitable for direct use, or perhaps it is not the correct length. Thus we want a process that will produce a derived key k of length l with $\min(e, l)$ bits of entropy. This means that it should require $O\left(2^{\min(e,l)}\right)$ work for an attacker that does not know S, or is unable to determine any partial information about k, to determine k. In other words, we desire a key derivation function such that whatever entropy is present in the input is evenly distributed over the output.

This is a reasonable and desirable property for a good key derivation function to have. Intuitively, it says that partial knowledge of k gives an adversary no significant advantage in determining any unknown bits in k.

We note that this property depends upon the source used for the input. For example, given a key derivation function, kdf, that produces strings of length 128 bits from inputs of length 256 bits, we could define a source that generates only those 256 bit inputs x such that $kdf(x)$ is the all 1's string. On average there will be around 2^{128} such inputs. Now, the function, when considered over all possible 256 bit inputs, may have our desired property. However, when considered over our modified input source, it certainly does not.

Thus, it is crucial to know the probability distribution P_S of the source that produces S and the interaction between the key derivation function and the source. It seems reasonable to assume however that most "natural" sources of random strings will not have such negative interactions with reasonably constructed key derivation functions, and that is what we have assumed in our constructions. We believe a necessary condition for a secure key derivation function is that the above property hold for all but a negligible number of sources for S.

We also note that the related problem of converting a string S from an arbitrary source with entropy e into a uniformly distributed string of entropy l has a provable solution that makes use of universal hash functions (see [11]). However, we desire a construction that does not use universal hash functions, but rather uses something with an efficiency similar to existing key derivation functions and uses any cryptographically secure hash function.

Let us now consider the performance of the following common construction of a key derivation function with respect to our desired property. Let $h()$ be any hash function of the form described in Section 2.1. In particular, $h()$ could be SHA-1. Let $n = \lfloor \frac{l-1}{hashlen} \rfloor + 1$ and let $[x]_l$ be the leftmost l bits of x. The symbol $||$ represents concatenation and $h(x, y) = h(x||y)$. Also let P_i be a known (e.g., standardized) string containing certain defined parameters of the key derivation function. These parameters must have the property that $P_i \neq P_j$ if $i \neq j$. A common way to accomplish this is for P_i to contain the value i. Let $kdf(S, l) = [h(S, P_1)||h(S, P_2)|| \cdots ||h(S, P_n)]_l$.

Now, assume that the length of S is a multiple of the hash function block length, $hashlen$. Thus, when computing $h(S, P_i)$, the string S will end on a block boundary. Now, consider the chaining variable H after processing just the string S. It has length $hashlen$ but is the only state within the hash function that depends upon S. Since the attacker knows the parameter string P_i, she can exhaust over all $2^{hashlen}$ values of H and determine all possible values of $h(S, P_i)$. Thus, if an attacker is given any particular $h(S, P_i)$ she can determine the value of H after just the string S was processed (which is the same regardless of which parameters will be processed next) with $2^{hashlen}$ work, by exhausting over all values of H and producing candidates for $h(S, P_i)$ for each value of H. Once the correct value of H is determined, she can use that to determine $h(S, P_j)$ for $j \neq i$, and hence determine the remaining bits of the output of $kdf(S, l)$. Therefore, this key derivation function does not distribute the input entropy evenly over the output string if $l > hashlen$ and $e > hashlen$ since knowledge of $hashlen$ bits of k, along with $2^{hashlen}$ work, is sufficient to reveal all remaining bits of k, regardless of the length of k. Notice that this could commonly be the case in systems that wish to generate keys for AES-256 [8], but support only the SHA-1 hash function (i.e., 2^{160} work reveals the full 256-bit key).

We note that this attack on the defined key derivation function does not appear to be new. It seems to be known or at least hinted at in various discussion groups and mail lists, but we have been unable to find a formal reference for it. Also, the above, general, flawed construction has repeatedly been used in national and international standards that require a key derivation function. See Section 4 for more details.

Now let us consider a slightly different key derivation function. With the same terminology and components as before, let us now define $kdf(S, l) = [h(P_1, S)||h(P_2, S)|| \cdots ||h(P_n, S)]_l$.

It appears that the attacker cannot now use the fact that S remains fixed for all applications of $h(P_i, S)$ since the chaining variable H depends upon P_i and will be different each time that the hash function begins processing S. However, let us now give our attacker the ability to influence the parameters P_i. This is not unreasonable since in many cases the parameters will contain identifiers for the parties that will have access to the derived key, identifiers for the applications or protocols in which the keys will be used, or other data that can be manipulated. Assume also that the length of P_i is a multiple of the hash function block length.

Now by the birthday paradox the attacker, with $2^{\frac{hashlen}{2}}$ work, can find two parameter strings P_i and P_j, $i \neq j$, such that the internal chaining variable H is the same after processing these parameter strings [20]. Since S remains fixed and is the only data processed by the hash function after this point, we get that

$h(P_i, S) = h(P_j, S)$. Thus, given $h(P_i, S)$ the attacker will know $h(P_j, S)$ and this construction does not have our desired property against an attacker that can influence the parameters, if $l > hashlen$ and $e > hashlen$.

What is the problem with these constructions and why are strong hash functions not providing us with the characteristics that we want? The answer to these questions lies in the underlying approach to the construction. Creating a *kdf* by varying the input to the hash function in a known way (i.e., by appending or prepending known parameter blocks) relies upon the property that knowing some portion of the input to a hash function reveals no information about its output. But cryptographic hash functions have exactly the opposite property: they are designed to be one way and collision resistant. That is, given the *output* it is hard to determine any information about the *input*.

Existing cryptographic hash functions were not designed to have the "partially-known input, unknown output" property. They were never designed to mix any particular bits of the input into the internal variables of the hash in such a way that the output could not be determined without the knowledge of those bits. Furthermore, it seems somewhat naïve to hope that these hash functions will have such a property by accident. Thus, if we wish to use existing hash functions as a building block for a key derivation function, we must design the *kdf* to rely upon only the properties that hash functions were designed to have. In particular, we must design the *kdf* to use the one wayness and collision resistance of cryptographic hash functions.

We note in passing that designing key derivation functions by modifying the input to a hash function seems like a very ad-hoc construction. What is required is a general construction that can be shown to be secure based only upon the designed properties of the underlying hash function. Then any hash function that has those properties can be used in this construction and the designer can be sure that the desired properties of the key derivation function have been obtained.

While the work factors given above (i.e., $2^{hashlen}$ and $2^{\frac{hashlen}{2}}$) will likely be acceptable security levels for some environments with some choices of hash function (e.g., SHA-512 [7]), the fact that existing, common constructions do not distribute the input entropy evenly over the output string is concerning. We would recommend that standards and applications transition to a key derivation function that provides more appropriate security guarantees as soon as it is feasible to do so.

2.2   Key Derivation Functions Using HMAC

The HMAC [14] construction is defined as $HMAC(k, data) = h(k \oplus opad || h(k \oplus ipad || data))$ where $h()$ is a cryptographic hash function (such as SHA-1), k is a secret key, and *ipad* and *opad* are inner and outer fixed strings, respectively, that are used to mask k.

Resulting from the definitions of *ipad* and *opad*, the strings $k \oplus ipad$ and $k \oplus opad$ each end on a block boundary for $h()$. Therefore, an attacker can, with $2^{hashlen}$ work, try all possible chaining variables that result from $h(k \oplus ipad)$ and also, with $2^{hashlen}$ work, try all possible chaining variables that result from $h(k \oplus opad)$. Consider the common kdf construction described above with $HMAC()$ used for the hashing operation, $kdf(S, l) = [HMAC(S, P_1)||HMAC(S, P_2)|| \cdots ||HMAC(S, P_n)]_l$. The $P_1 \ldots P_n$ are known, and an attacker is given (or somehow acquires) a subset of the key, k_{P_i} corresponding to $HMAC(S, P_i)$, for some i. The attacker can try all possible chaining variables that could result from $h(k \oplus ipad)$, continue the hashing operation from each chaining variable (using $h()$) over the known data P_i, and obtain a value X. For each such X, the attacker can try all possible chaining variables that could result from $h(k \oplus opad)$, continue the hashing operation from each of these chaining variables (using $h()$) over X, and compare the result with k_{P_i}. Once the attacker finds a match, she knows that the correct inner and outer chaining variables have been found. All other bits of the key can then be determined trivially using these variables, the hash function $h()$, and the known data P_i.

The work factor to break this form of HMAC-based kdf is therefore $2^{2*hashlen}$, where $hashlen$ is the output length of the HMAC hash function $h()$.

Thus, this common construction of a key derivation function from HMAC does not distribute the input entropy evenly over the output string either. Again, since the work factor here ($2^{2*hashlen}$) provides a security level which is likely sufficient for most applications, this is not an immediate (or even near-term) vulnerability. However, the lack of our desired property is again concerning and thus we recommend that HMAC should not be used in the construction of a key derivation function. We note that a similar attack is possible if $HMAC(P_i, S)$ is used instead of $HMAC(S, P_i)$.

3   Constructions That Overcome These Limitations

We supply two improved key derivation function constructions. The first does not distribute the input entropy evenly over the output string; however, it appears to be more secure than previous constructions. The second appears to have our desired property, but as yet we are unable to construct a rigourous proof that this is actually the case.

3.1   A Construction That Seems to Work

Going against the advice contained in Section 2.2, we provide an ad-hoc construction for which we have some concerns, but which appears to be more secure than the other constructions given. This construction may be referred to as a *computationally-secure kdf*, or *cs-kdf*, which may be appropriate for environments in which a more dedicated construction is undesirable or unnecessary.

Using the same notation as in Section 2.2, we define $kdf(S, l) = [h(S, P_1, S)|| h(S, P_2, S)|| \cdots ||h(S, P_n, S)]_l$.

Assume that S is a multiple of the hash function block length, B, and that the parameter strings are greater than B bits and can be influenced by the attacker. Now, for each of the $2^{hashlen}$ possible chaining variables resulting from the partial hash computation on the initial S, the attacker can attempt to find a collision in the parameters, as in Section 2.2. This would require now $2^{hashlen} *$ $2^{\frac{hashlen}{2}} = 2^{\frac{3*hashlen}{2}}$ work, with the result being that for each of the $2^{hashlen}$ possible chaining variables, if the attacker is given $h(S, P_i, S)$ for a particular i then she can determine $h(S, P_j, S)$ for some $j \neq i$.

The problem is that since the attacker does not know S, she does not know the correct value of the chaining variable H. Thus, she must be able to obtain $O(2^{hashlen})$ values of $h(S, P_i, S)$ and look for a match. If one is obtained, then she will likely be able to determine $h(S, P_j, S)$. Strictly speaking, this construction then does not achieve our desired property against an attacker that is able to influence the parameters. However, since the attack also requires a large number of known hash outputs (larger than is ever achievable in practice), this construction appears to provide higher security than those described in Section 2.2.

3.2   An Improved Construction

The construction given in this section may be referred to as an *entropy-secure kdf*, or *es-kdf*. As we saw in Section 2.1, we are considering hash functions that have an internal chaining variable, H, of length *hashlen*. In order to begin processing the first block, this chaining variable is usually initialized to a fixed value H^0. Let us consider, for this construction, the hash function h such that the initial value of the chaining variable is allowed to vary as a parameter to the function. Thus we define the hash function $h_X()$, where X is the value of the initial chaining variable. The usual computation of $h()$ is thus written as $h_{H^0}()$.

Again, with the notation as in Section 2.2, let us define $L_1 = h_{H^0}(S)$, and $L_i = h_{L_{i-1}}(S)$ for $i > 1$. Our key derivation function can then be described as $kdf(S, l) = [L_1||L_2|| \cdots ||L_n]_l$.

Notice that the output of the hash function depends solely upon the input string S and the number of times that the hash function has been applied, and that only the string S gets input into the hash function directly. There is no dependence upon formatting the input in any particular way, or upon any parameter blocks or counters in the input data. We believe that, based upon the results in Section 2.1, it is a mistake and a security vulnerability to introduce such specified inputs into the construction.

3.3   Security

Intuitively, the attacks described in Section 2.2 do not apply to this construction since each application of the hash function to the input string S is processed completely differently by virtue of the change in the initial chaining variable each time.

Slightly more formally, let S' be the input string S padded (using the padding rule specified by the hash function $h()$) to the next input block length for $h()$. Then, the L_i above may be equivalently written as $L_i = h(\overbrace{S'||S'||S'|| \cdots ||S'}^{i \text{ times}})$.

Thus, L_j, $j > i$, may be written as $L_j = h(\overbrace{S'||\cdots||S'}^{i \text{ times}}\,\overbrace{S'||\cdots||S'}^{j\text{-}i \text{ times}}) = h_{L_i}(\underbrace{S'||\cdots||S'}_{j\text{-}i \text{ times}}) = h_{L_i}(X)$, where $X = \overbrace{S'||\cdots||S'}^{j\text{-}i \text{ times}}$

Assuming that the initial value of the chaining variable does not affect the designed security properties of the hash function, given L_i, there are three ways to find L_j.

We can search for a collision that provides us with L_j. We could attempt to find $\overline{X}$ such that $h_{L_i}(\overline{X}) = L_j$ with $\overline{X} \neq X$. However, by assumption our attacker does not know L_j and thus finding this collision seems to be impossible. With $2^{\frac{hashlen}{2}}$ work though, our attacker can find a Y and $\overline{Y}$ such that $h_{L_i}(Y) = h_{L_i}(\overline{Y})$. This does not appear to be of any advantage since it is only with vanishing probability that $Y = X$ for some valid X corresponding to an L_j.

We can search for a pre-image of L_i. Assuming that S is generated by a process with e bits of entropy, there are at least 2^e possibilities for S. If $e \leq hashlen$ then determining other bits of the derived key from L_i is possible. If $e > hashlen$ then we would expect that there would still be at least $2^{e-hashlen}$ possible values for S that would provide the given L_i. Thus, this line of attack does not appear to provide any significant advantage in determining other bits of output of our key derivation function and therefore it still appears to have our desired property. Notice that the security of the full key derivation function output relies upon the entropy of S, which explains the name (es-kdf) of this construction.

We can find L_j through some other means from our knowledge of L_i. For example, perhaps it is possible that modifying the initial value of the chaining variable modifies the output of the hash function in some pre-determined way that is independent of the hash input. In other words, $h_{L_i}(Y) = f(h_{H^0}(Y))$ for all Y and some known $f()$. Then it would be possible to easily compute $L_{2i}, L_{3i}, \ldots$ simply from the knowledge of L_i. Given the flexibility that the presence of such a function would provide in choosing prefixes for known hashes, it seems that it may possibly allow a method for finding collisions (in which case such a function could not exist for collision-resistant hash functions). However, we are unable to prove that this is the case. Similarly, we do not know, and are unable to prove, whether it is possible to find L_j through any other means, given L_i.

With respect to the opposite direction, given L_j, it appears to be impossible to determine L_i. It seems reasonable that the presence of an algorithm to do so would violate the one-wayness of the hash function, but we do not yet have a proof for this conjecture.

An explicit proof that the es-kdf distributes the input entropy evenly over the output entropy is certainly desired and for further study. However, this construction does appear more amenable to a proof based upon solely the one-way and collision resistant properties of hash functions than previous constructions. Additionally, since it does not depend on formatting, parameter blocks, or counters, it appears to be superior to all previously proposed key derivation functions.

4 Commonly Used Key Derivation Functions

We now apply the analysis of Sections 2 and 3 to commonly used key derivation functions defined in popular standards.

4.1 The Concatenation Key Derivation Function

In the national and international standard specifications ANSI X9.42 [2], ANSI X9.63 [3], IEEE P1363a [12], ISO/IEC 18033-2 [13], and NIST Key Establishment Schemes [15], a construction referred to as the *Concatenation Key Derivation Function* is defined. Omitting some of the details (which may be found, for example, in X9.42 [2]), the construction can be described as follows. Compute $h_i = h(ZZ||Counter||[OtherInfo])$, where h_i is the ith computation of the hash function $h()$, ZZ is a bit string denoting a shared secret value, $Counter$ is the counter value i represented as an octet string, and $OtherInfo$ is an optional bit string representing some (known) information shared between the communicating entities (such as data to specify the intended use of the derived key). Then $KeyingData$ is defined to be the leftmost $keylen$ bits of $h_1||h_2||\ldots||h_d$, where $keylen$ is an integer representing the length in bits of the keying data to be generated, and $d = \lceil keylen/hashlen \rceil$.

This X9.42 *Concatenation* construction is clearly a specific implementation of the general form given in Section 2.2 above and so suffers from the non-ideal characteristics of that form. The improved construction presented in Section 3.2 may be a better choice for high-security environments and applications.

4.2 The ASN.1 Key Derivation Function

In the national and international standard specifications ANSI X9.42 [2], NIST Key Establishment Schemes [15], and IETF S/MIME [18], another key derivation function is defined, called the *ASN.1 KDF*. This KDF is almost identical to the previous Concatenation KDF except that the format of all input and output data is specified in ASN.1. Thus, $h_i = h(ZZ||OtherInfo)$, where $OtherInfo$ consists of an algorithm identifier, a counter and other arbitrary information all placed within a particular ASN.1 structure. Then, as above, $KeyingData$ is the leftmost $keylen$ bits of $h_1||h_2||\ldots||h_d$.

Again, this construction is simply a specific case of the general construction of Section 2.2, and the improved construction of Section 3.2 may be a better choice in some high-security applications.

4.3 The Key Derivation Function in PKCS-5

In the specification PKCS-5 [17], the key derivation function PBKDF2 is defined as follows. Let $T_i = F(P, S, c, i)$ for $i = 1, \ldots, d$, where P is a secret password, S is a salt value, and c is an iteration count. The function $F()$ is defined to be $F(P, S, c, i) = U_1 \oplus U_2 \oplus \ldots U_c$, where $U_1 = prf(P, S||i)$ and $U_i = prf(P, U_{i-1})$ for $i = 2, \ldots, c$. The derived key is then the first $keylen$ bits of $T_1||T_2||\ldots||T_d$.

The example pseudo-random function prf given in this specification is HMAC-SHA-1, although it is noted that a hash function $h()$ may also meet the requirements under certain assumptions. For the purposes of this paper, we note that this is just a specific version of the constructions in Sections 2.2 and 2.3. In particular, if the length of the secret password P is such that it lies on the block boundary of the underlying hash function (i.e., $h()$ or SHA-1), then the work factor to break the derived key, given an appropriate subset of the key, will be $2^{hashlen}$ if the prf is $h()$, or 2^{320} if the prf is HMAC-SHA-1. In such situations, it may be preferable to use the kdf described in Section 3.2, although this is not strictly necessary: as observed in the specification, with password-based cryptography the search space for a password is unlikely to be greater than 160 bits.

4.4   The Key Derivation Function in TLS

The Transport Layer Security (TLS) Version 1 protocol specified in IETF RFC 2246 [5] defines a key derivation function $prf()$ in two pieces. First, a function called P_hash is defined, where

$$P\_hash(secret, seed) = HMAC\_hash(secret, A(1)||seed) \;||$$
$$HMAC\_hash(secret, A(2)||seed) \;||\ldots$$

and $A()$ is defined as $A(0) = seed$ and $A(i) = HMAC\_hash(secret, A(i - 1))$. Second, an initial secret S is split into two pieces, S_1 and S_2, and the pseudo-random function is defined as $prf(secret, label, seed) = P\_MD5(S_1, label||seed) \oplus P\_SHA\text{-}1(S_2, label||seed)$ where $label$ is a pre-defined ASCII string. Keying material is produced by letting S be the $master\_secret$, $seed$ be the server's random value concatenated with the client's random value, and $label$ be the string "key expansion".

The use of HMAC to generate a long key stream can require $2^{2*hashlen}$ work to break, as discussed in Section 2.3. However, in the TLS construction, the use of both MD5 and SHA-1 means that the total work required to mount this type of attack will be at least $2^{2*128} * 2^{2*160} = 2^{576}$. Depending upon the entropy of the initial secret, the attacker may do better to simply try to guess the secret pieces S_1 and S_2. From the definitions of the MD5 and SHA-1 hash functions, these pieces may be up to 512 bits each, but for this specification they will be much smaller than this bound since the master secret is defined to be 48 bytes (384 bits) in length. The key derivation function defined for TLS, therefore, seems sufficiently strong for its purpose.

4.5   The Key Derivation Function in SPKM

The Simple Public-Key GSS-API Mechanism (SPKM) is specified in the IETF Proposed Standard RFC 2025 [1]. In this specification a k-bit key is generated as $rightmost\_k\_bits(OWF(context\_key||x||n||s||context\_key))$ where: x is the ASCII character C if the key is for a confidentiality algorithm, or the ASCII character I if the key is for a keyed integrity algorithm; n is the number of the algorithm in the appropriate agreed list of algorithms for the context; s is the *stage* of processing, which is always the ASCII character 0 unless the key length k is greater than the output size of the One-Way Function OWF, in which case the OWF is computed repeatedly with increasing ASCII values of *stage* (each OWF output being concatenated to the end of previous OWF outputs), until k bits have been generated; and OWF is any appropriate One-Way Function.

This key derivation function is an example of the general form given in Section 3.1 above. While this is deemed to be adequate for most requirements, high-security environments may instead wish to use the construction of Section 3.2.

4.6   The Key Derivation Function in IKE

The Internet Key Exchange (IKE) specification, IETF RFC 2409 [10], contains a key derivation function defined as follows. Let $N_e = prf(N, C)$, where N is a nonce, C is a cookie containing predefined information (from the ISAKMP header), and $prf(key, msg)$ is a suitable keyed pseudo-random function (such as HMAC). Then, to generate a *keylen*-bit key K_e when *keylen* is greater than *prflen* (the output size of the *prf*), set K_e to be the most significant *keylen* bits of K, where $K = K_1 || K_2 || \ldots || K_d$, $K_1 = prf(N_e, 0)$, and $K_i = prf(N_e, K_{i-1})$ for $i = 2, \ldots, d$. From this construction, the entropy of the process that generates K_e is at most *prflen*, since knowledge of either N and C, or N_e, suffices for an attacker to generate all of K. Equivalently, given any K_i, $0 \leq i < d$, a maximum of 2^{prflen} guesses at the value of N_e will allow an attacker to determine all subsequent bits of K (and therefore all subsequent bits of K_e). This clearly does not meet the goal of distributing the input entropy evenly over the output string. For environments that need *keylen* > *prflen*, then, it is recommended that the construction described in Section 3.2 be used directly on the N and C values.

5   Conclusion

We have examined the construction of key derivation functions based on cryptographic hash functions. A number of applications today require key sizes that are longer than the output length of commonly-used hash functions. In many implementations and in many national and international standard specifications, the hash function is iterated, with varying input data, to generate sufficient keying material. We have examined such constructions and found security flaws under certain conditions that may be concerning. We have also proposed new constructions and provided intuitive justifications for their security.

Acknowledgements. The authors would like to thank Hugo Krawczyk and the anonymous referees for their helpful comments.

References

1. Adams, C., "The Simple Public-Key GSS-API Mechanism (SPKM)", RFC 2025, October 1996.
2. ANSI X9.42-2001: *Public Key Cryptography For The Financial Services Industry: Agreement of Symmetric Keys Using Discrete Logarithm Cryptography*, Accredited Standards Committee X9, 2001.
3. ANSI X9.63-2002: *Public Key Cryptography for the Financial Services Industry: Key Agreement and Key Transport Using Elliptic Curve Cryptography*, Accredited Standards Committee X9, 2002.
4. Bellare, M., R. Canetti, and H. Krawczyk, "Pseudorandom Functions Revisited: The Cascade Construction and its Concrete Security", http://www-cse.ucsd.edu/users/mihir/papers/cascade.pdf (see also *Proceedings of the 37th Symposium on Foundations of Computer Science*, IEEE, 1996, for an abridged version).
5. Dierks, T., and C. Allen, "The TLS Protocol Version 1.0", RFC 2246, January 1999.
6. FIPS 46-3, "Data Encryption Standard (DES)", *Federal Information Processing Standards Publication 46-3*, 1999. Available from http://csrc.nist.gov/publications/fips/fips46-3/fips46-3.pdf.
7. FIPS 180-1, "Secure Hash Standard (SHS)", *Federal Information Processing Standards Publication 180-1*, 2002. Available from http://csrc.nist.gov/publications/fips/fips180-2/fips180-2.pdf.
8. FIPS 197, "Advanced Encryption Standard (AES)", *Federal Information Processing Standards Publication 197*, 2001. Available from http://csrc.nist.gov/publications/fips/fips197/fips-197.pdf.
9. Freier, A., Karlton, P., and P. Kocher, "The SSL Protocol Version 3.0", draft-freier-ssl-version3-02.txt, November 18, 1996 (work in progress). Available at http://wp.netscape.com/eng/ssl3/draft302.txt.
10. Harkins, D., and D. Carrel, "The Internet Key Exchange (IKE)", RFC 2409, November 1998.
11. Håstad, J., Impagliazzo, R., Levin, L., and Luby, M., "A pseudorandom generator from any one-way function", *SIAM Journal on Computing*, **28** (1999), pp. 1364-1396.
12. IEEE P1363A: *Standard Specifications for Public Key Cryptography: Additional Techniques*, Institute of Electrical and Electronics Engineers, July 16, 2003, Draft Version 12.
13. ISO/IEC 18033-2, *Information technology – Security techniques – Encryption algorithms – Part 2: Asymmetric Ciphers*, Committee Draft, June 10, 2003.
14. Krawczyk, H., Bellare, M., and R. Canetti, "HMAC: Keyed-Hashing for Message Authentication", RFC 2104, February 1997.
15. National Institute of Standards and Technology, Special Publication 800-56: Recommendation On Key Establishment Schemes, Draft 2.0, January 2003.
16. National Institute of Standards and Technology, Special Publication 800-57: Recommendation For Key Management – Part 1: General Guideline, Draft, January 2003.
17. PKCS #5 v2.0, *Password-Based Cryptography Standard*, March 25, 1999. Available from ftp://ftp.rsasecurity.com/pub/pkcs/pkcs-5v2/pkcs5v2-0.pdf.
18. Rescorla, E., "Diffie-Hellman Key Agreement Method", RFC 2631, June 1999.
19. Rivest, R., "The MD5 message-digest algorithm", RFC 1321, April 1992.
20. Yuval, G., "How to swindle Rabin", *Cryptologia*, **3** (1979), pp. 187-190.

Evaluating the Impact of Intrusion Detection Deficiencies on the Cost-Effectiveness of Attack Recovery

Hai Wang, Peng Liu, and Lunqun Li

Pennsylvania State University, University Park PA 16802, USA {haiwang, pliu}@ist.psu.edu, lunquan@psu.edu

Abstract. Traditional secure database systems rely on preventive controls and are very limited in surviving malicious attacks because of intrusion detection deficiencies. ITDB, a Intrusion Tolerant Database prototype system, has been proposed, which can detect intrusions, repair the damage caused by intrusions in a timely manner. In this paper, we evaluate ITDB using TPC-C benchmark. The performance measurements show that ITDB system is cost-effective within reasonable False Alarm Rate and Detection Latency ranges. Our experiment results also indicate that ITDB can achieve good survivability without being seriously affected by various intrusion detection deficiencies. It can provide essential database services in the presence of attacks, and maintain the desired essential (security) properties such as integrity and performance.

1 Introduction

Database security concerns the confidentiality, integrity, and availability of data stored in a database. A broad span of research addresses primarily how to protect the security of a database, especially its confidentiality. However, very limited research has been done on how to survive successful database attacks, which can seriously impair the integrity and availability of a database. Experience with data-intensive applications such as credit card billing, banking, and online stock trading, has shown that a variety of attacks do succeed to fool traditional database protection mechanisms. In fact, we must recognize that not all attacks-even obvious ones-can be averted at their outset. Attacks that succeed, to some degree at least, are unavoidable. With cyber attacks on data-intensive Internet applications, e.g., e-commerce systems, becoming an ever more serious threat to our economy, society, and everyday lives, attack resilient database systems that can survive malicious attacks are a significant concern.

One critical step towards attack resilient database systems is intrusion detection, which has attracted many researchers [10,14]. Intrusion detection systems monitor system or network activity to discover attempts to disrupt or gain illicit access to systems. However, intrusion detection makes the system attack-aware but not attack resilient; that is, intrusion detection itself cannot maintain the integrity and availability of the database in face of attacks. To overcome the

K. Zhang and Y. Zheng (Eds.): ISC 2004, LNCS 3225, pp. 146–157, 2004.
© Springer-Verlag Berlin Heidelberg 2004

inherent limitation of intrusion detection, a broader perspective is introduced, saying that, in addition to detecting attacks, countermeasures to these successful attacks should be planned and deployed in advance. In the literature, this is referred to as survivability or intrusion tolerance. [1,15] propose a database intrusion tolerance system and a set of attack recovery algorithms.

In this paper, we focus on evaluating the cost-effectiveness of Intrusion Tolerant Database prototype system (ITDB), an intrusion tolerant database system prototype developed by [15] recently, and especially, we are interested in understanding the impact of existing intrusion detection deficiencies, such as false alarm rate, detection rate and detection latency, on the cost-effectiveness of ITDB. Although a good number of survivable systems are recently developed in the literature, and although it is widely recognized that a quantitative understanding of the dependency of intrusion tolerant systems on intrusion detection performance is crucial and in urgent need, quantitative system-level evaluation of this dependency has been missing in the literature. In this paper, we take the first steps to do detailed, quantitative evaluation of the impact of intrusion detection deficiencies on the performance and survivability of ITDB.

The rest of the paper is organized as follows. In Section 2, we discuss the related work. In Section 3, we give an overview of the ITDB framework. In Section 4, we outline our evaluation plan. In Section 5, we present our evaluation test-bed. In Section 6, we show how we generate testing transactions. In Section 7, we do the evaluation and report the experiment results. In Section 8, we conclude the paper.

2   Related Work

ITDB, an intrusion tolerant database prototype system, builds itself upon several recent and ongoing research efforts to achieve its goal of transaction-level intrusion tolerance. First, ITDB exploits the recent advances in database intrusion detection. Second, several ideas of ITDB are motivated by the recent advances in survivability and intrusion tolerance.

The need for intrusion tolerance, or survivability, has been recognized by many researchers in such contexts as information warfare [5]. Recently, extensive research has been done in general principles of survivability [8], survivable software architectures [16], survivability of networks [13], survivable storage systems [18], etc. These researches are helpful for database survivability, but the techniques cannot be directly applied to build intrusion tolerant database systems.

Besides ITDB, some research has been done in database survivability. In [2], a fault tolerant approach is taken to survive database attacks where (a) several phases are suggested to be useful, such as attack detection, damage assessment and repair, and fault treatment, but no concrete mechanisms are proposed for these phases; (b) a color scheme for marking damage (and repair) and a notion of integrity suitable for partially damaged databases are used to develop a mechanism by which databases under attack could still be safely used.

Besides transaction level survivability, there are also some works on OS-level database survivability. In [12] a technique is proposed to detect storage jamming, malicious modification of data, using a set of special detect objects which are indistinguishable to the jammer from normal objects. Modification on detect objects indicates a storage jamming attack. In [3], checksums are smartly used to detect data corruption. In [11], a trusted database system built on untrusted storage is proposed where a trusted DBMS runs in a trusted processing environment, and a small amount of trusted storage is used to protect a scalable amount of untrusted storage.

3   Intrusion Tolerant System Model

ITDB is motivated by the following practical goal: "After the database is damaged, locate the damaged part and repair it as soon as possible, so that the database can continue being useful in the face of attacks." In other words, ITDB wants to provide sustained levels of data integrity and availability to applications in the face of attacks. The major components of ITDB are shown in Figure 1. Note that all operations of ITDB are on-the-fly without blocking the execution of (most) normal user transactions. The job of the Intrusion Detector is to identify malicious transactions.

ITDB contains mainly three parts: 1) transaction proxy subsystem; 2) intrusion detection subsystem; 3) attack recovery subsystem. In the rest of this section, we give an overview of the jobs that these ITDB components do.

3.1   Transaction Proxy Subsystem

The transaction proxy subsystem is a proxy between users and the database. When a user submits a transaction, the subsystem will transfer each operation and transaction processing call to the database system. And most important is that the subsystem will keep useful information about transactions and generate corresponding logs about transactions' read and write operations. Intrusion detection and attack recovery subsystems will identify and recover malicious and affected transactions using these logs. This part is the foundation of the whole ITDB system.

3.2   Intrusion Detection Subsystem

The intrusion detection subsystem has the responsibility to detect and report malicious transactions to the attack recovery subsystem. It uses the trails kept in the logs and some relevant rules to identify malicious transactions. The intrusion detection subsystem distinguishes itself from other intrusion detection systems in four aspects. (a) It is a database intrusion detection system. (b) It is application aware. (c) It is at transaction level. (d) Instead of developing new intrusion detection techniques, ITDB applies existing anomaly detection techniques, and instead focuses on the system support for flexible application-aware

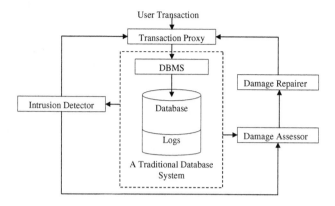

Fig. 1. Basic ITDB System Architecture

transaction-level database intrusion detection, and seamless integration of the
intrusion detection subsystem into the ITDB prototype.

3.3   Attack Recovery Subsystem

The attack recovery subsystem has the responsibility to perform on-the-fly damage assessment and repair. To do this job, first, the attack recovery subsystem
retrieves reported malicious transaction messages from the intrusion detection
subsystem. ITDB traces damage spreading by capturing the affecting relationship among transactions. In a history, a transaction T_i is dependent upon another
transaction T_j, if there exists an object x such that T_i reads x after T_j updates
it, and there is no committed transaction that updates x between the time T_j
updates x and T_i reads x. The dependent upon relation indicates the path along
which damage spreads. After assessing damage spreading, the subsystem repairs
the damage caused by both malicious transactions and affected transactions, using a special cleaning transaction which restores each contaminated data object
to its latest undamaged version.

4   ITDB Cost-Effectiveness Evaluation

Evaluations of developed technologies such as those used for intrusion tolerant
systems are essential to document existing capabilities, identity limitations, and
guide future research. The evaluation results will contribute substantially to
guide people to focus research on the technical problems that really matter, and
motivate researchers to build better systems, and explore alternative approaches.

Despite the importance and urgency of evaluating the dependency of intrusion tolerant systems on intrusion detection performance, quantitative system

level evaluation of such dependency has been largely missing in the literature. In this section, we will propose some experiments to evaluate the impact of intrusion detection deficiencies on the cost-effectiveness and survivability of ITDB. In particular, we will focus on three important components, the transaction proxy subsystem, the intrusion detection subsystem, and the attack recovery subsystem.

There are many works on evaluating intrusion detection systems [7,6]. ITDB builds its intrusion detection subsystem by applying existing anomaly detection techniques. So here, we will not put efforts into evaluating the performance of intrusion detection, instead focus on evaluating its impact on attack recovery.

The deficiencies of intrusion detection subsystem can be measured by three parameters: 1) False Alarm Rate (FAR), which indicates how accurate the detection subsystem is when an alarm is raised; 2) Detection Rate (DR), which indicates the portion of the malicious transactions the detection subsystem can detect; 3) Detection Latency (DL), which indicate the time that the detection subsystem needs to do intrusion detection. We will evaluate the cost-effectiveness and survivability of ITDB under different levels of deficiencies of intrusion detection.

4.1   Overhead Evaluation

The objective of overhead evaluation is to measure the system performance degradation caused by ITDB components and operations. It is important to enhance the ITDB system's performance. The overhead of the transaction proxy subsystem can be measured by one metric: the *average response time (or throughput)* degradation of user transactions, which indicate the negative impact of the transaction proxy on the execution of user transactions.

The overhead of the attack recovery subsystem can be measured by two metrics: 1) the average response time (or throughput) degradation of user transactions, which indicates the negative impact of the recovery subsystem on the execution of user transactions; 2) the average repair time, which indicates how efficient the recovery subsystem is at repairing damage.

4.2   Survivability Evaluation

Survivability is the capability of a system to fulfill its mission, in a timely manner, in the presence of attacks. Survivable systems must have some key properties. ITDB has some survivable characteristics such as recognition of attacks and the extent of damage, damage recovery after attack, and resistance to attacks.

Computer database is a whole set of related data objects with minimum redundancy. Attacks will damage the data objects and spread their damage within the database. If the attack recovery subsystem cannot control the damage spreading by repairing the affected transactions, the database will have a high degree of damage and will not be survivable in presence of attacks. To evaluate ITDB's survivability on maintaining database integrity, we measure the Damage Rate (DMR) under different levels of intrusion detection performance.

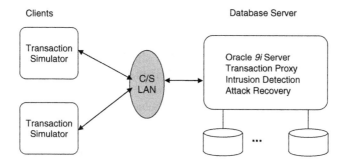

Fig. 2. Evaluation Test Bed Structure

5   Evaluation Test Bed

The approaches were initially explored to generate a corpus that could be widely distributed and that included both background traffic and attacks. The approach we followed was to recreate normal and attack traffic on a private network using real hosts, live attacks, and live background traffic based on TPC Benchmark C (TPC-C) [17].

For our test bed, we use Oracle 9i Server to be the underlying DBMS. TPC-C is in general DBMS independent, thus the corresponding transaction application can be easily adapted to tolerate the intrusions on a database managed by almost every "off-the-shelf" relational DBMS such as Microsoft SQL Server, Informix, and Sybase.

The Oracle Server runs on a Dell Intel Xeon 1.8 GHz CPU workstation with 512 MB memory. The transaction proxy, intrusion detection, and attack recovery subsystems also run on the Dell workstation. The Transaction Simulators run on a Dell Mobile Pentium 4 2.0 GHz CPU laptop with 512 MB memory and an IBM Pentium 4 2.4 GHz CPU desktop with 512MB memory. All the computers run Windows XP professional and are connected by a 10/100 Mbps switch LAN. Figure 2 shows a conceptual view of the evaluation test bed.

6   Background Transaction Generation

Background transactions are important for our experiments and may substantially affect the damage rate, false alarm rate, and detection rate of an ITDB system. We will generate our background transactions based on TPC-C benchmark. We pick TPC-C as the transaction processing application for several reasons. First, TPC-C provides a standard transaction processing scenario, which simulates a complete computing environment where users execute transactions against a database. Second, the TPC-C transactions are dependant upon each other to a large extent. Accordingly, the damage will be spread widely by some types of TPC-C transactions. Third, we set the number of warehouses to be 5. In this way, our experiments will handle millions of records.

We create a simulator process, called Transaction Simulator, to simulate TPC-C transactions automatically. Using the Transaction Simulator, we can define our parameters used in the experiments. They are: size of transactions, number of transactions, dependency degree, and number of concurrent users. All five types of TPC-C transactions are generated at each Transaction Simulator. The Transaction Simulator will randomly select a transaction type from a weighted distribution. The weights are chosen to achieve a minimum percentage of each type of transaction while meeting the TPC-C requirement of the transaction mix.

7   Evaluation Experiments

7.1   Overhead on System Performance

ITDB system is composed of several components [15]. In this section, we will focus on measuring the system throughput degradation caused by ITDB's transaction proxy and attack recovery subsystems.

We apply the TPC-C benchmark to evaluate the run-time performance of ITDB on the top of Oracle database server. The performance metric used by TPC-C is transactions per minute (tpmC). In reverse, we measure performance in response time per 100 transactions. The Transaction Simulator is used to compose and submit transactions to the database system continuously and automatically.

The response time is composed of several parts: a) Time used by the Transaction Simulator for preparing each statement in a transaction; b) Time used by the DBMS to process each statement; c) ITDB's overhead. In the following section, we will measure the response time increase caused by some ITDB components.

Transaction Proxy Overhead. The transaction proxy subsystem is an important component of ITDB. It provides services to clients for accessing database, and captures some important information about submitted transactions' behaviors. In this section, we will measure the system performance degradation caused by the transaction proxy subsystem.

Two important functions of the transaction proxy subsystem are transferring transactions to the database and keeping operation logs of transactions. It is necessary to measure the performance overhead by these two parts separately. Then we can analyze which is the primary reason for the performance. And then we can focus our research accordingly further to improve the system performance.

In our experiments, first, we will submit transactions without going through the proxy, which means we submit transactions directly to the database. Second, we will submit transactions through the proxy, but the proxy will not generate any log. Finally, we will submit transactions through the proxy, and it also generates logs.

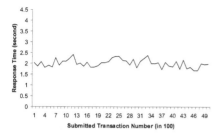

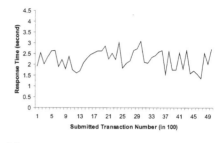

(a) Response Time per 100 Transactions without transaction proxy subsystem. The average response time per100 transactions (without proxy) is 2.011 second. The maximum response time of 100 transactions (without proxy) is 2.422 second.

(b) Response Time per 100 Transactions with transaction proxy. The average response time per100 transactions (without proxy) is 2.231 second. The maximum response time of 100 transactions (without proxy) is 3.079 second.

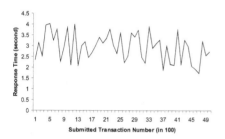

(c) Response Time per 100 Transactions with transaction proxy and logs. The average response time per100 transactions (without proxy) is 2.926 second. The maximum response time of 100 transactions (without proxy) is 4.015 second.

Fig. 3. Transaction Proxy Overhead

The results in Figure 3(a), 3(b), and 3(c) show that the performance is decreased when we send the transactions to database through the transaction proxy subsystem. And the degradation is not significant. The proxy part decreases the performance by 11%. The logging part decreases the system performance by 31%. These results show that the logging part is the primary component that impacts the performance in the ITDB's transaction proxy subsystem, although it is not very significant.

ITBD keeps several logs for submitted transactions, such as read operation logs, write operation logs, and transaction logs. These logs will be used for intrusion detection and attack recovery. The efficiency of keeping logs is important to

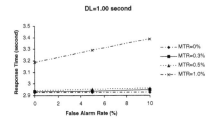
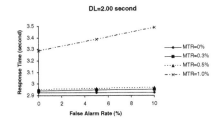

(a) Average Response Time Vs. False Alarm Rate under different Malicious Transaction Rate when Detection Latency is 1.00 second.

(b) Average Response Time Vs. False Alarm Rate under different Malicious Transaction Rate when Detection Latency is 2.00 second.

Fig. 4. Attack Recovery Overhead

the overall ITDB system. The experiment results suggest that further research should focus on developing a more efficient log system.

Attack Recovery Overhead. The attack recovery subsystem is to perform on-the-fly damage assessment and repair. For this part, we will measure the system throughput degradation caused by the attack recovery subsystem.

The overhead of the attack recovery subsystem on system throughput will be affected by several parameters. First, the attack recovery subsystem will heavily rely on intrusion detection. The performance of the intrusion detection subsystem can be captured by three parameters, namely FAR, DR, and DL. We will use these three parameters to represent the capability of ITDB's intrusion detection subsystem.

Second, the performance of the attack recovery subsystem will be affected by the malicious transaction arriving intensity. We use Malicious Transaction Rate (MTR) to represent this factor. MTR is the percentage of malicious transactions, not including affected transactions, among all the submitted transactions. In this experiment, we will measure the overhead of attack recovery on the system performance under different situations. First, we assume the DR of intrusion detection is 95%. Then MTR is increased gradually from 0.0% to 1.0%. Under different FARs, the increasing response time shows the decreasing of system throughput.

From Figure 4, first, we can easily see that the average response time is affected by the malicious transaction arriving intensity significantly. The average response time increases from 9% to 19% under different FARs and DLs when MTR is increased to 1%. Second, FAR and DL, which represent the performance of the intrusion detection subsystem, do not affect the throughput significantly, which means the system throughput is not influenced heavily by the intrusion detection system. These results demonstrate that ITDB system has reasonable performance within certain FARs and DLs range.

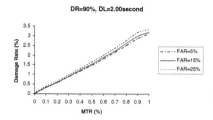

(a) Malicious Transaction Rate Vs. Damage Rate under different False Alarm Rate when Detection Latency is 2.00 second and Detection Rate is 90%.

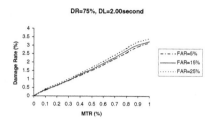

(b) Malicious Transaction Rate Vs. Damage Rate under different False Alarm Rate when Detection Latency is 2.00 second and Detection Rate is 75%.

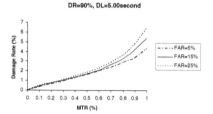

(c) Malicious Transaction Rate Vs. Damage Rate under different False Alarm Rate when Detection Latency is 5.00 second and Detection Rate is 90%.

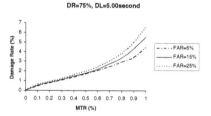

(d) Malicious Transaction Rate Vs. Damage Rate under different False Alarm Rate when Detection Latency is 5.00 second and Detection Rate is 75%.

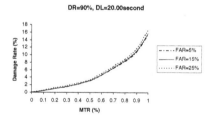

(e) Malicious Transaction Rate Vs. Damage Rate under different False Alarm Rate when Detection Latency is 20.00 second and Detection Rate is 90%.

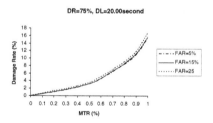

(f) Malicious Transaction Rate Vs. Damage Rate under different False Alarm Rate when Detection Latency is 20.00 second and Detection Rate is 75%.

Fig. 5. Influences on System Survivability

7.2   Influences on System Survivability

A survivable system can deliver essential services and maintain essential properties such as integrity, confidentiality, and performance, despite the presence of intrusions. In section 7.1, we already found that ITDB could provide its services under attacks and maintain its performance to some extent under reasonable FARs and DLs. We will evaluate ITDB's survivability on maintaining data integrity in this section.

Damage Rate (DMR) is a major metric to represent the database integrity level. In our experiments, Damage Rate is defined as the percentage of damaged transactions, which contain both malicious transactions and affected transactions, among all the submitted transactions. DMR is variable in the process of submitting transactions. It will increase as the damage is spreading. And it may decrease while the Attack Recovery subsystem is repairing the damage. The DMRs shown in the figures are the highest DMR in the whole process, through which we can know the worst situation of damage spreading and integrity degradation.

The DMRs in Figures 5(a) and 5(b) increase evenly while the MTR is increased. The experiment results show that ITDB can control the damage spreading and maintain data integrity with a good intrusion detection system. The highest DMR in Figure 5(c) and 5(d) is below 7%. This indicates that the ITDB has some capability to control the damage spreading by repairing the contaminated transactions and maintain data integrity with a not so good Intrusion Detection system. Figure 5(e) and 5(f) give some examples of bad Intrusion Detection systems which have a long Detection Latency. In these situations, damage is spread widely and damage rates are increased sharply in the long detection latency. Even in these worse cases, ITDB can repair all the damage eventually and maintain the database integrity in a long run. But high DMR is certainly a danger to the database, we should avoid these situations. All the results above show that ITDB can achieve good survivability without being seriously affected by various intrusion detection deficiencies.

8   Conclusion and Future Works

In this paper, we have evaluated the impact of intrusion detection deficiencies on the cost-efficiency of ITDB using TPC-C benchmark. The results show that (1) with reasonable ranges of false alarm rates and detection latency, ITDB can maintain reasonably good performance under attacks, and (2) when the false alarm rate is not so high and when the detection latency is not so long, ITDB can achieve good survivability.

During the experiments, we also found some problems of ITDB through the evaluation results. After ITDB is optimized during the evaluation, there are still some works for future research. First, it takes a relative long delay for the transaction proxy subsystem to keep logs. This suggests that further research should focus on developing an efficient log system. Second, building a more efficient attack recovery subsystem will decrease the damage spreading, decrease the recovery time, and increase the system performance accordingly.

Acknowledgement. This work was supported by DARPA F20602-02-1-0216, by NSF CCR-0233324, and by DOE Early Career PI Award.

References

1. Ammann, P., Jajodia, S., Liu, P.: Recovery from Malicious Transactions. IEEE Transactions on Knowledge and Data Engineering. **15** (2002) 1167–1185
2. Ammann, P., Jajodia, S., McCollum, C.D., Blaustein, B.T.: Surviving information warfare attacks on databases. In Proceedings of the IEEE Symposium on Security and Privacy. (1997) 164–174
3. Barbara, D., Goel, R., Jajodia, S.: Using checksums to detect data corruption. In Proceedings of the 2000 International Conference on Extending Data Base Technology. (2000)
4. Bishop, M., Cheung, S., et al.: The Threat from the Net. IEEE Spectrum. **38** (1997)
5. Graubart, R., Schlipper, L., McCollum, C.: Defending database management systems against information warfare attacks. Technical report, The MITRE Corporation. (1996)
6. Helman, P., Liepins, G.: Statistical foundations of audit trail analysis for the detection of computer misuse. IEEE Transactions on Software Engineering. **19** (1993) 886–901
7. Jagannathan, R., Lunt, T.: System design document: Next generation intrusion detection expert system (nides). Technical report, SRI International. (1993)
8. Knight, J., Sullivan, K., et al.: Survivability architectures: Issues and approaches. In Proceedings of the 2000 DARPA Information Survivability Conference & Exposition. (2000) 157–171
9. Luenam, P., Liu, P.: ODAR: An On-the-fly Damage Assessment and Repair System for Commercial Database Applications. Proc. 15th IFIP WG 11.3 Working Conference on Data and Application Security. (2001)
10. Lunt, T.F.: A Survey of Intrusion Detection Techniques. Computers & Security. **12** (1993) 405–418
11. Maheshwari, U., Vingralek, R., Shapiro, B.: How to Build a Trusted Database System on Untrusted Storage. Proc. USENIX Symposium on Operating Systems Design and Implementation (OSDI). (2000)
12. McDermott, J., Goldschlag, D.: Towards a model of storage jamming. In Proceedings of the IEEE Computer Security Foundations Workshop. (1996) 176–185
13. Medhi, D., Tipper, D.: Multi-layered network survivability- models, analysis, architecture, framework and implementation: An overview. In Proceedings of the 2000 DARPA Information Survivability Conference & Exposition. (2000) 173–186
14. Mukherjee, B., Heberlein, L.T., Levitt, K.N.: Network Intrusion Detection. IEEE Network. (1994) 26–41
15. Liu, P.: Architectures for Intrusion Tolerant Database Systems. Proc. 2002 Annual Computer Security Applications Conference. (2002) 311–320
16. Stavridou, V.: Intrusion tolerant software architectures. In Proceedings of the 2001 DARPA Information Survivability Conference & Exposition. (2000)
17. TPC-C benchmark, http://www.tpc.org/tpcc/
18. Wylie, J. J., Bigrigg, M. W., et al.: Survivable information storage systems. IEEE Computer. **8** (2000) 61–68

A Model for the Semantics of Attack Signatures in Misuse Detection Systems

Michael Meier

Brandenburg University of Technology Cottbus, Computer Science Department
P.O. Box 101344, 03013 Cottbus, Germany
mm@informatik.tu-cottbus.de

Abstract. Misuse Detection systems identify evidence of attacks by searching for patterns of known attacks (signatures). A main problem in this context is the modeling and specification of attack signatures. A couple of languages are proposed in the literature, which differ in the aspects of signatures that can be described. Some aspects that can be specified in one language cannot be expressed in another. In this paper we present a model for the semantics of attack signatures that systematically enumerates the different aspects that characterize attack signatures. The presented model represents a kind of a checklist for the development of a signature specification language or for the comparison of existing signature specification languages.

1 Introduction

In the area of computer security intrusion detection systems (IDSs) play an important and growing role for the automatic identification of attacks. In addition to preventive security mechanisms they provide post-mortem detection capabilities. A main problem for the detection of security violations using misuse detection systems is the modeling and specification of attack scenarios (signatures). For this purpose, different languages have been proposed. These languages differ in the set of aspects of signatures that can be described. Some aspects that can be specified in one language cannot be expressed in another. Thereby these languages offer different expressiveness, and therefore are only appropriate in distinct domains.

In the area of Active Databases the specification of triggers constitutes a similar problem domain. A number of different languages have been proposed for the description of events. Zimmer et al [7] have developed a Meta-Model for the semantics of complex events in Active Database systems. This model treats the different aspects of event semantics in a systematic way.

Inspired by the work of Zimmer et al we developed a model for the semantics of attack signatures. Instead of starting to build a new model from the scratch we tried to adapt Zimmer's model to benefit from already gained insights in the Active Database domain. Because of some differences between Active Database triggers and attack signatures we needed to modify and extend this model. In the paper we present the adapted model of the semantics of attack signatures, which systematically enumerates the different aspects that characterize attack signatures. These aspects are discussed in

K. Zhang and Y. Zheng (Eds.): ISC 2004, LNCS 3225, pp. 158–169, 2004.
© Springer-Verlag Berlin Heidelberg 2004

detail and their meaning in the context of misuse detection is demonstrated using examples.

The paper is organized as follows: After a short introduction of misuse detection concepts in Section 2 we give an overview of existing languages for the specification of complex events and discuss differences between event semantics in misuse detection and active databases in Section 3. Section 4 introduces some basic definitions that we use for the detailed presentation of the model in Section 5. Finally we draw some conclusions and give an outlook on future work.

2 Misuse Detection

Intrusions represent a set of related actions or events in a system, e.g. a sequence of system calls or network packets. The task of an audit function is to capture information about the execution of each of these security relevant actions by generating audit data records. Misuse detection systems try to detect sequences that correspond to known attacks by searching the audit data stream for patterns encoded in attack signatures.

The audit data records generated during an attack represent the *manifestation* (trace) of the attack. A *signature* of an attack describes the criteria (pattern) required to identify the manifestation of an attack in an audit data stream. It is possible that several attacks of the same type are executed simultaneously and proceed independently. Therefore it is necessary to be able to distinguish different instances of an attack. A *signature instance* is a set of criteria that clearly identifies the manifestation of one instance of an attack in the audit data stream.

One of the core problems in misuse detection is the development of attack signatures. This process is time consuming and requires expertise about system vulnerabilities, audit mechanisms, misuse detection analysis techniques and a clear understanding of the semantics of attack signatures. We believe that wrong understanding of the semantics of attack signatures is one of the main sources of false alerts or undetected attacks. There is a growing need for methods that simplify the process of signature generation and models that clarify the semantics of attack signatures. A more detailed discussion of the signature development process and our experiences in this area can be found in [5].

3 Event Description Languages

Events are used as abstraction in the context of misuse detection signatures as well as in the area of active databases. In this section we give an overview of languages for the description of events and discuss differences of event semantics in both areas.

Active database systems have been developed for applications that need an automatic reaction in response to certain conditions being satisfied or certain events occurring. Active database systems use rules to monitor situations of interest and to trigger a response when these situations occur. For example, such rules can be used to enforce integrity constraints, to compute derived data, and to calculate statistics. These rules typically follow the ECA-Paradigm (Event Condition Action) [10]. When a triggering event occurs the conditions of related rules are evaluated. If a condition is fulfilled the related action is executed. Typical examples for triggering events are data manipulation operations. To react on more sophisticated situations complex events can be used, which are defined using operators of the event algebra of the event language. A number of event languages have been proposed. Examples are HiPAC [10], SNOOP [11], NAOS [12] and ACOOD [1].

Detection languages for misuse detection are used to encode criteria for identifying manifestations of attack instances. A number of detection languages have been proposed but most of them are dedicated to the detection mechanisms used to analyze the audit data stream. Examples are STATL [1], LAMBDA [3], ADeLe [2], Sutekh [4] and SHEDEL [5]. While a number of detection languages have been developed, to our knowledge there is no model of general characteristics which describe the aspects of attack signatures relevant to their detection. Most languages differ regarding their expressiveness that is difficult to assess and outline without a set of common criteria.

As mentioned above rules for Active Databases typically follow the ECA-Paradigm. Attack signature specifications do not have this structure. Instead the three parts are combined in the complex event specification that represents the attack signature. In the context of misuse detection events only occur if they satisfy the specified condition. Further, actions may be executed also if no complex event has occurred yet. This can happen if an attack signature specifies that an action should be executed already after particular parts of the complex event have occurred. This allows responses to attacks that have not been finished yet.

Another important difference is the handling of partial, not completed complex events. These are events that partially have occurred but are not yet finished. We use the term *partial event instance* for these events. Active databases do not know the concept of partial event instances. This is because of a different method of instance creation (*late instance creation*). In active databases complex event instances are triggered by the final event that is part of the complex event. Thus there can never be a partial instance. In contrast, in misuse detection complex event instances are created by the first step that is part of the complex event (*early instance creation*). These instances are incomplete until all other events that are part of the complex event are occurred. It is also possible that a partial instance is never completed but is destroyed because an event occurs that make it impossible for the instance to be completed. Misuse detection systems follow this transition-oriented procedure because it allows responding to partial detected attacks (e.g. by raising a "yellow" alert).

4 Basic Definitions

This section introduces the relevant basic definitions for the introduction of the model. The terminology of [7] was adapted and extended to be applicable for the misuse detection domain.

Definition 1 (Event, Basic Event, Event Type, and Event Instance): An *event* is characterized by a set of features. There is a set of *basic events*, which represent the basic detectable units. A basic event is atomic and bound to a specific point in time. An *event type* describes the features that are common to occurrences of events of that type. When specifying an attack signature actually the corresponding event type is described. Each concrete occurrence of an event type is called *event instance*. This distinction between type and instance is similar to that of programming languages.

Definition 2 (Audit and Time Events): Basic events are divided into audit and time events. *Audit events* correspond to audit records that document security related actions. *Time events* are generated by a timer function. They describe specific points in time either absolutely (seven o'clock) or relative (15 minutes after action x).

Definition 3 (Complex Event, Step, and Parent Event Type): Complex events consist of a collection of events that we call subevents or *steps*. The steps of an event are in relationship to each other, temporally or by their features. The event type of a complex event that contains steps is called the *parent event type* of these steps. An instance of an event type can be used as step in several complex events i.e. an instance can have several parent event types.

Definition 4 (Event Trail): The *event trail* is a partially ordered set of event instances. Its order reflects the occurrence times of its event instances.

Definition 5 (Event Context, Intra-event condition, Inter-event condition): Context conditions define constraints regarding the context of an event. For the specification of complex events we distinguish intra-event conditions and inter-event-conditions. *Intra-event-conditions* consist of a Boolean formula with atoms being comparisons between features of a step and constants. They can be evaluated by merely inspecting some features of the corresponding step. *Inter-event conditions* are Boolean formulas with atoms that are comparisons between features of different steps.

Definition 6 (Initial, Interior, Final, and Exit Steps): Steps that are a first step of a complex event, according to the temporal relations, are called the *initial steps* of the complex event. The last step of an event is called the *final step*. After occurrence of a final step the complex event instance occurs. There are also steps that represent a kind of counter evidence for events. The occurrence of such a step, which we call *exit steps*, makes it impossible for a complex event instance to occur. When an exit step of an event instance occurs this instance is removed. All steps that are neither initial, final nor exit steps are named interior steps.

Notations: We use upper case letters to denote event types and lower case letters for event instances. For event instances we encode the event type in the letter and use a subscript to indicate the order of occurrence times of the event instances. For example the trail $\{a_1\, a_2\, a_3\}$ contains a sequence of three instances of event type A.

Axioms:
1. Basic events are generated by the audit function of the monitored system (or in the case of time events by a timer function). This means that basic events occur when the corresponding audit log entry is generated and the occurrence time is determined by the time component of the log entry.
2. The occurrence time of a final step of a complex event determines the occurrence time of the complex event.
3. Events can occur simultaneously i.e. different event instances may get the same occurrence time.

5 The Model

In this section we present the model for the semantics of signature events in misuse detection systems. Following the structure of Zimmer's model [7] the semantics of event descriptions are divided into three dimensions, whose semantic aspects are discussed in detail and demonstrated using examples.

5.1 Semantic Dimensions of Event Descriptions

Basically there are three questions that are to be answered by an event description to sufficiently define the semantics of the described event. From these questions a partitioning of event semantics in different dimensions can be derived [6].

Question 1 (Event Pattern): Which event instances of a trail cause the occurrence of a complex event? Several criteria have influence on the decision whether an instance is triggered by a given trail or not. For example the type, the order and number of event instances play a decisive role.

Question 2 (Step Instance Selection): Which event instances of a subtrail that cause the occurrence of a complex event are bound to the steps of the complex event and are available for further event correlation? Since there may be multiple matching event instances in such a subtrail that can be bound to a step, it may be ambiguous which one is to be bound to this step.

Example 1: Consider event description E_1 which describes a sequence of an event of type A followed by an event of type B followed by an event of type C and a trail $t_1 := \{b_1\ x_1\ a_1\ c_1\ y_1\ b_2\ x_2\ b_3\ y_2\ c_2\}$. Figure 1 exemplifies how the event pattern selects event instances from the trail that cause the occurrence of a complex event E_1. It also shows that there are alternatives for the selection of an event instance for the step of type B.

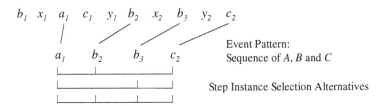

Fig. 1. Example Event Pattern and Step Instance Selection

Question 3 (Step Instance Consumption): Should already occurred steps of a (partial) complex event instance be correlated only with the first or with all matching occurrences of another step?

Example 2: Consider event description E_2 which searches for any sequence of the following events: a specific process p starts executing a program (event type A), process p creates a child process (event type B), and the child process starts executing a specific program (event type C). Since a process can create any number of child processes, in this scenario events of type B differ from events of type A and C in a distinct characteristic. After an event instance a_1 has occurred, any subsequent events of type B and C must be correlated with a_1. This is because the execution of a program by process p (event type A) establishes a state that is not consumed by the creation of a child process (event type B). Instead other child processes can be created by process p. Therefore event type B is *non-consuming* in this scenario; event instance a_1 is never consumed by an event of type B. A trail $t_2 = \{a_1\ b_1\ c_1\ b_2\ c_2\}$ triggers two instances $\{a_1\ b_1\ c_1\}$ and $\{a_1\ b_2\ c_2\}$ of the complex event E_2.

The above-mentioned questions characterizes distinct dimension of the event semantics that play a role in specifying complex events. In the sequel we discuss the characteristics of these dimensions in the context of misuse detection in detail.

5.2   Event Pattern

The event pattern of a complex event describes on an abstract level the search pattern, which is used to identify complex event instances within a trail. Five different aspects have to be considered by the event pattern, namely the type and order, repetition, continuity, concurrency and context conditions. Each aspect is discussed in the sequel.

Type and order. The frame of a complex event is formed by the underlying steps and their order. Steps can be of a complex or basic event type. The order of steps is defined by a set of operators. The model provides a *sequence (;)*, a *disjunction (OR)*, a *conjunction (AND)*, a *simultaneous (||)*, and a *negation (NOT)* operator.

The sequence operator is probably the most often used one. Instances have to occur in the order determined by the sequence operator. An instance of the type *(A; B; C; D)* occurs if the step instances of type A, B, C and D occur in the given order.

The disjunction operator can be used to describe patterns of attacks that can be completed by alternative actions. Instances of the type *(A OR B OR C)* occur if one instance of one of the given types occurs. Instead of describing each possible sequence of alternative actions, the use of the disjunction operator allows a more compact and concise description of signatures.

Some attacks are composed of sequences of actions, where some subsequences can be executed in arbitrary order. Instead of describing attack signatures for all possible combinations of these subsequences the conjunction operator allows to describe this concurrent behavior in an explicit and more compact way. Instances of the type *(A AND B AND C)* occur if instances of the types A, B and C have occurred, irrespective of their order.

An instance of the type *(A || B || C)* occurs if instances of type A, B and C have occurred and their occurrence times are identical. The simultaneous operator is useful when correlating complex events or events coming from different distributed sources, where actions can be executed simultaneously. Further one instance of the event type of a final step can trigger several instances of possibly different complex event types. Since complex events derive their occurrence time from the occurrence time of the final step, these events occur simultaneously. The simultaneous operator is useful to further correlate such events with respect to their simultaneous occurrence.

The negation operator only makes sense if applied to a time interval [6], which is specified as a sequence of at least to events. Instances of the event type *NOT(A, (B; C; ...; D))* occur if the specified sequence of events occur and no instance of type A

occurs between the instance of type B and the instance of type D. In the context of signature specifications the negation operator is mainly used to describe exit steps of an event.

Example 3: Assume an attack that consists of creating a specific process (event type A) which executes three distinct actions in a specific order (sequence of events of types B, C and D). The termination of the process (event type E) represents an exit step for this attack. Event description $F:=NOT(E, (A; B; C; D))$ matches successful occurrences of this attack.

Repetition. It is useful to be able to specify the number of event instances of a step that have to occur to satisfy the event pattern. This can be specified using a *delimiter* in front of a step declaration. The delimiter can be a number that describes how many step instances *exact* (n), *at-most* $(-n)$ or *at-least* $(n-)$ are required by the complex event pattern. A delimiter of the form *at-least n* and *at-most m*, with $n<m$, is also possible. If no delimiter is specified the delimiter $(1-)$ (at-least one) is assumed. The semantics of a delimiter for a step depends on whether the step instances have to occur in a distinct time interval or not. Such a time interval is defined by predecessor and the successor steps of this step. A step with an at-most delimiter has already occurred if no step instance occurs. Therefore it makes no sense to use an at-most delimiter without a time interval. Further, if used outside of a time interval the semantics of an at-least delimiter is equal to that of the exact delimiter i.e. an instance of event type ($(n-) B$) occurs when the nth instance of type B occurs.

Delimiters for steps inside a time interval are much more useful. An exact delimiter can be used to describe a distinct number of repetitions of a particular action. An instance of type $(A; (n) B; C)$ occurs if after an instance of type A, n instances of type B, and thereafter an instance of C occur. If the $(n+1)$th instance of B occurs before C is occurred, the partial complex event instance cannot be completed. The $(n+1)$th instance of B represents an implicit exit step for this event description. At-least and exact delimiters can be used to describe attacks that manifest themselves in a number of repetitions of an action that exceeds a particular threshold within a specified time interval. Example 4 discusses such an attack signature.

Example 4: A kind of attack, which we call doorknob-rattling attack, consists of a number of repetitive login actions. An attacker can use this procedure to guess the password of an account. As an indicator for the presence of such an attack we use the occurrence of at least six failed logins within 30 seconds. The time interval defined by the first and the last failed login is constrained using a condition to be at most 30 seconds long. Assuming that failed logins are represented as events of type A we can describe the corresponding attack signature using an exact delimiter as follows: $(A; (4) A; A)$. If we use explicit time events and an at-least delimiter to model this signature it looks as follows: $(T_0; (6-) A; T_{30})$. This event occurs when an event of type T_{30} occurs after at least six failed logins. For this example the event description $NOT(T_{30}, (T_0; (6) A))$ is more appropriate since an instance of this type already occurs when the sixth failed login occurs.

As mentioned earlier a step with an at-most delimiter has already occurred if no step instance occurred. An at-most delimiter does not model the occurrence of events but the non-occurrence of events or events that did not occur often enough. Example 5 discusses a useful application of this delimiter semantics.

Example 5: Our security policy states that encryption keys used to secure a communication link have to be changed three times a day. To be able to detect violations of this policy, key changes are documented by generating an event log entry (event type C). The signature to detect such policy violations looks as follows $(T_1; (-2) C; T_2)$. Instances of this event type are caused if two or less instances of type C (key changes) occur in the time interval defined by T_1 (00:00 a.m.) and T_2 (11:59 p.m.). An alternative description of this signature is *NOT((3-) C, $(T_1; T_2)$*. Any event description of the form *(A; (-n) B; C)* can be transformed to *NOT(((n+1)-) B, (A; C))*.

Continuity. The continuity aspect clarifies the semantics of the event pattern. For example assume an event type $E_2:= (A; B; C)$. Different people may interpret such a pattern in two different ways:
1. At least one step of type A is followed by at least one step of type B that is followed by at-least one step of type C.
2. At least one step of type A is followed by at least one step of type B that is followed by at least one step of type C and there is no event of type C between the steps of type A and B, and no event of type A between the steps of type B and C.

To clarify the meaning of such a pattern the model distinguishes two different continuity modes *non-continuous* (1. and the default) and *continuous* (2.).

Concurrency. The concurrency modes *overlap* (default) and *non-overlap* define whether the time intervals associated with the steps may overlap or not. For example consider the event types $X:= (A; B; C)$, $Y:= (D; E; F)$, $Z_1:= non\text{-}overlap (X; Y)$ and $Z_2:= overlap (X; Y)$. Event pattern Z_1 requires the event instances of type A, B, C, D, E, and F to occur in this order, while Z_2 also allows sequences of events of type A, B and C and the sequences of events of type D and E to occur interleaved. Note that there is a difference between Z_2 and $Z_3:= (X AND Y)$. Z_2 requires that step F of event type Y occurs after step C of event type X. In contrast Z_3 allows the step sequence of X and Y to occur completely interleaved. Figure 2 demonstrates the different semantics.

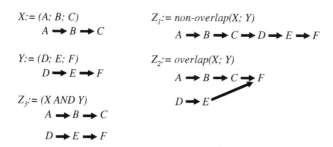

Fig. 2. Differences of concurrency operators

Context condition. Context conditions specify constraints on the context in which steps of a complex event occur. For each step a set of intra-event conditions can be specified. They can be used for example to constraint an audit event to be caused by a specific user or on a specific host. Further context restrictions can be defined using inter-event conditions. They are useful for example to constrain two or more steps to represent audit events caused by the same process or affecting the same object.

5.3 Step Instance Selection

When a complex event has occurred an event instance selection process has to bind the correct event instances to the steps of the complex event. Instance selection defines which step instances are kept for subsequent event correlations or actions to be executed in response to the occurrence of a complex event. Zimmer et al [7] proposes four different instance selection modes. In the context of misuse detection signatures we consider only three of them as useful.

Example 6: Consider event pattern $E_3 := (A; B; C)$ where events of type B correspond to log events that document the values of a performance counter e.g. the CPU or network load. Further assume a trail $t_2 := \{a_1\ b_1\ b_2\ b_3\ c_1\}$. Which instance of type B shall be selected? We distinguish the three modes *first* (default), *last* and *all* to control instance selection. If we use mode first for the event of type B, trail t_2 causes the instance $\{a_1\ b_1\ c_1\}$. If we use last instead of first, instance $\{a_1\ b_3\ c_1\}$ is caused by t_2. And if mode all is used, t_2 results in an instance $\{a_1\ b_1\ b_2\ b_3\ c_1\}$. All three modes are useful for specifying attack signatures. Mode first can be used if the caused complex event instance shall document the first exceeding of the threshold. If an alert and the occurring event instance shall contain the last (current) value of a counter, last is the appropriate mode. Mode all causes all instance of type B that occurred in the defined interval to be contained in the complex event instance.

5.4 Step Instance Consumption

Following to the occurrence of an instance a_1 of step A an instance b_1 of step B occurs and the partial complex event instance is further completed to $\{a_1\ b_1\ ...\}$. If now another instance b_2 of step B occurs, can this instance b_2 together with the instance $a1$ build another partial event instance $\{a_1\ b_2\ ...\}$ or not? The answer to this question can be controlled using the instance consumption modes. We distinguish two modes, which we call *consuming* (default) and *non-consuming* following the terminology of STATL [1]. If for step B the mode consuming is defined, then b_1 consumes a_1. In this case instance b_2 cannot build another partial event instance together with a_1. If step B is defined non-consuming, each instance of type B together with any instance of type A occurred before build an own partial event instance.

Example 7: Consider event $E_3 := (A; \text{non-consuming } B; C)$ and trail $t_3 := \{a_1\ a_2\ b_1\ b_2\}$. Trail t_3 results in four partial event instances of type E_4, which are $\{a_1\ b_1\ ...\}$, $\{a_2\ b_1\ ...\}$, $\{a_1\ b_2\ ...\}$ and $\{a_2\ b_2\ ...\}$.

Which mode has to be chosen for a step is typically defined by the action that is modeled by this step. For example for a complex event that must keep track of a system call sequence of a process the consumption mode of the steps can be derived from the semantics of the action modeled by a step. For example fork calls of a process (creation of a child process) are typically modeled as non-consuming steps, because a process can create multiple child processes that can complete the attack. Construction of system objects (e.g. file or process creation) is typically modeled as non-consuming step. The non-consuming mode is also often found for final steps if certain repeatable event should always trigger a complex event instance.

A process exit call is modeled as a consuming step since a process can be terminated only once. Consuming steps are typically used to describe steps that document object destructions (file deletion, process termination, etc.) or the change of object properties (file renaming). Exit steps are always consuming. The consuming mode is also used in cycles were features of steps are aggregated or passes are counted.

In counting loops (for example in a sequence of sensor events that document values of some performance counters) the semantics is a little bit more complex. We come back to the so-called doorknob-rattling attack. To simplify the discussion we modify the example and now search for three failed logins. Again we assume that an event of type A models a failed login. We discuss the semantics of $E_5 := $ *(consuming A; consuming A; consuming A)* and $E_6 := $ *(non-consuming A; non-consuming A; non-consuming)* for the trail $t_4 := \{a_1\, a_2\, a_3\, a_4\, a_5\, a_6\}$. Since the initial step of E_5 is of type A, for every event instance of trail t_4 a new partial instance of E_5 is created. The overall trail t_4 causes the following four instances of type E_5 $\{a_1\, a_2\, a_3\}$, $\{a_2\, a_3\, a_4\}$, $\{a_3\, a_4\, a_5\}$ and $\{a_4\, a_5\, a_6\}$ and leaves the following two partial instances $\{a_5\, a_6\, ...\}$ and $\{a_6\, ...\}$. E_5 describes all combinations (without repetitions) of three consecutive instances of type A. The number of instances caused by a trail can be calculated by $n\text{-}3\text{-}1$ where n is the number of events of type A in the trail. Figure 5 a) shows which combinations of the event instances of t_4 are correlated by E_5. Because of the non-consuming mode of the steps in E_6 much more instances of type E_6 are caused by trail t_4. This is because E_6 describes all combinations (without repetitions) of three (consecutive or not) instances of type A. Here the number of complex event instances of type E_6 caused by a trail containing n event instances of type A is determined by the binomial coefficient n *choose 3*, which is 20 in our case. Figure 5 b) shows which combinations of event instances of t_4 are correlated by E_6.

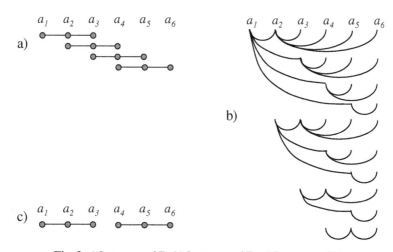

Fig. 3. a) Instances of E_5. b) Instances of E_6. c) Instances of E_7.

The above discussion shows that we have to determine via the consumption mode, which combinations should result in an alert. Specifically for the signature discussed in example 4 one may argue that none of consumption modes results in the appropriate event instances since in the described situation only the two event instances $\{a_1\, a_2\, a_3\}$ and $\{a_4\, a_5\, a_6\}$ should be released. Therefore we need further semantics of *disjoint instances* of consuming step chains, where each step is only involved in one event instance. To support these semantics we introduced the concept of *exclusive steps*. An event instance that was already bound to a step of any event instance cannot be bound to an exclusive step. Further we assume that if an event instance is checked to be bound to a step, partial complex event instances are always checked before initial steps of new (empty) complex event instances are checked. This means that an event instance can only be bound to an exclusive initial step, if it cannot be bound to a step of any partial events. Using this concept the event that signals a doorknob rattling attack looks as follows: $E_7 := $ *(exclusive consuming A; consuming A; consuming A)*. Instances of E_7 caused by t_4 are shown in figure 5 c).

6   Conclusions and Future Work

In this paper we have presented a model for the semantics of attack signatures that adapts Zimmer's model for event semantics in active database systems [7]. The model divides the semantics in the three dimensions event pattern, step instance selection and step instance consumption. The event pattern specifies the point in time events occur, the step instance selection defines which events are bound to a complex event. Step instance consumption controls, whether already occurred steps of a (partial) complex event instance have to be correlated only with the first or with all matching occurrences of another step.

Since the model presented in this paper systematically treats the semantic aspects of attack signatures, it contributes to the ongoing work in the area of misuse detection systems in several ways:

- The model provides a solid and in-depth understanding of properties of complex signature events.
- It explicitly mentions and distinguishes the different aspects of signature descriptions and thereby supports a systematic development of attack signatures.
- It offers a solid basis for the development of detection languages.
- It can be used as kind of checklist for a systematic comparison of detection languages regarding their expressiveness in distinct aspects of signatures.

Further we have discussed some semantic aspects of attack signatures, which have not been taken into account by existing detection languages. Only a few languages provide a conjunction operator for the definition of the event pattern. To our knowledge Lambda [3] is the only language that supports a concept similar to the simultaneous operator. The dimension step instance consumption was first considered by the language STATL [1] and the language of the IDIOT IDS [9], but in a restricted sense. None of the existing languages supports different step instance selection modes and none of these languages allows the specification of the doorknob-rattling attack signature using disjoint instances semantics as discussed in Section 5.4.

We have not presented a complete formal syntax for the specification of the semantics of complex signatures, since the syntactical constructs used in this paper are intended for explanation purposes only. A challenging task for future work is to develop a controllable and comfortable detection language that supports all aspects of semantics of complex events.

References

1. Eckmann, St. T.; Vigna, G.; Kemmerer, R. A.: STATL: an Attack Language for State-based Intrusion Detection, in Proc. of the ACM Workshop on Intrusion Detection, Athens, Greece, November 2000.
2. Michel, C.; Me, L.: ADeLe: an Attack Description Language for Knowledge-based Intrusion Detection, in Proc. of the Internat. Conference on Information Security, Kluwer, June 2001.
3. Cuppens, F.; Ortalo, R.: LAMBDA: A Language to Model a Database for Detection of Attacks. In: Proc. of the Third International Workshop on Recent Advances in Intrusion Detection, LNCS 1907, Springer, 2000, pp. 197-216.
4. Pouzol, J.-P.; Ducassé, M.: From Declarative Signatures to Misuse IDS. In: Proc. of the Fourth International Symposium on Recent Advances in Intrusion Detection, LNCS 2212, Springer, 2001, pp. 1-21.
5. Meier, M.; Bischof, N.; Holz, T.: SHEDEL - A Simple Hierarchical Event Description Language for Specifying Attack Signatures. In: Proc. of the 17th International Conference on Information Security. Kluwer, 2002, pp. 559-571.
6. Zimmer, D.: A Meta-Model for the Definition of the Semantics of Complex Events in Active Database Management Systems (in German). PhD Thesis, University of Paderborn, Shaker-Verlag, ISBN: 3-8265-3744-0, 1998.
7. Zimmer, D.; Unland, R.: On the Semantics of Complex Events in Active Database Management Systems. In Proc. of the 15th International Conference on Data Engineering, IEEE Computer Society Press, 1999, pp. 392-399.
8. Vigna, G.; Eckmann, S. T.; Kemmerer, R. A.: Attack Languages, in: Proc. of the IEEE Information Survivability Workshop, Boston, MA, October 2000.
9. Kumar, S.: Classification and Detection of Computer Intrusions, PhD Thesis, Purdue University, 1995.
10. Dayal, U.; Buchmann, A.; Chakravarthy, S.: The HiPAC Project. In: Active Database Systems. Morgan Kaufmann, ISBN: 1-55860-304-2, 1996.
11. Chakravarthy, S.; Krishnaprasad, V; Anwar, E.; Kim, S.: Composite Events for Active Databases: Semantics, Contexts and Detection. In Proc. of the 20th International Conference on Very Large Databases, 1994, pp. 606-617.
12. Collet, C.; Coupaye, T.: Composite Events in NAOS. In Proc. of the seventh International Conference on Database and Expert Systems Applications. 1996, pp. 475-481.
13. Berndtsson, M.: ACCOD: An approach to an Active Object-Oriented DBMS. Master thesis, University of Skövde, 1991.

Detection of Sniffers in an Ethernet Network

Zouheir Trabelsi and Hamza Rahmani

The University of Tunisia
The College of Telecommunications (SupCom)
Cité Technologique des Communications
Route de Raoued Km 3,5 – 2083 El Ghazala, Ariana, Tunisia
trabelsi.zouheir@supcom.rnu.tn

Abstract.. On a local network, security is always taken into consideration. When plain text data is being sent onto the network, it can be easily stolen by any network user. Stealing data from the network is called sniffing. By sniffing the network, a user can gain access into confidential documents and cause intrusion into anyone's privacy. Many 0freely distributed software on the Internet provides this functionality. Despite the easiness of sniffing, sniffers are usually difficult to detect, since they do not interfere with the network traffic at all. System administrators are facing difficulties to detect and deal with this type of attack. Several antisniffers programs can be used to detect sniffers. However, sniffers are becoming very advanced so that current antisniffers are unable to detect them.

This paper explains a new technique used by SupCom AntiSniffer, a tool that can effectively scan sniffers on an Ethernet network. The proposed technique uses three phases to detect the sniffing hosts in an Ethernet network. In the first phase, the ARP caches of the sniffing hosts are corrupted. In the second phase, TCP SYN request connections packets are sent to each host in the network using fake IP and MAC source addresses. Finally, by analyzing the responses of the hosts, all hosts running sniffers are detected. Four anti-sniffers, PMD [18], PromiScan [17], L0pht AntiSniff [19] and SupCom anti-sniffer, are tested and the evaluation results show that SupCom AntiSniffer succeeded to detect more sniffing hosts than the other antisniffers.

1 Introduction

In the local network, the act of sniffing has been a big thread. Malicious users can easily steal confidential documents and anyone's privacy by sniffing the network. Sniffing can be done simply by downloading free sniffer software (sniffers) from the Internet and installing them into personal computers. Using sniffers can have extremely grave consequences. Indeed, information gathered by a sniffer can include passwords, e-mail messages, encryption keys, TCP packets sequence numbers, etc. The sniffing attack on a network is usually difficult to detect, since it does not interfere with the network traffic at all. System administrators are facing difficulties to detect and deal with this attack.

Because Ethernet networks are shared communication channels, the network interface of a computer on such a network sees all the packets transmitted on the segment it resides on. Each packet has a header indicating the recipient of the packet.

K. Zhang and Y. Zheng (Eds.): ISC 2004, LNCS 3225, pp. 170–182, 2004.

Under normal operating procedures, only the machine with that proper address is supposed to accept the packet. However, the Network Interface Card (NIC) can be set to a special mode called promiscuous mode to receive all packets on the wire. A sniffer is a special program or piece of code that put the NIC in the promiscuous mode. Then the NIC will blindly receive all packets and pass them to the system kernel. Packets that are not supposed to arrive to that computer are no longer blocked by the NIC. Many basics services, such as FTP, Telnet and SMTP [9], send clear text data in the packets. The sniffer captures all packets and displays their contents on the hacker's computer screen, for examples the passwords used to authenticate during an FTP session, or the message of an email in SMTP packets.

This paper discusses a new detection technique based on ARP cache poisoning attack. The technique includes mainly three phases. Based on this technique, a tool, called SupCom Anti-Sniffer, is implemented. SupCom anti-sniffer gives automatically system administrators a better helping hand regarding the detection of sniffers in an Ethernet network. Four anti-sniffers, PMD[18], PromiScan[17], L0pht AntiSniff [19] and SupCom anti-sniffer, are tested and the evaluation results show that SupCom anti-sniffer gives a better detection performance than the others.

2   Related Works

There are mainly three well-known techniques used to detect sniffing hosts in an Ethernet network, namely the ARP detection technique, the DNS detection technique and the RTT detection technique. Most current anti-sniffers, such as PMD [18], PromiScan [17] and L0pht AntiSniff [19], are based on these detection techniques. However, the techniques present many limits so that advanced sniffers are designed in such a way they can stay undetectable by current anti-sniffers.

2.1   The RTT Detection Technique

The RTT (Round Trip Time) is the time of the round trip of a packet sent to a host. That is the time that a packet took to reach the destination, plus the time that a response took to reach the source. It is expected that the measurement of the RTT increases considerably when a host is in the promiscuous mode, since all packets are captured.

The idea behind the RTT detection technique ([16] and [13]), is first to send to a host, with a particular OS, a number of request packets, and wait for the responses packets, in order to take the RTT measurements. Then, the host is set to the promiscuous mode. And, the same request packets are sent again to the host, and the corresponding RTT measurements are collected. The RTT averages, the standard deviations, and the percentage of changes of the collected RTT measurements are computed. The RTT averages, standard deviations, percentage of changes are called the training data.

The samples of the collected RTT measurements represent two different populations, called the normal mode population and the promiscuous mode population. To show that the two averages of the samples RTT measurements are statistically different enough and therefore represent two different populations (the normal mode and the promiscuous mode populations), the z-statistics [1] model is used. The z-statistics model allows making a judgment about whether or not a host's NIC is set to the promiscuous mode.

In the real world, the system administration has to identify first the OS of the suspicious host. This can be done by several available tools, such as Nmap [15]. Then, a number of request packets should be sent to the suspicious host in order to collect the corresponding RTT measurements.

The suspicious host can be either in the normal mode or in the promiscuous mode. Two z-statistics are computed. The first one, called the normal mode z-statistics, uses the training data related to the OS of the suspicious host for the normal mode, as the first population, and the collected data in the real world, as the second population. The second z-statistics, called the promiscuous mode z-statistics, uses the training data related to the OS of the suspicious host for the promiscuous mode, as the first population, and the collected data, as the second population. If the normal mode z-statistics is less than the z value (which is 2.36), then we may conclude that the host's NIC is almost 99% set to the normal mode, else, the host's NIC is set to the promiscuous mode.

The limits of the RTT detection technique: The RTT detection technique is a probabilistic technique. Many known and unknown factors, such as the operating system of the suspicious host, and the LAN traffic, may affect considerably the results generated by any anti-sniffer based on this technique. When the LAN is under heavy traffic, this probabilistic technique may generate false decision regarding whether the suspicious host's NIC card is set to the promiscuous mode or to the normal mode. This is due mainly on the RTT measurements taken which may lead to a false decision. In addition, an advanced sniffer may attempt to put heavy traffic in the network in order to let the anti-sniffer generates misleading results.

The RTT detection technique attempts to send heavy traffic to a suspicious host on a particular open port, usually the FTP port (21). However, it is not common to have always the FTP port (21) open in each host in the network. Finally, to work appropriately, this technique needs to send heavy traffic on the network and then takes the RTT measurements. Such an action may cause some damage to the network's hosts and services, such as denial of service attacks.

2.2 The DNS Detection Technique

The DNS detection technique [13] works by exploiting a behaviour common to many sniffers. Current sniffers are not truly passive. In fact, current sniffers do generate network traffic, although it is usually hard to distinguish whether the generated network was from the sniffer or not. It turns out that many sniffers do reverse DNS lookup (that is looking up a hostname by an IP address) on the traffic that it sniffed. Since this traffic is generated by the sniffer program, the trick is to detect this DNS lookup some how and distinguish it from normal DNS lookup requests.

Do that, we can generate fake traffic to the Ethernet segment with a source address of some unused IP address. Then, since the traffic we generate should normally be ignored by the hosts on the segment, if a DNS lookup request is generated, we know that there is a sniffer on the Ethernet segment. And by sniffing the packets on the Ethernet segment, we can detect which hosts are sending the DNS lookup requests.

The limits of the DNS detection technique: This technique can be quickly side stepped. Sniffers can easily be changed to not perform the reverse DNS lookup. Furthermore, hackers will become more intelligent so as to never perform the reverse DNS lookup either. This will render the technique completely useless.

2.3   The ARP Detection Technique

The ARP detection technique is described more in detail in our paper [16]. However, we need to describe it again here since; this paper uses some of its results.

2.3.1   MAC Addresses Types

All the NIC's on the Ethernet are represented by a 6-byte hardware address. The manufacturer assigns this address such that each address is unique in the whole world. All communications on the Ethernet are based on this hardware address. The NIC, however, can set up different filters (called hardware filter) in order to receive different kinds of packets. The following are a list of hardware filters:

➤ *Unicast*: Receive all packets having the same destination address as the hardware address of the NIC.
➤ *Broadcast*: Receive all broadcast packets. Broadcast packets have destination address FF:FF:FF:FF:FF:FF. The purpose of this mode is to receive the packets which are supposed to arrive at all nodes existing on the network.
➤ *Multicast*: Receive all packets which are specifically configured to arrive at some multicast group addresses. Only packets from the hardware multicast addresses registered beforehand in the multicast list can be received by the NIC.
➤ *All Multicasts*: Receive all multicast packets. Since this mode may also correspond to other high level protocols other than IPv4, all Multicast will receive all packets that have their group bit set (01:00:00:00:00:00).
➤ *Promiscuous*: Receive all packets on the network without checking the destination address at all.

2.3.2   Detection Mechanism

The ARP detection technique consist into checking whether or not a suspicious host responds to ARP request packets that are not supposed to be treated by the suspicious host. Since the sniffing host receives all the packets, including those that are not targeting to it, it may make mistakes such as responding to a packet, which originally is supposed to be filtered by the host's NIC. Therefore, the detection is performed by checking the responses of ARP reply packets, when ARP request packets are sent to all hosts on the network.

On an Ethernet linked by IP addresses, packets are in fact sent and received based on hardware addresses (MAC address). Packets cannot be sent by just using an IP address. Therefore, the Ethernet needs a mechanism that converts IP addresses into hardware addresses. At this time, ARP packets are used. ARP packets belong to the link layer, which is the same layer as IP, so ARP packets do not affect the IP layer.

Since IP addresses resolving is always available on an IP network, ARP packets become suitable packets for testing the response of the hosts when detecting promiscuous mode.

It is important to mention that there is nothing specifying that there must be some consistency between the ARP header and the Ethernet header. That means you can provide uncorrelated addresses between these two headers. For example, the source MAC address in the Ethernet header can be different from the source MAC address in the ARP message header.

2.3.3 Promiscuous Mode Detection

When the NIC is set to promiscuous mode, packets that are supposed to be filtered by the NIC are now passed to the system kernel. Therefore, if we configure an ARP packet such that it does not have broadcast address as the destination address, send it to every host on the network and discover that some hosts respond to it, then those hosts are in promiscuous mode.

In this example, the ARP packet destination hardware address is set to an address that does not exist, for example 00-00-00-00-00-01. When the NIC is in normal mode, this packet is considered to be "to other host" packet, so it is refused by the hardware filter of the NIC. However, when the NIC is in promiscuous mode, the NIC does not perform any filter operation. Then this packet is able to pass to the system kernel. The system kernel assumes that this ARP requests packet arrives because it contains the same IP address as that machine, so it should respond to the packet. However, this is not true. There exists some sort of software filter in the kernel, called the Software Filter, because a packet is actually filtered again by the system kernel. The software filter depends on the operating system kernel (Figure 1).

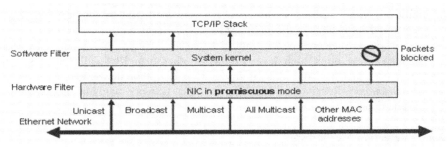

Fig. 1. The NIC is set to the promiscuous mode

2.3.4 Software Filtering Based Detection

It is unnecessary to sent ARP packet with MAC addresses that do not exist, since the software filter will block such packets. However, we need to send ARP packets with MAC addresses that may pass the software filter. So that, we can understand the mechanism used by the software filter to filter packets based on their MAC addresses. The following are the list of hardware MAC addresses used to send ARP request packets, when the NIC is in the promiscuous mode (the hardware filter do not filter packets):

- FF:FF:FF:FF:FF:FF broadcast address : All nodes should receive this kind of packets and respond because it is a broadcast address. A usual ARP request packet uses this address.

- FF:FF:FF:FF:FF:FE fake broadcast address : This address is a fake broadcast address missing the last 1 bit. This is to check whether the software filter examines all bits of the address and whether it will respond.

- FF:FF:00:00:00:00 fake broadcast 16 bits : This address is a fake broadcast address in which only the first 16 bits are the same as the broadcast address. This may be classified as a broadcast address and replied when the filter function only checks the first word of the broadcast address.

- FF:00:00:00:00:00 fake broadcast 8 bits : This address is a fake broadcast address in which only the first 8 bits are the same as the broadcast address. This may be classified as a broadcast address and replied when the filter function only checks the first byte of the broadcast address.

- F0:00:00:00:00:00 fake broadcast 4 bits : This address is a fake broadcast address in which only the first 4 bits are the same as the broadcast address. This may be classified as a broadcast address and replied when the filter function only checks the first 4 bits of the broadcast address.

- 01:00:00:00:00:00 group bit address: This is an address with only the group bit set. This is to check whether this address is considered as a multicast address as Linux does.

- 01:00:5E:00:00:00 multicast address 0: Multicast address 0 is usually not used. So we use this as an example of a multicast address not registered in the multicast list of the NIC. The hardware filter should reject this packet. However, this packet may be misclassified to be a multicast address when the software filter does not completely check all bits. The system kernel thus may reply to such packet when the NIC is set to promiscuous mode.

- 01:00:5E:00:00:01 multicast address 1: Multicast address 1 is an address that all hosts in the local network should receive. In the other word, the hardware filter will pass this kind of packets by default. But it is possible that the NIC does not support multicast mode and does not respond, but this hypothesis was not available because all the available cards on the market bear multicasting. So this is to check whether the host supports multicast addresses.

- 01:00:5E:00:00:02 multicast address 2: Multicast address 2 is used to all routers in the local networks. So we use this as an example of a multicast address not registered in the multicast list of the NIC. The hardware filter should reject this packet and also is not accepted by the software filter. The system kernel check the hardware result and one notices while the software filter always comes after the hardware filter, from which for the addresses multicast, if an address was rejected by the hardware filter she is therefore rejected by the software filter.

- 01:00:5E:00:00:03 multicast address 3: Multicast address 3 is not assigned. So we use this as an example of a multicast address not registered in the multicast list of the NIC. The hardware filter should reject this packet and also is not accepted by the software filter. The system kernel check the hardware result and one notices while the software filter always comes after the hardware filter, from which for the addresses multicast, if an address was rejected by the hardware filter she is therefore rejected by the software filter.

2.3.5 Experiences and Results

The tests are performed against a number of operating systems (Windows 9x, ME, 2000/NT and XP, Linux 2.4x and FreeBSD 5.0). As expected, all kernels respond to the broadcast address and multicast address 1 when the NIC is in normal mode. The test results using the hardware addresses listed in the previous section are listed in Table 1. However, when the NIC is set to the promiscuous mode, the results are OS dependent.

Table 1. Promiscuous mode detection results using trap ARP request packets

Operating Systems		Windows XP		Windows 2k/NT		Linux 2.4.x & FreeBSD 5.0	
Hardware Addresses		Norm.	Prom.	Norm.	Prom.	Norm.	Prom.
FF:FF:FF:FF:FF:FF	Br	O	O	O	O	O	O
FF:FF:FF:FF:FF:FE	B47	--	X	--	X	--	X
FF:FF:00:00:00:00	B16	--	X	X	X	--	X
FF:00:00:00:00:00	B8	--	--	--	--	--	X
01:00:00:00:00:00	Gr	--	--	--	--	--	X
01:00:5E:00:00:00	M0	--	--	--	--	--	X
01:00:5E:00:00:01	M1	O	O	O	O	O	O
01:00:5E:00:00:02	M2	--	--	--	--	--	X
01:00:5E:00:00:03	M3	--	--	--	--	--	X

O: **Legal response**, X: **Illegal response**, --: **No response**

Microsoft Windows:
➢ In the case of Windows XP and Windows 2000/NT, they respond to fake broadcast B47 and B16. Hence, their software filters determine the broadcast address by checking only the two first bytes. Since Windows 2000/NT responds to the fake broadcast B16 in the normal mode also, therefore, only the address B47 can be used to verify whether a NIC card is set to a promiscuous mode or not. However, for Windows XP, the two fake broadcast addresses B47 and B16 can be used to verify whether a NIC card is set to a promiscuous mode or not.

Linux and FreeBSD:
➢ In the case of Linux 2.4x and FreeBSD 5.0, it responds to all fake broadcast and to all addresses with the group bit set. Therefore, any fake broadcast addresses can be used to verify the promiscuous mode. In addition, any address with the group bit set can be used to verify the promiscuous mode, excluding the multicast address M1. Since, Multicast address M1 is an address that all hosts in the local network should receive.

Based on the results shown in Table 1, it is important to notice that if the destination MAC address in the Ethernet header of a packet is the fake broadcast address B47 (FF:FF:FF:FF:FF:**FE**), then any host, with any OS, set to the promiscuous mode will accept the packet and send it to the TCP/IP stack for processing.

2.3.6 The Limits of the ARP Detection Technique

The main limits of this detection technique is that if a host does not generate any ARP reply messages while sniffing, then this technique becomes useless. Because this detection technique relies on the ARP reply messages generated by the sniffing host. Consequently, any anti-sniffer based on this detection technique is unable to detect the sniffing hosts that do not generate ARP reply messages.

3 A Sniffer Detection Technique Based on ARP Cache Poisoning Attack

3.1 Updating the ARP Cache

Each host in a network segment has a table, called ARP cache, which maps IP addresses with their MAC addresses. New entries in the ARP cache can be created or already existing entries can be updated by ARP request or reply messages.

Create a new entry: When an ARP reply message arrives in a host, an entry in the ARP cache should be created. If the entry exists already, then it should be updated. In addition, when a host receives an ARP request message, it believes that a connexion is going to be performed. Hence, to minimize the ARP traffic, it creates a new entry in its ARP cache and puts there the addresses provided in the ARP request message. It is important to mention that sending an ARP request message in unicast is totally RFC compliant. They are authorized to let a system checks the entries of its ARP cache.

Update an entry: When an ARP reply message or an ARP request message arrives in a host, if the entry exists already, then it will be updated by the addresses (the source MAC address and the source IP address) provided in the ARP message.

3.2 ARP Cache Poisoning Attack

ARP cache poisoning attack is the malicious act, by a host in a LAN, of introducing a spurious IP address to MAC address mapping in another host's ARP cache. This can be done by manipulating directly the ARP cache of a target host, independently of the ARP messages sent by the target host. To do that, we can either:
  ➤ add a new fake entry in the target host's ARP cache
  ➤ or, update an already existing entry by fake addresses (IP and/or MAC addresses).

Create a fake new entry: To do that, we send an ARP request message to a target host, with fake source IP and MAC addresses. When the target host receives the ARP request message, it believes that a connexion is going to be performed, and then, creates a new entry in its ARP cache and puts there the fake source addresses (IP and/or MAC) provided in the ARP request message. Consequently, the target host's ARP cache becomes corrupted.

Update an entry with a fake entry: To do that, we just have to send an ARP reply message to a target host with fake IP and MAC addresses. Thus, even if the entry is already present in the target host's ARP cache, it will be updated, with the fake entries.

3.3   The Detection Mechanism

The proposed mechanism used to detect sniffing hosts is based mainly on the ARP cache poisoning attack. It consists of three different phases:

- In the first phase, we attempt to corrupt the ARP cache of each sniffing host in the LAN, with a fake entry, using ARP cache poisoning attack. We will demonstrate that only the ARP caches of the hosts running sniffers will be corrupted, and this attack on the ARP caches will not make any damage to the attacked hosts.
- In the second phase, we attempt to establish a TCP connexion with each host in the LAN on any port, whether it is an open port or a closed one.
- In the third phase, we sniff the LAN in order to capture any packet containing the fake entry. We will demonstrate that the hosts that sent TCP packets containing the fake entry are running sniffers. However, the hosts that sent ARP request packets are not running sniffers.

The following sub-sections describe in detail the three phases. We assume that we use a host in the LAN, called the testing host, to do all the actions needed in the three phases.

3.3.1   Phase 1: ARP Cache Poisoning

The aim of this phase is to corrupt only the ARP caches of the sniffing hosts in a LAN. First, we send an ARP request message, with fake source IP and MAC addresses (IP-X and MAC-X), to all hosts in the LAN.

The ARP request message sent to the hosts has an Ethernet header and an ARP message header. Hence, we need to choose the values of the fields in each header, in order to let only the sniffing host processes the ARP request message. If we choose the destination MAC address in the Ethernet layer header as a broadcast address (*FF:FF:FF:FF:FF:FF*), then all the ARP caches of the hosts in the LAN will be corrupted by the ARP cache poisoning attack. Such a destination MAC address is discarded because it does not allow us to detect which hosts are sniffing.

However, if the destination MAC address is the fake broadcast address B47 (*FF:FF:FF:FF:FF:**FE***), then any host, with any OS, set to the promiscuous mode will accept the ARP request message and send it to the ARP layer (refer to section 2.3.5). If the host is set to the normal mode, this ARP request message will be blocked at the Ethernet layer, since the destination MAC address is not a unicast address, a broadcast address nor a multicast address. Consequently, the values of the main fields of the ARP request packet used to corrupt only the ARP caches of the sniffing hosts are:

> **Ethernet header:**
> o Source MAC address = *Any MAC address*
> o Destination MAC address = *FF:FF:FF:FF:FF:**FE** (B47)*
> o Ethernet Type = *0x0806 (ARP message)*
> **ARP message header:**
> o Source IP address = *Fake IP address (IP-X)*
> o Source MAC address = *Fake MAC address (MAC-X)*
> o Destination IP address = *IP address of a target host in the LAN*
> o Destination MAC address = *00:00:00:00:00:00*
> o Operation code: *1 (ARP request)*

3.3.2 Phase 2: Establishing TCP Connections

Then, for each host in the LAN, we will attempt to establish a TCP connection. To do that, we need to send TCP packets with the bit SYN set, from the testing host, to each host in the LAN. However, the source IP address in the IP header of the TCP packets is not the source IP address of the testing host. But, it is that fake IP address (IP-X). Each host in the LAN will process the received TCP packet.

The values of some important fields of the TCP packet used to establish a TCP connexion with each host in the LAN are:

> **Ethernet header:**
> o Source MAC address = *The Testing host's MAC address*
> o Destination MAC address = *Target host's MAC address*
> **IP header:**
> o Source IP address = *Fake IP address (IP-X)*
> o Destination IP address = *IP address of a target host*
> **TCP header:**
> o *Destination Port = Any number between 1 and 65535 (for example: 40000)*
> o *Source Port = Any number*
> o *Bit SYN = 1*

3.3.3 Phase 3: Detection of the Sniffing Hosts

Just following the request for establishing a TCP connexion with each host in the LAN, we expect three types of possible replies packets come from the hosts.

- The first type can be a TCP SYN/ACK packet indicating that the connexion can be done (the SYN and ACK bits are set).
- The second type can be a TCP RST packet indicating that the connexion cannot be established because the port destination is inaccessible (the RST, reset, bit is set).
- The third type can be an ARP request message sent by a host to look for the MAC address of the fake source IP address IP-X.

The hosts that generate any TCP packets with the fake addresses IP-X and MAC-X as the destination addresses in the IP header are consequently running sniffers. Because, those host's ARP caches are corrupted with the fake IP and MAC addresses (IP-X and MAC-X) and are able to provided the MAC address MAC-X of the IP address IP-X. It is important to indicate again that during the first phase we used the ARP cache poisoning attack to corrupt only the ARP caches of the sniffing hosts, with the fake entry (IP-X and MAC-X).

We use a sniffer to capture any TCP packet on the LAN that has those fake IP and MAC addresses (IP-X and MAC-X) as the destination addresses, and has been sent by a host. All hosts that sent such TCP packets are consequently running sniffers, and their IP addresses can be easily identified.

However, any host whose ARP cache is not corrupted would generate an ARP request message in order to get the MAC address of the fake IP address IP-X. This MAC address will be used later to send the reply message which is expected to be a TCP packet. Therefore, any host in the LAN that will send ARP request message looking for the MAC address of the IP address IP-X are not running sniffers.

4   SupCom AntiSniffer

Based on the proposed detection technique, an anti-sniffer with a Graphical User Interface (GUI), called SupCom Anti-Sniffer, has been developed using Visual C++6.0 and WinpCap Library. SupCom Anti-Sniffer integrates a TCP and ARP packet generator and a sniffer with filtering capabilities. SupCom Anti-Sniffer allows generating ARP request packet with fake source IP and MAC addresses. In addition, it is able to sniff the network and capture packets based on filtering rules defined by the users.

SupCom Anti-Sniffer uses the three phases discussed in the previous sections, to detect the sniffing hosts in a LAN. SupCom Anti-Sniffer is able to detect hosts running even advanced sniffers. Advanced sniffers are sniffers that do not send any ARP request and reply messages, ICMP messages and DNS messages, in order to stay undetected by current anti-sniffers.

5   Detection Performances of the Anti-sniffers

Current detection techniques rely on the DNS, the ARP and the ICMP messages generated by the sniffing hosts. The proposed detection technique does not rely on such messages. In a LAN, even an advanced sniffer cannot stay undetectable by an anti-sniffer based on the proposed detection technique. Unless the sniffer stops all types of traffic directed to and issued from the sniffing host. In such a situation, the sniffer becomes useless, since no other networking activities can be done while the sniffer is working.

Four anti-sniffers, PromiScan [17], PMD [18], L0pht AntiSniff [19], and SupCom Anti-Sniffer are used to detect sniffing hosts in a LAN, during two tests. In the first test, the sniffing hosts can generate ARP reply messages. The following table shows that all the four anti-sniffers are able to detect all the sniffing hosts. In the second test, the hosts are running an advanced sniffer that does not generate any ARP messages and reverse DNS lookup messages. The following table shows that only SupCom Anti-Sniffer was able to detect all the sniffing hosts. This experience demonstrates clearly that SupCom anti-sniffer is more efficient than current anti-sniffers, particularly when detecting advanced sniffers.

Table 2. Detection performance of some anti-sniffers

Anti-Sniffers	Test 1: simple sniffer (1)	Test 2: advanced sniffer (2)
PromiScan, PMD and L0pht AntiSnff	All sniffing hosts detected	No sniffing hosts detected
SupCom anti-sniffer	All sniffing hosts detected	**All sniffing hosts detected**

(1) *Simple sniffer*: is a sniffer that allows the sniffing host to generate all type of ARP, ICMP, TCP, UDP, and reverse DNS lookup packets.

(2) *Advanced sniffer*: is a sniffer that does not allow the sniffing host to generate ARP packets and reverse DNS lookup packets, in order to avoid detection by current anti-sniffers.

6 Conclusions

This work discusses a technique for detecting malicious sniffers in Ethernet networks, based on the ARP cache poisoning attack. Even though sniffers are difficult to detect, the proposed technique can provide system administrator with a consistent decision. Current anti-sniffers use many detection techniques, mainly the RTT detection technique, the DNS detection technique, and the ARP detection technique. These techniques have many limits, so that well designed and implemented sniffers can stay undetectable by current anti-sniffers. When the sniffing hosts do not generate any reply ARP and DNS messages, or put heavy traffic on the network, these detection techniques become useless.

However, by combining many detection techniques in a single anti-sniffer, systems administrators will have more results that confirm whether or not a target host is running a sniffer.

References

1. Freedman, Pisani, Purves and Adhikari, "Statistics – Second Edition", W.W. Norton & Company, Inc. 1991.
2. Grundshober, S. "Sniffer Detector Report", Global Security Analysis Lab., Zurich Research Laboratory, IBM Research Division, June 1998.
3. Hornig, C., "A Standard for the Transmission of IP Datagrams over Ethernet Networks", RFC-894, Symbolics Cambridge Research Center, April 1984.
4. Jacobson, V. Leres, C., and Mc-Canne S., "The Tcpdump Manual Page", Lawrence Berkley Laboratory.
5. Postel, J., "Internet Protocol", RFC-791, USC/Information Science Institute, Sempter 1981.
6. Postel, J., "Transmission Control Protocol", RFC-793, USC/Information Science Institute, Sempter 1981.
7. Postel, J., "Internet Control Message Protocol", RFC-792, USC/Information Science Institute, Sempter 1981.
9. Richard Stevens – "TCP/IP Illustrated : Volume 1", 2001.

10. Security Software Inc., "Antisniff", Technical Report 2000, "http://www.securitysoftwaretech.com",
11. S. Grundschober. "Sniffer Detector Report", Diploma Thesis, IBM Research Division, Zurich Research Laboratory, Global Security Analysis Lab, June 1998.
12. J. Drury., "Sniffers: What are they and how to protect from them", November 11, 2000., http://www.sans.org/.
13. D. Wu and F. Wong., "Remote Sniffer Detection". Computer Science Division, University of California, Berkeley. December 14, 1998.
14. Daiji Sanai, "Detection of Promiscuous Nodes Using ARP Packets", http://www.securityfriday.com/.
15. Nmap Tools, http://securityfocus.com.
16. Trabelsi Zouheir, and all, "Malicious Sniffing Systems Detection Platform", The IEEE/IPSJ 2004 International Symposium on Applications and the Internet (SAINT2004)", Tokyo, Japan, January 26-30, 2004.
17. PromiScan anti-sniffer: "http://www.securityfriday.com".
18. PMD (Promiscuous Mode Detector): "http://webteca.port5.com".
19. L0pht AntiSniff: "http://www.l0pht.com/antisniff/".

Using Greedy Hamiltonian Call Paths to Detect Stack Smashing Attacks

Mark Foster, Joseph N. Wilson, and Shigang Chen

Department of Computer and Information Sciences and Engineering
University of Florida
Gainesville, Florida 32611
mfoster@cise.ufl.edu

Abstract. The ICAT statistics over the past few years have shown at least one out of every five CVE and CVE candidate vulnerabilities have been due to buffer overflows. This constitutes a significant portion of today's computer related security concerns. In this paper we introduce a novel method for detecting stack smashing and buffer overflow attacks. Our runtime method extracts return addresses from the program call stack and uses these return addresses to extract their corresponding invoked addresses from memory. We demonstrate how these return and invoked addresses can be represented as a directed weighted graph and used in the detection of stack smashing attacks. We introduce the concept of a Greedy Hamiltonian Call Path and show how the lack of such a path can be used to detect stack-smashing attacks.

1 Introduction

The term buffer overflow refers to copying more data into a buffer than the buffer was designed to hold. A buffer overflow attack takes places when a malicious individual purposely overflows a buffer to alter a program's intended behavior. The most common form of this attack deals with the attacker intentionally overflowing a buffer on the stack so that the excess data overwrites the return address that resides just below the buffer on the stack. Thus when the current function returns, control flow is transferred to an address chosen by the attacker. Commonly, this address is a location on the stack where the attacker has injected his/her own malicious code inside the same buffer. This type of buffer overflow attack is also referred to as a stack smashing attack since the buffer resides on the stack. Stack smashing attacks are one of the most common forms of buffer overflow attacks due to their simplicity of implementation.

Buffer overflow attacks have been a major security issue for a number of years. Wagner et al. [1] extracted statistics from CERT advisories showing that between 1988 and 1999 buffer overflows accounted for up to 50% of the vulnerabilities reported by CERT. Wagner cites several other statistics showing where buffer overflows were at a minimum of 23% of the vulnerabilities in different databases. A more recent look at the ICAT statistics shows that a significant number of the CVE and CVE candidate vulnerabilities were due to buffer overflows. For the years 2001, 2002 and 2003 buffer overflows accounted for 21%, 22%, and 23% of the vulnerabilities respectively [2]. In addition, SecurityTracker.com released statistics for the

K. Zhang and Y. Zheng (Eds.): ISC 2004, LNCS 3225, pp. 183–194, 2004.

time period between April 2001 and March 2002. These statistics show that buffer overflows were the cause behind 20% of the vulnerabilities reported by Security-Tracker [3]. These more recent statistics reinforce the case made by Wagner et al. Buffer overflows are a significant issue for system security.

The purpose of this paper is to introduce a new method for detecting stack smashing and buffer overflow attacks. While much work has been focused on detecting stack-smashing attacks, few approaches use the program call stack to detect such attacks. We propose a new method of detecting stack smashing attacks that relies solely on intercepting system calls and information that can be extracted from the program call stack and process image. Upon intercepting a system call, our method traces the program call stack to extract return addresses. These return addresses are used to extract what we refer to as *invoked addresses*. In the process image, return addresses are preceded by *call* instructions. These *call* instructions are what placed the return addresses on the stack and then transferred control flow to another location. An address that was invoked by a *call* instruction is referred to as an *invoked address*. We use the return and invoked addresses to create a weighted directed graph. We have found that the graph constructed from an uncompromised process always contains a Greedy Hamiltonian Call Path (GHCP). This allows us to use the lack of a GHCP to indicate the presence of a buffer overflow or stack smashing attack.

The rest of this paper is organized in the following manner. In Section 2 we discuss related work. In Section 3 we introduce our new method and prove its correctness using induction. Sections 4 and 5 discuss the limitations and benefits of our proposed method. Our conclusions from this study are stated in Section 6.

2   Related Work

One of the most notable approaches to detecting and preventing buffer overflow attacks is referred to as StackGuard [4]. Cowan et al. created a compiler technique that involves placing a *canary* word on the stack next to the return address. When a function returns, if the canary word has been modified, it implies that the return address has also been modified. The only downfall of Stackguard is that programs are only protected if they have been recompiled with a specially enhanced compiler.

Baratloo et al. proposed two new methods referred to as Libsafe and Libverify [5]. Libsafe uses the saved frame pointers on the stack to act as upper bounds when writing to a buffer. Libverify uses a similar approach to Stackguard in that a return address is verified before a function is allowed to return. Libverify does this by copying each function into the heap and overwriting the original beginning and end of each function with a call to a wrapper function. One downfall of this method is that the amount of space in memory required for each function is double that of what the process would require if not using Libverify.

One approach proposed by Feng et al. is VtPath [6]. VtPath is designed to detect anomalous behavior but would also work well in detecting buffer overflow attacks. VtPath is unique in that it uses information from a program's call stack to perform anomaly detection. At each system call VtPath takes a snapshot of the return addresses on the stack. The sequence of return addresses found between two system calls creates what is referred to as a virtual path. A training phase is used to learn a program's normal virtual paths. When online, virtual paths not experienced in the training phase are considered an anomaly.

3 Overview of Technique

We propose a new method of detecting stack-smashing attacks that deals with checking the integrity of the program call stack. The proposed method operates at the kernel-level. It intercepts system calls and checks the integrity of the program call stack before allowing such system calls to continue. To check the integrity of a program's call stack we extract the return address and invoked address of each function that has a frame on the stack. Using the list of return addresses and invoked addresses we can create a weighted directed graph. We have found that a properly constructed weighted directed graph of a legitimate process always has the unique characteristic of a Greedy Hamiltonian Call Path (GHCP). We refer to this as a call path since it corresponds to the sequence of function calls that lead us from the entry point of a given program to the current system call. This call path is greedy because when searching for this path within our weighted directed graph, we always choose the minimum weight edge when leaving a vertex. Furthermore, this path is Hamiltonian because every vertex must be included *exactly once*. Most significantly, we have found that the lack of such a path can be used to indicate that there has been a stack smashing or buffer overflow attack.

3.1 Constructing the Graph

The task of constructing a weighted directed graph from the program call stack involves five major steps. We demonstrate these five steps on an example program. The functions, their source code, starting and ending addresses in memory for the example program are shown in Table 1.

The five major steps include:

Step 1 - Collect Return Addresses. Using the existing frame pointer, trace through the program call stack to extract the return address from each stack frame.

Step 2 – Collect Invoked Addresses. For each return address extracted from the stack, find the *call* instruction that precedes it in memory. Extract the invoked address from that *call* instruction. At this point we can create a table of return address/invoked address pairs. For the program shown in Table 1, the return and invoked addresses in Table 2 would be extracted.

In Table 2 it is easy to see how the addresses that start with 0x0804... correlate to the addresses in Table 1. The addresses that start with 0x420... are simply the addresses of C library functions that are used by our program. The last address, 0xc78b1dc8 is the kernel address of the system call function *execve()*. Addresses such as 0x420b4c34 and 0x420b4c6a correspond to the system call wrapper in our C library. The additional addresses at the beginning of the table (i.e. 0x08048321, 0x42017404 and 0x42017499) are the addresses corresponding to _start and __libc_start_main. The purpose of these functions is not pertinent to this paper.

Table 1. Example program we use to demonstrate graph construction.

Function Name	Starting Address in Memory	Ending Address in Memory	Function's Code
f3()	0x08048400	0x0804842a	execve(...);
f2()	0x0804842c	0x08048439	f3();
f1()	0x0804843c	0x08048449	f2();
main()	0x0804844c	0x0804845f	f1(); return 0;

Table 2. Return Address/Invoked Address Pairs.

Return Address	Invoked Address
0x08048321	0x42017404
0x42017499	0x0804844c
0x08048457	0x0804843c
0x08048447	0x0804842c
0x08048437	0x08048400
0x08048425	0x420b4c34
0x420b4c6a	0xc78b1dc8

Step 3 - Divide Addresses into Islands. Once the values in Table 2 have been obtained we can begin construction of our weighted directed graph. Our final graph contains a node for each of the addresses in Table 2. However, before we can make each address into a node we must first categorize our addresses into what we refer to as islands. Our addresses are divided into islands based on their locations in memory. For example, addresses that begin with 0x0804... are part of a different island from addresses that begin with 0x420.... Addresses are further divided on whether they are a return address or an invoked address. In this example we have four islands. These islands are show in the Figure 1.

Note that the address 0xc78b1dc8 was not placed into an island. This is because this address represents the first instruction of our system call. It represents a unique node later on. We add this address' node when we begin adding edges. The address 0x08048300, the first instruction in the _start_ procedure, was added even though it is not in Table 2. This address is part of an ELF header and is loaded into memory, thus it can be extracted at runtime. Every program must have an entry point and therefore can be part of our graph.

Step 4 – Adding Edges. Recall the return address/invoked address pairs we have listed in Table 2. Each of these pairs are connected with a zero weight edge leading from the return address to the invoked address. At this time we can add a node for the address 0xc78b1dc8, and subsequently add a zero weight edge to it from it's corresponding return address. All of the edges added thus far are part of our final GHCP.

To complete this step, we attempt to give each invoked address node an edge to every return address node in the same memory region. These edges are weighted with the distance in memory between the two nodes. For example, the node with address 0x0804842c has a directed edge with weight 1b leading to the node with address

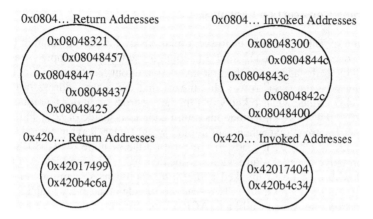

Fig. 1. Example program's addresses divided into islands.

0x08048447. In addition, the node with address 0x0804842c also has a directed edge leading to 0x08048457 with a weight of 2b. The edges leading from invoked address node 0x0804842c to every return address node of the same memory region are shown in Figure 2.

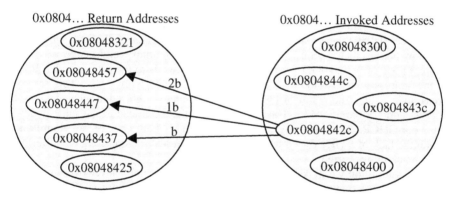

Fig. 2. Edges leading from Invoked Address node 0x08048418.

Note that the node 0x0804842c was not given an edge to nodes 0x08048321 and 0x08048425. This is because these edges would have resulted in negative weights which we do not allow in the graph. This concept is explained more thoroughly in the next subsection.

Once all of the appropriate edges have been added, the graph is complete. We have omitted the drawing of our completed graph due to the crowded nature of a graph of such a simple program.

3.2 Graph Construction Explained

Inspection of Table 2 allows us to see a relationship between a value in the ith row of column one and the $(i-1)^{th}$ row of column two. For example, we know that 0x0804842c is the address of the first instruction in our *f2()* function. Let the row with this address be the $(i-1)^{th}$ row. This means that the return address in the ith row is 0x08048437. Since we also know that the last instruction in our *f2()* function is at address 0x08048439, we know that this return address is inside of *f2()*. Furthermore, we can see in Figure 2 that when a minimum weight edge leaving the address node of 0x0804842c is chosen, it leads to the return address node of 0x08048437. Stated more formally, if we let return addresses be denoted with ω and invoked addresses be denoted with α, a given invoked address, α_i, should have a minimum weight edge leading to return address, ω_{i+1}. This leads to the idea that every graph's GHCP is no different from the Actual Call Path (ACP) of the progrm.

It turns out, this is exactly what we need. All programs that have not fallen victim to a stack smashing or buffer overflow attack posses this ACP. We can find this ACP by searching for a GHCP. Our method must be greedy to insure that we chose the minimum weight edge when leaving a given node. In addition, since our path must include each vertex exactly once, our path is Hamiltonian. If we are unable to find such a GHCP, then we know that our ACP has been disrupted. This implies the likely occurrence of a stack smashing or buffer overflow attack.

To demonstrate why this works, suppose the function *f2()* were vulnerable to a buffer overflow attack. Suppose the attack overwrites the return address of *f2()* with the address 0x0804844a. This results in the edge from Figure 2 that was labeled with '*b*', now being labeled with a '*1e*'. Thus when a minimum weight edge leaving the address node of 0x0804842c is chosen, it no longer leads to the proper node. It leads to the address node 0x08048447, whose edge is labeled with a '*1b*'. This same address node is also the result of choosing a minimum weight edge when leaving the address node of 0x0804843c. Having two edges that both lead to the same node disrupts our GHCP. There no longer exists a path that is both Greedy and Hamiltonian. When the lack of a GHCP is detected, we know that a stack smashing or buffer overflow attack has occurred.

One assumption we make is that two functions in memory never overlap and that the initial instruction of a function is always the invoked address. We realize that some programs written in assembly may not abide by this assumption. However, all compiled programs and most assembly programs will satisfy this constraint.

To summarize, our ACP represents the expected GHCP. However, we provide multiple paths leaving a given invoked address to give that invoked address a choice when determining our GHCP. By providing a choice, it allows the other return addresses to act as upper bounds. The upper bounds created by other return addresses limit the potential range of addresses that a given return address can been overwritten and modified to by an attacker. There already exists an inherent lower bound since we do not include negative weight edges. Recall that invoked addresses are likely the address of the first instruction for a given function. Thus it makes sense that unaltered execution flow of a given function should never lead to an instruction that resides at a lower memory address than the first instruction of that function.

3.3 Proof by Induction

In order for us to rely on the nonexistence of a GHCP to indicate the presence of a stack smashing attack we must first prove that a GHCP exists for all uncompromised programs. In this section, we consider the case in which there are no recursive function calls. Knowing that our graph has two types of edges, those leaving return addresses and those leaving invoked addresses, we can simplify this proof. Since there is always exactly one edge leaving a given return address, we know this edge is always part of our GHCP. We can exploit this feature of our graph to simplify our proof. With this feature, we now only need to prove that in the ACP each invoked address always has a minimum weight edge leading to its corresponding return address. We prove, using induction that this holds true for all unobjectionable programs. Our formal inductive hypothesis is as follows:

Theorem 3.1 *For all unobjectionable programs in which n different functions have been called, where $n \geq 1$, every invoked address α_i, for $i < n$, has a minimum weight edge leading to the return address ω_{i+1}.*

With this stated we must first prove our base case.

Base Case. In this case there is one active function and no other calls have been made. Our assertion that α_i, for $i < n$, has a minimum weight edge leading to return address ω_{i+1}, is vacuously true. Alternatively, we can say that the GHCP corresponds to the ACP, because they are both null.

Inductive Case. For our inductive case we must prove that if the GHCP corresponds to the ACP for n calls, it corresponds to the ACP when the $(n+1)^{st}$ call is made. Stated more formally, we assume the following to be true:

$$GHCP_n = ACP_n = \alpha_1, \omega_2, \alpha_2, \omega_3, \alpha_3, \omega_4 \ldots \omega_n, \alpha_n$$

Thus we must prove the following to be true:

$$GHCP_{n+1} = ACP_{n+1} = \alpha_1, \omega_2, \alpha_2, \omega_3, \alpha_3, \omega_4 \ldots \omega_n, \alpha_n, \omega_{n+1}, \alpha_{n+1}$$

The $(n+1)^{st}$ call results in adding the two additional nodes, ω_{n+1} and α_{n+1}, to our graph. This also results in the additional edges, (α_i, ω_{n+1}) and (α_n, ω_{i+1}), being added to our graph. Since we know that GHCP = ACP, as long as every invoked address α_i, has a minimum weight edge leading to the it's corresponding return address ω_{i+1}, we must prove the following proposition.

Proposition: *For each i, where $i < n$, $weight(\alpha_i, \omega_{i+1}) < weight(\alpha_i, \omega_{n+1})$*

Before proceeding any further we must define some variables.

Table 3. Variables for the induction proof.

L_i	Length in bytes of the ith function.
α_i	Address of the first byte of the ith function.
$r\alpha_i$	The offset to the return address inside the ith function. $(r\alpha_i = \omega_{i+1} - \alpha_i)$

We also assume that two separate functions loaded into memory never overlap. Therefore, we must prove our proposition for two different scenarios namely, $\alpha_i < \alpha_n$ and $\alpha_n < \alpha_i$.

We can construct an abstract version of our graph as it would exist the moment our $(n+1)^{st}$ call is made. This version of our graph, Figure 3, illustrates the relationship between the function that made the $(n+1)^{st}$ call and any other invoked/return address pairs.

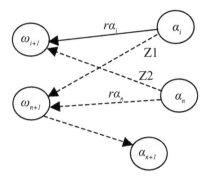

Fig. 3. Abstract graph once $(n+1)^{st}$ call is made. A solid line represents an existing edge. A dotted line represents a new edge.

Now we prove our proposition holds for both scenarios. For the scenario
$$\alpha_i < \alpha_n,$$
we know the following must also be true
$$\omega_{i+1} < \omega_{n+1}.$$
Therefore we can conclude
$$weight(\alpha_{i,} \omega_{i+1}) = ra_i = \omega_{i+1} - \alpha_i < \omega_{n+1} - \alpha_i = Z1 = weight(\alpha_{i,} \omega_{n+1}).$$
Thus our proposition holds true for our first scenario. Given the second scenario
$$\alpha_n < \alpha_i,$$
we know the following must also be true
$$\omega_{n+1} < \omega_{i+1}.$$
Therefore we can conclude
$$weight(\alpha_{i,} \omega_{n+1}) < 0,$$
and since our graph does not contain negative edges, our proposition still holds true.

It might seem logical to conclude that we also need to prove a second proposition. This second proposition is stated below.

Proposition 2: *For each i, where i < n, $weight(\alpha_{n,} \omega_{n+1}) < weight(\alpha_{n,} \omega_{i+1})$*

Proving this proposition for the first scenario we find
$$weight(\alpha_{n,} \omega_{i+1}) < 0.$$
Once again, since our graph does not contain negative edges, our proposition still holds true. With the second scenario we find
$$weight(\alpha_{n,} \omega_{n+1}) = ra_n = \omega_{n+1} - \alpha_n < \omega_{i+1} - \alpha_n = Z2 = weight(\alpha_{n,} \omega_{i+1}).,$$
Thus we can prove that our 2nd proposition also holds for both scenarios. However, if Proposition 1 holds, then this second proposition is unneccessary. When we arrive at the point where we must choose an edge leaving α_n, since we are searching for a GHCP, our only feasible choice is ra_n leading to ω_{n+1}. If the first proposition holds, every ω_{i+1} for $i < n$, has already been visited. Thus the only choice that maintains a Hamiltonian path is ω_{n+1}.

In conclusion, we have proven that when the $(n+1)^{st}$ call is made, every invoked address α_i, still has a minimum weight edge leading to it's corresponding return address ω_{i+1}. This in turn proves that if the GHCP corresponds to the ACP for n calls, it corresponds to the ACP when the $(n+1)^{st}$ call is made. Therefore we know that the lack of a GHCP demonstrates that some form of stack smashing or buffer overflow attack has occurred.

3.4 Recursion

Recursion is the case where $\alpha_i = \alpha_n$ for some $i < n$. When this is the case, we have two different scenarios that may create a problem.

- $\omega_{i+1} = \omega_{n+1}$
- $\omega_{i+1} > \omega_{n+1}$

The first scenario creates a problem because α_i has two equal weight edges leading to ω_{i+1} and ω_{n+1}. Subsequently, these two equal weight edges are also the minimum weight edges leaving α_i. When searching for a GHCP, we won't know which edge to choose. The second scenario creates a problem because α_i has a minimum weight edge leading to ω_{n+1}. To address these scenarios we add a new theorem to our graph construction.

Theorem 3.2: *If $\alpha_i = \alpha_n$ for some i, where $i < n$, we don't allow the edge (α_i, ω_{n+1}) in our graph.*

With this theorem being stated, we must now prove that our GHCP still coresponds to our ACP even with this condition. We now revisit each case of our induction proof in the previous section.

It is important to note that we are not concerned about the scenario where $\omega_{i+1} < \omega_{n+1}$, for the same reasons we were not concerned about the Proposition 2 in Theorem 4.1.

Base Case (n = 1). Since this case has only one active function, the new condition has no affect on it. Once again, the GHCP corresponds to the ACP, because they are both null.

Inductive Case (n > 1). For our inductive case we must prove that if the GHCP corresponds to the ACP for n calls, it corresponds to the ACP when the $(n+1)^{st}$ call is made even when our new condition is applied. We know that GHCP$_n$ still corresponds to ACP$_n$. We know this because before the $(n+1)^{st}$ call is made, α_n is the last node in our ACP$_n$. Hence, ω_{n+1} does not exist yet and neither of our scenarios create a problem yet.

Once the $(n+1)^{st}$ call is made, we must still prove that when our additional condition is followed that GHCP$_{n+1}$ corresponds to ACP$_{n+1}$. Fortunately, we know the following:

$$If\ i < n,\ then\ i \ \ n$$

Thus,

$$(\alpha_i, \omega_{n+1})\ \ (\alpha_i, \omega_{i+1})$$

Since the edge (α_i, ω_{i+1}) is never the same edge as (α_i, ω_{n+1}) we can safely remove (α_i, ω_{n+1}) from our graph and our GHCP is not affected. Since (α_i, ω_{i+1}) is always left unmodified, we know that our GHCP still exists. Figure 4 shows our abstract graph when the $(n+1)^{st}$ call is made for when $\alpha_i \ \ \alpha_n$ and $\alpha_i = \alpha_n$.

Figure 4 illustrates that when the $(n+1)^{st}$ call is made, regardless of whether $\alpha_i \ \ \alpha_n$ or $\alpha_i = \alpha_n$, GHCP$_{n+1}$ still corresponds to the ACP$_{n+1}$. Our new condition never alters our (α_i, ω_{i+1}) edges.

To summarize, we use other function's return addresses to perform bounds checking on a specific function, say $f()$. We do not allow multiple invocations of $f()$ to create bounds criteria for itself.

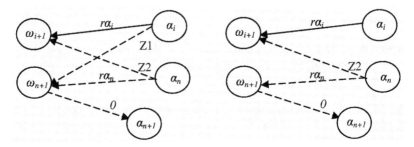

Fig. 4. Abstract graph when recursion is present, once the $(n+1)^{st}$ call is made. Left: $\alpha_i \quad \alpha_n$, Right: $\alpha_i = \alpha_n$.

4 Limitations

One limitation of our GHCP analysis is that it depends on the existence of a valid frame pointer. In most cases when the return address is overwritten, the frame pointer is also overwritten. Without a valid frame pointer, there is no way to trace through the stack to extract return addresses. However, in the case where there is no valid frame pointer, we already know that some form of buffer overflow or stack smashing attack is underway. A system that implements our proposed method would detect, before even generating a graph, that no valid frame point exists. A system that only tests for the ability to trace up a stack is too easily evaded by an attacker to warrant a stand alone buffer overflow detection system. However, due to the prevalence of attacks that could be detected with such a test, we believe it should be incorporated.

There are two methods with which an attacker might be able to evade detection of a system using GHCP analysis. The first method an attacker could use to evade detection is to perform a buffer overflow attack that overwrites a return address to a new return address but leaves the frame pointer unmodified. The second method an attacker could use to evade detection, is to perform a buffer overflow attack that overwrites the return address and frame pointer and also injects code onto the stack. The first few instructions of this injected code must restore the return address and frame pointer to their original values. The injected code would then jump to preexisting code the attacker wants to execute. Both of these methods could work, but they exhibit a major limitation. The new return address or the preexisting code jumped to by the injected code must reside in the same function as the original return address. Recall that each invoked address must have a minimum weight edge to its corresponding return address. If the new return address is inside of another function, the attacker risks destroying the minimum weight edge between the invoked address and the original return address. Likewise for the second method. When a system call is made, a return address is placed on the stack. Thus, if the injected code has jumped to a piece of code in another function, the attacker risks this return address not having a minimum weight edge from its corresponding invoked address. While both methods are possible, the challenges facing the attacker are much more rigorous than without GHCP analysis.

Another limitation of our method is its ability to deal with function pointers. Currently, we use return addresses to trace through memory and find a corresponding invoked address. These invoked addresses are part of a *call* instruction in memory. The bytes in memory representing a *call* instruction include an address or offset to an address. In either case we can extract the address invoked by this *call* instruction. In the case of function pointers, the *call* instruction is often calling an address that is in a register. We have no way to determine what address was in this register when this *call* instruction executed. However, we propose one could easily modify a compiler to store invoked addresses on the stack. This would give us the ability to always be able to determine a return address' corresponding invoked address. Function pointers would no longer be a limitation.

5 Benefits

A system designed for buffer overflow detection using GHCP analysis has a number of benefits. First, our system does not require access to a program's source code. Secondly, it does not require that a program be compiled with any specially enhanced compiler or even have the executable binary file rewritten unless wants to verify call through pointers to functions. In addition, our system does not require linking with any special libraries or place any additional burden on the application programmer. Many intrusion detection systems also rely on a training phase with a program to learn it's normal behavior. After a training phase, the system can monitor a program to ensure that it doesn't deviate from the behavior observed during the training. Our system does not require any training phase.

Our method is similar to a nonexecutable stack because it makes it extremely difficult for an attacker to execute malicious code on the stack. However, our method provides a number of benefits the executable stack does not. For example, in addition to stack smashing attacks, our method can also detect heap smashing attacks. Furthermore, it is likely to also detect a similar attack that uses the bss or data segment. Our method would also detect most attempts to rewrite a return address to another location in preexisting code. A nonexecutable stack would not detect such an attack. Lastly, our method allows code with a legitimate stack trace to execute code on the stack. In cases where an uncompromised process needs to execute code on the stack, the nonexecutable stack would not allow such a process to proceed.

Our method also provides the framework for even more concise buffer overflow detection system. Currently, one of the limitations of our method is that we rely on other functions in the call path for our bounds checking criteria for a given function. A compiler could easily be modified to inject a dummy function in between every function in a given program. The code for the ith dummy function would consist of only the code required to call the $(i+1)^{st}$ dummy function. By calling the sequence of dummy functions before starting *main()* we would place the necessary bounds checking criteria on the stack that we need for any function in our program. The cost of this is in the compilation and start up times of the program. In addition, computation of the GHCP would only require time proportional to the number of active functions.

6 Conclusions

In this paper we have introduced a novel method for detecting stack smashing and buffer overflow attacks. We have shown how the return addresses extracted from the program call stack can be used along with their corresponding invoked addresses to create a weight directed graph. We have also introduced the concept of a Greedy Hamiltonian Call Path (GHCP) that exists in such a graph for all unobjectionable programs. Thus, the lack of a GHCP can be used to indicate the existence of a stack smashing or buffer overflow attack.

In addition, our work has laid the framework for an even more concise detection system for stack smashing and buffer overflow attacks. Using our methods in conjunction with an enhanced compiler could remove the limitations experienced by our system involving function pointers and programs with few active functions. An existing compiler could be easily modified to include the necessary modifications.

We have begun implementing a prototype for our method. Early results show a promising outlook for low overhead. Future work includes continued development of our prototype with more exhaustive testing of overhead and compatibility with items such as setjmp/longjmp calls. We expect such items to be compatible with our method but it remains unconfirmed and beyond the scope of this paper.

References

1. D.Wagner, J. Foster, E. Brewer, A. Aiken, "A First Step Towards Automated Detection of Buffer Overrun Vulnerabilities", In Proceedings 7th Network and Distributed System Security Symposium, Feb, 2000.
2. ICAT Vulnerability Statistics, Downloaded at:
   http://icat.nist.gov/icat.cfm?function=statistics
3. SecurityTracker.com Statistics, Found at:
   http://www.securitytracker.com/learn/securitytracker-stats-2002.pdf
4. C. Cowan, C. Pu, D. Maier, H. Hinton, J. Walpole, P. Bakke, S. Beattie, A. Grier, P. Waggle, Q. Zhang, "StackGuard: Automatic Adaptive Detection and Prevention of Buffer-Overflow Attacks", Proceedings of the 7th USENIX Security Conference, San Antonio, TX, 1998.
5. A. Baratloo, N. Singh, "Transparent Run-Time Defense Against Stack Smashing Attacks", In Proceedings of the 2000 USENIX Technical Conference, San Diego, CA, Jan, 2002.
6. H. H. Feng, O. M. Kolesnikov, P. Fogla, W. Lee, W. Gong, "Anomaly Detection Using Call Stack Information", IEEE Symposium on Security and Privacy, Berkeley, CA, May, 2003.

Securing DBMS: Characterizing and Detecting Query Floods

Elisa Bertino[1], Teodoro Leggieri[2], and Evimaria Terzi[3]

[1] CERIAS and Department of Computer Sciences,
Purdue University, West Lafayette, IN, USA
bertino@cerias.purdue.edu
[2] Department of Computer Sciences
University of Milano, Italy
leggieri@dico.unimi.it
[3] HIIT and Department of Computer Science
University of Helsinki
Helsinki, Finland
terzi@cs.helsinki.fi

Abstract. Current multi-tiered Web-based applications are very often characterized by the use of a database system. Database systems are thus not any longer confined to well-protected environments. In this paper, we focus on a specific type of attack, known as query flood. Under such an attack, a subject, or a colluding set of subjects, floods the database with a very large number of requests thus making the database unable to serve, with adequate response time, requests from honest subjects. The approach we propose is based on modeling access profiles and using these profiles to detect unusual behaviors in the subjects accessing the database. Our approach supports varying granularities in that one can build a single profile for the entire database or build specialized profiles for each table in the database. We employ our techniques both in misuse and anomaly detection settings. An evaluation of the proposed approach has been carried out and some preliminary experimental results are reported.

1 Introduction

A database system is usually a core-component of modern web-based applications since it is in charge of storing the application-relevant data that need to be made available, acquired and managed through the Web. The exposure of databases on the web increases the security risks to which data are exposed. This explains the large research effort towards developing sophisticated data protection techniques [4]. Whereas there is a variety of techniques addressing data confidentiality and integrity, the problem of database protection against denial-of-service (DoS) attacks has not been addressed. A typical DoS attack against a DBMS may occur through a *query flood*, that is, when a subject or a set of colluding users imposes a large number of queries and/or updates against the database with the intention to hinder other people from being serviced.

K. Zhang and Y. Zheng (Eds.): ISC 2004, LNCS 3225, pp. 195–206, 2004.
© Springer-Verlag Berlin Heidelberg 2004

The goal of the work reported in this paper is to develop techniques and methodologies able to address query flood attacks against relational database systems. Our approach is characterized by three key aspects: (a) We address the problem of DoS attacks both from the point of view of misuse and anomaly detection. (b) We provide a characterization which is time-dependent and parameter-free. Some of the techniques we use are borrowed from standard time series and sequence analysis (see for example [10,3,7,5]). However we enhance them with features adequate to serve our purposes. (c) We provide different protection granularities so that the database administrator may decide to protect the entire database using just a single global access profile for the entire database or protect single relations by building specific profiles for each table.

Related work: Intrusion Detection (ID) has been a very active area of research. There are two main techniques towards ID, namely *anomaly detection* and *misuse detection*. A taxonomy and an overview of the existing ID Systems (IDS) is presented in [2]. In general, anomaly detection identifies activities that vary from established patterns for users or group of users. Anomaly detection typically involves the creation of knowledge bases (containing the profiles of the monitored activities), whereas misuse detection involves the comparison of the users activities with the (known) behaviors of attackers (attempting to penetrate a system). DoS attacks have been considered in many previous research efforts as for example reported in [11,12,13]. Classes of models and tools that can become core components in intrusion detection systems have been extensively discussed in [8,9]. However, those approaches mainly focus on network and operating system layer attacks. Additionally, the data mining and machine learning tools they use for constructing the models are completely different from those proposed here. The only work that deals with DoS attacks at application layer is the work presented in [6]. In this work flooding-based DoS attacks in Peer-to-Peer (P2P) systems have been investigated. The authors propose simple techniques to deal with the problem depending on the topology of the network formed by the distributed nodes that handle the arriving requests. However, such technique is very coarse and is not able to model time-dependent access patterns.

Contribution: In this paper we focus on the detection of query floods within the database system at the application level. To the best of our knowledge this is the first comprehensive and articulated approach dealing with query flood attacks considering application-layer log information. There are two main reasons why application layer attacks should be dealt with separately. First of all, actions malicious for an application are not necessarily malicious for the network as well. Additionally, network and application layer intrusion detection parts may cooperate with each other. Therefore, intrusion detection mechanisms that may be too time consuming and computationally expensive for network routers, for example, can very well be handled by an application layer mechanism. Database tables play a key role in our approach as they are considered as central entities around which the security model is built. The main tools used for handling the database log files are borrowed from information theory.

2   Preliminaries

2.1   Minimum Description Length (MDL) Principle

MDL principle is a major tool that has been used to scale down the ideas behind the Kolmogorov complexity in order to make them applicable into practical settings. In brief MDL states the following: Assume two parties A and B, that want to communicate with each other. More specifically assume that A wants to send data D to B using as less bits as possible. In order for A to achieve this minimization of communication cost it has to select a model M, from a class of models $\mathcal{M}$, such that M best describes A's data. The model M is selected from the class of models $\mathcal{M}$ with probability $P(M)$ while the data D (observations) have been generated by M with probability $P(D \mid M)$. Based on the Shannon's Information Theorem the number of bits needed to encode the data D is $L(D) = -\log(P(D))$, where $P(D)$ is the probability of the data. Given that we have selected model M for describing our data then the encoding length in bits will be $L(D \mid M) = -\log(P(D \mid M)P(M)) = -\log(P(D \mid M)) - \log(P(M))$. So the goal of the MDL principle is to find the model $M \in \mathcal{M}$ such that the number of bits needed to encode the data (namely $L(D \mid M)$) is minimized. In our case, we have considered the set of segmentation models for modeling the data. A a segmentation of a sequence of events is a set of successive non-overlapping intervals that cover the whole sequence. Each interval is characterized by its starting and ending points and its level that corresponds to the average intensity of the sequence in the segment.

2.2   Notation

For the rest of the paper we consider a database $U = R_1, R_2, .., R_n$ consisting of n relations. Each relation R_i consists of set of attributes A_i with $A(i) = \{a_1^i, a_2^i, ..., a_{n_i}^i\}$. Also we consider a sequence of log files LF_τ ordered with respect to time τ and denote with LF_τ^r the series of log files that contain SQL commands that have included relation R_r. These log files have been separated from the global LF_τ after a preprocessing step.

The set of usable SQL commands is denoted by Cmd, with $cmd_i \in Cmd$ to correspond to a single such command.

3   Misuse Detection of DoS Attacks in DBMS

Assume a sequence of τ log files LF_τ consisting of commands of different types. Each such log file corresponds to logs over the same time line T (say daily logs) and consists of a set of transaction log-records. Each record contains the command used, the time this command was issued as well as other information.

198 E. Bertino, T. Leggieri, and E. Terzi

Mining each such log file is a relatively easy task and can be done by defining sliding windows of length w along time-line T, and for each such sliding window counting the frequency of commands or combinations of commands of specific type.

Counting the frequency of commands or sets of commands is similar to the frequent episode mining problem. The mining algorithm we use is based on the frequent set mining algorithm (Apriori) [1]. For the sake of completeness we give the definitions of *k-command set(i)* and *frequent k-command set(i)* that are in complete agreement with the definitions of (frequent) itemsets and (frequent) episodes.

Definition 1. *A* **k-command_set** *is a set of k distinct commands that appear together in at least one sliding window in LF_τ.*

Definition 2. *A* **frequent k-command_set** *is a set of k distinct commands that appear together in at least* **freq** *sliding windows in LF_τ, where* **freq** *is the frequency threshold used in the mining process.*

In the context of misuse detection the goal is the following: Given the sequence of log files FL_τ we need to identify a segmentation S over τ with respect to the probability of appearance of a specific *command_set* $Cmd_i \subseteq Cmd$ throughout LF_τ.

For simplicity consider first the 1-command_set example. In this case the only parameter of the model is the probability of appearance (or average frequency) of each command within segment s, denoted by p_s. The goal is to find a segmentation S of the τ logs with respect to $p_s \forall s \in S$. More specifically, from the class of all possible segmentation models $\mathcal{M}$ over τ we need to identify a model $M \in \mathcal{M}$ such that $L(M) + L(D|M)$ (i.e. the length in bits of encoding the model and the data given the model) is minimized. The model itself is the value of p_s over the different segments s. If we assume that we have l segments for calculating the cost of the model we need to add up (a) the cost of encoding the parameter p_s for each segment and (b) the cost of encoding the l block boundaries. Since p_s is a real number its encoding cost will be $\rho = \frac{1}{2}\log(|s_k|)$, with $|s_k|$ being the length of segment s_k. Calculating the cost of (b) is easy because each block boundary is a natural number between 1 and τ and therefore for each one of them we need $\log \tau$ bits. The total cost of the model in the case of 1-command_sets is:

$$L(M) = \sum_{k=1}^{l} \frac{1}{2}\log(|s_k|) + l \log \tau \qquad (1)$$

The cost of encoding the data given the model $L(D|M)$ is given by:

$$L(D|M) = \sum_{s=1}^{l} -\log p_s \cdot P_{\mathcal{D}}(D(s)) \qquad (2)$$

where $P_{\mathcal{D}}$ corresponds to the distribution that the patterns (here denoted by D) follow and $D(s)$ to the data in segment s.

Multiple Command Types: In the multiple command case we need to determine segmentation points over τ with respect to the probability of appearance of a *k-command_set*. For the description of each of the *k-command_sets* we need to define the probability of appearance of each one of the k commands in the set and therefore our model consists of these k probabilities. These commands may not necessarily be dependent, and therefore the space of models that cover all possible dependencies grows exponentially. For example in the 3-command case there are $7 = \sum_{i=1}^{3} \binom{3}{i}$ possibilities of combinations of dependencies between the corresponding 1-command_sets. However notice that once one has found the best model for the case of 2-command_sets then one does not have to search the space of all the possible models for the 3-command_set case. It is enough to consider only the subset of models that are compatible with the one selected for the 2-command_set case. This observation proves useful for pruning the space of models.

Algorithm for finding the best segmentation The best segmentation can be found using dynamic programming with the following set of equations: Let $s = [a, b]$ be a temporal interval. The cost associated with interval s is:

$$f(a, b) = -\log P_D(D(s) + \frac{1}{2}\log(|s|) + \log \tau$$

Therefore, the optimal segmentation S_{opt} is the one that minimizes such cost, that is, we require that:

$$L(S_{opt}) = min_S \sum_{[a,b] \in S} f(a, b)$$

where S includes all possible segmentations in $[1, \tau]$. If additionally we denote with $F(k)$ the cost of the optimal segmentation from 1 up to k, then the total dynamic programming equation is as follows.

$$F(k) = min_{1 \leq i \leq k}(F(i-1) + f(i, k))$$

where $F(0) = 0$.

Reporting DoS attacks: For separating the surprising patterns that may be indicators of attacks we need to define measures for quantifying "suspiciousness" of a pattern. Some natural definitions of the **suspicion factor** of a pattern are the following:

Definition 3. *The* **"diff"** *suspicion factor gives an estimate of how suspicious the fluctuation of a pattern, in our case a command_set, is. Therefore it is defined as follows:*

$$SF_{diff}(cmd\_set) = |p(cmd\_set)^{obs} - p(cmd\_set)^{est}|$$

Alternatively, one can consider the ratio of estimated probabilities. This results in the "ratio" suspicion factor defined below.

Definition 4. *The "**ratio**" suspicion factor gives an estimate of how suspicious the fluctuation of a pattern, by considering the ratio of observed versus expected probabilities of appearance of commands. Thus:*

$$SF_{ratio}(cmd\_set) = \frac{p(cmd\_set)^{obs}}{p(cmd\_set)^{est}}$$

What the above definitions say is that the difference (definition 3) and the ratio (definition 4) of the observed probability of the patterns and the estimated probability based on our MDL approach give an estimate of how suspicious a segment is. When $SF(cmd\_set) \geq sT$, where sT is a pre-specified suspicion threshold, then the cmd_set is said to show a suspicious fluctuation.

Determining the threshold is crucial. For this we have employed a randomization test. More specifically we have generated a large number of random pairs of p parameters. For each one of these pairs we have taken their difference and ratio and we have sorted them. Values of the differences and thresholds occurring in the large extreme (very large values) are a good candidates for thresholds that will guarantee high accuracy.

3.1   Identifying DoS Attacks at Multiple Degrees of Granularity

The method described in the previous subsection allows for the identification of suspicious patterns given a set of log files LF_τ. Depending on the granularity at which the DB Administrator (DBA) wants to enforce the misuse detection method he/she can follow one of the two approaches proposed below:

– *Schismatic Approach:* In this case, each relation R_r is considered separately and the corresponding sequence of its logs LF_τ^r is evaluated independently. Information that in the same command a user may refer to more than one relation is not considered. Commands of the form *select a_1^1 from R_1*, and *select a_2^1 from R_1* are considered similar since they are both selections and they refer to the same relation R_1. In the above setting this means that we consider a sequence of τ log files each corresponding to commands referring relation R_i.
– *Catholic Approach:* In this case the database log LF_τ is considered as a whole. Given two commands **cmd1:** cmd_1 on R_i and **cmd2:** cmd_2 on R_j appearing in the log files one can proceed using one of the following two alternatives:
  • **cmd1** and **cmd2** are considered the same if $cmd_1 = cmd_2$ and different otherwise.
  • **cmd1** and **cmd2** are considered the same if $cmd_1 = cmd_2$ and $R_i = R_j$.

4   Anomaly Detection of DoS Attacks

In the anomaly detection we need: (a) to provide models and methods to describe the normal profiles; (b) to define measures of deviation from the given profile in order to identify behaviors that are suspicious.

4.1   Building the Model of Normal Behaviors

Assume again a series of τ training log files LF_τ, each one logging events on time-line T consisting of $|T|$ time units. Further assume that none of these log files contain an intrusion [1]. Time-line T can correspond to any real-life time-line (e.g. a single day, a week, a month etc.). with respect to which events, which in our case are query commands, occur. The goal here is to build a model that best describes the activities of normal users captured in all the τ log files.

From experience and common sense we know that users' activity usually follows some patterns. For example, we can expect their activity to be similar in all mornings as well as in all evenings of the weekdays and to differentiate during the mornings and evenings of the weekends. Additionally, probably all nights, no matter the days, show similar behavior. However, these observations do not generalize so well. For example, Sunday evenings are expected to be much different from Saturday evenings, and also Friday evenings much different from other weekday evenings. Furthermore, the observed patterns may be completely different during holiday days. Therefore, forming a framework that models the set of acceptable behaviors of the users is a rather challenging task. We need a model that really captures all those variations, without being very tolerable so as to ignore possible occurrences of attacks.

We again adopt a segmentation-based model. The goal here is to find groups of log files with identical or similar segmentation points. The input in this case consists of τ sequences of observations of length $|T|$. Therefore the data can be represented as a matrix of dimension $\tau \times |T|$, namely $LF^r_{\tau \times T}$, with $LF^r(i, j)$ corresponding to observations in log file LF^r_i at time point j. We assume that the data follow a generic data distribution $\mathcal{D}$, with $P_\mathcal{D}$ as probability function. The segmentations of the normal log files are build using one of the alternatives presented in the sequel.

Loose Group Segmentation (LGS): In this case we consider the τ log files corresponding to the same time line T and the same relation R_r. The goal is to divide the set of time lines LF^r into segments in such a way that time lines of events with similar segmentation points are going to be assigned to the same cluster. The algorithmic steps for performing LGS are the following:

1. For each time line i that corresponds to log file LF^r_i compute a segmentation S_i using the method described in section 3.
2. Cluster the τ available time lines using the following similarity measure between segmentations S_i and S_j:

$$\text{sim}(S_i, S_j) = \sum_{p \in S_i} \min_{q \in S_j}(|p - q|) + \sum_{q \in S_j} \min_{p \in S_i}(|q - p|) \qquad (3)$$

---

[1] Since there is no way one can guarantee in practice that log files not to contain intrusions, we assume that LF_τ is a sequence of log files obtained by observing the user accesses and from which the suspicious elements of the sequences have been removed by following the approach that we proposed in the previous section.

where p, q run all the segmentation points of segmentations S_i and S_j respectively.

3. For each cluster randomly obtain l_c sequences to be considered as the most representative behaviors of the cluster. Behaviors that deviate from the representative descriptions are not well described by the cluster and therefore correspond to suspicious actions.

Strict Group Segmentation (SGS): A formal specification of the SGS problem is the following. Given a set of τ log files $LF^r_{\tau \times |T|}$ referring to a specific relation $R_r \in U$ identify a common segmentation $S = \{1, 2, ..., I\}$ of the τ time-lines of length $|T|$, consisting of I non-overlapping time-intervals in such a way that for each one of these non-overlapping intervals the set of all τ observations in this interval can be adequately described by a small set of classes. Again MDL is used for finding the best segmentation of the sequences. The way we proceed here is somehow different, due to the inherent difference of the setting. We need to simultaneously segment τ sequences and we require them to have the same segmentation points. Therefore, we are trying to find a global segmentation $S = \{[b_1, e_1][b_2, e_2]...[b_I, e_I]\}$ consisting of I non-overlapping segments, where each segment $s \in S$ is characterized by its beginning and ending points b_s and e_s respectively. Additionally, for each segment $s \in S$ there are n_s centers that can adequately describe the data appearing in all the τ sequences in segment s. Each such center is a real number representing the intensity level at this segment. The intensity, as before, is the estimated probability of the occurrence of of an even at that segment. Given the above segmentation S the cost, in bits, of encoding this segmentation is determined by: (a) the cost for specifying the block boundaries $(I \log(|T|))$; (b) the cost for specifying the number of representatives per segment $(I \log \tau)$; (c) the cost for coding each such representative. Note that a representative corresponds to an intensity level, and thus to a real number. Given that we have n_s representatives in segment $s \in S$ the total cost for encoding them will be $n_s \rho$. Again ρ is the cost of encoding a real number. For segment s_k the cost is $\rho(k) = \frac{1}{2} \log(|s_k|)$ with $|s_k|$ representing the length of the segment. Therefore the total cost of the model of segmentation S in bits is given by the following expression:

$$L(S) = I \log(|T|) + I \log \tau + \sum_{k=1}^{I} n_{s_k} \rho(k) \qquad (4)$$

Consider again a single segment $s = [b_s, e_s]$ and the time-line l with $1 \leq l \leq \tau$, LF^r_l whose values within s are denoted by $LF^r_l(s, j)$ with $b_s \leq j \leq e_s$. Additionally, consider that segment s has n_s representative centers forming the set C_s. Assume a single such center $c_s \in C_s$. Then the probability of the data $LF^r_l(s)$ is given by $P(LF_l(s)|c_s) = P_D(LF_l(s, j))$, under the assumption that neighboring events are independent.

Therefore the cost of coding the data is equal to the sum of $-\log(P(LF_l(s)|c_s))$ for all segments $s \in S$ and for all time-lines $l \in [1, \tau]$, and of the cost for identifying for each segment the center that best describes the data, which is $\log(n_s)$. The way to proceed in order to construct the segmentation is the same as the one described in the previous section using dynamic programming. The main difference between the case we have considered in Section 3 and the case we consider here is that we additionally need to specify for each segment s the set of segment centers C_s that best describe the data in this segment. To this purpose we employ the k-means clustering algorithm for k varying from 1 to 5.

Combining LGS and SGS in an iterative fusion we obtain the alternative algorithm of *Combined Group Segmentation (CGS)*.

4.2   Detecting Anomalous Behaviors

Assume now that a new set of events e, out of the possible set of observations $\mathcal{E}$, has been logged involving relation R_r. The goal here is to identify whether the occurrence of the set e or of any subset of it is enough for raising an alarm. The set of events in e defines a time interval $i_e = [B_e, E_e]$, which has a position over the time line T. In order to be able to identify whether e contains a query flood attack or not we need to define a class of "deviation" functions $\mathcal{F}$ that allow the comparison between $e \in \mathcal{E}$ and the segmentation model $S \in \mathcal{S}$ that has already been specified from the set of all possible segmentations $\mathcal{S}$. Therefore each function $f \in \mathcal{F}$, is defined as $f : [\mathcal{E}, \mathcal{S}] \to \Re$. If there exists $f \in \mathcal{F}$ such that $f(e, S) \geq iT$, where iT is a pre-specified intrusion threshold, then a query flood attack is highly probable to exist within e.

Definition 5. *The **deviation function** f_1 is a mapping from $[\mathcal{E}, \mathcal{S}] \to \Re$, from the set of possible observed sequences of events $\mathcal{E}$ and segmentation models $\mathcal{S}$ to the set of real numbers. Given an event $e \in \mathcal{E}$ and a segmentation model $S \in \mathcal{S}$, $f_1(e, S)$ is defined as follows:*

$$f_1(e, S) = \sum_{i=1}^{E_e - B_e + 1} (e(i) - min\_c_s)$$

where min_c_s is the value of the segment center c of segment $s \in S$ that overlaps with s and which has the smallest partial distance for the subset of events in e that overlap with s.

Alternatively, given the segmentation S we determine for each segment $s \in S$ the upper threshold for this segment. More specifically:

Definition 6. *The **upper threshold** ($Upper\_T(s)$) of a segment $s \in S$, containing n_s centers that define the set C_s is defined as*

$$Upper\_T(s) = max_{c_s \in C_S} c_s$$

Definition 7. *The **upper threshold** ($Upper\_T(S)$) of a segmentation $S \in \mathcal{S}$, containing I segments $\{s_1, s_2, ..., s_I\}$, is defined as:*

$$Upper\_T(S) = \sum_{j=1}^{I} Upper\_T(s_j)$$

5   Experimental Evaluation

Here we present experiments on simulated data where accuracy is measured in terms of false positives and false negatives. A false positive occurs when the system raises an alarm for a DoS attack while there was not such an attack in the sequence. A false negative refers occurs when the system does not raise an alarm while it should have done so. Misuse and anomaly detection have been analyzed separately.

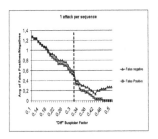 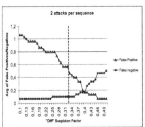 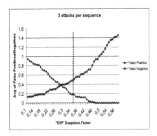

Fig. 1. Accuracy results for "diff" suspicion factor

5.1   Misuse Detection

For the misuse detection experiments we have generated a set of sequences, each consisting of segments of data following Bernoulli distributions with varying parameters p. The parameter p used for generating the data in each segment was selected to be below a random threshold, when the threshold was containing no attack and above the random threshold otherwise. Within each sequence we have incorporated one, two or three attacks.

The results for the "diff" suspicion factor are reported in Figure 1. The plots summarize the accuracy results (the values are averages over 100 runs) of our method when using the "diff" and the "ratio" suspicion factors. The y-axis corresponds to the average number of false positives/negatives (over 100 runs) while the x-axis to the different values of the suspicion factor. In all cases we achieve high accuracy results. The lines parallel to the y-axis in the figures correspond to the optimal thresholds for the suspicion factor ("diff" or "ratio") as output by the randomization test. A general observations from the plots is that the model selection is a trade off between false positives and false negatives. Depending on the application the DBA needs to decide which of the two wants to avoid (favor) most. However, in any case the accuracy of our method is satisfactory enough to provide some accuracy guarantees for a quite wide range of suspicion factor values. The results for the "ratio" suspicion factor are similar, but omitted due to space limitations.

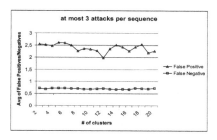

Fig. 2. LGS accuracy results wrt the number of clusters and deviation function f_1

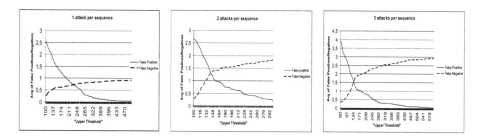

Fig. 3. SGS accuracy results with respect to the value of the "upper threshold"

5.2   Anomaly Detection

For the anomaly detection experimental evaluation we present the results for
LGS and SSG. The accuracy is measured by the average number of false positives
and false negatives over a number of runs. For the experiments we generated 100
normal sequences for training the model. For those sequences the probability of
occurrence of an event was below a certain threshold. For testing 100 normal
data sequences and 100 sequences containing artificial attacks were generated.
Figure 2 reports the accuracy results of the LGS-related experiments for the
case of sequences with at most 3 attacks. The trends for the case of 2 attacks
are similar and we omit them for sake of space. The accuracy results are again
averages over 100 runs. One can easily conclude that the number of clusters
hardly plays any role in the overall accuracy of the method. On the other hand,
as the values of the f_1 deviation function becomes larger the obtained accuracy
increases, since both the number of false positives and false negatives is low.
Figure 3 provides a summary of the results of the SGS experiment. Again the
threshold selection is critical, and constitutes a trade off between the number
of false negatives and false positives. Notice though that for high values of the
threshold value the number of false positives almost tend to zero whatever the
number of attacks (Figure 3).

6   Conclusions and Future Work

In this paper we have addressed the problem of query floods attacks to relational database systems. Some relevant features of our approach include access profiles incorporating time and variable protection granularity, in that one can associate a general access profile with the entire database or associate specific access profiles with specific tables. We have also evaluated our approach through some simulation and results show that our method is effective.

Indeed our methods are general and their applicability can also go beyond the DBMS. We are currently extending our work in various directions. In particular, we plan to develop a tool assisting the administrator in managing the profiles and the various parameters required by our approach. A second direction is related to investigating how different DBMS react with respect to query flood attacks and identify which features of such systems make them more vulnerable to such attacks. Finally, we plan to extend our approach to protect other types of systems, namely LDAP directories and UDDI registries for Web services.

References

1. R. Agrawal, T. Imielinski, and A. Swami. Mining association rules between sets of items in large databases. In *SIGMOD*, 1993.
2. S. Axelsson. Intrusion detection systems: A survey and taxonomy. In *Technical Report No 99-15, Dept. of Computer Engineering, Chalmers Univeristy of Technology, Sweden*, 2000.
3. R. Bellman. On the approximation of curves by line segments using dynamic programming. *Communications of the ACM*, 4(6), 1961.
4. E. Bertino and E. Ferrari. Information security. *Practical Handbook of Internet Computing, M.Singh ed., CRC Press*, 2003.
5. A. Cantoni. Optimal curve fitting with piecewise linear functions. *IEEE Transactions on Computers*, C-20(1):59–67, 1971.
6. N. Daswani and Hector Garcia-Molina. Query-flood attacks in gnutella. *Technical Report, Stanford University*, 2002.
7. E. Keogh, S. Chu, D. Hart, and M. Pazzani. An online algorithm for segmenting time series. In *ICDM*, pages 289 – 296, 2001.
8. Terran Lane and Carla E. Brodley. Temporal sequence learning and data reduction for anomaly detection. *ACM Trans. Inf. Syst. Secur.*, 2(3):295–331, 1999.
9. Wenke Lee and Salvatore J. Stolfo. A framework for constructing features and models for intrusion detection systems. *ACM Trans. Inf. Syst. Secur.*, 3(4):227–261, 2000.
10. W. Li. Dna segmentation as a model selection process. In *RECOMB*, pages 204 – 210, 2001.
11. D. Moore, G. Voelker, and S. Savage. Inferring internet denial of service activity. In *USENIX Security Symposium*, 2001.
12. C. Schuba, I. Krsul, M. Kuhn, E. Spafford, A. Sundaram, and D. Zamboni. Analysis of a denial of service attack on tcp. In *IEEE Symposium on Security and Privacy*, pages 208–223, 1997.
13. C. Yu and V. Gligor. A formal specification and verification method for the prevention of denial of service. In *IEEE Symposium on Security and Privacy*, pages 187–202, 1988.

An XML-Based Approach
to Document Flow Verification

Elisa Bertino[1], Elena Ferrari[2], and Giovanni Mella[3]

[1] CERIAS and CS Department, Purdue University,
Recitation Building, 656 Oval Drive, West Lafayette, IN 47907-2086
bertino@cerias.purdue.edu
[2] Dipartimento di Scienze della Cultura, Politiche e Informazione,
Università dell'Insubria, Via Valleggio, 11, 22100 Como, Italy
elena.ferrari@uninsubria.it
[3] Dipartimento di Informatica e Comunicazione,
Università degli Studi di Milano, Via Comelico, 39/41, 20135 Milano, Italy
mella@dico.unimi.it

Abstract. The paper proposes an XML-based approach for a controlled distribution of documents, that must be subject to distributed and collaborative updates. In particular, the approach we propose allows one to attach a *flow policy* to a document, that partially or totally specifies the list of subjects that have to receive the document. Flow policies associated with documents can be dynamically changed during document transmission. Such modifications are regulated by a set of *modification control rules*, specified according to a model that we present in this paper. A key feature of the proposed solution is that a subject, upon receiving a document can also locally verify the correctness of the path and of the modification operations possibly performed over it, without interacting with other parties. In the paper, besides presenting the language to specify flow policies and modification control rules, we describe the suite of protocols we have developed to perform the above-mentioned checks on document paths.

1 Introduction

Many of today advanced applications, such as collaborative e-commerce [9] and decentralized workflow systems [1], require secure transmission of documents among several parties, often distributed at different sites in a computer network, under different security domains, and belonging to different organizations. A key requirement is not only that of ensuring document integrity and authenticity, but also to ensure that documents are modified according to the access control policies agreed upon by the various parties. Moreover, if required by the application at hand, the documents could be actually transmitted to the parties according to a specified order. By a specified order, we mean that a specification is associated with the transmitted document stating the order according to which the document must be received by the involved parties. Such specification

K. Zhang and Y. Zheng (Eds.): ISC 2004, LNCS 3225, pp. 207–218, 2004.

can consist of the full list of all the subjects having to receive the document, or can be more flexible by allowing to specify only some of the subjects having to receive the document. Those subjects, if properly authorized, can in turn decide additionally subjects to which the document is to be transmitted. The involved subjects form a so-called *collaborative group*, that is, a set of subjects to which the document can be sent to be read and/or updated. In the remainder we refer to the flow policy specification as *flow policy attachment*. The development of a system supporting secure document distribution according to the stated flow policies entails addressing several issues. The first issue is the development of a suitable language for the specification of such policies. A second relevant issue is related to the development of techniques ensuring that the document is actually transmitted according to the stated flow policies. Finally, a subject should be able to recover a valid version of the document in case the received version of the document has flown through parties violating the stated flow policy or it is corrupted. In this paper, we address the above requirements by proposing an XML-based language for flow policy specification and by describing the algorithms needed to verify the correctness of document flow. In this paper, we do not deal with the problem of verifying the correctness of the updates performed on the document wrt the stated access control policies, since this issue has been considered in a previous paper by us [4]. The remainder of this paper is organized as follows. Section 2 surveys related work. Sect.3 gives a general overview of our approach, whereas Sect.4 presents the concept of *flow policy attachment*. In Sect.5 we present the modification control model we have defined. Section 6 deals with authoring certificates which are used by a subject to properly modify a flow policy attachment, whereas in Sect.7 we present the protocols supported by our approach. Finally, Sect.8 presents the assessment of our approach, whereas Sect.9 concludes the paper.

2   Related Work

The problem of secure distributed and cooperative updates of XML documents is new and to the best of our knowledge it has not been addressed by other researchers before. However, several approaches have been recently proposed dealing with integrity and authenticity mechanisms for XML documents.[1] Related work also includes the Security Assertion Markup Language (SAML) standard proposed by the Organization for the Advancement of Structured Information Standards (OASIS) [8]. SAML supports the specification of requests and responses to be exchanged during a distributed transaction to obtain for example authorization or authentication assertions that a subject needs to verify in order to access a particular resource. The architecture underlying SAML relies on three parties: a subject (S), that wishes to access a particular resource (r), a Relying Party (RP), that manages the requested resource and needs to authenticate S to grant/deny access to r, and an Asserting Party (AP) that can assert that S has been authenticated. A major difference of our approach with respect to

---

[1] See [7] for an updated overview of work related to XML security.

SAML is that our approach uses a decentralized mechanism to locally check the satisfaction of receiver profiles, composing a flow policy, and the authenticity of receiver information, without contacting any other party. Our approach is thus better suited for peer-to-peer systems. The problem considered in this paper has been already partially addressed in some previous papers by us [2,5]. Our current paper extends our previous proposals from two different points of view. First, it proposes a comprehensive language to specify flow policies for documents. Second, the present paper proposes a more efficient approach to integrity verification.

3   General Overview

The exchange and collaborative updates of a document must be supported by a proper infrastructure. We believe that two are the main requirements of such an infrastructure. The first is the development of a high level language for flow policies specification. Such a language has to enable a subject, denoted in the following as the *originator* of a flow policy, to declare all the characteristics that have to be possessed by a receiver. Further such a language has to enable an originator to directly specify into a flow policy whether a receiver can or cannot perform the insertion of a new *sub-policy*, thus modifying the path that the document must follow. The updates to the original flow policy must be regulated by proper *modification control rules*, that state which subjects can modify which portions of that flow policy and in which mode. The generation of these rules is managed by the originator of that flow policy, according to our authorization model.[2] A subject knows which privileges it can exercise and over which portions of a flow policy because it receives from the originator of a flow policy some certificates,[3] generated according to the specified modification control rules, attesting the rights it possesses on the flow policy. The possibility of modifying a flow policy requires the generation of some *control information* to properly exercise the privileges supported by the modification control model and to make possible for a subject to check the integrity of a flow policy associated with a received XML document. This control information together with its corresponding flow policy form the so-called *flow policy attachment*. Finally, an XML document and its flow policy attachment form the *document package*.[4] The architecture supporting such a controlled document flow management is shown in Fig.1, and consists of three main components. A flow policy is first processed by the *Control Information Generator* module that generates a flow policy attachment formed by the flow policy received in input and the corresponding generated control information. The generated flow policy attachment is then composed with an XML document by the *Dispatcher* module to form the document package, that is sent by this module to the first subject, specified in

---

[2] See Sect.5 for more details.

[3] More details about the specification of a certificate are given in Sect.6.

[4] The package also contains additional control information required to properly modify the document content.

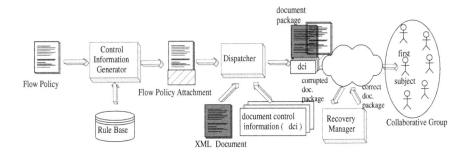

Fig. 1. Document flow management: overall schema

the flow policy attachment. Whenever a subject detects that the flow policy integrity was violated, it sends a recovery request to the *Recovery* module to obtain the last correct version of that flow policy and the associated XML document.

4   The Flow Policy Attachment

In this section we give more details on the flow policy attachment by presenting its specification language (Sect.4.1), its XML encoding (Sect.4.2), and the control information needed to properly modify a flow policy and to check its integrity (Sect.4.3).

4.1   Flow Policy Specification Language

A flow policy is basically a sequence of receiver specifications denoting the subjects that must receive the document. Each of these specifications contains a set of alternative profiles to be satisfied by a subject to be a valid receiver. Additionally each alternative profile is associated with information explicitly specifying whether a subject, that satisfies that profile, is enabled to extend a flow policy by inserting a sub-policy. To support a flexible specification of the profiles, each subject is associated with one or more *credentials* [10] against which profiles are specified. A credential is a set of characteristics qualifying a subject, relevant for security purposes. Credentials are encoded in an XML-based language as shown in Fig.2. Credentials are certified by the Certification Authority (CA) that issued them. In what follows we denote with the term *credential expression* each condition specified over credentials using an XPath-compliant language [11]. Table 1 presents the main components of a flow policy, whereas Table 2 gives their semantics.

Example 1. *An example of flow policy is the following:*
```
<{("//manager[@Department="CTS"]", subpath), ("//secretary[@Department=
  "CTS"]", nosubpath)}, {("//notary[@law_firm="GDC"]", subpath)},
  {("//company_management_director", subpath)}>
```

```
<manager credID= "154", CIssuer= "CA10">
  <RSAKeyValue> ... </RSAKeyValue>
  <name>
    <Fname> Tom </Fname>
    <lname > Miller </lname>
  </name>
  <age> 42 </age>
  <department> CTS </department>
  <salary> 8,000 </salary>
  <category > Top Executive </category>
</manager>
```

```
<secretary credID= "104", manager= "154",
          CIssuer= "CA22">
  <RSAKeyValue> ... </RSAKeyValue>
  <name>
    <Fname> Ann </Fname>
    <lname > Moore </lname>
  </name>
  <age> 30 </age>
  <department> CTS </department>
  <salary> 2,000 </salary>
  <level > third </level>
  <duty > manager secretary </duty>
</secretary>
```

Fig. 2. Examples of XML encoded credentials

*which specifies that the first receiver must be a manager or a secretary of the
"CTS" Department; the second receiver must be a notary of the "GDC" law firm;
whereas the third receiver must be a company management director. Moreover,
the flow policy specifies that whereas managers, notaries and company management directors are entitled to insert a new sub-policy into this flow policy,
secretaries are not enabled to do that.*

4.2   XML Encoding of a Flow Policy Attachment

A flow policy attachment is encoded using XML, thus allowing a uniform management of the protected document and the associated flow information. Figure
3(a) shows the DTD of a flow policy attachment.

A flow policy attachment consists of a set of nested elementary components.
We denote with the term *atomic flow policy attachment*, shown in Fig.3(b), an
XML flow policy attachment, instance of the DTD in Fig.3(a), that contains
only one *Fpa* element (the root element of that instance). An atomic flow policy
attachment mainly consists of a first portion containing a flow policy, and a second portion containing the corresponding control information. According to the
tree structure of a flow policy attachment, a Pre-Order, Depth-First, Left-to-
Right tree traversal (PO-DF-LR) gives the *order* in which the *FlowPolicyElement*
elements should be considered. Basic portions that compose the flow policy portion of an atomic flow policy attachment are called *atomic elements*. We can
formally define an atomic element as follows.

Definition 1. (Atomic Element). Let *a_fpa* be an atomic flow policy attachment. Let *e* be an element belonging to *a_fpa* and let id(*e*) be the value of the

Table 1. Flow policy main components

Component	Structure	Meaning
FlowPolicy	ordered list of FlowPolicyElement, one for each receiver specification	information generated by a subject to partially specify the path that a document must follow
FlowPolicyElement	set of CredentialSpec, one for each alternative profile to be satisfied by a receiver	information used by a subject to choose a valid next receiver
CredentialSpec	(*CredentialExpr, Ext*)	condition that composes a receiver profile

Table 2. Flow policy additional components

Component	Semantics
CredentialExpr	credential expression that must be satisfied by a receiver
Ext	value in the set {subpath|nosubpath} stating whether a receiver is authorized (subpath) or not (nosubpath) to insert a sub-policy in a given flow policy

```
                                              <Fpa Id = ''F1'' version = ''V1''>
                                               <FlowPolicyElement Id = ''1''>        Flow policy portion
                                                <CredentialSpec Id = ''2''>
                                                 <CredentialExpr Id = ''3''>
                                                  ''//manager[Department=''CTS'']"
                                                 </CredentialExpr>
                                                 <Ext Id = ''4''>
<!DOCTYPE Fpa                                      subpath
 [                                               </Ext>
 <!ELEMENT Fpa (FlowPolicyElement+, ControlInfo)>  </CredentialSpec>
 <!ELEMENT FlowPolicyElement (NextSbj?,          <CredentialSpec Id = ''5''>
            CredentialSpec+, CredentialInfo?,     <CredentialExpr Id = ''6''>
            Fpa?)>                                 ''//secretary[Department=''CTS'']"
 <!ELEMENT NextSbj (#PCDATA)>                      </CredentialExpr>
 <!ELEMENT CredentialSpec (CredentialExpr, Ext)>   <Ext Id = ''7''>
 <!ELEMENT CredentialExpr (#PCDATA)>                nosubpath
 <!ELEMENT Ext (#PCDATA)>                          </Ext>
 <!ELEMENT CredentialInfo (#PCDATA)>             </CredentialSpec>
 <!ELEMENT ControlInfo (ModifiableInfo?,        </FlowPolicyElement>
            StaticInfo, Signature+)>            <FlowPolicyElement Id = ''8''>
 <!ELEMENT ModifiableInfo (Mod_el+, hcslast-1,   <CredentialSpec Id = ''9''>
            sighcslast-1, slast-1,                <CredentialExpr Id = ''10''>
            hcslast, sighcslast, slast, hserv-1,   ''//notary[law_firm=''GDC'']"
            hserv)>                                </CredentialExpr>
 <!ELEMENT Mod_el (full, h_me)>                   <Ext Id = ''11''>
 <!ELEMENT full (Signature)>                       subpath
 <!ELEMENT h_me (DigestMethod, DigestValue)>       </Ext>
 <!ELEMENT DigestMethod (#PCDATA)>               </CredentialSpec>
 <!ELEMENT DigestValue (#PCDATA)>               </FlowPolicyElement>
 <!ELEMENT hcslast-1 (prevdig, prev2dig,        <FlowPolicyElement Id = ''12''>
            certificates, ringlast-1)>           <CredentialSpec Id = ''13''>
 <!ELEMENT sighcslast-1 (Signature)>              <CredentialExpr Id = ''14''>
 <!ELEMENT slast-1 (#PCDATA)>                      ''//company_management_director"
 <!ELEMENT hcslast (lastdig, last2dig,            </CredentialExpr>
            certificates, ringlast)>              <Ext Id = ''15''>
 <!ELEMENT sighcslast (Signature)>                 subpath
 <!ELEMENT slast (#PCDATA)>                        </Ext>
 <!ELEMENT hserv-1 (Signature)>                  </CredentialSpec>
 <!ELEMENT hserv (Signature)>                   </FlowPolicyElement>
 <!ELEMENT prevdig (DigestMethod, DigestValue)> ...
 <!ELEMENT prev2dig (DigestMethod, DigestValue)> <ControlInfo>                  Control Information portion
 <!ELEMENT certificates (certificate*)>          <ModifiableInfo>
 <!ELEMENT certificate (#PCDATA)>                 <Mod_el Id = ''AE1'' type = ''tags'' at_el = ''1''>...</Mod_el>
 <!ELEMENT ringlast-1 (#PCDATA)>                  <Mod_el Id = ''AE2'' type = ''tags'' at_el = ''2''>...</Mod_el>
 <!ELEMENT lastdig (DigestMethod, DigestValue)>  <Mod_el Id = ''AE3'' type = ''tags'' at_el = ''3''>...</Mod_el>
 <!ELEMENT last2dig (DigestMethod, DigestValue)> <Mod_el Id = ''AE4'' type = ''dc'' at_el = ''3''>...</Mod_el>
 <!ELEMENT ringlast (#PCDATA)>                    <Mod_el Id = ''AE5'' type = ''tags'' at_el = ''4''>...</Mod_el>
 <!ELEMENT StaticInfo (Originator, FirstReceiver, <Mod_el Id = ''AE6'' type = ''dc'' at_el = ''4''>...</Mod_el>
            ring)>                                ...
 <!ELEMENT Originator (ANY)>                      <Mod_el Id = ''AE9'' type = ''dc'' at_el = ''6''>...</Mod_el>
 <!ELEMENT FirstReceiver (ANY)>                   ...
 <!ELEMENT ring (#PCDATA)>                        <Mod_el Id = ''AE11'' type = ''dc'' at_el = ''7''>...</Mod_el>
 <!ELEMENT Signature (...)>                       ...
 <!ATTLIST Fpa Id ID #REQUIRED version CDATA      <Mod_el Id = ''AE15'' type = ''dc'' at_el = ''10''>...</Mod_el>
            #REQUIRED>                            ...
 <!ATTLIST FlowPolicyElement Id ID #REQUIRED>     <Mod_el Id = ''AE17'' type = ''dc'' at_el = ''11''>...</Mod_el>
 <!ATTLIST CredentialSpec Id ID #REQUIRED>        ...
 <!ATTLIST CredentialExpr Id ID #REQUIRED>        <Mod_el Id = ''AE21'' type = ''dc'' at_el = ''14''>...</Mod_el>
 <!ATTLIST Ext Id ID #REQUIRED>                   ...
 <!ATTLIST Mod_el Id ID #REQUIRED type (dc|tags)  <Mod_el Id = ''AE23'' type = ''dc'' at_el = ''15''>...</Mod_el>
            at_el IDREF>                          ...
 <!ATTLIST certificate setofelements IDREFS> ]  </ModifiableInfo>
                                                <StaticInfo>
                                                 <Originator> ... </Originator>
                                                 <FirstReceiver> ... </FirstReceiver>
                                                 <ring>0</ring>
                                                </StaticInfo>
                                                <Signature> ... </Signature>
                                               </ControlInfo>
                                              </Fpa>
```

Fig. 3. (a) DTD of a flow policy attachment and (b) an example of XML atomic flow policy attachment

identifier associated with e. The set $\mathcal{AE}(a\_fpa)$ of atomic elements of a_fpa is defined as follows: 1) for each element e, id(e).tags $\in \mathcal{AE}(a\_fpa)$, where id(e).tags denotes the tags of e together with its attributes; 2) for each element e, such that e contains data content, id(e).dc $\in \mathcal{AE}(a\_fpa)$, where id(e).dc denotes the data content of e.

Example 2. *Example of atomic elements in the atomic flow policy attachment in Fig.3(b) are:*
a) 1.tags = *"<FlowPolicyElement Id = "1"> </FlowPolicyElement>";*
b) 5.tags = *"<CredentialSpec Id = "5"> </CredentialSpec>";*
c) 3.dc = *"//manager[@Department = "CTS"]".*

A receiver subject can modify only the atomic elements in a flow policy attachment for which it possesses proper authorizations.

4.3   Flow Policy Enforcement

In this section we present in detail the control information over which our approach for verifying flow policy enforcement relies. First of all, we introduce two control information, denoted as *CredentialInfo* and *NextSbj*, that each receiver must insert in the flow policy attachment. *CredentialInfo* control information must contain one receiver's credential, whereas *NextSbj* control information must contain the public key of the next receiver subject to which the receiver sends the document package. Because flow policies can be modified different control information must be generated for modifiable and non-modifiable portions. This information, consisting of some hash values and digital signatures and contained in the *ControlInfo* element, is organized into three main portions: *modification control information* (*ModifiableInfo* element); *static control information* (*StaticInfo* element); and a set of digital signatures (*Signature* element).

We start by describing the *StaticInfo* element, which contains an *Originator* element (the originator's public key), a *FirstReceiver* element (the public key of the first receiver of the package) and a *ring* element, used to prevent a receiver from inserting in the flow policy an old version of its content. By contrast, *ModifiableInfo* element contains for each modifiable atomic element m_ae, a *Mod_el* sub-element. Each *Mod_el* element contains the type of m_ae (in *type*), the identifier of the element referred by this m_ae (in *at_el*) and some additional information (*full* and *h_me*).

In particular, the *full* element specifies whether m_ae was deleted or not. The *h_me* element contains a hash value computed over the portions of the element referred by attribute *at_el* and specified in the attribute *type*. *ModifiableInfo* element also contains some hash values and digital signatures generated by the last two subjects (*slast-1* and *slast*) that have modified and/or verified modifiable portions. Such hash values are maintained in the *hcslast-1* and *hcslast* elements respectively, to make a subject able to check the integrity of the modifiable portions. To perform this check, the subject has to verify that, starting from the last but one state of those portions and locally executing the last declared modification operations, it obtains the current state of those portions. Finally, the *ModifiableInfo* element contains information on which portions have been modified by the last subject that has operated on the flow policy. The third element, *Signature*, contains two different types of digital signatures.[5] A *receiver signature* is computed by the ith receiver over its current FlowPolicyElement element

---

[5] Signatures are compliant with the W3C standard [11].

and over the non-modifiable information of an atomic flow policy attachment, if inserted in that FlowPolicyElement element. An *originator signature* is computed by the originator of a flow policy attachment, at the beginning of the update process and whenever the update of ring element is required, over the receiver signatures inserted in the flow policy attachment up to that point and over the following portions of an atomic flow policy attachment: a) StaticInfo element and its sub-elements; b) all the non-modifiable atomic elements; c) all the Mod_el elements, without their sub-elements (full and h_me); d) Fpa element and its attributes. In what follows, with the term *current flow policy attachment*, we denote the flow policy attachment received by the current receiver, whereas the term *free FlowPolicyElement* denotes a FlowPolicyElement element that does not contain both the CredentialInfo and NextSbj element, that is, it denotes a receiver specification not yet associated with a subject. We denote with the term *current FlowPolicyElement* the first *free FlowPolicyElement* element encountered executing a `PO-DF-LR` traversal of the graph representation of the current flow policy attachment.

5   Modification Control Model

In this section, we introduce the model according to which rules to modify atomic flow policy attachments can be specified. In particular, we focus on the main components of a rule, that is how subjects and protection objects are qualified in the rules, which privileges our model supports, and, finally which types of propagation options we provide.

Subjects. In order to make more flexible the specification of the set of subjects to which a rule applies, modification control rules contain credential expressions.

Protection objects. A protection object in our model is a portion of an atomic flow policy attachment to which a modification control rule applies. With respect to the structure of an atomic flow policy attachment a modification control rule can only apply to the elements belonging to its flow policy portion, namely *FlowPolicyElement*, *CredentialSpec*, *CredentialExpr*, and *Ext* elements.

Privileges. In our model we support two distinct privileges: `update` and `delete`. The first one allows a subject s to modify only the data content of a *CredentialExpr* and/or *Ext* element of an atomic flow policy attachment. The second privilege gives a subject the possibility of deleting one or more *FlowPolicyElement* and/or *CredentialSpec* elements in an atomic flow policy attachment.

Propagation options. We support two types of propagation options: `NO_PROP` and `PROP`. The `NO_PROP` option means that a rule applies only to the protection objects specified in the rule itself, whereas the `PROP` option propagates the effect of a modification control rule to all the protection objects belonging to the subtrees rooted at the protection objects specified in the modification control rule itself. Similar to credentials, also modification control rules are encoded using XML. We denote with the term Rule Base ($\mathcal{RB}$) an XML file encoding a set of modification control rules.

```
<rule_base>
  <rule_spec pid="R1" cred_expr="//notary[@law_firm="GDC"]" target="Fpa_Mortage_deed.xml"
             path="//FlowPolicyElement[@Id="1"]" priv="delete" prop="PROP" />
  <rule_spec pid="R2" cred_expr="//secretary" target="Fpa_Mortage_deed.xml" path="" priv="update" prop="PROP" />
  <rule_spec pid="R3" cred_expr="//vice_company_management_director" target="Fpa_Mortage_deed.xml"
             path="//FlowPolicyElement/CredentialSpec" priv="delete" prop="NO_PROP" />
  <rule_spec pid="R4" cred_expr="//director[@Department="CTS"]" target="Fpa_Mortage_deed.xml"
             path="//FlowPolicyElement/CredentialSpec/CredentialExpr" priv="update" prop="NO_PROP" />
</rule_base>
```

Fig. 4. An example of *Rule Base*

Example 3. *Figure 4 shows a rule base referring to the atomic flow policy attachment reported in Fig.3(b). According to the rules in Fig.4 notaries working in the GDC law firm are entitled to delete the element with Id 1 and all its subelements; secretaries are enabled to modify all the data contents belonging to each CredentialExpr/Ext element; vice company management directors can delete all the CredentialSpec elements, whereas directors working in the "CTS" Department are entitled to modify all the CredentialExpr elements.*

6   Authoring Certificates

Authoring certificates are used by a subject, that has modified a flow policy attachment portion, to prove its right to modify that portion to the subsequent receivers of the package. An authoring certificate consists of a privilege p, the public key (p_key) of a subject that can exercise p, and the set of protection objects (set_of_objs) on which the subject can exercise p. Authoring certificates containing the privilege `delete` allow a subject to delete all the objects specified within set_of_objs component, whereas `update` certificates allow a subject to update one or more of the objects specified in the set_of_objs component.

Example 4. *Consider two users Ann and Tom, whose credentials are shown in Fig.2. Consider moreover the atomic flow policy attachment constituted by the portions in Fig.3(b), and the rules in Fig.4. Then: (F1, update, PK(Ann),[6] {AE4, AE6, AE9, AE11, AE15, AE17, AE21, AE23}) is a valid certificate, since Ann is authorized to update the atomic elements: 3.dc, 4.dc, 6.dc, 7.dc, 10.dc, 11.dc, 14.dc and 15.dc. By contrast, (F1, delete, PK(Tom), {AE2, AE3, AE4, AE5, AE6})) is not a valid certificate, since Tom is not authorized to delete the atomic elements: 2.tags, 3.tags, 3.dc, 4.tags and 4.dc.*

7   Protocols

Three are the main protocols we have developed: 1) the integrity check protocol, that verifies the integrity of the flow policy associated with the received document, 2) the update protocol, that allows a subject to modify a flow policy, and, finally, 3) the recovery protocol, that takes care of building the last correct version of a corrupted package. The first two protocols are executed by the receivers, whereas the third is executed by the document originator. Due to lack of space we focus only on those executed by a receiver.

---

[6] With PK(s) we denote the public key associated with subject s.

7.1 Integrity Check Protocol

The integrity check protocol analyzes the flow policy attachment contained in the received package and if an error occurs it sends a recovery request to the document originator, otherwise it returns the correct analyzed flow policy attachment. The protocol starts validating the received flow policy attachment with respect to its corresponding DTD. Then, it verifies that the sequence of subjects associated with the *non-free* FlowPolicyElement elements are valid receivers and that inserted sub-policies have been added by authorized subjects. All FlowPolicyElement elements, after the first one found free, must be free too and they must not contain an atomic flow policy attachment, because they cannot be associated with any subject. The next checks are applied to each atomic flow policy attachment. The protocol checks the integrity of the signatures inserted by the subjects that have already received the package up to that point. Then, the protocol verifies the correct correspondence between the value of ring in the StaticInfo element and the last one received by the originator of that atomic flow policy attachment. Finally, the protocol checks the integrity of modifiable atomic elements, verifying also that the operations executed by the last subject that has modified them were executed over atomic elements that follow the one corresponding to the FlowPolicyElement element associated with that subject.

7.2 Update Protocol

After the integrity check protocol has been executed a subject s can update the received flow policy attachment according to its authorizations, and then updates the control information associated with the updated modifiable atomic elements. In particular, such information is updated in each atomic flow policy attachment to which at least an updated modifiable atomic element belongs to. The update protocol inserts into the current FlowPolicyElement a NextSbj element, containing the public key of the chosen next receiver, and a CredentialInfo element containing a credential owned by s and satisfying the conditions specified in at least one CredentialExpr element (ce) of the current FlowPolicyElement element itself. Then, the protocol enables s to add a new atomic flow policy attachment in its current FlowPolicyElement element if the Ext element associated with ce contains the value *subpath*. Finally, the protocol generates and then inserts in the flow policy attachment the receiver signature. The next receivers are thus ensured that the current subject is a valid receiver and it has the right to insert a new atomic flow policy attachment.

8   Assessment of the Proposed Approach

In the following we remark some relevant properties of our approach in terms of originality, flexibility, and detection of subject malicious behaviours.

1. The presence and the content of the NextSbj and CredentialInfo elements assure the following properties:

Possession of a proper credential in order to qualify as a valid receiver: the matching between the content of the CredentialInfo element and the conditions specified in the CredentialExpr elements assures that a receiver is a valid receiver in a particular position within the flow policy attachment.

Authenticity of the information contained in a CredentialInfo element: since the CA that generates the credentials signs them, the signature computed over a credential makes it possible to check the integrity and therefore the authenticity of the information it contains.

No substitutions of chosen receivers: the content inserted in the NextSbj element ensures that a malicious subject is not able to replace the chosen receiver with another one without being detected.

No use of credentials of other subjects: the correspondence between the content of a NextSbj element and the public key in the corresponding CredentialInfo element assures that a chosen receiver does not insert/use a credential that refers to another subject.

Ownership of a credential by the chosen receiver: the correspondence between the content of a NextSbj element and the public key in the corresponding CredentialInfo element, together with the verification that the signature computed over the FlowPolicyElement element that contains such CredentialInfo element has been actually generated by the subject specified in it, assures that the inserted credential belongs to that specified subject.

2. The receiver signature assures the following properties:

   No alteration to the content of a given FlowPolicyElement element: the signature computed over a given FlowPolicyElement element assures that no subject is able to modify the content of that FlowPolicyElement element without being detected by the subsequent receivers.

   No deletion or substitution of an atomic flow policy attachment executed by subjects different from its originator: the receiver signature is computed by a receiver also over some information belonging to the atomic flow policy attachment inserted in its current FlowPolicyElement element; thus deletion or substitution of that atomic flow policy attachment can be detected.

9   Concluding Remarks

In this paper we have presented an approach for the controlled flow of documents that must be subject to distributed and collaborative updates. We plan to extend this work along several directions. First, we plan to extend our modification control model to enable partial disclosure of flow policy attachments. Furthermore, we are interested in addressing the problem of assuring anonymity of all or part of the subjects that receive the package. Another issue that we intend to address is the possibility, for a receiver, of entering, in the flow policy attachment, only the information needed to guarantee that it is a valid receiver, instead of a whole credential. Finally, we plan to implement a prototype system and test the performance and the overhead implied by our solution.

References

1. V. Atluri, Soon Ae Chun, P. Mazzoleni, "A Chinese wall security model for decentralized workflow systems", *Proc. of the 8th ACM conference on Computer and Communications Security*, Philadelphia, PA, USA, 2001, pp 48-57.
2. E. Bertino, G. Correndo, E. Ferrari, and G. Mella. "An Infrastructure for Managing Secure Update Operations for XML Data", *Proc. of the 8th ACM Symposium on Access Control Models and Technologiesz*, Villa Gallia, Como, Italy, June 2-3, 2003.
3. E. Bertino, and E. Ferrari. "Secure and Selective Dissemination of XML Documents". *ACM Transactions on Information and System Security (TISSEC) 5(3): 290-331 (2002)*.
4. E. Bertino, E. Ferrari, G. Mella, "A Framework for Distributed and Cooperative Updates of XML Documents", *Proc. of the 16th Annual IFIP WG 11.3, Working Conference on Data and Application Security*, Cambridge, UK, July 2002, pp 211-227.
5. E. Bertino, E. Ferrari, G. Mella. "Flow Policies: Specification and Enforcement", *Proc. of the Workshop on Information Assurance, WIA2004, yeld in conjunction with the 23rd IEEE International Performance Computing and Communications Conference*, Phoenix, Arizona, April, 14 - 17, 2004.
6. E. Damiani, S. De Capitani di Vimercati, S. Paraboschi, and P. Samarati. "Securing XML Documents". In *Proc. 6th International Conference on Extending Database Technology*, Konstanz, Germany, March 2000, pages 121-135.
7. C. Geuer Pollmann. The XML Security Page. http://www.nue.et-inf.uni-siegen.de/g̃euer-pollmann/xml_security.html
8. Security Assertion Markup Language, SAML v1.1 Standard Specification set (2 September 2003): OASIS Standard. Available at: `http://www.oasis-open.org/committees/tc_home.php?wg_abbrev=security`
9. B. Thuraisingham, A. Gupta, E. Bertino, E. Ferrari, "Collaborative Commerce and Knowledge Management", Knowledge and Process Management, 9(1):43-53 (2002).
10. M. Winslett, N. Ching, V. Jones, I. Slepchin. "Using Digital Credentials on the World Wide Web". *Journal of Computer Security*, 7, 1997.
11. World Wide Web Consortium. Available at: `http://www.w3.org/`

Model-Checking Access Control Policies

(Extended Abstract)

Dimitar P. Guelev[1], Mark Ryan[1], and Pierre Yves Schobbens[2]

[1] School of Computer Science, University of Birmingham
Edgbaston, Birmingham B15 2TT, UK
[2] Institut d'Informatique, Facultés Universitaires de Namur
Rue Grandgagnage 21, 5000 Namur, Belgium

Abstract. We present a model of access control which provides fine-grained data-dependent control, can express permissions about permissions, can express delegation, and can describe systems which avoid the root-bottleneck problem. We present a language for describing goals of agents; these goals are typically to read or write the values of some resources. We describe a decision procedure which determines whether a given coalition of agents has the means (possibly indirectly) to achieve its goal. We argue that this question is decidable in the situation of the potential intruders acting in parallel with legitimate users and taking whatever temporary opportunities the actions of the legitimate users present. Our technique can also be used to synthesise finite access control systems, from an appropriately formulated logical theory describing a high-level policy.

1   Introduction

In a world in which computers are ever-more interconnected, *access control systems* are of increasing importance in order to guarantee that resources are accessible by their intended users, and not by other possibly malicious users. Access control systems are used to regulate access to resources such as files, database entries, printers, web pages. They may also be used in less obvious applications, such as to determine whether incoming mail has access to its destination mailbox (spam filtering), or incoming IP packets to their destination computers (firewalls).

We present a model of access control which has, among others, the following features:

- Access control may be dependent on the data subject to control. This is useful in certain applications, such as the conference paper review system described below, or stateful firewalls, databases, etc. In [5], this is called *conditional authorisation*.
- Delegation of access control is easily expressed. This helps to avoid the root bottleneck, whereby root or the owner of a resource is required in order to make access control changes, and the insecurity caused by investing too much power in a single agent.
- Permissions for coalitions to act jointly can be expressed.

K. Zhang and Y. Zheng (Eds.): ISC 2004, LNCS 3225, pp. 219–230, 2004.

A key feature of our model is that *permissions* are functions of *state variables*, and therefore may change with the state. Because the ability to change the state is itself controlled by permissions, one can, in particular, express *permissions about permissions*. This allows us easily to devolve authority downwards, thus avoiding the root bottleneck, and to express delegation.

A potential problem of sophisticated access control systems, such as those which can be described using our model, is *indirect paths*. It might be that the system denies immediate access to a resource for a certain agent, but it gives the agent indirect possibilities by allowing it to manipulate permissions. Hence, there could be a sequence of steps which the agent can execute, in order to obtain access to the resource. We are interested in verifying access control systems to check whether such indirect paths exist.

Example 1. Consider a *conference paper review system*. It consists of a set of papers, and a set of agents (which may be authors, programme-committee (PC) members, etc). The following rules apply:

- The chair appoints agents (if they agree to it) to become PC members. PC members can resign unilaterally.
- The chair assigns papers for reviewing to PC members.
- PC members may submit reviews of papers that they have been assigned.
- A PC member a may read b's review of a paper, if the paper has not been assigned to a, or the paper has been assigned to a, and she has already submitted her own review.
- PC members may appoint sub-reviewers for papers which they have been assigned. Sub-reviewers may submit reviews of those papers. The PC member can withdraw the appointment of sub-reviewers.
- Authors should be excluded from the review process for their papers.

Each of these rules is a read access or a write access by one or more agents to a resource. We formalise this example in the next section, and use it as a running example through the paper. Statements 3 and 4 illustrate the dependency of write access and read access (respectively) on the current state. Statement 5 shows how permissions about permissions are important; here, the PC member has write permission on the data expressing the sub-reviewers' write permission on reviews.

Model checking such an access control system will answer questions such as: *can an author find out who reviewed her paper? Can a reviewer of a paper read someone else's review, before submitting his own?* We answer the second question in Example 5.

The main part of this paper presents a simple language for programming access, a propositional language for specifying access goals, and an accessibility operator which denotes that a given goal is achievable by means of a program in the programming language and can be used to formulate access control policies. In the full version of the paper [7] we propose axioms which lead to the expressibility of this operator in propositional logic and to decision procedures for it. These procedures allow access control policies to be checked and behaviour that violates them to be proposed as counterexample to imperfect implementations of policies. Furthermore, the propositional expressibility of the accessibility operator entails that implementations of policies formulated with it can be automatically synthesised. In the full version of the paper [7] we also show that it is decidable whether the execution of a certain program by one coalition provides another coalition with temporary opportunities that are sufficient for the achievement of a certain goal, given that the second coalition can interleave its actions with the actions of the first one. A Prolog implementation of one of the possible decision procedures for our accessibility operator (together with examples) is available on the web [6].

Structure of the paper. We first define our model of access control formally, show how Example 1 can be encoded in it and point to some properties of our model known to be important from the literature. Then we introduce the simple programming language which expresses the procedures that coalitions of agents can use to access systems and define a class of goals that can be pursued by coalitions of agents. For every concrete system it is decidable whether a coalition can achieve a given goal of this class by running a program. In the full version of the paper [7] we argue that the techniques developed in detail for the simple programming language can be straighforwardly extended to more general settings, which include some forms of concurrent access and languages based on high-level access actions. In the concluding section we explain how these techniques lead to algorithms for model checking access control policies on existing systems and synthesising systems which implement given policies.

2   Access Control Systems

We denote the set of propositional formulas φ built using the variables p from some given vocabulary P by $\mathbf{L}(P)$. We adopt $\Rightarrow$ and $\bot$ as basic in the construction of these formulas and regard $\top$, $\neg$, $\wedge$, $\vee$ and $\Leftrightarrow$ as abbreviations. We denote the set of the variables occurring in a formula $\varphi \in \mathbf{L}(P)$ by $\mathrm{Var}(\varphi)$.

Definition 1. *An* access control system *is a tuple* $S = \langle P, \Sigma, \mathbf{r}, \mathbf{w} \rangle$*, where* P *is a set of propositional variables as above,* Σ *is a set of* agents, *and* $\mathbf{r}$ *and* $\mathbf{w}$ *are mappings of type* $P \times \mathcal{P}_{fin}(\Sigma) \to \mathbf{L}(P)$*, where* $\mathcal{P}_{fin}(\Sigma)$ *stands for the set of the finite subsets of* Σ*. The mappings* $\mathbf{r}$ *and* $\mathbf{w}$ *are required to satisfy*

$$A' \subset A \text{ implies } \vdash \mathbf{r}(p, A') \Rightarrow \mathbf{r}(p, A) \text{ and } \vdash \mathbf{w}(p, A') \Rightarrow \mathbf{w}(p, A). \qquad (1)$$

The requirement (1) reflects that a coalition A has the abilities of all of its subcoalitions A'.

The state of an access control system $S = \langle P, \Sigma, \mathbf{r}, \mathbf{w} \rangle$ is determined by the truth values of the variables $p \in P$, denoted by 0 and 1. States are models for $\mathbf{L}(P)$ as a propositional logic language. We represent the states of S by the subsets of P, $s \subseteq P$ representing the state at which the variables which evaluate to 1 are those in s. We denote the truth value of formula φ at state s by $\varphi(s)$. Truth values of formulas are defined in the usual way.

Given $p \in P$, $A \subset_{fin} \Sigma$ and $s \subseteq P$, coalition A has the right to read or overwrite p at state s iff $\mathbf{r}(p, A)(s) = 1$ or $\mathbf{w}(p, A)(s) = 1$, respectively. The definitions of r and w are assumed to be known to all agents $a \in \Sigma$. Agents, however, may lack the permission to access variables in the formulas that r and w produce, and therefore be unable to decide what is permitted at certain states.

Example 2. Consider the Conference paper review system again. Let Papers and Agents be fixed sets, let the function

$$\texttt{author} : \texttt{Papers} \times \texttt{Agents} \rightarrow \{\bot, \top\}$$

be fixed, and the constant $c : \texttt{Agents}$ denote the chairperson of the programme committee. Let P contain the variables

pcmember(a)	a is a PC member
reviewer(p, a)	paper p is assigned to PC member a
subreviewer(p, a, b)	paper p is assigned to sub-reviewer b by PC member a
submittedReview(p, a)	a review of p has been submitted by sub-reviewer a
review(p, a)	the review of p from sub-reviewer a

for each $a \in \texttt{Agents}$ and $p \in \texttt{Papers}$, and assume that pcmember(c) holds (initially). Here follow the definitions of r and w for propositional variables of the form reviewer$(p, a), A)$:

$$\texttt{r}(\texttt{reviewer}(p, a), \{x\}) \rightleftharpoons \texttt{pcmember}(x) \wedge \neg\texttt{author}(p, x)$$

$$\texttt{w}(\texttt{reviewer}(p, a), A) \rightleftharpoons \left(\begin{pmatrix} \texttt{pcmember}(a) \wedge \{a, c\} \subseteq A \wedge \\ \neg\texttt{author}(p, a) \wedge \neg\texttt{reviewer}(p, a) \end{pmatrix} \vee \\ \begin{pmatrix} (a \in A \vee c \in A) \wedge \texttt{reviewer}(p, a) \\ \wedge \neg \bigvee_{b \in \texttt{Agents}} \texttt{subreviewer}(p, a, b) \end{pmatrix} \right)$$

The full definition of r and w for this example can be seen in [7]. The purpose of the example is to illustrate our model and syntax. It becomes clear in Example 5 that the design of the system specified above is not flawless. It admits violating some well-established practices of conference management.

We extend r to a mapping from $\mathbf{L}(P) \times 2^{\Sigma}$ to $\mathbf{L}(P)$ by putting $\mathbf{r}(\varphi, A) \rightleftharpoons \bigwedge_{p \text{ occurs in } \varphi} \mathbf{r}(p, A)$.

An access control system $\langle P, \Sigma, \mathbf{r}, \mathbf{w} \rangle$ is *finite*, if P and Σ are finite. In this paper we study finite access control systems. We only consider systems whose resources are sets of boolean variables; for example, the review of a paper was represented as a boolean, which is more crude than the reviews from most conferences.

2.1   Comparison with Other Models

Several formal models of access control have been published. The influential early work [9] proposed a model for access control with a matrix containing the current rights of each agent on each resource in the modelled system. The actions allowed include creating and destroying agents and resources and updating the matrix of the access rights. The possibility to carry out an action is defined in terms of the rights as described in the matrix. Given the generality of that model, it is not surprising that the problem of whether an agent can gain access to a resource, called the *safety problem*, is not decidable. This can be largely ascribed to the possibility to change the sets of agents and resources in the model. Restrictions on the model and on this possibility in particular have allowed to identify decidable cases in [8,11,13]. In our model, the sets of agents and resources are fixed.

The formulas $r(p, A)$ and $w(p, A)$ may be considered as the values of the cells of an access matrix

		Coalition A	
$\ldots$	$\ldots$	$\ldots$	$\ldots$
Resource p	$\ldots$	$r(p, A), \; w(p, A)$	$\ldots$
	$\ldots$	$\ldots$	$\ldots$

which for each particular state s of the modelled system corresponds to a matrix of the form from [9] describing the rights of reading and writing at that state. Unlike [9], entries in the matrix are updated by actions specifically for that purpose, whereas in our model coalitions update *general purpose* state variables, which in turn affect the value of the formulas $r(.,.)$ and $w(.,.)$. This allows the modelling of *automatic* dependencies between the contents of the access control system, if viewed as a database, and the rights of its users. The special case in which every particular right can be manipulated by a dedicated action can be modelled in our system by choosing a dedicated propositional variable $q_{x,p,A}$ for each triple $x \in \{r, w\}$, $p \in P$ and $A \subseteq \Sigma$ and defining $x(p, A)$ as $q_{x,p,A}$. Then changing the right x of coalition A on p can be made independently for each triple x, p, A. In this case, however, special care needs to be taken to avoid infinite digressions like $q_{x,p,A}, \; q_{y,q_{x,p,A},B}, \; q_{z,q_{y,q_{x,p,A},B},C}, \; \ldots$

An analysis of formal models is given in [5]. Desirable properties highlighted in the literature include:

- *Conditional authorisations* [5]. Protection requirements may need to depend on the evaluation of conditions. As shown by the example above, this is a central feature of our model.
- *Expressibility of joint action* [10,1]. Some actions require to be executed jointly by a coalition of agents, such as the appointment of an agent to the programme committee in the example above, which requires the willingness both of the chair and the candidate.
- *Delegation mechanisms.* In particular, permission to delegate a privilege should be independent of the privilege [3]. Delegation mechanisms may be classified according to permanence, transitivity and other criteria [4].
- *Support for open and closed systems* [5]. In open systems, accesses which are not specified as forbidden are allowed. Thus, the default is that actions are allowed. In closed systems, the default is the opposite: actions which are not expressly allowed are forbidden.

- *Expressibility of administrative policies* [5]. Administrative policies specify who may add, delete, or modify the permissions of the access control system. They are "one of the most important, although less understood" aspects of access control, and "usually receive little consideration" [5]. In our model, they are fully integrated, as the conference paper review example shows.
- *Avoidance of root bottleneck.* Called 'separation of duty' in [5], this property refers to the principle that no user should be given enough privilege to misuse the system on their own. Models should facilitate the design of systems having this property.
- *Support for fine-and coarse-grained specifications* [5]. Fine-grained rules may refer to specific individuals and specific objects, and these should be supported. But allowing *only* fine-grained rules would make a model unusable; some coarse-grained mechanisms such as roles must also be supported. Our model supports fine-grained rules. It relies on a higher-level language such as the language of predicates used in the example above to express coarse-grained rules.

Our model satisfies all these properties, except the last one. It is not meant to be a language for users. It represents a low-level model of access control, which we can use to give semantics to higher-level languages such as RBAC [14], OASIS [2], and the calculus of [1].

3   Programs in Systems with Access Control

In this section we introduce a simple language which can be used to program access to systems as we described above. Programs α in it have the syntax

$$\alpha ::= \texttt{skip} \mid p := \varphi \mid \texttt{if } \varphi \texttt{ then } \alpha \texttt{ else } \alpha \mid (\alpha; \alpha) \tag{2}$$

and the usual meaning. It can be shown that adding a *loop* statement, e.g. while φ do α to this language would have no effect on its ultimate expressive power. This follows from our choice to model only finite state systems. We do not include loops in (2), because our concern is the mere existence of programs with certain properties.

3.1   Semantics of Programs

We define the semantics of programs in (2) as functions from states to states. This can be regarded as a *denotational semantics* for (2), as known from the literature (see, e.g., [12]). The ingredient of this semantics that is specific and most important to our study is a mapping describing executability of programs as the subject of access restrictions. The notation below is introduced to enable the concise definition of the semantics. Let $S = \langle P, \Sigma, \mathtt{r}, \mathtt{w} \rangle$ be a fixed access control system for the rest of this section.

Definition 2. *Substitutions are functions of the type* $P \to \mathbf{L}(P)$. *We record substitutions* f *in the form* $[f(p)/p : p \in P]$. *We often write* $[f(p)/p : p \in Q]$ *where* $Q \subset P$ *to denote* $\lambda p.\mathbf{if}\ p \in Q\ \mathbf{then}\ f(p)\ \mathbf{else}\ p$. *If* $Q = \{p_1, \ldots, p_n\}$, *then we sometimes denote* $[f(p)/p : p \in Q]$ *by* $[f(p_1)/p_1, \ldots, f(p_n)/p_n]$.

A substitution f *is extended to a function of type* $\mathbf{L}(P) \to \mathbf{L}(P)$ *by the clauses* $f(\bot) = \bot$ *and* $f(\varphi \Rightarrow \psi) = f(\varphi) \Rightarrow f(\psi)$. *We omit the parentheses in* $f(\varphi)$ *for* $\varphi \in \mathbf{L}(P)$. *Given substitutions* f *and* g, fg *denotes* $[fg(p)/p : p \in P]$. $\exists p\varphi$ *stands for* $[\bot/p]\varphi \vee [\top/p]\varphi$. $\forall p\varphi$ *stands for* $\neg \exists p \neg \varphi$. *If* $\mathrm{Var}(\varphi) = \{p_1, \ldots, p_n\}$, *then* $\exists \varphi$ *and* $\forall \varphi$ *stand for* $\exists p_1 \ldots \exists p_n \varphi$ *and* $\forall p_1 \ldots \forall p_n \varphi$, *respectively.*

Let $\mathbf{P}$ be the set of all programs in P. The function $[\![.]\!] : \mathbf{P} \to (P \to \mathbf{L}(P))$ is defined by the clauses:

$$[\![\mathbf{skip}]\!] = [p/p : p \in P] = [\ ]$$
$$[\![p := \varphi]\!] = [\varphi/p]$$
$$[\![\mathbf{if}\ \varphi\ \mathbf{then}\ \alpha\ \mathbf{else}\ \beta]\!] = [(\varphi \wedge [\![\alpha]\!](p)) \vee (\neg\varphi \wedge [\![\beta]\!](p))/p : p \in P]$$
$$[\![(\alpha; \beta)]\!] = [\![\alpha]\!][\![\beta]\!]$$

Proposition 1. *If* S *grants all the access* α *attempts, then the run of* α *from state* $s \subseteq P$ *takes* S *to state* $\{p : ([\![\alpha]\!](p))(s) = 1\}$.

Every particular step of the execution of a program can be carried out only if the respective coalition has the necessary access rights. E.g., for an assignment $p := \varphi$ to be executed, the coalition needs the right to overwrite p and read the variables occurring in φ. We define this by means of the function $[\![.,.]\!] : 2^{\Sigma} \times \mathbf{P} \to \mathbf{L}(P)$. $[\![A, \alpha]\!]$ evaluates to a formula which expresses whether the coalition A may execute the program α. $[\![.,.]\!]$ is defined by the clauses:

$$[\![A, \mathbf{skip}]\!] = \top$$
$$[\![A, p := \varphi]\!] = \mathbf{r}(\varphi, A) \wedge \mathbf{w}(p, A)$$
$$[\![A, \mathbf{if}\ \varphi\ \mathbf{then}\ \alpha\ \mathbf{else}\ \beta]\!] = \mathbf{r}(\varphi, A) \wedge (\varphi \Rightarrow [\![A, \alpha]\!]) \wedge (\neg\varphi \Rightarrow [\![A, \beta]\!])$$
$$[\![A, (\alpha; \beta)]\!] = [\![A, \alpha]\!] \wedge [\![\alpha]\!][\![A, \beta]\!]$$

Proposition 2. S *will grant coalition* $A \subseteq \Sigma$ *to execute program* α *from state* s *iff* $[\![A, \alpha]\!](s) = 1$.

Despite its ultimate simplicity, the language (2) can describe every deterministic and terminating algorithm for access to a system the considered type, as long as it is assumed that a failed access attempt can only bring general failure, and cannot be used to, e.g., draw conclusions on the state of a system for the purpose of further action. This restriction can be lifted. See the more general setting outlined in the full version of the paper [7].

3.2 Programs Which Obtain Access

Let $S = \langle P, \Sigma, \mathbf{r}, \mathbf{w} \rangle$ be a fixed access control system again, and let $\mathbf{P}$ be the set of programs (2) in the vocabulary P. Given a state $s \subseteq P$ and a $p \in P$, the truth values $r(p, A)(s)$ and $w(p, A)(s)$ indicate whether A can read and write p, respectively, *in state* s. However, it may be that A currently does not have some permission, but that A can change the state in order to obtain it. In this section we define $R_A\varphi$ and $W_A\varphi$, which denote A's ability to read/write φ by a possibly lengthy sequence of steps. Such sequences can be encoded as programs of the form (2). The ultimate ability for A to obtain the truth value of $\varphi \in \mathbf{L}(P)$ can be understood as the ability of A to run a program $\alpha \in \mathbf{P}$ that works out the value of φ and copies it into some variable p_0 such that $r(p_0, A) = w(p_0, A) = \top$. It can be expressed in terms of $[\![\alpha]\!]$ and $[\![A, \alpha]\!]$ as follows:

$$R_A\varphi \rightleftharpoons (\exists \alpha \in \mathbf{P})\forall([\![A, \alpha]\!] \wedge ([\![\alpha]\!](p_0) \Leftrightarrow \varphi)) \tag{3}$$

Similarly, the ability of A to drive the system into a state where some $\varphi \in \mathbf{L}(P)$ has a truth value of A's choosing, can be expressed by the formula

$$W_A\varphi \rightleftharpoons (\exists \alpha_\top, \alpha_\perp \in \mathbf{P})\forall([\![A, \alpha_\top]\!] \wedge [\![A, \alpha_\perp]\!] \wedge [\![\alpha_\top]\!]\varphi \wedge [\![\alpha_\perp]\!]\neg\varphi) \tag{4}$$

The universal closures $\forall$ in (3) and (4) express that α, $\alpha_\top$ and $\alpha_\perp$ are runnable and produce the stated results from all initial states. Note that R_A and W_A allow for destructive behaviour of the programs involved. Obtaining the desired goal may involve changing the state, possibly in a way which A cannot undo. In the next section, we consider a more expressive goal language in which we restrict the search to programs which are not destructive.

The formulas (3) and (4) determine the ability of A to execute a program which would achieve the goal of reading or writing φ. Quantifier prefixes like $(\exists \alpha \in \mathbf{P})$ make it hard to evaluate (3) and (4) directly. However, if S is finite, these formulas have purely propositional equivalents, and therefore can be computed mechanically, because there are only finitely many different programs in the vocabulary P modulo semantical equivalence. Of course, the enumerating all these programs in order to evaluate $(\exists \alpha \in \mathbf{P})$ is very inefficient. In Section 4 we treat R_A and W_A as special cases of a more general accessibility operator. In an appendix of [7] we describe a way to evaluate this operator, and consequently, R_A and W_A, without resorting to quantifier prefixes of the form $(\exists \alpha \in \mathbf{P})$, which is more efficient.

4   A General Accessibility Operator

Extracting information and driving a system into a state with some desired property are only the simplest goals of access. One goal cannot be treated without regard for others, because achieving a goal may have destructive side effects which prevent another goal from being achieved. That is why achieving composite goals sometimes needs to be planned with all their subgoals in mind at the same time. In this section, we consider a language for describing more refined kinds of access. Our language allows us to express boolean combinations of goals. Expressible goals include preserving the truth value of some formulas while reading or setting the truth values of others. Preservation is understood as restoring the original value of the formula in question upon the end of activities, and not necessarily keeping the value constant throughout the run of a program.

The accessibility operator in this language is written in the form $A(\Phi, \psi)$ where A is a coalition, Φ is a list of formulas in $\mathbf{L}(P)$ that A wants to read, and ψ is a *goal formula* with the syntax

$$\psi ::= \bot \mid \top \mid \mathbf{p} \mid \psi \wedge \psi \mid \psi \vee \psi \tag{5}$$

where $\mathbf{p}$ denotes an atomic goal of one of the following forms:

- $\overline{\varphi}'$, where $\varphi \in \mathbf{L}(P)$; this is the goal of making φ true.
- $\overline{\varphi}$, where $\varphi \in \mathbf{L}(P)$; this is the goal of "realising" that φ is true.

$\top$ and $\bot$ stand for a trivial goal, which calls for no action, and an unachievable goal, respectively. The goal $\psi_1 \vee \psi_2$ is regarded as achieved if either ψ_1 or ψ_2 are. The goal $\psi_1 \wedge \psi_2$ is achieved if both ψ_1 and ψ_2 are. Atomic goals of the form $\overline{\varphi}$ may fail even if A manages to obtain the truth value of φ, in case it turns out to be 0. On the other hand a goal of the form $\overline{\varphi} \vee \overline{\neg\varphi}$ can be assumed achieved without any action.

Example 3. The expression $A(\langle p \rangle, (\overline{q} \wedge \overline{q}') \vee (\overline{\neg q} \wedge \overline{\neg q}'))$ denotes that A wants to read p and *preserve* the truth value of q. If $\mathbf{r}(p, A) = q$ and $\mathbf{r}(q, A) = \mathbf{w}(q, A) = \top$, then A can achieve its goal by means of the program

```
if q then p0:=p else (q:=⊤; p0:=p; q:=⊥)
```

where p_0 is a variable dedicated to storing the value of p. Note that the program restores the value of q after temporarily setting it to 1 in order to gain access to p in the else clause of the conditional statement. The goal described by the simpler expression $A(\langle p \rangle, \top)$, which does not require q to be restored, can be achieved by the simpler program $(q:=\top; p_0:=p)$.

The formula ψ in $A(\Phi, \psi)$ can express an arbitrary relation

$$R(\overline{p_1}, \dots, \overline{p_n}; \overline{p_1}', \dots, \overline{p_n}')$$

between the initial values $\overline{p_1}, \dots, \overline{p_n}$ and the final values $\overline{p_1}', \dots, \overline{p_n}'$ of the variables $p_1, \dots, p_n$ of the system as a requirement for A to satisfy. The main difficulty in implementing the relation R in our setting is not in computing R, but to the planning of the actions needed to access the variables.

Example 4. Let $P = \{p_1, p_2, p_3\}$, $A \subseteq \Sigma$, $\mathbf{r}(p_1, A) = \neg p_2$, $\mathbf{w}(p_1, A) = p_2$, $\mathbf{r}(p_2, A) = \mathbf{w}(p_2, A) = \top$, $\mathbf{r}(p_3, A) = p_1$ and $\mathbf{w}(p_3, A) = \neg p_1$. *From any state, can A achieve a state in which the value of p_3 is inverted?* Yes; for example, this program samples the variables in order to determine what it can do, and inverts the value of p_3. A can run it from any state.

```
if p2 then (
    p1:=⊤;
    if p3 then (p1:=⊥; p3:=⊥) else (p1:=⊥; p3:=⊤)
)
```

```
else if p1 then
    if p3 then (p2:=⊤; p1:=⊥; p3:=⊥) else (p2:=⊤; p1:=⊥; p3:=⊤)
else (
    p2:=⊤; p1:=⊤;
    if p3 then (p1:=⊥; p3:=⊥) else (p1:=⊥; p3:=⊤)
)
```

The program (except for the formatting) was produced by our implementation [6].

In general, the goal $A(\Phi, \psi)$ expresses the ability of the coalition A to execute a program which reads the values of formulas in Φ, while changing the values of formulas in order to make the relation represented by ψ hold. The simple goals expressed by $R_A\varphi$ and $W_A\varphi$ can be expressed in this language:

$$R_A\varphi \Leftrightarrow A(\{\varphi\}, \top), \qquad W_A\varphi \Leftrightarrow A(\emptyset, \overline{\varphi}') \wedge A(\emptyset, \overline{\neg\varphi}').$$

In the appendix of [7] we show that the possibility (for A) to achieve $A(\Phi, \psi)$ can be decided mechanically and, if $A(\Phi, \psi)$ is achievable, a program which can be used (by A) to achieve it can be synthesised.

To demonstrate this, we add the superscripts V, T, K to goal expressions. $A^{V,T,K}(\Phi, \psi)$ expresses the existence of a program α which A can execute to read the formulas from Φ and enforce the relation represented by ψ, *provided that the initial state s of the system satisfies $s \cap V = T$* and *without going through any of the states in the list of states K*. We use the superscript triple V, T, K to express achievability of *subgoals* which can arise after some action that brings partial knowledge of the state of the system has already been taken. The list K is used to prevent considering moving to states which have already been explored. Now the original form $A(\Phi, \psi)$ can be viewed as the special case $A^{\emptyset,\emptyset,\emptyset}(\Phi, \psi)$, in which nothing is assumed about initial states. Further details are given in an appendix of [7].

Sometimes goals involve enabling the achievement of further goals. A natural way to formulate and to enable reasoning about such goals is to allow *nested occurrences* of the accessibility operator A in goal formulas ψ:

$$\psi ::= \bot \mid \top \mid \mathbf{p} \mid A(\Phi, \psi) \mid \psi \wedge \psi \mid \psi \vee \psi \tag{6}$$

Example 5. For the conference paper review system, the question of whether reviewer a of paper p can read reviewer b's review before submitting his own, may be written as:

$$\{a, b, c\}(\emptyset, \overline{\texttt{submitted}(p, b) \wedge \neg\texttt{submitted}(p, a)}' \wedge \{a\}(\langle\texttt{review}(p, b)\rangle, \overline{\texttt{submitted}(p, a)}')).$$

This formula asks: *is it possible for a, b and the chair c to reach a state s in which b has submitted his review of p but a has not yet submitted hers, and from there a may read b's review and then submit hers?* If this formula holds, we can synthesise a program for $\{a, b, c\}$ to enable $\{a\}$ to achieve $(\langle\texttt{review}(p, b)\rangle, \overline{\texttt{submitted}(p, a)}')$ from such an s. Surprisingly, the answer is "yes". PC member a can read b's review, then become appointed a subreviewer by c and submit her own review.

Since we define the achievability of a goal by a coalition as its ability to plan its actions for achieving the goal in the form of a program, one coalition can enable another coalition to achieve a goal by taking the system to a state which allows the second coalition to achieve the goal and, most importantly, passing the second coalition the knowledge of this state needed to justify its plan for achieving the goal. If Φ is the empty list $\langle \rangle$, then $A^{V,T,K'}(\Phi, B(\Phi', \psi'))$ means that A can reach a state s in which A's knowledge of s will be sufficient for B to achieve (Φ', ψ'). In case $\Phi' \neq \langle \rangle$, we assume that it is possible to achieve $A^{V,T,K'}(\Phi, B(\Phi', \psi'))$ by (I) A *sharing with B its knowledge* of a reached s described by appropriate V and T upon passing the control to B and then (II) B reading the formulas from Φ *for A*. That is why we have

$$B^{V,T,\{T\}}(\Phi' * \Phi, \psi') \Rightarrow A^{V,T,K'}(\Phi, B(\Phi', \psi'))$$

where $\Phi' * \Phi$ denotes the concatenation of Φ' and Φ. Since K is irrelevant to the description of the knowledge of coalition A on S, it does not appear on the left of $\Rightarrow$ above. Appendix A of [7] covers the extended syntax (6).

5   Conclusions

We conclude by listing some problems whose solutions can be derived from the techniques developed in this paper.

Model checking (Synthesis of attacks). Given a concrete access control system of the form $\langle P, \Sigma, \mathbf{r}, \mathbf{w} \rangle$ a recursive equation for $A(\Phi, \psi)$ from the appendix of [7] provides an algorithm to calculate the ability of a coalition A to achieve a general goal combining reading and writing variables, and, if there is such ability, to synthesise a program for A to achieve the goal. Hence it can be checked whether the system permits various forms of legitimate access, leak of data or attacks which can be written as goals of the form (Φ, ψ).

Synthesis of access control systems. Given a set of propositional variables P, a set of agents Σ and an access control policy formulated as a logical theory about $A(.,.)$ for $A \subseteq \Sigma$ on systems which have their state described in terms of the variables from P, it can be decided whether an access control system of the form $\langle P, \Sigma, \mathbf{r}, \mathbf{w} \rangle$ which implements this policy exists and, if so, definitions for its remaining components $\mathbf{r}$ and $\mathbf{w}$ can be proposed. This can be done by developing the equation from [7] into full propositional definitions of the instances of $A(.,.)$ involved in the formulation of the policy and establishing the satisfiability of the policy with respect to the applications of $\mathbf{r}$ and $\mathbf{w}$ at the respective states of the system treated as propositional variables. If the policy turns out to define a satisfiable restriction on $\mathbf{r}$ and $\mathbf{w}$, any particular pair of mappings $\mathbf{r}$ and $\mathbf{w}$ which satisfies this restriction can be chosen to complete the access control system in a way which implements the given policy.

The results from Sections 3-4 can be reproduced for systems of a general form where access is based on an arbitrary set of high-level actions. A representation of the respective access operator $A(.,.)$ like that in the appendix of [7] for the basic case can be assembled from the components used in this basic case. We proposed a way to reason about goals which involve enabling some further goals to be achieved.

The algorithms which follow from the appendix of [7] are not optimal. Results on the complexity of the problems on the class of all access control systems of the considered form might be practically unrepresentative, because instances of extreme complexity usually have little in common with typical real cases. That is why it would be interesting to describe subclasses which exhibit the kinds of regularity typical for real access control systems first.

Acknowledgements. The authors thank the anonymous referees for their helpful comments.

References

1. Martín Abadi, Michael Burrows, Butler Lampson, and Gordon Plotkin. A calculus for access control in distributed systems. *ACM Transactions on Programming Languages and Systems*, 15(4):706–734, September 1993.
2. Jean Bacon, Ken Moody, and Walt Yao. Access control and trust in the use of widely distributed services. *Lecture Notes in Computer Science*, 2218:295+, 2001. Also: *Software Practice and Experience* 33, 2003.
3. O. Bandmann, M. Dam, and B. Firozabadi. Constrained delegations. In *Proc. IEEE Symposium on Security and Privacy*, pages 131–142, 2002.
4. E. S. Barka. *Framework for Role-Based Delagation Models*. PhD thesis, George Mason University, 2002.
5. Sabrina De Capitani di Vimercati, Stefano Paraboschi, and Pierangela Samarati. Access control: principles and solutions. *Software Practice and Experience*, 33:397–421, 2003.
6. D. P. Guelev. Prolog code supporting "Model-checking access control policies". http://www.cs.bham.ac.uk/~dpg/mcacp/, November 2003.
7. D. P. Guelev, M. D. Ryan, and P. Y. Schobbens. Model-checking access control policies. http://www.cs.bham.ac.uk/~dpg/fullaclpaper.ps/, April 2004.
8. M. Harrison and W. Ruzzo. Monotonic protection systems. In *[?]*. Academic Press, New York, 1978.
9. Michael A. Harrison, Walter L. Ruzzo, and Jeffrey D. Ullman. On protection in operating systems. In *Proceedings of the fifth symposium on Operating systems principles*, pages 14–24. ACM Press, 1975.
10. Butler Lampson, Martín Abadi, Michael Burrows, and Edward Wobber. Authentication in distributed systems: Theory and practice. *ACM Transactions on Computer Systems*, 10(4):265–310, 1992.
11. R. Lipton and L. Snyder. On synchronization and security. In *[?]*. Academic Press, New York, 1978.
12. H. Riis Nielson and F. Nielson. *Semantics with Applications: A Formal Introduction*. Wiley, 1992.
13. R. Sandhu. The typed access matrix model. In *Proceedings of the IEEE Symposium on Research in Security and Privacy*, pages 122–136. IEEE Computer Society Press, 1992.
14. Ravi S. Sandhu, Edward J. Coyne, Hal L. Feinstein, and Charles E. Youman. Role-based access control models. *IEEE Computer*, 29(2):38–47, 1996.

A Distributed High Assurance Reference Monitor[*]

Extended Abstract

Ajay Chander[1], Drew Dean[2], and John Mitchell[3]

[1] DoCoMo Communications Laboratories USA, San Jose, CA 95110
[2] Computer Science Laboratory, SRI International, Menlo Park, CA 94025
[3] Computer Science Department, Stanford University, Stanford, CA 94305

Abstract. We present DHARMA, a distributed high assurance reference monitor that is generated mechanically by the formal methods tool PVS from a verified specification of its key algorithms. DHARMA supports policies that allow delegation of access rights, as well as structured, distributed names. To test DHARMA, we use it as the core reference monitor behind a web server that serves files over SSL connections. Our measurements show that formally verified high assurance access control systems are practical.

1 Introduction

One of the major landmarks in computer security research was the definition of the reference monitor as a central location for access control decisions, and the associated notion of a Trusted Computing Base (TCB)[23,38]. The classic definition of a reference monitor has three properties: (1) It is always invoked (equivalently, is unbypassable). (2) It is tamper-proof. (3) It is verifiable. Much research over the last thirty years has been done on the first [37] and second properties, but comparatively little research has appeared on the verifiability of reference monitors. Given the importance of reference monitor correctness, this state of affairs is highly regrettable. Bugs in the reference monitor have a high probability of directly compromising the security goals of the system, as they are in the control flow path for every access control decision. While a reference monitor for a file system or other resource is often part of the TCB, recent trends in extensible operating kernels [16] and proof-carrying code [30] suggest that it may be possible to move some portions of traditional reference monitor functionality out of the TCB, as long as computations done outside the TCB can be checked within the TCB.

Formal methods can be difficult and time-consuming to use, and are considered impractical for many applications. Because of the difficulty of using formal

[*] This work is supported by DARPA through SPAWAR contract N66001-00-C-8015 and by DOD University Research Initiative (URI) program administered by the Office of Naval Research under Grant N00014-01-1-0795.

K. Zhang and Y. Zheng (Eds.): ISC 2004, LNCS 3225, pp. 231–244, 2004.

methods, alternative assurance techniques have been developed [39]. Unfortunately, alternative techniques do not provide the same confidence in correctness as formal, machine-checked, proofs. That formal methods remain the "gold standard" can be seen, for example, in the Common Criteria. The paucity of general purpose operating systems evaluated at EAL7 (under any protection profile) shows the rarity of formally-verified reference monitors.

In earlier work, we presented the design of a distributed reference monitor, along with its formal verification [10]. In this paper, we use the PVS theorem proving system [32] to turn our formalization into a mechanically-generated *verified* distributed reference monitor *implementation*, that provides access control in credential chain check and search modes. As a result, our implementation provably meets a formally specified definition of security, namely, soundness and completeness *w.r.t.* a semantic access control model. We use the PVS compiler, which takes a substantial subset of the PVS specification language and generates Common Lisp.

To test the performance and functionality of the automatically generated reference monitor, we manually wrote the code to link the reference monitor with cryptographic libraries and administrative interfaces. These components were then integrated into a HTTP server. While building the test system around the verified reference monitor was not conceptually challenging, it was necessary to make a number of modifications and extensions to the tools and utilities we used. In addition to providing a working system that confirms our belief in the potential for verified components of a trusted computing base, we also produced improvements in a standard web server and cryptographic library interface that will be useful for other projects.

2   Distributed Reference Monitor Architecture

The two fundamental concepts in our policy language are access control lists (ACLs) and bounded delegation. Every resource has an associated ACL, which is a list of (subject, right, delegation bound) tuples. An ACL grants some subject a right on some object, and also specifies how far (if at all) that subject can delegate this right by specifying a non-negative integral delegation depth. As shown in previous work, the combination of ACLs and delegation depth provides an attractive compromise between revocability and decentralized control of rights [9]. Moreover, since delegation chains can be viewed as proofs certifying access to a resource, we will use the terms "proof search" and "proof check" for the delegation chain search and chain validity algorithms respectively.

Our policy supports structured distributed names. Names can refer to principals in policies, and are generated by a grammar that is independent of the authorization constructs. In particular we support linked local name spaces as defined in SPKI/SDSI [15,36], such as Alice's Bob's Doctor, which we denote by Alice.Bob.Doctor. Names compile to keys, which may appear directly in policies and proofs submitted by clients. With the addition of names, our policy language is expressive enough to subsume the core authorization and naming primitives of SPKI/SDSI.

Shared reference monitor: operational modes. Our verified reference monitor DHARMA is parameterized over a finite set of rights whose meanings are not interpreted by the reference monitor. The monitor can be used both in proof search and proof check mode. In proof check mode, the reference monitor ensures that the given evidence is sufficient to allow the requested access. In proof search mode, the reference monitor tries to construct a proof of access from the given policy.

A system deployed in a distributed setting will not know the identities of its users in advance, or have all the evidence required to generate the needed proof of access. A proof search procedure needs to access policy statements made by several resource owners (or principals). For this, we need guarantees on the validity of local policy statements, when used elsewhere in the system. While some systems use signed certificates to authenticate policy statements, DHARMA supports the authentication of principals through SSL, and allows for the collection of policy statements through secure HTTP connections. Finally, name resolution for linked local names is done through remote procedure calls over SSL. These calls are handled by "nameobjects", which contain local name definitions for the principal owning the nameobject. For example, to resolve the name `Alice.Bob` in the current context, a secure RPC call to the nameobject for `Alice` returns the key for `Alice.Bob`. Nameobjects and the name resolution function are specified within PVS, from which executable versions are automatically generated.

Access graphs: a general semantic model. The semantic model of access for this architecture is a forest of weighted, directed graphs, whose nodes are principals and edges capture policy statements (credentials). Each graph is rooted at the associated resource. The weights represent delegation depths. Given an access graph, a subject s can access a resource (o, r) if a path p exists in the graph from the node corresponding to o to the node corresponding to s, labeled with policy statements for the right r, such that the length of each subpath from a node in p down to s is no larger than the weight associated with that node. The weight condition must be satisfied at every node in the path, meaning that if d_i and d_{i+1} are weights of two consecutive nodes, then $d_{i+1} \leq d_i - 1$.

Proof engines for access. We implement the access control model using a proof system that is sound and complete for the weighted graph semantics [10]. We *prove* that subject s can access the resource (o, r), by constructing a *proof* of the assertion $\mathsf{Access}(s, o, r, d)$. Proofs start from the access policy and proceed using the proof rules in Table 1, where $\vdash$ denotes provability in the system. Access policies are expressed with similar assertions. The policy assertion $\mathsf{ACL}(A, B, r, d)$ adds A to the ACL for right r on object B, with further delegation ability d. The assertion $\mathsf{Del}(A, B, r, C, d)$ allows A to delegate a right r on object B, to principal C with further delegation depth d.

The inference rules are essentially straightforward. For example, rule (*Delegation*) can be read as: if A can access right r on resource B with the ability to delegate it further at most $(d+1)$ times, and delegates the same right to C with a delegation bound of d, then C can access right r on B and can delegate it further up to a depth of d. The last two rules are needed for completeness: if you have the ability to delegate a right n times, you can also delegate that right k times, for any $k < n$.

Structured, distributed names. Our policy language also provides support for linked local names, in the manner of SPKI/SDSI. In earlier work, we showed that soundness and completeness for an access control system that includes naming follows logically from a commutativity theorem [10] between authorization and naming constructs. Linked local names are a special case of a general approach to composition, captured by the commutativity theorem, that supports other policy constructs such as groups, roles, etc.

Our PVS effort includes a specification of linked local names and name resolution, using which we formally prove the commutativity theorem. This allowed us to formally demonstrate the soundness and completeness of the name-extended proof system, increasing confidence in an implementation that uses them directly. We note also that as a result of the commutativity theorem, policies that contain names can first be compiled into a policy containing only keys, to which the rules in Table 1 can then be applied.

Table 1. Logical rules for access judgments

(*RootACL*)	$\mathsf{ACL}(A, B, r, d) \vdash \mathsf{Access}(A, B, r, d)$
(*Delegation*)	$\mathsf{Access}(A, B, r, d+1), \mathsf{Del}(A, B, r, C, d) \vdash \mathsf{Access}(C, B, r, d)$
(*Ord1*)	$\mathsf{Access}(A, B, r, d+1) \vdash \mathsf{Access}(A, B, r, d)$
(*Ord2*)	$\mathsf{Del}(A, B, r, C, d+1) \vdash \mathsf{Del}(A, B, r, C, d)$

3   Formal Verification of Reference Monitor Using PVS

The first set of proofs within PVS ensure the soundness and completeness of our proof rules *w.r.t.* the semantic model of access graphs. These theorems relate *provability* within the proof system, denoted by $\vdash$, to *truth* in the access graph semantic model, denoted by $\models$. Formally, we capture the set of local policies relevant to the access control decision by the *world state*. We denote the minimal access graph model corresponding to a world state w by $M(w)$. Given a world state w, access graph G, subject s, object/right pair (o, r), we use the following notation:

$w \vdash s \rightarrow (o, r) \equiv$ there exists a proof of s accessing (o, r) using the logical rules
$w \models s \rightarrow (o, r) \equiv s$ can access (o, r) in the access graph model
$\quad\quad G \models w \equiv$ all accesses provable in w are also true of the access graph G

Given this, soundness and completeness can be stated as follows:

$$\text{(S)} \qquad w \vdash s \to (o, r) \Rightarrow \forall G.(G \models w) \Rightarrow G \models s \to (o, r)$$
$$\text{(C)} \quad \forall G.[G \models w \Rightarrow G \models s \to (o, r)] \Rightarrow w \vdash s \to (o, r)$$

In other words, soundness states that for any given world state w, subject s, and resource (o, r), if one can *prove* that s can access the right r on object o within the proof system, then in all semantic models (access graphs) that satisfy the world state, subject s can access the resource (o, r). Completeness can be understood as follows: let us assume that for all access graphs G, whenever G satisfies the given world state w, subject s can access resource (o, r) in the access graph. Then there exists a *proof* of $s \to (o, r)$ within the proof system. These formally verified properties increase confidence in any implementation of a reference monitor that uses these rules.

Correctness of algorithms. We obtain a verified implementation of our verified model by specifying the proof search and check algorithms in PVS, from which PVS extracts equivalent Lisp code. Thus, we avoid the implementation errors often associated with hand-coded implementations of verified models (e.g., [2]). Either algorithm can be invoked by the server or the client. Ideally, the client would use proof search (verified or otherwise) to ensure that it can access the desired resource, and the server would validate this proof using the verified proof check algorithm. This setup provides the same efficiency benefits as proof-carrying code [29,3]; instead of executable code sent by the client, we have a verifiable proof corresponding to an access request.

Soundness for the proof check (equivalently, chain validation) algorithm ensures that the logical proof of an allowed access will correspond to a valid path in the access graph. Completeness for this algorithm ensures that whenever there exists a valid path in the access graph, the proof check algorithm will validate the corresponding logical proof. Formally, given an access graph G that is a model of the world state w, $(G \models w)$, if there exists a path t of G that is equivalent to a logical proof $p \equiv w \vdash s \to (o, r)$, then soundness and completeness for this algorithm can be stated as:

$$\text{(PC\_S)} \qquad \text{check}(w, p, s, o, r) \Rightarrow \forall G.(G \models w) \Rightarrow \exists t.G \models_t s \to (o, r)$$
$$\text{(PC\_C)} \ \forall G.(G \models w) \Rightarrow \exists t.G \models_t s \to (o, r) \Rightarrow \exists p.\text{check}(w, p, s, o, r)$$

where $G \models_t s \to (o, r)$ denotes that s can access the resource (o, r) in the access graph G via the well-defined path t.

The proof search algorithm returns a proof-tree that can be checked against Table 1, thereby ensuring soundness. Completeness of this algorithm shows that if the procedure fails, then no path exists in the access graph for the access request. Using the same terminology as above, soundness and completeness for this algorithm can be stated as:

$$\text{(PS\_S)} \ \text{search}(w, s, o, r) = \text{witness}(p) \Rightarrow \forall G.(G \models w) \Rightarrow \exists t.G \models_t s \to (o, r)$$
$$\text{(PS\_C)} \qquad \text{search}(w, s, o, r) = \text{failed} \Rightarrow \forall t.\neg(G(w) \models_t s \to (o, r))$$

Soundness and completeness imply that the PVS algorithms will match our expectation of when an access should be allowed. We refer the reader to [10] for more details.

Code extraction from verified specification. A large subset of the PVS specification language can be seen as a functional language, supporting common data types such as lists and records, higher order functions, parametrization, and additional features such as dependent types, that greatly simplify proof construction. From version 2.3, PVS can generate Lisp code from the corresponding functional specification, which is guaranteed to meet the specifications if all proof obligations have been discharged. We use this capability to generate implementations of the proof check and proof search algorithms in DHARMA from their verified PVS specification. In addition to soundness and completeness, type correctness condition proofs ensure the termination of the recursively defined proof check and search functions.

4   A Policy-Driven Web-Based File Server

Our PVS specification allowed us to automatically generate the verified reference monitor DHARMA. To study its applicability, we instrumented a HTTP server with DHARMA. The enhanced server allows for editing of local policies, remote management of policy databases, and access control via proof check and proof search.

Infrastructure. We chose Franz's Allegro Common Lisp and AllegroServe HTTP server [21] as our research infrastructure. Due to AllegroServe's provision of a hook for the authorization of each HTTP request, integrating DHARMA was easy to do. We enhanced the Allegro Common Lisp OpenSSL binding to support client authentication.

Enhancing the server with DHARMA. We use AllegroServe's authorizer framework to integrate DHARMA with AllegroServe. Files are published in AllegroServe by associating one or more entities with the file. An entity is a Common Lisp object which handles *all* requests for the file, and can have a number of attributes related to pre-loading, caching, the time-out for serving the file, etc. Each entity also has a hook for an authorizer object, which can be any Lisp function. When a client connects to the port on which AllegroServe is listening, AllegroServe passes that connected socket to a free worker thread that has access to the local policy. The worker thread locates the entity that is associated with the request; if an entity is found and has an authorizer, it calls the authorizer function to decide if this client should be allowed to access the selected file.

We instantiated the authorizer functions for the entities of each published resource with our verified DHARMA proof search and proof check functions. Based on whether or not the client has presented a proof, the appropriate function (proof check and proof search, respectively) is invoked. The client's public key, name, and URI of the requested resource are passed to the function. We also need to authenticate the client, and perform distributed name resolution when the presented proof contains linked local names.

Leveraging AllegroServe's request protocol in this manner allows us to express the security guarantees provided by the web server in terms of the security properties of the reference monitor DHARMA. The fact that AllegroServe is programmed in a functional style in Lisp allowed us to quickly audit its source code and assure ourselves that DHARMA is invoked before *any* resource is served by the enhanced web-server. This source code audit is, of course, far short of a formal proof of security for the DHARMA-enhanced AllegroServe. Such a proof would be important for production use of a high-assurance system; however, it is outside the scope of this work. We also note that the context in which AllegroServe operates may be vulnerable to other attacks; for example, an attacker may gain root access to the machine and replace the DHARMA-enhanced web server with an insecure server. The research described here is focused on providing assurance for a critical software component, the reference monitor, even as we remain cognizant of other attacks on the larger system containing DHARMA.

Managing local policy databases. A resource owner may not have all the certificates required to decide on an access request. We provide the ability to add delegation policy statements to a *local* policy database after authenticating the signer of the statement against the subjects mentioned in the body of the statement. For example, to add the statement which says that A adds B to its ACL for a particular right, it must be signed by A. Checking signatures in this manner is equivalent to implementing the logical operator "says" used in other treatments [1] of distributed authorization. DHARMA supports this by using a POST method over a SSL-secured HTTP connection. In addition to such peer exchange of credentials, a resource host can edit its own local policy as reflected in the files and their authorizers published through AllegroServe.

Distributed name resolution. As mentioned earlier, our policy language supports linked local names. Local name resolution is provided via nameobjects that are generated automatically from their PVS specification. Since PVS doesn't have native support for remote procedure calls, we provided this by means of a *semantic attachment* to the PVS specification. A semantic attachment is an external piece of code that is declared but not defined within a PVS specification. The hand-written implementation of the semantic attachment is linked with the PVS code generated for the nameobjects at the different peer sites. This hand-written code was a few lines that set up Allegro Lisp RPC sockets, connecting the PVS-generated local name resolution function on one nameobject to the same function running on another nameobject. Our handling of nested RPC calls, such as those involved in resolving the name $A.B.C$, is iterative; this allows us to detect if a specific nameobject is unresponsive, and provides a way of caching keys corresponding to intermediate names such as $A.B$.

Table 2. Baseline performance (requests served / second) for AllegroServe and Apache

		Size of file		
Protocol	Server	1B	8KB	100KB
HTTP	AllegroServe	613	430	90
	Apache	431	417	104
HTTPS	AllegroServe	128	101	38
	Apache	101	95	54
ACL	AllegroServe	125	99	38
	Apache	96	92	52

5   Measurements

To measure the cost of adding DHARMA to a HTTP server, we performed a series of measurements. First, to get a baseline, we compared the performance of AllegroServe to Apache, both with and without SSL support. Then, we measured the cost of adding either proof check or proof search while handling file requests. Finally, we measured the cost of resolving linked local names in a distributed setting, as part of checking the proof presented with the access request. This series of measurements allowed us to identify the costs of individual additions to the original web server, and point to performance limits as well as areas where optimization would produce the most benefit. All measurements were performed on a dual Xeon machine, with 2GB of RAM, running at 2.8GHz with hyperthreading enabled. The machine was running Redhat Linux 7.3, kernel version 2.4.18. We used AllegroServe version 1.2.26, and Apache version 2.0.47 with the mod_ssl module. Measurements used version 0.8 of the httperf tool [28] that was slightly modified to support sending client certificates as per [35].

Distributed name resolution. We found AllegroServe to be a well-architected, high-performance web-server that performed well on our tests. We made three representative measurements, for file sizes of 8Kbytes (text page), 100Kbytes (image), and 1byte (minimal HTTP payload processing time). Table 2 shows the throughput for the different servers, for serving files of different sizes over HTTP and HTTPS connections.

To estimate the relative cost of adding a Lisp reference monitor to AllegroServe with a C-based one, we compared the performance for DHARMA-enhanced AllegroServe that does proof search over a policy database containing only ACLs, and ACL-based access control in Apache using SSLRequire directives. For a set of 100 credentials, we measured a 2.4% performance hit for AllegroServe, and 3.8% for Apache. These numbers suggest that our measurements in the following sections reflect the intrinsic cost of the algorithms, rather than the choice of Lisp for the reference monitor.

Adding proof check. Figure 1 measures the cost of verified proof check in DHARMA-enhanced AllegroServe. This is a crucial measurement, as it is a fundamental guarantee of assurance. A proof presented by a client will have to be

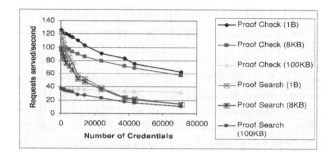

Fig. 1. Requests per second for DHARMA-enhanced AllegroServe

validated by the verified proof check code, irrespective of the algorithm used for proof search.

For our measurements, we varied the number of principals and the number of credentials (policy statements) in the generated policy database. The proof check algorithm checks every step of the presented proof against this database, in addition to checking whether each pair of successive steps represents a valid application of one of the rules in Table 1. The policy database is represented as lists within PVS; we can see the effect of searching through longer lists as the number of credentials increases.

Our measurements show that verified proof check using DHARMA scales very well. For access control scenarios in corporations with up to 5000 credentials, the expected performance hit is only 5% for an average file size of 8KB. If the average resource size is higher, then even more credentials can be supported with the same penalty. An optimization is to specify the policy database as a hashtable within PVS, which would allow for nearly constant proof check time.

Adding proof search. Proof search is the most expensive operation in DHARMA. Figure 1 measures the times for verified proof search for different combinations of policy and file sizes. Our proof search algorithm is equivalent to a breadth first search on the size of the access graph, and thus is linear in the number of credentials which may grow as $\Theta(N^3)$ in an access graph with N principals. In our measurements for both proof search and proof check, we generated a policy database by limiting the degree of nodes in the access graph to between 3 and 20, depending on the total number of principals. The degree estimates how many other principals a given principal would add to an ACL for a resource controlled by itself, and to how many principals it would pass on a delegated access. In other words, a principal may have upto 20 other principals on its ACL, *and* pass on rights to 20 principals for resources it doesn't own.

In contrast with proof check, proof search over a database of 5000 credentials has an expected performance penalty of about 40%. The contrast is more pronounced with higher policy sizes; 15000 credentials corresponds to only a 17% performance penalty for proof check in DHARMA, but 110% for proof search. These numbers for verified proof search correspond to the best known algorithm for proof search in policies without extended names [13], and thus reflect the complexity of the underlying algorithm, as opposed to the performance of the generated code.

Adding name resolution via RPC. Finally, we considered the cost of resolving linked local names through remote procedure call, when they appear in the proof presented by the client. Setting up an SSL-secured channel over RPC incurred significant cost; for scenarios in which the presented proof contained *only one* linked local name, where each name resolution request is handled by a different server, DHARMA was only able to handle 11 requests per second initiated by an individual client. The other extreme, when all name resolution requests are handled by a single server using the same secured RPC channel, results in DHARMA being able to handle 80 requests per second. Recall that in the absence of names, DHARMA can handle 125 requests per second.

Our measurements show that name resolution during proof check imposes a significant penalty, in the absence of a central name server. Thus, when using DHARMA with a different proof search algorithm that can handle names in credentials, we suggest compiling the final proof containing names to one that has only keys. This compiled proof can then be validated against a database that contains the equivalent name-resolved credentials, without compromising security.

Discussion. Our experience with DHARMA shows that the TCB can be augmented with a verified reference monitor that provides proof check functionality, without significant penalties. In addition to intranet scenarios discussed earlier, this benefit scales well to wide-area services such as electronic subscription-based publishing as only the sizes of local policy tables *in the presented proof* affect the cost of proof check. However, adding proof search to the TCB has significant cost, as a result of the complexity of the proof search algorithm. For the case of credentials that contain names, the optimal search algorithms are cubic in the number of *credentials* [13,24], which would further worsen performance if included in the TCB. If the result returned by the search algorithm is validated by the verified proof checker, then the search algorithm itself doesn't provide any additional assurance. Given the lower bounds on these search algorithms, we suggest implementing the search algorithm as efficiently as possible outside the TCB, and validating the result by the verified proof checker inside the TCB.

We notice from the name resolution measurements that there is a significant penalty for making remote calls for name resolution. A system with greater delegation depth in policies may have longer proofs of access on the average, which would multiplicatively increase this name resolution cost. Since search algorithms with named credentials are already more expensive, we suggest providing name-resolved proofs to the server while accessing a resource. One option for the infrastructure to support this is for the principals in the system to attach name resolution credentials together with the authorization credentials as part of the proof of access presented with the request. SPKI/SDSI-style name credentials that attest to the (local name, key value) binding in a nameobject, can be directly used for this purpose. Servers may also advertise "recency requirements" on credentials that they are willing to accept, which can guide the rate at which principals refresh their credentials. Another observation is that performance is much improved by having a single name server, since the cost of secure channel setup is shared amongst several name resolution requests. This points to an architecture with a few back-end "resolution servers" available to all DHARMA-enhanced web servers.

6   Related Work

Early work in formal methods, such as the Stanford Pascal Verifier [26], and Ina Jo [25] employed separate specification and implementation languages. Gypsy [18] was an early system that provided separate specification and implementation languages, and a compiler from its implementation language to executable code. Approaches such as Sannella's Extended ML system [22] integrate axiomatic specifications with Standard ML programs. The Design/CPN tool has been used to compile a colored Petri net specification of a centralized access control system into ML code [27], but lacks full verification support. Some recent work in model checking system code [11,12] has approached the problem by extracting specifications from actual code.

There is a rich history of security kernel designs from the late 1970s and early 1980s, including the provably secure operating system PSOS [31] and the kernelized secure operating system (KSOS), which was implemented in Modula-2,and specified *separately* as a finite state machine. The PSOS-inspired KSOS went through several future generations, and begot SCOMP [17] (KSOS-6), KSOS-11 [5], VIKING [20], and the Secure Ada Target [8]. Gutmann presents the verification of a reference monitor based kernel [19] using assertion-based testing tools and hierarchical design methods; in comparison, we provide provable compliance to a formal definition of security.

Several access control systems with support for decentralized policies have been built, though none provide strong assurance guarantees or report performance studies. The two best known are PolicyMaker [7] and KeyNote [6], with SPKI/SDSI [36,15] being the most analyzed. Clarke [14] integrated an existing C language implementation of SPKI/SDSI into the Apache HTTP server, but didn't provide actual system measurements. We note that a very early version of linked local names appears in Reed's Ph.D. thesis [34]; his implementation is very similar to our implementation of nameobjects and name resolution (see Section 4.) Proof-carrying authentication [3,4] provides a general-purpose higher-order *undecidable* logic for distributed access control, and is implemented in the proof-checker Twelf[33], but is not formally verified.

7   Conclusions

Building on our previous work on the formal analysis of access control policies, we used PVS to generate a *verified* reference monitor. We then *integrated* this monitor into a web server that checks SSL certificates, resolves names against a set of hierarchical local namespaces, and determines whether to allow an access request. The timing results in Section 5 show that the verified system has acceptable performance in proof check mode when certificate chains are supplied as input. For greater efficiency, we can replace the verified proof search function with hand-coded C, since the output of the search process is a certificate chain that is checked by our verified reference monitor. The results of Section 5 suggest that an architecture with a few public name resolution servers mitigates the cost of setting up per-name secure connections in a distributed access control system, making the performance of the verified chain validation acceptable in the presence of linked local names.

References

1. Martín Abadi, Michael Burrows, Butler Lampson, and Gordon Plotkin. A calculus for access control in distributed systems. *TOPLAS*, 15(4):706–734, September 1993.
2. James P. Anderson. Computer security technology planning study. Technical Report ESD-TR-73-51, U.S. Air Force, Electronic Systems Division, Deputy for Command and Management Systems, HQ Electronic Systems Division (AFSC), L. G. Hanscom Field, Bedford, MA 01730 USA, October 1972. Volume 2, pages 58–69.
3. Andrew W. Appel and Edward W. Felten. Proof-carrying authentication. In *ACM Conference on Computer and Communications Security*, pages 52–62, 1999.
4. Lujo Bauer, Michael A. Schneider, and Edward W. Felten. A general and flexible access-control system for the web. In *Proc. of the 11th USENIX Security Symposium*, San Francisco, CA, August 2002.
5. T.A. Berson and G.L. Barksdale. KSOS: Development methodology for a secure operating system. In *National Computer Conference*, pages 365–371. AFIPS Conference Proc., 1979. Vol. 48.
6. M. Blaze, J. Feigenbaum, and A. D. Keromytis. KeyNote: Trust management for public-key infrastructures. In *Proc. of the 1998 Security Protocols Workshop*, volume 1550 of *Lecture Notes in Computer Science*, pages 59–63, 1999.
7. Matt Blaze, Joan Feigenbaum, and Jack Lacy. Decentralized trust management. In *Proc. of the 1996 IEEE Symposium on Research in Security and Privacy*, pages 164–173, Oakland, CA, May 1996.
8. W. E. Boebert, R. Y. Kain, W.D. Young, and S.A. Hansohn. Secure Ada target: Issues, system design, and verification. In *Proc. of the 1985 IEEE Symposium on Security and Privacy*, pages 176–190, Oakland, CA, May 1985.
9. Ajay Chander, Drew Dean, and John Mitchell. A state-transition model of trust management and access control. In *Proc. of the 14th IEEE Computer Security Foundations Workshop*, pages 27–43, June 2001.
10. Ajay Chander, Drew Dean, and John C. Mitchell. Reconstructing trust management. *Journal of Computer Security*, 12(1):131–164, 2004.
11. Hao Chen and David Wagner. MOPS: An infrastructure for examining security properties of software. In *Proc. of the 9th ACM Conference on Computer and Communication Security*, pages 235–244, Washington D.C., November 2002.
12. Hao Chen, David Wagner, and Drew Dean. Setuid demystified. In *Proc. of the 11th USENIX Security Symposium*, pages 171–190, San Francisco, CA, August 2002.

13. D. Clarke, J.-E. Elien, C. Ellison, M. Fredette, A. Morcos, and R.L.Rivest. Certificate chain discovery in SPKI/SDSI. *Journal of Computer Security*, 9(4):285–322, 2001.

14. Dwaine E. Clarke. SPKI/SDSI http server / certificate chain discovery in SPKI/SDSI. Master's thesis, Massachusetts Institute of Technology, 2001.

15. C. Ellison, B. Frantz, B. Lampson, R. Rivest, B. Thomas, and T. Ylonen. SPKI certificate theory. RFC 2693, September 1999.

16. Dawson R. Engler, M. Frans Kaashoek, and James O'Toole Jr. Exokernel: an operating system architecture for application-level resource management. In *Proc. of the 15th ACM Symposium on Operating Systems Principles (SOSP '95)*, pages 251–266, Copper Mountain, CO, December 1995.

17. L. J. Fraim. SCOMP: A solution to the multilevel security problem. *IEEE Computer*, 16(7):26–34, July 1983.

18. Donald I. Good, Ralph L. London, and W. W. Bledsoe. An interactive program verification system. *IEEE Transactions on Software Engineering*, 1(1):59–67, March 1975.

19. Peter Gutmann. *The Design and Verification of a Cryptographic Security Architecture*. PhD thesis, Department of Computer Science, University of Auckland, August 2000.

20. Bret Hartman. A Gypsy-based kernel. In *Proc. of the 1984 IEEE Symposium on Security and Privacy*, pages 219–225, Oakland, CA, May 1984.

21. John Foderaro. AllegroServe – A Web Application Server (Franz. Inc.). `http://allegroserve.sourceforge.net/`.

22. S. Karhs, D. Sannella, and A. Tarlecki. The definition of Extended ML: a gentle introduction. *Theoretical Computer Science*, 173:445–484, 1997.

23. Butler Lampson. Protection. In *Proc. of the 5th Annual Princeton Conference on Information Sciences and Systems*, pages 437–443, Princeton University, 1971.

24. Ninghui Li, Will Winsborough, and John C. Mitchell. Distributed credential chain discovery in trust management. *Journal of Computer Security*, 11(1):35–86, 2003.

25. R. Locasso, J. Scheid, D. V. Schorre, and P. R. Eggert. *The Ina Jo Specification Language Reference Manual*. System Development Corporation, Santa Monica, CA, November 1980.

26. D. C. Luckham, S. M. German, F. W. von Henke, R. A. Karp, P. W. Milne, D. C. Oppen, W. Polak, and W. L. Scherlis. Stanford Pascal Verifier user manual. CSD Report STAN-CS-79-731, Stanford University, Stanford, CA, March 1979.

27. Kjeld H. Mortensen. Automatic code generation method based on coloured petri net models applied on an access control system. In *Lecture Notes in Computer Science: 21st International Conference on Application and Theory of Petri Nets (ICATPN 2000), Aarhus, Denmark, June 2000*, volume 1825, pages 367–386. Springer-Verlag, 2000.

28. David Mosberger and Tai Jin. httperf: A tool for measuring web server performance. In *First Workshop on Internet Server Performance*, pages 59–67. ACM, June 1998.

29. George C. Necula. Proof-carrying code. In *Conference Record of POPL '97: The 24th ACM Symposium on Principles of Programming Languages*, pages 106–119, Paris, France, Jan 1997.

30. George C. Necula and Peter Lee. Safe kernel extensions without run-time checking. In USENIX, editor, *2nd Symposium on Operating Systems Design and Implementation (OSDI '96), October 28–31, 1996. Seattle, WA*, pages 229–243, Berkeley, CA, USA, 1996. USENIX.

31. Peter G. Neumann, Robert S. Boyer, Richard J. Feiertag, Karl N. Levitt, and Lawrence Robinson. A provably secure operating system: The system, its applications, and proofs. Technical Report CSL-116, 2nd Ed., SRI International, May 1980.

32. S. Owre, N. Shankar, J. M. Rushby, and D. W. J. Stringer-Calvert. *PVS Language Reference, Version 2.3*. SRI International, September 1999. http://pvs.csl.sri.com/.

33. Frank Pfenning and Carsten Schürmann. System description: Twelf — A metalogical framework for deductive systems. In *Proc. of the 16th International Conference on Automated Deduction (CADE-16)*, pages 202–206, Trento, Italy, 1999. Springer-Verlag LNAI 1632.

34. D. P. Reed. Naming and synchronization in a decentralized computer system. Technical Report MIT/LCS/TR-205, Massachusetts Institute of Technology, September 1978. Also Ph.D. thesis.

35. Eric Rescorla. An introduction to OpenSSL programming, Part I. Originally appeared in the Linux Journal; http://www.rtfm.com/openssl-examples/part1.pdf, 2001.

36. Ron Rivest and Butler Lampson. SDSI–A Simple Distributed Security Infrastructure. http://theory.lcs.mit.edu/~rivest/sdsi11.html, October 1996.

37. John Rushby. Noninterference, transitivity, and channel-control policies. Technical Report SRI-CSL-92-02, SRI International, December 1992.

38. U.S. D.O.D. *Trusted Computer System Evaluation Criteria ('Orange Book')*. 1983.

39. Gary Vecellio and Willian Thomas. Issues in the assurance of component-based software. In *Proc. of the 2000 Workshop on Continuing Collaborations for Successful COTS Development (ICSE2000)*, Limerick, Ireland. wwwsel.iit.nrc.ca/projects/cots/icse2000wkshp/Papers/14.pdf.

Using Mediated Identity-Based Cryptography to Support Role-Based Access Control[*]

D. Nali, C. Adams, and A. Miri

School of Information Technology and Engineering (SITE)
University of Ottawa, Canada
{deholo,cadams,samiri}@site.uottawa.ca

Abstract. We suggest a scheme to cryptographically support *role based access control* (*RBAC*) in large organizations where user roles change frequently. To achieve this, we propose a secure method to manage role keys and we extend a recent pairing-based mediated identity-based cryptographic scheme to allow the enforcement of possession of multiple roles to access certain documents. We also design an architecture and a set of algorithms which cryptographically enforce *RBAC* and allow for role addition, revocation, and delegation. Finally, we briefly discuss the space requirements and security of our scheme.

1 Introduction

Providing information confidentiality and privacy based on highly dynamic user roles and privileges is a major current challenge for large organizations. To deal with this challenge, we show, in this paper, how to support role-based access control by the use of pairing-based mediated identity-based cryptography.

1.1 Background Information

This section motivates our research contributions. We present an overview of role-based access control (*RBAC*), mediated identity-based public-key cryptography, and the concept of pairing-based virtual keys, arguing that the last two can suitably support *RBAC*.

Role-Based Access Control. Role-based access control (*RBAC*) [4] is a methodology to manage the access to resources of a system. The well-known efficiency of RBAC relies on the insightful suggestion that users having identical privileges be grouped in classes called *roles*. *RBAC* also suggests that roles be organized in a hierarchy, in order to support privilege inheritance. Moreover, *RBAC* allows for roles and privileges to be activated and deactivated. Thus, access privileges can be given only when required. Furthermore, role activation

---

[*] This work was partially supported by Canada's National Sciences and Engineering Research Council.

K. Zhang and Y. Zheng (Eds.): ISC 2004, LNCS 3225, pp. 245–256, 2004.

246 D. Nali, C. Adams, and A. Miri

makes it possible to require that users deactivate certain roles before exercising others (thereby realizing the so-called *Separation-of-Duty* principle).

Typically, *RBAC* is used as follows: users of a system interact with an access control manager (*ACM*) which enforces predefined access control policies. Thus, the *ACM* verifies users credentials and, when the credentials are both trustworthy and sufficient, the *ACM* sends cleartext copies of confidential information to users. One disadvantage of such a pure-policy-based implementation of *RBAC* is that the *ACM* must perform the role-based credential verification at each confidential information request. Another disadvantage is the absence of protection against eavesdropping of protected information sent by the *ACM* to users.

Mediated Identity-Based Public-Key Cryptography. Public-key cryptography can be used to improve the above access control scheme. In this alternative paradigm, a private-public key pair is assigned to each role. The *ACM* encrypts confidential documents with the public keys of the roles required to access the documents. Then, the *ACM* sends copies of the encrypted documents to users. Finally, each user receives her roles' private keys, and uses them to decrypt confidential documents which she is authorized to access.

Since traditional public key schemes (such as *RSA* and *ElGamal*) require the use of (seemingly random) public keys, certain data structures called *digital certificates* are typically used to bind role identifiers with public keys. However, it is well known that the generation, storage and management of revoked and non-revoked digital certificates can be extremely cumbersome. Consequently, the use of identity-based public-key cryptographic schemes has been suggested to address the challenges induced digital certificates. Indeed, identity-based public keys can take arbitrary string values, including role identifiers. Thus, the need for digital certificates can be avoided.

Another issue to consider when cryptographically supporting *RBAC* is the so-called *ex-role-membership* problem. This problem arises when, after a user role r is revoked, the user can still access confidential information requiring r (because she may still hold the decryption key associated with r). To address this issue, mediated cryptography has recently been suggested by Boneh et al. [3,2]. The suggestion is that each decryption require the active cooperation of a user and an online trusted entity called the *security mediator* (*SEM*). *SEMs* are created by a central authority (denoted PKG^1), assigned a set of users, and given a secret share of these users' decryption keys, while the complementary shares are given to the users. Thus, users are grouped around *SEMs* with which they must interact during decryption. When the central authority wants to revoke a user, it simply notifies the appropriate *SEM* to stop interacting with the user. Thus, mediated cryptography supports *instantaneous* user privilege revocation, unlike architectures where multiple authorities deliver full decryption keys to users. Recently, Libert and Quisquater [5] suggested a pairing-based[2] mediated

---

[1] *Private Key Generator*

[2] The term *pairing-based* reflects the fact that the mediated identity-based scheme of Libert and Quisquater uses a Bilinear map also known as *pairing*.

identity-based scheme allowing *SEMs* to be *semi-trusted* entities, in the sense that their compromise only affects the security of the partial keys which they hold. This scheme (henceforth denoted *IB-mBF*) improves a previous one (denoted *IB-mRSA*) in which the compromise of a *SEM* caused a total security failure of the underlying cryptosystem [3,2].

Consequently, pairing-based mediated identity-based cryptography can suitably be used to support *RBAC*, since arbitrary role identifiers can be used as public keys, and since user decryption capabilities can be instantaneously revoked by the *ACM*. In particular, remark that, while *fast* revocation of security privileges may be sufficient in many contexts, fine-grained *instantaneous* revocation of security capabilities is crucial for *RBAC* to support dynamic *separation of duty*. Hence, pairing-based mediated cryptography is extremely suitable for *RBAC*.

Virtual Keys and *RBAC*. Also helpful in the cryptographic support of *RBAC* are pairing-based virtual keys. Introduced recently by Chen et al. [1], pairing-based virtual keys exploit the additive property of keys in pairing-based identity-based cryptographic schemes. Among the various applications of virtual keys, one -called *legal hoop jumping*- is particularly suitable for *RBAC*. *Legal hoop jumping* essentially refers to the enforcement of multiple conditions determined by multiple *PKGs*, in a pairing-based identity-based cryptosystem. To achieve this, an encryptor uses the sum of these *PKGs*' public keys as the public-key encryption component. Then, the decryptor must interact with the same *PKGs* and add the corresponding decryption keys in order to recover the original plaintext. Thus, since document access often requires multiple roles in *RBAC*, virtual keys are suitable to this context.

As a consequence, both pairing-based mediated identity-based public key cryptography and pairing-based virtual keys are suitable for *RBAC* support.

1.2 Outline

The sequel is organized as follows: section 2 outlines our contributions; section 3, presents our *RBAC*-supporting scheme; section 4 briefly discusses various aspects of our scheme, and section 5, concludes the paper.

2 Contributions

Our main contribution is the proposal of a scheme which cryptographically supports *RBAC* by the use of pairing-based identity-based mediated cryptography.

To achieve this, we proceed as follows: first, we propose an assignment of role key shares to *SEMs* which minimizes the security threats of *SEM* corruption; second, we use the concept of virtual keys to extend Libert and Quisquater's scheme [5], in order to enforce the possession of multiple roles for the access of certain documents; third, we architecturally and functionally describe an infrastructure which cryptographically supports *RBAC* and allows for role addition, revocation, and delegation.

2.1 Key Assignment

Our first contribution is the suggestion of a role key assignment which is robust against *SEM* compromise. In the following paragraphs, we justify the benefits of our choice.

Recall that the *SEM* architecture was originally proposed as a solution to instantaneously revoke users of a public key cryptosystem. Then, it was pointed out that the *SEM* architecture may also be used to revoke fine-grained user security capabilities. In this sense, the *SEM* architecture is directly applicable to *RBAC*. Let us then make this direct application more explicit.

Role keys are used instead of user keys. Moreover, with each local group of users is associated a (*semi-trusted*) *SEM* which holds shares of all these users's role (decryption) keys. As a consequence, the compromise of *SEM* by any of its users allows the attacker to hold *SEM* key shares of potentially many roles he or she did not have. These *SEM* key shares may then be used by the attacker, when he or she illicitly acquires the corresponding user key shares. Moreover, by impersonating the compromised *SEM*, the attacker may deny decryption capability to many users who want to access documents requiring the compromised roles. To address this security concern, we suggest an alternative role key assignment to *SEMs*.

Our suggestion is that each role be associated with a *collection* of (*semi-trusted*) *SEMs*, each of which holds a secret share of the corresponding role's (decryption) key. Moreover, we recommend that each group of local users be assigned to a set of local *SEMs* in such a way that each user is associated with the *SEMs* corresponding to its top[3] roles. Furthermore, each *SEM* is suggested to manage both its role and sub-roles. Thus, if a *SEM* is broken into, only the corresponding role and its sub-roles are compromised.

Note that this alternative key assignment combines the following three benefits: *Locality of SEMs* (since users only deal with *local SEMs*), *Interaction with a minimal number of SEMs* (since users only interact with *SEMs* representing their *top* roles), and *Robustness against SEM compromise* (since the compromise of *SEM* only affects the corresponding role and its sub-roles).

As a consequence, our role key assignment enables a more secure use of pairing-based identity-based mediated cryptography to support role-based access control. However, this alternative key assignment brings the necessity that users simultaneously deal with multiple *SEMs* when they need to access a document which requires the possession of multiple roles. Therefore, the original scheme of Libert and Quisquater [5] needs to be extended accordingly, as we explain next.

---

[3] Recall that, in the context of *RBAC*, it can be assumed that roles are organized in a partially ordered hierarchy, so that each user has a set of maximal roles (also called *top roles*).

2.2   Extended Cryptographic Scheme

Our second contribution is the extension of Libert and Quisquater's mediated scheme [5] to handle the case in which a user must interact with many *SEMs* in order to decrypt a document. Such a situation is likely to happen often in *RBAC* since, in this context, document access often requires many roles.

As a remark, note that our extension of *IB-mBF* may have other applications than the cryptographic support of *RBAC*.

In order to handle the case of cooperative interaction with multiple *SEMs* for decryption purposes, we make use of the concept of virtual keys. Indeed, we saw in section 2 that virtual keys exploit the additive property of the key space in pairing-based cryptographic schemes. More precisely, virtual keys are sums of keys. Thus, note that key shares also can be added to form *virtual key shares*. What is even more interesting is that *partial SEM decryptions* may also be added and used to complete the decryption process, without any malicious malleability security concern.

This absence of malleability security concern is due to the fact that, in the decryption completion process of *IB-mBF*, the partial decryption token is applied to a cryptographic Hash function.

As a result, the observation that not only decryption keys, but also partial decryptions can be added to form *virtual decryption keys* and *virtual partial decryption* leads to an extension of Libert and Quisquater's scheme. This extended scheme is then used as a convenient way to handle cooperative decryption when *RBAC* is supported by pairing-based identity-based mediated cryptography. In fact, such an extension would also be required in order to handle multiple access requirements, even if the straightforward role key assignment was used.

In section 2.3, we show how our key assignment and our extension of *IB-mBF* can be used in a scheme which cryptographically supports the various features of *RBAC*.

2.3   *RBAC* Scheme

Our third contribution is the design of a scheme which comprehensively and cryptographically supports *RBAC*.

In particular, there is a need to propose an access control architecture and a set of processes which handle not only access control, but also role addition, revocation and delegation.

In the next section, we describe such an access control architecture, explaining how to implement our key assignment. We also describe an access control scheme, using our extension of *IB-mBF*. Finally, we present a set of procedures to handle role management, distinguishing individual user role changes from role changes which affect all users of a system. In particular, we describe algorithms for role addition, revocation and delegation.

3   Suggested RBAC Scheme

In this section, we present a scheme which cryptographically and comprehensively supports $RBAC$ using pairing based identity-based mediated cryptrography.

3.1   Architectural Description

Our $RBAC$ scheme makes use of two main components: a Role Manager (RM) and a Database Manager (DBM).

Role Manager. The RM is responsible for maintaining the role hierarchy of a given organization. When role or privilege changes are to be made, the adjustments are performed at the RM's level. The RM also maintains, for each role, a collection of security mediators ($SEMs$). The RM assigns each system user to a set of local $SEMs$ associated with the user's top roles. Moreover, each SEM is responsible for both its role and descendant roles.

Database Manager. The DBM is responsible for managing the system's database. In particular, the DBM publishes a *description table* (DT) of all (protected) resources accessible by system users. This DT points to the actual resources and indicates, for each resource, the roles required to access it. The specification of these roles is a responsibility of the DBM. Finally, the DBM maintains a *cipher table* (CT) of all ciphered data recently sent to users.

3.2   Functional Description

Our scheme is specified by a *System Setup* algorithm, a *Role-Based Access Control* procedure, and a set of *Role Management* methods dealing with role addition, revocation and delegation. In the following sections, we describe each of these functions.

System Setup. The RM has the role of the PKG in a pairing-based identity-based mediated cryptographic scheme. It first generates system-wide parameters, as done in the *Setup* algorithm of Libert and Quisquater [5]:

> Given a security parameter k, the RM chooses groups $\mathcal{G}_1$ and $\mathcal{G}_2$ of prime order q, a generator P of $\mathcal{G}_1$, a bilinear map $\hat{e} : \mathcal{G}_1 \times \mathcal{G}_2$ and a master-key $s \in F_q^*$. It then computes $P_{pub} = sP$ and chooses hash functions
> $$\mathcal{H}_1 : \{0,1\}^* \to \mathcal{G}_2, \qquad \mathcal{H}_2 : \mathcal{G}_2 \to \{0,1\}^n$$
> $$\mathcal{H}_3 : \{0,1\}^n \times \{0,1\}^n \to Z_q^*, \quad \mathcal{H}_4 : \{0,1\}^n \to \{0,1\}^n$$
> where n denotes the size of plaintexts. The system's public parameters are
> $$\mathcal{P} = (P, n, P_{pub}, \mathcal{H}_1, \mathcal{H}_2, \mathcal{H}_3, \mathcal{H}_4)$$
> (and must be certified by a CA) while the master-key s is kept secret by the RM.

Then, for each role ID_i, the RM generates a key $d_{ID_i} = s\mathcal{H}_1(ID_i)$ and a pair $(d_{ID_i,sem}, d_{ID_i,user})$ of key shares, where $d_{ID_i,user}$ is randomly chosen in $\mathcal{G}_1^*$ and $d_{ID_i,sem} = d_{ID_i} - d_{ID_i,user}$.

The RM also creates, for each role, a collection of security mediators ($SEMs$). Thus, the RM assigns each system user to a set of local $SEMs$ associated with the user's top roles. For each role ID_i, the RM gives both $d_{ID_i,sem}$ and its sub-role decryption key shares to the $SEMs$ associated with ID_i; moreover, the RM gives $d_{ID_i,user}$ to the users entitled to ID_i. As a consequence, each user obtains a key share of his/her roles, and each SEM obtains the key shares of both its role and sub-roles.

Role-Based Access Control. When a user $\mathcal{A}$ wants to access a protected document m, the following steps take place:

1. $\mathcal{A}$ looks up m in the DBM's DT and requests m from the DBM.
2. The DBM obtains, from the RM, the keys of all roles required to access m and encrypts m using these role keys. This is done, by creating *virtual identifier*, as follows:
   Let $ID_{i_1}, \cdots, ID_{i_k}$ be the roles required to access m, and $d_{ID_{i_1}}, \cdots, d_{ID_{i_k}}$ the corresponding keys. Then the DBM:
   a) Computes $Q_{ID_{i_j}} = \mathcal{H}_1(ID_{i_j}) \in \mathcal{G}_1 \ \forall j \in \{1, \cdots, k\}$
   b) Computes the virtual identifier $Q_{1,\dots,k} = \sum_{j=1}^k Q_{ID_{i_j}}$.
   c) Chooses a binary string $\sigma \leftarrow_R \{0,1\}^n$ and computes $r = \mathcal{H}_3(\sigma, M)$.
   d) Computes $U = rP \in \mathcal{G}_1$, $g = \hat{e}(P_{pub}, Q_{1,\dots,k})^r \in \mathcal{G}_2$.
   e) Obtains the ciphertext

$$C = (U, V, W) = (rP, \sigma \oplus \mathcal{H}_2(g), M \oplus \mathcal{H}_4(\sigma))$$

3. The DBM stores, in the CT, a copy of C and sends it to $\mathcal{A}$.
4. a) $\mathcal{A}$ obtains, from the DBM's DT, the list of roles required to access m.
   b) $\mathcal{A}$ elects, among its $SEMs$, a minimum number of $SEMs$ whose roles are all ancestors of the roles required to access m; to those $SEMs$, $\mathcal{A}$ sends both C and the list of roles.
   c) The $SEMs$ use their shares of the roles keys and compute their partial decryption of C. This is done concurrently by computing virtual decryption keys, as follows:
   Assume[4] that $\mathcal{A}$ sent C to SEM_1 and SEM_2. Assume also that, SEM_1 is responsible for the roles $ID_{i_1}, \cdots, ID_{i_b}$, while SEM_2 is responsible for the roles $ID_{i_{b+1}}, \cdots, ID_{i_k}$. Then:
   – SEM_1:
     i. Checks whether the recipient's identity or any of the role identifiers is either revoked or would break an $RBAC$ separation of duty rule when activated. If any of these conditions is satisfied, SEM_1 returns an annotated error message.
     ii. Computes the virtual key[5] $d_{sem_1} = \sum_{j=1}^b d_{ID_{i_j},sem_1}$.

---

[4] The generalization to an arbitrary number of $SEMs$ is straightforward
[5] Note that, a priori, the probability to compute such a virtual key is $\frac{1}{q}$, which can be made arbitrarily low by the choice of the group size q.

iii. Computes $g_{sem_1} = \hat{e}(U, d_{sem_1})$ and sends it to the user.
- SEM_2:
    i. Checks whether the recipient's identity or any of the role identifiers is either revoked or would break an $RBAC$ separation of duty rule when activated. If any of these conditions is satisfied, SEM_2 returns an annotated error message.
    ii. Computes the virtual key $d_{sem_2} = \sum_{j=b+1}^{k} d_{ID_{i_j},sem_2}$.
    iii. Computes $g_{sem_2} = \hat{e}(U, d_{sem_2})$ and sends it to the user.
d) Finally, $\mathcal{A}$ uses its shares of the role keys to complete the decryption of C. This is done by computing a virtual key, as follows:
    i. $\mathcal{A}$ computes the virtual decryption key $d_{user} = \sum_{j=1}^{k} d_{ID_{i_j},user}$.
    ii. $\mathcal{A}$ computes $g_{user} = \hat{e}(U, d_{user})$.
    iii. Upon reception of g_{sem_1} and g_{sem_2} from the $SEMs$, $\mathcal{A}$ computes
    $g = g_{sem_1} g_{sem_2} g_{user}$.
    iv. $\mathcal{A}$ computes $\sigma = V \oplus \mathcal{H}_3(g)$ and then $M = W \oplus \mathcal{H}_4(\sigma)$.
    v. $\mathcal{A}$ checks the ciphertext's validity: $U = r'P$ with $r' = \mathcal{H}_3(\sigma, M)$.
5. $\mathcal{A}$ recovers m, if $\mathcal{A}$ has all required roles and privileges.

Role Management

Role Addition

System Roles:
When a role ID_i is added to the hierarchy maintained by the RM, the RM:
1. Generates a new key d_{ID_i} for the role.
2. Generates a new set of $SEMs$ associated with the role.
3. Generates a new key share pair $(d_{ID_i,sem}, d_{ID_i,user})$, where $d_{ID_i,user}$ is randomly chosen in $\mathcal{G}_1^*$ and $d_{ID_i,sem} = d_{ID_i} - d_{ID_i,user}$.
4. Sends a copy of $d_{ID_i,sem}$ to the new $SEMs$ and to all $SEMs$ associated with an ancestors of ID_i.
5. Sends a copy of $d_{ID_i,user}$ to each user entitled to ID_i. In order to do so, the RM selects all the users associated with a SEM whose role is either ID_i or an ancestor of ID_i.

User Roles:
When a user is given a new role ID_i (already existing in the role hierarchy), the RM:
1. Associates ID_i with a SEM whose role is ID_i.
2. Instructs the SEM to interact freely with the new user, according to the system policies.
3. Sends, to the user, a copy of $d_{ID_i,user}$ and of all its descendants.

Role Revocation

System Roles:
When a role ID_i is revoked from the hierarchy maintained by the RM, the RM:

1. Removes ID_i from the hierarchy.
2. Notifies all *SEMs* associated with either ID_i or one of its ancestors to stop performing decryption tasks involving ID_i.
3. Notifies all users entitled to ID_i that this role has been removed.
4. If the system policy specifies it
    a) The children of ID_i each become a new child of ID_i's parents.
    b) All *SEMs* corresponding to either ID_i or one of its ancestors are notified of this change (during Step 2).
    c) All users entitled to ID_i are notified of this change (during Step 3).

User Roles:
When a user role ID_i is revoked, the *RM*:
1. Associates ID_i with a *SEM* whose role is ID_i.
2. Instructs the *SEM* associated with ID_i and the user to stop interacting with this user in tasks involving ID_i and all its descendants.
3. Notifies the user of the change.

Role Delegation

When a user $\mathcal{A}$ wants to delegate to a user $\mathcal{B}$ one of his/her role ID_i, the following steps take place:

1. $\mathcal{A}$ notifies the *RM* of its delegation intent, sending the public key of ID_i .
2. The *RM* ensures that $\mathcal{B}$ does not already have ID_i and that $\mathcal{A}$ possesses both ID_i and the right to delegate it to $\mathcal{B}$. Otherwise, the delegation fails and $\mathcal{A}$ is notified.
3. If $\mathcal{B}$ does not have ID_i, then:
    a) The *RM* sends $d_{ID_i,user}$ to $\mathcal{B}$.
    b) If ID_i is a top role of $\mathcal{B}$, then $\mathcal{B}$ is associated with a new *SEM* corresponding to ID_i.
4. $\mathcal{A}$ is notified of the delegation success.

Note that we only considered the type of delegation in which the delegatee does not already have the delegated role. This notion could be extended to the case in which the delegatee has the role but must exercise it on behalf of some entity. In this latter case, every such role (say $\hat{r}$) could be associated with two keys: one to identify the role and the other (named *behalf key*) to specify that the role is exercised on behalf of a trusted party. The *sum* of these keys would yield the role's decryption key. Thus, when the delegatee already has $\hat{r}$, the delegator would only send his/her share of the *behalf key* to the delegatee. Then, in order to compute his/her share of $\hat{r}$'s decryption key, the delegatee would *sum* his/her share of $\hat{r}$'s identifying key and $\hat{r}$'s behalf key.

4   Discussion

After having presented our scheme in the previous section, we now discuss two of its aspects, namely space requirements and security. We also present and discuss the benefits and shortcomings of two variants of our scheme.

4.1   Space Requirements

Role Manager. On top of role identifiers and system policies (including separation-of-duty rules, and others), the *RM* needs to store two key shares for each role.

Database Manager. On top of the *DB* per se, the *DBM* needs space for the *DT* and the *CT*. The *DT* has a size at least linear in the size of the *DB* - the extra storage being due to the space needed to store the required privileges of each protected document. The *CT*'s size is at most that of the *DB*.

SEM. Each *SEM* must store the key share of its role and that of all its descendant roles. Thus, with regard to this feature, the space requirement of a *SEM* grows linearly with respect to the height of its corresponding role in the system hierarchy. It would be convenient to be able to compute sub-role key shares from any given role key share, using a *mediated hierarchical identity-based* encryption scheme [6]. However, note that this would add a start-up computational overheard to both *SEMs* and users (assuming that the sub-role key share computation would also work with user keys).

Aside from key shares, each *SEM* also needs to store information concerning the each user's session. This information should in fact be shared with other *SEMs* to allow separation-of-duty to be enforced for each user.

User. Each user must store his/her shares of authorized privilege keys.

4.2   Security

This section briefly discusses the security of our *RBAC*-cryptographic-support encryption scheme.

Attack Model. Since our scheme is essentially a threshold scheme, the following attack model may be considered. Let $\mathcal{C}$ be an entity called the *Challenger*. Assume that a user U wants to decrypt a random ciphertext c, which requires U to interact with n_{tr} *SEMs*. Let $\mathcal{A}$ be an attacker who compromises $n_{tr} - 1$ of these *SEMs*. The goal of $\mathcal{A}$ is to decrypt c. Thus, if, for any challenger $\mathcal{C}$, no attacker polynomially bounded attacker $\mathcal{A}$ can be found that successfully decrypts c with non-negligible probability $\varepsilon(k)$, then our pairing-based mediated identity-based multi-*SEM* encryption scheme is said to be secure.

Security Guarantees. Using the above attack model, it can be shown (with an argument similar to the one provided for the proof of Theorem 3.1 of [5] -cf. [6]-) that, if the *Bilinear Diffie-Hellman* problem is difficult, then our scheme is secure. From a more practical point of view, one can say that the security of our scheme relies on the difficulty of compromising (high-privileged) roles. Indeed, the compromise of a *SEM* only affects the corresponding role and its descendants. As a consequence, the security of high-privileged *SEMs* should well protected.

4.3   Variant Scheme

In this section, we describe a variant of our scheme, and discuss its computational, storage, communication and security features.

Description. The alternative scheme will be henceforth referred to as the *re-encryption* scheme. In this scheme, the Role Manager (*RM*) continues to act like a *PKG*. However, it does not give users their shares of role decryption keys. Instead, the *RM* secretly sends role keys to their associated *SEMs*. Then, to decrypt a document, a user shows her credentials to one of her associated *SEMs*, and indicates all the roles required to decrypt de document. The *SEM* then interacts *SEMs* associated with the other required roles; this interaction consists in the other *SEMs* partially decrypting the ciphered document and sending back the partial decryptions to the requesting *SEM*. The requesting *SEM* then completes the decryption of the ciphertext (as users would do it in our mediated scheme) and *re-encrypts* it under the user's public key. The re-encrypted document is sent back to the user who can decrypt it using her private key, which must be sent by the *RM*, when the user joins the system.

Comparison. For comparison, remark that, in the *re-encryption* scheme the *RM* does not have to split and secretely distribute role key shares. This induces important computational, storage and communication savings for the *RM*; this also induces storage savings for the *SEMs* which, then, only need to store one role decryption key (instead of storing both a role key and all its descendant role keys). However, this forces *SEMs* to interact with all *SEMs* associated with their descendant-roles, thereby generating extra communication costs.

Another point of comparison is the communication overhead due to user-*SEM* interactions. This overhead is reduced to one *SEM* per user, instead of n_{tr}, where n_{tr} is the average number of top roles per user. However, note that each user-*SEM* interaction reduction is replaced by a *SEM*-*SEM* interaction. Assuming that *SEM* have, on average, greater computational power than users, it follows that the *re-encryption* scheme is computationally advantageous.

Note also that, in the mediated scheme, the *RM* is much more active than in the *re-encryption* scheme, and therefore potentially easier to compromise. With regard to this aspect, the variant scheme is thus advantageous.

Remark that, in both schemes, the compromise of a *SEM* does not compromise the security of other *SEMs*. However, note that, in the variant scheme, the compromise of *SEM* affects the decryption capability of all *SEMs* served by the compromised one.

Moreover, unlike our mediated scheme, the *re-encryption* scheme suffers from one main security weakness, namely the fact that the compromise of a *SEM* jeopardizes the confidentiality of encrypted documents sent by users to the *SEM*. This weakness is due to the fact that, unlike our mediated scheme, the variant scheme allows *SEMs* to have full decryption keys. One may argue that, since compromising a *SEM* is harder than compromising a user, the variant scheme is not substantially less secure than the mediated scheme.

Consequently, system engineers must decide whether they are ready to trade both the document confidentiality concerns (induced by *SEM* compromise), and the increased communication cost (induced by *SEM-to-lower-SEM* interactions), for the substantial computational and storage benefits of the *re-encryption* scheme. This decision will be influenced by the robustness of *SEMs* against active attackers and the value of confidential information secured by the system.

5   Conclusion and Future Work

In this paper, we have shown that pairing-based identity-based mediated cryptography is suitable for the cryptographic support of role-based access control. Moreover, we have proposed a scheme to effectively support *RBAC* cryptographically.

For our scheme, we devised a role key assignment which is robust against the compromise of certain key-managing entities called security mediators. Then, we extended a recent pairing-based mediated scheme in order to allow the enforcement of possession of multiple roles to access certain documents. Moreover, we designed an architecture and a set of algorithms which cryptographically enforce *RBAC* and allow for role addition, revocation, and delegation. Furthermore, we have discussed the space requirements and security of our scheme. To the best of our knowledge, our scheme is the best cryptographic-support scheme for *RBAC*.

One possible extension of this work is to design and investigate the applications of a mediated hierarchical identity-based encryption scheme [6]. Another option is to formally analyze the security of schemes which cryptographically support *RBAC*, including the security of our scheme.

References

1. Liqun Chen, Keith Harrison, Nigel Smart, and David Soldera, *Applications of Multiple Trust Authorities in Pairing Based Cryptosystems*, Infrastructure Security : InfraSec 2002 (G. Davida, Y. Frankel, and O. Rees, eds.), Springer-Verlag LNCS 2437, September 2002, pp. 260–275.
2. Gene Tsudik Dan Boneh, Xuhua Ding and C. Wong, *A Method for Fast revocation of Public Key Certificates and Security Capabilities*, Proceedings of the 10th USENIX Security Symposium, USENIX, 2001, pp. 297–308.
3. Xuhua Ding Dan Boneh and Gene Tsudik, *Identity-based Mediated RSA*, Proceedings of the third International Workshop on Information and Security Applications (WISA'02) (Jeju Island, Korea), 2002.
4. David F. Ferraiolo, Ravi Sandhu, Serban Gavrila, D. Richard Kuhn, and Ramaswamy Chandramouli, *Proposed NIST Standard for Role-Based Access Control*, ACM Trans. Inf. Syst. Secur. **4** (2001), no. 3, 224–274.
5. Benoît Libert and Jean-Jacques Quisquater, *Efficient Revocation and Threshold Pairing Based Cryptosystems*, Proceedings of the twenty-second annual symposium on Principles of distributed computing, ACM Press, 2003, pp. 163–171.
6. Deholo Nali, Ali Miri, and Carlisle Adams, *Mediated Hierarchical Identity-Based Cryptography*, In preparation, 2004.

Towards Human Interactive Proofs in the Text-Domain

Using the Problem of Sense-Ambiguity for Security

Richard Bergmair[1] and Stefan Katzenbeisser[2]

[1] University of Derby in Austria
A-4060 Leonding, rbergmair@acm.org
[2] Technische Universität München
Institut für Informatik
D-85748 Garching, skatzenbeisser@acm.org

Abstract. We outline the linguistic problem of word-sense ambiguity and demonstrate its relevance to current computer security applications in the context of Human Interactive Proofs (HIPs). Such proofs enable a machine to automatically determine whether it is interacting with another machine or a human. HIPs were recently proposed to fight abuse of web services, denial-of-service attacks and spam. We describe the construction of an HIP that relies solely on natural language and draws its security from the problem of word-sense ambiguity, i.e., the linguistic phenomenon that a word can have different meanings dependent on the context it is used in.

Keywords: HIP, CAPTCHA, text, natural language, linguistic, lexical, word-sense ambiguity, learning

1 Introduction

As networking technology is making progress and society finds ever more efficient ways of sending information around the globe, our attitude towards the way we make information available is rapidly changing; this change is mainly taking us into one direction: automation. If we want to make information or services available on the net, then we actually use a computer that offers services to other computers. When we gather information from the net, then we have a computer that obtains this information for us from other computers. It is important to recognize that the act of sending information to or receiving information from the net is usually automated. This phenomenon lies at the heart of many highly security-critical situations. Although automation drives the progress of the IT industry, there are situations where too much automation is undesirable. For example, consider the following scenarios:

- *Abuse of web-services:* While free e-mail services should be available to subscribers, web bots that subscribe to thousands of accounts in order to send spam are obviously unwanted guests. In a similar scenario, online polls should

K. Zhang and Y. Zheng (Eds.): ISC 2004, LNCS 3225, pp. 257–267, 2004.
© Springer-Verlag Berlin Heidelberg 2004

only accept votes from humans, not from web bots aiming at manipulating the poll by stuffing the ballot box with thousands of invalid votes [20].

- *Fighting spam and worms:* We want to accept e-mails from our friends and colleagues, but not from automated mass-mailers distributing spam. For this purpose, it would be highly desirable to have a device that can decide whether an e-mail originated from a human or from an automated bot (the company *www.spamarrest.com* is already marketing this idea) [12,20].
- *Privacy issues:* Personal data can be made available to humans without high risk if the recipients are trusted. However, we want to prevent sensitive data from being replicated, indexed, or otherwise analyzed at a large scale, for example by web-spiders of search-engines or web-advertisers.
- *Denial-Of-Service:* Online services have to process requests issued by legitimate human users, but, in order to prevent denial-of-service attacks, they need to refuse processing requests made by malicious scripts for the sole purpose of putting load on the system [10].
- *Dictionary Attacks:* Computer systems could try to process only login attempts by human users, but refuse to process login attempts originating from a bot running a dictionary attack [13].
- *Protecting Business Interests:* Online shops may want to offer their services only to humans, but not to bots for comparative shopping [12].

The core component that would be needed to protect against any of the aforementioned security threats is a device allowing us to distinguish between humans and computers in communication systems. This problem is investigated in the context of Human Interactive Proofs (HIPs) [19]. The computer security community only recently discovered the power of HIPs for solving practical security problems.

To our knowledge, the earliest appearance of HIPs in the literature is an unpublished manuscript by Moni Naor [12], dating back to 1997. He suggested the inclusion of a test into a communication system that can easily be passed by humans, but that cannot be passed by computers, similar in setup to Turing's test [18]. Turing's test evaluates whether or not a machine shows intelligent behavior by having an interrogator communicate to the machine and to another human. In his test-setup both the computer and the human are hidden from the interrogator, interacting with him through the same interface. If the interrogator is unable to distinguish between the computer and the human when talking to them over the interface, then we could in fact attribute intelligent behavior to the machine. On the other hand, if we agree that the machine is not "intelligent" enough (i.e., there are some questions of the interrogator that can be solved by a human but not by the machine), we can devise a test that distinguishes the human from the machine—in essence, this amounts to an HIP.

In January 2002, the *First Workshop on Human Interactive Proofs* was held at Xerox PARC [22]. One year later, von Ahn et. al. [20] proposed the notion of the "Completely Automated Public Turing Test to Tell Computers and Humans Apart" (CAPTCHA). While Turing's original version of the test requires a human interrogator to judge the answers received from the testee, the "completely automated" Turing test substitutes the human interrogator for a computer program, which is able to automatically generate and grade the tests passed on to and received from the testee. Furthermore, adhering to Kerckhoffs' principle, this computer program is assumed to be public knowledge.

Von Ahn et. al. [20] implemented, and investigated in further detail, image-based CAPTCHAs. Generally, their systems rely on the difficulty of recognizing the semantic content of images. For example, their OCR-based CAPTCHA, called *GIMPY*, produces images by typesetting words from a dictionary in the generation phase. *BONGO* draws geometric shapes, and *PIX* employs a public database of images labeled by humans with an identification of their content. In any case, the output of this phase is an image, and a symbolic representation of the semantics that would be assigned to it by a human. The image is then distorted in such a way that humans would still be able to recognize the image content, but state-of-the-art algorithms known to the AI-community would not. Although all programs and databases used by these systems are assumed public knowledge, the distortion depends on a private source of randomness. During the testing phase, the testee is asked to identify the content of the image (e.g., read a word typeset by *GIMPY*); the syntactic representation of this content is then checked against the representation of the intended semantics produced in the generation phase. Other treatments of OCR-based CAPTCHAs can be found in [3,17].

The security of the system depends heavily on the assumption that a computer program cannot "pass" the test. This assumption is usually justified by the lack of appropriate AI algorithms for this purpose. However, this does not mean that such algorithms cannot exist in general. For example, Malik and Mori [11] have developed a program that can recognize *GIMPY* images with a success rate of 92%. This shows that a constant evaluation of the security of existing HIPs as well as the construction of various new HIPs is an important topic. In particular, it is important to have CAPTCHAs operating on many different kinds of media, for example ones that can be used by the visually impaired. CAPTCHAs concentrating on the sound-domain, for example, were investigated by [1,2].

The medium of interest in this paper will be natural language text. We discuss the major problems that arise when constructing an HIP in the text domain in Sections 2 and 3. Constructions for HIPs are proposed in Sections 4 and 5. We will show that it is indeed possible to construct an HIP based on natural language texts. Finally, future research directions are outlined in Section 6.

2   HIPs in the Text-Domain

The idea of HIPs operating in a text-domain is near at hand, since computational linguistics is one of the most prominent research disciplines in artificial intelligence. The construction of an HIP (or CAPTCHA) in the text-domain is often cited as an important open problem [20,21,14,8]. To our knowledge, the only attempt to create text-based CAPTCHAs was made by Godfrey [8].

In his first approach, he randomly selected a word from a piece of text taken from a datasource of human-written text, and substituted it by another word selected at random, in the hope that it would be easy for humans to pick that word (because it didn't fit in the context), but difficult for computers. However he could write a program that had considerable success-rates in "cheating" the test by taking into account statistic characteristics of natural language.

In a second approach, he used a statistic model to generate essentially meaningless text in order to get a "bad" sentence, and selected a "good" sentence from a repository of human-written text. The idea was that, after applying random transformations to both, a human should still be able to distinguish between the good and the bad sentence, which turned out not to be the case.

Godfrey concluded his contribution with a discussion of why text was so much more problematic a medium for the construction of CAPTCHAs than images or sounds. He attributed this to the fact that humans are more often exposed to distorted images and sounds than to distorted text, and, as a result, it is more difficult for humans to recognize distorted text. However, we believe that the problem is actually due to the types of text-manipulations studied so far.

A linguistic HIP cannot work if, on one hand, we rely on a human's ability to assign meaning to a meaningful text as the very distinction between humans and computers, and, on the other, we carry out semantically significant distortions, thereby presenting meaningless text to the testees. It is not surprising that a human has no true advantage over a computer in handling text, where semantic content has been destroyed, e.g. by randomly replacing or shuffling words or otherwise manipulating the text by statistical models that treat words as meaningless symbolic black-boxes.

In this paper we will present a kind of text-manipulation that uses a model of natural language semantics to ensure that semantic content is preserved thoughout all distortions applied to a text. In particular, we will use lexical semantics to construct an HIP that draws its security from the problem of *word-sense ambiguity*, i.e., the phenomenon that a single word can have different meanings and that different words can have the same meaning, depending on the context in which a word is used. This issue has been thoroughly studied both in computational and theoretical linguistics. Computer Science has been facing this problem, ever since the first computers were to be used for natural language translation in the early 1950s, but it has remained a major gap between humans' and computers' ability to understand natural language.

3   The Problem of Sense-Ambiguity

The problem of word-sense ambiguity is closely linked to the notion of synonymy, defined by Miller et. al. [9] in the following way:

> "According to one definition (usually attributed to Leibniz) two expressions are synonymous if the substitution of one for the other never changes the truth value of a sentence in which the substitution is made. By that definition, true synonyms are rare, if they exist at all. A weakened version of this definition would make synonymy relative to a context: two expressions are synonymous in a linguistic context C if the substitution of one for the other in C does not alter the truth value."

	move	impress	strike	motion	movement	work	go	run	test
s_1	1	1	1	0	0	0	0	0	0
s_2	1	0	0	1	1	0	0	0	0
s_3	1	0	0	0	0	0	1	1	0
s_4	0	0	0	0	0	1	1	1	0
s_5	0	0	0	0	0	0	0	1	1
...									

Fig. 1. A lexical matrix.

Roughly, a *linguistic context* can be seen as the surrounding of a word in the text in which it appears, helping to determine the word's meaning. We can use this definition of synonymy to organize words into synonymy-sets or *synsets* for short. A synset contains words that can *sometimes* (i.e., in a linguistic context) be substituted for each other. Using this approach, we can infer the meanings of words from their organization into synsets (such models for meaning are called differential theories of semantics). The association between a word and its meaning is referred to as *word-sense*.

For example, *move*, in a sense where it can be replaced by *run* or *go*, has a different meaning than *move*, in a sense where it can be replaced by *impress* or *strike*. If we wanted our dictionary to model semantics explicitly, we would have to formulate statements of the form "use *move* interchangeably with *run* or *go* if *you want to express that* something goes through a process" or "use *move* interchangeably with *impress* or *strike* if *you want to express that* something has an emotional impact on you". However, in differential approaches to semantics, as adopted in this paper, we do not represent meaning explicitly, because representing the *"if you want to express that..."*-part of the above phrases is very difficult, if not impossible. All we do is to formulate statements of the form "there exists *one* sense for *move*, in which it can be interchanged by *run* or *go*" and "there exists *another* sense for *move*, in which it can be interchanged by *impress* or *strike*". This yields two synsets {*move, run, go*} and {*move, impress, strike*}.

Miller et. al. [9] used the *lexical matrix* to demonstrate the relation between words and their senses; an example is given in Figure 1. If we wanted to look up the meaning of a word, say *run*, we would get multiple senses s_3, s_4, and s_5. This ambiguity is called *polysemy*. Inversely, if we want to look up the word for a specific meaning we have "in mind", say s_2, we would get multiple words: *move, motion* and *movement*. This ambiguity is called *synonymy*. Alternatively, we can represent the phenomenon by a VENN diagram in the space of word-meanings (see Figure 2), displaying words as sets of meanings they express. Sense-ambiguity is the phenomenon that these sets overlap.

The problem of sense-ambiguity in natural language texts can be used in an HIP to tell computers and humans apart. As expressed by Miller et. al. in the paragraph quoted earlier, we have to think of word-sense as being resolved by a linguistic context, i.e., by clues inherent to the actual use of a word in a sentence or paragraph. An interesting property of linguistic context is that humans seem to have no problem in using it to resolve sense ambiguity, whereas computers have constantly struggled with the issue.

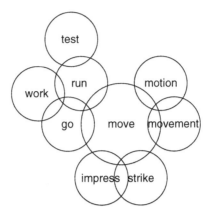

Fig. 2. Ambiguity of words in the space of meanings.

In order to clarify the role of context, we turn back to our example. In a sentence like *Today's sermon really moved me*, the word *move* can be replaced by *impress* or *strike*. When we use the same word in a sentence like *The speech has to move through several more drafts*, then we use it in a linguistic context, where it can be replaced by *go* or *run*. The sentences *Today's sermon really ran me* or *The speech has to impress through several more drafts* are clearly incorrect. However it will be very difficult for a computer—using differential models for semantics—to judge whether these sentences are correct, as the word *move* appears in the two synsets {*move, run, go*} and {*move, impress, strike*}. Unless a computer is able to solve the problem of sense-ambiguity, it cannot decide which synset contains the correct substitutions of the word *move*. Therefore the test shown in Figure 3 will be very difficult for a computer, but trivial for a human native speaker of the language.

A human can tell from the context which of the words are correct replacements, and which of the words are not. Making a computer do so is studied in the context of Word-Sense Disambiguation (WSD). Current approaches to WSD are nowhere near completely solving the problem of lexical ambiguity. State-of-the-art WSD systems operate at a precision of up to 65% [16], whereas human annotators agree about word-sense in 90% of the cases [15,4]. We believe that the gap of 25% is large enough to construct a reliable HIP if we repeat the test

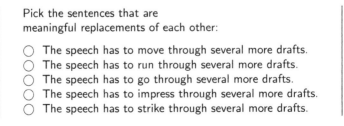

Fig. 3. A task that is difficult for a computer but trivial for a human.

several times independently in order to reduce the error probability. In addition, the performance of 65% is achieved only for test-scenarios that capture typical text in everyday written-language. By selecting word-senses that are especially difficult to disambiguate, eventually checking whether a test can be passed by any of the well-known techniques before presenting it to the testee, we can make work much harder for WSD systems.

4   Constructing HIPs

For the construction of an HIP based on sense-ambiguity, we need a *corpus* C, which is a collection of correct natural language sentences. Furthermore we need a *lexicon* consisting of the set of words W and the organization of these words into synsets $S_1, \ldots, S_n$ with $S_i \subseteq W$ for $1 \le i \le n$. Denote the set of all synsets by $S = \{S_1, \ldots, S_n\} \subseteq 2^W$. Both the corpus and the lexicon can safely be assumed public wisdom. However we need to rely on a private database establishing a mapping $sa : C \times W \mapsto S$, which we will refer to as the *secret annotation*.

The Public Lexicon: The set W is a table containing words, represented by character-coded strings. The set S is stored as a table associating words and symbolic tokens in such a way that each group of words assigned to the same symbolic token is a semantic equivalence-class relative to some linguistic context (similar to the intuitive picture of synsets presented in the previous section).

The Public Corpus: Each sentence $c \in C$ contains at least one word w_c that is contained in at least two distinct synsets $S_a, S_b \in S$, so that $w_c \in S_a \cap S_b$. Thus, looking up the word w_c in the table representing S yields multiple symbolic tokens, indicating that w_c has different meanings.

The Secret Annotation: If two synsets S_a and S_b contain word w_c, the annotation sa resolves this conflict from the linguistic context. For example, if S_a contains the correct replacements for w_c in the sentence c, we have $sa(c, w_c) = S_a$. This mapping will have to be established by a table, or by tagging the sentences in C via control-symbols, but in any case it needs to be based on data that (initially) has been entered by humans. The security of the scheme presented herein relies on the fact that no computer will be able to compute the annotation using state-of-the-art WSD algorithms with low error probability.

A database containing such knowledge could be initialized from available word banks, such as WordNet. Princeton's WordNet [7,9] is a lexicon containing 139 786 English words organized into 111 222 synsets. 15 892 of these words are useful for our purposes, because they are contained in multiple synsets, each of which contains multiple words[1]. WordNets for most other important languages

---

[1] The actual number will be slightly smaller, because in WordNet, synsets are assigned with regard to semantic considerations. A word can be assigned to multiple synsets, that have distinct identifiers, but the same elements. Of course these should be counted only once, for our purposes.

are readily available or currently under construction. If they were not public, the sample sentences contained in the WordNet glossaries or the SemCor [5,6] corpus could be used to initialize the corpus.

We can now characterize the set $R(c)$ which contains correct replacements of a sentence c, and the set $Q(c)$ containing sentences that cannot be distinguished from correct replacements of a sentence c without solving the problem of sense-ambiguity. Let the function $subst(c, w_c, w_s)$ denote the result of substituting the word w_c in the sentence c for another word[2] w_s. We write $w_c \in c$ if w_c occurs in c. Formally, we define $Q(c)$ and $R(c)$ for any $c \in C$ as follows:

$$Q(c) = \{subst(c, w_c, w_s) \mid w_c \in c, S_c \in S, w_c \in S_c, w_s \in S_c\},$$
$$R(c) = \{subst(c, w_c, w_s) \mid w_c \in c, S_c = sa(c, w_c), w_c \in S_c, w_s \in S_c\}.$$

In other words, given a sentence $c \in C$ and synonymy-sets S, the sentences originating from *correct* substitutions are given by $R(c)$; here, a sentence $c' \in R(c)$ originates from c by substituting a word $w_c \in c$ with one of those synonyms which are contained in the annotated synset. In $Q(c)$ the word w_c is replaced with a word w_s that appears in *any* synset that also contains w_c. Note that an automated adversary can correctly reproduce $R(c)$ only if he can solve the WSD problem.

The human interactive proof is carried out in several phases:

1. In the generation phase, the tester composes n test instances $t_1, \ldots, t_n$, where n acts as security parameter. Each instance t_i consists of all sentences in $Q(c)$ for a randomly selected sentence $c \in C$ in random order. All test instances are then presented (in a human-readable form and in a random arrangement) at once to the testee.
2. In the testing phase, the testee solves the problem, by selecting the sentences that are meaningful replacements of each other in each test-instance. The testee returns the selections to the tester.
3. In the verification phase, the hypothesis "For each test instance t_i, the testee could distinguish sentences chosen from $Q(c)$, from sentences chosen from $R(c)$" is confirmed or rejected by the tester. More precisely, the tester checks for each test instance t_i, whether the testee selected all sentences in $R(c)$ and no sentences in $Q(c) \backslash R(c)$. The tester accepts, if the testee answered all instances t_i correctly.

5   Learning HIPs

A basic problem is that any resource used by a machine to automatically generate test instances will allow an adversary to solve them. For example, using WordNet-glossaries for C is *not* a good idea from a strategic point of view, since they are public, and would therefore allow the adversary to solve the test in the

---

[2] Strictly speaking, there could be multiple appearances of w_c in c. In this case we consider only the first occurrence of w_c.

same way an answer to the test is evaluated. In particular, the annotation sa must remain secret (which violates Kerckhoffs' principle).

However, we believe that—in practice—relying on such a private datasource is not a great limitation, if we see it as a dynamic component that grows as the system is being used, and only needs to be seeded with initially private hand-annotated data.

For any $c \in C$, let

$$P(c) = \{subst(c, w_c, w_p) \mid w_c \in c, w_p \in W\}$$

be the set of sentences originating from c by substituting w_p for w_c, where w_p is chosen randomly from the set of all words W.

We can use answers received from a human testee to learn new annotations. For this purpose, we present sentences from $Q(c)$ to the testee as above in order to judge whether he is a human. In addition, we present randomly chosen sentences $p \in P(c)$ together with all the sentences from $Q(p)$. This second batch of sentences will be used to train the HIP for future tests.

Figure 4 shows an example. By random choice we have replaced *send* by *cough*, and the resulting sentence d makes no sense. However, we might just as well end up with a replacement that yields a meaningful sentence, as is the case with sentence p, where *send* has been replaced by *take*. Unfortunately, at this point we don't know which sense the word *take* is used in, since it is contained in two synsets: {*take, rent, hire*} as in *We took a sailing boat* or {*take, accept*} as in *We will gladly take your orders*. This is why the sentences from $Q(p)$ need to be presented as well. A human user will come to the conclusion that p_2 makes no sense; this allows the tester to conclude that the synset $S_p = \{take, accept\}$ contains the correct substitutions for the word $w_p = take$ in the linguistic context imposed by $p = We'll\ take\ your\ order\ tomorrow$. Thereby the tester can learn a new annotation by remembering the sentence p together with its annotation $S_p = sa(p, w_p)$ for future use. Of course, this should be done only if the tester collected evidence in the verification phase that the testee was in fact human.

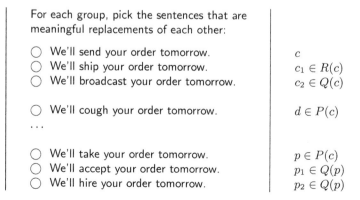

Fig. 4. The HIP can learn from these answers.

4. In the learning phase, sentence $p \in P(c)$ can be added to the corpus C, if the (human) testee considered it meaningful. An association $sa(p, w_p) = S_p$ can be added to the annotation, if each sentence originating from the substitution of w_p by any $w_x \in S_p$ in p was considered a correct replacement by the testee.

If we think of large-scale scenarios such as free e-mail providers telling humans from web-robots that register for free email accounts, we know that such a resource would grow very fast, and we could therefore rely on a highly sophisticated lexical resource originating from a very well trained language learner. A user in the scale of a business that relies on web-robots to sign up for free e-mail accounts, on the other hand, is very unlikely to succeed in outperforming such a linguistic resource.

6   Conclusions and Future Research

In this contribution we have identified word-sense ambiguity as a very promising linguistic phenomenon to build a secure text-based HIP upon. We presented the details of a construction, allowing us to distinguish computers from humans via purely textual interfaces in a fully automatic way. We also showed that it is possible to use answers provided by humans as part of the test for training the linguistic model that serves as a back-end of the HIP.

Although we cannot claim to have solved the problem of creating a CAPTCHA in the text-domain (in the sense of a facility that does not rely on any private resources but a randomness-source), we showed that the learning nature of our HIP helps us to overcome limitations arising from a private linguistic model.

Transformations that provide for a serious computational obstacle to anyone trying to reverse them, paralleling the construction of current image-based CAPTCHAs, have not yet been found for the text-domain. However, we hope to have identified a direction where to look for them, by pointing out the relevance of natural language semantics to the topic. Lexical models provide only for the tip of the iceberg of natural language semantics, so we believe it will be fruitful to investigate the application of other linguistic models as well.

References

1. Tsz-Yan Chan. http://drive.to/research.
2. Tsz-Yan Chan. Using a text-to-speech synthesizer to generate a reverse turing test. In *Proceedings of the 15th IEEE International Conference on Tools with Artificial Intelligence*, page 226. IEEE Computer Society, 2003.
3. Allison L. Coates and Richard J. Fateman. Pessimal print: A reverse turing test. In *Sixth International Conference on Document Analysis and Recognition (ICDAR '01)*, 2001.
4. Philip Edmonds. Introduction to Senseval. *ELRA Newsletter*, 2002. Available electronically: http://www.senseval.org/publications/senseval.pdf.
5. Miller et. al. SemCor 1.6.
ftp://ftp.cogsci.princeton.edu/pub/wordnet/semcor16.tar.gz, 1998.

6. Miller et. al. and Rada Mihalcea. Semcor 2.0.
   http://www.cs.unt.edu/~rada/downloads/semcor/semcor2.0.tar.gz, 2004.
7. Christiane Fellbaum, editor. *WordNet, An Electronic Lexical Database*. MIT Press, 1998.
8. Philip Brighten Godfrey. Text-based CAPTCHA algorithms. In *First Workshop on Human Interactive Proofs*, 2002. Unpublished Manuscript. Available electronically: http://www.aladdin.cs.cmu.edu/hips/events/abs/godfreyb_abstract.pdf.
9. George A. Miller, Richard Beckwith, Christiane Fellbaum, Derek Gross, and Katherine Miller. Introduction to WordNet: An on-line lexical database. http://www.cogsci.princeton.edu/~wn/5papers.ps, August 1993.
10. William G. Morein, Angelos Stavrou, Debra L. Cook, Angelos D. Keromytis, Vishal Misra, and Dan Rubenstein. Using graphic turing tests to counter automated ddos attacks against web servers. In *Proceedings of the 10th ACM Conference on Computer and Communication Security*, pages 8–19. ACM Press, 2003.
11. Greg Mori and Jitendra Malik. Recognizing objects in adversarial clutter: Breaking a visual CAPTCHA. In *Conference on Computer Vision and Pattern Recognition (CVPR '03)*, volume I, 2003.
12. Moni Naor. Verification of a human in the loop or identification via the turing test. Unpublished Manuscript. Available electronically: http://www.wisdom.weizmann.ac.il/~naor/PAPERS/human.ps, 1997.
13. Benny Pinkas and Tomas Sander. Securing passwords against dictionary attacks. In *Proceedings of the 9th ACM Conference on Computer and Communications Security*, pages 161–170. ACM Press, 2002.
14. Bartosz Przydatek. On the (im)possibility of a text-only CAPTCHA. In *First Workshop on Human Interactive Proofs*, 2002. Unpublished Abstract. Available electronically: http://www.aladdin.cs.cmu.edu/hips/events/abs/bartosz_abstract.pdf.
15. Philip Resnik. Selectional preference and sense disambiguation. In *Proceedings of the ACL SIGLEX Workshop on Tagging Text with Lexical Semantics: Why, What, and How?*, April 1997.
16. Senseval. http://www.sle.sharp.co.uk/senseval2/Results/all_graphs.xls, 2001. accessed March 6, 2004.
17. Patrice Y. Simard, Richard Szeliski, Josh Benaloh, Julien Couvreur, and Iulian Calinov. Using character recognition and segmentation to tell computer from humans. In *Seventh International Conference on Document Analysis and Recognition*, volume I, 2003.
18. Alan M. Turing. Computing machinery and intelligence. *Mind*, 49:433–460, 1950.
19. Luis von Ahn, Manuel Blum, Nicholas J. Hopper, and John Langford. Hips. http://www.aladdin.cs.cmu.edu/hips/.
20. Luis von Ahn, Manuel Blum, Nicholas J. Hopper, and John Langford. CAPTCHA: using hard ai problems for security. In *Advances in Cryptology, Eurocrypt 2003*, volume 2656 of *Springer Lecture Notes in Computer Science*, pages 294–311, May 2003.
21. Luis von Ahn, Manuel Blum, and John Langford. Telling humans and computers apart automatically. *Communications of the ACM*, 47(2):56–60, 2004.
22. Xerox PARC. *First Workshop on Human Interactive Proofs*, January 2002.

Image Recognition CAPTCHAs[*]

Monica Chew and J.D. Tygar

UC Berkeley
{mmc,tygar}@cs.berkeley.edu

Abstract. CAPTCHAs are tests that distinguish humans from software robots in an online environment [3,14,7]. We propose and implement three CAPTCHAs based on naming images, distinguishing images, and identifying an anomalous image out of a set. Novel contributions include proposals for two new CAPTCHAs, the first user study on image recognition CAPTCHAs, and a new metric for evaluating CAPTCHAs.

1 Introduction

We want to distinguish Internet communications originating from humans from those originating from software robots. Alan Turing's celebrated "Turing Test" paper [13] discussed the special case of a human tester who attempts to distinguish humans and artificial intelligence computer programs. However, the situation is far harder when the tester is a computer. Recent interest in this subject has spurred a number of proposals for CAPTCHAs: *Completely Automated Public Tests to tell Computers and Humans Apart* [14,3]. This interest is motivated in large part by a variety of undesirable behavior associated with software robots, such as sending bulk unsolicited commercial e-mail (spam), or inflating ratings on a recommender system by rating the same product many times. Paypal and Yahoo already require CAPTCHAs in order to provide services. However, sufficiently advanced computer programs can break a number of CAPTCHAs that have been proposed to date.

Integrating a CAPTCHA into a software system raises a question which straddles the fields of *human computer interactions* (HCI) and *computer security*: how do we develop an effective CAPTCHA that humans are willing to take? This paper examines three proposals for image recognition CAPTCHAs and finds merits and weaknesses associated with each of them. Since CAPTCHAs straddle HCI and computer security, we need to apply techniques drawn from both fields to analyze them. This paper concentrates not only on the underlying security issues raised by these CAPTCHA proposals, but also on their usability. We validate our results with serious user tests.

CAPTCHAs must satisfy three basic properties. The tests must be

– Easy for humans to pass.

---

[*] This work was supported in part by the National Science Foundation and the US Postal Service. The opinions here are those of the authors and do not necessarily reflect the opinions of the funding sponsors.

K. Zhang and Y. Zheng (Eds.): ISC 2004, LNCS 3225, pp. 268–279, 2004.

– Easy for a tester machine to generate and grade.
– Hard for a software robot to pass. The only automaton that should be able to pass a CAPTCHA is the one generating the CAPTCHA.

The first requirement implies that user studies are necessary to evaluate the effectiveness of CAPTCHAs. The second and third requirements push us in a different direction. We must find a test with a new property: the test must be easy to generate but intractable to pass without special knowledge available to humans and not computers. Image recognition seems to be such a problem. Humans can easily identify images, but to date, image recognition appears to be a hard problem for computers.

Generating tests is also a challenge. Unless the number of potential tests is huge or the material being tested is highly dynamic, one runs the risk of an adversary generating all possible tests and using a hash function to look up the answer in a precomputed database.

Note that CAPTCHAs need not be 100% effective at rejecting software robots. As long as the CAPTCHA raises the cost of using a software robot above the cost of using a human, the CAPTCHA can still be effective.

Several types of CAPTCHAs already exist. The types of tasks they require include: image recognition, text recognition, and speech recognition. All of the CAPTCHAs in use are either broken or insufficiently studied. The idea of using image recognition for CAPTCHAs is not new, but no previous formal study of such CAPTCHAs exists. There are two prototypes of image recognition CMU's CAPTCHA website [3]. Both of them use small, fixed sets of images and responses. Text-based CAPTCHAs alternatively require the user to transcribe an image of a word, but seem to be easy to break [10,4].

1.1   Contributions of This Work

A number of researchers [3] have proposed the image recognition-based *naming CAPTCHA*, where the test subject is asked to identify a word associated with a set of images. We propose two variations on this approach:

– Asking the test subject to determine if two subsets of images are associated with the same word or not (the *distinguishing CAPTCHA*);
– Showing the test subject a set of images where all but one image is associated with a word and asking the test subject to identify the *anomalous* image (the *anomaly CAPTCHA*).

In this paper, we propose a new metric for evaluating CAPTCHAs, implement all three approaches, evaluate them both theoretically and in user studies, and find that anomaly identification appears to be the most promising approach. Preliminary results indicate that 100% of users can pass the anomaly CAPTCHA at least 90% of the time. We also help expand the literature on the intersection between HCI and computer security by discussing a number of unique HCI issues that arise in the evaluation of CAPTCHAs.

The naming CAPTCHA   **The anomaly CAPTCHA**

Fig. 1. The figure on the left is the naming CAPTCHA. (Answer: *astronaut*.) The right figure illustrates the anomaly CAPTCHA. Five images are of *moose*, top middle anomalous image is of *weave*.

2   Image Recognition CAPTCHAs

We use the following three tasks to construct our CAPTCHAs.

1. **The naming images CAPTCHA.**
   The *naming CAPTCHA* presents six images to the user. If the user correctly types the common term associated with the images, the user passes the round. Figure 1 shows an example of one round of the naming CAPTCHA. The common term illustrated in the figure is *astronaut*.

2. **The distinguishing images CAPTCHA.**
   The *distinguishing CAPTCHA* presents two sets of images to the user. Each set contains three images of the same subject. With equal probability, both sets either have the same subject or not. The user must determine whether or not the sets have the same subject in order to pass the round. For example, of six images, the subject of the top three images could be *briefcase*, and the subject of the bottom three images could be *plate*.

3. **The identifying anomalies CAPTCHA.**
   The *anomaly CAPTCHA* presents six images to the user: five images are of the same subject, and one image (the anomalous image) shows a different subject. The user must identify the anomalous image to pass the test. Figure 1 shows five images of *moose* and one image of *weave*.

To make an image recognition CAPTCHA, we need a database of labelled images, several images for each label in a dictionary. Since it will be easy for humans to guess the label and hard for machines, we can use this database to create CAPTCHAs.

Dictionary. For the labels, we use a dictionary of 627 English words from Pdictionary [12]. Pdictionary is an pictorial dictionary, so every word in it is easy to illustrate. Easily illustrated or visualized words are important; pictures of abstract nouns such as *love* or *agony* are difficult to identify.

Images. For the images, we collect the first 20 hits from Google's image search on each word in the dictionary, using moderate safe search (a content filter). After culling broken links and potentially offensive images, 10116 images remain.[1] For this study, we pre-fetched the images to minimize latency when presenting the user with a round (in order to get more accurate timing information) and to ensure that no images are offensive. However, one could easily fetch the images dynamically to take advantage of changes in Google's image index.

2.1 Problems Affecting Human CAPTCHA Performance

Each of the three above tasks (naming images, distinguishing images, identifying an anomalous image) incur potential problems that might lower test scores for humans. A problem lowers the probability that a human user will pass. A potential problem might hurt or help human performance. Below, × indicates a problem, ○ a possible problem.

Task	Misspelling	Synonymy	Polysemy	Mislabelling
Naming images	×	×	○	×
Distinguishing images			○	×
Identifying anomalies			○	×

Misspelling. The human user may misspell a word.

- *The naming CAPTCHA*: The human user must type the word associated with the images. The user may misspell a word, failing the CAPTCHA even though the user knows the correct label of the image. *Solution*: We do not require an exact string match between the answer and the query in order for the user to pass. We choose Oliver's similarity score, a good metric that is also available as a PHP built-in function [11].
- *The distinguishing CAPTCHA and the anomaly CAPTCHA*: Misspelling is not a problem, since the user does not have to type anything.

Synonymy. One word may have multiple correct definitions.

- *The naming CAPTCHA:* Synonymy will lower user scores. For example, a user may label a picture of a mug as a *cup* or a *mug*. Both answers are correct, but the *cup* answer will cause the user to fail. *Solution*: The CAPTCHA could use a thesaurus, and accept all synonyms of the expected answer. The problem with this solution is that an adversary also has a greater chance of passing if there is more than one correct answer.

  Another solution is to allow the user to fail some rounds: a CAPTCHA could be composed of m rounds, and a user would only have to pass k of them. We choose this solution and discuss picking the optimal k and m in Section 3.

---

[1] Google has since added a strict content filter, which might help weed out more offensive images.

- *The distinguishing CAPTCHA and the anomaly CAPTCHA:* Synonymy is not a problem since the user does not have to type anything.

Polysemy. One word may correspond to multiple definitions. For example, a mouse is both a rodent and an electronic pointing device.

- *The naming CAPTCHA:* Polysemy might cause lower test scores, or it might raise them. On one hand, polysemy may provide more hints to the user. In the example above, if the user were only shown the picture of the rodent, the user might answer *rat* or *mouse*. However, if the picture of the pointing device is included, the user could rule out *rat* and give the correct answer. On the other hand, if the user does not know the alternate definition of mouse, the picture of the pointing device may be confusing.
- *The distinguishing CAPTCHA:* Polysemy could be a problem. For example, suppose the word is *mouse*. If the first set of images is of a rodent, and the second set is of a pointing device, the user will be confused. However, we expect this to be negligible in practice.
- *The anomaly CAPTCHA:* Polysemy could be a problem, if the user does not know the secondary definition of a word.

Solution: In each of the three CAPTCHAs, if polysemy is a problem, we can allow the user to fail some rounds.

Mislabelling. Google indexes images by the name of the image. Some images on Google are labelled incorrectly. The label may have a meaning to the author of the web page, but no discernible connection to the image content to anyone else. For example, someone might have a pet cat whose name is Pumpkin, and thus an image search of the word pumpkin might produce pictures of a cat.

- *The naming CAPTCHA:* Mislabelling confuses the user.
- *The distinguishing CAPTCHA:* The distinguishing CAPTCHA presents two sets of images to the user, each set containing three images. Mislabelling will confuse the user, especially if the majority of images in a set are mislabelled.
- *The anomaly CAPTCHA:* A mislabelled image is indistinguishable from an anomalous image. Suppose the two labels are *pumpkin* and *briefcase*, and there is a pet cat named Pumpkin. There might be four easily identifiable pictures of a pumpkin and two anomalous images: one picture of Pumpkin the cat and a picture of a briefcase.

Solution: In each of the three CAPTCHAs, we can allow the user to fail some rounds. Additionally, in the naming CAPTCHA, we present six images of the same query to the user, with the hope the majority of the images are labelled correctly and the user will be able to guess the correct response.

Allowing the human user to fail some rounds alleviates all of these problems; we turn to the question of the total number of rounds the user must take, and the number of those the user must pass.

3 CAPTCHA Metrics

In this section we choose two metrics for evaluating CAPTCHAs: a metric that allows us to measure CAPTCHA efficacy with respect to the number of rounds, and a metric measuring the expected time for a human user to take a CAPTCHA.

We can optimize a variety of CAPTCHA parameters:

1. **Type of task.** We can choose the nature of the tasks: naming the common element in a set of images, distinguishing images, and identifying an anomalous image.
2. **Number of images shown.** We can choose the number of images shown in each round. We chose to show six images, based on favorable response during the first round of experiments (Section 5).
3. **Number of rounds.** We can consider the number of rounds that compose a single CAPTCHA, and the minimum (threshold) number of rounds that a subject must pass to pass the CAPTCHA.
4. **Attack models.** We consider different attack models for a computer program attempting to pass the CAPTCHA. Section 4 discusses the effect of programs with good image identification ability which could do better than chance.

We consider several factors in choosing optimal values for the number of rounds and the threshold number of rounds that a subject must pass. First, human subjects have limits of how many rounds they are willing to tolerate. A human subject may find five rounds acceptable but is unlikely to agree to five hundred rounds. Second, computers have a speed advantage over humans. A computer can guess more quickly than a human can take a test. Below, we assume that within the time it takes for a human to complete one round, a computer can complete n rounds.[2]

CAPTCHA efficacy metric. We propose a new metric for CAPTCHA efficacy: the probability that in the time it takes a human to take a CAPTCHA, the human will pass and a computer will not. Let p be the probability that a human user will pass a round, q be the probability that a computer will pass a round, n be the number of times faster a computer is than a human, m be the number of rounds, and k be the threshold number of rounds. Then the efficacy metric G is

$$G = \sum_{i=k}^{m} \binom{m}{i} p^i (1-p)^{m-i} \cdot \left[1 - \sum_{i=k}^{m} \binom{m}{i} q^i (1-q)^{m-i} \right]^n$$

We also consider the expected time to complete a CAPTCHA. Short-circuit grading allows us to grade the CAPTCHA sometimes before all m rounds are complete. For a derivation of efficacy metric G and expected time to complete (pass or fail) a CAPTCHA with short-circuit grading, see the full version of the paper [5].

4   Attacking CAPTCHAs

Machine vision is a hard problem [1,2,6,9]. A computer program is unlikely to correctly identify a previously unseen image without good training data. How-

---

[2] Some might argue that choosing any value n unnecessarily limits the computer program, but we could apply other countermeasures, such as temporarily disabling IP blocks if too many attempts fail in a particular period of time.

ever, instead of the random-guessing attack model, a computer program could try the following attacks:

1. Build a database of labelled images from Google using our dictionary.
2. Search the database for the images presented in a round.

We can adopt the following countermeasures:

1. Use a large database of images.
   a) Increase the size of the dictionary, so the image database is harder to maintain. Although the current dictionary (an online picture dictionary) was hand-picked by humans, adding more words to the dictionary does not necessarily require human intervention. For example, the most frequently-used search terms on Google's image search might be good candidates for inclusion in the dictionary.
   b) Increase the number of images per word. For the user study, we prefetched the first 20 hits for each word in the dictionary. There is no reason not to increase this to, say, 100.
2. Use a dynamic database. Google updates its index of images frequently. There is no guarantee that an image in the database today will be there tomorrow. Also, recall that any attacker who indexes the entire Google image database is outside of our threat model, as we consider such attacks prohibitively expensive. Unlike the attacker, we do not have to maintain the database, since Google does it for us — the only advantage of prefetching images is speed.
3. Degrade the images, so searching for an exact match is no longer possible. This strategy might have the effect of lowering human performance. However, as long we maximize the gap between human performance and computer performance, we can still distinguish between the two. In addition, degrading the images is bound to have a negative effect on any kind of machine vision performance (both q and n). This is the first formal study of image recognition CAPTCHAs. We chose not to degrade the images in order to test the canonical *naming CAPTCHA*.

Recall that a CAPTCHA does not have to be 100% resistant to computer attack. If it is at least as expensive (due to database maintenance issues or image manipulations) for an attacker to break the CAPTCHA by machine than it would be to pay a human to take the CAPTCHA, the CAPTCHA is secure. Since these countermeasures are probably sufficient to deter current machine vision attacks, for the rest of the paper we only consider the random-guessing model.

5   First Round of Testing

We performed two rounds of user testing. The first round had 4 users and was small and informal; the second round had 20 users who each completed 100 rounds of naming images and 100 rounds of identifying anomalies. This section is restricted to discussing the first, preliminary round of testing.

We had several goals in the first, informal round of user testing:

1. Parameterize CAPTCHAs and check for practical considerations.

a) Estimate p for the general population. If p for any task is too low, we reject that task.
b) Using p, find the optimal m and k as in Section 3.
c) Estimate the time to complete a round for the general population.
d) Using p, m, and k, and round timing measurements, estimate the expected time to take a CAPTCHA. If the expected time for any CAPTCHA is too high, we reject that CAPTCHA.

2. Identify user interface problems.
3. Identify problems with the dictionary and database of images.

All tests were conducted on a web browser in the same location. Questions, answers, and timing measurements were logged on a `mysql` database on a single computer. During the testing, we received continuous feedback about user interface issues and difficulty of the tests.

Grading the naming CAPTCHA: For the naming images task, the Oliver similarity score is the best metric. We picked a minimum score of 80% to pass a round. For the preliminary test results, this lower bound allowed all the pluralization errors of the preliminary testers, and allowed no obviously wrong answers (no false positives). It did exclude a few obviously correct answers, but we wanted to be conservative to reduce the possibility of false positives. [3]

Problems with the dictionary and images: Mislabelled images were the most common problem. There are several mislabellings for surprising cultural reasons. For example, the word *cleaver* returns many pictures of cutting implements, and some pictures of the Cleaver family from the television program "Leave it to Beaver."

Optimal CAPTCHA parameters: We found the the the optimal m and k for the experimentally determined values of p. For the naming CAPTCHA, the adversary is assumed to know the dictionary and guess randomly, so $q = 1/627$. For the distinguishing images CAPTCHA, the adversary picks uniformly at random whether or not the sets are same, so $q = 1/2$. For the anomaly CAPTCHA, the adversary picks the anomaly uniformly at random from a set of 6 images, so $q = 1/6$. Likewise, for the distinguishing CAPTCHA, $q = 1/2$.

We let $n = 100$ and searched exhaustively over values of m and k until $G \geq 95\%$ and m was minimized, as in Section 3. Although the optimal number of rounds (m) for the naming images varies between 4 and 6, the threshold number of rounds (k) that a user must take is 2. For the anomaly CAPTCHA, $m = 10$ and $k = 7$, an acceptable number of rounds. Unfortunately, for the distinguishing CAPTCHA, $m = 26$ and $k = 22$. Based on these rough timing measurements, completing one CAPTCHA should take no more than 2 minutes, even with the maximum number of rounds. (The formal testing shows that both CAPTCHAs take less than one minute.)

The distinguishing CAPTCHA is impractical: We no longer considered the distinguishing images CAPTCHA, since it requires 26 rounds to be effective.

---

[3] In the dictionary, no two words have a similarity score greater than 12%. Since the metric obeys the triangular inequality, there are no words that are 80% similar to two words in the dictionary. Therefore, the dictionary still has size 627 using this similarity score.

Table 1. Average percent of 100 rounds passed (pass rate) by each user. The range in the optimal m column corresponds to the 95% confidence limits of the pass rate, and the number in parentheses indicates the optimal m for the mean pass rate. For example, the mean pass rate for anomaly detection rounds is 91%, with the 95% confidence interval 77.8-100%. The optimal m for the mean is 10, for the lower bound is 15, and for the upper bound is 7. Columns t_{cor} and t_{inc} correspond to the median number of seconds to pass or fail a round. $E[t]$ is the expected number of seconds to take the CAPTCHA with short-circuit grading.

Test type	Median (%)	Mean (%)	Optimal m	Optimal k	t_{cor}	t_{inc}	$E[t]$
Anomaly ID	91	91.4 ± 12.3	7–15 (10)	6–9 (7)	6	13	51
Image ID	76.5	74.0 ± 19.2	3–8 (5)	2	8	11	24

6   Second Round of Testing

20 users participated in the study ($N = 20$). The statistical significance of performance results varies with $\sqrt{N}$ and p. Based on results from the first round of testing, to achieve a 95% confidence interval of $\pm 3\%$ on p, we would have had to test nearly 1000 subjects, an infeasible number of subjects given financial and personnel constraints. We recruited the users on an Internet bulletin board and with paper fliers. The users varied in age from 18 to 60, in education from 11th grade to PhD, and in frequency of computer usage from 0.5 to 40 hours a week. Four of the users are non-native speakers.

The performance results from a sample of 20 users may not predict of the performance of the entire population, in this case, the population of Internet users. The educational demographics of the sample is approximately the same as the demographics of the Internet from the most recent comprehensive survey, GVU's 10th WWW survey of 5022 users [8]. The GVU survey did not cover frequency of computer usage in hours per week, but we believe our sample is not skewed towards frequent computer usage. The median number of hours on a computer per week is 17.5, or 2.5 hours a day. Given that 20% of the participants used a computer on the job (40 hours/week) and this time includes email, web-surfing, shopping, word processing, 17.5 is a plausible median for the population.

The users were paid $10-$15 for completing 100 image identification rounds and 100 anomaly identification rounds, about the number of rounds that could be completed in an hour.The users rated the difficulty of each test, on a scale from 1 (easiest) to 5 (hardest). The rating process was not included in the timing measurements of each round. The users rated the test before the answer is revealed to prevent bias. The tests were conducted in the same location to eliminate network latency and variation in setup.[4] The users were also videotaped. After the tests, the users completed an exit interview.

We can learn several things from this graph of pass rates (Figure 2).

1. **The anomaly CAPTCHA is better than the naming CAPTCHA.**
   All but one person were better at identifying anomalies than naming images

---

[4] Two users completed the testing at their home, but their timing results are excluded.

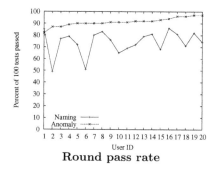

Round pass rate

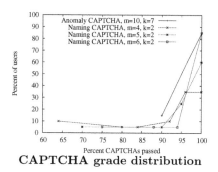

CAPTCHA grade distribution

Fig. 2. The graph on the left gives the percent of 100 rounds passed (pass rate) by each user. The x axis corresponds to the user ID, and the y axis corresponds to the percent of rounds they passed for each type of test. For example, user 20 passed 97% of the anomaly detection rounds and 74% of the naming images rounds. The graph on the right gives the distribution of percent of CAPTCHAs passed. The x axis corresponds to percent of CAPTCHAs passed, and the y axis corresponds to the percent of users who passed that many CAPTCHAs.

because of mislabelled images and an imperfect grading scheme. Figure 3 illustrates that a lower similarity score cutoff would not help much. Either the subject knew the correct label but might have made one or two mistakes in spelling or pluralization (resulting in a sufficiently high similarity score), or the subject guessed the wrong label, occasionally because of synonymy. Improving the grading scheme requires solving the synonymy problem.

2. **CAPTCHA performance is not uniform across CAPTCHA types.** Subjects who were good at identifying anomalies are not necessarily good at naming images, and vice versa. This means that if user does poorly at one kind of CAPTCHA, we can switch to the other kind in hopes they do better. This switch should not benefit adversarial computer programs, since the parameters for both CAPTCHAs result in similar computer failure rates.

3. **No discrimination against a particular educational or technical level.** Occupation, computer skills, technical background and education do not seem to be very good indicators of performance based on our sample of $N = 20$ users. For example, of the two highest scorers (97%) in anomaly detection, one completed high school, and the other had a PhD. Although our sample is small, these results suggest that the two CAPTCHAs do not discriminate against a particular educational or technical skill level.

4. **The anomaly CAPTCHA is language-independent.** Speaking English natively seems to be a pretty good indicator of performance in the naming CAPTCHA, but not in the anomaly CAPTCHA.

Table 1 gives the median and mean percent of 100 rounds passed by each user (pass rate) for image and anomaly identification rounds. The upper and lower bounds denote the 95% confidence limits for $N = 20$. Table 1 also shows the upper and lower bounds for the revised m and k, given the 95% confidence limits.

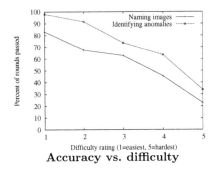
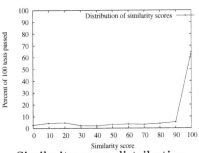

Accuracy vs. difficulty   **Similarity score distribution**

Fig. 3. The figure on the left gives accuracy vs. difficulty rating. The x axis corresponds to the difficulty rating, with 1 being the easiest rating and 5 the most difficult. The y axis is the mean pass rate for rounds with that rating. The figure on the right gives distribution of similarity scores. The x axis corresponds to the similarity score. The y axis is the proportion of naming images rounds in that bucket of scores. Each bucket is 10% wide, except the 100% bucket, which is 1% wide. We recommend a minimum similarity score of 80% to pass a round.

Note that the new values for m and k are identical to the old ones calculated after the preliminary testing.

Figure 2 shows the results of grading the rounds according to the parameters m and k. Using short-circuit grading produces nearly identical results (Section 3). From Figure 2, we see that 85% of the users passed the anomaly detection CAPTCHA 100% of the time with $m = 10, k = 7$, and 100% of the users passed the CAPTCHA at least 90% of the time. 85% of the users passed the anomaly detection 100% of the time with $m = 6, k = 2$. Table 1 shows the expected number of rounds and expected time to take a CAPTCHA. Figure 3 shows accuracy versus difficulty rating.

6.1   Lessons Learned

At the end of the testing, each subject completed an exit interview. Mislabelled images were the most common complaint.

The anomaly CAPTCHA is the best choice for the following reasons:

1. 90% of the users prefer it to the naming CAPTCHA.
2. 100% of the users pass the CAPTCHA at least 90% of the time, with $m = 10, k = 7$.
3. The expected time to take this CAPTCHA is 51 seconds.
4. Most people are willing to spend at least 2 minutes on a CAPTCHA.
5. The anomaly CAPTCHA is language-independent. Non-native speakers did equally well as native English speakers.

7   Open Problems

CAPTCHAs are still a new research area. Open problems include

- The mislabelling problem. Of all the problems discussed in Section 2.1, mislabelling causes the most human errors. We may be able to solve this using collaborative filtering, where known human users rate images according to how well they evoke their label.
- Optimizing CAPTCHA parameters. We can present more images per round in the anomaly detection CAPTCHA to deflate computer performance.
- Testing other image recognition CAPTCHAs. For example, we could require the human user to locate Waldo in an image filled with background clutter and other Waldo-shaped objects.
- Improving usability. Because of the CAPTCHA "annoyance factor," not everyone in the study was willing to take a CAPTCHA, even in exchange for free services. Rounds rated difficult (primarily because of the mislabelling problem) are both more onerous and difficult to pass.

References

1. K. Barnard, P. Duygulu, D. Forsyth, N. de Freitas, D. Blei, and M. Jordan. Matching words and pictures. *Special Issue on Text and Images, Journal of Machine Learning Research*, 3:1107–1135, 2002.
2. Kobus Barnard and David Forsyth. Learning the semantics of words and pictures. In *International Conference on Computer Vision*, volume 2, pages 408–415, 2001.
3. Manuel Blum, Luis A. von Ahn, John Langford, and Nick Hopper. The CAPTCHA Project. http://www.captcha.net, November 2000.
4. Monica Chew and Henry Baird. Baffletext: A human interactive proof. In *Document Recognition and Retrieval X*, 2003.
5. Monica Chew and J. D. Tygar. Image recognition captchas. Technical Report UCB//CSD-04-1333, UC Berkeley, 2004.
6. A. Goodrum. Image information retrieval: An overview of current research. *Informing Science*, 3(2):63–66, February 2000.
7. Nicholas J. Hopper and Manuel Blum. Secure human identification protocols. In *Asiacrypt*, pages 52–66, 2001.
8. Colleen Kehoe, Jim Pitkow, Kate Sutton, Gaurav Aggarwal, and Juan D. Rogers. Gvu's 10th world wide web user survey. http://www.gvu.gatech.edu/user_surveys/survey-1998-10/, 1999.
9. Sharon McDonald and John Tait. Search strategies in content-based image retrieval. In *Proceedings of the 26th annual international ACM SIGIR conference on Research and development in informaion retrieval*, pages 80–87. ACM Press, 2003.
10. Greg Mori and Jitendra Malik. Recognizing objects in adversarial clutter: Breaking a visual CAPTCHA. In *Computer Vision and Pattern Recognition*, 2003.
11. J. J. Oliver. Decision graphs - an extension of decision trees. In *Proceedings of the Fourth International Workshop on Artificial Intelligence and Statistics*, pages 343–350, 1993.
12. Pdictionary. The internet picture dictionary. http://www.pdictionary.com, 2004.
13. Alan Turing. Computing machinery and intelligence. In *Mind*, pages 433–60, 1950.
14. L. von Ahn, M. Blum, N. Hopper, and J. Langford. Captcha: Using hard AI problems for security. In *Eurocrypt*, 2003.

A Hierarchical Key-Insulated Signature Scheme in the CA Trust Model

Zhengyi Le, Yi Ouyang, James Ford, and Fillia Makedon

Department of Computer Science, Dartmouth College, USA
{zhengyi.le, yi.ouyang, James.Ford, Filia.Makdon}@dartmouth.edu

Abstract. In key-insulated cryptography, there are many private keys with different indexes and a single, fixed public key. When the trust model includes multiple Certification Authorities (CAs), it can be used to shorten the verification path and mitigate the damage caused by the compromise of a CA's private key. Existing work requires that the total number of CAs be fixed and that a trusted keystore store all private keys. This paper presents a hierarchical key-insulated signature scheme, called HKI, which converts existing key-insulated methods to a hierarchical scheme. Our scheme allows the system to repeatedly generate a new private key for a new CA and also provides two important features, namely a shortened verification path and mitigated damage. By basing our approach on a general key-insulated scheme, we have made it possible to take advantage of any future improvements in computation complexity, key length, or robustness in current key-insulated methods.

1 Introduction

A CA is a trusted third-party organization that issues digital certificates which are signed messages specifying a name and the corresponding public key. The role of the CA is to guarantee that an individual granted a unique certificate is who he or she claims to be. The individual's certificate is signed by the CA's private key; a verifier can verify it by using the CA's public key. In the real world, a CA is trusted by a subset of people, called the *trust domain* of this CA, instead of by everyone. If a verifier and a certificate holder are in different subsets, the verifier cannot verify the certificate issued by a CA who he doesn't trust. When creating the trust relationships among CAs, the traditional cryptography requires every CA have its own key pair. This means that a verifier must go through the *trust path* to verify a certificate issued in a different trust domain and that the compromise of a CA's private key will affect some trust paths.

This paper suggests a solution to this problem, *the Hierarchical Key-Insulated Signature scheme* called HKI. It shortens the verification path in multiple-CA models and mitigates the damage caused by the compromise of a CA's private key. The basis of our scheme is *Key-Insulated Signature (KIS)* cryptography. In KIS, there are many private keys with different indexes and a single, fixed public key. This property makes it possible that all the CAs share one public key but hold their own private keys. The most closely related work in the literature is

K. Zhang and Y. Zheng (Eds.): ISC 2004, LNCS 3225, pp. 280–291, 2004.

[13]; however, this scheme uses KIS straightforwardly, assuming a fixed number of CAs, and it needs a trusted keystore to store private keys (which must all be generated beforehand). Our scheme can achieve the same goal but has none of these deficiencies.

Since there are variants of KIS, such as [6] and [11], we limit ourselves to general constructions based on KIS so as to make our work independent of KIS progress. This should ensure that any improvement to the underlying KIS cryptography will benefit our scheme.

Section 2 summarizes existing CA trust models with the traditional cryptography and also surveys related cryptography. Section 3 describes our goal, presents our hierarchical key-insulated signature scheme with a correctness proof, and discusses issues related to primes and revocation. Section 4 presents the conclusion and future work.

2   Related Work

2.1   CA Trust Models

There are three fundamental categories of CA trust models (the oligarchy model and the fully connected mesh model can be grouped together as extreme variants of the anarchy model):

Monopoly model. There is only one CA globally. This single CA is self-certified. A verifier can use the monopoly CA's public key to verify any user's certificate. But this is impractical—the number of global users is huge and keeps increasing. The workload is too heavy for a single CA. Furthermore, in case the CA's private key is compromised, all the certificates should be revoked and re-signed.

Anarchy model. There are multiple CAs. Each CA has its own key pair and is self-certified. The workload of global certificate issuance is distributed. Any two CAs can perform *cross-certification*[1]to create a bilateral trust relationship. A verification procedure needs a *trust path*, also called *verification path* or *CA chain*, from a verifier to a certificate holder through certain cross-certifications if they are in different trust domains. The length of the verification path is the total of cross-certifications between them. This model eliminates monopoly pricing, but increases the burden on verifiers. The verifier needs to verify each CA's certificate and cross-certificate on the trust path. When a CA's private key is compromised, only those certificates issued by this CA and those related cross-certificates need to be revoked. In addition, it introduces another problem: the existence of a trust path doesn't necessarily imply that the trust relationship is always transitive.

Hierarchical model. This model organizes CAs hierarchically. Every CA has its own key pair. The root CA is self-certified and every subCA's certificate is signed by its parent CA (each CA has two kinds of users: common users and subCAs.). The root CA's trust domain is global. A subCA's trust domain is a

---
[1] A cross-certification is defined in the X.509 specification [1].

subdomain of its parent. The workload of global certificate issuance is distributed to subCAs. The length of the verification path is the distance from a certificate holder to the nearest common ancestor of the certificate holder and verifier.

In this model the registration of a new CA should be permitted by a higher-level CA. Each CA self-governs its trust domain and is the supervisor of all its subdomains. The drawbacks of this model are (1) the increased burden on verifiers; (2) revocation of the certificates of a CA's common users, as well as those of all its subCAs, when a CA's private key is compromised.

2.2   Related Cryptography

Forward secure public-key cryptography. The first Forward Secure Signature (FSS) scheme was designed by Bellare and Miner [3]. Their idea is as follows. Time is divided into periods: $0, 1, 2, \ldots, T$. With a fixed public key PK, the private key evolves every period: SK_0, SK_1, SK_2,..., SK_T. The key-evolving algorithm is a one-way function so that forward security is provided. In period i, $(0 \leq i \leq T)$, a message M is signed by SK_i. When someone wants to verify the signature S of M, he inputs $\langle PK, i, S, M \rangle$. Following that work, many improvements and similar forward secure schemes have been published (e.g., [2,10,14, 15,12,5,4]). However, FSS cannot provide backward security; the cryptographic algorithms are public, and once an attacker successfully compromises SK_i he can evolve the key by himself so that he can forge future signatures.

Key-insulated cryptography. A strong key-insulated signature scheme was designed by Dodis *et al.* [6], which can provide both forward and backward security. It was improved with forward secure cryptography and provable security by Itkis and Reyzin [11]. The general idea of KIS is similar to that of FSS—the difference is that KIS uses a physically secure device to store a master key MK. When a user needs to update his private key, the device generates a partial secret from its master key and then sends the partial secret to the user. The user generates the next private key from the partial secret and his current private key. Thus, the key update cannot be performed without the interaction of the device. Since we assume the device is physically secure, the exposure of the current private key doesn't allow the attacker to derive the private key in any other time period.

Here we give an overview of a general KIS, which is the basis of our proposed scheme. KIS is a 5-tuple of poly-time algorithms $(Gen, Upd^*, Upd, Sign, Vrfy)$:

- *Gen*: the key generation algorithm. $Gen(k, t) \to (PK, MK, SK_0)$, where k and t are two security parameters, SK_0 is the private key of period 0.
- *Upd**: the device key update algorithm. $Upd^*(i, j, MK) \to SK'_{i,j}$, where i and j are the time period indexes. This algorithm returns a partial secret $SK'_{i,j}$ which will be sent to the user to update the user's current private key SK_i to SK_j.
- *Upd*: the user private key update algorithm. $Upd(SK_i, SK'_{i,j}) \to SK_j$. The user uses the partial secret received from the device and his current private key of period i to generate a new private key of period j.

- *Sign*: the signing algorithm. $Sign(M, i, SK_i) \rightarrow \langle i, S \rangle$. S is the signature. i indicates the time period in which S is signed.
- *Vrfy*: the verification algorithm. $Vrfy(PK, M, \langle i, S \rangle) \rightarrow true/false$.

3   The Hierarchical Key-Insulated Signature Scheme

While the hierarchy model is the most desirable of its properties, it unfortunately still has deficiencies. Thus, a worthwhile goal is to use recent cryptographic advances to address weaknesses in the hierarchical model by shortening the verification path and mitigating the damage caused by the compromise of a CA's private key.

Koga *et al.* noted that one public key has many matched private keys in FSS and KIS. Therefore, they suggested two constructions [13] to achieve this goal based on an interweaving FSS and a plain KIS, respectively. In their constructions, all CAs share one fixed public key but each CA holds a different private key. Thus, the verification path is short (a verifier uses the fixed public key to verify certificates issued by any CA) and an attacker cannot derive other CAs' private keys with a compromised CA's private key. However, their constructions require that the number of CAs be fixed and that all the private keys be generated during a system initialization phase. Because of these limitations, dynamically adding a subCA is impossible in their models. Furthermore, their constructions are linear, instead of being hierarchical.

Our work focuses on removing these limitations, and allowing the dynamic addition of a new CA within a hierarchical model while also achieving the overall goals of shortened verification path and damage limitation. In contrast to FSS, KIS supports an unbounded number of periods and a compromised private key cannot be used to derive any other private key without the help of a device. We therefore have selected KIS as the basis for our approach. The principal challenge addressed in this paper is the construction of a hierarchical scheme using KIS, since each layer may have an unbounded number of CAs and the number of layers is also unbounded.

3.1   Constructions and Proofs

In the desired hierarchical tree, the size of layer zero is 1; the size of layer one is N, where N is the size of the set of the natural numbers; the size of layer two is $N * N$; and the size of layer i is N^i. It seems that the hierarchical structure has the size of $\lim_{N \to +\infty} \sum_{i=0}^{N} N^i$. This number is equal to $\lim_{N \to +\infty} \frac{N^N - 1}{N - 1}$, which is close to N^{N-1}. However, since the total number we can assign in KIS is N, our design challenge becomes in essence how to map the N private keys to $\sum_{i=0}^{N} N^i$ CAs such that no two CAs share the same private key.

Since all CAs share one public key, the length of the verification path is always one. Furthermore, in KIS there is only one physically secure device. If our hierarchy has only one such device, it may be very inconvenient to add new CAs, since each addition will require use of the same device. Therefore, we give each subCA a subdevice. A desired property of these subdevices is that even if a subCA's private key is compromised and its device captured, an attacker should not be able to generate any other existing CA's private key.

Our constructions are based on two well-known number theorems:

Theorem 1. *The number of primes is infinite.*

Theorem 2. *Every positive integer (greater than 1) is a product of prime numbers, and its factorization into primes is unique up to the order of the factors.*

We give some definitions that are helpful in explaining our constructions.

Definition 1. $L = \{[x_1 \cdot x_2 \cdots x_n] : n \in N \text{ and } \forall i(1 \leq i \leq n)x_i \in N\} \bigcup \{\phi\}$

L is the union of the set of all lists of natural numbers with $\{\phi\}$.

Definition 2. *A CA's position in the hierarchical tree is defined by a $[x_1 \cdot x_2 \cdots x_t] \in L$. The $CA_{[x_1 \cdot x_2 \cdots x_t]}$ is in layer t; its ancestors are $\{[x_1 \cdot x_2 \cdots x_i] : 1 \leq i < t\}$; it is the x_tth child of its father $CA_{[x_1 \cdot x_2 \cdots x_{t-1}]}$. The position of the root CA is an empty list, denoted by CA_ϕ.*

For instance, the CAs in layer one are $CA_{[1]}, CA_{[2]}, \ldots, CA_{[i]}, \ldots$. The subCAs of $CA_{[i]}$ are $CA_{[i\cdot 1]}, CA_{[i\cdot 2]}, \ldots, CA_{[i\cdot j]}, \ldots$. Since each CA has its own device, the devices could be also denoted by the same list of numbers, *i.e.* $Dev_{[x_1 \cdot x_2 \cdots x_t]}$.

Definition 3. p_i *is the ith prime number.*

For example, $p_1 = 2, p_2 = 3, p_3 = 5, p_4 = 7, \ldots$.

Definition 4. ϖ_k *is the total of $k - bit$ primes.*

In prime number theory there is a well-known quantity $\pi(x)$ that specifies the number of primes less than some integer x. We can derive

$$\varpi_k = \pi(2^k - 1) - \pi(2^{k-1} - 1) = \pi(2^k) - \pi(2^{k-1}) \tag{1}$$

since 2^k and 2^{k-1} are not primes (for $k > 2$).

Definition 5. f *is defined as $f : \forall X \in L \to f(X) \in N$.*

f maps each position in the hierarchy to a unique natural number.

Definition 6. *Dev is a forward secure device of KIS. First, it is physically secure, i.e., it is a functional black box, unbreakable but capturable. Second, it is forward secure, i.e., it is stateful, and at each invocation it outputs a certain partial secret as a function of the current state and then deletes the old state, never repeating previous partial secrets.*

The device described in [11], which is protected by forward security technique, can provide these properties.

Now, the remaining work is to (1) create an f and (2) design the matched *Dev* to achieve the aforesaid goals .

Construction I. We construct the f function as follows (see Figure 1):

$$f_1([x_1 \cdot x_2 \cdots x_n]) = \prod_{i=1}^{n} p_{(\Sigma_{j=1}^{i} x_j)-i+1} \tag{2}$$

For instance, $f_1([i]) = p_i$. This means the $CA_{[i]}$ ($i \geq 1$) holds the $p_i th$ private key of KIS. $f_1([i \cdot j]) = p_i * p_{i+j-1}$. This means the $CA_{[i \cdot j]}$ holds the $p_i * p_{i+j-1}th$ private key of KIS. In this way, each CA is assigned a natural number so that it holds the corresponding KIS private key. In addition, we define $f_1(\phi) = 1$. This means the root CA_ϕ holds SK_1.

For example, $f_1([4]) = p_4 = 7$ so that $CA_{[4]}$ holds SK_7, the $7th$ KIS private key; $f_1([4 \cdot 2]) = p_4 * p_{4+2-1} = p_4 * p_5 = 7 * 11 = 77$ so that $CA_{[4 \cdot 2]}$, which is the 2nd child of $CA_{[4]}$, holds SK_{77}.

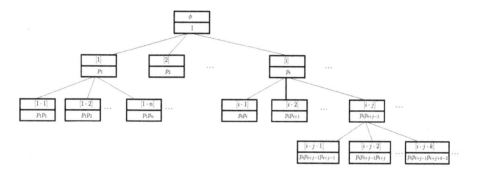

Fig. 1. Construction I

Theorem 3. $f_1 : L \to N$ is a one-to-one function, i.e., no two CAs share the same private key.

Proof. It is obvious that every member in L has a unique f_1 value in N, i.e. $\forall [x_1 \cdot x_2 \cdots x_n] \in L$, there is a unique product $\prod_{i=1}^{n} p_{(\Sigma_{j=1}^{i} x_j)-i+1} \in N$.

Then we prove that every member in N has a unique f_1^{-1} value in L, $f_1^{-1} : N \to L$. Theorem 2 says that $\forall y \in N$, $y \geq 2$, y can be factored uniquely:

$$y = p_{a_1}^{b_1} \cdot p_{a_2}^{b_2} \cdots p_{a_n}^{b_n} \tag{3}$$

where $n \in N$, $a_1 < a_2 < \cdots < a_n$ and $b_i \in N (1 \leq i \leq n)$. From (2) we have:

$$f_1^{-1}(y) = [a_1 \cdot \underbrace{1 \cdot 1 \cdots 1}_{b_1-1} \cdot (a_2 - a_1 + 1) \cdot \underbrace{1 \cdot 1 \cdots 1}_{b_2-1} \cdots (a_n - a_{n-1} + 1) \cdot \underbrace{1 \cdot 1 \cdots 1}_{b_n-1}] \tag{4}$$

For example, $f_1^{-1}(189) = f_1^{-1}(3^3 * 7) = f_1^{-1}(p_2^3 * p_4) = [2 \cdot 1 \cdot 1 \cdot 3]$. We can see every y must have a unique f_1^{-1} value since its $\{(a_1,b_1),(a_2,b_2),\ldots,(a_n,b_n)\}$ is unique. In addition, since $f_1(\phi) = 1$, $f_1^{-1}(1) = \phi$. □

It follows that any node of this tree (*i.e.*, $CA_{[x_1 \cdot x_2 \cdots x_n]}$) is mapped to a unique natural number (*i.e.*, a unique private key of KIS) and that every private key of KIS (except SK_0) has a unique position in this tree. In this way, we convert the linear structure of KIS to a hierarchical one. In addition, Theorem 1 guarantees that this tree could have infinite layers and that each node could create unlimited children as required.

A remaining problem is specifying the function of the devices used in KIS. Assume every CA has a *Dev*. $Dev_{[x_1 \cdot x_2 \cdots x_n]}$ stores three parameters: MK, $[x_1 \cdot x_2 \cdots x_n]$, and i, where i indicates how many children this CA has created. At each invocation, $Dev_{[x_1 \cdot x_2 \cdots x_n]}$ does the following:

- replace i with $i + 1$.
- run $Upd^*(f_1([x_1 \cdot x_2 \cdots x_n]), f_1([x_1 \cdot x_2 \cdots x_n \cdot i]), MK)$. (The description of Upd^* is in Section 2.2.)
- output a partial secret $SK'_{f_1([x_1 \cdot x_2 \cdots x_n]), f_1([x_1 \cdot x_2 \cdots x_n \cdot i])}$.

$CA_{[x_1 \cdot x_2 \cdots x_n]}$ derives $SK_{f_{[x_1 \cdot x_2 \cdots x_n \cdot i]}}$ from this partial secret and its private key $SK_{f_{[x_1 \cdot x_2 \cdots x_n]}}$ and then gives this new private key to its *ith* child $CA_{[x_1 \cdot x_2 \cdots x_n \cdot i]}$. Furthermore, as noted in Definition 6, every *Dev* is both physically secure and forward secure: it is infeasible to either break it and reconstruct MK or to invoke it to output a past partial secret. It only outputs the next partial secret, as intended, sequentially at each invocation.

In brief, this construction allows all the CAs to share one public key so that the verification path is shortened, and also allows every CA to create infinite children so that the hierarchy is dynamically scalable. Section 3.2 will discuss the issue of revocation.

In addition, we also can use Gödel numbers [9] to construct f:

$$f_G([x_1 \cdot x_2 \cdots x_n]) = \prod_{i=1}^{n} p_i^{x_i} \tag{5}$$

This f_G can also map any list of numbers to a unique natural number—for example, $f_G([2 \cdot 3 \cdot 2]) = p_1^2 * p_2^3 * p_3^2 = 2^2 * 3^3 * 5^2 = 2700$, but there are some numbers in N for which we cannot find corresponding number lists—for example, those natural numbers whose factors are not consecutive primes, say $33(= 3 * 11 = p_2 * p_5)$, we can never find a list with a matching f_G value (here, 33). Thus, while f_G would assign every CA a unique KIS private key, not every private key would be assigned to a CA (that is, some private keys are unused).

Construction II. We first introduce a pseudo random prime generator, which is embedded in every *Dev*.

Definition 7. *Prpg(k) is a pseudo random prime generator. At each invocation, it generates a random $k-bit$ prime. It is not feasible either to make it regenerate any previous random prime or to predict any future prime.*

We construct function f as follows:

$$f_2([x_1 \cdot x_2 \cdots x_n]) = f_2([x_1 \cdot x_2 \cdots x_{n-1}]) \cdot Prpg(k) \tag{6}$$

where $f_2(\phi) = 1$, $\forall x_1 \in N$, $f_2([x_1]) = Prpg(k)$, and k could be 1024.

The root CA_ϕ holds SK_1 of KIS. Its child, $CA_{[i]}$, holds $SK_{f_2([i])}$. $CA_{[i \cdot j]}$, the child of $CA_{[i]}$, holds $SK_{f_2([i]) \cdot Prpg(k)}$. Note that f_2 is not a one-to-one function from L to N. The following Theorem 4 guarantees that f_2 nonetheless works.

Lemma 1. *Let Pr' be the probability that a new CA is assigned the same private key as any other existing CA by f_2. When the depth of the hierarchy is not greater than ϖ_{1024}, $Pr' \le \frac{1}{\varpi_{1024}}$.*

Proof. In our hierarchy, f_2 guarantees that CAs in different layers never share the same private key. Therefore, a new CA may only share a private key with CAs in the same layer.

In the ith layer, when a new CA is being added, let Pr'_i be the probability that this new CA shares the same private key with any given CA. We can derive

$$Pr'_1 = \frac{1}{\varpi_{1024}}, Pr'_2 = \frac{2!}{\varpi_{1024}^2} - \frac{1}{\varpi_{1024}^3}, Pr'_3 = \frac{3!}{\varpi_{1024}^3} - \frac{9}{\varpi_{1024}^4} + \frac{4}{\varpi_{1024}^5}, \cdots$$

Note that Pr'_i becomes more complicated with increasing i since $Prpg(1024)$ might choose any ϖ_{1024}-bit prime more than once. However, we can find an upper bound: $Pr'_i \le \frac{i!}{\varpi_{1024}^i}$. The numerator is not greater than $i!$ since the value of a product cannot be affected by the order of its factors.

Furthermore, $\forall i$, $1 \le i \le \varpi_{1024}$, we have

$$\frac{i!}{\varpi_{1024}^i} \le \frac{(i-1)!}{\varpi_{1024}^{i-1}} < \cdots < \frac{1}{\varpi_{1024}} \tag{7}$$

So, we have $\forall i$, $1 \le i \le \varpi_{1024}$, $Pr'_i \le \frac{1}{\varpi_{1024}}$, i.e. $Pr' \le \frac{1}{\varpi_{1024}}$.   □

In traditional cryptography with a hierarchical model, each CA has its own public/private key pair, such as an RSA key pair. A parent vouches for the private keys of its children. We know that a RSA private key is decided by its modulus and public key, and that RSA is no less secure if public keys are always chosen to be the same number (in the real world the default public key is always 65537 in OpenSSL). Assuming all RSA users use the default number, it is possible that two of them share the same private key and modulus.

Theorem 4. *In the traditional method, let Pr be the probability that a new CA generates a RSA prime couple identical to that in use by another CA. When the depth of the hierarchy is not greater than ϖ_k, we have $Pr' < Pr$.*

Proof. Assume the modulus of RSA is 1024-bit so that the two big primes in RSA are 512 bit each. In our hierarchy, we assume $k = 1024$.

Step 1: Compute ϖ_{512} and ϖ_{1024}. (1) suggests that we need to obtain $\pi(2^{512})$, $\pi(2^{511})$, $\pi(2^{1024})$ and $\pi(2^{1023})$ first[2]. Dusart [7] showed:

$$\frac{x}{\ln x}(1+\frac{0.992}{\ln x}) \leq \pi(x) \leq \frac{x}{\ln x}(1+\frac{1.2762}{\ln x}) \tag{9}$$

where the lower bound holds for $x > 598$ and the upper bound holds for $x > 1$. The results of using (9) are

$$2^{502.5288} \leq \varpi_{512} \leq 2^{502.5323} \tag{10}$$

$$2^{1013.5288} \leq \varpi_{1024} \leq 2^{1013.5305} \tag{11}$$

Step 2: In the traditional method, for any existing CA, its two primes could be identical with the probability of $\frac{1}{\varpi_{512}}$ and be different with the probability of $\frac{\varpi_{512}-1}{\varpi_{512}}$. So, we have

$$Pr = \frac{1}{\varpi_{512}}(\frac{1}{\varpi_{512}}\cdot\frac{1}{\varpi_{512}}) + \frac{\varpi_{512}-1}{\varpi_{512}}(\frac{1}{\varpi_{512}}\cdot\frac{1}{\varpi_{512}}\cdot 2) = \frac{2}{\varpi_{512}^2} - \frac{1}{\varpi_{512}^3} \tag{12}$$

From (10) and (12), we can derive $Pr > \frac{1}{\varpi_{512}^2} \geq \frac{1}{2^{1005.0646}}$. From (11) and Lemma 1, we can likewise derive $Pr' \leq \frac{1}{\varpi_{1024}} \leq \frac{1}{2^{1023.5288}}$. So, $Pr' < Pr$.   □

Thus, any node of this tree is mapped to a natural number by f_2, and this tree is dynamically scalable. However, it is not the case either that every KIS private key is assigned to a CA or that every private key is assigned to a unique CA. Theorem 4 guarantees that the probability that any two CAs share a KIS private key is less than the probability that any two RSA users share a prime couple.

To summarize the function of the KIS device, each $Dev_{[x_1 \cdot x_2 \cdots x_n]}$ stores three parameters, MK, $[x_1 \cdot x_2 \cdots x_n]$ and child counter i, and also embeds a $Prpg(k)$. At each invocation, $Dev_{[x_1 \cdot x_2 \cdots x_n]}$ accomplishes the same steps as in Construction I, but by calling f_2 instead of f_1.

Construction III. We can construct function f using $Prpg(k)$ in another way:

$$f_3([x_1 \cdot x_2 \cdots x_n]) = Prpg(1023 + n) \tag{13}$$

The supporting theorem is as follows:

---

[2] The latest research [16] gives $\pi(x) = \int_2^x \frac{dx}{\ln x} + O(xe^{-\frac{A(\ln x)^{3/5}}{(\ln \ln x)^{1/5}}})$ for some constant A. But generally we can approximate

$$\pi(x) \sim \frac{x}{\ln x - 1} \tag{8}$$

The results of using this formulas are $\varpi_{512} \sim 2^{502.5300}$ and $\varpi_{1024} \sim 2^{1013.5293}$.

Theorem 5. *If each CA is assigned a private key of KIS by f_3, let Pr'' be the probability that a new CA is assigned the same private key as another CA. We have $Pr'' < Pr$, where Pr is the same as in Theorem 4.*

Proof. Step 1: It is easy to see that CAs in different layers can never share the same private key. Let Pr_i'' be the probability that a new CA of layer i shares the same private key with any other CA in the same layer, $Pr_i'' = \frac{1}{\varpi_{1023+i}}$.

Step 2: We begin by proving Pr_i'' is nonincreasing. If ϖ_k is nondecreasing, Pr_i'' is nonincreasing. Thus, we prove that ϖ_k is nondecreasing, where $k \geq 1024$.

$$\varpi_k \geq \varpi_{k-1}$$

$$\overset{(1)}{\Leftrightarrow} \pi(2^k) - \pi(2^{k-1}) \geq \pi(2^{k-1}) - \pi(2^{k-2})$$

$$\overset{(8)}{\Leftrightarrow} \frac{2^k}{k \ln 2 - 1} - \frac{2^{k-1}}{(k-1)\ln 2 - 1} \geq \frac{2^{k-1}}{(k-1)\ln 2 - 1} - \frac{2^{k-2}}{(k-2)\ln 2 - 1}$$

$$\Leftrightarrow \frac{4}{k \ln 2 - 1} + \frac{1}{(k-2)\ln 2 - 1} \geq \frac{3}{(k-1)\ln 2 - 1} + \frac{1}{(k-1)\ln 2 - 1}$$

$$\Leftarrow \frac{4}{k \ln 2 - 1} > \frac{3}{(k-1)\ln 2 - 1}$$

$$\Leftrightarrow k > 4 + \frac{1}{\ln 2}$$

So, we have when $i \geq 1$, $k \geq 1024 \Rightarrow k > 4 + \frac{1}{\ln 2} \Rightarrow \varpi_k \geq \varpi_{k-1} \Rightarrow Pr_i'' \leq Pr_{i-1}''$.

Step 3: We already know that $\frac{1}{\varpi_{1024}} < Pr$, i.e., $Pr_1'' < Pr$ (see the proof of Theorem 4). So, $\forall i, i > 1$, $Pr_i'' < Pr_1'' < Pr$, i.e., $Pr'' < Pr$.   □

The function and discussion of *Dev* for Construction III is identical to that in Construction II.

3.2   Discussion

Primes. Construction I can infinitely expand but its actual scalability depends on how many available primes we have. It requires that the device used generate the next prime when needed. If the scale of the hierarchy is very large, recent research shows that Construction I will have trouble. The current world record[3] found the largest known value of $\pi(n)$: $\pi(4 * 10^{22})$ which is 783,964,159, 847,056,303,858. Since $4 * 10^{22} = 2^{75.0824}$, it is computationally challenging that the device is required to compute the next prime for a 75-bit prime.

Construction II and III cannot infinitely expand but we have proved that the probability that a new CA might share a same private key with an existing CA is smaller than the probability that two CAs share a same prime couple in the traditional RSA construction. Judging whether a number is prime can be done much faster than counting the number of primes less than that number or generating the next prime. The largest known prime[4] is $2^{20996011} - 1$ which has 6320430 digits. So, generating a larger prime is also a challenge.

---

[3] http://numbers.computation.free.fr/Constants/Primes/countingPrimes.html
[4] http://www.utm.edu/research/primes/notes/by_year.html

Revocation. We classify the types of compromises that are possible. Note that the security proof to KIS is outside the scope of our work.

First, an attacker only compromises a CA's private key. In the traditional hierarchical model, if a CA's private key is compromised, we need to revoke (1) this compromised private key, (2) all of its subCAs' private keys, and (3) all the users' certificates issued by this CA and its subCAs. However, in our scheme since the device is physically secure, the exposure of any CA's private key will not allow the attacker to derive any other private key. We only revoke (1) this compromised private key and (2) the common users' certificates signed by this CA's private key. Its subCAs' private keys are all still valid, as are any user certificates signed by its subCAs. This CA will be added as a new CA by its parent and these revoked certificates will be re-signed using its new private key.

Second, the attacker only captures a CA's device. Since the device only generates partial secrets, the attacker cannot derive any private key. So, we needn't revoke anything—what we need to do is to give this CA a new device.

Third, the attacker compromises a CA's private key and captures its device. Since the *Dev* is both physically secure and forward secure, the attacker only can derive future private keys which haven't been assigned to any existing subCA. So, the private keys of existing CAs are still secure and valid. We need to revoke (1) this CA's private key and (2) all the common users' certificates issued by this CA. This CA will be re-added as a new CA by its parent and will re-issue these revoked certificates.

If this compromised CA is the root CA, we can re-initialize a HKI scheme for it and its old childrens' private keys are still safe and valid. If so, we will have two HKI systems, *i.e.*, two HKI public keys; therefore, we use another method. Construction I only has one unused private key, SK_0 (because $f_1(\phi) = 1$ and $f_1([1]) = p_1 = 2$). Therefore, the root CA only has one backup private key, which is SK_0. We could assign $SK_{f_1([1])}$ to the root CA as its initial private key so that $SK_{f_1([i])}$, $i \geq 2$, is the backup of $SK_{f_1([1])}$; then every layer in Construction I is shifted one-layer lower. Construction II and III have many unused private keys which could be the backups of the root CA's private key.

Note that in *Hierarchical ID-based cryptography* [8] if any of those private key generators is broken, the attacker can generate any private key of its domain. However, in our constructions if the physically secure device is captured, the attacker cannot generate any private key without an exposed private key. Even if he also has an exposed private key, the newly generated private keys are different from any existing CA's.

4   Conclusion and Future Work

This hierarchical key-insulated signature scheme shortens the verification path using the KIS property that many private keys with different indexes share one fixed public key; it mitigates the damage of the exposure of a CA's private key because our *Dev* is forward secure; and it allows the hierarchy to add new CAs dynamically and without bound, which is the main problem not addressed by existing work on the previous points. In addition, our constructions are built on a general KIS scheme, allowing improvements in key length, computation complexity, or robustness for KIS to directly benefit our scheme as well.

This paper has focused on providing a functional description based on a new forward secure *Dev*. The implementation of *Dev*, in hardware or software, is our next work. Furthermore, there are several aspects of our scheme that we hope to improve; for example, Construction II and III have many unused private keys, and the key length in Construction II grows quickly with increasing depth in the hierarchy. The scheme does not effectively scale. It would be desirable to come up with a scheme that computes the i-th private key with time complexity independent of i.

References

1. Internet X.509 Public Key Infrastructure Certificate and CRL profile. *RFC3280*, April 2002.
2. Michel Abdalla and Leonid Reyzin. A New Forward-Secure Digital Signature Scheme. *Advances in Cryptology-ASIACRYPT'00*, pages 116–129, Dec 2000.
3. Mihir Bellare and Sara K. Miner. A Forward-Secure Digital Signature Scheme. *Advances in Cryptology-CRYPTO'99*.
4. Mihir Bellare and Bennet Yee. Forward-Security in Private-Key Cryptography. *Topics in Cryptology-CT-RSA*, 2003.
5. Ran Canetti, Shai Halevi, and Jonathan Katz. A Forward-Secure Public-Key Encryption Scheme. *Advances in Cryptology - Eurocrypt'02*.
6. Yevgeniy Dodis, Jonathan Katz, Shouhuai Xu, and Moti Yung. Strong Key-Insulated Public-Key Schemes. *Workshop on Public Key Cryptography (PKC)*, Jan 2003.
7. Pierre Dusart. The kth prime is greater than $k(\ln k + \ln\ln k - 1)$ for $k \geq 2$. *mc*, 68(225):411–415, January 1999.
8. Craig Gentry and Alice Silverberg. Hierarchical ID-Based Cryptography. *Proceedings of Asiacrypt'02*.
9. Kurt Gödel. *On Formally Undecidable Propositions of Principia Mathematica and Related Systems*. Dover Publications, INC., 1992.
10. Gene Itkis and Leonid Reyzin. Forward-Secure Signatures with Optimal Signing and Verifying. *Advances in Cryptology-CRYPTO'01*.
11. Gene Itkis and Leonid Reyzin. SiBIR: Signer-Base Intrusion-Resilient Signatures. In *Advances in Cryptology - CRYPTO 2002*, volume 2442 of *Lecture Notes in Computer Science*. Springer, 2002.
12. Jonathan Katz. A Forward-Secure Public-Key Encryption Scheme. *Cryptology eprint archive Report 2002/060*, May 2002. http://eprint.iacr.org/2002/060/.
13. Satoshi Koga and Kouichi Sakurai. Decentralization Methods of Certification Authority Using the Digital Signature Schemes. In *Proceedings of 2nd Annual PKI Research Workshop*, 2003.
14. Anton Kozlov and Leonid Reyzin. Forward-Secure Signatures with Fast Key Update. *3rd Conference on Security in Communication Networks*, 2002.
15. Hugo Krawczyk. Simple Forward-Secure Signatures From Any Signature Scheme. *7th ACM Conference on Computer and Communication Security*, 2000.
16. Hans Riesel. The Remainder Term in the Prime Number Theorem. *Prime Numbers and Computer Methods for Factorization (Progress in Mathematics, Vol 126)*, 1994.

Certificate Recommendations to Improve the Robustness of Web of Trust*

Qinglin Jiang, Douglas S. Reeves, and Peng Ning

Cyber Defense Lab
Departments of Computer Science and Electrical and Computer Engineering
N. C. State University, Raleigh, NC 27695-8207 USA
{qjiang,reeves,pning}@ncsu.edu

Abstract. Users in a distributed system establish webs of trust by issuing and exchanging certificates amont themselves. This approach does not require a central, trusted keyserver. The distributed web of trust, however, is susceptible to attack by malicious users, who may issue false certificates. In this work, we propose a method for generating certificate *recommendations*. These recommendations guide the users in creating webs of trust that are highly robust to attacks. To accomplish this we propose a heuristic method of graph augmentation for the certificate graph, and show experimentally that it is close to optimal. We also investigate the impact of user preferences and non-compliance with these recommendations, and demonstrate that our method helps identify malicious users if there are any.

Keywords: Authentication, certificates, PGP keyrings, graph connectivity.

1 Introduction

Authenticating a user's public key is a very basic requirement for public key cryptography. In large-scale systems, this function is usually provided by public key infrastructures, such as X.509 [25] and PGP [27]. Generally speaking, in these systems public keys are authenticated by means of certificates. A certificate is a signed message in which an authority speaks about a user's public key.

Obviously, the correctness of a user's public key information in a certificate relies on the certificate issuer or authority. In X.509, certificates can only be issued by an entity referred to as a certificate authority, or CA. A CA is usually secured and trusted, so it is safe to believe all certificates contain truthful information. Systems like this are referred to as *hierarchical trust* systems, with CAs as roots of the hierarchy. In PGP, each user becomes an authority, and issues certificates to each other. Systems like this are referred to as *web of trust*

---

* This work is partially supported by the U.S. Army Research Office under grant DAAD19-02-1-0219, and by the National Science Foundation under grant CCR-0207297.

K. Zhang and Y. Zheng (Eds.): ISC 2004, LNCS 3225, pp. 292–303, 2004.

systems. In such systems, it is unrealistic to expect every user to be fully secure and trustworthy. If users can be malicious, or their computers can be compromised, it is risky to accept all the certificates they provide without question. For this reason, a method of measuring the robustness of web of trust systems would be very useful. Very intuitively, several researchers have suggested the use of redundancy, i.e., the agreement of multiple users to authenticate the same key information. Following this method, investigation of existing PGP keyrings shows that most of them do not provide a high degree of assurance in the validity of key information[14]. These previous works have mainly addressed the issue of how to *measure* robustness. In this paper, our focus is on how to *enhance* robustness in web of trust systems.

The paper is organized as follows. Section 2 discusses related work on using redundancy to measure the robustness of web of trust. Section 3 defines the research problems and our assumptions. Section 4 describes an algorithm for efficiently enhance the robustness of web of trust. Section 5 illustrates the performance of our solutions on both actual and generated web of trust using experiments. Section 6 investigates the impact of users' willingness and users' preference on the recommendations, respectively. Section 7 discusses and shows how our recommendation method may be used to help users to detect attacks and identify malicious users. The final section concludes our work, and presents some open problems.

2   Related Work

First we briefly mention some existing public key infrastructures. X.509 [25] is centralized and has a hierarchical structure composed of many CAs. PGP [27] is distributed, and is popular in personal communications. Some other public key infrastructures, such as SPKI/SDSI [8], Delegation Networks [2] and Policy-Maker [5] mainly focus on access control issues. Most of the methods [24,18,4,17], or so called "trust metrics" measure the robustness of web of trust based on the trust profile established for each user. A new concept of insurance is introduced in [21] and a maximum flow approach is presented in [16]. A different approach is presented in [22] which computes the assurance by counting the number of public key-independent certificate chains. The method of [14] is similar to [22] but investigates the case that each user may possess multiple public keys. It also shows practical PGP keyrings provides poor assurance on users' key information and investigates certificate conflicts. Certificate conflicts were first pointed out to be very important in [22] and is analyzed in [14]. However, while these methods provide a way to measure the robustness of web of trust, they do not address how to enhance it.

The next section presents the definitions and assumptions of the research problem.

3   Problem Statement

First we briefly introduce some notions in web of trust systems. A *user* is an entity who participates in web of trust and who will receive our recommendations. He or she may be represented by a *name*, such as "Bob" and "Alice". The set of all names is denoted by U. A *public key certificate* is a signed name-to-key binding represented by a triple $\langle x, k_x, s(k_y) \rangle$, where x is a name, k_x is a public key, and $s(k_y)$ is a digital signature (generated using the private key corresponding to k_y) over the binding of x and k_x. The set of all certificates are usually stored and collected in one or more public known locations, i.e. *keyservers* or *repositories*.[1]

In all methods of authenticating public keys [24,18,4,17,21,22,16,14], multiple certificate chains represent high assurance for the name-to-key binding in question. More specifically and accurately, [22] has shown multiple disjoint certificate chains is an essential measurement of the assurance of name-to-key bindings.

In the rest of this paper we use *certificate graphs* as the model to represent the collection of certificates. A certificate graph G is a simple graph and consists of a set V of vertexes and a set E of arcs (directed edges). In this graph, a vertex labeled k in V represents the public key k. There is an arc labeled x from vertex k_y to vertex k_x if and only if there exists a certificate $\langle x, k_x, s(k_y) \rangle$. That is, the key k_y is used to sign a certificate binding x to k_x. A certificate chain is represented by a directed path in the certificate graph, starting from a key in a known correct name-to-key binding. [2]

From the above, if there are q vertex-disjoint paths in the certificate graph, each starting from user x's own key and all ending at the same target name-to-key binding, the *assurance* of the target name-to-key binding for x is defined to be q. That is, x would be able to say that the target name-to-key binding is resistant to attacks on less than q keys as shown in [22,16]. The number of vertex disjoint paths can be computed by a maximum flow algorithm using an vertex-splitting technique[1]. There are various maximum flow algorithm available, such as those in [1].

we introduce the following notions in a certificate graph. Let $K_x(G)$ represent the set of all *correct* name-to-key bindings whose keys are reachable from vertex k_x (x's own key) in the certificate graph G. Let $K_x^T(G, l)$ represent the set of name-to-key bindings whose assurance are greater or equal to a predefined threshold l (for user x, binding x/k_x and the name-to-key bindings x directly certifies are correct, thus their assurance is set to be infinite). Then for user x the *robustness* of the certificate graph G at assurance l is defined to be

$$\mathcal{A}(x, G, l) = \frac{\mid K_x^T(G, l) \mid}{\mid K_x(G) \mid}$$

---

[1] The issue of how users distribute certificates among themselves, when there are no public repositories, is out of the scope of this paper.

[2] The set of known correct name-to-key bindings for each user is different. It is a general knowledge that user x's known correct name-to-key bindings include her own binding x/k_x and those that are directly certified by herself.

We define the total, or aggregate, robustness of a certificate graph G at assurance l for all users to be

$$\mathcal{A}(G, l) = \frac{\sum_{x \in U} |K_x^T(G, l)|}{\sum_{x \in U} |K_x(G)|}$$

It is straightforward to see this robustness represents the percentage of name-to-key bindings whose assurance is at least l, thus robustness can range from a minimum of 0% (worst) to 100% (best).

We can now formally state the problem addressed by this paper. Given a directed certificate graph G and a value l representing a desired level of assurance, add the minimum number of arcs (i.e., additional certificates) to this graph so that robustness $\mathcal{A}(G, l)$ of whole certificate graph reaches 100%. It is worthwhile to minimize the number of additional certificates because it may reduce users' efforts that are required to yield the desired robust keyrings.

The next section presents a method for accomplishing the goal.

4   Enhancing Certificate Graphs

From the preceding discussion, assurance is enhanced when the number of vertex-disjoint paths between pairs of vertexes is increased. By Menger's theorem [12], vertex-disjoint paths correspond to graph connectivity. Specifically, a graph is q-connected iff every pair of vertexes is joined by at least q vertex-disjoint paths, or to say, there does not exist a set of q or fewer vertexes whose removal disconnects the graph [12]. The key requirement in achieving our goal is therefore to make the directed certificate graph G q-connected, where $q \geq l$ and l is the desired level of assurance for all users and all name-to-key bindings.

The problem of increasing the connectivity of a graph by adding a minimal number of edges is referred to as the *graph connectivity augmentation* problem. There are a number of solutions to this problem and a quite complete survey has been done both in [20] and [9]. Among the numerous solutions to this problem, [10,3,11] are the candidates to augment the vertex-connectivity in directed graphs. Unfortunately these may not be the practical solutions. For example, [10] relies on the ellipsoid method [19] which is well known to be impractical. [3] points out its practical efficient implementations require oracle choices. [11] requires a very expensive running time of $O(|V|^6 f(k))$ where $|V|$ is the number of vertexes, $f(k)$ is a super-exponential function of k and k is the required connectivity.

To efficiently solve this problem, we propose a heuristic for the graph augmentation problem. First we introduce some notations. Let $G = (V, E)$ be the given certificate graph. The *in-degree* $\Delta_i(v)$ of a vertex v in V is defined as the number of arcs in G whose terminal is v, while the *out-degree* $\Delta_o(v)$ of v is defined as the number of arcs in G whose initial is v. Let $\lambda_i^q(v)$ be the in-degree q-*deficiency* of vertex v, i.e., the minimum value to be added to make $\Delta_i(v)$ greater than or equal to q, and $\lambda_o^q(v)$ is similarly defined for the out-degree. The *minimum degree* of a graph G is represented as $\delta(G)$, and is defined as

$$\delta(G) = min\{\Delta_i(v), \Delta_o(v)|v \in V\}$$

The heuristic has two phases, and is shown as Algorithm 2. In Phase 1, arcs are added between vertexes with the smallest in- or out-degrees. The purpose is to increase $\delta(G)$ to reach q by adding a minimum number of arcs. In Phase 2, each vertex's in- and out-degree is at least q but G may not be q-connected. To make G q-connected, algorithm 1 is used to detect critical pairs of vertexes whose connectivities are lower than q, then arcs are directly added between them.

Algorithm 1 q-connectivity algorithm

---

input: digraph G

output: vertex connectivity $q(G)$

1: select a vertex u with the minimum $\{\Delta_i(u) + \Delta_o(u)\}$
2: compute $c_1 = \min\{q(u,v) \mid v \in V - \{u\}, (u,v) \notin E\}$
3: compute $c_2 = \min\{q(v,u) \mid v \in V - \{u\}, (v,u) \notin E\}$
4: compute $c_3 = \min\{q(x,y) \mid x \in P(u), y \in O(u), (x,y) \notin E\}$
5: $q(G)=\min\{c_1, c_2, c_3\}$

Algorithm 2 *Graph connectivity augmentation algorithm*

---

input: $G(V, E)$, l

output: $G'(V, E')(l - connected)$

1: $G'(V, E') = G(V, E), q = l$

Phase 1

2: construct an arc list $L = \{(u,v) \mid u \in V, v \in V, (u,v) \notin E', (\Delta_o(u) < q \vee \Delta_i(v) < q)\}$
ordered by $\text{SUM}(\Delta_o(u) + \Delta_i(v))$
3: **while** $\delta(G') < q$ **do**
4:     choose the first arc e in L
5:     add arc e to E'
6:     update L
7: **end while**

Phase 2

8: run algorithm 1 and construct the arc list $L = \{(u,v) \mid q(u,v) < q, u \in V, v \in V\}$
ordered by $q(u,v)$.
9: **while** $q(G') < q$ **do**
10:     choose the first arc e in L
11:     add e to E'
12:     run algorithm 1 and update L
13: **end while**

Due to space reasons, we only briefly explain algorithm 1 and 2. Details of these algorithms may be found in [13]. First we explain algorithm 1. Denote the vertex connectivity between two nodes u and v as $q(u,v)$. The vertex connectivity $q(u,v)$ between u and v can be computed by a maximum flow algorithm [1] using vertex-splitting techniques in time $O(|V||E|\log(\frac{|V|}{|E|}))$. The vertex connectivity

$q(G)$ of G, is the minimum vertex connectivity of any pair of vertexes in graph G, i.e.,

$$q(G) = min\{q(u,v)|\text{ ordered pair } u, v, (u,v) \notin E\}.$$

$q(G)$ can be easily determined by computing the maximum flow for every ordered pair of vertexes in G and taking the minimum. However, we propose algorithm 1 as a faster means of computing $q(G)$. This algorithm follows some insights from an approach in [1] for computing edge connectivity of a directed graph. The set $P(v)$ of predecessors of vertex v is defined as $P(v) = \{u|(u,v) \in E\}$, and the set $O(v)$ of successors of vertex v is defined as $O(v) = \{u|(v,u) \in E\}$. Algorithm 1's main purpose is to check $q(G)$ by checking the connectivity of a set of $2|V|+q^2$ pairs of vertexes. The connectivity of each pair of vertexes is checked using maximum flow algorithm and algorithm 1 requires to run maximum flow $2|V| + q^2$ times.

In algorithm 2, phase 1 is to make $\delta(G) \geq q$ by adding a minimum number of arcs. It is simple to see that in a q-connected graph, any vertex's in- and out-degree must be at least q (We refer to this as the $q - degree$ requirement). Thus the number of arcs needed to be added to make $\delta(G) \geq q$ is at least

$$max(\sum_{v \in V} |\lambda_i^q(v)|, \sum_{v \in V} |\lambda_o^q(v)|).$$

Our heuristic successfully achieve this goal by adding an arc from the vertex with the minimum out-degree to the vertex with the minimum in-degree each time. In phase 2, if algorithm 1 tells us G is already q-connected, then algorithm 2 can simply stop because the goal of making G q-connected is already completed. Otherwise, algorithm 1 would tell us which pair of vertexes has a connectivity lower than q, and our heuristic's choice is to simply add an arc directly between them.

The complexity of our heuristic is discussed as follows. Phase 1 only needs to check and sort each vertex's degree and requires $O(|V|log(|V|))$ time. In phase 2, suppose a total number of ε additional arcs are needed to make the graph q-connected, then algorithm 1 needs to be called ε times. Algorithm 1 itself needs to run maximum flow $2|V| + q^2$ times. The running time of phase 2 is $O(\varepsilon \cdot |V|^2|E| log(\frac{|V|}{|E|}))$ which is also the running time for algorithm 2.

With this method, we can now address the goal of increasing the robustness of a certificate graph to 100%. For any arbitrary level of assurance l, the certificate graph is enhanced or augmented to be q-connected$(q \geq l)$ using the above method. The method is guaranteed to terminate, and the enhanced certificate graph is guaranteed to have an robustness of 100%. The arcs added by the method represent recommendations of certificates to add to the certificate graph. These recommendations may be directly sent to users by email[3] or be provided by running web service.

We have described heuristic methods for accomplishing our goal. In the next section, we examine the performance of the heuristic on actual web of trust: PGP keyrings.

---

[3] In PGP, each user's email address can be directly obtained from their certificates.

Table 1. PGP keyrings used in this experiment

KR25	PGP keyrings with 67 keys and 209 certificates
KR105	PGP keyrings with 105 keys and 245 certificates
KR588	PGP keyrings with 588 keys and 5237 certificates
KR1226	PGP keyrings with 1226 keys and 8779 certificates
SKR588	Synthetic keyrings simulating KR588
SKR1226	Synthetic keyrings simulating KR1226

5   Experimental Results

The effectiveness and practicality of the proposed methods depend on the data to which it is applied. The best examples of web of trust that are widely available are PGP keyrings[7]. We therefore used these for purposes of experimental validation. The PGP keyrings we use in experiments are downloaded from PGP keyservers and the keyanalyze [23] tool was used to extract many strongly-connected components. The PGP keyrings used in this experiment are listed in table 1.

In the first set of experiments, we attempted to enhance the robustness of the actual keyrings KR588 and KR1226. We used algorithm 2 to enhance its robustness to 100% for varying levels of assurance l. We compared the performance with a method which randomly adds arcs to the graph. Any reasonable heuristic should of course perform better than the random method. We also computed a lower bound for the number of arcs which must be added by *any* method in order to achieve q-connectivity. It is very intuitive to see that by the q-degree requirement, the minimum number of arcs that must be added to make G q-connected is at least

$$max(\sum_{v \in V} |\lambda_i^q(v)|, \sum_{v \in V} |\lambda_o^q(v)|).$$

The performance of our method (total number of arcs after addition) relative to the random method, and to this lower bound, is shown in Table 2 for the actual keyrings KR588 and KR1226. It is clear that our heuristic performs much better than the random method. In addition, our method is very close to optimal for these two keyrings; in all cases, the difference between the lower bound and our method is no greater than 0.7%.

To increase confidence that these results are representative, we also synthetically generated keyrings using the model of [6]. In this experiment, we generate two sets of keyrings, i.e. SKR588 and SKR1226. For each set of keyring, 50 synthetic keyrings were generated, based on the method of [6]. The results are shown in Table 3. Each value shown in this graph is the average of 50 synthetic instances and has been rounded to the nearest integer, and has a 99% confidence interval of ±5 certificates. The results show our method consistently performs close to optimal, and much better than a random method.

Table 2. Number of certificates needed to reach 100% robustness for PGP keyrings

PGP keyrings	Different methods	Total number of arcs needed at different levels of assurance								
		$l=2$	$l=3$	$l=4$	$l=5$	$l=6$	$l=7$	$l=8$	$l=9$	$l=10$
KR588	lower bound	5343	5523	5754	6029	6351	6706	7085	7484	7907
	our method	5349	5524	5754	6030	6352	6710	7086	7484	7907
	random method	8168	8877	9864	10505	11959	13991	14654	14901	15267
KR1226	lower bound	9147	9720	10403	11187	12034	12931	13846	14781	15744
	our method	9203	9769	10458	11223	12061	12960	13876	14827	15796
	random method	17369	20385	24679	24709	26717	31507	32350	33352	33372

Table 3. Number of certificates needed to reach 100% robustness for synthetic keyrings

Synthetic keyrings	Different methods	Total number of arcs needed at different levels of assurance								
		$l=2$	$l=3$	$l=4$	$l=5$	$l=6$	$l=7$	$l=8$	$l=9$	$l=10$
SKR588	lower bound	5409	5598	5814	6077	6376	6713	7077	7469	7880
	our method	5409	5598	5815	6077	6377	6714	7078	7469	7881
	random method	9289	10255	11324	12376	13157	14219	15132	15841	16787
SKR1226	lower bound	9286	9874	10528	11284	12102	12973	13874	14808	15763
	our method	9287	9875	10530	11285	12103	12974	13875	14809	15763
	random method	18466	20989	23524	25923	27565	29635	31379	33448	35217

These experiments also yield useful insights into existing PGP keyrings. First, it may be seen that the "cost" (additional certificates) to achieve 100% robustness for a lower level of assurance is small (e.g., less than 10% additional certificates with no more than assurance 4). However, the overhead grows steadily, and for a higher level of assurance (e.g., greater than 10) it may be expected this overhead is substantial.

Our experiments also show the practical running time for algorithm 2. Practical experiment data tells us that algorithm 1 is called by algorithm 2 for only a few times. In all cases, ε is no greater than $\frac{|V|}{50}$. The heuristic is implemented in Java and C and the test environment is Linux Fedora Core 1 on a PC with a 2.4GHz Pentium IV processor and 512MB of memory. For the PGP keyring KR588 and KR1226, in all cases algorithm 2 requires less than 2 and 30 minutes to complete, respectively.

6   User Preferences (Constraints)

In our discussion of the problem we termed the addition of certificates *recommendations*. This is an acknowledgment that certificates are generated by people, frequently for personal reasons. We propose that user preferences be incorporated into the method for enhancing certificate graphs, in the form of constraints. The many forms such preferences can take is outside the scope of this short discussion. We only intend to indicate two approaches and show that our heuristic is feasible even under such constraints. For these purposes, we propose to model user preferences as *user compliance* and *buddy lists*, respectively. By user compliance, we mean some users may choose to follow only part of our recommendations instead of all of them. In buddy lists, a user would not issue certificates to users other than those on her buddy list. One consequence of user compliance and buddy lists (and of user preferences in general) is that it is no longer possible to guarantee that the enhancement method will always terminate with a robustness of 100%. Experiments for these two types of user preferences have been done and are shown as below.

User compliance. To investigate how user compliance may affect the performance of our method, we ran the following experiments. First we applied algorithm 2 and produced all the recommendations that are needed to reach a 100% robustness at assurance levels from 2 to 10. With all these recommendations, a fraction t of users are randomly chosen to follow all of our recommendations and the rest users will randomly choose to follow a part(from 0% to 99.99%) of our recommendations. The results are shown in Figure 1 for different values of t.

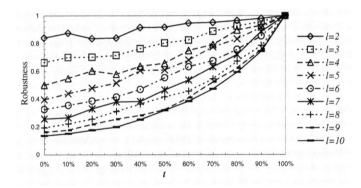

Fig. 1. Robustness of KR588 under different percentage of users' compliance

From this figure, we can see that the robustness is always higher than t for small levels of assurance($l < 5$). When l goes higher, the robustness can't keep up with t. One of the reasons is that for lower l, the number of recommendations is small, thus the users who don't comply with recommendations have little impairment on the resulting robustness of keyrings.

Buddy lists. Practical data of buddy lists, such as MSN, Yahoo Messenger and AOL Messenger are not available to us for obvious reasons. Instead, we artificially generated the buddy lists by utilizing the small world graph generator of [6]. Small world phenomena has been frequently found in social networks [26], World Wide Webs [15] and PGP web of trust [6]. Specifically, the users' buddy lists may be represented by a small world graph, where a vertex represents a user and an arc represents the buddy relationship. We generated 9 different sets of user preferences (sets of buddy lists), for values of b from 2 to 10. For each set of user preferences, we measured the achievable robustness with our method at different levels of assurance from 2 to 10. Incorporating the constraint of buddy lists into algorithm 2 is simple. In this algorithm, when building the candidate arc list L, we simply exclude those arcs (u, v) where v is not in u's buddy list. The results for algorithm 2 with buddy lists constraints are shown in Figure 2.

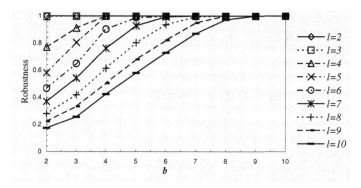

Fig. 2. Robustness of KR588 under different buddy lists

From this figure it can be seen that robustness increase roughly linearly with the increase of b, the minimum size of buddy list. The rate of increase of robustness decreases as b goes up. And a 100% robustness is achieved once b becomes the same as the level of assurance.

7   Certificate Conflicts and Suspect Set

Certificate conflict was first caught attention in [22] and being analyzed in [14]. It is defined to be a pair of certificates in which the two name-to-key bindings have the same name but different keys. The definition is also extended to the case that each user may have multiple keys by associating a sequence number with each key[14]. Certificate conflicts may be used to detect malicious behavior and it is possible to construct *suspect set* to identify malicious users [14]. A suspect set is defined to be a set of names in which at least one belongs to a malicious user. Or to say, there is at least one malicious user in each suspect set. For details on how suspect sets may be constructed and used, we refer to [14].

One impact of our recommendation method is that it may be used for the purpose of constructing suspect sets. To see how this purpose may be served, we ran the following experiment on KR588. Note this experiment is just an illustration of our method's application to identify malicious users. No proof or data about the general effectiveness or optimality of the method are presented. First we randomly chose 9 colluding malicious users and each of them certifies an incorrect name-to-key binding to a victim newly added to the keyring. Second we apply our recommendation method to this keyring with $l = 10$. Note in this experiment, all malicious users are not supposed follow our recommendations simply because they may not like to do so. The results are as following. Before applying our method, no certificate conflicts can be detected and no suspect set can be constructed. After applying our method, all users are able to detect the conflicts and over 99% users are able to construct suspect sets with size as small as three. If users may spend more efforts on the certificate conflicts, e.g. by contacting the victim, and find out which certificate contains the incorrect name-to-key binding, then over 99% users would be able to construct 9 suspect sets with size one. Or to say, almost all users would be able to identify all the 9 malicious users.

8   Conclusions and Future Work

In this paper we described how distributed web of trust can be made more robust against malicious attacks. The problem is modeled as a graph theory problem, i.e. increasing vertex connectivity of a certificate (directed) graph, which is a known problem with optimal but expensive solutions. Our heuristic for this problem runs fairly efficient and experimental results indicate that the robustness of PGP keyrings can be greatly increased with only a small increase in the number of certificates. In addition, we addressed the issue of user behavior and the constraints that adds. We investigate the impact of users' compliance and users' preference of our recommendations on the robustness of PGP keyrings. Moreover, the application of our method may also serve as a determent to malicious attacks because of user's ability to detect these attacks and identify malicious users. Future work will focus on how to integrate this method with PGP keyrings, in the form of recommendations to users about the certificates they are issuing.

References

1. R. Ahuja, T. Magnanti, and J. Orlin. *Network flows : theory, algorithms, and applications.* Prentice Hall, Englewood Cliffs, N.J., 1993.
2. Tuomas Aura. On the structure of delegation networks. In *Proc. 11th IEEE Computer Security Foundations Workshop*, pages 14–26, Rockport, MA, June 1998. IEEE Computer Society Press.
3. András A. Benczúr. Pushdown-reduce: an algorithm for connectivity augmentation and poset covering problems. *Discrete Applied Mathematics*, 129(2-3):233–262, 2003.
4. Thomas Beth, Malte Borcherding, and Birgit Klein. Valuation of trust in open networks. In *Proceeding of the 3rd European Symposium on Research in Computer Security (ESORICS 94)*, pages 3–18, 1994.
5. Matt Blaze, Joan Feigenbaum, and Jack Lacy. Decentralized trust management. In *Proceedings of the 1996 IEEE Symposium on Security and Privacy*, pages 164–173, Oakland CA USA, 6-8 May 1996.
6. Srdjan Capkun, Levente Buttyán, and Jean-Pierre Hubaux. Small worlds in security systems: an analysis of the pgp certificate graph. In *Proceedings of the 2002 workshop on New security paradigms*, pages 28–35. ACM Press, 2002.
7. Darnell D. Pgp or pki? the future of internet security. *EDI Forum: The Journal of Electronic Commerce*, 12(1):59–62, 1999.

8. C. Ellison, B. Frantz, B. Lampson, R. Rivest, B. Thomas, and T. Ylonen. RFC 2693: SPKI certificate theory, September 1999.
9. A. Frank. Connectivity augmentation problems in network design. *Mathematical Programming: State of the Art 1994*, pages 34–63, 1994.
10. A. Frank and T. Jordan. Minimal edge-coverings of pairs of sets. *Journal of Combinatorial Theory, Series B*, 65(1):73–110, 1995.
11. Andras Frank and Tibor Jordan. Directed vertex-connectivity augmentation. *Mathematical Programming*, 84(3):537–553, 1999.
12. Frank Harary. *Graph Theory.* Addison-Wesley, Reading, Mass., 1969.
13. Qinglin Jiang, Douglas S. Reeves, and Peng Ning. Certificate recommendations to improve robustness of webs of trust. Technical Report TR-2004-04, Department of Computer Science, N.C. State University, January 2004.
14. Qinglin Jiang, Douglas S. Reeves, and Peng Ning. Improving robustness of PGP by conflict detection. In *The Cryptographers Track at the RSA Conference 2004*, volume 2964 of *Lecture Notes in Computer Science*, pages 194–207. Springer, 2004.
15. Jon Kleinberg. The small-world phenomenon: an algorithm perspective. In *Proceedings of the thirty-second annual ACM symposium on Theory of computing*, pages 163–170. ACM Press, 2000.
16. R. Levien and A. Aiken. Attack-resistant trust metrics for public key certification. In *Proceedings of the Seventh USENIX Security Symposium*, 1998.
17. Ueli Maurer. Modelling a public-key infrastructure. In *Proceedings of the Fourth European Symposium on Research in Computer Security (ESORICS 96)*, pages 324–350, 1996.
18. S. Mendes and C. Huitema. A new approach to the X.509 framework: Allowing a global authentication infrastructure without a global trust model. In *Proceedings of the Symposium on Network and Distributed System Security, 1995*, pages 172–189, San Diego, CA , USA, Feb 1995.
19. M.Grotschel, L.Lovasz, and A.Schrijver. The ellipsoid method and its consequences in combinatorial optimization. *Combinatorica*, 1:169 –197, 1981.
20. Hiroshi Nagamochi and Toshihide Ibaraki. Graph connectivity and its augmentation: applications of ma orderings. *Discrete Appl. Math.*, 123(1-3):447–472, 2002.
21. M. Reiter and S. Stubblebine. Toward acceptable metrics of authentication. In *IEEE Symposium on Security and Privacy*, pages 10–20, 1997.
22. M. Reiter and S. Stubblebine. Resilient authentication using path independence. *IEEE Transactions on Computers*, 47(12), December 1998.
23. M. Drew Streib. Keyanalyze - analysis of a large OpenPGP ring. http://www.dtype.org/keyanalyze/.
24. Anas Tarah and Christian Huitema. Associating metrics to certification paths. In *Computer Security - ESORICS 92, Second European Symposium on Research in Computer Security, Toulouse, France, November 23-25, 1992, Proceedings*, volume 648 of *Lecture Notes in Computer Science*, pages 175–189. Springer Verlag, 1992.
25. Int'l Telecommunications Union/ITU Telegraph & Tel. ITU-T recommendation X.509: The directory: Public-key and attribute certificate frameworks, Mar 2000.
26. D. Watts and S. Strogatz. Collective dynamics of small-world networks. *Nature*, 393:440, 1998.
27. Philip Zimmermann. *The official PGP user's guide.* MIT Press, Cambridge, Mass., 1995.

Universally Composable Secure Mobile Agent Computation*

Ke Xu and Stephen R. Tate

University of North Texas, Denton, TX 76203, USA
{kxu,srt}@cs.unt.edu

Abstract. We study the security challenges faced by the mobile agent paradigm, where code travels and performs computations on remote hosts in an autonomous manner. We define universally composable security for mobile agent computation that is geared toward a complex networking environment where arbitrary protocol instances may be executing concurrently. Our definition provides security for all the participants in the mobile agent system: the originator as well as the hosts. Finally, under the assumption of a universally composable threshold cryptosystem, we present universally composable, multi-agent protocols with provable security against either static, semi-honest or static, malicious adversaries, according to our definition, where in the latter case we need to provide access to a common reference string.

1   Introduction

Mobile agents are goal-directed, autonomous programs capable of migrating from host to host during their execution. From the security point of view, this execution model gives rise to some unique and interesting issues. Mobile agent computation is a distributed computing process, where the participants are the originator who launches the agents and the remote hosts who receive and execute the agents. It is natural to assume no party (i.e., the originator or any of the hosts) trusts anyone else, and mobile agents can be the perfect means for one party to attack another. For example, the agents may try to steal private information from the hosts, or the hosts could manipulate the agents so as to obtain favorable results at the expense of the originator or other hosts' interests. Therefore, the centerpiece of secure mobile agent computation is maintaining the honesty of the agents and the hosts on which they execute. This turns out to be a non-trivial task as the goal may appear to be self-conflicting: The hosts want to monitor the agents' behavior as much as possible, while the originator (and other hosts) wants the agents to have enough privacy and protection to avoid malicious manipulation.

Traditionally, security in mobile agents has been considered along the two separate lines of either protecting the hosts against agent attacks or vice versa, with each having (potentially negative) implications on the other. A recent direction of applying cryptographic protocols from secure multi-party computation

---

* This research is supported in part by NSF award 0208640.

K. Zhang and Y. Zheng (Eds.): ISC 2004, LNCS 3225, pp. 304–317, 2004.

to mobile agents has shown the promise of a complete solution that could benefit both sides [16,5,2,17]. Specifically, the results of [5,2,17] are all based on Yao's two-party secure function evaluation protocol [19]. This approach has several advantages over the previous ones. First of all, it looks at the whole picture of mobile agent computation, and aims at providing security for all parties in the system — the originator and the hosts — at the same time. Thus, the assumption is that any party may become malicious and malicious parties can collude with each other, including collusion between the originator and some hosts in the attempt to attack other hosts. Second, it has a solid theoretical basis. In particular, the secure function evaluation problem has been studied extensively in theory and provably sound results exist — from the definition of security [14, 6] to universal protocols for evaluating any polynomial-time function [19,13,4, 11]. Harvesting these existing results enables one to study the mobile
    agent security problem in a well thought-out theoretic context and obtain formally provable solutions, which is the purpose of this paper.

1.1   Universally Composable Security for Mobile Agents

Essentially, mobile agent computation is a distributed computing process, and for many applications it is a process of evaluating a sequence of two-party functions between the originator and each of the hosts. For example, a shopping agent takes the originator's buying criteria and compares it with the offers from different hosts. A search agent matches the information provided by each host against the search phrase from the originator. Often, the result from evaluating one function is used as the input to the next function on the next host. Hence, the functions computed by the agents takes two inputs: one is the current *agent state* which represents the result from the computation on the previous host, and the other is the input provided by the current host. The outcome is a new agent state that will be taken to the next host, and optionally the host may also receive some output from the function, which we refer to as the *local output*. Eventually, the agent goes back to the originator who obtains its desired result from the agent's final state.

Universally composable (UC) security was proposed by Canetti [6] to address the problem of preserving secure protocols in a complex environment, where an unbounded number of protocol instances are executed arbitrarily (i.e., sequentially or concurrently). It is a realistic model for today's networking environment. The contribution of Canetti's work is that it presents a way to study cryptographic protocols which is similar to the previous approach of viewing the protocols as "stand-alone" computation, but the achieved security is geared toward the more complex environment. To this end, in addition to the parties directly involved in the protocol, a new entity called the *environment* is added into the system. Intuitively, the environment represents everything outside of the protocol in question. It provides inputs to the parties and reads their outputs. It also may exchange information freely with the adversary. However, the environment does not see the internals of the protocol execution — messages sent by the parties or the internal states of the parties. Security is defined from the environment's point of view such that no environment can distinguish the execution of the real protocol and a simulation in the ideal model, where an imaginary trusted ideal functionality performs the computation on behalf of all the parties. A *universal composition* theorem asserts such security is preserved when the protocol is executed arbitrarily with other protocols including serving as a subroutine in a larger protocol.

1.2   Our Results

The theme of this work is to treat computing with mobile agents as a secure function evaluation (SFE) problem between the originator and the hosts, with the goal of obtaining universally composable, secure protocols for mobile agent computation. Toward this goal, we first define UC security for mobile agents. Based on the definition, we present two agent protocols. The first one is secure against static, semi-honest adversaries, while the second one adds security against malicious attacks. In both cases we require a universally composable non-interactive threshold cryptosystem, which has not yet been discovered, but several promising advances have been made in this direction [8,1]. In the case of malicious adversaries, we also augment the model by introducing a common reference string as required by the techniques of [10].

Although there already exist general protocols for two-party and multi-party SFE with UC security [10], one unique restriction in mobile agents prohibits directly applying those results. The autonomous property of mobile agents implies no interaction should happen between the agents and the originator. In other words, the originator should be assumed offline after sending out the agents. On the other hand, all the general results of [10] require continuous communication among the parties[1].

Our technique is based on the two-party SFE protocol due to Yao [19]. In Yao's protocol, one party, Alice, creates an *encrypted circuit* for computing the desired function and sends it to the other party, Bob. Bob evaluates the circuit and obtains the output. However, evaluating the encrypted circuit does not reveal any information about Alice's input other than what the output implies. Cachin et al. [5] first proposed implementing the code of mobile agents as encrypted circuits, a result which was improved by [2,17]. In particular, Tate and Xu [17] presented a secure multi-agent protocol that does not rely on a trusted third party or trusting any agent or host in the system.

Our results extend this multi-agent protocol with provable UC security, which are lacked by all the prior work. It turned out to be non-trivial to add provable security to the multi-agent protocol. A prerequisite is a formal definition of security in the UC framework, which had not been done before. The cryptographic tools used in the previous protocol have to be reconsidered for UC security. Furthermore, additional techniques are employed in our results so that the resulting security can be proved according to the definition.

---

[1] In fact, if using the general results, we would not need mobile agents at all, whose sole purpose is to represent the originator and do computation with the hosts.

In Section 2, we formally define the security for mobile agent computation under the UC framework. Section 3 describes the cryptographic tools used in our protocols. UC-secure mobile agent protocols against static, semi-honest and malicious adversaries are presented in Sections 4 and 5, respectively.

2   Secure Mobile Agent Computation — Definitions

We impose the following requirements on the mobile agent computation.

1. The agent computation can be modeled as the evaluation of a sequence of two-party functions between the originator and each of the hosts, as described in Section 1.1.
2. The hosts can be partitioned into *disjoint* subsets, and accordingly the evaluation can be broken down into subproblems, where each problem involves one subset of hosts and can be computed concurrently with the other subproblems. As a result, the originator dispatches one agent to each host subset, and later combines the final states of all the agents into the final result.
3. The participating hosts are predetermined before the protocol starts, as is the partition of the hosts, which determines the total number of agents needed.

Although not every real-world mobile agent application meets these requirements, this is still a fairly general model. (One open problem is to remove the restriction that hosts have to be predetermined, to accommondate free-roaming agents.) We define the notation for host identity and agent functions as follows.

Definition 1. *Assume there are a total of ℓ hosts and n agents in the system, where $n \leq \ell$. The hosts are partitioned into n disjoint subgroups, each group to be visited by exactly one agent. We use the combination of the group id, i, for $i = 1, \ldots, n$, and the host id within that group, j, for $j = 1, \ldots, m_i$ and $\sum_{i=1}^{n} m_i = \ell$, to identify a particular host, noted as $H_{(i,j)}$.*

Definition 2. *Let $f^{(i,j)} : \{0,1\}^* \times \{0,1\}^* \to \{0,1\}^* \times \{0,1\}^*$, for $i = 1, \ldots, n$, $j = 1, \ldots, m_i$, and $\sum_{i=1}^{n} m_i = \ell$, denote the (probabilistic) polynomial-time agent function computed by a mobile agent on host $H_{(i,j)}$. The first parameter is the current agent state, and the second parameter is the input from the host. The function outputs a new agent state as well as a local output to the host. Furthermore, for $i = 1, \ldots, n$, let $x_{(i,0)}$ denote the initial state of mobile agent MA_i and $y_{(i,j)}$ be the input from host $H_{(i,j)}$. Visiting hosts $H_{(i,1)}, \ldots, H_{(i,m_i)}$, agent MA_i computes function $f^{(i,j)}$ at host $H_{(i,j)}$ with the current agent state and the host's input, and obtains the following outputs:*

$$(x_{(i,j)}, z_{(i,j)}) = f^{(i,j)}(x_{(i,j-1)}, y_{(i,j)}) \text{ for } 1 \leq j \leq m_i.$$

$x_{(i,j)}$ *is the updated agent state, and $z_{(i,j)}$ is the local output to host $H_{(i,j)}$.*

Finally, all n agents return to the originator O with final states $x_{(i,m_i)}$, which are combined to give O's final output, denoted by $\xi = g(x_{(1,m_1)}, \ldots, x_{(n,m_n)})$, where $g(\cdots)$ is the combination function.

2.1   Definition of Security

We define an ideal model for mobile agent computation which captures the desired security properties, as well as a real model in which the secure agent protocol executes. In both models, the parties include the originator, the hosts, an adversary, and the environment. Interactions between the parties in both models follow the general description in [6]. The ideal model uses a trusted ideal functionality defined as follows, to compute the agent functions.

Definition 3. $\mathcal{F}_{\mathrm{MA}}$ *proceeds as follows, interacting with originator O, ℓ hosts whose ids are defined as in Definition 1, and adversary $\mathcal{S}$.*

1. *Upon receiving the initial agent states $x_{(1,0)}, \ldots, x_{(n,0)}$ with session id "sid" from O, store them in a buffer. Send a notification (O_input, sid) to $\mathcal{S}$, where "O_input" is just a text message containing no information about the input value.*
2. *Upon receiving input $y_{(i,j)}$ from host $H_{(i,j)}$, send notification $(H_{(i,j)}\_input, sid)$ to $\mathcal{S}$. If $x_{(i,j-1)}$ has not been created, save $y_{(i,j)}$. Otherwise, compute $x_{(i,j)}$ and $z_{(i,j)}$, store $x_{(i,j)}$ and return $z_{(i,j)}$ to $H_{(i,j)}$. In addition, if there are saved $y_{(i,k)}$ for $k = j+1, j+2, \ldots$, continue computing the corresponding $x_{(i,k)}$ and $z_{(i,k)}$, returning $z_{(i,k)}$ to host $H_{(i,k)}$, until there are no more buffered inputs.*
3. *Upon receiving a request to reveal intermediate result $x_{(i,j-1)}$ from both O and host $H_{(i,j)}$, send $x_{(i,j-1)}$ to $\mathcal{S}$.*
4. *Once all final agent states $x_{(1,m_1)}, x_{(2,m_2)}, \ldots, x_{(n,m_n)}$ have been computed, combine them using function $g(\cdots)$ as defined in Definition 2, and return the result ξ to O. If a request to reveal the final agent states is received from O, send all the final agent states to $\mathcal{S}$. Halt after this step is done.*

We consider static adversaries who can corrupt the originator and/or the hosts, but only before the protocol starts. In other words, the adversary's choice of which party to corrupt does not depend on the execution of the protocol. Furthermore, we distinguish two types of adversaries: A semi-honest adversary strictly follows the protocol but tries to infer more knowledge from the information it obtained legally, while a malicious adversary may exhibit arbitrary (Byzantine) behavior. As introduced before, the environment reads the outputs of the originator and the hosts. It can also communicate freely with the adversary, and in the end, the environment outputs a binary value.

Definition 4. *Let $\stackrel{c}{\approx}$ denote computational indistinguishability [12]. Mobile agent protocol π **securely realizes** $\mathcal{F}_{\mathrm{MA}}$ **against static, semi-honest (or malicious) adversaries under condition** t, if for any such adversary $\mathcal{A}$ interacting with the real-model execution of π and corrupting parties subject to condition t, there exists a corresponding adversary $\mathcal{S}$ corrupting the same set of parties in the ideal model, such that the running time of $\mathcal{S}$ is polynomial in the running time of $\mathcal{A}$ and for all environments $\mathcal{Z}$ we have*

$$\mathrm{REAL}_{\pi,\mathcal{A},\mathcal{Z}} \stackrel{c}{\approx} \mathrm{IDEAL}_{\mathcal{F}_{\mathrm{MA}},\mathcal{S},\mathcal{Z}}. \tag{1}$$

where $\mathrm{REAL}_{\pi,\mathcal{A},\mathcal{Z}}$ *and* $\mathrm{IDEAL}_{\mathcal{F}_{\mathrm{MA}},\mathcal{S},\mathcal{Z}}$ *denote the ensembles of* $\mathcal{Z}$ *'s binary outputs when it is interacting with the real model execution of* π *and the ideal model agent computation, respectively.*

Due to the Universal Composition Theorem of [6], a complex protocol can be broken into subproblems and each subproblem can be studied separately. Once a secure protocol for a subproblem is obtained, executing the subprotocol in the larger protocol can be treated as running an ideal process with the ideal functionality for the subproblem. This so called *hybrid model* largely reduces the complexity of analyzing the overall protocol, and is used extensively in our work. We begin by introducing the building blocks of our mobile agent protocol and their secure implementations. The first agent protocol is then presented in a hybrid model where the parties have access to the ideal functionalities for the primitives.

3   Cryptographic Tools

The basic idea of the multi-agent protocol of [17] can be summarized as follows. The originator creates n agents each visiting a disjoint subset of hosts. For each host, the originator creates an *encrypted circuit* to compute the agent function for that host. The originator also sets the initial agent states, in the form of *signals* recognizable to the encrypted circuits. Once a host receives an agent, it conducts *oblivious threshold decryption* with enough remote agents to obtain the signals corresponding to its input. Then the host evaluates the encrypted circuit with the current agent state and its own input. The host receives the local output from the circuit, and sends the agent with a new state, which is in the form of signals recognizable by the next encrypted circuit, to the next host in the same subset. In the end, the originator receives back all the agents and combines their final states into the final result. In this section, we describe under the UC framework the building blocks of the multi-agent protocol.

3.1   Encrypted Circuits

Encrypted circuits were introduced by Yao as the centerpiece of his two-party SFE protocol, and are a scrambled form of boolean circuits in which the signals on the wires are random binary strings that represent boolean values. The mappings from the random strings, referred to as the "signals," to their corresponding boolean values, known as the "semantics," are hidden from the evaluator of the circuit. With correctly constructed truth tables for the gates, the encrypted circuit can be evaluated by one who has no knowledge of the semantics of the input signals. Moreover, the output is also in the form of signals, and therefore evaluation does not reveal any information about the input, the output, or any intermediate result within the circuit.

Currently there are several implementations of the encrypted circuit [18,15, 3]. The result of [18] is particularly appealing due to its full proof of security, which establishes the following.

Theorem 1. *To an evaluator who knows the signals for at most one instance of input and the semantics of the signals for the output it is entitled to learn (if any), real encrypted circuits are computationally indistinguishable from fake encrypted circuits which can be generated in polynomial-time with only the knowledge mentioned above.*

Theorem 2. *Assume an encrypted circuit in which the length of every signal is k. Define the signals obtained on each wire in the evaluation with a particular instance of input as the "on-path" signals for that input, and the rest of the wire signals as the "off-path" signals. For every probabilistic polynomial-time evaluator A with the specific input, every positive polynomial $p(\cdot)$, and sufficiently large k, the probability that A correctly guesses the off-path signal for any given wire in the circuit is strictly less than $\frac{1}{2^k} + \frac{1}{p(k)}$.*

3.2   Oblivious Threshold Decryption

Oblivious threshold decryption (OTD) is a process where a user sends a pair of ciphertexts to enough decryption servers, but receives only one plaintext, while no server learns which plaintext the user receives. It is a combination of oblivious transfer and threshold decryption. In the multi-agent protocol, the agent functions are implemented as encrypted circuits, and each host is an evaluator. The agent functions take inputs from the hosts, and the way for a host to obtain the signals corresponding to its input is essential to the security of the protocol, because both Theorems 1 and 2 rely on the vital assumption that the evaluator holds the signals for only one instance of input, i.e., one signal per input wire. Through OTD, a host receives only the signals for its input and nothing else, and its private input is not revealed to any other party in the system. We define the ideal functionality of OTD to capture both security requirements. Our definition is based on a similar definition for traditional (i.e., non-threshold) public-key encryption from [6].

Definition 5. *Ideal Functionality $\mathcal{F}_{\mathrm{OTD}}$ is defined with a threshold parameter $m \le n$ and security parameter k for participants $P_1, \ldots, P_n$ and adversary $\mathcal{S}$:*

Key Generation: *On the first activation, expect to receive a message* (KeyGen, sid, $\mathcal{DS}$) *from some party P_i, where $\mathcal{DS}$ is a set of at least m parties (the "decryption servers"). Then do:*

1. *Hand* (KeyGen, sid) *to $\mathcal{S}$.*
2. *Receive a value e from $\mathcal{S}$, record e, and hand e to P_i.*

Encryption: *Upon receiving a message* (Encrypt, sid, e', w) *from a party $P_{i'}$:*

1. *Hand* (Encrypt, sid, e', $|w|$) *to $\mathcal{S}$. (If $e' \ne e$ or e is not yet defined then hand also the entire value w to $\mathcal{S}$.)*
2. *Receive a tag c from $\mathcal{S}$ and hand c to $P_{i'}$. If $e' = e$ then record the pair (c, w). (If c appears in a previously recorded pair then halt.)*

Oblivious Decryption Request: *Upon receiving* (DecryptRequest,*sid*, c_0, c_1, b) *from a party* P_j, *where* $b \in \{0,1\}$, *record the request as* (DecryptRequest, *sid*, c_0, c_1, b, P_j) *and return control to* $\mathcal{S}$. *We refer to* P_j *as the "decryption user" for this ciphertext pair.*

Oblivious Decryption Assist: *Upon receiving* (DecryptAssist, *sid*, c_0, c_1) *from a party* $P_k \in \mathcal{DS}$, *where* (c_0, c_1) *is a ciphertext pair from a previously recorded DecryptRequest and* P_k *has not yet given a DecryptAssist message for this ciphertext pair:*

1. *Record* (DecryptAssist, *sid*, c_0, c_1, P_k) *to track requests for* (c_0, c_1).
2. *If this is the mth recorded DecryptAssist for ciphertext pair* (c_0, c_1), *then:*
   If an encryption request has recorded a pair (c_b, w_b), *then return* w_b *to* P_j *(the party that made the corresponding DecryptRequest); otherwise, hand* (DecryptRequest, *sid*, c_b) *to the adversary, receive a value* w *from the adversary, and hand* w *to* P_j.

$\mathcal{F}_{\mathrm{OTD}}$ can be securely realized with non-interactive threshold decryption and oblivious transfer. The ideal functionality $\mathcal{F}_{\mathrm{TD}}$ (for threshold decryption) is very similar to $\mathcal{F}_{\mathrm{OTD}}$ except with only a single ciphertext being provided in the decryption phase, and the ideal functionality $\mathcal{F}_{\mathrm{OT}}$ for oblivious transfer is defined by Canetti et al. in [10] (we are only interested in 1-out-of-2 OT instead of the more general 1-out-of-ℓ OT).

Canetti et al. [10] presented secure realizations of $\mathcal{F}_{\mathrm{OT}}$ in the presence of static and adaptive adversaries. However, to our knowledge, currently there is no published, provably secure implementation of $\mathcal{F}_{\mathrm{TD}}$. The non-interactive threshold cryptosystem of Canetti and Goldwasser [8] is a likely candidate, pending formal proof under the UC model [7]. In light of this, we describe the implementation of $\mathcal{F}_{\mathrm{OTD}}$ in a general sense.

Suppose there exists a non-interactive threshold cryptosystem, NITD, that securely realizes $\mathcal{F}_{\mathrm{TD}}$ (when converted in the obvious way) in the real model through four basic operations.

- Key Generation: This is done by a trusted dealer or through a multi-party protocol by the decryption servers. As a result, the public key is made known to the encryption user, and each server gets its share of the decryption key secretly.
- Encryption: The encryption user runs the encryption algorithm on a plaintext with the encryption key. This is a process involving only the encryption user.
- Decryption: A decryption server applies the decryption algorithm with its share of the decryption key on a ciphertext. The result is a decryption share. Obtaining a decryption share involves only the current server and requires no interaction with the decryption user or any other server.
- Share Combination: After collecting m decryption shares, the decryption user combines them using the combination algorithm and obtains the plaintext. We require no interaction with the servers in this phase.

Then, $\mathcal{F}_{\mathrm{OTD}}$ can be implemented in the $\mathcal{F}_{\mathrm{OT}}$-hybrid model (i.e., assuming access to $\mathcal{F}_{\mathrm{OT}}$ is available) as follows.

Protocol 1. *Oblivious Threshold Decryption in The $\mathcal{F}_{\mathrm{OT}}$-Hybrid Model*

1. *Key Generation: Run the* Key Generation *phase of NITD, giving decryption key shares to all parties in $\mathcal{DS}$.*
2. *Encryption: Run the* Encryption *operation of NITD.*
3. *Oblivious Decryption Request: The decryption user P_j has a bit b and a pair of ciphertexts (c_0, c_1), sends the pair of ciphertexts to m other parties from $\mathcal{DS}$, and then invokes a copy of $\mathcal{F}_{\mathrm{OT}}$ with each such party.*
4. *Oblivious Decryption Assist: Each party invoked in the previous step obtains decryption shares (c_0^i, c_1^i) through the* Decryption *operation of NITD, and completes the $\mathcal{F}_{\mathrm{OT}}$ with P_j. Thus P_j receives c_b^i. Applying* Share Combination *of NITD, P_j combines the m shares it has received to obtain the plaintext corresponding to c_b.*

Lemma 1. *If non-interactive threshold decryption scheme NITD securely realizes ideal functionality $\mathcal{F}_{\mathrm{TD}}$ in the presence of a static, semi-honest adversary that corrupts up to t decryption servers, where $t < m$, then Protocol 1 securely realizes $\mathcal{F}_{\mathrm{OTD}}$ against a static, semi-honest adversary that corrupts up to t servers in the $\mathcal{F}_{\mathrm{OT}}$-hybrid model.*

Proof (Sketch): The goal is to demonstrate for a given real-model adversary $\mathcal{A}$ an adversary $\mathcal{S}_{\mathrm{OTD}}$ in the ideal model, such that no environment can computationally distinguish the ideal process from the execution of Protocol 1. Since NITD securely realizes $\mathcal{F}_{\mathrm{TD}}$, there exists an ideal adversary $\mathcal{S}_{\mathrm{TD}}$ running with $\mathcal{F}_{\mathrm{TD}}$ that simulates protocol NITD. Since the Key Generation and Encryption of Protocol 1 are the same as in NITD, and their counterparts in the corresponding ideal functionalities are also the same, $\mathcal{S}_{\mathrm{TD}}$ can be directly used to simulate these two operations.

For Oblivious Decryption, first notice share collecting is done through ideal oblivious transfer. Therefore, party P_j receives shares for only one ciphertext, and the decryption servers receive only notifications. As a result, if P_j is not corrupted, the view of adversary $\mathcal{A}$ is just the same as what the adversary in NITD sees except there are two ciphertexts. Because of the semantic security of the encryption, there is no distinguishable relation between the two ciphertexts even if their corresponding plaintexts are related. Thus, the simulation is basically running the corresponding part of $\mathcal{S}_{\mathrm{TD}}$ twice to simulate two separate ciphertexts. By corrupting P_j, the adversary would also obtain the decryption shares including those from the honest servers for one ciphertext. This is still simulatable because the ideal adversary $\mathcal{S}_{\mathrm{OTD}}$ gets to generate the public key as well as shares of the decryption key, playing either as the trusted dealer or on behalf of the honest servers, when it simulates the Key Generation phase. Therefore, $\mathcal{S}_{\mathrm{OTD}}$ has the key shares of the honest servers and can obtain their decryption shares for any ciphertext.   ∎

3.3 Public-Key Encryption

We also employ standard, non-threshold public-key encryption in our multi-agent protocol. A definition of ideal public-key encryption, $\mathcal{F}_{\text{PKE}}$, can be found in [6]. A following paper [9] has proved that for non-adaptive adversaries, this definition is equivalent to CCA security. Hence, a CCA-secure PKE scheme can be trivially turned into a secure realization of the ideal PKE functionality.

4 Mobile Agents with Static, Semi-honest Adversaries

In this section we present a multi-agent protocol that securely realizes $\mathcal{F}_{\text{MA}}$ against static, semi-honest adversaries, in the hybrid model with access to $\mathcal{F}_{\text{OTD}}$ and $\mathcal{F}_{\text{PKE}}$.

Protocol 2. *Mobile Agent Computation in The $\mathcal{F}_{\text{OTD}}$, $\mathcal{F}_{\text{PKE}}$-Hybrid Model*
The parties are an originator O and ℓ hosts, partitioned into n subsets as described above. The size of each agent's state is n_x bits, and the size of every host input is n_y bits.

1. *Each host $H_{(i,j)}$, upon receiving its input $y_{(i,j)}$ from the environment, sends a notification of this event to the originator O.*
2. *Every host invokes a copy of ideal functionality $\mathcal{F}_{\text{PKE}}$ to generate a public key e, and broadcasts this key to all other hosts and O. In the following, we use the host id (i,j) to identify its corresponding copy of $\mathcal{F}_{\text{PKE}}$.*
3. *Having received its input $(x_{(1,0)}, \ldots, x_{(n,0)})$ from the environment, as well as the input notifications and the public keys from all hosts, O invokes the Key Generation operation of ideal functionality $\mathcal{F}_{\text{OTD}}$.*
4. *For each host $H_{(i,j)}$, O creates an encrypted circuit $(\mathcal{C}^{(i,j)}, \mathcal{L}^{(i,j)}, \mathcal{K}^{(i,j)}, \mathcal{U}_x^{(i,j)}, \mathcal{U}_z^{(i,j)})$ to compute function $f^{(i,j)}$, where $\mathcal{C}^{(i,j)}$ is the description of the circuit, $\mathcal{L}^{(i,j)}$ is the list of signals for the input wires corresponding to the agent state, $\mathcal{K}^{(i,j)}$ is the list of signals for the host input, and $\mathcal{U}_x^{(i,j)}$ and $\mathcal{U}_z^{(i,j)}$ are the lists of signals for the two outputs — the new agent state and the local output to the host, respectively. In all these lists, the two signals for each wire are grouped together as a pair, e.g., $(L_{k,0}^{(i,j)}, L_{k,1}^{(i,j)})$, where the signal with semantics 0 is the first element and the signal with semantics 1 is the second element. In addition, O invokes ideal functionality $\mathcal{F}_{\text{OTD}}$ to encrypt each signal in $\mathcal{K}^{(i,j)}$. Denote the encrypted signals as $\overline{\mathcal{K}}^{(i,j)} = ((\overline{K}_{1,0}^{(i,j)}, \overline{K}_{1,1}^{(i,j)}), \ldots, (\overline{K}_{n_y,0}^{(i,j)}, \overline{K}_{n_y,1}^{(i,j)}))$.*
5. *O creates n mobile agents: For agent $\mathcal{MA}_i$, $i = 1, \ldots, n$, its code includes the encrypted circuits $\mathcal{C}^{(i,j)}$, the encrypted signals $\overline{\mathcal{K}}^{(i,j)}$, and $\mathcal{U}_z^{(i,j)}$, for all the hosts in subset i. O also sets, for $k = 1, \ldots, n_x$, $L_k'^{(i,1)} = L_{k,x_{(i,0),k}}^{(i,1)}$, where $x_{(i,0),k}$ is the k-th bit of $x_{(i,0)}$, as the initial state of $\mathcal{MA}_i$. Following our convention, denote this list of signals by $\mathcal{L}'^{(i,1)}$. Then O invokes ideal functionality $\mathcal{F}_{\text{PKE}}^{(i,1)}$ to encrypt the initial agent state. Denote the encrypted agent state by $\overline{\mathcal{L}}'^{(i,1)}$.*

6. O sends out $\mathcal{MA}_i$ with its encrypted state to $H_{(i,1)}$, for $i = 1, \ldots, n$.

7. Every host $H_{(i,j)}$, upon receiving agent $\mathcal{MA}_i$, sends the encrypted agent state $\overline{\mathcal{L}}'^{(i,j)}$ to $\mathcal{F}_{\mathrm{PKE}}^{(i,j)}$ and receives the decryption $\mathcal{L}'^{(i,j)}$.

8. Next, $H_{(i,j)}$ sends the encrypted input signal list $\overline{\mathcal{K}}^{(i,j)}$ to m agents including $\mathcal{MA}_i$, the agent on this host. Then $H_{(i,j)}$ and the m agents engage with $\mathcal{F}_{\mathrm{OTD}}$ to obliviously decrypt one signal from each pair in $\overline{\mathcal{K}}^{(i,j)}$. Specifically, $H_{(i,j)}$ makes the DecryptRequest, and the m agents are the decryption servers. For each OTD, the pair of ciphertexts is $(\overline{K}_{k,0}^{(i,j)}, \overline{K}_{k,1}^{(i,j)})$, for $k = 1, \ldots, n_y$, and the selection bit that determines which ciphertext $H_{(i,j)}$ will actually decrypt, is $y_{(i,j),k}$.

9. From $\mathcal{F}_{\mathrm{OTD}}$, $H_{(i,j)}$ receives the signals corresponding to its input $y_{(i,j)}$. Denote this list of host input signals as $\mathcal{K}'^{(i,j)}$.

10. $H_{(i,j)}$ evaluates the encrypted circuit $\mathcal{C}^{(i,j)}$ using the input signals $\mathcal{L}'^{(i,j)}$ and $\mathcal{K}'^{(i,j)}$, recovers the value of its own local output using the corresponding $\mathcal{U}_z^{(i,j)}$ vector, and sends the agent (consisting of the encrypted circuits and the various signal lists for the following hosts, as well as the updated agent state, which is in the form of signals and encrypted by $\mathcal{F}_{\mathrm{PKE}}^{(i,j+1)}$ using host $H_{(i,j+1)}$'s public key) to the next host $H_{(i,j+1)}$. If this is the last host in the subset, then the agent is returned back to the originator with its state not encrypted. If the transfer was to a different host, that host repeats steps 7 – 10.

11. After all n agents return back to O with their final states. O recovers the values they represent and uses function g to combine the results into the final result.

12. Every host outputs its local output from the circuit evaluation, and O outputs the result from function g.

Theorem 3. *Protocol 2 securely realizes ideal functionality $\mathcal{F}_{\mathrm{MA}}$ in the $\mathcal{F}_{\mathrm{OTD}}$, $\mathcal{F}_{\mathrm{PKE}}$-hybrid model against a static, semi-honest adversary who corrupts parties with the following restrictions: if the adversary corrupts hosts only, then it is limited to corrupting hosts from up to $m - 1$ out of the n subsets of hosts, where m is the threshold parameter of $\mathcal{F}_{\mathrm{OTD}}$; or the adversary can corrupt the originator and any number of hosts.*

Proof (Sketch): It is easy to verify that Protocol 2 correctly implements the functionality of $\mathcal{F}_{\mathrm{MA}}$ when every party follows the protocol, which is the case with a semi-honest adversary. Therefore, after the protocol execution is over, the originator and the hosts will output the correct results, and so the main task now is constructing an ideal-model adversary $\mathcal{S}$ to simulate the interaction between the environment and the adversary $\mathcal{H}$ in the hybrid model. $\mathcal{S}$ runs a copy of $\mathcal{H}$ internally and forwards the messages from the environment to the internal $\mathcal{H}$. In addition, $\mathcal{S}$ simulates the view $\mathcal{H}$ expects, as explained below. As a result, the internal $\mathcal{H}$ produces the same messages back to the environment as a real $\mathcal{H}$ does, which are forwarded by $\mathcal{S}$ to the environment.

The UC framework assumes open communication channels, and so the view of $\mathcal{H}$ includes the inputs and outputs of the corrupted parties as well as all the messages sent in the system except those between the ideal functionalities and the honest parties. By corrupting the same set of parties in the ideal model, $\mathcal{S}$ can provide the internal $\mathcal{H}$ with the corrupted parties' inputs and outputs. The messages seen by $\mathcal{H}$ include the input notifications from the hosts to the originator, the hosts' public keys, all the agents travelling from one host to another, the encrypted input signals $\overline{\mathcal{K}}^{(i,j)}$ sent by a host to remote agents for decryption, and the messages from the ideal PKE and OTD to the corrupted parties. Simulating these messages depends on what parties $\mathcal{H}$ corrupts.

If only the hosts are corrupted and the corrupted hosts are from at most $m-1$ different subsets, adversary $\mathcal{H}$ is not able to control enough agents to invoke $\mathcal{F}_{\mathrm{OTD}}$ to decrypt the encrypted host input signals of its choice. Therefore, for any encrypted circuit contained in an agent, $\mathcal{H}$ knows signals for only one instance of host input to that circuit if the circuit is for a corrupted host, and no input signal at all if the circuit is for an honest host. Furthermore, only the semantics of the signals for local host outputs are known to $\mathcal{H}$, and the agent states, in the form of signals, make no sense to $\mathcal{H}$. Therefore, applying Theorem 1, $\mathcal{S}$ can construct agents containing fake encrypted circuits that are indistinguishable to $\mathcal{H}$, based on the local outputs to the corrupted hosts. To simulate encrypting the lists of host input signals and the agent states, as well as OTD for the corrupted parties at various stages of Protocol 2, $\mathcal{S}$ plays the role of ideal functionality $\mathcal{F}_{\mathrm{OTD}}$ and $\mathcal{F}_{\mathrm{PKE}}$, and interacts with $\mathcal{H}$ accordingly.

Once the originator is corrupted, there is no need to maintain the limit on corrupted hosts, since it is now the adversary $\mathcal{H}$ who creates the agents. Thus, controlling enough agents to decrypt any chosen signals for host input wires becomes irrelevant. In fact, there is no need to simulate the encrypted circuits at all. The new issue, however, is that the agent states, which are represented by signals and previously make no sense to $\mathcal{H}$, now can be easily interpreted, simply because it is $\mathcal{H}$ that creates the circuits and selects the signals and their semantics. Therefore, $\mathcal{S}$ has to obtain from $\mathcal{F}_{\mathrm{MA}}$ the intermediate state of an agent when it comes to a corrupted host. (If the host is not corrupted, the agent state is still unreadable to $\mathcal{H}$ as it is encrypted by the uncorrupted host's public key.) This can be done by sending a request on behalf of O and the corrupted host to $\mathcal{F}_{\mathrm{MA}}$ for revealing the particular intermediate result. The same can be done for revealing the final agent states, which $\mathcal{H}$ sees by controlling O. ∎

Substituting ideal functionalities $\mathcal{F}_{\mathrm{OTD}}$ and $\mathcal{F}_{\mathrm{PKE}}$ with their secure realizations in the real model, we can transfer Protocol 2 into a real-model protocol. Security is preserved by the Universal Composition Theorem. However, if the implementation of $\mathcal{F}_{\mathrm{OTD}}$ is secure against t corrupted servers, for $t \leq m - 1$, the real-model adversary has to be restricted to corrupting hosts in at most t subsets if the originator is not corrupted.

5   Mobile Agents with Static, Malicious Adversaries

For security against arbitrary malicious attacks, we apply the *universally composable compiler* presented in [10] to Protocol 2. The UC compiler is a general result that transforms a secure protocol with regard to semi-honest adversaries to one secure against malicious adversaries. The basic idea is to force a malicious adversary to behave semi-honestly. For this purpose, the UC compiler begins with having all parties in the protocol jointly generate a uniformly random tape for each party. After this phase, each party obtains a private random tape for use in the protocol, while every other party holds a commitment for the random tape. Next, all parties start execution of the original protocol which is secure against semi-honest adversaries, with the following additional steps. First, when a party receives an input from the environment, it commits the input to everyone else using a functionality known as "commit-and-prove", denoted by $\mathcal{F}_{CP}$. Second, whenever a party wants to send a message as required by the protocol, it uses the same $\mathcal{F}_{CP}$ to prove that the message is correctly generated based on the party's committed input, its random tape obtained in the setup phase, and the genuine messages it has received so far. Notice that these three components together uniquely determine the message that should be sent by the party if it is honest. Third, all messages in the system are broadcast through an *authenticated broadcasting channel* to every party, even though it is not intended for everyone. Upon receiving a message, one checks the validity of the message to ensure it was generated based on the three components mentioned before. This is possible because every party holds the commitments of other parties' inputs and random tapes, and all the messages are sent to everyone. As a result, any malicious attacks will be detected by an honest party when a cheating message for the attack is received.

Implied in the description of the compiler is the requirement that every party receives every message sent in the system. This, however, is not possible for the originator, who does not receive any messages after sending out the agents except for receiving the agents back. (The hosts can all stay online and follow the steps required by the compiler.) This restriction can be worked around due to the security of the encrypted circuits (Theorem 2). In brief, the only messages intended for the originator are the agents coming back. As long as the OTD is secure during the agent computation, which is guaranteed by the hosts following the compiler, it is infeasible for a malicious adversary to modify the final agent states, which have to be represented by valid signals.

Protocol 3. *Assuming that the originator and all the hosts share a common reference string, apply the universally composable compiler of [10] to Protocol 2 as follows.*

1. *All participants including the originator O carry out the* random tape generation *phase. Then everyone starts execution of Protocol 2 with additional steps required by the compiler as described above, with every message broadcast to all parties.*
2. *After sending out the agents (i.e., step 6 of Protocol 2), O is excluded from all broadcast messages other than an agent's coming home. All the hosts continue to behave according to Protocol 2 and the compiler.*
3. *When O receives an agent back from the hosts, it checks the validity of the agent's final state. That is, it checks if the strings that represent the agent state are valid signals for the corresponding wires. If not, O ignores this message. Otherwise, it treats the agent according to Protocol 2.*

Theorem 4. *Protocol 3 securely realizes ideal functionality $\mathcal{F}_{MA}$ against a static, malicious adversary with the same assumption about the adversary's selection of corrupted parties as in Theorem 3.*

References

1. Abe, M., Fehr, S.: Adaptively Secure Feldman VSS and Applications to Universally-Composable Threshold Cryptography. To appear in: CRYPTO 2004.
2. Algesheimer, J., Cachin, C., Camenisch, J., Karjoth, G.: Cryptographic security for mobile code. In: Proc. of the IEEE Symposium on Security and Privacy. (2001) 2–11
3. Beaver, D.: Correlated pseudorandomness and the complexity of private computation. In: Proc. of the 28th Annual ACM Symposium on Theory of Computing. (1996) 479–488
4. Ben-Or, M., Goldwasser, S., Wigderson, A.: Completeness theorems for non-cryptographic fault-tolerant distributed computation. In: 20th STOC. (1988) 1–10
5. Cachin, C., Camenisch, J., Kilian, J., Müller, J.: One-round secure computation and secure autonomous mobile agents. In: Proc. of the 27th ICALP. (2000) 512–523
6. Canetti, R.: Universally composable security: A new paradigm for cryptographic protocols. In: Proc. of the 42nd FOCS. (2001) 136–145
7. Canetti, R.: Personal communication (2003)
8. Canetti, R., Goldwasser, S.: An efficient threshold public key cryptosystem secure against adaptive chosen ciphertext attack. In: EuroCrypt'99. (1999) 90–106
9. Canetti, R., Krawczyk, H., Nielsen, J.B.: Relaxing chosen-ciphertext security. In: Advances in Cryptology — Crypto 2003. (2003) 565–582
10. Canetti, R., Lindell, Y., Ostrovsky, R., Sahai, A.: Universally composable two-party and multi-party secure computation. In: 34th STOC. (2002) 494–503
11. Chaum, D., Crépeau, C., Damgård, I.: Multiparty unconditionally secure protocols. In: Proc. of the 20th ACM Symposium on Theory of Computing (STOC). (1988) 11–19
12. Goldreich, O.: Foundations of Cryptography, Volume 1 Basic Tools. Cambridge University Press (2001)
13. Goldreich, O., Micali, S., Wigderson, A.: How to play any mental game or a completeness theorem for protocols with honest majority. In: 19th STOC. (1987) 218–229
14. Micali, S., Rogaway, P.: Secure computation. In: Crypto'91. (1991) 392–404
15. Naor, M., Pinkas, B., Sumner, R.: Privacy preserving auctions and mechanism design. In: 1st ACM Conference on Electronic Commerce. (1999) 129–139
16. Sander, T., Tschudin, C.F.: Protecting mobile agents against malicious hosts. In: Mobile Agents and Security. LNCS Vol. 1419. Springer (1998) 379–386
17. Tate, S.R., Xu, K.: Mobile agent security through multi-agent cryptographic protocols. In: 4th International Conference on Internet Computing. (2003) 462–468
18. Tate, S.R., Xu, K.: On garbled circuits and constant round secure function evaluation. Technical report, University of North Texas (2003) Available from http://cops.csci.unt.edu/publications/ (Journal version under preparation).
19. Yao, A.C.: How to generate and exchange secrets. In: Proc. of the 27th IEEE Symposium on Foundations of Computer Science (FOCS). (1986) 162–167

Re-thinking Security in IP Based Micro-Mobility

Jukka Ylitalo, Jan Melén, Pekka Nikander, and Vesa Torvinen

Ericsson Research NomadicLab, 02420 Jorvas, Finland.
{first-name.surname}@ericsson.com

Abstract. Security problems in micro-mobility are mostly related to trust establishment between mobile nodes and middle-boxes, i.e. mobile anchor points. In this paper, we present a secure micro-mobility architecture that scales well between administrative domains, which are already using different kind of network access authentication techniques. The trust between the mobile nodes and middle boxes is established using one-way hash chains and a technique known as secret splitting. Our protocol protects the middle-boxes from traffic re-direction and related Denial-of-Service attacks. The hierarchical scheme supports signaling optimization and secure fast hand-offs. The implementation and simulation results are based on an enhanced version of Host Identity Protocol (HIP). To our knowledge, our micro-mobility protocol is the first one-and-half round-trip protocol that establishes simultaneously a trust relationship between a mobile node and an anchor point, and updates address bindings at the anchor point and at a peer node in a secure way.

1 Introduction

Authentication, Authorization and Accounting (AAA) and Public Key Infrastructures (PKI) can be used to establish a security association between a mobile node and middle-boxes. The operators must have cross signed certificates or common roaming agreements to support inter-domain hand-offs. However, once the mobile node changes a trust domain, AAA and PKI based systems have scalability problems that results in long hand-off times. To solve that problem, we present a secure micro-mobility architecture that can be used between different administrative domains.

Heterogenous networks and a multi-operator environment set limits to micro-mobility when a mobile node makes a hand-off between different operator networks. Current trust models are not designed to establish a trust relationship between mobile users and middle-boxes locating between two operator networks. In addition, the access networks may belong to small hot-spot providers without global roaming agreements. The hot-spot providers may want to offer signaling optimization for mobile users without having initial assurances of the users. All the issues are related to obtaining fast and secure key-sharing between mobile nodes and middle-boxes supporting signaling optimization.

In our approach, the trust between a mobile node and a middle-box is based on an initial trust relationship between the mobile node and its peer. In the

K. Zhang and Y. Zheng (Eds.): ISC 2004, LNCS 3225, pp. 318–329, 2004.

basic case, the peer node may be a rendezvous server[1] that has initially shared a secret with the mobility node. The middle-box learns the identity and establishes a trust relationship with the mobile node during a macro-mobility exchange. The trust relationship is required to authenticate mobility management messages at the middle-box during micro-mobility. Our hierarchical micro-mobility scheme does not necessitate middle-boxes to access to public keys, or require them to perform computationally expensive operations.

The rest of this paper is organized as follows. Section 2 contains the problem statement. Section 3 defines the essential cryptographic techniques. Section 4 describes our mobility management protocol applying those techniques. In Section 5 we present simulation results and an instantiation of our architecture based on Host Identity Protocol (HIP). Finally, Section 6 concludes the paper.

2 Problem Statement

A middle-box supporting micro-mobility must be able to verify that address binding updates come from an authentic mobile node. However, the middle-box cannot verify the validity of the new locators without a secure binding between the IP addresses and a host. In other words, the middle-boxes and the peer nodes need evidence that an IP address belongs to the specific mobile node. Unverified address binding update messages open several security vulnerabilities. A malicious node can cause packets to be delivered to a wrong address. This can compromise secrecy and integrity of communication and cause DoS both at the communicating parties and at the address that receives the unwanted packets[1].

Mobile nodes, on the other hand, have to verify messages sent by middle-boxes to protect from Man-in-the-Middle (MitM) attackers. Mobile nodes trust anchor points, like in NAT devices, to translate the network addresses correctly. Moreover, the peer nodes cannot trust address update messages without making an end-to-end reachability test whenever a mobile node arrives to a new middle-box region.

Cellular IP[2], HAWAII [3], TIMIP[4] and HMIP[5] are examples of IP based micro-mobility schemes. They all use Mobile IP(v4)[6] / IPv6[7] for macro-mobility. Basically, the main security problems in all micro-mobility protocols are related to authenticating local address binding updates between mobile nodes and middle-boxes. Typically, security issues are mentioned only incidentally in different protocol proposals. Eardley et.al.[8] present an evaluation criteria framework for regional IP mobility protocols. However, their framework does not focus on security aspects in detail.

The Hierarchical Mobile IP (HMIP)[5] micro-mobility protocol is currently under development at IETF[9]. HMIP uses optionally IPSec to protect the local address binding updates. According to Soliman et.al. [9], the IPSec SAs can be created with any key establishment protocol, e.g., with IKE. However, in a typical case there is no initial trust relationship between the mobile node and

---

[1] E.g. a Mobile IP Home-Agent.

a middle-box, i.e., called Mobility Anchor Point (MAP)[2]. Thus, according to our understanding, the only realistic way to create the SAs is opportunistic authentication[3].

Many of the current problems with the micro-mobility protocols are related to making security and configuration efficient. For example, the mobile node must send twelve (12) messages when it changes securely the MAP region in HMIP using IKE. In addition, the operators have to make a careful analysis of the network topology, and configure router advertisement policies for the MAP devices. In the mobile node, the optimal selection between different MAPs requires some sophisticated algorithm.

Several security problems in micro-mobility are basically related to scalable key-sharing. Mink et. al[10] analyze different approaches to implement key management, in Mobile IP[6], between a mobile node and a middle-box in a foreign network. However, their Key Distribution Center (KDC) approach requires pre-configured security associations between networks. They have continued the work in [11] by presenting a Firewall-Aware Transparent Mobility Architecture (FATIMA).

3   Cryptographic Techniques

Middle-boxes supporting public key based authentication are typically vulnerable for CPU related Denial-of-Service attacks. In our approach, we use both Lamport *one-way hash chains* [12][13] and *secret splitting* techniques [14][15] to authenticate mobility management messages between mobile nodes and middle-boxes.

The protocol is based on an assumption that the end-points have established a mutual security association before the mobility exchange takes place. Once the mobile node wants to inform its peer about its new location, it constructs a hash chain, encrypts one of the successor hash values and sends it to the peer. As a result both end-points possess part of the same Lamport hash chain. The messages sent by both peers are protected with Hashed Message Authentication Codes (HMACs) using the hash values of the same hash chain. Basically, we protect HMACs with one-time passwords.

We apply a similar kind of authentication mechanism that is used in TESLA[16]. In our hierarchical micro-mobility model, there can be several middle-boxes on the communication path between the end-points. The middle-boxes support message buffering to implement delayed authentication for the the mobility management messages. In other words, a middle-box is able to verify a message only after it has received the successor message. Using the Lamport hash chains the middle-boxes are also able to verify that the messages belong together. A mobile node must always get a reply to its message, before sending the next message. This protects the hosts from MitM attacker trying to delay

---

[2] Alternatively, the trust could be based on using the AAA infrastructure, as is planned to be done in HMIP.

[3] The nodes blindly trust each other during the initial key-exchange, e.g., like in SSH.

packets to learn hash values. The basic idea of the delayed authentication is illustrated with the following protocol:

$A \Rightarrow$ (Middle-box)$\Rightarrow B : IDs, Enc(H_{i+2}), H_i, HMAC(H_{i+1}, IDs||Enc(H_{i+2}))$
$A \Leftarrow$ (Middle-box)$\Leftarrow B : IDs, H_{i+1}, HMAC(H_{i+2}, IDs)$
$A \Rightarrow$ (Middle-box)$\Rightarrow B : IDs, H_{i+2}$

The middle-boxes learn the anchor hash value, H_i, during the end-to-end exchange. The authentication is based on an assumption that the middle-box does not need to care about the actual owner of the hash chain as long as the hash chain values are valid during the communication context lifetime (see Section 2). Thus, the only problem related to initial bootstrapping is that an attacker can establish a state using own hash chain with a spoofed identifier, e.g., a home-address of the mobile node. This results into a situation where the authentic mobile node cannot create a state with the middle-box using its identifier. The problem can be solved by hashing the identifier with a random number. The mobile node sends its identifier and the random number to the peer. If a middle-box has already a context for the specific hash, the mobile node just generates a new random number and restarts the exchange with a new hash.

Another design issue is related to hash chain bootstrapping. Basically, the bootstrapping message can be authenticated using public key cryptography. In our approach, the peers do not authenticate the bootstrapping message with signatures, but they link together two independently created one-way hash chains with HMAC computation. A value of the first one-way hash chain is used to authenticate the anchor value of the new chain. The old anchor value is replaced with the new anchor value after the exchange.

$A \Rightarrow$ (Middle-box)$\Rightarrow B : H_0^{new}, H_i^{old}, HMAC(H_{i+1}^{old}, H_0^{new}))$
$A \Leftarrow$ (Middle-box)$\Leftarrow B : H_{i+1}^{old}$

4   Mobility Management Protocol

In our context, a logical *end-point* is a participant in an end-to-end communication[17]. Each end-point is identified with a global *End-point Identifier (EID)*. A location name, i.e. *a locator*, defines the topological point-of-attachment of an end-point in the network. When the locators are separated from end-point identifiers, an end-point may change its location without breaking the transport layer connection. The binding, between EIDs and locators, may be simultaneously dynamic and one-to-many, providing mobility and multi-homing, respectively [6][7][18].

When we separate the location names from the end-point identifiers, we obtain a new name space that can be used as static identifiers. An EID multiplexed NAT device associates a connection state with the EIDs. It is able to multiplex several connections on a single IP address based on the end-point identifiers.

REA: EIDs, SHA1(K_{1xor2}), $Enc_{K_{e2e}}$ ($K_2\|H_{i+2}$), $Enc_{K^{old}_{1xor2}}$ ($K_2\|H_{i+2}$), H_i ,$[H^{new}_0$], K_1 ,SPIs

$$HMAC(H_{i+1} ,SHA1(...))$$

AC: EIDs, K_2, H_{i+1} , SPIs, HMAC(H_{i+2} , SHA1(EIDs $\| K_2\|H_{i+1}$))

ACR: EIDs, H_{i+2} , HMAC(K_{1xor2}, EIDs$\|H_{i+2}$), HMAC(K_{e2e} , EIDs$\|H_{i+2}$)

Fig. 1. Micro and macro-mobility exchanges use common packet structures. $K_1 = 1^{st}$ key piece, $K_2 = 2^{nd}$ key piece, $K_{1xor2} = K_1 \oplus K_2, K^{old}_{1xor2} = K^{old}_1 \oplus K^{old}_2, K_{e2e} =$ shared end-to-end key,$Enc_K =$ encrypted with K,$H_k = k^{th}$ hash value.

This makes network address translation similar to routing, since now IP address translation can be logically based on the static end-point identifiers. An EID multiplexed NAT device supporting dynamic address bindings is called a *regional anchor point*. An anchor point maintains a state for each mobile node inside its region.

When a mobile node arrives to a new anchor point region and the anchor point does not have a state for the mobile node, it forwards mobility management messages to the peer. During this macro-mobility exchange the anchor points in the hierarchy learns the anchor hash value. In addition, the nearest anchor point in the hierarchy learns a symmetric key. It is the only anchor point that knows the symmetric key and can reply to messages sent by the mobile node during micro-mobility. Other anchor points in the hierarchy authenticate the address binding update messages with the hash chain values before forwarding packets to the peer. After the initial macro-mobility exchange, the anchor point hides mobility signaling from the peer node. The micro-mobility approach is transparent to the mobile nodes.

The trust model between the mobile node and the anchor points is based on a flow of trust. The flow start from the initial security association (SA) established between the mobile node and the other end-point (e.g. a rendezvous server). During the macro-mobility exchange the other end-point plays the peer role, but when the micro-mobility takes place the old anchor point, knowing the shared secret, becomes the peer. Basically, the mobile node trusts its peer to faithfully decrypt and reply to all packets sent to it.

Both the micro- and macro-mobility exchange use similar kind of three-way handshake. The protocol consists of re-address (REA), address check (AC) and address check reply (ACR) packets (See Figure 1). The mobile node informs its peer about its IP addresses using the REA packet. The peer responds with AC packet, verifying that the mobile node is indeed at the claimed location. The ACR message contains the answer to the challenge. The purpose of the AC/ACR message pair is to prevent legitimate mobile nodes from inducing flooding attacks [1].[4]

---

[4] It corresponds the Mobile IPv6 Return Routability (RR) test[7].

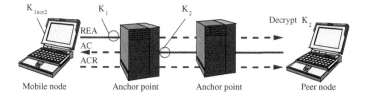

Fig. 2. Using secret splitting to share a key between a mobile node and an anchor point.

4.1   Message Authentication at an Anchor Point

The mobile node generates a hash chain containing n items to be used in several subsequent protocol runs. During the initial macro-mobility exchange the mobile node bootstraps a hash chains by revealing H_i (i=0) in the REA message. Each exchange consumes three hash values, and each hand-off inside an anchor region triggers a new exchange. The first micro-mobility REA message reveals the hash value, H_{i+3}, and so on. The hash chain binds the subsequent re-addressing exchanges to each other. Finally, when the mobile node is running out of hash items (n = 3) it must bootstrap a new hash chain by revealing a new anchor value H_0^{new}. The bootstrapping and authentication follows the procedures presented in Section 3. An anchor point must always forward a packet containing a new anchor value to the peer node. In other words, each bootstrapping results in a macro-mobility exchange. In this way, the other anchor points in the hierarchy keep in synchrony with the hash chains. During the bootstrapping procedure the anchor points between the peers must verify that H_{i+k} in the received REA is a successor value of already known anchor value H_i.

As described in Section 3, the hash value, H_{i+2}, is encrypted with a symmetric key in the REA message. The protocol uses the existing security association between the peers to encrypt the value. Once the peer receives the REA packet it decrypts the H_{i+2} value and constructs the same hash chain with the mobile node. As a result, both peers know the values of the same hash chain. Each regional anchor point in the hierarchy verifies the first message after the second packet arrives, and the second packet after the third packet arrives. If a MitM sends a spoofed AC message, the mobile node just drops the message based on the invalid HMAC and resends a new REA packet. On the other hand, the anchor points drop ACR packets with incorrect H_{i+2} values, until they receive a valid one. The REA packets are protected from reply attacks with an increasing message counter.

4.2   Sharing a Key Between a Mobile Node and an Anchor Point

The hash chains are used to update address binding and to bootstrap hash chains at anchor points in the hierarchy. The key splitting technique [14][15], in turn, is used to protect the communication between the mobile and the nearest anchor point in which region the mobile node is. A shared secret, K_{1xor2}, is divided into two pieces, K_1 and K_2.[5] The REA packet contains a plaintext key piece and an encrypted piece (Figure 1). The nearest anchor point zeros the plain key piece, K_1, before forwarding the packet to the peer (Figure 2). The HMAC cannot be computed over the K_1, because otherwise the peer could not verify the REA message. Instead, a hash of the full shared key, $SHA1(K_{1xor2})$, is covered by the HMAC.

Once the peer receives a re-addressing packet it decrypts the second key piece, K_2, and sends it back as plaintext in the reply message. The nearest anchor point to the mobile mobile validates the second key piece using the hash of the shared key. Before forwarding the AC reply packet to the mobile node, the anchor point zeros also the second key piece. As a result, it remains the only Man-in-the-Middle knowing the both key pieces. After the initial macro-mobility exchange, the anchor point runs the reachability test by replying to incoming REA messages with AC message. Both the challenge (AC) and challenge reply (ACR) are authenticated with hash chain values known only by the mobile node and the anchor point.

The protocol is vulnerable for two kind of MitM attacks. In the first case, the MitM pretends to be the nearest anchor point towards the mobile node. The operator may moderate the attack by tagging its leaf anchor points. If the authentic leaf anchor point does not find the K_1 value in the packet it knows somebody is pretending to be the leaf anchor point. In such a case, the authentic leaf anchor point must zero the K_2 when it arrives in the AC message. As result, the attacker will not find the K_{1xor2}, but each following hand-off results in macro-mobility exchange. In the other attack, two MitM attackers must locate on both sides of the anchor point to learn the key pieces and replace the packets containing the hash chain values to successfully implement an attack. On the other hand, the current Mobile IPv6 Return Routability (RR) test is also vulnerable for this kind of attack.

Each subsequent micro-mobility exchange updates the security association between the mobile node and the anchor point. The old shared key, K_{1xor2}^{old}, is replaced by the new K_{1xor2}. The anchor point uses the old shared key to decrypt the second key piece of the new shared key. This is an important property during the regional hand-off (Section 4.3). The anchor point uses the H_{i+2} hash value instead of K_{1xor2} to protect the AC message. The reason for this is that an anchor point knowing the shared secret can play the peer role in the hierarchical model during hand-off. The other anchor points on the path are able to authenticate messages as described in the next Section.

4.3   Micro-Mobility Management Inside Hierarchy

Basically, it is easier to implement security in micro-mobility using soft hand-offs than hard hand-offs. However, several wireless technologies do not currently support soft hand-offs. We have focused on solving fast hand-off problems related

---

[5] $\exists(K_1, K_{1xor2} \in nonce); (K_2 = K_{1xor2} \oplus K_1) \Rightarrow (K_{1xor2} = K_1 \oplus K_2)$

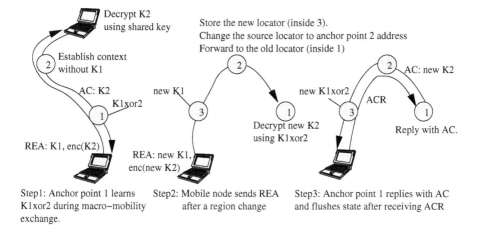

Step1: Anchor point 1 learns K1xor2 during macro–mobility exchange.

Step2: Mobile node sends REA after a region change

Step3: Anchor point 1 replies with AC and flushes state after receiving ACR

Fig. 3. A mobile node attaches to a network inside the anchor point 1 region. Later, it makes a regional hand-off and moves to anchor point 3 region.

to hard hand-offs between anchor point regions. Different micro-mobility hand-off schemes are analyzed, e.g., by Ghassemian and Aghvami[19].

The presented three-way handshake protocol (Figure 1) supports deep anchor point hierarchies. In our approach the anchor points locate on the communication path, like NAT devices. As a result, the micro-mobility communication is transparent to the mobile node. Figure 3 illustrates a situation when a mobile node moves inside a two-level anchor point hierarchy. We assume that the mobile node has earlier established a security association with the other end-point. If an anchor point does not have a context for the mobile node it forwards the packets to the peer. During the macro-mobility exchange the anchor points 1 and 2 establish a context, and learn the current location of the mobile node. The nearest anchor point 1, in the hierarchy, learns also the shared key, K_{1xor2}. Later, the mobile node changes to the anchor point 3 region.

The hand-off triggers a new re-addressing exchange. As a result, the mobile node generates fresh key pieces and sends a REA packet to the other end-point. The anchor point 3 learns the first key piece in the normal way. Once the root[6] anchor point 2 receives the REA packet, it verifies that the hash value is a successor value of the earlier received anchor value and updates the context with the new hash value. Furthermore, it forwards the REA packet back to the mobile node's old location, stored in the context. However, before forwarding the packet, the anchor point 2 changes the source IP address with its own. Otherwise, the anchor point 1 might route the packet directly to mobile node, instead of routing it via the anchor point 2. In this way, the anchor point may verify the REA and AC messages, and update its context.

---

[6] The first anchor point on the path that has a context for the mobile node, but does not know the shared key works as a root during the region change.

After receiving the REA message, the anchor point 1 decrypts the new key piece, K_2, using the earlier learned shared key, K_{1xor2}, and includes the decrypted key piece to the AC reply message. The anchor point 2 verifies the REA message, and forwards the AC packet back to the mobile node's new location. The anchor point 3 learns the new shared secret, known only by it and the mobile node. The mobile node replies with ACR message that is routed again via anchor point 2 to the anchor point 1. Each anchor point verifies the ACR and updates its context with the mobile node's new location. The anchor point 1 also flushes its state. It is good to notice that every re-addressing exchange initializes a new shared secret. Thus, the old anchor point 1 cannot send spoofed messages after the mobile node has established a context with the anchor point 3.

5   Implementation

Our implementation is based on the Host Identity Protocol (HIP)[20][18]. HIP separates end-point identifiers from locators by defining a new cryptographical name space. The translation between the EIDs and locators happens at a logical layer between transport and networking layers. HIP consists of a base exchange and a re-addressing exchange. The base exchange is basically a two-round-trip end-to-end authenticated Diffie-Hellman key exchange protocol. We have replaced the original re-addressing exchange with the new version, presented in this paper, and implemented the regional anchor point functionality. The implementation is based on the FreeBSD 5.2 operating system.

The end-point identifiers are not present in the regular traffic between the hosts. However, each packet must logically include both the end-point identifiers and IP addresses of the sender and recipient. The IPSec Security Parameter Index (SPI) values, together with IP addresses, can be used as *indices for end-point identifiers*, resulting in packets that are syntactically similar to those used today [18]. A regional anchor point learns the SPIs together with the EIDs during re-addressing exchanges. The anchor point uses the SPIs to properly demultiplex any packets arriving to a shared IP address, i.e., implementing SPI multiplexed NAT (SPINAT) (see anchor point definition, Section 4). Basically, SPINAT works in the same way as port multiplexed NAT (NAPT) [21], but with SPI values. This means that the SPI values in the exchanges cannot be encrypted or included into signatures. The security properties of SPINAT are discussed in more detail in [22].

5.1   Simulation Results

In our simulation, a mobile node negotiated the HIP end-to-end base exchange once with a web-server using IPv4. When it arrived to a new anchor point region it negotiated macro-mobility exchange with a web-server via an anchor point.[7]

---

[7] The mobile node had 1.4 GHz Mobile Pentium processor, while the anchor point and the web-server had 2 GHz Pentium 4 processors.

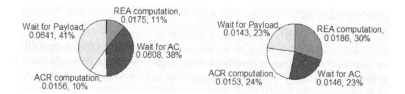

Fig. 4. Left: Macro-mobility exchange between the mobile node (MN) and the web-server in seconds (total 0.162 sec). Right: Micro-mobility exchange between the MN and the anchor point in seconds (total 0.062 sec). From MN viewpoint.

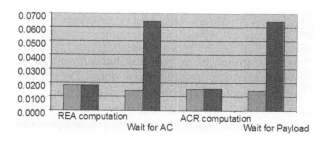

Fig. 5. Micro (left) and macro-mobility (right) hand-offs. Delay in seconds.

After a successful exchange, the mobile node moved inside the anchor point region sustaining the connection.

We ran our simulation 100 times to get statistically valid results. We simulated the latency[8] when the mobile node and anchor point located in Finland (nomadiclab.com) and communicated with a web-server at White House (www.whitehouse.gov). The mobile node was attached to the local network using 802.11b. The average Round-Trip-Time (RTT) between mobile node and the anchor point was 2.4ms. The simulated end-to-end RTT over the Internet was 55ms.

Figure 4 illustrates the hand-off times during macro-mobility and when a mobile node moves inside an anchor point region. The first slice in both figures describes the total computation time of a REA packet. The lower layer delays, caused by e.g. 802.1x authentication, are not included in the figures. They are considered to be the same in both cases. The second slice illustrates the network latency and AC computation time at the peer node. The third slice contains the ACR processing time. The exchange ends when the mobile node receives the first payload packet from the server.

Figure 5 compares the micro and macro-mobility hand-off times. When a mobile node changes an anchor point region it negotiates macro-mobility exchange once with its peer. The micro-mobility scheme does not increase the amount of signaling nor computation time compared to macro-mobility. The

---

[8] Freebsd 5.2 ipfw property.

actual packet processing times are similar in both cases. However, the network latency causes most of the delay in the macro-mobility. In our case, the micro-mobility scheme allows 2.6 times faster hand-offs (micro-mobility 62ms vs. macro-mobility 162ms). The obtained benefit depends directly on the total network latency between mobile node and the server, because the anchor point does not cause extra signaling.

A good reference protocol is IKE with OAKLEY Quick-mode using 1536 MODP group that is run after HMIP MAP region exchange (Section 2). The exchange took over 1 second to complete between the mobile node and the anchor point using our IKE installation.

6   Conclusion

In this paper, we have presented a three-way handshake that is used both for micro and macro-mobility to update address bindings. The trust between the mobile node and the anchor point is established applying Lamport hash chains with delayed authentication and secret splitting techniques. The key-sharing model scales well between administrative domains and makes possible to implement fast hand-offs between anchor point regions.

The presented protocol is vulnerable for certain Man-in-the-middle attacks. While the security provided by our protocol is relatively low, it is sufficient to prevent the new attacks enabled by the addition of micro-mobility to the Internet mobility protocols. We believe that a scalable reachability test in micro-mobility may turn out be as important thing as the return routability protocol has been for macro-mobility protocols.

The presented simulation results show that it is possible to build simultaneously secure and fast micro-mobility architecture. The architecture does not require an anchor point discovery protocol, which makes network configuration easy. In addition, the mobile node does not need to make complex routing desicions. As a result, the presented secure micro-mobility architecture is easy to deploy.

Acknowledgments. The authors would like to thank Tuomas Aura, Mats Naslund, Goran Schultz, Tommi Linnakangas, Miika Komu, Mika Kousa and Kristian Slavov for their valuable comments.

References

1. Aura, T., Roe, M., Arkko, J.: Security of Internet Location Management. In Proc. Asia-Pacific Computer Systems Architecture Conference, ACSAC'02, Monash University, Melbourne, Australia. Feb. 2002.
2. Campbell, A., Gomez, J., Kim, S., Valko, A., Wan, C., Turanyi, Z.: Design, implementation, and evaluation of Cellular IP. IEEE Personal Commun. Mag., vol. 7, no. 4. Aug. 2000.

3. Ramjee, R., Porta, T., Salgarelli, L., Thuel, S., Varadhan, K.: IP-based Access Network Infrastructure for next Generation Wireless Data Networks. IEEE Personal Commun. Mag., vol. 7, no.4. Aug. 2000.
4. Grilo, A., Estrela, P., Nunes, M.: Terminal Independent Mobility for IP (TIMIP). IEEE Commun. Mag. Dec. 2001.
5. Castelluccia, C.: HMIPv6: A Hierarchical Mobile IPv6 Proposal. ACM Mobile Computing and Communication Review (MC2R). Apr. 2000.
6. Perkins, C.: IP Mobility Support. RFC 2002. 1996.
7. Johnson, D., Perkins, C., Arkko, J.: Mobility Support in IPv6. RFC 3775. 2004.
8. Eardley, P., Mihailovic, M., Suihko, T.: A Framework for the Evaluation of IP Mobility Protocols. In Proc. the 11th IEEE International Symposium on Personal, Indoor and Mobile Radio Communications (PIMRC'00). Sept. 2000.
9. Soliman, H., Castelluccia, C., El-Malki, K., Bellier, L.: Hierarchical Mobile IPv6 mobility management (HMIPv6). Internet Draft, work in progress. June 2004.
10. Mink, S., Pahlke, F., Schafer, G., Schiller, J.: Towards Secure Mobility Support for IP Networks. In Proc. IFIP International Conference on Communication Technologies (ICCT). Aug. 2000.
11. Mink, S., et.al.: FATIMA: A Firewall-Aware Transparent Internet Mobility Architecture. In Proc. the 5th IEEE Symposium on Computers and Communications (ISCC). July 2000.
12. Lamport, L.: Password authentication with insecure communication. Commun. Mag. of ACM, 24 (11), pp. 770-772. 1981.
13. Hu, Y.-C., Perrig, A., Johnson, D.: Efficient Security Mechanism for Routing Protocols. In Proc. Network and Distributed Systems Security Symposium (NDSS'03). Feb. 2003.
14. Shamir, A.: How to Share a Secret. Comm. of the ACM, 22(11):612- 613. Nov. 1979.
15. Blakely, G: Safeguarding Cryptographic Keys. In Proc. AFIPS National Computer Conference. pp. 313-317. 1979.
16. Canetti, R., Song, D., Tygar, D.: Efficient Authentication and Signing of Multicast Streams over Lossy Channels. In Proc. IEEE Security and Privacy Symposium SP2000. May 2000.
17. Saltzer, J., Reed, D., Clark, D.: End-To-End Arguments in System Design. ACM Transactions on Computer Systems, vol. 2. Nov. 1984.
18. Nikander, P., Ylitalo, J., Wall, J.: Integrating Security, Mobility, and Multi-Homing in a HIP Way. In Proc. Network and Distributed Systems Security Symposium (NDSS'03). Feb. 2003.
19. Ghassemian, M., Aghvami, A.: Comparing different handoff schemes in IP based Micro-Mobility Protocols. In Proc. IST2002. Nov. 2002.
20. Moskowitz, R., Nikander, P., Jokela, P., Henderson, T.: Host Identity Protocol. Internet Draft, work in progress. June 2004.
21. Srisuresh, P. Holdrege, M.: IP Network Address Translator (NAT) Terminology and Considerations. RFC 2663. 1999.
22. Ylitalo, J., Nikander, P.: BLIND: A Complete Identity Protection Framework for End-points. In Proc. the Twelfth International Workshop on Security Protocols. Apr. 2004.

Shared-Key Signature and Its Application to Anonymous Authentication in Ad Hoc Group

Qianhong Wu[1,4], Xiaofeng Chen[2], Changjie Wang[3], and Yumin Wang[4]

[1] Key Lab. of Computer Networks and Information Security,
Ministry of Education, Xidian University, Xi'an 710071, P. R. China
woochanhoma@hotmail.com
[2] School of Information Science and Technology,
Sun Yat-sen University, Guangzhou 510275, P. R. China
isschxf@zsu.edu.cn
[3] Department of Computer Science and Engineering,
Chinese University of Hong Kong, Hong Kong, P. R. China
cjwang@cse.cuhk.edu.hk
[4] State Key Lab. of Integrated Service Networks,
Xidian University, Xi'an 710071, P. R. China
ymwang@xidian.edu.cn

Abstract. We formalize the notion of shared-key signatures, which makes it possible to anonymously sign any message with verification by a shared common public key. Unlike group signatures, shared-key signatures require no group manager or other third party to help the group members to generate signing keys. Also unlike ring signatures, shared-key signatures have no special structure such as a ring and the signing and verification procedures are the same as those of the ordinary signatures. In addition, they can be easily transformed into interactive authentication protocols while the ring signatures cannot. A concrete construction of such signatures is proposed based on Weak Dependence Problem (WDP). Since WDP is NP-complete and many researchers believe that NPC problems are intractable even in the quantum computation model, our scheme may be used to sign the documents requiring a longer-term validity with anonymity.

1 Introduction

Anonymity has been a main concern in cryptography for years. Several approaches have been proposed to realize it in cryptographic community including group signatures, witness indistinguishable signatures, ring signatures, and etc. In this paper, we propose a novel cryptographic primitive, i.e., shared-key signature, to achieve it.

1.1 Related Works

Anonymity was first realized by Chaum *et al* in 1991 with group signatures [1]. Cramer *et al* implemented anonymity in 1994 with witness indistinguishable signaturess [2]. Recently, the notion of ring signature [3] was introduced by Rivest,

K. Zhang and Y. Zheng (Eds.): ISC 2004, LNCS 3225, pp. 330–341, 2004.

et al in 2001 to achieve anonymity. This notion has attracted much attention since it was formalized. Abe *et al* [4] presented a ring signature based on discrete logarithms and showed another scheme with the mixture of the RSA public key and Schnorr key. Zhange *et al* [5] suggested a ring signature scheme from pairs. Wong *et al* [6] proposed a new approach to construct a ring signature scheme. They obtained the new ring signature scheme from the observation of the equivalency between the erasure correction technique of the Reed-Solomon (RS) code [7] and the polynomial interpolation. Actually, all the known (threshold) ring signatures can be more or less considered as instantiations of witness indistinguishable signature due to Cramer *et al* [2].

Compared with the related concept of group signatures [1], which allows a registered member of a predefined group to produce anonymous signatures on behalf of the group, ring signatures may enjoy the following additional advantages. (1) Set-up free. Ring signatures require no managers to initialize the system. All the signers publish their public keys to form a public-key list and then the ring signatures can be generated. Any player wishing to generate a ring signature later appends his own public key to the list and can generate a valid ring signature. Therefore, ring signatures are especially suit for ad hoc group in which all the members are equal in privileges and status and no group manager exist. (2) Cooperation-free. It refers to the capability of having a ring member produce a ring signature for any message independently. Hence, a ring signature requires no interactions among ring members and it is very useful when the other members do not agree to cooperate. (3) Unconditional anonymity. It means that it is infeasible for the unbounded adversaries to determine the identity of the real signer with probability greater than $1/n$ (Some ring signatures may be of computational anonymity). Hence it is essential when anonymity is a critical concern. (4) A natural designated verifier signature introduce by Jakobsson *et al* [8]. A signer can generate a designated verifier signature by producing a ring signature using its own private key and public key together with the intended verifier's public key. The intended verifier can verify the signature and the signer cannot repudiate it while any other third party cannot identify the true author of the signature because of signer-ambiguity. This may be useful in special applications.

1.2 Motivations and Contributions

However, ring signatures have some limitations. Firstly, the complexity grows linearly with the number of possible signers. Most of such schemes require many inefficient modular exponentiations. For instance, for a group of one hundred members, it may requires hundreds of modular exponentiations, which is unbearable in practice. Secondly, a ring signature cannot be converted into an interactive authentication protocol (i.e., an interactive zero-knowledge proof) because the prover must start from the point at which it knows its private key. Such an interactive proof is required if the prover and verifier do not want any other party to see what happens between them. Thirdly, a ring signature cannot be constructed from some signatures using the Fiat-Shamir heuristic [9], for instance, the Blum knowledge signature based on Hamilton Graph Problem [10] and the Goldreich knowledge signature based on Graph 3-colourablity Problem

[11]. Finally, to the best of our knowledge, all the existing ring signatures are based on the intractability of factorization or discrete logarithms. Unfortunately, it has been shown by Shor [12] that they are tractable in the quantum computation model. Hence, we need new anonymous signatures based on more *difficult* problems. However, based on such problems, it is often difficult to construct ring signatures or the constructions will be of unbearable complexity.

Motivated by these, we formalize the notion of shared-key signatures in which n players have n independent secret signing keys but only one shared common public key. The signing and verification procedures are the same as those of the corresponding ordinary signature with one secret key and one public key. Obviously, such a shared-key signature is of signer-ambiguity and in principle, its complexity does not grow with the number of the possible signers. Compared with group signatures and ring signatures, shared-key signatures require no group manger and have no special signature structure such as a ring. We propose such a scheme base on an NP-complete problem, the Weak Dependence Problem. It has all the advantages of ring signatures: no setup procedure, no group managers, no revocation procedures, and no coordination. It is also a designated verifier signature when the public key is shared by two players. In addition, it can be easily transformed into an interactive authentication protocol.

While Shor's result demonstrates the positive side of the power of the quantum computation model [12], other results indicate its limitation. Bennett *et al* show that relative to an oracle chosen uniformly at random with probability 1, class NP cannot be solved in the computation model in time $O(2^{n/2})$ [13]. Although this result does not rule out the possibility that NP$\subseteq$ BQP, which represents problems that can be solved by a QTM (quantum Turing machine) in polynomial time at worst with probability greater than $2/3$, i.e., in $1/3$ cases the computer may return an erroneous result, many researchers consider that it is hard to find a probabilistic polynomial-time algorithm to solve an NP-complete problem even in the quantum computation model [14]. Hence, our scheme based on Weak Dependence Problem is plausibly secure against quantum attackers, and especially fit to sign important documents of a longer-term validity with anonymity.

The rest of the paper is organized as follows. Section 2 formalizes the definitions of shared-key signature and exemplifies the notion with two simple shared-key signatures. We propose a shared-key signature based on WDP in section 3. The proposals are analyzed in detail in section 4, followed by the concluding remarks in section 5.

2 Definitions and Simple Examples

2.1 Shared-Key Signatures

We call a signature a *shared-key signature* if all the possible signers have independent secret signing keys but share a common public key and the signing and verification procedures are the same as those of the corresponding single secret key signature.

To produce such a cryptographic system, the possible signers may be required to (cooperatively) generate their own secret keys and the agreed public key, that is, the system can be either setup free or not. Hence, shared-key signatures usually consist of the following three algorithms:

- **key-generation**(l): a (an interactive) probabilistic polynomial-time algorithm which takes security parameter l and outputs $(s_1, s_2, \cdots, s_n)$ and K, where $s_1, s_2, \cdots, s_n$ are independent private singing keys and K is the shared public key.
- **sign**(m, K, i, s_i): a probabilistic polynomial-time algorithm which outputs a shared-key signature σ for the message m, public key K, together with the secret key s_i of the i-th member (who is the actual signer). Here, the signing algorithm is the same as that of an ordinary signature.
- **verify**(m, K, σ): a deterministic polynomial-time algorithm which outputs *accept* or *reject* for a given message m and its signature σ, together with the shared public key K. Here, the verification algorithm is also the same as that of an ordinary signature.

The security definitions are the same as the ordinary signatures except for the singer-ambiguity, that is, the verification must satisfy the usual soundness and completeness conditions, but in addition we want the signatures to be signer-ambiguous in the sense that the verifier should be unable to determine the identity of the actual signer with probability greater than $1/n$. This limited anonymity can be either computational or unconditional.

2.2   Two Mini Shared-Key Signatures

From a simple observation, to generate a ring signature based on Hamilton Graph Problem or Graph 3-colourability Problem, a signer has to show some graphs are isomorphic to one of the previously generated graphs, which is the possible signers' public keys. An unbounded adversary can determine which one it is by exhaustively search. Hence, it is impossible to construct a ring signature based on the Hamilton Graph Problem or Graph 3-colourability Problem with unconditional signer-ambiguity. Even for computational anonymity, it is also difficult because, to generate such a ring signature, one is required to solve the following problem: Given a Hamilton graph or 3-colourable graph G, and a random bit string $(c_1, c_2, \cdots, c_s)$, for $i = 1, 2, \cdots, s$, if $c_i = 0$, generate a graph H such that G and H are isomorphic; else generate a Hamilton graph or a 3-colour graph H such that there exists no (probabilistic) polynomial-time algorithm to determine whether or not H and G are isomorphic. When $c_i = 0$, the problem is easy. However, when $c_i = 1$, it seems difficult because there are many known efficient necessary conditions to determine that two graphs are isomorphic and a signer has to generate a graph not satisfying any known necessary condition. Hence, even if such a ring signature scheme were constructed, it would be extremely inefficient in practice. However, we will use these two problems to exemplify the notion of a shared-key signature.

Except an additional interactive key generation procedure to generate a shared public key, the following shared-key signatures are exactly the Blum knowledge signature [10] and Goldreich knowledge signature [11] transformed from the original interactive zero-knowledge proofs using the Fiat-Shamir heuristic [9].

2.2.1 A Shared-Key Signature Based on Hamilton Graph Problem

Assume that a mini ad hoc group consists of Alice and Bob, and they want to sign some message m anonymously using the Blum knowledge signature. Let $H(\cdot) : \{0,1\}^* \rightarrow \{0,1\}^s$ be a cryptographic hash function, where s is a security parameter. Alice can generate such an anonymous signature as follows.

– **Key agreement**: Alice randomly selects a v-vertex graph H with an Hamilton circle A (denoted by $A \subseteq H$) and sends it to Bob. After receiving H, Bob runs an efficient probabilistic polynomial time algorithm to generate a new Hamilton graph G by adding edges to H until he finds a Hamilton circle B. Bob publishes the new Hamilton graph G. Notice that A is also a Hamilton circle of G. Now Alice and Bob share a Hamilton graph G with a Hamilton circle A known only by Alice and a Hamilton circle B known only by Bob. G is the shared public key. Alice's private signing key is A and Bob's is B.
– **Signature generation**: For message m, Alice randomly selects s permutations on $G : \pi_1, \cdots, \pi_s$, and computes $c = (c_1, \cdots, c_s) = H(m||G||\pi_1(G)|| \cdots ||\pi_s(G))$. For $i = 1, \cdots, s$, if $c_i = 0$, she computes $\sigma_i = \pi_i(A)$; else she computes $\sigma_i = \pi_i$. The resulting signature is $\sigma = (\pi_1(G), \cdots, \pi_s(G); \sigma_1, \cdots, \sigma_s)$.
– **Signature verification**: Given the message m and its signature σ, a verifier verifies it as follows. For $i = 1, \cdots, s$, if $c_i = 0$, the verifier checks whether σ_i is a Hamilton circle of $\pi_i(G)$; else the verifier checks whether $\sigma_i(G) = \pi_i(G)$. Accept if all the checks hold. Reject, otherwise.

The above signature is transformed from the known Blum zero-knowledge proof using the Fiat-Shamir heuristic. The only modification is an additional key-generation procedure. The scheme is unconditional anonymous if an attacker does not know the original Hamilton graph H generated by Alice because the signatures generated by Alice and Bob have the same distribution (but the signature is linkable for a unlimited adversary, that is, an unbounded attacker can determine whether two signatures are generated by the same singer or not). However, if the original graph H is known, the scheme degrades to computational anonymity. In this case, notice that the Hamilton circle known by Bob has some edges not in H and hence it is not a Hamilton circle of H. An unbounded adversary can attack as follows. For some $c_i = 0$, the adversary compute π_i from $\pi_i(G)$ and G and check whether $\pi_i^{-1}(\sigma_i)$ is a Hamilton circle of H. If it is, the unbounded attacker is convinced that the signature is generated by Alice. Otherwise, the signature is generated by Bob. Clearly, *the complexity of the signature does not grow with the number of possible signers*.

2.2.2 A Shared-Key Signature Based on Graph 3-Colourablity Problem

It is similar to the above scheme. In this case, Alice and Bob only need replace the Hamilton graph by a 3-colour graph and in the key generation procedure,

Bob will delete edges of the original graph generated by Alice rather than add edges. We omit the detailed specification.

The above schemes have two disadvantages. Firstly, the schemes are not setup free and require the possible signers to cooperatively agree on a graph with some property. Secondly, as the number of possible signers increase, the security of the schemes degrades. For instance, in the Blum version, as the graph grows with added edges, it may become less difficult to find a Hamilton circle in it. With such a Hamilton circle, any one can forge a valid signature. This problem can be addressed by initializing with a graph in a larger size, that is, *the complexity slightly grows with the number of possible signers.*

3   Proposed Shared-Key Signature/Authentication

3.1   Weak Dependence Problem (WDP)

Problem: Given positive integers k, l, and an integer-entity vector $a = (a_1, \cdots, a_k) \in \{1, 2, \cdots, 2^l\}^k$, find a vector $x = (x_1, \cdots, x_k) \in \{0, \pm1\}^k \setminus \{0^k\}$ such that $\langle a, x \rangle = x_1 a_1 + x_2 a_2 + \cdots + x_k a_k = 0$ or show that there exists no such a vector, where $\langle \cdot, \cdot \rangle$ is the Euclid inner product of two vectors.

In our following construction, we will also use the slight variation of the problem: Given positive integers k, l, b, and an integer-entity vector $a = (a_1, \cdots, a_k) \in \{1, 2, \cdots, 2^l\}^k$, find a vector $x = (x_1, \cdots, x_k) \in \{0, \pm1\}^k \setminus \{0^k\}$ such that $\langle a, x \rangle = x_1 a_1 + x_2 a_2 + \cdots + x_k a_k = b$ or show that there exists no such a vector. Obviously, this variation is as difficult as the original problem. In the general case, WDP is NP-complete [15] and its difficulty depends on two factors: k and k/l. Roughly speaking, the larger k and k/l are, the more difficult the problem is. This problem can also be reduced to another NPC problem, the Shortest Vector Problem in lattice [16]. In order not to introduce some undesirable features in the problem, in our construction we will use the random instances, that is, the WDP instances are generated by flipping a fair coin. To the best of our knowledge, when $k > 300$, $k/l > 1$, such a random instance cannot be efficiently solved using the available computation techniques. NPC problems are the most difficult ones in class NP and no argument has been shown that it can be solved in the quantum computation model. Hence, our construction based on WDP may provide a better security basis against quantum adversaries in the case that factorization and discrete logarithms are tractable in the quantum computation model.

3.2   System Settings

- **Public system parameters**: Secure parameters $s, l, k \in Z$. $H : \{0,1\}^* \to \{0,1\}^s$ is a publicly available cryptographic collusion-resistant hash function. $a = (a_1, \cdots, a_k) \leftarrow \{1, 2, \cdots, 2^l\}^k$ is a random vector, where $a \leftarrow S$ denotes that a element is randomly chosen from the set S and assigned to a.
- **Historical public/private keys**: Let an *ad hoc* group consist of members $1, 2, \cdots, n$. Suppose that player j among n players has a secret key $X_j \in_U \{0, \pm1\}^k \setminus \{0^k\}$ and a public key $b_j = \langle X_j, a \rangle$, where $a \in_U S$ means that a is

a random element in the set S. We assume that all the players' public keys have been certificated by some authority.
- **Shared public key**: Let n players have the certificated public keys $b_1, \cdots, b_n$, respectively. The shared public key is $\alpha = (a, b)$, where $b = (b_1, \cdots, b_n)$. Their private keys remains unchanged.

3.3 Signing and Verification Algorithms

Assume that Alice (indexed by j for $1 \leq j \leq n$) wants to anonymously produce a shared-key signature for message m with her private X_j and the shared public key $\alpha = (a, b)$, where $b = (b_1, \cdots, b_n)$ and b_j is her contributing public key component. Now her private key X_j is rewritten as $X = (X_j, 0, \cdots, 0, -1, 0, \cdots, 0) = (x_1, \cdots, x_k, 0, \cdots, 0, -1, 0, \cdots, 0) = (x_1, \cdots, x_{k+n})$, where the last n entities are all 0's except that $x_{k+j} = -1$. The following shared-key signature uses the Fiat-Shamir heuristic and the cut-and-choose technique.

[**Signing procedure**]

- For $i = 1, 2, \cdots, s$, select a random matrix $A_i \leftarrow M_{k+n,k+n}\{0, \pm 1\}$ and a random vector $Y_i = (y_{1,i}, \cdots, y_{k+n,i}) \leftarrow \{0, \pm 1\}^{k+n} \backslash \{0^{k+n}\}$ such that $Y_i A_i = X$, where $M_{k+n,k+n}\{0, \pm 1\}$ denotes the matrices of order $(k+n) \times (k+n)$ with entities in $\{0, \pm 1\}$ and $Y_i A_i$ is the multiplication of the vector Y_i and the matrix A_i.
- For $i = 1, 2, \cdots, s$, compute $\delta_i^T = (\delta_{1,i}, \cdots, \delta_{k+n,i})^T = A_i \alpha^T$, where α^T is the transposition of α.
- Compute $c = (c_1, \cdots, c_s) = H(m||\alpha||\delta_1|| \cdots ||\delta_s)$.
- For $i = 1, 2, \cdots, s$, if $c_i = 0$, compute $f_i = Y_i$; else if $c_i = 1$, compute $f_i = A_i$.
- Output the resulting signature $(\delta_1, \cdots, \delta_s, f_1, \cdots, f_s)$.

[**Verification procedure**]

- Compute $c = (c_1, \cdots, c_s) = H(m||\alpha||\delta_1|| \cdots ||\delta_s)$.
- For $i = 1, 2, \cdots, s$, if $c_i = 0$, check $\langle \delta_i, f_i \rangle = 0$ and $f_i \in \{0, \pm 1\}^{k+n} \backslash \{0^{k+n}\}$; else if $c_i = 1$, check $\delta_i^T = f_i \alpha^T$ and $f_i \in M_{k+n,k+n}\{0, \pm 1\}$.
- Accept if all the checks hold. Reject, otherwise.

When a player wants to join into such an *ad hoc* group, he can just append his public key component to the existing public key and then produce a shared-key signature as above. If a signer is to be deleted from the group, the only work is to delete his public-key component and the deleted signer can no longer sign any message as a legitimate member.

3.4 Transform to Interactive Anonymous Authentication

As we mentioned before, a ring signature cannot be transformed to an interactive anonymous authentication because a ring member must start from the point at which it knows the private key and then a verifier can link the prover with the identity. However, our proposed shared-key signature can easily be converted into an interactive anonymous authentication scheme.

Consider the same settings as the above. Let a prover want to anonymously show to a verifier that it is a legitimate *ad hoc* group member. They can run the following protocol.

- The prover selects a random matrix $A \leftarrow M_{k+n,k+n}\{0, \pm 1\}$ and a random vector $Y = (y_1, \cdots, y_{k+n}) \leftarrow \{0, \pm 1\}^{k+n} \setminus \{0^{k+n}\}$ such that $YA = X$, and sends vector $\delta^T = A\alpha^T$ to the verifier.
- The verifier selects a random challenge $c \in \{0, 1\}$ and sends it to the prover.
- If $c = 0$, the prover sends Y to the verifier, else it sends A to the verifier.
- If $c = 0$, the verifier verifies $\langle Y, \delta \rangle = 0$ and $Y \in \{0, \pm 1\}^{k+n} \setminus \{0^{k+n}\}$, else it verifies $\delta^T = A\alpha^T$ and $A \in M_{k+n,k+n}\{0, \pm 1\}$.
- If the verification does not hold, the verifier aborts the protocol.
- The prover and verifier repeat the above protocol s times. The verifier accepts the prover's proof.

4   Analysis of the Proposed Scheme

In this section we consider the security and efficiency of the proposed shared-key signature/authentication scheme.

4.1   Security of the Scheme

Since the signature scheme can also be considered as converted from the interactive authentication using Fiat-Shamir heuristic, which transforms a secure verifier-honesty zero-knowledge proof to a secure signature, we only analyze the securities of the authentication scheme. The following results hold in the signature scheme without additional proofs.

Theorem 1. *(Completeness) If the prover follows the protocol, the proof will always be accepted.*

Proof. If $c = 0, \langle Y, \delta \rangle = \langle Y, A\alpha^T \rangle = YA\alpha^T = X\alpha^T = \langle X, \alpha \rangle = x_1 a_1 + x_2 a_2 + \cdots + x_k a_k + 0 \cdot b_1 + \cdots + 0 \cdot b_{j-1} - b_j + 0 \cdot b_{j+1} + \cdots + 0 \cdot b_n = x_1 a_1 + x_2 a_2 + \cdots + x_k a_k - b_j = 0$. If $c = 1, \delta^T = A\alpha^T$ and $A \in M_{k+n,k+n}\{0, \pm 1\}$ trivially hold. Hence, the verification always succeeds.

Theorem 2. *(Soundness) If WDP is intractable and the verifier chooses the challenge $c = 0$ (or 1) with probability $1/2$, the prover cannot succeed in cheating the verifier with probability more than 2^{-s}, no matter what strategy it chooses.*

Proof. Assume that the prover does not know any of the private keys. Since it cannot guess the verifier's challenge $c \in \{0, 1\}$, it has only two strategies to choose.

1. It prepares with non-zero vectors δ and Y such that $\langle \delta, Y \rangle = 0$, where $Y \in \{0, \pm 1\}^{k+n} \setminus \{0^{k+n}\}$ and sends δ to the verifier.

2. It prepares with a random matrix $A \in M_{k+n,k+n}\{0,\pm1\}$, and then computes and sends $\delta^T = A\alpha^T$ to the verifier.

If the verifier's challenge is 0 and the prover uses the first strategy, it cheats successfully. However, if it uses the second strategy, it has to determine a vector $Y \in \{0,\pm1\}^{k+n} \setminus \{0^{k+n}\}$ satisfying $\langle \delta, Y \rangle = 0$, which is a random instance of WDP and intractable for the prover. Hence, in this case, it fails to cheat. Similarly, if the verifier's challenge is 1 and the prover uses the second strategy, it cheats successfully, but it fails to cheat if it uses the first strategy.

Let P_1, P_2 be the probabilities that the prover uses the first strategy and the second one, and Q_0, Q_1 be the probabilities that the verifier chooses challenge $c = 0$ and $c = 1$, respectively. Therefore, in each round of the protocol, the prover succeeds in cheating with probability $P = P_1 Q_0 + P_2 Q_1 = (P_1 + P_2) \times 1/2 = 1/2$. After repeating the protocol s times independently, the prover succeeds to cheat with exact probability 2^{-s}.

Theorem 3. *(Zero-knowledge) The above protocol is zero-knowledge.*

Proof. When $c = 0$, the verifier knows Y satisfying $YA = X$, which is the one-time-one-padding of X using the Hill encryption and the matrix A satisfies $\delta^T = A\alpha^T$ and $A \in M_{k+n,k+n}\{0,\pm1\}$. However, there are about $(3^{n+k}/2^{l+\log(n+k)})^{n+k}$ such matrices. Hence, the verifier does not learn any information about X. when $c = 1$, the verifier knows A satisfying $YA = X$ and Y is unknown. Indeed, there are about $3^{n+k}/2^{l+\log(n+k)}$ vectors Y satisfying $Y \in \{0,\pm1\}^{k+n} \setminus \{0^{k+n}\}$ and $\langle \delta, Y \rangle = 0$. Furthermore, it is computationally infeasible to find any of such vectors. Hence, in this case, the verifier learns also no information about Alice's private key X. It is straightforward to prove this theorem using the standard simulation techniques.

Theorem 4. *(Anonymity) The above protocol is anonymous if WDP is difficult.*

Proof. Notice that in the authentication protocol, a prover only shows that it knows a solution $X \in \{0,\pm1\}^{k+n} \setminus \{0^{k+n}\}$ such that $\langle X, \alpha \rangle = 0$ and any one knowing such a solution can finish the proof. In order to determine whether the prover has some public key component, say b_j, an attacker has to respectively solve the following problems when $c = 0$ and $c = 1$.

Problem 1. Given $a = (a_1, \cdots, a_k)$, $b = (b_1, \cdots, b_n)$, $Y \in \{0,\pm1\}^{k+n} \setminus \{0^{k+n}\}$ and vector δ, determine whether there exist $X_j \in_U \{0,\pm1\}^k \setminus \{0^k\}$, $A \in M_{k+n,k+n}\{0,\pm1\}$ such that

$$\begin{cases} \langle X_j, a \rangle = b_j & (1) \\ YA = X & (2) \\ \delta = A\alpha^T & (3) \end{cases}$$

where $X = (X_i, 0, \cdots, 0, -1, 0, \cdots, 0) = (x_1, \cdots, x_{k+n})$ in which the last n entities are all 0's but $x_{k+j} = -1$. In the above equation systems, (1) has about $3^k/2^{l+\log k}$ solutions and (3) has about $(3^{n+k}/2^{l+\log(n+k)})^{n+k}$ solutions. Furthermore, one has to solve WDP to obtain one of such solution. It is easy to find a solution to (2). However, it has about $(3^{n+k}/(n+k))^{n+k}$ solutions. In addition, these three equations can also be considered as an random instance of $\{0, \pm 1\}$-Programming Problem, which is also NP-Complete. Therefore, it is difficult to solve Problem 1.

Problem 2. Given $a = (a_1, \cdots, a_k), b = (b_1, \cdots, b_n), A \in M_{k+n,k+n}\{0, \pm 1\}$ and vector δ, determine whether there exist $X_1 \in_U \{0, \pm 1\}^k \backslash \{0^k\}$, and $Y \in \{0, \pm 1\}^{k+n} \backslash \{0^{k+n}\}$ such that

$$
\begin{cases}
\langle X_j, a \rangle = b_j & (4) \\
YA = X & (5) \\
\langle Y, \delta \rangle = 0 & (6)
\end{cases}
$$

In the above equation systems, (4) has about $3^k/2^{l+\log k}$ solutions and (6) has about $3^{n+k}/2^{l+\log(n+k)}$ solutions. They are both instances of WDP and it is difficult to find such a solution. (5) is easy but it has exponentially solutions. The equations (4), (5) and (6) are an random instance of $\{0, \pm 1\}$-Programming Problem. Hence, it is also difficult to solve problem 2.

Since Problem 2 may have no solution and this convinces adversaries that the prover is not the j-th player, the protocol is computationally anonymous.

4.2 Performance of the Scheme

Now we consider the performance of the signature scheme. The authentication version has similar efficiency. The main cost of the signing procedure is s computations of $A_i \alpha^T$ which require about $2(n+k)^2/3$ l-bit integer additions. Hence, the average signing procedure complexity is $2ls(n+k)^2/3$. Similarly, the average verification computation complexity is about $ls(n+k)^2/3$. The length of the shared-key signature is about $\log_2 3 \times s(n+k)^2/2$ bits. The following tables compare our scheme with the typical ring signatures in details, where the complexity of DL-based ring signature and RSA ring signature are from [4].

Table 1. Comparison of the length of the anonymous signatures (bits)

	Length of signature	Typical value
DL-ring signature	$L(DL) \times n$	$160 \times n = 1.6 \times 10^4$
RSA-ring signature	$(L(RSA) + 160) \times (n+1)$	$1184 \times (n+1) \approx 1.2 \times 10^5$
shared-key signature	$\log_2 3 \times s(n+k)^2/2$	$130 \times (n+300)^2 \approx 2.0 \times 10^7$

Table 2. Comparison of the signing complexity (arithmetic operation)

	Signature generation	Typical value
DL-ring signature	$T(DL) \times 5/4 \times n$	$2.0 \times 10^8 \times n = 2.0 \times 10^{10}$
RSA-ring signature	$T(RSA^{-1}) + T(RSA) \times n$	$10^9 + 1.6 \times 10^7 \times n = 2.6 \times 10^9$
shared-key signature	$2ls(n+k)^2/3$	$10700 \times (300+n)^2 \approx 1.8 \times 10^9$

Table 3. Comparison of verification complexity (arithmetic operation)

	Signature generation	Typical value
DL-ring signature	$T(DL) \times 5/4 \times n$	$2.0 \times 10^8 \times n = 2.0 \times 10^{10}$
RSA-ring signature	$T(RSA) \times n$	$1.6 \times 10^7 \times n = 1.6 \times 10^9$
shared-key signature	$ls(n + k)^2/3$	$5400 \times (300 + n)^2 \approx 9.0 \times 10^8$

Table 4. Securities against quantum adversaries

	Soundness	Signer-ambiguity
DL-ring signature	Forgeable	Unconditional
RSA-ring signature	Forgeable	Unconditional
shared-key signature	Unforgeable	Computational

Here, $L(DL)$ is the length of exponent of DL signature, and is typically 160-bit. $L(RSA)$ is the length of modulus of RSA signature, and is typically 1024-bit. $T(DL)$, $T(RSA^{-1})$ and $T(RSA)$ are the computational costs of modular exponentiation, inverse RSA function and RSA function, respectively. For our shared-key signature, we suggest that $l = 100, k = 300, s = 160$ because the lattice Shortest Vector Problem is considered difficult when the dimension of the lattice is more than 300. From the table, we can see that the length of our signature is about 200 times more than that of the RSA ring signature for a group of 100 members. Hence, our scheme is less efficient in terms of bandwidth consumption. However, our scheme is the most efficient in terms of the computation complexities.

Because prime factorization and discrete logarithms are tractable in the quantum computation model, the DL-based ring signature and the RSA ring signature are forgeable for quantum adversaries although they are unconditionally signer-ambiguous. Since there is no argument shown that the NPC problems are tractable and many researchers consider it is infeasible even in the quantum computation model, our scheme may keep valid even the quantum computers are implemented in the future.

5   Conclusions and Further Works

In this paper, we introduce the notion of shared-key signatures, which makes it possible to anonymously sign any message with verification by a shared common public key. Although the complexity of our proposed scheme grows with the number of possible signers, in principle, the complexity of shared-key signatures may keep constant as the number of possible signers increases. Hence, shared-key signatures are deserved further research. In addition, one of the main advantages of the existing ring signature schemes is that they can be used with popular public key types that users are likely to already have been available. This will not be the case with a scheme that does not provide encryption. Hence, a general problem about our system is the lack of an encryption scheme. Especially, a shared-key encryption may be interesting because it implements broadcast public-key encryption naturally and efficiently.

Acknowledgement. We would like to thank the anonymous referees for their detailed comments and valuable suggestions. We are grateful to Dr. Fangguo Zhang for his correction of some mistakes in our preparing version of this paper.

This work is supported by the 973 National Important Project of China (No. G1999035801) and the Natural Science Foundation of China (No. 60073052).

References

1. D. Chaum and E. van Heyst. Group signatures. In Proc. of Eurocrypt'91, LNCS 547, pp. 257-265, Springer-Verlag, 1992.
2. R. Cramer, I. Damgård and B. Schoenmakers. Proofs of partial knowledge and simplified design of witness hiding protocols. In Proc. of Crypto'95, LNCS 839, pp. 174-187, Springer- verlag, 1994.
3. R. L. Rivest, A. Shamir, and Y. Tauman. How to leak a secret. In Proc. of Asiacrypt'01, LNCS 2248, pp. 552-565, Springer-Verlag, 2001.
4. M. Abe, M. Ohkubo, and K. Suzuki. 1-out -of-n Signatures from a Variety of Keys. In Proc. In Proc. of Asiacrypt'02, LNCS 2501, pp. 415-432, Springer-verlag, 2002.
5. F. Zhang and K. Kim. ID-Based blind signature and ring signature from pairings. In Proc. of Asiacrypt'02, LNCS 2501, pp. 533-547, Springer-Verlag, 2002.
6. D. S. Wong, K. Fung, J. K. Liu and V. K. Wei. On the RS-code construction of ring signature schemes and a threshold setting of RST. In Proc. of ICICS'03, LNCS 2836, pp. 34-46, Springer-verlag, 2003.
7. I. S. Reed and G. Solomon. Polynomial Codes over finite field. SIAM J. Applied Math., 8: 300-304, June 1960.
8. M. Jakobsson, K. Sako, and R. Impagliazzo. Designated verifier proofs and their applications. In Proc. of Eurocrypt'96, LNCS 1070, pp. 143-154, Springer-Verlag, 1996.
9. A. Fiat and A. Shamir. How to prove yourself: practical solutions of identification and signature problems. In Proc. of Crypto'86, LNCS 263, pp. 186-194, Springer-Verlag, 1987.
10. M. Blum. How to prove a theorem so no one else can claim it. In Proc. of the International Congress of Mathematicians, Berkeley, CA, pp. 1444-1451, 1986.
11. O. Goldreich, S. Micali and A. Wigderson: How to prove all NP statements in zero- knowledge and a methodology of cryptographic protocol design. In Proc. of Crypto'86, pp. 171-185, Springer-verlag, 1987.
12. P.W. Shor. Polynomial-time algorithm for prime factorization and discrete logarithms on a quantum computer. SIAM Journal of Computing, 26: 1484-1509,1997.
13. C. H. Bennett, E. Bernstein, G. Brassard, and U. Vazirani. Strengths and weaknesses of quantum computing. SIAM J. Comput. 26, 5, pp. 1510-1523, 1997.
14. T. Okamoto, K. Tanaka, and S. Uchiyama. Quantum Public-Key Cryptosystems, In Proc. of Crypto'00, LNCS 1880, pp. 147-165, Springer-Verlag 2000.
15. C. Dwork. Lattices and their application to cryptography. Stanford University, Springer Quarter Press. 1998.
16. A. K Lenstra, Jr. H. W. Lenstra, and Lovasz. Factorization polynomials with rational coefficients, Mathematische Annalen, 261, pp. 515-534, 1982.

Prevent Online Identity Theft – Using Network Smart Cards for Secure Online Transactions

HongQian Karen Lu and Asad Ali

Axalto, 8311 North FM 620 Rd, Austin, TX 78726, USA
{karenlu, amali}@axalto.com

Abstract. This paper presents a novel method that can be used to prevent online identity theft and thereby ensure secure online transactions. In particular, the method combats online identity theft mechanisms that capture information on the computer before the information is encrypted. The key feature of this method is the use of secure network smart cards to establish secure connections between the smart card and remote Internet nodes. Using this end-to-end secure connection, one can securely exchange confidential information between the smart card and a trusted remote server. Any intermediate node, including the host computer to which the smart card is connected, cannot compromise this secure connection.

1 Introduction

According to the Federal Trade Commission, in the year 2002 alone, there were 9.9 million identity theft victims, resulting in a loss of $47.6 billion to businesses and $5 billion in out-of-pocket expenses to individuals [1]. Online identity thefts are methods of stealing network identities used for Internet online transactions. Examples of network identity include, but are not limited to, Personal Identity Number (PIN) for bank cards, credit card numbers, Social Security numbers (SSN), online passwords, and driver's license numbers. The attackers can use the stolen identities to do many things including accessing the victims' online accounts or opening new accounts.

In a typical online transaction, a user uses a keyboard to type in confidential personal information, such as a credit card number. This information flows in clear text from the keyboard to the computer and may be displayed on the screen. One form of online identity theft is the use of a keystroke logger to log individual keystrokes; and another form is to capture a user's screen. The malicious program either stores the captured information on the machine for later retrieval or transmits it through the Internet to the attacker's computer. The attacker extracts network identities from the captured information. Two well-known cases of such attacks are the Kinko case in New York City and the Boston College case [2, 3]. As Internet online transactions become more pervasive, so does the threat of online identity theft.

A variety of software tries to combat keystroke loggers and screen capturers. Most of these products detect and fight against known malicious programs. However, because developers of malicious programs continually add anti-detection mechanisms into their software, this approach is not reliable.

K. Zhang and Y. Zheng (Eds.): ISC 2004, LNCS 3225, pp. 342–353, 2004.

Encrypting online sessions alleviates the security problem but cannot completely solve it. This is particularly true when using a publicly-accessible machine because confidential information can be compromised before the security layer has had a chance to encrypt it. Therefore, network security protocols, such as SSL/TLS, are necessary, but not sufficient. What is needed is a mechanism for augmenting this network security so that online transactions can be performed from un-trusted PCs. This paper describes such a mechanism that uses network smart cards.

The network smart card supports standard mainstream networking and security protocols like TCP/IP and SSL/TLS. With such smart cards, the un-trusted PC can be pushed outside the security boundary. We establish a secure connection between the network smart card and a trusted remote Internet server. Confidential information flows from the smart card directly to the remote server. This eliminates the need to manually type confidential information where it can be compromised by malicious software. This end-to-end security mechanism combats identity theft mechanisms that capture the information on the computer before it is encrypted, and thereby enhances the security of online transactions.

2 Related Work

This section describes some of the existing Internet security mechanisms that assist online transactions. Some are built to enhance the security of online transactions, while others are simply agents of convenience.

Smart Card. A smart card is a tamper-resistant, secure, and portable microprocessor card. It has been used for security in a variety of applications [4]. Relevant to this work, the smart card is a security token for computer and network access, and for secure communications. When in use, the smart card is connected to a host computer. Using Public Key Infrastructure (PKI) to secure communication, the card holds the private key of its owner and performs data encryption/decryption algorithms on the card. However, if a keystroke logger compromises the user's computer, the logger could capture sensitive data before the smart card encryption mechanism is applied.

Another approach is to store the user's confidential information on the smart card. For online transactions, the middleware (a special software) running on the computer gets the information from the smart card and fills in the appropriate fields in a web form. This method provides convenience but does not provide any more security than manual entry of the web form, because the confidential information is in an unencrypted form in the web browser.

Identity Federation. One of the most important issues for Internet services is authentication, which proves that an entity (a user, a client, or a server) is who it claims to be. One growing trend in authentication is identity federation (also called federation of authentication). Such a system provides authentication for client and server applications and the convenience of a single sign-in for the user. Once a user is authenticated, she or he can access services provided by different servers in the federation without having to log on to each server individually. The best-known protocol for such a system is Kerberos [5]. The Microsoft Passport [6] uses Kerberos to provide Passport single sign-in services. The Liberty Alliance is a consortium of 160 technology and consumer-oriented organizations [7]. The *Liberty Identity*

Federation Framework (ID-FF) of the Liberty Alliance aims to establish a standardized, multi-vendor, web-based single sign-on with simple federated identities in its first phase. The ID-FF overcomes some of the shortcomings of Microsoft Passport, such as using cookies for tickets and centralized identity server.

The above approaches focus on how an identity server provides authentication services to multiple service providers on the Internet. However, the implementation of Microsoft Passport and Liberty architecture is based on HTTP re-direction, which is susceptible to middleman attacks [7,8].

Virtual Credit Card Numbers. In an effort to stem the growth of credit card fraud during online transactions, several credit card companies (e.g., Citibank) provide virtual credit card numbers. These numbers are for one-time use only, which protects the user's actual credit card number during an online transaction. The user enters the virtual number when shopping online. Even if the virtual number is stolen, it is of little use because it cannot be reused after the first transaction.

Although helpful, this approach has two drawbacks. First, it is limited to credit card numbers and cannot be extended to other confidential information. Secondly, in order to get a one-time use virtual card number, the user must authenticate himself to the bank. This online authentication process can be a weak link. Attackers can impersonate the user and get virtual credit card numbers on his behalf. In this scenario, the user's actual credit card number is secure, but his identity is not.

The work presented in this paper focuses on securely passing information from the network smart card to an Internet server. This model presents an end-to-end security paradigm, which is absent from existing approaches.

3 Framework

A network smart card is a smart card that is an Internet node [9, 10, 11, 12, 13, 14]. The network smart card we have developed [12] is a *secure* Internet node, which sets the security boundary inside the card using SSL/TLS. A secure HTTPS connection can be established between the card and an Internet node. In the rest of this paper, the network smart card or Internet smart card means a smart card that is a network node and has the security boundary inside the card.

3.1 Method Overview

Online identity theft using a logging mechanism is possible because unencrypted confidential information is present in the computer for some duration, however small. The attacker could gain access to this information before any security mechanism is applied. The logging mechanism will not work if the confidential information never appears in clear text in the computer. This is the basic idea behind the method presented in this paper. We propose to use the network smart card to store confidential personal information. When needed and authorized by the owner, the information flows securely from the card to the remote Internet client or server. The encryption and decryption happen inside the card. Although the information still passes through the computer used for the online transaction, the information is encrypted and, hence, secure. From the network's perspective, the user's computer is just another router on the network.

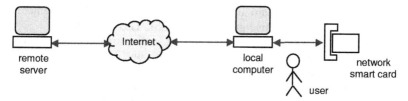

Fig.1. The physical connections among the entities.

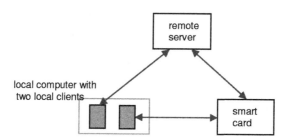

Fig. 2. Logical Internet connection among the Internet smart card, the remote server, and the local client applications.

A network smart card can combat the logging-based identity theft problem because it is a portable secure network node. In order to use the card, one must physically own the card and have its Card Holder Verification (CHV), which may be a PIN, a password, biometrics, or a combination of these. The CHV is securely stored in the smart card.

To conduct a secure online transaction, the user establishes a secure Internet connection between his smart card and the remote secure server of a service provider, for example, a bank. Through a web browser, the user decides which information is entered manually and which information the card sends directly to the server. Non-critical information can still be typed in and sent to the remote server. However, all confidential information flows securely and directly from the network smart card to the remote server.

To access the network smart card, the user still needs to enter the CHV. However, even if the host computer is compromised and the CHV is captured, the CHV itself is useless without physical access to the card. Even with network access to the card, the attacker still has to match the captured CHV with the card, which would be difficult, if not impossible.

Figure 1 illustrates the physical configuration of our method. The remote server runs on a remote computer. The local client, a web browser application, runs on a local computer that the user is using. Both computers are connected to the Internet. The network smart card connects to the Internet either by connecting to the local computer, which acts as a router, or, by connecting to another device. The connection to the Internet might be wired or wireless.

Figure 2 illustrates the logical connection. The local computer, the remote server, and the network smart card are all Internet nodes. On the local computer, the user uses two web browsers: one connects to his network smart card, and the other connects to the remote server. The smart card also has a direct connection with the remote server. All connections described in this figure represent SSL/TLS connections.

This mechanism applies to various kinds of online transactions; for example, creating a new account and accessing an existing account. The card owner determines what personal information to keep inside the card; for example, the card may contain passwords, SSN, and credit card numbers. Because the information is encrypted/decrypted inside the smart card or inside the remote secure server, the information is concealed from the user's local computer. Keystroke logging or other logging mechanisms cannot get the information.

The key features of this mechanism are to establish a secure Internet connection between the smart card and the remote server of a service provider, and to send encrypted information between the card and the server directly via the secure connection. It is an implementation and network configuration choice for the card to send data to the remote server or for the remote server to get data from the card.

The method presented here is not limited to the form of secure network smart cards. It also applies to other secure tokens that are Internet nodes and have their security boundaries inside the tokens. In addition, the method also prevents screen capture-based online identity theft.

3.2 Functions of the Players

Network Smart Card. A network smart card is a smart card that is an Internet node and is accessible from the Internet. User information is stored on the smart card. The smart card only gives out information to the trusted client or server at the user's authorization. The smart card can establish and maintain secure Internet connections with another Internet node, which can be a web server or a web browser.

It is important that mutual authentication be performed when the network smart card is connected. With SSL, client authentication is optional. However, with network smart card as a server, client authentication is mandatory. Otherwise, if only server authentication is performed, the client is protected, but the smart card is not protected.

Internet Client Application. The web browser is an Internet client application. The user uses a web browser to access services provided by an Internet service provider. Our technique does not require any changes to the standard web browsers, such as Internet Explorer, Netscape, or Mozilla. The web browser must support HTTPS connections. The user uses one instance of the web browser to connect to a remote server of a service provider. He uses another instance of the web browser to connect to his network smart card.

Remote Secure Server. The remote secure server runs the applications of the service provider, for example, a bank. It provides online services to the user. To use the network smart card to prevent online identity theft, the remote secure server must provide the following new features in addition to its existing functionalities:

1.   Maintain the association of a user and the corresponding smart card.
2.   Accept secure direct input from the network smart card.
3.   Enable the user, through the web browser, to request the remote secure server to get or wait for information from the network smart card.

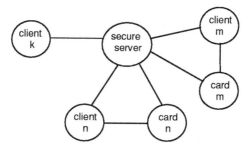

Fig. 3. Topology of the logical secure connections among the sever, client applications, and smart cards. The edges represent secure connections.

3.3 Association

Typically the remote server of a service provider can simultaneously service multiple client applications from different Internet nodes. Hence, the remote server may connect to multiple network smart cards at the same time. Figure 3 illustrates the topology of the secure logical connections among the server, clients, and smart cards. The nodes of the graph represent the server, a client, or a smart card. The edges of the graph represent secure connections between the nodes. Each node knows and only knows those edges that connect to the node. The questions are:

1. How does the remote secure server associate client n with card n?
2. How is the client node k prevented from asking the server node to associate with card n?

To resolve this association issue, we define a *Shared Association Secret* (SAS). The SAS is a secret that the user selects and is stored in his network smart card. The user may select an SAS for each of the trusted service providers stored in the card.

We also introduce the concept of a *three-way authentication* to form a triangle of trust among the user, the smart card, and the remote server. The user authenticates himself to the smart card using his CHV. He requests his smart card (card n) to initiate a secure connection with a remote server. The card will then send the user's login credential and the corresponding SAS to the remote server. The remote server uses the information to establish an association between the user and his smart card. When the user accesses the remote server via the web browser (client n), he enters the SAS to authenticate to the server. This enables the remote server to associate the client n with the user and his smart card (card n). The attacker, client k, may try to connect to the server and associate to card n, but he does not have the SAS and cannot establish the association. (More discussions will be presented in Section 5.) The information flow of this three-way authentication is illustrated in Figure 4.

The SAS acts as a shared secret between the user and the remote server during a session. The remote server keeps the SAS for one session only. The user-client-card association that includes the SAS is removed when the session is finished. For security, this SAS should be different from the smart card CHV.

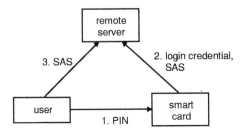

Fig. 4. Information flow of the three-way authentication.

If the user is on a public PC that is compromised, any keystroke he types may be captured and stored without his knowledge. The conventional username and password persist on the remote server. The attacker can use the captured username and password to log in to the user's account at the remote server. The SAS, on the other hand, is a one-time secret from the remote server's perspective. It is more secure because it can only be used with the network smart card. For added security, the user can use different a SAS for each different service providers and change SAS often.

The remote server must ensure that there are no identical SAS entries in its association map. The server can accomplish this by rejecting the connection request from a network smart card if an identical SAS is already present in the association map. Although SAS may not be unique, the probability of SAS collision is very small. For example, if the SAS is 8 characters long, the chance of collision is about 1 in 2×10^{13}. In case of a collision, the user can try to connect later.

4 Workflow

There are two possible workflow scenarios:

1. The network smart card connects to remote server and sends confidential information. This is called the *Push* model.
2. The remote server connects to the network smart card and requests confidential information. This is called the *Pull* model.

The Push model can be used in most network configurations where the network smart card has an IP address and is connected to the Internet. However, the Pull model can be used only if the network smart card is globally-accessible from outside the LAN. The following describes the Push model.

Figure 5 illustrates the Push model and describes the interaction of three key elements in this model: local computer, the network smart card, and the remote server of a service provider. All arrows indicating inter-element interactions represent HTTPS connections using SSL/TLS protocol.

1. The user starts a web browser on a local computer. This instance of the web browser is later referred to as B1.
2. From B1 the user connects to the network smart card and authenticates himself via his CHV over a secure HTTPS connection.

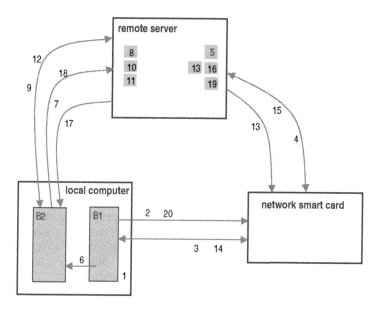

Fig. 5. Push model of using a local computer to securely get data from network smart card. The card itself pushes the requested data to remote server.

3. Once authenticated, he is presented with a list of trusted service providers. The user picks a service provider and asks the network smart card to establish a secure connection with this service provider.

4. The network smart card knows the URL of the selected service provider. It establishes a secure connection with the remote server of the service provider and sends the following data stored on the smart card to the remote server: (a) Login credentials, for example, the user's username and password for his account at the remote server; (b) the hash value H of a random number or string generated by his network smart card; and (c) the SAS, the shared association secret that provides an additional level of authentication when the user actually initiates a session with the remote server.

5. After receiving the data sent to it in step 4, the remote server first checks if the SAS and the hash value H are identical to those in an existing entry of the internal association map. If the answer is "no", the server creates a new entry in the association map, which contains the smart card's specific information, the user's login credentials, the hash value H, and the SAS. This associates the smart card with the user. If the answer is "yes", the association fails. The server informs the smart card, which informs the user. The smart card disconnects from the remote server. Subsequent steps listed below become irrelevant.

6. The user now clicks on a link in B1 to launch another instance of the web browser with the URL set to the authentication page of the remote server. A parameter in this URL is the hash value H. This new browser instance is referred to as B2.

7. B2 connects to the remote server to request a new session.

8. After receiving the new session request from B2, the remote server extracts the hash value H from the connection request. It then marks the corresponding entry in the association map as "connected", but not yet "authorized". Once any entry is marked as "connected" the server does not accept any other connections for this entry.

9. To authorize the current session with B2, the remote server asks the user to enter the SAS corresponding to this connection.

10. If the SAS entered by the user matches the SAS in an entry of the association map and the entry is in the "connected" state, the remote server changes this entry to the "authorized" state. This associates B2 with the user and the smart card, and the user is logged in. The workflow can now continue with step 12.

11. If, however, the SAS entered by user does not match any SAS in the association map, the remote server closes this client connection. Access is denied. If the SAS matches with the SAS in an entry in the association map, which has already been marked as "authorized", the new connection is closed. The remote server warns the previous connection corresponding to this entry of the potential threat. The true owner of the smart card might decide to disconnect. Subsequent steps listed below become irrelevant.

12. After access is granted, the user can access the services provided by the remote server through B2. One step in this interaction can be to request that some confidential information (e.g., user's credit card number and expiration date) be retrieved from the network smart card instead of being typed manually. The user indicates to the remote server that the network smart card will send this information.

13. The remote server now waits for this confidential information to arrive from the network smart card. The transaction, as well as the UI on web browser B2, will be in waiting mode.

14. The user now switches to browser B1, which is connected to the web server running on the network smart card. He interacts with the card to select the confidential information that should be sent to the remote server. This is the same information that the remote server is waiting for. Once selected, the user instructs the network smart card to forward this information to the remote server.

15. The smart card sends the selected information to the remote server and reads the response from the remote server. The response may include the status of the transaction and any additional information that the remote server wants to send back.

16. The remote server uses this information to complete the transaction that was put in a waiting state in step 13.

17. The remote server updates the UI on browser B2 to indicate that the requested transaction has been completed.

18. The user logs out from the remote server.

19. After receiving the user logout request, the remote server deletes the corresponding entry in association map. This prevents subsequent transactions from being sent to the smart card.

20. The user logs out from his network smart card and removes the smart card from the reader.

During an active session, the remote server may periodically check the existence and validity of the network smart card. The server may also do this kind of checking when the user navigates from one secure web page to another.

The only two pieces of confidential information manually entered by a user are his CHV to authenticate himself to the smart card, and the SAS to authenticate to the remote server. Neither action compromises the current session in any way. Even if captured, they are not useful without physical access to the network smart card. Furthermore, both of these values can be easily changed after the user returns to a secure environment.

In a typical usage scenario, the user carries the network smart card with him. The card can be connected to the network via any PC. The PC itself may be in a public location and may not be secure, but it can still be used to connect the network smart card to the Internet for secure online transactions. This scenario provides the added security of the "what you have" paradigm. The network smart card should be removed from the network after a transaction is complete. No malicious code can now mount any attack on the network smart card.

5 Security Analysis

This section analyzes the security of the proposed method. The first issue relates to the uniqueness of the shared association secret (SAS) and the smart card CHV (if not biometrics). Although the chance is very small, it is possible that one user's SAS and PIN are the same as another user's SAS and PIN for the same service provider. If both users are trying to access the service provider at the same time, the one who connects later will be rejected. The rejected user can try to connect later. The user can also change the SAS or the CHV (if changeable) in a secure environment.

The second issue is that the user must remember two things to conduct an online transaction: the CHV (if not biometrics) to authenticate to the network smart card, and SAS to authenticate to the service provider. This, however, is the trade-off between security and convenience. The technique may be less convenient for the user, but provides enhanced security.

The third issue is that the hash value H is passed from B1 to B2, and can be intercepted. The attacker may capture the hash value H and use H to request a connection before the actual user's request arrives. In this case, the remote server marks the corresponding entry in the association map as "connected". This prevents the actual user from connecting, but does not give the attacker access to the user's account, because the connection cannot be authorized without the SAS.

The fourth issue is that the attacker may capture the SAS as the user types it in B2. The attacker, however, cannot access the true user's account because he does not have the smart card. Even if the user's smart card is online, the attacker cannot connect to the remote server because the corresponding entry in the association map has already been marked as "connected". Even in the extreme case that the attacker gets connected to the remote server before the owner of the smart card does, the remote server would reject the owner. In this case, the owner must immediately remove his network smart card from the network to avoid damage.

The fifth issue is the possibility of attacking (or hijacking) the connection. Our method requires secure HTTPS connections using SSL/TLS. TLS is a well-tested protocol that provides a high level of network security. It has safeguards against various kinds of possible attacks, including man-in-the-middle attack and replay attacks. TLS assumes that the two end points of a TLS connection are secure. The end points keep the shared secret, which is used to regenerate session keys for each roundtrip communication between the two end points. It is not possible to guess the shared secret by monitoring the encrypted traffic on the network. TLS protocol was designed to prevent this kind of attack. The only way to break a TLS connection is to compromise one of the two end points, for example, the web server or the web browser.

In our scenario the two end points for passing confidential information are the network smart card and the trusted remote server. The smart card is a secure physical token carried by its owner. The user trusts that the remote server is secure; otherwise, he should not do business with it. Therefore, the two end points are secure and so is the HTTPS connection between them.

As a further safeguard, the network smart card can be set up to work in two modes: a trusted mode and an untrusted mode. In the trusted mode, the card owner can do many things with the card. In the untrusted mode, the card can only send confidential information, when the owner requests, to one of the trusted merchants that are specified in the smart card. The card cannot change passwords, create new accounts, modify existing ones, or send information to a merchant that is not on its trust list. This further limits the damage that an attacker can do.

6 Conclusions

Network smart cards can be used to prevent online identity theft and to secure online transactions. This new method establishes a secure Internet connection between the network smart card and the service provider. The network smart card stores the personal information. For online transactions, the user can authorize the network smart card to send selected information securely and directly to the service provider. Thus, no confidential personal information goes through the local computer in clear (unencrypted) format. This combats the identity theft mechanism that can capture the information on the computer before it is encrypted. This method extends the reach of secure online transactions to publicly-accessible computers.

References

1. Federal Trade Commission, "Federal Trade Commission Identity Theft Survey Report," September 2003, page 7, http://www.ftc.gov/os/2003/09/synovatereport.pdf.
2. Jesdanun, A., "Thief captures every keystroke to access accounts," *Seattle Post*, July, 2003, http://seattlepi.nwsource.com/national/131961_snoop23.html.
3. Poulsen, K., "Guilty Plea in Kinko's Keystroke Caper," *SecurityFocus*, July 18, 2003, http://www.securityfocus.com/printable/news/6447.
4. Jurgensen, T.M. and Guthery, S.B., *Smart Cards*, Pearson Education, Inc., 2002.
5. "Kerberos: The Network Authentication Protocol," http://web.mit.edu/kerberos/www/.
6. *Microsoft .Net Passport*, Microsoft Corporation, http://www.passport.net/.
7. *Liberty Alliance Project*, Liberty Alliance Consortium, http://www.projectliberty.org/.

8. Kormann, D.P. and Rubin, A.D., "Risks of the Passport Single Sign-on Protocol," *Computer Networks*, Elsevier Science Press, Volume 33, pages 51-58, 2000.
9. Urien, P., "Internet card, a smart card as a true Internet node," *Computer Communication*, Vol. 23, pp 1655-1666, 2000.
10. Rees, J., and Honeyman, P., "Webcard: a Java Card Web Server," Univ. of Michigan, http://www.citi.umich.edu/projects/smartcard/webcard/citi-tr-99-3.html.
11. Guthery, S., Kehr, R., and Posegga, J., "How to Turn a GSM SIM into a Web Server," http://www.scdk.com/websim.pdf.
12. Montgomery, M., Ali, A.M., and Lu, H.K., "Secure Network Card – Implementation of a Standard Network Stack in a Smart Card," Six Smart Card Research and Advanced Application IFIP Conference, France, August 2004.
13. Giesecke & Devrien, "Internet Smart Card," http://cebit.gi-de.com/eng/main/cebit-special/4_7_N.php4.
14. Muller, C. and Deschamps, E., "Smart Cards as First-Class Network Citizens," http://www.gemplus.com/smart/r_d/publications/pdf/MD02gdcc.pdf.

Provable Unlinkability Against Traffic Analysis Already After $\mathcal{O}(\log(n))$ Steps!*

Marcin Gomułkiewicz, Marek Klonowski, and Mirosław Kutyłowski

Institute of Mathematics, Wrocław University of Technology,
Wybrzeże Wyspiańskiego 27
50-370 Wrocław, Poland
{gomulkie,klonowsk}@im.pwr.wroc.pl, Miroslaw.Kutylowski@pwr.wroc.pl

Abstract. We consider unlinkability of communication problem: given n users, each sending a message to some destination, encode and route the messages so that an adversary analyzing the traffic in the communication network cannot link the senders with the recipients. A solution should have a small communication overhead, that is, the number of additional messages should be kept low.

David Chaum introduced idea of mixes for solving this problem. His approach was developed further by Simon and Rackoff, and implemented later as the onion protocol. Even if the onion protocol is widely regarded as secure and used in practice, formal arguments supporting this claim are rare and far from being complete. On top of that, in certain scenarios very simple tricks suffice to break security without breaking the cryptographic primitives. It turns out that one source of difficulties in analyzing the onion protocol's security is the adversary model. In a recent work, Berman, Fiat and Ta-Shma develop a new and more realistic model in which only a constant fraction of communication lines can be accessed by an adversary, the number of messages does not need to be high and the *preferences* of the users are taken into account. For this model they prove that with high probability a good level of unlinkability is obtained after $\mathcal{O}(\log^4 n)$ steps of the onion protocol where n is the number of messages sent.

In this paper we improve these results: we show that the same level of unlinkability (expressed as variation distance between certain probability distributions) is obtained with high probability already after $\mathcal{O}(\log n)$ steps of the onion protocol. Asymptotically, this is the best result possible, since obviously $\Omega(\log n)$ steps are necessary. On top of that, our analysis is much simpler. It is based on path coupling technique designed for showing rapid mixing of Markov chains.

Keywords: anonymity, unlinkability, mix network, Markov chain, rapid mixing, path coupling

* Partially supported by the EU within the 6th Framework Programme under contract 001907 (DELIS).

K. Zhang and Y. Zheng (Eds.): ISC 2004, LNCS 3225, pp. 354–366, 2004.
© Springer-Verlag Berlin Heidelberg 2004

1   Introduction

One of the main privacy problems in public computer networks is lack of anonymity: TCP/IP packets reveal both their origin and destination. Standard secure communication protocols protect the data fields only, while the packets can be read while they are processed through intermediate nodes. In some situations it should be kept secret that two parties are exchanging messages – this is crucial in many business contacts.

In order to avoid these problems a message might be encoded so that the source and destination are not revealed while the message is processed through an insecure communication link. However, this security measure may be insufficient due to "traffic analysis": an adversary can deduce source and destination information by tracing the number of messages on the communication links without understanding them.

A fundamental idea of protecting against traffic analysis due to Chaum [6] is based on *mixes*: messages arriving at a mix node are recoded and sent further so that an external observer cannot find which outcoming message corresponds to a given incoming message. If we apply a cascade of mixes, then a certain degree of anonymity can be achieved. Another famous technique are Dining Cryptographers networks introduced in [7]. This protocol guarantees anonymity even against computationally unrestricted attackers. However, it is rather impractical due to communication overhead and scalability problems.

Onion protocol. The next milestone was design of the onion protocol [11]. Later, the same idea was used as a core of Onion Routing protocol [10]. Its main goal is to protect against traffic analysis. The protocol routes each message through a path of randomly chosen intermediate nodes. Each user has a public and a private key, all public keys are widely accessible. The simplest version of the onion protocol looks as follows: in order to send a message M to node D, node S chooses at random intermediate nodes, say $J_1, \ldots, J_\lambda$, and encodes M as an *onion* (Enc_X means encryption with the public key of X):

$$\mathrm{Enc}_{J_1}(\mathrm{Enc}_{J_2}(\ldots(\mathrm{Enc}_{J_\lambda}(\mathrm{Enc}_D(M), \text{"to D"}), \text{"to } J_\lambda\text{"})\ldots), \text{"to } J_3\text{"}), \text{"to } J_2\text{ "}) .$$

This onion is sent by S to J_1. Node J_1 decrypts the message - the plaintext obtained consists of two parts: the second one is J_2, the first one is an onion

$$\mathrm{Enc}_{J_2}(\ldots(\mathrm{Enc}_{J_\lambda}(\mathrm{Enc}_D(M), \text{"to D "}), \text{"to } J_\lambda\text{ "})\ldots), \text{"to } J_3\text{"})$$

with one layer less than the original one. Then J_1 sends this onion to J_2. Nodes J_2 to J_λ work similarly, and the onion is "peeled off" until it finally arrives at D.

The general idea is that a node processing an onion (and an adversary tracing the traffic) cannot read the contents of an onion, but simultaneously decoding with the private key gives each intermediate node sufficient information to route the message.

The onion protocol acts as a network of mixes: if two onions enter the same node simultaneously, the adversary cannot determine the relation between incoming and outcoming onions (this is the key observation for the vertex mixing technique, briefly described later.) The onions meet frequently if there are many onions processed in the network.

Security of the onion protocol. Even if at the first glance such protocols seem to provide anonymity, formal security proofs are rather rare. Proving that the destination of a *single* message is untraceable might be insufficient, since from an adversary's point of view messages are *not* traveling independently. For example, consider the case when two messages enter a node, and leave the node after recoding. The mentioned protocols are based on the principle that it is impossible to find out which outcoming message corresponds to a given incoming message. However, if we guess which outcoming message corresponds to the first incoming message, we know which outcoming message corresponds to the second one. For that reason, while proving unlinkability, one should show a stronger property: probability distribution for configuration of destinations of *all* messages computed using traffic information should be very close to probability distribution computed when only the source nodes and delivery nodes are known.

The main question concerning the onion protocol is how large the λ parameter should be. It should be as small as possible (to minimize the communication overhead and time delay necessary to route the message), but not too small, since the anonymity obviously improves when λ grows.

Previous results. A significant progress in analyzing security of the onion protocol is due to Berman *et al.* [4]. They change adversary model and assume that an (non-adaptive) adversary can eavesdrop at most a constant fraction of all communication links and can corrupt only a constant fraction of all nodes. In such a situation they prove that n messages become unlinkable with high probability for $\lambda = \mathcal{O}(\log^4 n)$. This result is obtained for the original onion protocol, the number of messages n might be much smaller than the number of nodes N, and finally, probability distribution for a destination of a packet sent from a given node need not to be a uniform one. So at a price of assuming a slightly weaker (and more realistic) adversary, one can get much stronger anonymity result.

Onion protocol was considered also as a tool for hiding communication channels that consist of more than just a single message. In this case the attacks are numerous (see for instance [1]) and providing anonymity remains an open question.

New results. In this paper we improve the bound on the required length of the onion paths shown by Berman *et al.* While according to [4] onion paths of length $\mathcal{O}(\log^4 n)$ guarantee anonymity of n messages, we show the same security level is achieved for paths of length $\mathcal{O}(\log n)$ only. In general, this is the optimal result. Apart from the theoretical interest, this brings the bound to the level where it becomes interesting for real-world applications.

2   Adversary Model of Berman *et al.*

2.1   General Idea of "Layer Mixing"

Considering onion routing we usually think about a graph in which vertices represent servers and links stand for connections. In the classical approach [11] it is assumed that all links and some vertices are under adversary control. Information is hidden by "vertex mixing" (see Fig. 1): if two or more onions enter the same honest vertex they become indistinguishable when leaving this vertex. The problem is that probability of "meeting" of two onions in the same vertex is low, when the number of onions is small compared to the number of vertices. However, as was pointed out in [4], the protocol has to provide anonymity even if just a few users are active.

BEFORE MIXING   AFTER MIXING

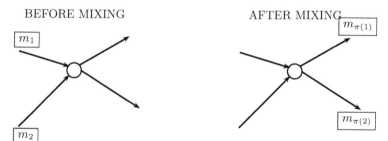

Fig. 1. Vertex mixing: what an adversary can see

To solve the problem of rare conflicts in the classical approach Berman *et al.* introduced "layer mixing", which occurs more likely than "vertex mixing". They assume that a constant fraction f of links remain secure, i.e. they cannot be eavesdropped by an adversary. In this approach traffic ambiguity is achieved in a different way. Namely, messages m_1 and m_2 are mixed when they pass through a so called *crossover structure* [4] (see Fig 2). Such a structure consists of four honest servers S_1^t, S_2^t, S_1^{t+1}, S_2^{t+1} with four secure links (S_1^t, S_1^{t+1}), (S_1^t, S_2^{t+1}), (S_2^t, S_1^{t+1}), (S_2^t, S_2^{t+1}) connecting them.

2.2   Berman's *et al.* Work in Details

Network. We assume that the network consisting of N servers is fully connected - a message can be sent directly between each pair of nodes. All servers' public keys are known. There are n messages to be delivered, the source (and destination) nodes of these messages are fixed but arbitrary. For each message an answer should be sent. There is no fixed relationship between N and n.

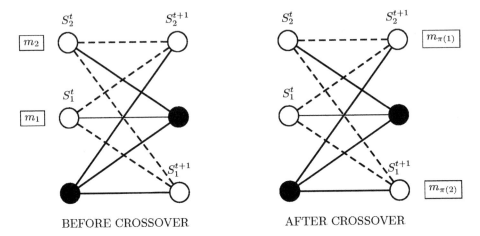

Fig. 2. Layer mixing: solid lines and filled depict links and servers controlled by an adversary; dashed lines and empty circles are "honest"

Onions. Berman *et al.* consider a variant of the onion protocol. Let us recall its simplified version: If server A wants to send a message a to server B and get an answer b it chooses at random $\lambda - 1$ nodes $v_1, v_2 \ldots v_{\lambda-1}$; let us use the notation $A = v_0$, $B = v_\lambda$. Moreover, server A chooses independently at random strings r_i and z_i, for $i \leq \lambda$. Let E_i denote encryption with a public key of server v_i. For $i \in 0 \ldots \lambda - 1$ let:

$$\alpha_i = E_{i+1}(r_{i+1}, z_{i+1}, v_{i+2}, E_{i+2}(\ldots E_{\lambda-1}(r_{\lambda-1}, z_{\lambda-1}, v_\lambda, E_\lambda(r_\lambda, a)) \ldots)) \; .$$

The way from A to B: server A sends (v_0, z_0, α_0) to v_1. Similarly, v_i sends (v_i, z_i, α_i) to v_{i+1}. Then v_{i+1} decrypts α_i and sends $(v_{i+1}, z_{i+1}, \alpha_{i+1})$ to v_{i+2}. It also records $v_i, v_{i+2}, z_i, z_{i+1}$ and r_{i+1} for the later use. Of course server $v_\lambda = B$ can easily recognize that it is a recipient of the message a.

The way back: server $B = v_\lambda$ sends $(z_{\lambda-1}, b_\lambda)$ to $v_{\lambda-1}$ where $b_\lambda = b \oplus r_\lambda$ (symbol $\oplus$ denotes bitwise XOR operation). In general, v_i receives a message (z_i, b_{i+1}). Then v_i recognizes the value z_i, the link (v_{i-1}, v_i) and the values r_i, z_{i-1} that are associated with it. Then it sends (z_{i-1}, b_i), where $b_i = b_{i+1} \oplus r_i$ to v_{i-1}. Finally, $A = v_0$ receives (z_0, b_0). The value b is reconstructed using equality $b = b_0 \oplus r_1 \oplus r_2 \oplus \ldots \oplus r_\lambda$.

Details are described later, since they are not crucial for the proof of our main result.

Adversary Model. Berman's *et al.* assume that an adversary can control (eavesdrop) a constant fraction of nodes and a constant fraction of links. That is, she can distinguish every packet that comes in and out of a corrupted node, and observe transmission over a corrupted link (which may connect honest nodes).

The nodes and links under attack must be determined in advance, but it is possible that for each step the adversary controls a different set of nodes and links. So, according to the literature, it is a "global passive adversary". (Berman *et al.* use a term "adaptive adversary" and also admit initiating messages not according to the protocol by corrupted servers; however, we believe that in such case a simple repetition attack would compromise the system – dishonest node can send a copy of a message some time later, and look for occurrences of messages known from the previous protocol execution, such occurrences leak information about the path of one message.)

A-Priori Knowledge. In their work Berman *et al.* point out existence of what they call *a-priori knowledge*. Intuitions are simple: some of the nodes may be more "popular" than the rest, and/or some of the nodes may have certain preferences. There are many cases where such preferences do exist; indeed, knowing them can be very helpful for an adversary.

One of the main results in [4] is that in order to prove unlinkability in presence of a-priori knowledge it suffices to prove unlinkability in a simple case (where the messages are sent at random, with uniform distribution), and double the number of steps. It is quite intuitive: one can observe messages at their origin (a new message appears) and at their destination (a message ceases to roam). If it is impossible to trace it from the beginning to the middle, and impossible to trace it backwards, from the end to the middle, an adversary cannot "join" the two paths. However, a mathematically sound proof is tricky and goes through information-theoretic arguments [4].

We shall prove unlinkability in $\mathcal{O}(\log n)$ steps in absence of a-priori knowledge. Due to the result from [4] just mentioned, the same asymptotic bound $\lambda = \mathcal{O}(\log n)$ suffices to hide connection in presence of a priori information.

Other Features. The model assumes discrete timing and synchronization. Berman *et al.* suggest that a rough synchronization between the nodes and an appropriate, small delays suffice for the protocol to work. This is the case for our proof as well, however we skip discussion on this issue due to space constraints.

3   Unlinkability

The main goal of any mix-network (whether based on onion-routing or not) is to hide as much information as one can. Obviously, not all information can be hidden: if no message enters a node no message can be delivered there. Therefore we focus on "additional information" one can get through traffic analysis. The point is that the conditional probability distribution in the presence of traffic information should be "close enough" to the a priori probability distribution.

3.1   Definitions of Unlinkability

Although many plausible definitions of unlinkability may be proposed, Berman *et al.* show that the most important definitions are (up to some factor) equivalent; details can be found in [4]. As we use different techniques for our proof, we need one definition only. Let us recall that the total variation distance between probability distributions μ_1 and μ_2 defined over space X of elementary events equals

$$\|\mu_1 - \mu_2\| = \frac{1}{2} \sum_{x \in X} |\mu_1(x) - \mu_2(x)| \ .$$

Let C denote a random variable describing adversary's knowledge on traffic during protocol execution, c is the actual value of C. Let Π be the uniform distribution over a space of all possible bijections between the onions sent by the source servers and the onions delivered to the destination servers. We shall show that the total variation distance

$$\|(\Pi|C = c) - \Pi\|$$

is small for overwhelming majority of all c. It can be easily seen that it roughly corresponds to Berman's *et al.* definition number 2.

3.2   Lower Bound

The lower bound is straightforward. For the sake of simplicity assume that $n < N^{1/4}$. Then it is easy to see that the probability that two onion meet at some node during k steps is less than $kn \cdot \frac{n}{N} < \frac{k}{n^2} < \frac{1}{2}$. Now assume that the onions never meet and consider a single message. During a single step the route chosen for processing this message is controlled by an adversary with a constant probability f. Hence after k steps the adversary can see the whole path made by the message with probability at least f^k. Hence $\mathcal{O}(\log n)$ steps are necessary to get it below $\frac{2}{n}$.

4   Coupling Based Unlinkability Proof

In our approach we treat mixing process as a very particular stochastic process, namely a Markov chain. Then we can use some advanced tools tailored for Markov chains to show *convergence rate* of the mixing process. To provide rigid proof of unlinkability we apply so-called *delayed path coupling* method. This technique, invented in [9], is an extension of well-known *coupling* and *path coupling* by Bubley and Dyer [5] (we shall describe it briefly below). This approach combined together with some technical lemmas from the original paper [4] turns out to be very efficient.

4.1   Onion Routing as a Markov Chain

Our key-observation is the fact that from passive adversary's point of view mixing process can be treated as a non-homogeneous Markov chain. A step of the protocol corresponds to a step of this Markov chain. The chain is defined for a fixed but random adversary (meaning that it is fixed in advance which nodes and which links are corrupted by the adversary) and the traffic information gained by the adversary during protocol execution (presence or absence of packets at corrupt links, recoding and routing done at corrupt nodes.)

For the sake of simplicity of presentation we assume that the adversary can observe each node and see how many onions are processed there at each step. Despite this additional information revealed to the adversary we show the unlinkability result. For each step, we assign the numbers 1 through n to the positions of the onions. The numbering is arbitrary, but note that since more than one onion can be found at a single node, the number of the "positions" assigned to a node might be greater than one.

The state of the Markov chain after step i is a permutation π_i over $\mathbb{S}_n$. It means that the jth message is included in the onion which is at position $\pi_i(j)$.

The transition function of the Markov chain is defined as follows. If after step i the chain is in state π, then π_{i+1}, the state after step $i+1$ is chosen uniformly at random over the set of all permutations $S \subseteq \mathbb{S}_n$ that are consistent with π and the information gained by the adversary. For instance, if there is a corrupted link from a node A holding a single onion (position u) to a node B that holds a single onion after step (position v), and the adversary observed an onion sent through this link, then we know that the same message is in node B at step $i+1$ as in node B at step i. In other words, $\pi_i^{-1}(u) = \pi_{i+1}^{-1}(v)$.

Stationary Distribution. Each step of the Markov chain is described by a permutation from $\mathbb{S}_n$ - this is a permutation chosen according to the traffic information seen by the adversary. The probability distribution describing this choice need not to be uniform. In fact, there are quite many relationships involved and they are not easy to describe.

Now assume that the initial state of the chain is described by the uniform distribution over the set of all permutations from $\mathbb{S}_n$. We may easily see that this is a stationary distribution, that is, no matter how the traffic information influences the single steps, after each step the probability distribution of the possible states are uniform over $\mathbb{S}_n$. Indeed, assume that permutations $\eta_1, \ldots, \eta_u$ describe a step i. After step i the state of the chain is a permutation π, if for some j after step $i-1$ the state is described by $\pi \circ \eta_j^{-1}$ and permutation η_j is applied at step i. Due to stochastic independence of step i from the previous state we get that the probability of getting π equals

$$\sum_{j=1}^{u} \left(\Pr(\pi \circ \eta_j^{-1}) \cdot \Pr(\eta_j) \right) = \sum_{j=1}^{u} \left(\frac{1}{n!} \cdot \Pr(\eta_j) \right) = \frac{1}{n!} \ .$$

4.2 Rapid Mixing via Coupling Techniques

We shall show that our Markov chain converges quickly to the stationary distribution. We use *path coupling* technique, so first we briefly describe original *coupling* and its extensions. Technical details (with formal proofs) can be found in [5].

Let us start with some definitions. Let $\mathbf{M} = (\mathcal{Y}_t)_{t \in \mathbb{N}}$ be a discrete-time (possibly non-homogeneous) Markov chain with a finite state space $\mathbf{S}$ that has a stationary distribution μ. Let $\mathcal{L}_Y(\mathcal{Y}_t)$ denote the probability distribution of $\mathcal{Y}_t$, given that $\mathcal{Y}_0 = Y$ (where Y might be a random variable as well). The standard measure of the convergence is *mixing time*, defined as:

$$\tau_{\mathbf{M}}(\varepsilon) = \min \left\{ T : \forall_{Y \in \mathbf{S}}, \forall_{t \geq T} \, \|\mathcal{L}_Y(\mathcal{Y}_t) - \mu\| \leq \varepsilon \right\} .$$

Delayed Path Coupling. A *coupling* [2] for a Markov chain $(\mathcal{Y}_t)_{t \in \mathbb{N}}$ is a stochastic process $(Y_t, Y_t^\star)_{t \in \mathbb{N}}$ on the space $\mathbf{S} \times \mathbf{S}$. The initial state of Y_0 is chosen according to the probability distribution of $\mathcal{Y}_0$, while the initial state of $Y_0^\star$ is chosen according to the stationary distribution μ. Each process Y_t and $Y_t^\star$ considered separately is a faithful (in terms of transition probabilities) copy of $\mathcal{Y}_t$. That is, $\mathcal{L}(Y_t) = \mathcal{L}(\mathcal{Y}_t)$ and $\mathcal{L}(Y_t^\star) = \mathcal{L}(\mathcal{Y}'_t)$, where $\mathcal{Y}'$ is the same Markov chain as $\mathcal{Y}$ except that the initial state is chosen according to distribution μ.

Lemma 1. *[9] Let δ be a positive integer and Δ be a metric function on $\mathbf{S}$ with values $\{0, 1, \ldots, D\}$. Let $(Y_{t+1}, Y_{t+1}^\star)_{t \in \mathbb{N}}$ be a coupling for $\mathbf{M}$ such that for every $t \in \mathbb{N}$ and every $(Y_{t\delta}, Y_{t\delta}^\star)$ with $\Delta(Y_{t\delta}, Y_{t\delta}^\star) = 1$, it holds*

$$\mathbf{E}[\Delta(Y_{(t+1)\delta}, Y_{(t+1)\delta}^\star)] \leq \beta$$

for some $\beta < 1$. Then,

$$\tau_{\mathbf{M}}(\varepsilon) \leq \delta \left\lceil \log(D\varepsilon^{-1}) / \log \beta^{-1} \right\rceil .$$

In particular, it follows from Delayed Path Coupling Lemma that if

$$\mathbf{E}[\Delta(Y_{(t+1)\delta}, Y_{(t+1)\delta}^\star)] \leq c$$

for some constant $c < 1$, constant δ, and $D = \mathcal{O}(n)$, then

$$\tau_{\mathbf{M}} \left(\tfrac{1}{n} \right) \leq \mathcal{O}(\log n) .$$

Hence to provide a proof of convergence rate of a Markov chain to a stationary distribution, it is enough to find an appropriate metric and build two copies of the stochastic process under consideration. Moreover, it suffices to consider both processes in the states such that the distance between them equals 1. Fact that we deal with two copies of one process (i.e. having the same transition function) does not mean that they are independent. In fact, we must construct dependence between these processes so that the expected distance between them drops below 1 in δ steps. What is more, any coupling with any metric would work! Usually the moves of the second process are adjusted to the moves of the first process, which works "freely." The relationship might be deterministic or involve some randomization.

A Toy Example. Consider random walk in $(\mathbb{Z}_2)^k$. The possible states are k-bit long bitstrings, the distance is a Hamming weight of (mod 2) difference of the bitstrings, the space diameter D is equal to k. At each step the process may perform one step in a random direction: we can think it chooses uniformly at random one of its k coordinates and sets it randomly, i.e. with probability $\frac{1}{2}$ it walks along some, randomly chosen, edge of a k-dimensional hypercube. It is obvious that regardless of the initial state, after sufficiently many steps, each state shall be almost equally probable. The only question is how many steps are required for the actual distribution to get close (no farther than ε) to the stationary distribution. To answer that, we construct a coupling in the following way: consider two processes $Y = Y_t$ and $Y^* = Y_t^*$, assume that they differ at l-th position, i.e. their distance is one. We let the first process move freely, and adjust the movement of the second process. Say that Y has chosen the mth coordinate for a potential change; let Y^* also choose the mth coordinate. If $m \neq l$ let Y^* mimic behavior of Y: if Y stays, then Y^* stays, if Y moves, then Y^* also moves. If $m = l$, let Y^* disobey with Y: if Y stays, then Y^* moves, if Y moves, then Y^* stays. It can be easily seen that, although Y^* is completely determined by Y, it is still a faithful copy of the original process, that is all transition probabilities are the same. Also note, that expected distance after one step ($\delta = 1$) is $\leq \beta = \frac{k-1}{k} < 1$; hence, all is properly set-up to use Lemma 1.

4.3   Other Important Facts

As in [4] we use the following lemma due to Noga Alon [3, Corollary 2.1]:

Lemma 2. *Let $G = (V, E)$ be a graph with $|E| \geq \binom{|V|}{2} \cdot \gamma$. Let us choose randomly and independently four vertices $a, b, c, d \in V$. Then*

$$\Pr\left(\{\{a, c\}, \{a, d\}, \{b, c\}, \{b, d\}\} \subseteq E\right) \geq \gamma^4 .$$

For each $\pi_1, \pi_2 \in \mathbb{S}_n$ we define function $\Delta(\pi_1, \pi_2)$ as a minimal number of transpositions necessary to obtain π_2 from π_1. Obviously $\Delta(\cdot, \cdot)$ is a metric and diameter of $\mathbb{S}_n$ with this metric function is equal to $n - 1$.

4.4   Construction of a Coupling

In this section we prove that with high probability the distribution of the messages observed by a passive adversary after $T = \mathcal{O}(\log(n))$ steps is very close to the uniform one.

Let $M = \{\mathcal{Y}_t\}_{t \in \mathbb{N}}$ be a Markov chain that represents a permutation of messages on the positions after t steps. We build a coupling for $\mathcal{Y}_t$, say a pair of processes (Y_t^*, Y_t). By Lemma 1, it is enough to consider the case that $\Delta(Y_t^*, Y_t) = 1$.

Let us imagine that messages are represented by balls painted with different colors. By definition of Δ, one can obtain the state of Y_t from the state of Y_t^* by transposing two balls, say a black one and a white one.

Now we consider the transitions at steps $t + 1$ and $t + 2$. We do not interfere with the first process, we only adjust the moves of the second one to the choices made by the first process. First, we move all balls except the white and black ones in the second process exactly the same way as they move in the first one. Now our attention is focused on the movement of the black and white balls. At step $t+1$ the white ball of the second process moves exactly as the black ball of the first process and the black ball of the second process moves as the white ball of the first process. Say, they go to servers S_1 and S_2. Obviously, the distance between the processes remains to be 1. The point is that the servers S_1, S_2 are chosen at random by the first process. This will give us a fair chance to succeed to *couple* the processes at step $t+2$.

Let during step $t+2$ the black and white balls of the first process go to servers S_3 and S_4, respectively. Now we need some luck – we wish that the servers S_1, S_2, S_3 and S_4 form a *crossover structure*. We have such a structure (see Fig. 3) if

- none of the servers S_1, S_2, S_3 and S_4 is corrupted by the adversary,
- the links between servers S_1, S_2 and servers S_3 and S_4 are not monitored by the adversary at this step.

In this case we may couple both processes easily without violating the view of an adversary and the marginal probabilities of both processes. Namely, for the second process the black ball goes from S_2 to S_3 and the white ball goes from from S_1 to S_4 (see Fig. 3).

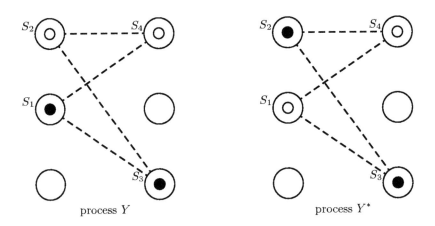

process Y process Y^*

Fig. 3. The case with a crossover structure

When the servers S_1, S_2, S_3, S_4 do not form a crossover structure (see Fig. 4) we do not attempt to couple both processes: if for the first process one ball goes from S_1 to S_3 and one from S_2 to S_4, then we make the second process do the same (but with balls of different colors). In this way a difference between both processes at servers S_1 and S_2 changes into a difference at servers S_3 and S_4, the distance between the states of Y_{t+2} and Y^*_{t+2} remains to be 1.

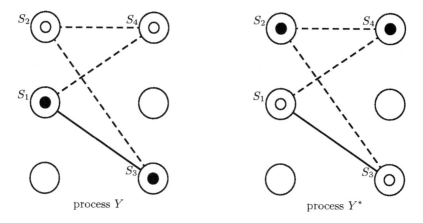

Fig. 4. The case with no crossover structure

It easy to see that the coupling definition does not violate transition probabilities of Y_t^*. Indeed, there is a symmetric event, which differs from the case described in a way that the first process sends the black and white balls, respectively, from S_1 to S_4 and from S_2 to S_3. Of course, since the balls chose their paths at random, uniformly and independently, this event has the same probability. Then the second process, according to the rules defined, sends the black and white balls, respectively, from S_2 to S_4 and from S_1 to S_3. By Lemma 2, we know that with a probability greater than ρ, for some constant $\rho > 0$, servers S_1, S_2, S_3 and S_4 form a crossover structure. So

$$E(\Delta(Y_{t+2}^*, Y_{t+2})) \leq 0 \cdot \rho + 1 \cdot (1 - \rho) = 1 - \rho$$

Hence, by Lemma 1:

$$\tau_M(\varepsilon) \leq \delta \left\lceil \log((n-1)\varepsilon^{-1}) / \log^{-1}(1 - \rho) \right\rceil .$$

So for $\varepsilon = 1/n$ we obtain $\tau_M(1/n) = \mathcal{O}(\log n)$.

4.5   Conclusions and Open Problems

Apart from the constants hidden in the big "$\mathcal{O}$" notation the case of a passive adversary and the fixed routes of messages seems to be settled in the adversary model considered.

An active adversary may easily compromise the system: for instance by duplicating the messages. Building schemes resistant to all attacks of this kind seems to be very hard at the moment. However, our proof technique seems to be well suited to analyze security of future solutions.

Acknowledgment. We thank Berthold Vöcking for bringing our attention to the adversary model introduced in [4].

References

1. Adler, M., Levine, B.N., Schields, C., Wright, M.: Defending Anonymous Communication Against Passive Logging Attacks. IEEE Symp. on Security and Privacy, 2003

2. Aldous, D.: Random Walks of Finite Groups and Rapidly Mixing Markov Chains. In: Azéma, J., Yor, M. (eds.): Séminare de Probabilités XVII 1981/82. Lecture Notes in Mathematics 986. Springer-Verlag, Berlin (1983) 243-297

3. Alon, N.: Testing Subgraphs in Large Graphs. ACM-SIAM FOCS '2001, 434-439

4. Berman, R., Fiat, A., Ta-Shma, A.: Provable Unlinkability Against Traffic Analysis. Financial Cryptography'2004

5. Bubley, B., Dyer, M.: Path Coupling: a Technique for Proving Rapid Mixing in Markov Chains. ACM-SIAM FOCS '1997, 223-231

6. Chaum, D.: Untraceable Electronic Mail, Return Addresses, and Digital Pseudonyms. CACM 24(2) (1981), 84-88

7. Chaum, D.: The Dining Cryptographers Problem: Unconditional Sender and Recipient Untraceability. Journal of Cryptology 1.1 (1988), 65-75

8. Czumaj, A., Kanarek, P., Kutyłowski, M., Loryś K.: Distributed Stochastic Processes for Generating Random Permutations. ACM-SIAM SODA'99, 271-280

9. Czumaj, A., Kutyłowski, M.: Delayed Path Coupling and Generating Random Permutations. In: Random Structures and Algorithms 17(3-4) (2000), 238-259

10. Goldschlag, D.M., Reed, M.G., Syverson, P.F.: Hiding Routing Information. Information Hiding '1996, Lecture Notes in Computer Science 1174, Springer-Verlag, 137-150

11. Rackoff, C., Simon, D. R.: Cryptographic Defense Against Traffic Analysis. ACM STOC'1993, 672-681

An Efficient Online Electronic Cash with Unlinkable Exact Payments

Toru Nakanishi*, Mitsuaki Shiota, and Yuji Sugiyama

Dept. of Communication Network Engineering, Okayama Univ., Japan
nakanisi@cne.okayama-u.ac.jp

Abstract. Though there are intensive researches on off-line electronic cash (e-cash), the current computer network infrastructure sufficiently accepts *on-line* e-cash. The on-line means that the payment protocol involves with the bank, and the off-line means no involvement. For customers' privacy, the e-cash system should satisfy unlinkability, i.e., any pair of payments is unlinkable w.r.t. the sameness of the payer. In addition, for the convenience, exact payments, i.e., the payments with arbitrary amounts, should be also able to performed. In an existing off-line system with unlinkable exact payments, the customers need massive computations. On the other hand, an existing on-line system does not satisfy the efficiency and the perfect unlinkability simultaneously. This paper proposes an on-line system, where the efficiency and the perfect unlinkability are achieved simultaneously.

1 Introduction

To solve privacy problem in electronic payments, many electronic cash (e-cash) systems have been proposed. In e-cash systems, a customer withdraws electronic *coins* from a bank, and the customer *anonymously* pays the coins to a vendor. The vendor deposits the paid coins in the bank. The important properties are the *unlinkability* and *exact payments*. The unlinkability is the strong anonymity, and it means that any other one except the trusted third party cannot determine whether two payments are made by the same customer. In linkable anonymous e-cash systems, the linked payments enable the other one to trace the payer by other means (i.e., correlating the payments' locality, date, frequency, etc.). In practice, exact payments, i.e., payments of arbitrary amounts, are desirable.

E-cash systems are classified into two types: *on-line* and *off-line*. In the on-line type, the payment protocol, where a customer pays a coin to a vendor, involves with the bank. Thus, note that the deposit protocol is unnecessary. On the other hand, in the off-line one, the customer communicates with only the vendor during the payment protocol. A lot of off-line systems have been proposed so far (e.g., [3,13,8,14]). The merits of the off-line type are that the payment communications are distributed, and that the payments are performed without a global communication channel. However, under the current state, a

---

* This work was partially supported by TAF in Japan.

K. Zhang and Y. Zheng (Eds.): ISC 2004, LNCS 3225, pp. 367–378, 2004.
© Springer-Verlag Berlin Heidelberg 2004

lot of powerful servers can deal with the burst communications, and the wireless network enables us to utilize Internet anywhere. Furthermore, the on-line e-cash system has the big advantage that over-spending is completely prevented: The bank can detect and stop over-spending during the payment protocol. On the other hand, in the off-line system, after over-spending was caused, it can be just detected. Therefore, on-line systems are sufficiently attractive.

For off-line exact payments, divisible e-cash systems have been proposed (e.g, [8]), where a customer divides a withdrawn coin into sub-coins and pays part of them. The recent system proposed in [14] satisfies the unlinkability of all the payments. However, the payment protocol needs inefficient zero-knowledge proofs of knowledge with the binary challenge. Let N be (the total coin amount)/(minimum divisible unit amount), i.e., the divisibility precision. Then, for example, in the usual case of $N = 100,000$ (i.e., the total coin amount is \$1000 and the minimum divisible unit amount is 1 cent), the payment protocol needs about 600 exponentiations. Additionally, the deposit protocol also needs massive computations including $O(N)$ exponentiations.

On the other hand, an on-line e-cash system with unlinkable exact payments using anonymous change is proposed [4]. In the system, before a payment, a customer anonymously pays coins with more than paid amount to the bank, and is returned changes, i.e., new coins with the exact paid amount in different denominations. However, this approach requires the complexity that is linear in the number of the coins. A simple way to reduce coins is to introduce many denominations. Consider that denominations for all possibly amounts are set up. Then, it weakens the unlinkability: In payment transaction T_1, a customer obtains a coin with the paid amount a and another coin with the remainder b. In the next T_2, he offers the coin with b. Though a blinding can make the latter coin and T_1 unlinkable, the amount b itself links T_1 and T_2. Thus, if transactions with b rarely occur, T_1 and T_2 are linked. Since there are a lot of denominations, such a rare amount may occur. Next, consider another case, where denominations for the amount 2^i ($0 \le i \le \lfloor \log N \rfloor$) are set up. Then, a payment needs $O(\log N)$ coins, which is about 17 in the example of $N = 100,000$. Since the payment in [4] requires about 10 multi-exponentiations per a coin, the total cost is massive. Moreover, for less denominations set up, more coins are needed. Thus, this does not achieve the efficiency and unlinkability simultaneously.

This paper proposes an on-line e-cash system with unlinkable exact payments, where both the efficiency and unlinkability are achieved. Our scheme adopts an approach similar to the previous on-line system [4] using anonymous change. A coin is a digital signature w.r.t. the bank's key. In the previous system, the public key of the signature indicates the denomination, namely the amount of the coin. This causes the link of transactions via the paid amount. In our scheme, the amount information is signed as a message. Furthermore, during the payment, the signed message is concealed by an encryption and an efficient zero-knowledge technique. Thus, linking transactions via the amount is infeasible. On the other hand, since a single coin indicates arbitrary amount, the number of the paid coin is always 1 and the complexity of a payment transaction is also $O(1)$ w.r.t. N.

2   Model and Requirements

We adopt the model of e-cash system with *trustees-based revocable anonymity* [4,13,8,14] to protect illegal acts of anonymous customers. In this model, trusted third parties, called trustees, participate in the system. The trustees cooperatively can revoke the anonymity of payments to protect the illegal acts as money laundering and so on. Though, in this paper, one trustee has the authority of the revocation for simplicity, it is easily extended into the the model of multiple trustees by using the threshold cryptosystems.

Our model consists of 6 protocols: In advance, *setup* protocol sets up the keys of the bank and trustee. By *establishment* protocol, a customer opens his account in the bank, and withdraws an initial coin. Using *withdrawal* protocol, the customer obtains a coin with the amount $a + b$, where a is the amount that he owns before this protocol and b is the amount withdrawn from his account. *Payment* protocol allows the customer who owns a coin with an amount c to pay an amount d to a vendor via the bank, where the paid amount d ($d \leq c$) is deposited in the vendor's account and the customer finally obtains a coin with the amount $c - d$. The remaining are *owner tracing* and *coin tracing* protocols below.

The requirements for on-line e-cash systems with unlinkable exact payments are as follows:

Unforgeability: Coins cannot be forged. Furthermore, anyone without a coin cannot perform withdrawals and payments.

Consistency: From the bank, a customer can obtain only consistent coins, i.e., the coins with the amount $a + b$ in the withdrawal, and with the amount $c - d$ in the payment, where a, b, c, d are the amounts introduced above.

No over-spending: An over-spender can be prevented and identified. Over-spending means that a coin is spent twice or more, and additionally that a coin is spent for the payment whose amount is more than the coin's amount.

No swindling: No one except the owner of a coin can spend the coin.

Anonymity: No one except the payer and the trustee can trace the payer from the payment.

Unlinkability: No one except the payer and the trustee can determine whether any pair of payments is executed by the same customer, unless the payments cause over-spending.

Amounts secrecy: Both the amounts of the currently spent coin and the consequently obtained coin in every withdrawal and payment are kept secret.

Anonymity revocation: Anonymity of a transcript of a payment can be revoked only by the trustee and when necessary, where the following revocation procedures should be accomplished:

Owner tracing: To identify the payer of a targeted payment.

Coin tracing: To link a customer's identity to the payments made by the customer.

Only the transcript for which a judge's order is given must be de-anonymized.

Exact payments: A customer can pay arbitrary amount up to the monetary amount of an unspent coin.

3   Preliminaries

3.1   Assumptions and Cryptographic Tools

Our system utilizes Camenisch and Lysyanskaya's signature scheme whose security is based on the strong RSA assumption. Let $n = pq$ be an RSA modulus for safe primes p, q (i.e., $p = 2p' + 1, q = 2q' + 1$, and p, q, p', q' are prime), and let $QR(n)$ be the set of quadratic residues modulo n, that is, the cyclic subgroup of $\mathbb{Z}_n^*$ generated by an element of order $p'q'$. The strong RSA assumption on $QR(n)$ means that finding $(u \in QR(n), e \in \mathbb{Z}_{>1})$ s.t. $u^e = z$ (mod n) on inputs $(n, z \in QR(n))$ is infeasible. Furthermore, note that $QR(n)$ also satisfies the DDH assumption. Including the signature scheme, we use cryptographic tools on $QR(n)$ as follows. Hereafter, we use notations: Let $[a, a+d]$ be the integer interval of all integers int such that $a \leq int \leq a+d$, for an integer a and a positive integer d. Let $[a, a+d)$ be the integer interval of all int such that $a \leq int < a+d$, and let $(a, a + d)$ be the interval for all int such that $a < int < a + d$.

Camenisch-Lysyanskaya signature scheme for blocks of messages.

Key generation: Let $\ell_n, \ell_m, \ell_s, \ell_e, \ell$ be security parameters s.t. $\ell_s \geq \ell_n + \ell_m + \ell$ and $\ell_e \geq \ell_m + 2$, where ℓ controls the statistical closeness of the distribution simulated in the security proof of the Camenisch-Lysyanskaya signature scheme to the actual distribution (in practice, $\ell \approx 160$) [6]. The secret key consists of safe primes p, q, and the public key consists of $n = pq$ of length ℓ_n and $a_1, \ldots, a_L, b, c \in_R QR_n$, where L is the number of blocks.

Signing: Given messages $m_1, \ldots, m_L \in [0, 2^{\ell_m})$, choose $s \in_R [0, 2^{\ell_s})$ and a random prime e from $(2^{\ell_e - 1}, 2^{\ell_e})$. Compute v s.t. $v = (a_1^{m_1} \cdots a_L^{m_L} b^s c)^{1/e}$. The signature is (s, e, v).

Verification: Given messages $m_1, \ldots, m_L$ and the signature (s, e, v), check $v^e = a_1^{m_1} \cdots a_L^{m_L} b^s c$ and $e \in (2^{\ell_e - 1}, 2^{\ell_e})$.

As proved in [6], this scheme is existentially unforgeable against the adaptive chosen messege attack.

Commitment scheme. A commitment scheme on $QR(n)$ is proposed by Damgård and Fujisaki [10], whose security is based on the strong RSA assumption. The following is a slightly modified version due to Camenisch and Lysyanskaya [6].

Key generation: The public key consists of a secure RSA modulus n of length ℓ_n, h from $QR(n)$, and g from the group generated by h.

Commitment: For the public key, input m of length ℓ_m, and randomness $r \in_R \mathbb{Z}_n$, the commitment C is computed as $C = g^m h^r$.

ElGamal cryptosystem. As well as [1], we adopt the ElGamal cryptosystem on $QR(n)$.

Key generation: Let ℓ_n, n, g be common to the above schemes. The secret key is $x \in \mathbb{Z}_n$ and the public key consists of n, g and $y = g^x$.

Encryption: For the public key, input $m \in QR(n)$ and randomness $r \in_R \mathbb{Z}_n$, the ciphertext (Y, G) is computed as $Y = y^r m$ and $G = g^r$.
Decryption: The ciphertext (Y, G) is decrypted by $m = Y/G^x$.

Paillier cryptosystem. We furthermore adopt Paillier cryptosystem [15] using the modulus of a composite number, but its security is based on another assumption, called the decisional composite residuosity assumption [15,11].

Key generation: Let ℓ_n be a security parameter. The secret key consists of safe primes p, q, and the public key consists of $n = pq$ of length ℓ_n, and g, where g is a random element of $\mathbb{Z}_{n^2}^*$ with the order devided by n.
Encryption: For the public key, input $m \in \mathbb{Z}_n$ and randomness $r \in_R \mathbb{Z}_n$, the ciphertext P is computed as $P = g^m r^n \bmod n^2$.
Decryption: The ciphertext P is decrypted by $m = L(P^{\Lambda(n)} \bmod n^2) / L(g^{\Lambda(n)} \bmod n^2) \bmod n$, where $L(x) = (x - 1)/n$ and $\Lambda(n) = \mathrm{lcm}(p - 1, q - 1)$.

3.2 Zero-Knowledge Proofs of Knowledge

As main building blocks, we use honest-verifier zero-knowledge proofs of knowledge, abbreviated as PKs. The proofs used in our scheme show the relations among secret representations of elements in the group $QR(n)$, as follows:

PK of representation. This proves the knowledge of a representation of $C \in QR(n)$ to the bases $g_1, g_2, \ldots, g_t \in QR(n)$, that is, $\alpha_1, \ldots, \alpha_t$ s.t. $C = g_1^{\alpha_1} \cdots g_t^{\alpha_t}$. This protocol is due to [10]. The computation cost is one multi-exponentiation for the prover and the verifier, respectively. Furthermore, PKs of two representations, where a part in one representation is equal to another part in the other representation, can be easily constructed.

PK of representation with parts in intervals. Consider an interval $[a, a + d]$ for integers a, d $(d > 0)$. This PK proves the knowledge of $\alpha_1, \ldots, \alpha_t$ s.t. $C = g_1^{\alpha_1} \cdots g_t^{\alpha_t}$ and $\alpha_i \in [a, a + d]$ for some i. For this PK, two types are known. One is due to Boudot [2], where it is assured that the knowledge exactly lies in the interval. However, this PK needs the computations of about 10 normal PKs of a representation. Another type appears in [7] for example, where the integer the prover knows in fact lies in the narrower interval than the interval the proved knowledge lies in. However, its efficiency is comparable to that of the normal PK, and this is why we use the later type. For $\alpha_i \in [a, a+d]$ in fact, this PK proves the knowledge in $[a - 2^{\tilde{\ell}}d, a + 2^{\tilde{\ell}}d]$, where $\tilde{\ell}$ is a security parameter derived from the challenge size and from the security parameter controlling the statistical zero-knowledge-ness (in practice, $\tilde{\ell} \approx 160$).

PK of representation with non-negative part. This PK proves the knowledge of a representation of $C \in QR(n)$ to the bases $g_1, \ldots, g_t \in QR(n)$, where the i-th part is a non-negative integer. Since we need to prove that the knowledge is exactly 0 and over, we adopt the PK due to Boudot [2]. The computation cost is 7 and 4 multi-exponentiations for the prover and the verifier, respectively.

Furthermore, we need a PK proving that the message in a Paillier ciphertext is equal to a message in a commitment on $QR(n)$.

PK for connection between commitment and Paillier ciphertext. Let (n, g, h) be the public key of the above commitment on $QR(n)$, and let (n', g') be that of Paillier cryptosystem. This PK proves the knowledge of m, r, r' s.t. $C = g^m h^r$ (mod n) for $m \in [0, 2^{\ell_m})$ and $r \in \mathbb{Z}_n$, and $P = g'^m r'^{n'}$ (mod n'^2) for $r' \in \mathbb{Z}_{n'}$. This PK is described in [12], and is the combination of a PK of a representation on $QR(n)$ and a PK for Paillier encryption [9,11].

We often use notations for PKs, as $PK\{(\alpha, \beta, \ldots) : R(\alpha, \beta, \ldots)\}$, which means the PK to prove the secret knowledge $\alpha, \beta, \ldots$ satisfying the relation $R(\alpha, \beta, \ldots)$.

4   Proposed System

4.1   Idea

The base of our system is the Camenisch-Lysyanskaya signature scheme. Let $Sign(m_1, m_2, m_3)$ be the signature on three messages m_1, m_2, m_3. Furthermore, this scheme equips two types of protocols. By using one type, a receiver sends commitments of m_1, m_2, m_3 to a signer and obtains $Sign(m_1, m_2, m_3)$ without revealing the messages to the signer. The other protocol allows the owner of the signature to prove the knowledge of the messages and the signature in the zero-knowledge fashion. We remark that this signature scheme is generalization of certificates in [1,5], which correspond to the version of $Sign(m_1)$.

Our system regards bank's signature $Sign(x, y, m)$ as a coin, where x, y are customer's secrets, and m is the amount of the coin. In the withdrawal, a customer with a coin $Sign(x, y, m)$ obtains a new coin $Sign(x, y', m')$ from the bank, while the difference $d = m' - m$ is charged the customer's account. In the payment, the customer with the coin $Sign(x, y', m')$ obtains a new coin $Sign(x, y'', m'')$ for the paid amount $d' = m' - m''$, while the paid amount d' is deposited in the vendor's account. During both protocols, the Camenisch-Lysyanskaya protocols allow the customer to prove the ownership of the old coin and to obtain a new coin without revealing the secrets x, y, y', y'' and the amounts m, m', m''. In addition, $d = m' - m$ and $d' = m' - m''$ are proved by PKs for the consistency, and $m'' \geq 0$ is checked by a PK to protect over-spending. On the other hand, both withdrawal and payment protocols force the customer to send $f(y)$ with the verifiability, where f is a DL (discrete log) type of one-way function. This allows the bank to detect whether the same coin is spent twice or more. Moreover, the secret x is common to all coins, and is linked to identity of the payer. This information is used for anonymity revocation.

4.2   Proposed Protocols

We describe the details of proposed protocols. Let $\mathcal{B}, \mathcal{T}, \mathcal{C}, \mathcal{V}$ denote a bank, a trustee, a customer, and a vendor, respectively.

Setup: In advance, $\mathcal{B}$ sets up the Camenisch-Lysyanskaya signature scheme and the commitment scheme, and $\mathcal{T}$ sets up the ElGamal cryptosystem and Paillier cryptosystem, as follows: Let ℓ_n be a security parameter. Then, $\mathcal{B}$ computes two $(\ell_n/2)$-bit primes $p = 2p' + 1$ and $q = 2q' + 1$, where p' and q' are primes, and then sets $n = pq$. $\mathcal{B}$ also chooses $a_1, a_2, a_3, b, c \in_R QR(n)$. Furthermore, he sets up the commitment scheme on $QR(n)$ by generating g and h. He publishes $(n, a_1, a_2, a_3, b, c, g, h)$ as the public key, and keeps the factorization of n as the secret key. On the other hand, $\mathcal{T}$ chooses a secret key $x_T \in_R \mathbb{Z}_n$ and computes the public key $y_T = g^{x_T}$ on the ElGamal cryptosystem. Additionally, for the Paillier cryptosystem, $\mathcal{T}$ computes another RSA modulus n' of length ℓ_n, and chooses $g' \in_R \mathbb{Z}_{n'^2}^*$ with the order devided by n'. $\mathcal{T}$'s public key is (y_T, n', g') and the secret key consists of x_T and the factorization of n'.

Let ℓ_x, ℓ_y, ℓ_m be the lengths of customers' secrets x, y and coin amount m, respectively, where values x, y, m are messages signed in the Camenisch-Lysyanskaya scheme. Then, for security parameters ℓ_s, ℓ_e in the scheme, we need the relationship $\ell_e \geq \max(\ell_x, \ell_y, \ell_m) + 2$ and $\ell_s \geq \ell_n + \max(\ell_x, \ell_y, \ell_m) + \ell$, where ℓ is also a security parameter for the security of the scheme, as mentioned in Section 3.1.

We need another security parameter $\tilde{\ell}$ that is for PK of intervals as shown in Section 3.2. To simplify the description, we introduce interval notations as follows: Define $\mathcal{X} = [0, 2^{\ell_x})$, $\mathcal{Y} = [0, 2^{\ell_y})$, $\mathcal{M} = [0, 2^{\ell_m})$, $\mathcal{N} = [0, 2^{\ell_n})$, $\mathcal{S} = [0, 2^{\ell_s})$, and $\mathcal{E} = (2^{\ell_e - 1}, 2^{\ell_e})$. Since the proposed protocols adopt the efficient PK of the intervals, we need to prepare the narrower intervals $\tilde{\mathcal{X}} = [2^{\ell_x - 1}, 2^{\ell_x - 1} + 2^{\ell_x - 2 - \tilde{\ell}}], \tilde{\mathcal{Y}} = [2^{\ell_y - 1}, 2^{\ell_y - 1} + 2^{\ell_y - 2 - \tilde{\ell}}], \tilde{\mathcal{M}} = [2^{\ell_m - 1}, 2^{\ell_m - 1} + 2^{\ell_m - 2 - \tilde{\ell}}], \tilde{\mathcal{N}} = [2^{\ell_n - 1}, 2^{\ell_n - 1} + 2^{\ell_n - 2 - \tilde{\ell}}], \tilde{\mathcal{E}} = [2^{\ell_e - 1} + 2^{\ell_e - 2}, 2^{\ell_e - 1} + 2^{\ell_e - 2} + 2^{\ell_e - 3 - \tilde{\ell}}]$ of $\mathcal{X}, \mathcal{Y}, \mathcal{M}, \mathcal{N}, \mathcal{E}$, respectively. If $x \in \tilde{\mathcal{X}} = [2^{\ell_x - 1}, 2^{\ell_x - 1} + 2^{\ell_x - 2 - \tilde{\ell}}]$ in fact, the knowledge proved by the PK lies in expanded $[2^{\ell_x - 1} - 2^{\ell_x - 2 - \tilde{\ell}} 2^{\tilde{\ell}}, 2^{\ell_x - 1} + 2^{\ell_x - 2 - \tilde{\ell}} 2^{\tilde{\ell}}]$, that is, $[2^{\ell_x - 1} - 2^{\ell_x - 2}, 2^{\ell_x - 1} + 2^{\ell_x - 2}]$. Thus, it is confirmed that the knowledge lies in $[0, 2^{\ell_x}) = \mathcal{X}$. This is the same in cases of $(\mathcal{Y}, \tilde{\mathcal{Y}})$, $(\mathcal{M}, \tilde{\mathcal{M}})$ and $(\mathcal{N}, \tilde{\mathcal{N}})$, and is similar to the case of $(\mathcal{E}, \tilde{\mathcal{E}})$.

A real coin amount is in $[0, MAX]$, where MAX means the maximum of available amounts. However, due to the limitation of the above PK, the information representing the amount should be chosen from $\tilde{\mathcal{M}} = [2^{\ell_m - 1}, 2^{\ell_m - 1} + 2^{\ell_m - 2 - \tilde{\ell}}]$. Thus, we introduce a 1-1 function $F(m) = m + 2^{\ell_m - 1}$. Assume that ℓ_m is selected s.t. the maximum of available amounts is less than $2^{\ell_m - 2 - \tilde{\ell}}$. Then, for all amounts m, $F(m) \in \tilde{\mathcal{M}}$.

Structure of a coin. A coin of a customer $\mathcal{C}$ is (s_i, e_i, v_i) on his secrets x, y_i and a coin amount m_i s.t.

$$v_i^{e_i} = a_1^x a_2^{y_i} a_3^{F(m_i)} b^{s_i} c, x \in \mathcal{X}, y_i \in \mathcal{Y}, F(m_i) \in \mathcal{M}, s_i \in \mathcal{S}, e_i \in \mathcal{E}.$$

Then, (s_i, e_i, v_i) is the Camenisch-Lysyanskaya signature on messages $(x, y_i, F(m_i))$. Note that $s_i \notin \mathcal{S}$ is also permitted, since $|s_i|$ has only to be larger than $\ell_n + \max(\ell_x, \ell_y, \ell_m) + \ell$. Thus, in the verification of the signature, check of $s_i \in \mathcal{S}$ is omitted.

Establishment: When a customer $\mathcal{C}$ opens his account in $\mathcal{B}$, $\mathcal{C}$ obtains an initial coin (s_0, e_0, v_0) from $\mathcal{B}$. For this, $\mathcal{C}$ performs the following protocol with $\mathcal{B}$ via an authenticated channel:

1. $\mathcal{C}$ computes $C_1 = a_1^x$ and $C_2 = a_2^{y_0} b^{r_0}$, where $x \in_R \tilde{\mathcal{X}}$, $y_0 \in_R \tilde{\mathcal{Y}}$, and $r_0 \in_R \tilde{\mathcal{N}}$, and computes a Paillier ciphertext $P = g'^x r' \bmod n'^2$, where $r' \in_R \mathbb{Z}_{n'}$. $\mathcal{C}$ sends C_1, C_2, P to $\mathcal{B}$, and proves the knowledge of the secrets by

$$PK\{(\alpha, \beta, \gamma, \delta) : C_1 = a_1^\alpha \wedge C_2 = a_2^\beta b^\gamma \wedge P = g'^\alpha \delta^{n'}$$
$$\wedge \alpha \in \mathcal{X} \wedge \beta \in \mathcal{Y} \wedge \gamma \in \mathcal{N}\}.$$

This PK shows $C_1 = a_1^x$, $C_2 = a_2^{y_0} b^{r_0}$, $P = g'^x r' \bmod n'^2$, $x \in \mathcal{X}$, $y_0 \in \mathcal{Y}$ and $r_0 \in \mathcal{N}$.

Furthermore, $\mathcal{C}$ requests an initial coin with an amount m_0.

2. For the amount m_0, $\mathcal{B}$ computes $v_0 = (C_1 C_2 a_3^{F(m_0)} b^{t_0} c)^{1/e_0}$, where $t_0 \in_R \mathcal{S}$ and e_0 is a random prime from $\tilde{\mathcal{E}}$, and sends (t_0, e_0, v_0) to $\mathcal{C}$. $\mathcal{B}$ charges $\mathcal{C}$'s account the requested amount m_0.

3. $\mathcal{C}$ obtains the initial coin (s_0, e_0, v_0) on his secrets x, y_0 and amount m_0 s.t. $v_0^{e_0} = a_1^x a_2^{y_0} a_3^{F(m_0)} b^{s_0} c$, where $s_0 = r_0 + t_0$.

Withdrawal: Assume that $\mathcal{C}$ owns an unspent coin $(s_{i-1}, e_{i-1}, v_{i-1})$ on his secrets x, y_{i-1} and an amount m_{i-1}. Then, $\mathcal{C}$ can obtain a new coin with an amount m_i via an authenticated channel with $\mathcal{B}$, as follows:

1. At first, $\mathcal{C}$ announces the withdrawn amount $\bar{m}_i$ (i.e., $\bar{m}_i = m_i - m_{i-1}$). Then, $\mathcal{C}$ computes $C_i = a_1^x a_2^{y_i} a_3^{F(m_i)} b^{r_i}$ and $D_{i-1} = g^{y_{i-1}}$, where $y_i \in_R \tilde{\mathcal{Y}}$ and $r_i \in_R \tilde{\mathcal{N}}$. Additionally, $\mathcal{C}$ computes $C_{v_{i-1}} = g^{w_i} v_{i-1}$, $C_{w_i} = g^{w_i} h^{r_{w_i}}$, where $w_i, r_{w_i} \in_R \mathbb{Z}_n$. $\mathcal{C}$ sends $(C_i, D_{i-1}, C_{v_{i-1}}, C_{w_i})$ to $\mathcal{B}$, and proves the knowledge of the old coin $(s_{i-1}, e_{i-1}, v_{i-1})$ in addition to the secrets x, y_i for an new coin, and proves the correctness of D_{i-1} and the amount relationship $m_i = m_{i-1} + \bar{m}_i$, by

$$PK\{ (\alpha, \beta, \gamma, \delta, \epsilon, \zeta, \eta, \theta, \iota, \kappa, \lambda, \mu) :$$
$$C_i = a_1^\alpha a_2^\beta a_3^\gamma b^\delta \wedge \alpha \in \mathcal{X} \wedge \beta \in \mathcal{Y} \wedge \gamma \in \mathcal{M} \wedge \delta \in \mathcal{N}$$
$$\wedge c = C_{v_{i-1}}^\epsilon / a_1^\alpha a_2^\zeta a_3^\eta b^\theta g^\iota \wedge 1 = C_{w_i}^\epsilon / g^\iota h^\kappa \wedge C_{w_i} = g^\lambda h^\mu$$
$$\wedge D_{i-1} = g^\zeta \wedge C_i / a_3^{\bar{m}} = a_1^\alpha a_2^\beta a_3^\eta b^\delta \wedge \epsilon \in \mathcal{E} \wedge \zeta \in \mathcal{Y} \wedge \eta \in \mathcal{M}\}.$$

This PK proves $v_{i-1}^{e_{i-1}} = a_1^x a_2^{y_{i-1}} a_3^{\dot{m}_{i-1}} b^{s_{i-1}} c$, $x \in \mathcal{X}$, $y_{i-1} \in \mathcal{Y}$, $\dot{m}_{i-1} \in \mathcal{M}$ and $e_{i-1} \in \mathcal{E}$ (i.e., the correctness of the own coin), in addition to $C_i = a_1^x a_2^{y_i} a_3^{\dot{m}_i} b^{r_i}$, $D_{i-1} = g^{y_{i-1}}$, $y_i \in \mathcal{Y}$, $\dot{m}_i \in \mathcal{M}$, $r_i \in \mathcal{N}$ and $\dot{m}_i = \dot{m}_{i-1} + \bar{m}_i$ (cf. Lemma 1 and 2). As shown in Theorem 1 (Consistency), $\dot{m}_i = \dot{m}_{i-1} + \bar{m}_i$ implies $m_i = m_{i-1} + \bar{m}_i$, where $\dot{m}_{i-1} = F(m_{i-1})$ and $\dot{m}_i = F(m_i)$.

2. $\mathcal{B}$ checks whether the currently sent D_{i-1} was used in all the past withdrawal and payment transcripts. If it was used, $\mathcal{B}$ stops this protocol, due to double-spending. Otherwise, $\mathcal{B}$ computes $v_i = (C_i b^{t_i} c)^{1/e_i}$, where $t_i \in_R \mathcal{S}$ and e_i is

a random prime from $\tilde{\mathcal{E}}$, and sends (t_i, e_i, v_i) to $\mathcal{C}$. $\mathcal{B}$ charges $\mathcal{C}$'s account the requested amount $\bar{m}_i$.

3. $\mathcal{C}$ obtains the new coin (s_i, e_i, v_i) on his secrets x, y_i and amount m_i such that $v_i^{e_i} = a_1^x a_2^{y_i} a_3^{F(m_i)} b^{s_i} c$, where $s_i = r_i + t_i$.

Payment: Similarly, assume that $\mathcal{C}$ owns an unspent coin $(s_{i-1}, e_{i-1}, v_{i-1})$ on his secrets x, y_{i-1} and an amount m_{i-1}. Then, $\mathcal{C}$ can spend an amount $\bar{m}_i$ to a vendor $\mathcal{V}$ and instead obtain a new coin with an amount $m_i = m_{i-1} - \bar{m}_i$ via an *anonymous* channel with $\mathcal{B}$ and $\mathcal{V}$, as follows:

1. At first, $\mathcal{C}$ announces the spent amount $\bar{m}_i$. Then, as well as Step 1 of the withdrawal protocol, $\mathcal{C}$ computes $(C_i, D_{i-1}, C_{v_{i-1}}, C_{w_i})$. Further-more, as the tracing information, $\mathcal{C}$ computes $\tilde{G}_i = \tilde{g}_i^x$ for $\tilde{g}_i \in_R QR(n)$, and $Y_i = y_T^{u_i} a_1^x$ and $G_i = g^{u_i}$ for $u_i \in_R \mathbb{Z}_n$. Then, $\mathcal{C}$ sends $(C_i, D_{i-1}, C_{v_{i-1}}, C_{w_i}, \tilde{g}_i, \tilde{G}_i, Y_i, G_i)$ to $\mathcal{B}$, and proves the knowledge of the old coin $(s_{i-1}, e_{i-1}, v_{i-1})$ in addition to the secrets x, y_i for an new coin, and proves the correctness of $D_{i-1}, \tilde{G}_i, (Y_i, G_i)$ and the amount relationship $m_i = m_{i-1} - \bar{m}_i$ and $m_i \geq 0$, by

$$PK\{ (\alpha, \beta, \gamma, \delta, \epsilon, \zeta, \eta, \theta, \iota, \kappa, \lambda, \mu, \nu, \xi) :$$
$$C_i = a_1^\alpha a_2^\beta a_3^\gamma b^\delta \wedge \alpha \in \mathcal{X} \wedge \beta \in \mathcal{Y} \wedge \gamma \in \mathcal{M} \wedge \delta \in \mathcal{N}$$
$$\wedge c = C_{v_{i-1}}^\epsilon / a_1^\alpha a_2^\zeta a_3^\eta b^\theta g^\iota \wedge 1 = C_{w_i}^\epsilon / g^\iota h^\kappa \wedge C_{w_i} = g^\lambda h^\mu$$
$$\wedge D_{i-1} = g^\zeta \wedge \tilde{G}_i = \tilde{g}_i^\alpha \wedge C_i a_3^{\bar{m}} = a_1^\alpha a_2^\beta a_3^\delta b^\delta \wedge C_i / a_3^{2^{\ell_m - 1}} = a_1^\alpha a_2^\beta a_2^\nu b^\delta$$
$$\wedge Y_i = y_T^\xi a_1^\alpha \wedge G_i = g^\xi \wedge \epsilon \in \mathcal{E} \wedge \zeta \in \mathcal{Y} \wedge \eta \in \mathcal{M} \wedge \nu \geq 0\}.$$

In addition to the statements proved by the PK of the withdrawal protocol, except $\dot{m}_i = \dot{m}_{i-1} + \bar{m}_i$, this PK proves $\dot{m}_i = \dot{m}_{i-1} - \bar{m}_i$, $\dot{m}_i \geq 2^{\ell_m - 1}$, $\tilde{G}_i = \tilde{g}_i^x$, $Y_i = y_T^{u_i} a_1^x$ and $G_i = g^{u_i}$. As well as the withdrawal, $\dot{m}_i = \dot{m}_{i-1} - \bar{m}_i$ implies $m_i = m_{i-1} - \bar{m}_i$, and $\dot{m}_i \geq 2^{\ell_m - 1}$ implies $m_i \geq 0$ (cf. Theorem 1 (consistency and no over-spending)). Note that (Y_i, G_i) is an ElGamal ciphertext on a_1^x.

2. As well as Step 2 of the withdrawal protocol, after checking the correctness of D_{i-1}, $\mathcal{B}$ computes and sends (t_i, e_i, v_i) to $\mathcal{C}$. The spent amount $\bar{m}_i$ is deposited in $\mathcal{V}$'s account. Additionally, $\mathcal{B}$ issues the certificate of this payment to $\mathcal{V}$ (e.g., by a digital signature).

3. $\mathcal{C}$ obtains the new coin (s_i, e_i, v_i) on his secrets x, y_i and amount m_i such that $v_i^{e_i} = a_1^x a_2^{y_i} a_3^{F(m_i)} b^{s_i} c$, where $s_i = r_i + t_i$.

4. After receiving the certificate, $\mathcal{V}$ permits this payment.

Owner tracing:

1. From the targeted payment transcript, $\mathcal{B}$ sends (Y_i, G_i) to $\mathcal{T}$.
2. $\mathcal{T}$ decrypts (Y_i, G_i) by $C_1 = Y_i / G_i^{x_T}$ to return C_1 to $\mathcal{B}$, and prove the correctness by $PK\{\alpha : Y_i / C_1 = G_i^\alpha \wedge y_T = g^\alpha\}$.
3. $\mathcal{B}$ can identify the owner by searching $C_1 = a_1^x$ in all the establishment transcripts.

Coin tracing:

1. From the establishment transcript of the targeted customer, $\mathcal{B}$ sends P to $\mathcal{T}$.
2. $\mathcal{T}$ decrypts P by $x = L(P^{\Lambda(n')} \bmod n'^2)/L(g'^{\Lambda(n')} \bmod n'^2) \bmod n'$ to return x to $\mathcal{B}$.
3. $\mathcal{B}$ can verify the correctness by checking $C_1 = a_1^x$ in the targeted establishment transcript. Then, for any anonymous payment transaction, $\mathcal{B}$ can check $\tilde{G}_i = \tilde{g}_i^x$ to detect the transaction of this customer.

5 Discussion

5.1 Security

To show the security, we prepare the following lemmas.

Lemma 1. *Both PKs in the withdrawal and payment protocols prove the knowledge* $(x, y_{i-1}, \dot{m}_{i-1}, s_{i-1}, e_{i-1}, v_{i-1})$ *s.t.* $v_{i-1}^{e_{i-1}} = a_1^x a_2^{y_{i-1}} a_3^{\dot{m}_{i-1}} b^{s_{i-1}} c$, $x \in \mathcal{X}$, $y_{i-1} \in \mathcal{Y}, \dot{m}_{i-1} \in \mathcal{M}$ *and* $e_{i-1} \in \mathcal{E}$, *i.e., the knowledge of the old coin* $(s_{i-1}, e_{i-1}, v_{i-1})$, *the secrets* x, y_{i-1} *and the embedded amount information* $\dot{m}_{i-1}$.

Lemma 2. *For the knowledge* $x, \dot{m}_{i-1}$ *in Lemma 1, the PK in the withdrawal also proves the knowledge of* $y_i \in \mathcal{Y}, \dot{m}_i \in \mathcal{M}, r_i \in \mathcal{N}$ *s.t.* $C_i = a_1^x a_2^{y_i} a_3^{\dot{m}_i} b^{r_i}$, *and* $\dot{m}_i = \dot{m}_{i-1} + \bar{m}_i$. *On the other hand, the PK in the payment proves the knowledge* $y_i \in \mathcal{Y}, \dot{m}_i \in \mathcal{M}, r_i \in \mathcal{N}$ *s.t.* $C_i = a_1^x a_2^{y_i} a_3^{\dot{m}_i} b^{r_i}$, $\dot{m}_i = \dot{m}_{i-1} - \bar{m}_i$ *and* $\dot{m}_i \geq 2^{\ell_m - 1}$.

In addition, note that the PKs in the establishment, withdrawal and payment prove the correctness of $C_1, C_2, P, D_{i-1}, \tilde{G}_i, Y_i, G_i$. The proof is straightforward. For the unforgeability, we prepare the following.

Lemma 3. *Under the security of the Camenisch-Lysyanskaya signature scheme, coins* (s_i, e_i, v_i) *in our system are unforgeable against any adversary that adaptively obtains valid coins from* $\mathcal{B}$.

These lemmas can be proved as [6]. Now, we discuss the properties of the proposed system.

Theorem 1. *The proposed system satisfies the requrements in Section 2.*

Proof sketch.

Unforgeability: From Lemma 3, a coin is existentially unforgeable, even if valid coins are adaptively obtained from the bank.
From Lemma 1, the PKs in the withdrawal and the payment protocol prove the knowledge of the coin and the corresponding secrets and amount. Thus, withdrawals and payments cannot be performed without a coin.

Consistency: In the withdrawal, for $\dot{m}_{i-1}$ (resp., $\dot{m}_i$) of an old coin (resp., the new coin) and withdrawn amount $\bar{m}_i$, the PK ensures $\dot{m}_i = \dot{m}_{i-1} + \bar{m}_i$, from Lemma 2. Similarly, in the payment, the PK ensures $\dot{m}_i = \dot{m}_{i-1} - \bar{m}_i$, for the paid amount $\bar{m}_i$. On the other hand, the establishment ensures that $\dot{m}_0 = F(m_0) = m_0 + 2^{\ell_m-1}$ is embedded in the initial coin, for the known initial amount m_0. Thus, for all i, $\dot{m}_i = \dot{m}_{i-1} + \bar{m}_i$ in the withdrawal and $\dot{m}_i = \dot{m}_{i-1} - \bar{m}_i$ in the payment implies $m_i = m_{i-1} + \bar{m}_i$ and $m_i = m_{i-1} - \bar{m}_i$, respectively, where $m_i = F^{-1}(\dot{m}_i) = \dot{m}_i - 2^{\ell_m-1}$. Therefore, the customer cannot obtain inconsistent coins.

No over-spending: When a coin $(s_{i-1}, e_{i-1}, v_{i-1})$ for secrets x, y_{i-1} is spent to obtain a new coin (s_i, e_i, v_i), $D_{i-1} = g^{y_{i-1}}$ is revealed with the verifiability by the PK. Since y_{i-1} is proper to the old coin $(s_{i-1}, e_{i-1}, v_{i-1})$, spending the old coin twice or more can be detected via the sameness of D_{i-1}, and the transaction is blocked. Then, the over-spender can be traced by the owner tracing.

Moreover, from Lemma 2, in the payment, the PK ensures $\dot{m}_i \geq 2^{\ell_m-1}$. Thus, for $m_i = F^{-1}(\dot{m}_i) = \dot{m}_i - 2^{\ell_m-1}$, the inequation $m_i \geq 0$ holds. Thus, the customer cannot pay the amount $\bar{m}_i > m_{i-1}$, due to $m_i = m_{i-1} - \bar{m}_i < 0$.

No swindling: When spending a coin $(s_{i-1}, e_{i-1}, v_{i-1})$ for the secrets x, y_{i-1}, the customer has to prove the knowledge y_{i-1}. However, the PK of y_{i-1} does not reveal y_{i-1}. Additionally, $D_{i-1} = g^{y_{i-1}}$ does not also reveal y_{i-1}. In the establishment, withdrawal, and payment, the coin issue process does not also reveal y_i. This is because y_i is concealed by $C_2 = a_2^{y_0} b^{r_0}$, $C_i = a_1^x a_2^{y_i} a_3^{\dot{m}_i} b^{r_i}$ and the PK. Thus, any other one including $\mathcal{B}$ cannot spend the coin.

Anonymity: In every protocol, the PK does not reveal the information. Additionally, since P and (Y_i, G_i) are ciphertexts, they also reveal no information. Since $C_2, C_i, C_{v_{i-1}}, C_{w_i}$ are commitments, they are statistical hinding. The remaning information consists of $C_1 = a_1^x$ in the establishment, $D_{i-1} = g^{y_{i-1}}$ in withdrawals and payments, and $\tilde{G}_i = \tilde{g}_i^x$ in payments. Anonymity of the payment can be compromised by linking from $C_1 = a_1^x$ to $\tilde{G}_i = \tilde{g}_i^x$. However, this link is infeasible due to the DDH assumption.

Unlinkability: As well as the anonymity, compromizing the unlinkability between payments requires linking between $\tilde{G}_i = \tilde{g}_i^x$ and $\tilde{G}_j = \tilde{g}_j^x$ $(i \neq j)$. However, this link is also infeasible due to the DDH assumption.

Amounts secrecy: Similarly, since the commitment $C_i = a_1^x a_2^{y_i} a_3^{\dot{m}_i} b^{r_i}$ and the PK have no infomation on m_i, m_{i-1}, the amounts secrecy holds.

The other properties hold clearly.   □

5.2   Efficiency

We concentrate in the withdrawal and payment that are frequently executed by customers. Note that both protocols have the complexity that is independent from the divisibility density N, since the customer spend a single coin in a transaction. Closely, the withdrawal needs 10 multi-exponentiations for the customer, and the payment needs about 20 multi-exponentiations. This is sufficiently efficient, compared with the previous payment protocol [4], which requires more

than 100 multi-exponentiations in the case of the binary denominations and
$N = 100,000$.

Finally, we discuss a bottleneck on the scalability. In the proposed system,
$\mathcal{B}$ must manage a database of D_{i-1}, whose size is in proportion to the number
of all coins of all customers. That is the number of withdrawal and payment
transactions of all customers, since each transaction uses only one coin. On the
other hand, the previous systems [4,8,14] also require this type of database,
whose size is in proportion to the number of all coins of all customers. However,
there is a difference that the previous systems need multiple coins (or devided
sub-coins) in a payment. Therefore, the database in our system is less than that
in the previous systems, which is another advantage of our system.

References

1. G. Ateniese, J. Camenisch, M. Joye, and G. Tsudik, "A practical and provably
   secure coalition-resistant group signature scheme," CRYPTO 2000, LNCS 1880,
   pp.255–270, 2000.
2. F. Boudot, "Efficient proofs that a committed number lies in an interval," EURO-
   CRYPT 2000, LNCS 1807, pp.431–444, 2000.
3. S. Brands, "Untraceable off-line cash in wallets with observers," CRYPTO '93,
   LNCS 773, pp.302–318, 1994.
4. E. Brickell, P. Gemmell, and D. Kravitz, "Trustee-based tracing extensions to
   anonymous cash and the making of anonymous change," SODA '95, pp.457–466,
   ACM, 1995.
5. J. Camenisch and A. Lysyanskaya, "An efficient system for non-transferable anonymous credentials with optional anonymity revocation," EUROCRYPT 2001, LNCS
   2045, pp.93–118, 2001.
6. J. Camenisch and A. Lysyanskaya, "A signature scheme with efficient protocols,"
   SCN '02, LNCS 2576, 2002.
7. J. Camenisch and M. Michels, "Separability and efficiency for generic group signature schemes," CRYPTO '99, LNCS 1666, pp.413–430, 1999.
8. A. Chan, Y. Frankel, and Y. Tsiounis, "Easy come - easy go divisible cash," EU-
   ROCRYPT '98, LNCS 1403, pp.561–575, 1998.
9. R. Cramer, I. Damgård, and J.B. Nielsen, "Multiparty computation from threshold
   homomorphic encryption," EUROCRYPT 2001, LNCS 2045, pp.280–299, 2001.
10. I. Damgård and E. Fujisaki, "A statistically-hiding interger commitment scheme
    based on groups with hidden order," ASIACRYPT 2002, LNCS 2501, pp.125–142,
    2002.
11. I. Damgård and M. Jurik, "A generalisation, a simplification and some applications
    of paillier's probabilistic public-key system," PKC 2001, LNCS 1992, pp.119–136,
    2001.
12. I. Damgård and M. Jurik, "Client/server tradeoffs for online elections," PKC 2002,
    LNCS 2274, pp.125–140, 2002.
13. G. Davida, Y. Frankel, Y. Tsiounis, and M. Yung, "Anonymity control in e-cash
    systems," FC '97, LNCS 1318, pp.1–16, 1997.
14. T. Nakanishi and Y. Sugiyama, "Unlinkable divisible electronic cash," ISW 2000,
    LNCS 1975, pp.121–134, 2000.
15. P. Paillier, "Public-key cryptosystems based on composite degree residuosity
    classes," EUROCRYPT '99, LNCS 1592, pp.223–238, 1999.

Modifiable Digital Content Protection in P2P*

Heejae Park and Jong Kim

Department of Computer Science and Engineering
Pohang University of Science and Technology(POSTECH)
San 31, Hyoja-dong, Pohang, Kyungbuk, South Korea
{myphj, jkim}@postech.ac.kr

Abstract. Today, the Internet and digital technologies lead to illegal reproduction and spread of digital content. Since a copy of digital content is identical with the original, it is difficult to protect the copyright of its creator. In addition, P2P applications like Napster, Gnutella, KaZaA, and so on have accelerated the illegal sharing of digital content. Moreover, a user in P2P can not only be the reader of content, but also the creator and the writer of content. But current technologies like digital watermarking and digital right management does not meet these characteristics, because of their weaknesses such as the allowance of unauthorized viewing in digital watermarking and targeting only the unmodifiable content in digital right management.

In this paper, we propose a framework for copyright protection of digital content in a P2P environment. We present a framework where anyone can create and modify a digital content and has the copyright of his contribution with maintaining the copyrights of previously participated contributors. The proposed framework is compared with previous related works such as digital watermarking, XML security, and digital right management.

1 Introduction

As the Internet becomes faster and more widespread, digital content sharing among computer users become easier and faster. The market of digital content has suffered by illegal sharing of commercial digital content. In recent years, by the introduction of peer-to-peer (P2P) applications like Napster, Gnutella, and KaZaA [1,2,3], the number of users illegally sharing content grows rapidly. Because P2P applications are based on an architecture where transmission between users is self-decided without the intervention of the server[1], the users can download any content from another peer freely. Nowadays, the more distributed prevalent P2P application, the lower profit of commercial digital content. Hence the field of digital content goes shrinking quantitatively and qualitatively largely due to illegal sharing using P2P applications.

The service architecture in the Internet is currently changing from the server-client architecture to the P2P architecture since every user is now the content

---

* This research was supported by the University IT Research Center Project of Korea.
[1] The server to help locating other peers may exist in P2P architecture.

K. Zhang and Y. Zheng (Eds.): ISC 2004, LNCS 3225, pp. 379–390, 2004.
© Springer-Verlag Berlin Heidelberg 2004

producer as well as the content consumer. The fact that *blog* [4], which is an abbreviated word of weblog, is very popular in these days shows that users want to participate to create and modify digital content. According to this fact, some users want to have their rights on the blocks created or modified by them. Therefore, the framework that can not only protect the digital content from illegal distribution but also protect modifier's copyright on the modification block in the content is needed.

The current technologies about copyright protection such as digital watermarking [5], digital right management [6,10] have been studied but they have some weaknesses like the allowance of unauthorized viewing in digital watermarking and targeting only the unmodifiable multimedia content in digital right management. The method of securing XML documents [15] focuses only the access based on the right and does not propose the fundamental solution.

Therefore in this paper, we propose a framework where anyone can create content and distribute it and any authorized users can read and modify it in a P2P environment. The proposed framework has functionalities such that the user with the right to modify that content has the copyright about his modification part, and the copyright and modification content can not be deleted or modified.

This paper is organized as follows. In Section 2, we examine previous works related to copyright protection and their weaknesses. In Section 3, we explain the requirements, design goals and system model of this work, and we propose our framework in Section 4. In Section 5, we explain the functionalities of the framework and finally conclude in Section 6.

2   Related Works

Previous works related to copyright protection include digital watermarking, XML document encryption, *PCMHoDC*, which is copyright protection scheme of modification block, and some digital right management systems.

Digital watermarking is used to determine who has the copyright of content by adding some markings to the contents [5]. And Securing document with XML enables every user to make and sign the content with a different level [15]. But these method can not stop the legal user redistributing the content itself.

PCMHoDC [16] is another study of managing the copyright and modification history of content. In the study, a user requests content to the server and if he has a right to modify and wants to modify, he sends modification information to the server. Although the copyright and modification history of content are maintained in the server and only legal users can read the content, the single point failure problem and the traffic bottleneck in the server side exist in this system because of the server–client architecture.

Digital right management (DRM) is the integrated technology that can protect content and maintain the copyright of the content creator [6,10]. This technology guarantees that the contents are not disclosed while it is stored in the client side and is transmitted. However, since content producers and content consumers are fixed, content is scarcely modified and the modification history is not managed.

Further DRM systems related to our approach are found in the lists of the US Patent [11,12,13,14]. Stefik proposed the system which manages the derivative works in DRM [11]. However, he assumes that content is located in the trustworthy repository and the system does not support multiple repositories so that it is not scalable. Johnson proposed the system which manges the content and its right centrally [12]. This system has the problem of single point of failure. Schneck proposed the DRM system which can cover the derivative work [13]. However, this system also has the problem that it cannot be applied to multiple repositories. Kahn suggests the overall, specific, and detail structure of DRM system [14]. Having the central registration server and the right management server is the problem of the system because all creators and modifiers have to contact with the central servers. Consequently, the structure of the system is not fully decentralized.

3   Preliminaries

3.1   Threats and Requirements in P2P to Modifiable Digital Content

When modifiable digital content is maintained in a P2P environment, various threats can be considered. They are disclosure of content, illegal reproduction and distribution of unprotected content, unauthorized modification, forgery, destruction of copyright information, and deletion. The main goal of our frame is to defeat the above threats in any way. The threats such as disclosure of content, illegal reproduction and distribution of unprotected content, unauthorized modification are prevented by using a framework. Also, the threats such as forgery, alteration, and destruction of copyright information are detected at the very beginning of the access in the framework. The deletion threat is handled by having replicated copies in a P2P environment.

The requirements needed in the framework to handle all the threats in an environment that a user can modify content and manage its copyright such as e-book and *blog* are as follows : (1) only a legal user can read, (2) even a legal user can not distribute content without copyright protection, (3) copyright is managed for each created or modified block, (4) modification history and its copyright of content is maintained, and (5) no server managing content is needed. Table 1 shows that all previous models do not support all requirements. So in this paper, we propose a new framework that satisfies all these requirements.

3.2   Goals

- Modifiable content can be stored in a P2P environment.
- Content can be modified by a user resided in a P2P environment, and the modifier of content has the copyright for the block he modified.
- Content can be accessed with the right to read and modify, and only the rightful user can perform a legal action.

Table 1. Characteristics of Related works

	Only a legal user can read.	A legal user can't distribute content as decrypted.	Copyright of content can be managed.	Modification history of content can be managed.	No server managing content is needed.
Watermarking	X	X	O	X	O
XML Security	O	X	X	O	O
PCMHoDC	O	O	O	O	X
D Classic	O	O	O	X	X
R Stefik's method	O	O	O	O	X
M Johnson's method	O	O	O	O	X
Kahn's method	O	O	O	O	X

3.3 System Model

Figure 1 shows the system model of the proposed framework in the view of each content. The *MMAP(Modification Manager Application Program)* is the user level special program in order to protect the illegal modification and reproduction of content. The *MMAP* has a secret key unknown to the outside, which can be implemented by various software protection methods [7,8,9] like code obfuscation, tamper–proofing, and so on. If a user wants to read or modify content, he gives his identifier and his private key to his MMAP. And when a connection between the user and the MMAP is closed, the MMAP does not use the private key of the user any longer. *Content Creator* is the user who creates content using the MMAP. Anyone in a P2P environment can create content and distribute it so that other users can view it. *Content Creator* must appoint the *Content Right Holder* unless he will not do that role. *Content Right Holder* is the user that gives the right about the content and is assigned by the *Content Creator*. Whoever wants to read or modify content must contact the *Content Right Holder* and get the right from him. So, its creator should let a trustful and high available user be its right holder. Since some peers act just like servers and others just like clients in P2P [17], the creator must assign one of server-like peers for the right holder of content. *Content Viewer* and *Content Modifier* are

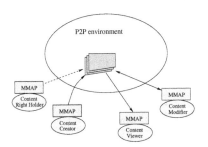

Fig. 1. System Model

Table 2. Notations

$cid(C)$	the identifier of content C
id_u	the identifier of user u
$create\_time(C,k)$	the creation time of kth block of content C
$rh(C)$	the right holder of content C
$cr(C)$	the creator of content C
sk_{MMAP}	the secret key of the MMAP
pu_u	the public key of user u
pr_u	the private key of user u
$H(a)$	the hash value of a
ES_A	the encryption with symmetric key A
EP_A	the encryption with private or public key A
$M(C,k)$	the kth modification data of content C
$sk_{bl(C,k)}$	the secret key of kth block of content C
$modi(bl(C,k))$	the modifier of the kth block of content C
$right(bl(C,k),u)$	the right of a user u about the kth block of content C
$bl(C,k)$	the kth modification block of content C
$ar(u,C,k)$	the user u's right to access the kth modification content C

consumers in this system. They can find the content he wants to read or modify by another path like Web. Next, they must contact their MMAP and sends the content information to it. If the user does not have the corresponding right, his MMAP first contacts to its right holder. The *Content Right Holder* can give the right to the user, and that user acquires the right. *Content Viewer* is the user who can read it and *Content Modifier* is the user who can modify it.

Anyone in a P2P environment has his own identifier, private key, and matching public key and can be a *Content Creator*, a *Content Right Holder*, a *Content Viewer*, and a *Content Modifier*. In this framework, it is allowed that one user acts more than one roles for the same content.

Table 2 represents the notations used in this paper.

4   Proposed Framework: Modifiable Digital Content Protection in P2P

In this section, we define content and access right structures in order to satisfy the above requirements. Next, based on these structures, we propose communication protocols when content is created, read, and modified.

4.1   Structures of Content and Access Right Table

There is a list of users that can access the content with their rights. If the list is put in the content itself, the content must be modified whenever the right of a user is added in the list. This is highly inconvenient. So we separate them so that a content and the matching users' list are managed separately. And these two structures are tightly coupled by a pre-defined content right holder.

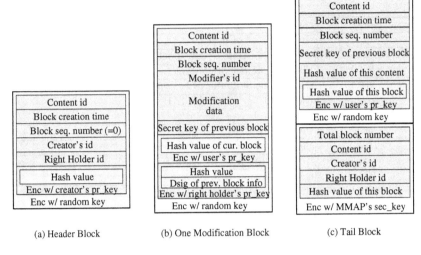

(a) Header Block   (b) One Modification Block   (c) Tail Block

Fig. 2. Structure of each block

Structure of Content. Content is composed of one header block and one tail block, and more than one modification block. A header block, which is created by the content creator, has the overall information of the content. This block can not be removed unless the content does not need protection. A modification block has the content information and is appended every time the content is modified. As content is modified frequently, the number of modification blocks increases and more space to store them is needed. A tail block is used to preserve the content integrity. The last modifier re-creates this block. Unlike a header block, this block can and must be modified when a modification process is executed. Each block is encrypted with a random secret key made by the user who creates that block. The detail block structures are shown in Figure 2.

A header block, of which sequence number is 0, is made by the content creator. This block is never modified and deleted until the content does not need any more protection. The information in this block is reflected in the first modification block. The detail structure of header block is shown in Figure 2(a).

A header block of content C, $bl(C,0)$, is

$$bl(C,0) = ES_{sk_{bl(C,0)}}\{ \; cid(C) \; || \; create\_time(C,0) \; || \; 0 \; || \; id_{cr(C)} \; || \; id_{rh(C)}$$
$$|| \; EP_{pr_{cr(C)}}\{H(cid(C)||create\_time(C,0)||0||id_{cr(C)}||id_{rh(C)})\} \; \}$$

A header block includes the content identifier, the creation time of this header block, sequence number 0, the identifier of the content creator, and the identifier of the content right holder. The hash value of all these information is encrypted with the private key of the content creator, which guarantees the integrity of this block.

A modification block contains the modification information and is created by the content modifier. This block must have the copyright evidence related to the modifier and be encrypted so that only a legal user can read. The modification information, the signature of the modifier, and the information of chaining with previous block, are included in this block. Figure 2(b) shows the detail structure of a modification block.

The kth modification block of content C, $bl(C, k)$, is

$$bl(C, k) = ES_{sk_{bl(C,k)}}\{block\_main(C, k) \mathbin{||} modifier\_sign(C, k)$$
$$\mathbin{||} rh\_verifi(C, k)\} \qquad if(k > 0)$$
$$block\_main(C, k) = cid(C) \mathbin{||} create\_time(C, k) \mathbin{||} k \mathbin{||} id_{modi(bl(C,k))}$$
$$\mathbin{||} M(C, k) \mathbin{||} sk_{bl(C,(k-1))}$$
$$modifier\_sign(C, k) = EP_{pr_{modi(bl(C,k))}}\{H(block\_main(C, k))\}$$
$$rh\_verifi(C, k) = EP_{pr_{rh(C)}}\{ H(block\_main(C, k)||modifier\_sign(C, k))$$
$$\mathbin{||} dsig\_block\_info(C, k - 1)\}$$
$$dsig\_block\_info(C, k) = EP_{pr_{modi(bl(C,k))}}\{cid(C) \mathbin{||} create\_time(C, k) \mathbin{||} k$$
$$\mathbin{||} id_{modi(bl(C,k))}\} \qquad if(k > 0)$$
$$dsig\_block\_info(C, k) = EP_{pr_{modi(bl(C,k))}}\{cid(C) \mathbin{||} create\_time(C, k) \mathbin{||} k$$
$$\mathbin{||} id_{cr(C)}\} \qquad if(k = 0)$$

As shown in the above equations, a modification block has three parts, which are the modification information, $block\_main(C, k)$, the signature of the modification information by the modifier, $modifier\_sign(C, k)$, and the signature of the content right holder, $rh\_verifi(C, k)$.

The $block\_main(C, k)$ contains the content identifier, the block creation time, the block sequence number k, the modifier identifier, the modification data, and the secret key of the previous block. Including the secret key of the previous block means that if someone decrypts one block, he can decrypt all of its previous block successively. It makes the secret key of the last block be the entire content key, which leads to the simple key management.

The $modifier\_sign(C, k)$ contains the hash value of $block\_main(C, k)$. It is used to determine whether this block is valid or not and to verify the copyright of the modifier. Whoever read this block can find this signature and recognize the modifier to make this block.

The $rh\_verifi(C, k)$ is the part on which the content right holder contributes by public key encryption. To write this part, the modifier first sends the hash value of previous information on the block, $block\_main(C, k)$ and $modifier\_sign(C, k)$, to the right holder. The right holder encrypts the hash value and $dsig\_block\_info(C, k)$, which represents the signature of the previous modifier about the previous block, with his private key and returns the encrypted data to the modifier. Then the modifier inserts the received encrypted data into the block. The purpose of this information is to chain the current block to the previous block and not to make the version tree of that content due to the management of the right holder.

After the last modifier modifies the content, he re-creates the tail block. This block also links with the previous block, the last modification block, so that someone cannot delete this block. The detail structure of the tail block is shown in Figure 2(c).

The tail block of kth modification content C, $bl(C, k+1)$, is

$$bl(C, k+1) = tail\_bl\_main(C, k) \parallel content\_info(C, k)$$
$$tail\_bl\_main(C, k) = ES_{sk_{bl(C,(k+1))}}\{tail\_bl\_info(C, k) \parallel tail\_bl\_sign(C, k)\}$$
$$tail\_bl\_info(C, k) = cid(C) \parallel create\_time(C, (k+1)) \parallel (k+1) \parallel sk_{bl(C,k)}$$
$$\parallel H(\ bl(C, 0) \parallel bl(C, 1) \parallel \dots \parallel bl(C, k)\ )$$
$$tail\_bl\_sign(C, k) = EP_{pr_{modi(C,k)}}\{\ tail\_bl\_info(C, k)\ \}$$
$$content\_info(C, k) = ES_{sk_{MMAP}}\{\ (k+1) \parallel cid(C) \parallel cr(C) \parallel rh(C)$$
$$\parallel H(\ (k+1) \parallel cid(C) \parallel cr(C) \parallel rh(C)\ )\ \}$$

A tail block is composed of two parts, which are the block information, $tail\_bl\_main(C, k)$, and the whole content information, $content\_info(C, k)$.

The $tail\_bl\_main(C, k)$ is also encrypted with a secret key and this key becomes the actual key of the entire content. The right holder knows this key and locks it so that only legal users can unlock. The $tail\_bl\_main(C, k)$ keeps the tail block information and its hash value. The tail block information is made up of the content identifier, the tail block creation time, the sequence number $k + 1$, the secret key of the previous block, the hash value of all previous blocks for an integrity check, and the signature of the last modifier. The $content\_info(C, k)$ has only the content information. Because it is encrypted with only the secret key of the MMAP, anyone can see it if he approaches with the MMAP. Removing it means removing only the tag of the content, which does not destruct the content and its integrity.

Structure of Access Right Table. An access right table contains the users' rights to access content. This is created by the content right holder and distributed in P2P as like digital content. Each record of this table is encrypted with the public key of the targeted user. Next, it is encrypted with the secret key of the MMAP, so that only the user with a right for content can access it. This table is composed of several access rights. The user u's right to access the kth modification content C, $ar(u, C, k)$, is

$$ar(u, C, k) = id_u \parallel ES_{sk_{MMAP}}\{\ E_{pu_u}\{\ sk_{bl(C,k+1)} \parallel right(bl(C, k+1), u)$$
$$\parallel E_{pr_{rh(C)}}\{H(sk_{bl(C,k+1)} \parallel right(bl(C, k+1), u))\}\ \}\ \}$$

A user identifier, id_u, which represents the targeted user, is not encrypted and can be removed, but it has no influence. Since the hash value for integrity is encrypted with the private key of the right holder, it is proved that this access right is made by him.

4.2   Communication Protocols

A user in P2P can create, read, and modify content and the right holder can give the access right of a user when the user requests it. Therefore, communication protocols are needed. We present the protocols of content creation, content reading, content modification, content deletion, and content access right production. By default, the transmitted data for these protocols is encrypted with the opposite public key so that others can not know its meaning.

Content Creation. The step of content creation is as follows. First, a user u connects his MMAP as giving his private key and creates content C and specifies to whom he wants to give the right. Also, he appoints the content right holder and receives the confirm message from the right holder. And then, the MMAP creates the header block information and the user's unique content identifier $(cid(C))$. Content can be determined by the creator's identifier and the content identifier. The MMAP also creates the random key, $sk_{bl(C,0)}$, and encrypts the header block information with $sk_{bl(C,0)}$. and sends the signature of the header block information, $dsig\_block\_info(C, 0)$, to the right holder. Content creation means the first content modification. So content creation process can be a part of content modification. At this point, *Content modification* protocol, explained later, is used. Using the protocol, the MMAP makes a modification block and the tail block and sends the secret key of the tail block, $sk_{bl(C,2)}$, and his signature of this block information, $dsig\_block\_info(C, 1)$, to the right holder. Finally, the MMAP distributes the content to peers in P2P and gives the users' list to access the content to the right holder. Then, the right holder makes the access right table and distributes it to peers in P2P, too.

Content Reading. Content reading starts as a user u connects his MMAP as giving his private key. The user finds the content C he wants to read, gets the content identifier, $cid(C)$, and the creator identifier, $cr(C)$, and requests it to the MMAP. The MMAP finds the last version of the content in P2P and gets it. The MMAP decrypts the part of the whole content information, $content\_info(C, k)$, in the tail block and checks whether the information is the same as the user wants to read. And the MMAP gets the total block number. And the MMAP can know the modification number of the content by subtracting two from the total block number. Two means the sum of the number of header block and that of the tail block. The MMAP acquires the user's access right of the content, $ar(u, C, k)$, found in P2P. It decrypts $ar(u, C, k)$ with its secret key, decrypts the result with the private key of the user and calculates the hash value of the final result. And it decrypts the written hash value with the public key of the right holder and compares these two hash values. If they differ from each other, it means that the right holder is invalid or the user does not have the right to read. Next, the MMAP can acquire the secret key of the tail block from the decrypted access right and check whether the user can read the content. Finally, the MMAP decrypts and organizes the content in reverse order and shows the result to the user.

Content Modification. When a user u wants to make the kth modification of content C, the user first creates the kth modification block and then makes the tail block, which is dependent on all previous blocks. The process to make a modification block is as follows. A user u connects his MMAP as giving his private key. Applying the above *Content reading* protocol enables the user to read content with a right to read. And then, he modifies the content and gives modification data, $M(C, k)$, to the MMAP, which determines whether the user has a right to modify the content based on the access right table. The MMAP generates the modification information, $block\_main(C, k)$, which is composed of the content identifier, the block creation time, the block sequence number, the modifier identifier, the $M(C, k)$, and the secret key of the previous block, and creates the user's signature, $modifier\_sign(C, k)$, on $block\_main(C, k)$. At the same time, it sends the hash value of $block\_main(C, k)$ and $modifier\_sign(C, k)$ and the signature of this block, $dsig\_block\_info(C, k)$, which will be used in the next modification of the content, to the right holder. The content right holder encrypts the received hash value and the signature of the previous modification, $dsig\_block\_info(C, k-1)$, with his private key, which is $rh\_verifi(C, k)$. Also, he returns $rh\_verifi(C, k)$ to the original sender. The MMAP creates the random secret key, $sk_{bl(C,k)}$, and encrypts this block with it.

After creating the modification block, the tail block of the content must be generated. Its process is as follows.

The MMAP makes the tail block information, $tail\_bl\_main(C, k)$, which includes the content identifier, the block creation time, the sequence number, the key of the previous block, the hash value of the whole content except the tail block, and the signature of this block. In this process, the MMAP generates a random secret key, $sk_{bl(C,k+1)}$, and uses it as an encryption key. Next, it sends $sk_{bl(C,k+1)}$, which becomes the actual content key, to the right holder. The right holder creates the access right table based on the new secret key, $sk_{bl(C,k+1)}$, and distributes it into P2P. The MMAP encrypts the changed content information with its secret key, sk_{MMAP}, and appends it to the tail block.

That a user has modified the content does not mean he becomes the right holder of the content. He has only the copyright of his modification block. Therefore, modification does not give him the right to endow other users.

Content Deletion. Strictly speaking, content deletion can not be done. If someone wants to delete all the same content, he have to search it in all nodes of the P2P. It is impossible to do it. However, we can think content deletion is realized if the content right does not make a new right to access it any longer. Although it can be read or modified by the users who have already had the right to access it, no more modification occurs and its use will go down and it will disappear automatically.

Content Access Right Production. When a user requests a right to read or modify content to its right holder with sending his identifier and public key, the right holder decides if it is okay that he assigns the right to the user. If so, he creates the access right for the user, appends it into the access right table, and notifies the user of the access right creation. Simultaneously, he distributes the modified access right table to peers in the P2P, which enables the users who have already had the right to access content to do it without the right holder.

5   Functionalities

In this section, we will show the functionalities of proposed framework. Further details can be found in [18].

- The user without the right to read the content can not do so.
  A user can read all blocks if he decrypts the tail block. Because the key is encrypted with the secret key of the MMAP and the public key of the user who has a right to access, a user without any right to access the content can not acquire the key of the tail block in any path.
- Even a legal user can not distribute content without copyright protection.
  Since the MMAP has a secret key unknown to the outside, the content is always stored in an encrypted form by the aid of the MMAP. When a user requests content, the MMAP obtains the content and shows to the user as decrypted. The user cannot know the secret key of the content and it is impossible to distribute content as decrypted.
- The copyright is managed for each created or modified block.
  Because copyright information, $modifier\_sign(C, k)$, and data in the modification block are encrypted with the secret key, it is impossible to remove or alter only the copyright information. If someone does it, checking the hash value of the block tells the illegal modification of the block.
- It can detect if a modification block is removed or altered.
  Illegal modification means that a user accesses the content in another path without using the MMAP. We can expect the following cases.
  1. The case that nth modification block is deleted illegally.
  2. The case that the tail block is deleted illegally.
  3. The case that nth modification block is deleted and at the same time, the information of the tail block is altered illegally.
  4. The case that nth modification block is removed and replaced with a illegal modification block.
  5. The case that nth modification block is deleted and next, a new modification block is inserted and the tail block is modified.
  The first case can be easily detected with $content\_info(C, n)$ in the tail block. And the second case can be detected by checking if the tail block exists in the content before the MMAP reads or modifies content. The third and fourth cases can be also detected with checking the hash value of content. The final case can be detected by using the signature of the previous block, which included in the current block as encrypted form.
- This framework works well without the server managing content.
  When content is created or modified, all operations are done in a user side except the encryption process by the content right holder for linking with the previous block. Therefore, no special server managing content is needed.

6   Conclusion

In this paper, we proposed an integrated framework that can store the modifiable digital content in P2P. The proposed framework satisfies the several requirements which was not met in previous related works. These are that (1) only a legal user can read, (2) even a legal user can not distribute content without copyright protection, (3) copyright is managed for each created or modified block, (4) modification history and its copyright of content is maintained, and (5) no server managing content is needed so as not to have the single point failure and not to concentrate the load on the server.

References

1. http://www.napster.com
2. http://www.gnutella.com
3. http://www.kazaa.com
4. Lindahl, C., Blount, E., "Weblogs: simplifying web publishing," *IEEE Computer*, Volume: 36 , Issue: 11 , Nov. 2003 Pages:114 - 116
5. C.I. Podilchuk and E.J. Delp, "Digital watermarking: Algorithms and applications," *IEEE Signal Processing Magazine*, vol. 18, no. 4, pp. 33-46, July 2001.
6. http://www.microsoft.com/windows/windowsmedia/drm.asp
7. Christian Collberg and Clark Thomborson. "Watermarking, tamper-proofing, and obfuscation - tools for software protection." Technical Report TR00-03, The Department of Computer Science, University of Arizona, Feb 2000.
8. Chenxi Wnag, Jonathan Hill, John Knight, Jack Davidson, "Protection of Software-based Survivability Mechanisms," *International Conference of Dependable Systems and Networks*, Sweden, July 2001.
9. T. Sander and C. F. Tschudin, "On software protection via function hiding," *Lecture Notes in Computer Science*, 1525:111-123, 1998.
10. F. Hartung and F. Ramme, "Digital Rights Management and Watermarking of Multimedia Contents for M-Commerce Applications," *IEEE Communications Magazine*, vol. 38, no. 11, pp. 78-84, Nov. 2000, Invited paper.
11. Stefik, Merkle, and Pirolli, *US Patent 5634012*, 1997.
12. Johnson et al., *US Patent 5991876*, 1999.
13. Schneck et al., *US Patent 5933498*, 1999.
14. Kahn Robert E. et al, *US Patent 20030115143*, 2003.
15. E. Damiani, S. Vimercati, S. Paraboschi, and P. Samarati, "Securing xml document," *In Proceedings of the 2000 International Conference on Extending Database Technology(EDBT2000)*, pp 121–135, Konstan, Germany, March, 2000.
16. H. Park and J. Kim, "PCMHoDC: A Scheme to Protect Copyright and Modification History of Digital Contents," *18th IFIP International Information Security Conference*, 26-28 May 2003, Athens, Greece
17. S. Saroiu, P. Gummadi, and S. Gribble, "A measurement study of peer-to-peer file sharing systems," *In Proc. of the Multimedia Computing and Networking*, January 2002.
18. H. Park and J. Kim, "Modifiable Content Protection Scheme in P2P and Its Functionalities," *Technical report HPC-04-01, Dept. of CSE, POSTECH*, April 2004.

Survey on the Technological Aspects of Digital Rights Management

William Ku and Chi-Hung Chi

School of Computing, National University of Singapore
3 Science Drive 2, Singapore 117543, Republic of Singapore
{kucheech, chich}@comp.nus.edu.sg

Abstract. Digitalization of content is both a blessing and a curse. While it allows for efficient transmission and consumption, the ease of copying and sharing digital content has resulted in rampant piracy. Digital Rights Management (DRM) has emerged as a multidisciplinary measure to protect the copyright of content owners and to facilitate the consumption of digital content. In this paper, we survey the technological aspects of DRM. We present a discussion of DRM definitions, formulate a general DRM model and specify its various DRM components. We also evaluated emerging trends such as the use of P2P in DRM and DRM for personal access control, some noteworthy issues such as content reuse and granularity, as well as citing some future directions such as frequent content key upgrades.

1 Introduction

The Internet has emerged as a vibrant information and digital entertainment hub. Other than being a hyper distribution channel for its easy and efficient dissemination of content, it also facilitates the synergy of digital technologies to provide a richer user experience. However, it has some drawbacks. The ease of copying and sharing of digital content such as music, without any deterioration in quality, has resulted in rampant piracy. Consequently, the content owners stepped in to tap on the unlimited potential of the Internet as well as to curb this piracy with technological and legal measures. One of such measures is Digital Rights Management (DRM).

DRM is basically an aggregation of security technologies to protect the interests of the content owners so that they may maintain *persistent* ownership and control of their content. A DRM system essentially specifies, manages and enforces "rules" in all aspects of the digital content, in particularly in its usage and distribution. The nature of these restrictions is such that existing DRM systems are typically closed proprietary systems. Digital content is packaged in proprietary data formats ("containment[1]") or/and marked and only accessible by proprietary trusted hardware/software, resulting in exclusion of certain users and non-interoperability between different DRM systems. In addition, the restrictions may hamper legitimate uses such as accessing the digital content on multiple devices or doing a backup.

---

[1] We would focus on the "containment" approach.

K. Zhang and Y. Zheng (Eds.): ISC 2004, LNCS 3225, pp. 391–403, 2004.
© Springer-Verlag Berlin Heidelberg 2004

DRM systems do also present certain user issues such as privacy and the notion of fair use. Users may not be able to consume the digital content anonymously. In addition, DRM systems could be easily used to profile users' consumption behaviour.

Content reuse may be promoted in DRM but does the present infrastructure support it and if so, to what extent? How could the same content and DRM technologies cater to heterogeneous devices with varying computing capabilities. We hope to find out how DRM addresses these issues from a technological point of view.

2   Definition and Overview

In this section, we would first look at some definitions of DRM followed by an overview of a DRM system.

2.1   Definition

There is an apparent lack of a standard definition of DRM in current literature. Some definitions are:

- DRM refers to *controlling* and *managing* rights to digital intellectual property [27].
- DRM is the description, identification, trading, protection, monitoring and tracking of all forms of rights usages over both tangible and intangible assets including management of rights holders relationships [12].
- DRM must be about the "digital management of rights" not the "management of digital rights" [9,12].

The definition of DRM can be further classified into two categories namely *management* and *enforcement* [13,28]. Management has to do with the managing of digital rights. The rights holders have to be able to identify their content, provide the meta-data of the content (so that users can trace originality), specify the terms and conditions of usage and distribution of the content and etc. Enforcement is about the digital managing of the rights which is to ensure that the content is only used as stipulated in the terms and conditions associated with its usage.

2.2   Overview

Here, we present an overview of a typical DRM system. There are essentially three parties in the setup illustrated in Figure 1, namely the *Content Owner*, the *License Broker* and the *User*. The Content Owner usually owns all rights to the content. It may refer to a music label or a solo digital artiste. The License Broker handles all transactions, on behalf of the Content Owner, pertaining to the issue of a License that would specify exactly the permissions granted to an User on the use of the content, subject to certain terms and conditions. The User[2] here refers to a trusted hard-

---

[2]   We would also refer it as the End-User Player (or Viewer) in this paper.

ware/software that is a proxy to the user (consumer). It is trusted in the sense that it would not allow the user unauthorized access to the content. It would also enforce the terms and conditions of the usage of the content. We outline the process of this DRM system:

1. The Content Owner would input the Content to the DRM system for Content Protection. In some cases, the Content Owner may be required to encode the Content in some proprietary data format. Here, the Content Owner may want to insert a digital watermark into the Content for purposes of identification. The DRM system would then encrypt and packaged for distribution. The Content Owner would need to specify, using a Rights Expression Language (REL), all applicable usage rights or rules that apply to this content.
2. The DRM system would return a Protected Content and a License (or one set of Licenses). The License contains a key that is needed to decrypt the Protected Content and must be used as a whole to access the content.
3. The Content Owner disseminates the Protected Content through various distribution channels including but not limited to the Internet, physical mediums such as CDROM/DVD, Email, Instant Messaging and P2P file-sharing. Distribution through the latter three media forms the notion of Superdistribution [17].
4. The Content Owner sends the License(s) to the License Broker. The License Broker is a trusted clearinghouse which would handle all requests for content access.
5. The User retrieves the Protected Content from a distribution channel. It examines its meta-data to identify the required License in order to access the content and the (location of) License Broker(s) that could provide the License.
6. If the user (consumer) does not the have the required (or a valid) License, the User would contact a License Broker to request for a License and making the requisite payment.
7. After the user has made payment, the License Broker would issue a License to the User. Depending on what the user (consumer) has paid for, the User would allow the user to access the content in a controlled manner.
8. The License Broker would remit to the Content Owner the proceeds from the transaction.

3   Components of DRM Systems

In Figure 1, we have a Content Protection "black box" that could be deciphered as shown in Figure 2 which also illustrate the main components of existing DRM systems:

1. The content is tagged with an unique identifier (identification) together with descriptive meta-data (meta-data).
2. A digital *watermark* is inserted into the content to serve as a proof of ownership identity in the event of a dispute.
3. A digital *fingerprint* is generated from the content. In addition to its forensic application for authentication (like watermarking), it has uses such as automatic content identification. This fingerprint is then stored in a database.

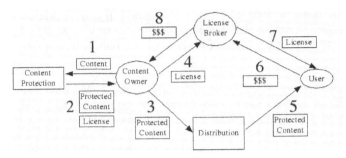

Fig. 1. Overview of a typical DRM system

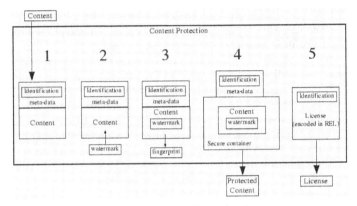

Fig. 2. The Content Protection Process

4. The content is enclosed by a *Secure Container* which would effectively prevent unauthorized access.
5. A License stating the rights and conditions of content usage is encoded in a Rights Expression Language (REL).

3.1   Content Identification and Meta-data

Before the rights of a content can be fully asserted, it has to be unambiguously identified so that users who want to access the content can purchase the usage rights of this content. The meta-data of the content may provide some non-sensitive information and may describe how to make use of the content identifier.

Content Identification. Other than being unambiguous, the content identifier has to be *persistent*. That is to say, even if the ownership of the content changes, the content identifier would remain the same. Existing uses of standard numbering schemes in DRM include ISBN, ISSN, ISAN and DOI [8].

Meta-data. Meta-data complements the use of the content identifier. The content identifier is likely to be an alphanumeric string which on its own, would not make any sense. The meta-data can provide more information on how to access the content. An example of a well-formed meta-data scheme is the <indecs> framework [14].

3.2   User Identification/Authentication

User identification/authentication is important in DRM as we would want only authorized users to be able to access the content. This is not an issue for certain closed systems such as mobile phone networks whereby the identity of the user is closely tied to his device but rather for semi-open networks such as the Internet. The significance here is that the difficulty in user identification resulted in most DRM systems for semi-open networks having to bind content to a specific device instead of to user.

User identification/authentication can be generally delegated to the License Brokers which could then use mature e-commerce technologies such as SSL to overcome user identification/authentication concerns.

Nevertheless, there are some work on user identification and authentication issues in the DRM context. [16,24] outline some sample applications where biometric technologies can successfully be applied to DRM applications. [7] presents a framework to hide the identity of an user by concealing the user's public key with a hash function.

3.3   Digital Watermarking

Watermarking is a technology that can be used for copy control, content identification and tracing. Most watermarking techniques use a spread spectrum approach which is essentially the insertion of a pseudo-noise signal with a small amplitude into the content (directly onto the content itself or onto its frequency domain). This watermark can be detected using correlation methods and often used in conjunction with a secret key so that the watermark can only be detected and removed by authorized parties.

In DRM, content is typically vulnerable to attacks at the end-user system. The content could be captured during its rendering (audio and video grabbing) or have its protection mechanism (its Secure Container) removed by direct attacks. Watermarking can be used to detect illegal copies of content that have been unprotected by such attacks. The basic requirements [11] of a watermark are:

- imperceptibility: the watermark must not affect the perceived quality of the content
- security: the watermark should only be accessible by authorized parties
- robustness: the watermark must be persistent and resilient to attacks

In the DRM context, the watermark must be able to survive indirect attacks such as audio and video grabbing. This requirement is not applicable in direct attacks since only the associated protection mechanism (the Secure Container) is removed but not the watermark. Nevertheless, the unprotected content at this junction could be subject to attacks to remove the watermark in it.

[3] provides an overview of data hiding in DRM. Firstly, in dealing with the proof of ownership, a watermark can be used to serve as a proof of ownership but is vulnerable to attacks such as average and collusion attacks. [33] highlights some possible collusion attacks and solutions. In addition to ensuring that a watermark cannot be removed, the DRM system has to ensure that a fake watermark cannot be inserted. [3] further discusses on how watermarking features in tracing and copy control mechanisms.

[1] introduces a formal framework that enables the rigorous assessment of the security of watermarks against protocol attacks. In addition, it shows how watermarking schemes can be secured against some protocol attacks by using a cryptographic signature of a trusted third party.

3.4   Content-Based Identification (Fingerprinting)

Content-based identification (Fingerprinting) refers to the characterization of the content based on its representation (signals or features) and matching it to an entry in a database. The term fingerprinting has been used interchangeably with watermarking in current literature and presents some confusion. We would differentiate these two terms here as tabulated in Table 1.

Table 1. Fundamental differences between watermarking and fingerprinting

Watermarking	*Fingerprinting*
Embeds a signal into content, altering the content.	Does not embed a signal into content and hence does not alter content.
Not a function of the content.	A function of the content.
Usually invisible for non-intrusion and to avoid detection by adversaries.	No such requirement. Non-intrusive.
Requires prior access to content.	Does not require prior access (other than for database entry). May be used for "legacy content".
Can watermark individual copies.	Does not have this capability.
Have to reprocess all copies in event of new technology.	No such requirement.
No additional treatment for new content.	Have to store fingerprints of new content in database.

Typically, fingerprinting has two processes. The first is the training phase whereby characteristic features of the content are extracted and compacted for entry into a database. The second process is the recognition phase which is essentially a pattern recognition process to match the fingerprint of a given content to an entry in the database. Some essential requirements of fingerprinting techniques are robustness and compactness. Robust fingerprinting techniques would be able to associate content derivations or deviations with the original content. By being compact, fingerprinting will allow for fast fingerprint extraction, search and matching.

Watermarking and fingerprinting are meant to complement one another. Fingerprinting may prove to be of assistance when attacks against watermarking succeeded (for example in audio and video grabbing) and the watermarks are removed. Robust fingerprinting techniques would still be able to identify the content so long as the characteristics features of the content remain. This is useful considering that illegal content are usually lossy copies of the original content.

Some applications of fingerprinting are broadcast monitoring and filtering. Broadcast monitoring refers to the automatic playlist generation of content in the various distribution channels for auditing purposes such as royalty collection. Filtering here refers to the identification of certain content for certain purposes. For example, Napster introduces a fingerprinting system to filter and remove copyrighted content in accordance with a court order.

Fingerprinting also has non-forensic uses. A popular use case in current literature is that of an user in a pub who likes the music being played, activates a personal device (possibly a mobile phone) to identify the music and to buy a copy of it. When the user goes back home, he would find the song downloaded (and billed for) into his digital music player.

Images. [18] presents a hash algorithm based on the observation that main geometric features in an image would remain approximately invariant under slight lossy changes.

Audio. Audio fingerprinting techniques fall into two main categories [31]. The first category refers to techniques that make use of the descriptive attributes of the content such as loudness, tempo, pitch etc while the second category includes approaches that are based on more intrinsic attributes of a recording with no explicitly identifiable descriptive qualities. An example technique of the first category is based on MPEG-7 [2]. Here, the *spectral flatness* (SFM) (related to the presence of tonal components within specified octave sub-bands) of the audio signal is used as a fingerprint. One example of an audio fingerprinting technique belonging to the second category is the MusicDNA system [30]. It essentially involves computing features from the time-frequency spectra of a recording. Further discussion of audio fingerprinting can be found in [4,5].

Text. Text fingerprinting have its roots in Natural Language Processing which has mature techniques for text and document feature characterization and classification. An example of text fingerprinting can be found in [30] which presents a way of fingerprinting text documents that can be used to identify content and expression similarities in documents, using surface, syntactic, and semantic features of documents. It claimed an accuracy of 90% and 67% for translated copies.

3.5   Secure Containers

Secure Containers are usually implemented in the use of cryptographic algorithms such as DES or AES. However, a combination of such algorithms (by way of obfuscation) may be used instead to provide further obscurity as shown in Microsoft audio DRM [29]. Coupled with the use of digital signatures and certificates, Secure Containers provides content confidentiality and integrity. The content integrity can be further enhanced by mechanisms generic to the content such as LAIR [9].

3.6   Rights Expression Languages

Rights Expression Languages (RELs) are used to articulate the usage rules of a content. These usage rules form the basis of the contract between the user and content owner pertaining to the use of the content. The usage of RELs can be mainly found in the meta-data of the content and its associated content. Thus, RELs have to be machine-readable (for interoperability) and extensible (in order to cater to all possible scenarios). Naturally, XML is the choice of language of existing RELs.

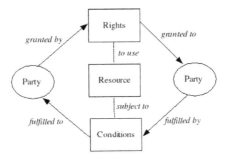

Fig. 3. Building blocks of the rights language concept in a REL

A REL has two distinct components: the *rights language concept* (syntax) and the *rights data dictionary* (semantics). The rights language concept refers to the grammar rules while the rights data dictionary refers to the ontology that provides meanings to the terms used in the grammar rules. Generally, the basic building blocks in the rights language concept of most RELs are enumerated as follows:

- Rights: the permissions allowed in the usage of the *resource*. This includes the *restrictions* of usage such as limited times of usage etc.
- Conditions: the prerequisites that need to be fulfilled before the *rights* can be exercised
- Resource: the content in question, which is to be unambiguously identifiable.
- Parties: the principals involved.

These basic building blocks and their relationships are illustrated in Figure 3.

Two widely accepted RELs are XrML [34] and ODRL [22]. XrML is being used by MPEG-21 [19], the OASIS Rights Language Technical Committee [21] and the Open eBook Forum [23] while ODRL is employed by the Open Mobile Alliance [25] as the standard REL for all mobile content.

License. A License can be generally encoded in a REL and contains the following elements:

- Content Identifier
- Optional user information
- Rights and restrictions: The exact terms and conditions of usage.
- Stateful information: To monitor the use of the content, possibly for the purpose of restrictions (for example limited number of access).
- Content key(s): To be kept secret.
- Authentication information: To provide for the decryption of the content key(s) and the binding of the License to the End-User Player. This may also allow the License to be modified by authorized parties. The integrity of the License is also based on this.

The License has to specify the rights accorded to the user, which have to be expressed in a REL. The License is to be bound to a device so that the License is not directly transferable across devices. Thus, individualization of the End-User Players is required so that Licenses can be constructed uniquely to the End-User Players.

The End-User Player

The End-User Player[3] (EUP) is a trusted unit in the DRM system (illustrated as the User in Figure 1) that enforces the rights of the content. With reference to Figure 3, the End-User Player assists the user to procure the *rights* to access the contents by getting the user to fulfill the required *conditions*. It also make sure that any *restrictions* to the *rights* are adhered to. It can be a hardware (for example Apple's iPod) or software (Microsoft Media Player). The key technical requirements for the EUP are:

- Closed specifications: It is proprietary by extension as the content data format is usually proprietary.
- Individualization: This would bound the EUP to the device and allow for ease of user identification/authentication as well as provides for Licenses to be uniquely bound to the EUP.
- Tamper-resistant: It should be difficult to reverse engineer and be able to resist manipulations.
- Security upgradeable: It should be easily upgraded for security fixes or new security mechanisms.
- Able to detect illegal content: The EUP should be able to detect illegal copies and refuse to render these illegal content.
- Separation of compliant and non-compliant EUPs: Non-compliant EUPs should not be able to render legal content.

We observed that there is little attention paid to the EUP in current literature, despite its relative importance in the DRM system.

4   Trends, Noteworthy Issues, and Future Directions

In this section, we look at some emerging trends in DRM, some noteworthy issues and cite some possible directions in future DRM research.

4.1   Mobile DRM

Mobile devices will form an integral backend for content consumption. There are several issues whereby DRM would have to address. Firstly, there is a wide spectrum of heterogeneous mobile devices that need to be able to interoperate with one another and with other devices such as the PC. Standardization of DRM would help here. Secondly, these mobile devices usually have limited and varying computing capabilities, content granularity (please see Section 4.5) becomes an issue. The DRM containment mechanism (Secure Container) essentially is a one-size-fit-all approach. Thus, what may be rendered in one device may not be similarly rendered in another device.

---

[3] It is also referred as the device in this paper.

However, mobile devices form a more tightly knitted network than the PCs/Internet. User identification/authentication is almost a non-issue as the mobile device (especially mobile phone) is usually bound to the user. They follow proprietary hardware specifications, making them more tamper-resistant than PCs. Their heterogeneous nature also means that attacks on one platform may not necessarily work on another platform. As such, DRM should be more easily enforced with mobile devices. There are already existing DRM implementations for mobile devices with more to come with the advent of the OMA and market forces.

4.2   DRM Integration with P2P

P2P provides DRM an excellent content delivery platform. There are some pioneer implementations that pave the way for this new paradigm. [26] presents the details of a P2P protocol based on broadcast encryption that supports and enforces renewable content protection for home networks and providing for a careful balance between the needs of content owners and consumers' expectations. [32] presents a similar P2P architecture of set-top boxes. The Potato system [20] is a DRM-enabled P2P system that provides incentives for users to redistribute content.

Integrating DRM into P2P systems is not a trivial exercise. [15] presents a study of some of the issues involved in such a setup. There is certainly much more work left in this aspect. Most probably, a DRM hybrid of P2P networks, the Internet and mobile networks would evolve.

4.3   DRM for Everyone

Existing DRM systems are set up for the benefits of large music labels, Hollywood movie studios and Fortune 500 content providers. There is no provision for the amateur artiste or any individual to make use of DRM to distribute their content.

DRM can be a great way to impose access control over personal content. For example, one may want to share his vacation photos and video among his friends. DRM can actually provide this functionality easily. Taking for instance a DRM-enabled P2P network, the user uploads his content and specifies some usage rules. He may specify that only his intimate friends may access certain photos and the video while others may view the rest. He passes the content to some friends who relay it to his other friends or even some strangers. Those who try to view the content would request for the license automatically. In this way, access control over personal content is achieved.

4.4   Content Reuse and Granularity

We look at the impact of DRM on content reuse and granularity. Content reuse refers the use of caches to minimize retrieval latency of the content while content granularity refers to the availability of the content in multiple resolutions.

Content reuse. Multimedia content accounts for only 20% of web content [6] although this percentage is expected to increase. Content owners often restrict distribution as they do not have access control over the content once it becomes available in the Internet. DRM offers a new dimension in content delivery both in the Internet and P2P in the notion of Superdistribution. With the assurance from DRM, content owners would release more content into the Internet and P2P, content reuse through the use of caches will have to be re-examined. These content would be large in size and caching large objects is expensive. How then are DRM and the web caches going to accommodate one another?

Content granularity. Granted that there is pervasive use of DRM, content granularity would play a significant role. It would not be practical to expect the Secure Container, a one-size-fits-all approach, to be able to cater to the wide spectrum of heterogeneous devices. For example, a handheld device with limited capabilities would not be able to render a large multimedia content. How can the device take it from there and locate a scaled-down version. Existing DRM systems do not address this. Conversely, a content received from a handheld device may not fully make use of the capabilities of a PC. One possibility is the use of the Content Identifier to locate other versions of the content..

The data format of the content would also play an important role as well. It has to be able to support multiple resolutions. It would not be practical to distribute a content of the highest quality so as to provide multiple granularity as the large file size of the content would impede its distribution (and availability to small devices).

4.5   Frequent Content Key Upgrades

DRM systems need frequent security upgrades. This could be easily done so for the various components so long as there is Internet access except for the Secure Container component. The Secure Container has a fixed content key. The distribution nature of the content makes it difficult to change its content key. Certainly, the same content could be protected with different keys but this not only complicate the retrieval of the correct content key, it does not solve the problem of the content having the same key for an indefinite period of time, providing fodder for a brute-force attack.

The paradigm of *forward security* can be applied here to alleviate the above issue. In a *forward-secure* scheme, secret keys are updated at regular periods of time. These keys are supposedly independent of one another such that knowledge of one key does not divulge the other keys. In the DRM context, the content key can be updated at certain time intervals, probably at point of access.

5   Conclusion

We hope we have presented a comprehensive survey of the technological aspects of DRM. We had looked at some definitions and examined a generic DRM model and dissect them into various components, each of which was individually discussed. We concluded by evaluating emerging trends, noteworthy issues and future directions.

References

1. ADELSBACH, A., KATZENBEISSER, S. and VEITH, H. 2003. Watermarking schemes provably secure against copy and ambiguity attacks, Proceedings of the 2003 ACM workshop on Digital rights management, 2003, pp. 111-119.
2. ALLAMANCHE, E., HERRE, J., HELMUTH, O., FRBA, B., KASTEN, T. and CREMER, M. 2001. Content-Based Identification of Audio Material Using MPEG-7 Low Level Description, Proceedings of the International Symposium of Music Information Retrieval, 2001.
3. BARNI, M. and BARTOLINI, F. 2004. Data hiding for fighting piracy, Signal Processing Magazine, IEEE, Volume 21, Issue 2, March 2004, , pp. 28- 39.
4. CANO, P., BATLLE, E., GMEZ, E., GOMES, L. DE C. T. and BONNET M. 2002. Audio fingerprinting: concepts and applications, Proceedings of 1st International Conference on Fuzzy Systems and Knowledge Discovery, Singapore, November 2002.
5. CANO, P., BATLLE, E., KALKER, T. and HAITSMA, J. 2002. A review of algorithms for audio fingerprinting, Proceedings of International Workshop on Multimedia Signal Processing, US Virgin Islands, December 2002.
6. CHI, C. H., WANG, H. and KU, W. 2003. Proxy-Cache Aware Object Bundling for Web Access Acceleration, Proceedings of Eighth International Workshop on Web Content Caching and Distribution, 2003.
7. CONRADO, C., KAMPERMAN, F., SCHRIJEN, G. J. and JONKER, W. 2003. Privacy in an identity-based DRM system, Proceedings of 14th International Workshop on Database and Expert Systems Applications 2003, 1-5 Sept. 2003, pp. 389-395.
8. DOI. The Digital Object Identifier (DOI) System. http://www.doi.org/
9. ERICKSON, J., IANNELLA, R. and WENNING, R. 2001. Workshop Report, W3C Workshop on Digital Rights Management for the Web, 22-23 January 2001.
10. GOODRICH, M. T., SHIN, M., STRAUB, C. D. and TAMASSIA, R. 2003. Distributed data authentication, Proceedings of DARPA Information Survivability Conference and Exposition 2003. Volume 2 , 22-24 April 2003, pp. 58-59.
11. HARTUNG, F. and RAMME, F. 2000. Digital rights management and watermarking of multimedia content for m-commerce applications, IEEE Communications Magazine, Volume 38, Issue 11, Nov. 2000, pp. 78-84.
12. IANNELLA, R. 2001. Digital Rights Management (DRM) Architectures, D-Lib Magazine, June 2001, Volume 7 Number 6, ISSN 1082-9873. http://www.dlib.org/dlib/june01/iannella/06iannella.html
13. IANNELLA, R. and HIGGS, P. 2003. Driving Content Management with Digital Rights Management, Apr 2003. http://www.iprsystems.com/whitepapers/CM-DRM-WP.pdf
14. INDECS. The <indecs> framework. http://www.indecs.org
15. IWATA, T., ABE, T., UEDA, Y. and SUNAGA, H. 2003. A DRM system suitable for P2P content delivery and the study on its implementation, Proceedings of The 9th Asia-Pacific Conference on Communications, APCC 2003, Volume 2, 21-24 Sept. 2003, pp. 806-811.
16. KANG, Y. K. and KIM, M. H. 2001. Real-time fingerprints recognition mechanism-based digital contents protection system for interaction on the Web, Proceedings of Pacific Rim International Symposium on Dependable Computing 2001, 17-19 Dec. 2001, pp. 304-309.
17. MORI, R. and KAWAHARA, M. 1990. Superdistribution: the concept and the architecture. Technical Report 7, Inst. of Inf. Sci. & Electron (Japan), Tsukuba Univ., Japan, July 1990.
18. MIHÇAK K. and VENKATESAN R. 2001. New Iterative Geometric Methods for Robust Perceptual Image Hashing, Security and Privacy in Digital Rights Management: Proceedings of ACM CCS-8 Workshop DRM 2001, Philadelphia, PA, USA, November 5, 2001, pp. 13-24.

19. MPEG-21. MPEG-21.
http://www.chiariglione.org/mpeg/standards/mpeg-21/mpeg-21.htm

20. NUTZEL, J. and GRIMM, R. 2003. Potato System and signed media format - an alternative approach to online music business, Proceedings of Third International Conference on Web Delivering of Music, 2003. 2003 WEDELMUSIC, 15-17 Sept. 2003, pp. 23-26.

21. OASIS. OASIS Rights Language Technical Committee.
http://www.oasis-open.org/committees/tc_home.php?wg_abbrev=rights

22. ODRL. Open Digital Rights Language (ODRL). http://www.odrl.net/

23. OEBF. Open eBook Forum. http://www.openebook.org/

24. OMA. Open Mobile Alliance (OMA). http://www.openmobilealliance.org/

25. ORTEGA-GARCIA, J., BIGUN, J., REYNOLDS, D., and GONZALEZ-RODRIGUEZ, J. 2004. Authentication gets personal with biometrics, Signal Processing Magazine, IEEE, Volume 21, Issue 2, March 2004, pp. 50- 62.

26. PESTONI, F., LOTSPIECH, J. B. and NUSSER, S. 2004. xCP: Peer-to-Peer content protection, Signal Processing Magazine, IEEE, Volume 21, Issue 2, March 2004, pp. 71- 81.

27. ROSENBLATT, B., TRIPPE, B. and MOONEY, S. 2001. Digital Rights Management: Business and Technology, John Wiley & Sons, 2001, ISBN 0764548891.

28. RUMP, N. 2003. Definition, Aspects, and Overview, E. Becker et al. (Eds.): Digital Rights Management, ISBN 3-540-40465-1, LNCS 2770, 2003, pp. 3-15.

29. "SCREAMER, B". 2001. "Beale Screamer"'s crack of Microsoft DRM Version 2.
http://cryptome.org/ms-drm.htm

30. UZUNER, Ö. and DAVIS, R. 2003. Content and expression-based copy recognition for intellectual property protection, Proceedings of the 2003 ACM workshop on Digital rights management, 2003, pp. 103-110.

31. VENKATACHALAM, V., CAZZANTI, L., DHILLON, N. and WELLS, M 2004. Automatic identification of sound recordings, Signal Processing Magazine, IEEE, Volume 21, Issue 2, March 2004, pp. 92- 99.

32. WALKER, J., MORRIS, O. J. and MARUSIC, B. 2003. Share it! - the architecture of a rights-managed network of peer-to-peer set-top-boxes, EUROCON 2003. Computer as a Tool. The IEEE Region 8, Volume 1, 22-24 Sept. 2003, pp. 251-255.

33. WU, M., TRAPPE, W., WANG, Z. J. and LIU, K. J. R. 2004. Collusion-Resistant Fingerprinting for Multimedia, Signal Processing Magazine, IEEE, Volume 21, Issue 2, March 2004, pp. 15- 27.

34. XRML. eXtensible rights Markup Language (XrML). http://www.xrml.org/

Detecting Software Theft via Whole Program Path Birthmarks

Ginger Myles and Christian Collberg

Department of Computer Science, University of Arizona, Tucson, AZ, 85721, USA
{mylesg,collberg}@cs.arizona.edu

Abstract. A software birthmark is a unique characteristic of a program that can be used as a software theft detection technique. In this paper we present and empirically evaluate a novel birthmarking technique — *Whole Program Path Birthmarking* — which uniquely identifies a program based on a complete control flow trace of its execution. To evaluate the strength of the proposed technique we examine two important properties: credibility and tolerance against program transformations such as optimization and obfuscation. Our evaluation demonstrates that, for the detection of theft of an entire program, Whole Program Path birthmarks are more resilient to attack than previously proposed techniques. In addition, we illustrate several instances where a birthmark can be used to identify program theft even when an embedded watermark was destroyed by program transformation.

Keywords: software piracy, copyright protection, software birthmark.

1 Introduction

Suppose Alice creates a program $\mathcal{A}$ which she sells to Bob. Subsequently, Alice discovers Bob is selling a program $\mathcal{B}$ which is remarkably similar to $\mathcal{A}$. Alice suspects Bob copied $\mathcal{A}$ and is reselling it under the new name. In order to take legal action, Alice needs to be able to prove that $\mathcal{B}$ is indeed a copy of $\mathcal{A}$. In this paper we will describe a technique known as *software birthmarking* which can be used to provide such proof.

A software birthmark is a unique characteristic, or set of characteristics, that a program possesses and which can be used to identify the program. The general idea is that if two programs p and q both have the same birthmark then it is highly likely that one is a copy of the other. There are two important properties of a birthmarking technique that must be considered: the detector should not produce false positives (i.e. it should not say that p and q originate from the same source, if, in fact, they do not), and it should be resilient to semantics preserving transformations (such as optimization and obfuscation) that an attacker may launch in order to defeat the detector. In this paper we propose and evaluate a new software birthmarking technique we call *Whole Program Path Birthmarks* (WPPB). WPPB is a *dynamic* technique, relying on the *execution pattern* of the program to detect the birthmark. This is in contrast to previously

K. Zhang and Y. Zheng (Eds.): ISC 2004, LNCS 3225, pp. 404–415, 2004.

proposed techniques which are *static*, i.e. they compute the birthmark based on the characteristics of the program source or binary code. We will show that the WPPB technique is more resilient to attacks by semantic-preserving transformations than published static techniques.

This paper makes the following contributions:

1. We introduce a new category of software birthmarks which we call *dynamic birthmarks*.
2. We propose and evaluate a new dynamic birthmarking technique based on *Whole Program Paths* [16].
3. We evaluate the four static birthmarking techniques proposed by Tamada, et al. [23,24] and show that they are easily defeated by current code obfuscation tools.
4. We provide an empirical evaluation between our WPPB technique and Tamada's birthmarks, and demonstrate that WPPBs are less vulnerable to attacks by semantics-preserving transformations.
5. Finally, we show that birthmarks can be used to identify program theft even when an embedded watermark has been destroyed by a program transformation.

2   Related Work

There are three major threats recognized against the intellectual property contained in software. *Software piracy* is the illegal reselling of legally obtained copies of a program. *Software tampering* is the illegal modification of a program to circumvent license checks, to obtain access to digital media protected by the software, etc. *Malicious reverse engineering* is the extracting of a piece of a program in order to reuse it in ones own.

A variety of techniques have been proposed to address these attacks. Each technique targets a different attack and can often be combined to produce a stronger defense. *Code obfuscation* [12] is a technique developed to aid in the prevention of reverse engineering. An obfuscation is a semantics-preserving transformation which makes the program more difficult to understand and reverse engineer. Probably the most well-known technique for detecting software piracy is *software watermarking* [7,9,11,14,17,20,22,25]. The basic idea is to embed a unique identifier in the program. Piracy is confirmed by proving the program contains the watermark.

A lesser known technique for the detection of theft is *software birthmarks*. Software birthmarks differ from software watermarks in two important ways. First, it is often necessary to add code to the application in order to embed a watermark. In the case of a birthmark additional code is never needed. Instead a birthmark relies on an inherent characteristic of the application to show that one program is a copy of another. Secondly, a birthmark cannot prove authorship or be used to identify the source of an illegal redistribution. Rather, a birthmark can only confirm that one program is a copy of another. A strong birthmark will be able to provide such confirmation even when code transformations have been applied to the code by the adversary in order to hide the theft.

One of the first occurrences of the use of the term birthmark was by Grover [15] where the term was used to mean characteristics occurring in the program by chance which could be used to aid in program identification. This term was distinguished from a fingerprint in that the characteristics used to embed the fingerprint are intentionally placed in the code. The general idea of a software birthmark is similar to that of a computer virus signature. An early example of the use of birthmarks was in an IBM court case [6]. In this case IBM used the order in which the registers were pushed and popped to prove that their PC-AT ROM had been illegally copied.

Tamada, et al. [23,24] have proposed four birthmarks that are specific to Java class files: constant values in field variables (CVFV), sequence of method calls (SMC), inheritance structure (IS), and used classes (UC). The CVFV birthmark extracts information about the variables declared in the class. For each variable the type t_i is extracted along with the initial value a_i. The birthmark is then the sequence $((t_1, a_1), (t_2, a_2), ..., (t_n, a_n))$. SMC examines the sequence of method calls as they appear in the class, but not necessarily in execution order. Because it is easy to change the names of the methods within the application only those method calls which are in a set of well-known classes are considered in the sequence. IS extracts the inheritance structure of the class. The birthmark is constructed by traversing the superclasses of the class back to `java.lang.Object`. All classes which are in the set of well-known classes are included in the sequence. The UC birthmark examines all classes which are used by a given class, i.e. they appear as a superclass of the given class, the return or argument types of a method, the types of fields, etc. All classes in the set of well-known classes are included in the sequence which is then arranged in alphabetical order. As we will see in Sect. 5 Tamada's birthmarks are easily defeated by applying simple code obfuscating transformations to the program.

Plagiarism detection is another area which is very similar to software birthmarking. A variety of plagiarism detection techniques have been proposed (e.g. Moss [5,21], Plaque [26], and YAP [27]) which have been quite successful at detecting plagiarism within student programs. Unfortunately, these systems compute similarity at the source code level. In many instances source code is unavailable. In addition, these systems do not consider semantics-preserving transformations and the effects of decompilation on the formatting of the source code. For example, it was shown by Collberg, et al. [10] that given the source code of a Java application, simply compiling then decompiling will cause Moss to indicate 0% similarity between the original and the decompiled source code.

3   Software Birthmarks

Before we can precisely define the idea of a birthmark we must define what it means for a program q to be a *copy* of another program p. The most obvious definition is where q is an exact duplicate of p. However, in order to hide the fact that copying has taken place an attacker might apply semantics-preserving transformations to q. For example, all of the identifiers in q might have been renamed or an optimizing register allocator might have been applied to q so that q and p now have different register assignments. In this case we would still like to be able to say that q is a copy of p. In addition, it is important that our definition reflects that if q is a copy of p then p and q should exhibit the same external behavior. (Note that the reverse of this property does not necessary hold. It is possible to find two programs which exhibit the same external behavior but are not copies. An example is iterative and recursive versions of the same function.)

The following definition of a software birthmark is a restatement of the definition given by Tamada, et al. [23,24].

Definition 1 (Birthmark). *Let p, q be programs. Let f be a method for extracting a set of characteristics from a program. Then $f(p)$ is a birthmark of p iff:*

1. *$f(p)$ is obtained only from p itself (without any extra information), and*
2. *q is a copy of $p \Rightarrow f(p) = f(q)$.*

As with software watermarking we can characterize a birthmark as either static or dynamic. A static birthmark extracts the set of characteristics from the statically available information in a program such as information about the types or initial values of the fields. A dynamic birthmark relies on information gathered from the execution of the application. A dynamic algorithm typically works at the program level whereas a static algorithm targets an entire program or individual modules within the program. The same distinction is true with static and dynamic watermarking algorithms. A dynamic algorithm can provide evidence if an entire program is stolen and a static algorithm may be able to detect the theft of a single module. The four birthmark techniques proposed by Tamada, et al. are characterized as static and target class-level theft. Definition 1 above defines a static birthmark.

Definition 2 (Dynamic Birthmark). *Let p, q be programs and i an input to these programs. Let f be a method for extracting a set of characteristics from a program. Then $f(p, i)$ is a dynamic birthmark of p iff:*

1. *$f(p, i)$ is obtained only from p itself by executing p with the given input i, and*
2. *q is a copy of $p \Rightarrow f(p, i) = f(q, i)$.*

The Whole Program Path Birthmark proposed in this paper computes the birthmark from the execution trace of the program. It is therefore, a dynamic birthmark designed to detect program level theft.

3.1   Evaluating Software Birthmarks

We would like a birthmark technique to satisfy the following two properties.

Property 1 (Credibility). Let p and q be independently written programs which accomplish the same task. Then we say f is a credible measure if $f(p) \neq f(q)$.

Property 2 (Resistance to Transformation). Let p' be a program obtained from p by applying semantics-preserving transformations $\mathcal{T}$. Then we say f is resilient to $\mathcal{T}$ if $f(p) = f(p')$.

Property 1 is concerned with the possibility of the birthmark falsely indicating that q is a copy of p. This could occur with independently implemented programs which perform the same task. It is highly unlikely that two independently implemented algorithms will contain all of the same details so the birthmark should be designed to extract those details which are likely to differ.

Property 2 addresses the issue of identifying a copy in the presence of a transformation. With the proliferation of tools for code optimization and obfuscation, for example [1,2,3,4], it is highly probable that an attacker will apply at least one transformation prior to distributing an illegally copied program. It is desirable that a birthmark be able to detect a copy even if a transformation has been applied to that program.

4   Whole Program Path Based Birthmarks

In the next section we present the first known dynamic birthmark technique. Through experiments we have performed on the four techniques proposed by Tamada, et al. we believe they are susceptible to a variety of simple program transformations. Thus, there are other characteristics of a program which could be used to construct a stronger birthmark technique.

4.1   Whole Program Paths

Whole Program Paths (WPP) is a technique presented in [16] to represent a program's dynamic control flow. The WPP is constructed by collecting a trace of the path executed by the program. The trace is then transformed into a more compact form by identifying its regularity, which is repeated code. To collect the trace the edges of the program's control flow graph are instrumented, by uniquely labeling each edge. As the program executes the edges are recorded, producing a trace. The trace is then run through the SEQUITUR algorithm which compresses it and reveals its inherent regularity [18,19]. The output of the SEQUITUR algorithm is a context-free grammar from which a directed acyclic graph (DAG) is produced. Each rule of the grammar is composed of a non-terminal and a sequence of symbols which the non-terminal represents. To construct the DAG representation of the grammar a node is added for each unique symbol. For each rule an edge is added from the non-terminal to each of the symbols it represents. The final DAG is the WPP.

The construction of the WPP is illustrated in Fig. 1. At ⓐ a control flow graph with 6 basic blocks and 8 edges is constructed from the input program. The control flow graph is instrumented so that each edge is labeled. At ⓑ the program is executed producing an edge trace. The trace is run through the SEQUITUR algorithm at ⓒ to produce the given context-free grammar. This grammar contains 3 unique non-terminals and 8 unique terminals. At ⓓ a DAG with 3 internal nodes, 8 leaf nodes, and 14 directed edges is constructed which represents the grammar.

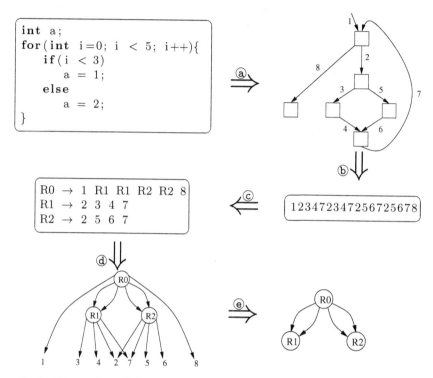

Fig. 1. An illustration of the stages involved in constructing a Whole Program Path (WPP). The construction begins with a program. A program control flow graph is constructed and instrumented. By executing the program on a given input an edge trace is constructed. This trace is run through the SEQUITUR algorithm to produce a context-free grammar. The grammar is then used to construct a directed acyclic graph which represents the WPP. All terminal nodes and corresponding edges are removed from the WPP to construct the WPP birthmark.

Our WPP birthmark is constructed in an identical manner as the WPP with the exception of the DAG in the final stage. An essential property of a birthmark is that it captures an inherent characteristic about the program which is difficult to modify through semantics-preserving transformations. The WPP birthmark captures the inherent regularity in the dynamic behavior of a program. Since we are only interested in the regularity we eliminate all terminal nodes in the DAG. It is the internal nodes which will be more difficult to modify through program transformations. Thus, the DAG in Fig. 1 is transformed into the birthmark of the example program at ⓔ.

4.2   Similarity of WPP Birthmarks

The WPP birthmark is in the form of a DAG. Suppose we have the birthmarks $f(p) = G_1$ and $f(q) = G_2$ for programs p and q. $f(p)$ and $f(q)$ are the same iff G_1 and G_2 are isomorphic. Since it is unlikely that q is an identical copy of p we would like to be able to say something about the similarity between $f(p)$ and $f(q)$. In other words, we would like to be able to conclude that q is a copy of p even in the presence of semantics-preserving transformations.

To compute similarity we use a slightly modified version of the graph distance metric in [8]. The similarity is based on finding a maximal common subgraph, G_3, between G_1 and G_2. The percentage of G_1 that we are able to identify in G_2 by finding the maximal common subgraph G_3 indicates the similarity between the two programs. The reason we are comparing the size of G_3 and G_1 instead of the maximum of G_1 and G_2 is that we are trying to identify a copy of p in q. We therefore want to know how much of G_1 is contained in G_2.

Definition 3 (Graph Distance). *The distance of two non-empty graphs* $G_1 = (V_1, E_1)$ *and* $G_2 = (V_2, E_2)$ *is defined as*

$$d(G_1, G_2) = \frac{|mcs(G_1, G_2)|}{|G_1|}$$

where $mcs(G_1, G_2)$ *is the maximum common subgraph of* G_1, G_2 *and* $|G| = |V| + |E|$.

Definition 4 (Similarity). *Let* $f(p) = G_1$ *and* $f(q) = G_2$ *be birthmarks extracted from programs* p *and* q. *The similarity between* $f(p)$ *and* $f(q)$ *is defined by:* $d(G_1, G_2) \times 100$.

5   Evaluation

To evaluate the effectiveness of the WPP birthmarking technique we examined its ability to satisfy the two properties from Sect. 3. We look at whether WPP birthmarks will produce false positives given two independently written applications which accomplish the same task and the tolerance of the birthmark against program transformations. As an additional evaluation we demonstrate how birthmarks can be used in conjunction with watermarking.

5.1   Credibility

To evaluate the credibility of WPP birthmarks we examined the ability to distinguish between two independently written applications which performed the same task. We looked at two problems: calculating a factorial and generating Fibonacci numbers. Each of these problems can be solved recursively and iteratively. The WPP birthmark found the factorial programs to be 50% similar and the Fibonacci programs 7% similar. From these results we are able to conclude that the recursive and iterative forms of the programs were probably written independently.

Tamada, et al. [23,24] state that their birthmark techniques are unable to distinguish between independently written applications which are small. This is true given the Factorial and Fibonacci programs. Using the four birthmarks proposed by Tamada, et al. the recursive and iterative versions are found to be 100% similar. The only exception was SMC on factorial which had a similarity of 16%. Thus, with respect to small applications and credibility the WPP birthmarks provide stronger results.

5.2 Resistance to Transformation

To evaluate the WPP birthmark's resistance to transformation we applied various obfuscations and optimizations to automatically transform our test program into an equivalent, but not identical program. To perform the transformations we used Zelix Klassmaster (ZKM) [4], Smokescreen [3], Codeshield [1], and SandMark [2]. ZKM, Smokescreen, and Codeshield all include name obfuscation, the elimination of debugging information, and some type of control flow obfucations. Additionally, Smokescreen supports dead code elimination and ZKM includes string encryption. Our test program was a Java program `wc.jar` that works like the UNIX wc program.

For each of the tools except SandMark we applied the tool with the strongest level of obfuscation. The SandMark tool permitted us to pick and choose which obfuscations were applied to the program. SandMark includes 31 obfuscation algorithms which we applied individually to `wc.jar` obtaining 31 obfuscated programs. In addition, we applied multiple obfuscations in succession to `wc.jar`.

We computed the WPP birthmark for each of the transformed applications, the 31 from SandMark plus the three additional, as well as the original `wc.jar`. In every case the similarity between the original and the obfuscated applications was found to be 100%.

We performed the same evaluation of the four techniques proposed by Tamada, et al. Table 1 shows a comparison of the results with our WPP birthmark using ZKM, Smokescreen, and Codeshield. The table shows that only WPP and IS compute 100% for each of the three obfuscated programs. Even though IS computes 100% similarity we believe the technique is not strong enough to be used on its own. The reason for this is that the technique could produce many false positives for independently implemented programs which both do and do not perform the same task.

We also tested the four static birthmarks against each of the 31 obfuscations included in the SandMark tool. For CVFV, SMC, and UC we were able to find obfuscations which cast doubt on the similarity between the original and obfuscated version. Using the CVFV birthmark a less than 100% similarity was detected for the obfuscations Bogus Fields (75%), Node Splitter (0%), Objectify (66%), Opaque Branch Insertion (75%), and Transparent Branch Insertion (75%). When all five of these obfuscations were applied in conjunction to wc.jar CVFV detected a 0% similarity. The SMC birthmark detected a less than

100% similarity on four obfuscations: Buggy Code (69%), Primitive Promoter (5%), Static Method Bodies (82%), and Transparent Branch Insertion (83%). A similarity of 1% was detected when all four obfuscations were applied. Four obfuscations also caused the UC birthmark to detect a less than 100% similarity: Objectify (92%), Opaque Branch Insertion (92%), Primitive Promoter (56%), and Transparent Branch Insertion (92%). The combination of the obfuscations yielded a 52% similarity. These initial results indicate that the WPP birthmark is stronger then the four techniques proposed in [23,24] when theft of an entire application is in question.

Table 1. Similarity percentage found using each birthmark technique on an original and obfuscated version of `wc.jar`.

	ZKM	Smokescreen	Codeshield
WPP	100%	100%	100%
CVFV	66.7%	83.3%	83.3%
SMC	25.0%	15.9%	100%
IS	100%	100%	100%
UC	100%	100%	45.0%

We do know of two attacks that the WPP birthmark is currently vulnerable to. The first is any loop transformation that alters the loop in ways similar to loop unrolling or loop splitting. Executing the loop backwards, however, will not effect the WPP birthmark. WPP birthmarks are also vulnerable to method inlining in certain instances. If the method call occurs inside of a loop then inlining will not alter the birthmark. On the other hand, if the method is a helper method which is called from various locations throughout the program, inlining the method call will have an effect on the birthmark similarity.

5.3   Birthmarks and Watermarks

One limitation of software birthmarks is that they provide weaker evidence than software watermarks. They are only able to say that one program is likely to be a copy of another not who the original author is or who is guilty of piracy. However, birthmarks can be used in instances where watermarking is not feasible such as applications where code size is a concern and the watermark would insert additional code. Birthmarks can also be used in conjunction with watermarking to provide stronger evidence of theft. One such example is the watermarking algorithm proposed by Stern, et al. [22] which provides a probability that a specific watermark is contained in the program. If the watermarking algorithm does not 100% guarantee that the watermark is contained in the program then a birthmark could be used as additional evidence of theft. There are also instances where watermarks fail, e.g. an attacker is able to apply an obfuscation which destroys the watermark. In these instances a birthmark may still be able to provide proof of program theft since the birthmark may be more resilient to transformations.

We were able to very easily construct three instances using the `wc.jar` program where a watermark is destroyed by an obfuscation, but WPP birthmarks still detect 100% similarity between the programs. In the first instance we used a very simple static watermarking algorithm which embeds the watermark by splitting it in half and using the first half to name a new field and the second in a name of a new method. We then applied an obfuscation which adds additional fields to the program. In the second instance the same watermarking algorithm is used but this time the obfuscation renames all of the identifiers in the program. In the third instance we watermarked the program using the algorithm proposed by Arboit [7] which encoded the watermark in opaque predicates [13] that are appended to various branches throughout the program. We then applied an obfuscation which adds opaque predicates to every boolean expression throughout the application. In each of these instance the watermark is destroyed which would have prevented piracy detection, but the WPP birthmark was able to detect 100% similarity.

6   Future Work

The most pressing future work is to conduct a more extensive evaluation of the WPP birthmark technique. The evaluation conducted in this paper was only preliminary and thus we would like to study the effectiveness on a larger set of test applications as well as more combinations of obfuscations.

As was discussed in Sect. 5.2 WPP birthmarks are susceptible to various loop transformations. To address this problem we want to evaluate the effectiveness of incorporating transformations, such as loop rerolling, in a preprocessing stage that would reverse the transformation. In addition, we would like to add functionality to the technique which would make it possible to target module level as well as program level theft. Once this functionality has been added we would like to evalute the effectiveness of WPP birthmarks in the detection of plagiarism within student programs.

Another interesting area of software birthmarks that should be explored is the combination of static and dynamic birthmarks. Unlike watermarks, where it is possible to destroy one watermark with another, two or more birthmarks can always be used in conjunction to provide stronger evidence of theft.

7   Summary

In this paper we expanded on the idea of software birthmarking by introducing dynamic birthmarks and in particular a specific dynamic birthmark called Whole Program Paths. We evaluated the technique with respect to two properties: credibility and resistance to transformation. In both evaluations the technique demonstrated promising results. WPP birthmarks did not falsely identify two independently written programs as being copies even though they perform the same task. Based on the test program, `wc.jar`, and the available obfuscations WPP birthmarks calculated a similarity of 100% between the original and the transformed program. We also demonstrated how birthmarks can be used in conjunction with watermarks and in some instances are able to detect piracy even when the watermark has been destroyed.

References

1. Codeshield java bytecode obfuscator. http://www.codingart.com/codeshield.html.
2. Sandmark. http://www.cs.arizona.edu/sandmark/.
3. Smokescreen java obfuscator. http://leesw.com.
4. Zelix klassmaster. http://www.zelix.com/klassmaster/index.html.
5. Alex Aiken. Moss – a system for detecting software plagiarism. http://www.cs.berkeley.edu/ aiken/moss.html.
6. Ross J. Anderson and Fabien A. P. Petitcolas. On the limits of steganography. *IEEE Journal of Selected Areas in Communications*, 16(4):474–481, May 1998. Special issue on copyright & privacy protection.
7. Geneviève Arboit. A method for watermarking java programs via opaque predicates. In *The Fifth International Conference on Electronic Commerce Research (ICECR-5)*, 2002.
8. H. Bunke and K. Shearer. A graph distance metric based on the maximal common subgraph, 1998.
9. C. Collberg, E. Carter, S. Debray, A. Huntwork, C. Linn, and M. Stepp. Dynamic path-based software watermarking. In *ACM SIGPLAN Conference on Programming Language Design and Implementation (PLDI 04)*, 2004.
10. Christian Collberg, Ginger Myles, and Mike Stepp. Cheating cheating detectors. Technical Report TR04-05, University of Arizona, 2004.
11. Christian Collberg and Clark Thomborson. Software watermarking: Models and dynamic embeddings. In *In Conference Record of POPL '99: The 26th ACM SIGPLAN-SIGACT Symposium on Principles of Programming Languages (Jan. 1999)*, 1999. http://citeseer.nj.nec.com/collberg99software.html.
12. Christian Collberg, Clark Thomborson, and Douglas Low. A taxonomy of obfuscating transformations. Technical Report 148, Department of Computer Science, University of Auckland, July 1997.
13. Christian Collberg, Clark Thomborson, and Douglas Low. Manufacturing cheap, resilient, and stealthy opaque constructs. In *Principles of Programming Languages 1998, POPL'98*, San Diego, CA, January 1998.
14. R.L. Davidson and N. Myhrvold. Method and system for generating and auditing a signature for a computer program. US Patent 5,559,884, Assignee: Microsoft Corporation, 1996. http://www.delphion.com/details?pn=US05559884__.
15. Derrick Grover. Program identification. In Derrick Grover, editor, *The Protection of Computer Software – Its Technology and Applications*, pages 122–154. Cambridge University Press, 1989.
16. James R. Larus. Whole program paths. In *ACM SIGPLAN Conference on Programming Language Design and Implementation (PLDI 99)*, 1999.
17. A. Monden, H. Iida, K. Matsumoto, Katsuro Inoue, and Koji Torii. A practical method for watermarking java programs. In *compsac2000, 24th Computer Software and Applications Conference*, 2000.

18. C. G. Nevill-Manning and I. H. Witten. Compression and explanation using hierarchical grammars. *The Computer Journal*, 40(2/3), 1997.
19. C.G. Nevill-Manning and I.H. Witten. Linear-time, incremental hierarchy inference for compression. In *Proceedings of the Data Compression Conference (DCC '97)*, 1997.
20. Gang Qu and Miodrag Potkonjak. Hiding signatures in graph coloring solutions. In *Information Hiding*, pages 348–367, 1999.
21. Saul Schleimer, Daniel Wilkerson, and Alex Aiken. Winnowing: Local algorithms for document fingerprinting. In *Proceedings of the 2003 SIGMOD Conference*, 2003.
22. Julien P. Stern, Gael Hachez, Francois Koeune, and Jean-Jacques Quisquater. Robust object watermarking: Application to code. In *Information Hiding*, pages 368–378, 1999. `http://citeseer.nj.nec.com/stern00robust.html`.
23. Haruaki Tamada, Masahide Nakamura, Akito Monden, and Kenichi Matsumoto. Detecting the theft of programs using birthmarks. Information Science Technical Report NAIST-IS-TR2003014 ISSN 0919-9527, Graduate School of Information Science, Nara Institute of Science and Technology, Nov 2003.
24. Haruaki Tamada, Masahide Nakamura, Akito Monden, and Kenichi Matsumoto. Design and evaluation of birthmarks for detecting theft of java programs. In *Proc. IASTED International Conference on Software Engineering (IASTED SE 2004)*, pages 569–575, Feb 2004.
25. Ramarathnam Venkatesan, Vijay Vazirani, and Saurabh Sinha. A graph theoretic approach to software watermarking. In *4th International Information Hiding Workshop*, Pittsburgh, PA, April 2001.
26. Geoff Whale. Identification of program similarity in large populations. *Computer Journal*, 33:140–146, 1990.
27. Micheal J. Wise. Detection of similarities in student programs: Yap'ing may be preferable to plague'ing. In *23rd SIGCSE Technical Symposium*, pages 268–271, 1992.

Effective Security Requirements Analysis: HAZOP and Use Cases

Thitima Srivatanakul*, John A. Clark, and Fiona Polack

Department of Computer Science, University of York,
Heslington, York, YO10 5DD, UK.
[jill,jac,fiona]@cs.york.ac.uk

Abstract. Use cases are widely used for functional requirements elicitation. However, *security* non-functional requirements are often neglected in this requirements analysis process. As systems become increasingly complex current means of analysis will probably prove ineffective. In the safety domain a variety of effective analysis techniques have emerged over many years. Since the safety and security domains share many similarities, various authors have suggested that safety techniques might usefully find application in security. This paper takes one such technique, HAZOP, and applies it to one widely used functional requirement elicitation component, UML use cases, in order to provide systematic analysis of potential security issues at the start of system development.

Keywords: HAZOP, requirement analysis, security analysis, use case

1 Background

Threats to computer systems and data grow as computer networking and literacy increase. To combat the rising number and severity of security risks, developers need to acknowledge the risks and analyse security with particular care. Security research has emphasised aspects or technologies that implement security mechanisms. Confidentiality properties, for example, have been formalised mathematically by many authors and there is much research into cryptography (see references in [12]). However, these are only partial solutions. Pre-defined solutions to past problems do not always suffice and ad hoc approaches to security leave too many loopholes. Subtlety is needed to determine in what security for a system should consist and how assurance can be gained that the developed system provides it. This is particularly so for complex or novel systems.

In the safety domain, analysts also deal with large, complex and novel systems, but have numerous simple but effective techniques for generating and recording evidence; their use is closely integrated with the development process. Fault Tree Analysis (FTA) [11] has inspired security Threat Trees [2] and Attack Trees [13]. These systematically decompose goals, representing findings in

---

* Thitima Srivatanakul is funded by the Royal Thai Government.

K. Zhang and Y. Zheng (Eds.): ISC 2004, LNCS 3225, pp. 416–427, 2004.

a tree structure. MOAT [6] is a security argumentation technique that uses FTA notations to express its assurance arguments. More sophisticated argumentation [8] is available via derivatives of the Goal Structured Notation [5].

Systematic deviational techniques such as HAZOP (Hazard and Operability Analysis) [10,9], successfully used in safety critical systems, are little used in security. The basic principle of HAZOP is that hazards take place due to deviations from normal or intended behaviours. Winther et.al. [16] has adapted HAZOP guidewords to generate guidelines specific to security attributes. However, the derived guidewords are not flexible enough to bring out the analysts' creativity. Perhaps the most significant deviational activity in security is the Flaw Hypothesis Method [15], one form of penetration testing. It uncovers weaknesses by hypothesising suspected flaws, thus providing a method for assessing vulnerabilities. However, the approach lacks rigour. The process, especially the flaw generation, relies heavily on analysts' domain expertise and skill; it does not encourage proactive analysis.

We have devised a HAZOP general approach for security. Specialising the technique for a particular domain may allow increased rigour and efficiency.

2   HAZOP-Based Security Analysis on Use Case Model

The use case technique [4], now popularised as part of the UML, describes behaviours of a system and actors from a user's perspective. In UML (and the related methods), use cases are usually used to capture and express functional requirements. They represent the system and its interactions, in a simple abstract form that is easily understood by the different parties involved. The expression of use cases is the foundation for subsequent development activities, as the captured requirements are fed into the specification and design process.

Recent work has applied use case modelling to requirements other than the purely functional. Abuse and misuse cases are proposed as (intuitive) means to capture and analyse security requirements [7,14] . Sindre [14] notes that both security and safety requirements can be elicited from use case diagram and scenarios. Douglass [3] shows that use case modelling can be used to document some non-functional requirements, for example, by annotating each action in use case scenarios with timing constraints. Allenby [1] uses HAZOP on use case scenarios to elicit and analyse safety requirements; the results, in a tabular form, describe possible catastrophic failures, their causes and effects.

Use, abuse and misuse cases are potentially useful for analysis of security requirements. The interface presented to an attacker can often be characterised by use cases. The attacker may 'stay within the rules' (but do so in a particularly clever way) or deviate from what is intended as acceptable behaviour. Attacks may be regarded as 'exceptional flows' in a use case. Current abuse case approaches do not offer a systematic way of generating such unusual deviations.

Our technique extends abuse cases, providing a more rigorous approach. By applying the principles of HAZOP, tailored to a security perspective, to an existing functional requirements representation (i.e. use cases), we systematically mutate the model and its elements, thus prompting identification of a wide range of threats and other non-functional requirements. HAZOP is thus used to generate alternative behaviours in a systematic way.

2.1   Use Case Elements and Their Security Deviations

Our technique applies HAZOP guidewords to elements of a use case that could be deviated in realisable ways. A key part of HAZOP analysis is to interpret the guidewords for the context of interest. We propose interpretations of guidewords for the attributes of each of the main elements of a use case that are subject to deviations (see Appendix A).

Actors are anything that needs to exchange information with the system [4]. An actor characterises the role that users or external systems have in relation to the system. Actors can represent individual or collective roles.

A person may play different roles and the roles of a person may be restricted. For example, the same person is not allowed to both process and approve a payment. Actor roles can be distinguished by their intent/action and capability. These determine deviations that are possible for each actor; the ways in which actors deviate from their normal role may have different impacts on the system. Deviations from intent or actions (deviations from goals), whether intentional or accidental, can reveal new threats to the system. New malicious actors may be identified by considering intentional deviation from expected actor behaviour. The intent of an actor is interesting – an actor may obey all security rules and participate in a seemingly innocuous interaction, when the real intent is to signal information via a covert channel.

The deviation of actors needs to take note of the potential resources and skills of individuals (or systems) playing the roles represented as actors. For example, a cyber-terrorist network usually has more ability to cause attacks than teenage hacker, in terms of access to resources and skills.

Associations of actors with use cases model the roles that interact with the system through the functionality modelled in the use case. The interaction may represent the exchange of information or invocation of system operations. In secure systems, access control depends on role; we need a clear idea of which actors should be able to access which use cases for what purpose. The significance of restricting operation access to a particular actor, and of assignment of access controls to particular users could be highlighted by this part of the analysis.

Use cases record intended associations for intentional interactions. It is intended that the associations model the only channels used by the actors. Covert channels can be thought of as unintended associations. For example an association implemented by a communications cable provides a point-to-point channel but physics implements an unintend channel, the emission of electromagnetic radiation that can be monitored by an eavesdropper. We try to identify such general concerns through our analysis.

Actors may have concurrent associations or engage in parallel instance of the same use case. It is possible also that uses cases executed in quick succession may cause problems. In on-line gambling, for instance, repeated sequential or parallel engagement may simply act as a denial of service mechanism, or may allow collusion among betters.

Use Cases represent tasks that the system must achieve on behalf of the associated actors. Use case documentation usually comprises at least pre-condition, post-condition and sequences of actions (scenarios), including variants.

In the execution of a scenario, deviant interactions could result in exceptions to the flow of events. We can address the causes and effects of variation by considering the deviations of each step in the use case. The use case pre- and post-condition represent states of the system at certain sets of times. Deviation from these normal states may be possible, and may affect security. Analysis must elicit possible causes of such deviant states.

2.2   Analysis Process

A HAZOP analysis is conducted by a team of analysts with varied backgrounds, led by a HAZOP leader. The team systematically investigates each use case element to identify deviation from requirements. Each deviant is further investigated for possible causes and effects. The process has the following steps:

1. From a use case, identify and record:
   - intent/action and capability of actors;
   - associations between actors and use cases;
   - components from use case description: pre-condition, main flow of events, alternative flow of events (i.e. normal but perhaps less likely and exceptional/error), post-condition.
2. Apply HAZOP guidewords with the appropriate interpretation, to each element identified in step 1, to suggest deviations.
3. Evaluate whether the identified deviations violate, or could violate, any security properties. Investigate possible causes of the deviations.
4. Identify consequences that may arise from the deviations (extract affected assets from the identified consequences).
5. Categorise the deviations identified, and generalise each group.
6. Provide recommendations on the identified problems/threats.

2.3   Deriving Use Case Deviants

The guidewords alone do not explain how to derive use case deviants. This section provides additional guidance for performing the HAZOP-based analysis, based on our experience of applying the technique.

Viewpoint considerations/stakeholders' interests – Stakeholders are individuals or organisations that have an interest in the system, even though they are not a direct part of the system, and may not directly interact with it. A viewpoint represents a stakeholder's interest in the system. Security analysis must take account of any conflicting viewpoints and the relative importance of stakeholders, but deviations from all stakeholder interests should be considered.

In addition, derivation of deviants considers as viewpoints the three fundamental security properties (confidentiality, integrity and availability).

Role/actor mapping – An actor characterises a role played in relation to the computer system. Individuals within roles are not distinguished, and an individual may play different roles. Deviation analysis must consider the possibility of unexpected interactions through shared and multiple roles. A multi-user role always has potential deviants in which the user in a role who initiates an interaction is not the same as the user receiving the response. The definition of actors and roles may be confused, allowing individuals to operate outside their intended or authorised roles.

Business rules define business constraints on a system, including policies and validation. When deriving the deviations, it is essential to consider what sort of business rules the system does or should enforce. In practice, security policies are often implicit. The use case analysis may help to make explicit the security policy, which may require system requirements to be modified so that functional requirements respect to the policy.

Common knowledge and security violations – Although the systematic HAZOP approach is a significant improvement on intuitive analyses, it is important not to ignore the existing 'checklists' of accumulated wisdom in security.

3   Example Application

This section presents a simple case study. An apparently-innocuous web ordering system, Figure 1, is systematically analysed to reveal threats.

A website hosts a company's product catalogue that anyone using the internet can access and browse. A customer is a person registered with the company who can order goods via the website. To order goods, the registered customer must

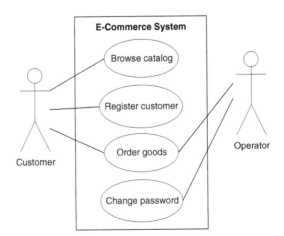

Fig. 1. Simple e-commerce system use case diagram

provide sufficient payment and delivery detail. If an un-registered contact wishes to place an order, the ordering facility provides an initial registration procedure. Orders are processed by an operator, logged on to the host system. The operator password can be changed as required.

Stakeholders' interests include:

1. Company owner - Interest in profits, and reputation of the company.
2. System manager - Interest in system's performance and operation of staff.
3. Developer - Interest in correct operation of the program.

The intents or goals of the Customer actor include *browse catalogue, register, order goods, pay for goods*. The operator's goal is to *process order goods*.

3.1   Analysis

We chose *order goods* to demonstrate how the technique is applied. The description of the use case is given in Table 1.

Table 1. *Order Goods* use case description

Use Case Name	Order goods
Goal:	To order goods from the system.
Actor(s):	Customer
	Operator
Preconditions:	1. The customer is registered to order goods.
	2. The customer has entered registration details e.g. user name (i.e. is logged on to the ordering section).
Main flow of events:	1. The customer enters Order Goods section.
	2. The system displays the customer's account detail.
	3. For each desired product, the customer enters its identity.
	4. The customer provides delivery details.
	5. The system calculates and displays the price of the goods ordered.
	6. The customer submits payment details.
	7. The system confirms the result of transaction.
	8. The operator collects the detail of the order.
	9. The operator processes the order.
Post conditions:	Order details are entered on the system and the order processed.

The use case description documents functional requirement for goods ordering, capturing the interactions between the actors and the system. It shows what functions the system needs, to satisfy the requirement.

From the use case and its description, we identify actor intent (customer – order goods, pay for goods; operator – process order), actor capability (customer – capability to order goods; operator – capability to process order), associations of customer and operator with *order goods* use case, pre- and post-conditions and the event sequence of *order goods*. Each element is subject to deviation.

3.2 Results

We provide a fragment of the analysis of *order goods*. Table 2 shows the results for the customer intent, Order Goods.

Results in Table 2 highlight potential threats to the system e.g. prank orders, impersonation or unauthorised access to the system by whatever means; deviations from the use case description also reveal issues. For example,

event 6 in the use case, *the customer submits payment detail* (Table 1), deviated using the OTHER THAN guideword, gives rise to *incorrect payment is sent (value or card number)*. This could be caused by an intruder modifying the message, message corruption, or simply by the customer entering incorrect details, perhaps due to distraction or poor interface design.

Applying the guideword, LATE, to event 7, we realise that, if the system does not confirm within a reasonable time, a customer might resubmit details and thus order more than once, a usability issue. A malicious attacker might delay network messages corresponding to event 6 to cause the customer to resubmit.

In the web-based example used here, the principals in transactions are distributed. The language in the use cases often obscures the underlying communications needed. Thus, *system presents to customer* involves sending the appropriate data across the web, though this is not stated. This abstraction hides attacks based on message interception/spoofing. We found in practice that we were prompted to address some communications security issues.

Another intriguing security issue was uncoverd by analysis of the registration process, during which a user is required to submit *details*. The use case checks that the details are not those of an already-registered customer. Applying OTHER THAN to *details*, it became apparent that a user could, maliciously or accidentally, obtain multiple identities if name or address details were subtly altered. This might compromise the company stakeholder's wishes to administer "one per customer" or "one per household" offers. This raises issues for the implementation detail-equality determination and the business offers policy.

In addition to exposing assumptions, the analysis raises a number of security-related requirements, such as checks on mandatory fields, and messages for acknowledgement and confirmation of details. From the discussion, other business-related issues emerge, such as the influence on sales results of different orderings of products in displayed lists.

4   Discussion

HAZOP provides a systematic approach to reasoning about the high-level security of a system modelled in use cases, and is thus a useful tool in the security analysis armoury. The study of which part is presented here allows us to draw conclusions on the utility of the general technique. Below we summarise our observations on the experience of applying HAZOP to the e-commerce example.

HAZOP helps the derivation of security requirements and policy. The analysis process is an effective means of teasing out security requirements.

Table 2. Analysis result from customer intent – Order Goods

Customer's intent	Order Goods
Guideword	**NO** - The customer does not order goods
Cause	Unsatisfied with the product selections/price Complicated interface Distraction by the company's opponent advertisement
Effects	Lose an opportunity to sell Customer's disappointment
Threats involved	Hacking
Recommendation	User friendly interface design Provision of mechanism to prevent unauthorised pop-up windows
Guideword	**MORE** - The customer excessively order goods
Cause	Not the owner of the account/or credit card Prank order with fake account
Effects	- The company sent order without getting paid later on. - The owner of the payment becomes furious when finds out that the order was not initiated by him. - Wasted time trying to verify payment detail for a fake card. - Increase workload to the company staff.
Threats involved	Obtain password and card detail (steal, bribery, social engineering). Impersonating as customer. Get access to other computer, while logging on to the system.
Recommendation	Consideration of policy on payment – before or after delivery.
Guideword	**LESS** - N/A
Guideword	**AS WELL AS** - The customer provides insufficient/incorrect detail when submitting order
Cause	Complicated interface Detail not available Typing mistake Distraction
Effects	- Processing of payment would be unsuccessful. - Customer's disappointment. - Increase workload to the company staff.
Threats involved	Steal/virus Distraction
Recommendation	Checks on mandatory field prior to accepting the request.
Guideword	**OTHER THAN** - The customer intends to achieve something other than to order goods.
Cause	Malicious intents
Effects	Wrong statistics data on the number of customer access Disruption on the service Increase workload
Threats involved	Flood/block the system Impersonating as customer
Recommendation	This raises the issues of whether to allow users to simultaneously log on using the same accounts.

Our illustration reveals issues on payment policy, and rules for simultaneous log-ins on one registration. At its simplest, the results provide additional functional requirements. However, we found that the analysis process often provoked discussion about higher-level policy issues. HAZOP prompts the analysis team to think in ways they would not otherwise have done. In some environments the security policy may be implicit and in many cases will be incomplete.

HAZOP highlights issues. HAZOP reveals problems and issues, not solutions. It forces the analyst to consider unusual scenarios. Sometimes the issues thrown up have no clear solution. Though strictly inapplicable at the use case level, in trying to interpret particular natural language descriptions, lower level design possibilities may be unearthed and recorded. Inevitably, much design is iterative with some degree of working ahead; working ahead with forethought should reduce misguided effort.

HAZOP can be applied to all use case elements. Once an element is identified it can be challenged by perturbation and the consequences considered. An assumption is typically made in use cases that the actor remains constant throughout a transaction. However, this assumption can be subjected to perturbation, leading to issues of masquerading and impersonation etc. The very existence of association as a concept leads to this sort of thinking.

Abstraction from communications hides threats. In our system the principals in transactions are distributed. The language in the use cases obscures the underlying communications needed. This abstraction hides attacks based on message interception/spoofing. Also, in uses cases, simple acknowledgement messages are often omitted. This too can hide or even create threats.

Viewpoint prompts are useful. We have found the use of stakeholder viewpoints useful. Considerations such as confidentiality, availability, integrity, accountability and timing also prompt the analysts to highlight issues in these areas. Analysts are free to generate viewpoints as appropriate.

There are more actors than you think. Determining what you have forgotten is hard. The analysts must consciously search for additional considerations. Thus, for example, cleaners did not appear in any of the previous analysis, and yet they may have physical access to terminals and servers.

Elicitation of attack patterns. The HAZOP based approach helps in elicitation of patterns of attack, as well as analysing and creating a process of developing a pattern library. For example, analysis reveals implicit protocols between the user and the system – and deviations from these protocols; this could form a pattern that can be applied generally.

The use of the technique itself is also observed. As a team-based analysis approach, the technique is more powerful than a single-user equivalent; creativity is encouraged and alternative views are discussed. However, there is a lot of repetition in the results. This is probably because the same guidewords are applied to each element of the use case, some of which are quite similar.

Most systematic approaches, including this one, are tedious and time consuming, but produce a thorough result. It is preferable to spend time and effort to identify what is significant to the system at an early stage of development.

The technique's results arise from deviating models or descriptions. Therefore, the thoroughness of the analysis depends on the quality of the model (the use case) and its level of abstraction.

5   Conclusion and Future Work

The role of security analysis is becoming increasingly important. Systems are becoming more complex and are operating in environments with higher risks. Consequences of system failure are of high concern. The method presented here provides a rigorous approach to security analysis. It is intended to supplement and integrate with other forms of analysis. Although not all security problems can be identified by consideration of perturbations of core use cases, the method does seem to yield useful information and prompts a systematic analysis.

The simple case study has demonstrated that it is possible and beneficial to adapt HAZOP (widely used in safety) to Use Cases (primarily used for capturing functional requirements) to provide a more systematic approach for security analysis. Future work in this area could include: (1) generation of attack patterns from the analysis results, (2) further application to other descriptive types (e.g. procedures, informal descriptions, protocols described using message sequence charts), (3) generalisation of threat results and (4) implementation of tool support.

References

1. K. Allenby and T.P. Kelly. Deriving safety requirements using scenarios. In *5th IEEE International Symposium on Requirements Engineering (RE'01)*. IEEE Computer Society Press, 2001.
2. E. Amoroso. *Fundamentals of Computer Security Technology*. Prentice-Hall, 1994.
3. B.P. Douglass. *Real-time UML (2nd ed.): Developing efficient objects for embedded systems*. Addison-Wesley Longman Ltd., 2000.
4. I. Jacobson, M. Christerson, P. Jonsson, and G. Overgaard. *Object-Oriented Software Engineering: A Use Case Driven Approach*. Addison-Wesley, 1992.
5. T.P. Kelly. *Arguing Safety - A Systematic Approach to Managing Safety Cases*. PhD thesis, Dept. of Comp. Science, University of York, UK, 1999.
6. D.M. Kienzle and W.A. Wulf. A practical approach to security assessment. In *Proc. of the 1997 New Security Paradigms Workshop, England*, 1997.
7. J. McDermott. Abuse-case-based assurance arguments. In *17th Annual Computer Security Applications Conference.*, 2001.
8. A.P. Moore. The JMCIS information flow improvement (JIFI) assurance strategy. Technical Report 500-190, Center for High Assurance Computer Systems Information Technology Division, Naval Research Lab., Washington, D.C., May 1997.
9. UK Ministry of Defence. Defence Standard 00-58: HAZOP Studies on Systems Containing Programmable Electronics. 1996.
10. F. Redmill, M. Chudleigh, and J. Catmur. *System Safety: HAZOP and Software HAZOP*. John Wiley & Sons, 1999.
11. N.H. Roberts, W.E. Vesely, D.F. Haasl, and F.F. Goldberg. *Fault Tree Handbook*. System and Reliablity Research Office of U.S. Nuclear Regulatory Commission, Washington, DC., 1981.
12. B. Schneier. *Applied Cryptography*. John Wiley & Sons, 1996.
13. B. Schneier. Attack Trees. *Dr. Dobb's Journal*, 1999.
14. G. Sindre and A.L. Opdahl. Eliciting security requirements by misuse cases. In *Proc. of TOOLS Pacific 2000*, pages 120–131, 2000.

15. C. Weissman. Security Penetration Testing Guideline: A Chapter of the Handbook for the Computer Security Certification of Trusted Systems. Technical report, NRL TM-8889/000/01, 1995.
16. R. Winther, O-A. Johnsen, and B.A. Gran. Security assessments for safety critical systems using hazops. In *Proc. of SAFECOMP 2001*, Budapest, Hungary, 2001.

A   Security HAZOP Guidewords for Use Case Model

A.1   Actors Guidewords

Action/Intent

- NO : The action/intent does not take place.
- MORE : More action is achieved. This may be one of the following:
  - Sequential Repeat - the same actions take place repeatedly.
  - Parallel Repeat - the same actions take place concurrently.
  - Extreme intent - some scalar attribute of the action is affected (e.g. extreme parameter values are used in service invocations).
- LESS : Less action is achieved than intended.
- AS WELL AS : Parallel action - as well as the intended or normal action, some unexpected supplementary actions occur or are intended.
- OTHER THAN : The action achieves an incorrect result. Alternatively, the actor may use facilities for purposes other than those intended, i.e. abuse of privilege.

Capability

- NO : Lack of the capability to perform the action.
- MORE : More general capability, allowing more to be achieved than intended.
- LESS : Less general capability, allowing less to be achieved than is required.
- PART OF : The actor has only part of, or is missing a specific part of the capability.
- AS WELL AS : As well as the specific capabilities required, the actor has other specific capabilities.

A.2   Association Guidewords

- NO : Association does not/can not take place.
- MORE : Superfluous - Interface permits greater functionality to a particular actor than is required. Association is not constrained as required. Further divisions are:
  - In-parallel with - More functionality is provided/occurs simultaneously with the permitted ones.
  - In- sequence with - More functionality provided/occurs before or after the permitted ones.
- LESS : Interface permits less functionality to a particular actor than is required. Association is over-constrained.
- AS WELL AS : Associations to a particular use case take place with other actors as well.
- REVERSE : Interaction takes place in the reverse direction.
- OTHER THAN : Wrong association is defined. Swapping roles - swapping of associations between actors or individuals.

A.3   Use Case Elements Guidewords

State (defined in a pre-condition or a post-condition)

- NO : The state or condition does not take place or is not detected.
- AS WELL AS : Additional conditions apply. This may mean that more stringent checks are made, or else a more restrictive state results than is strictly required. Errors of commission might be considered here.
- PART OF : Only a subset of the required conditions apply. This might for example, result from incomplete checks (e.g. access control checks or integrity checks), by incomplete implementation (a program doesn't do all it should), or because the consequences of system behaviour are not fully understood.
- OTHER THAN : An incorrect condition applies. Perhaps the wrong data is used.

Action

- NO : No action takes place.
- MORE : More action is achieved. This may be one of the following:
  - Repeat - the same actions take place repeatedly.
  - Superfluous - the system does additional actions to those intended or required.
- LESS : Less is achieved than intended. For example, an action is incomplete, or an action takes place for a shorter time than required, or an action stopped earlier than expected.
- OTHER THAN : An incorrect action takes place.

Sequence of Actions (scenarios)

- LESS : Less is achieved than intended. For example, *Drop* - miss one or more parts of action. Additionally, a sequence of action takes place for a shorter time than required.
- AS WELL AS : The sequence does the intended actions plus others.
- REVERSE : The sequence of actions take place in reverse order (and other out-of-order concepts).
- EARLY : The action sequence or its components takes place before it is expected (timing).
- LATE : The action sequence or its components takes place after it is expected (timing).
- BEFORE : The action sequence or its components happens before another action that is expected to precede it.
- AFTER : The action sequence or its components happens after another action that is expected to come after it.
- OTHER THAN : An incorrect action sequence takes place.

The Obfuscation Executive*

Kelly Heffner and Christian Collberg

Department of Computer Science
The University of Arizona
{kheffner,collberg}@cs.arizona.edu

Abstract. Code obfuscations are semantics-preserving code transformations used to protect a program from reverse engineering. There is generally no expectation of complete, long-term, protection. Rather, there is a trade-off between the protection afforded by an obfuscation (i.e. the amount of resources an adversary has to expend to overcome the layer of confusion added by the transformation) and the resulting performance overhead.

In this paper we examine the problems that arise when constructing an *Obfuscation Executive*. This is the main loop in charge of a) selecting the part of the application to be obfuscated next, b) choosing the best transformation to apply to this part, c) evaluating how much confusion and overhead has been added to the application, and d) deciding when the obfuscation process should terminate.

1 Introduction

A *code obfuscator* is a tool which—much like a code optimizer—repeatedly applies semantics-preserving code transformations to a program. However, while an optimizer tries to make the program as fast or as small as possible, the obfuscator tries to make it as *incomprehensible* as possible. Obfuscation is typically applied to programs in order to protect them from being reverse engineered or to protect a secret stored in the program from being discovered. In this paper we will describe the design of an *Obfuscation Executive* (OE), implemented within the SANDMARK [3] software protection research tool. The OE is the overall loop that applies obfuscation algorithms to parts of the program to be protected. In many ways the OE functions similar to a compiler's optimization pass: it reads and analyzes an application and repeatedly applies semantics-preserving transformations until some termination condition has been reached. Ideally, the executive should be able to pick an optimal set of transformations and an optimal set of program parts to obfuscate. The only necessary user interaction should be to indicate to the tool what "optimal" means: i.e. how much execution overhead the user can accept, how much obfuscation he wants to add, and which parts of the application are security- or performance-critical. The two major issues with this process is the order in which transformations should be applied (the

---

* This work was supported in part by the National Science Foundation under grant CCR-0073483 and the Air Force Research Lab under contract F33615-02-C-1146.

K. Zhang and Y. Zheng (Eds.): ISC 2004, LNCS 3225, pp. 428–440, 2004.

"phase-ordering-problem") and how to decide that the process should terminate. In the case of a code optimizer the order of transformations is usually fixed. The optimizer typically terminates when there are no more changes to the application or when all transformations have been tried at least once. As we will see from this paper, in the case of the OE neither phase-ordering nor termination is this simple.

For the sake of brevity, we refer to [5] for an introduction to code obfuscation and its uses. Obfuscating transformations are characterized by their *potency* (the amount of confusion they add), their *resilience* (the extent to which they can be undone by a *de-obfuscator*), and their *cost* (the performance penalty they incur on the obfuscated application) [6].

2   The Obfuscation Loop

At the heart of any OE is a loop that chooses a part of the application to obfuscate, chooses an appropriate obfuscating transformation from a pool of candidate algorithms, and then applies the transformation. After the transformation has completed, the loop computes how much the code has changed and decides if the process should continue. Unfortunately, there are a number of complications. First of all, neither the amount of protection we would like to achieve nor the amount of overhead we can accept are uniform over the application. Some subroutines may be performance-critical, others not. Some subroutines may be security-critical, others not. Secondly, given any non-trivial set of obfuscating transformations there will be restrictions on the order in which these should be applied. The reason is that an obfuscating transformation *destroys* structures in the application. This makes the obfuscated application more difficult to analyze, and, as a result, it might not be possible to apply any further transformations. Finally, not all obfuscations can be applied to all application objects. For example, obfuscations which rename classes [9] cannot be applied to classes that will be loaded dynamically by name. Also, if we are using obfuscations to hide a particular structure in the application (such as a watermark or a set of cryptographic keys) we cannot apply transformations that will destroy these structures.

2.1   Transformation Dependencies

SANDMARK's OE understands six types of dependencies between obfuscations and tools such as software watermarkers that use them. These are pre/post-suggestions, pre/post-requirements, and pre/post-prohibitions:

Pre-/postrequirement: Assume a software watermarking algorithm (such as CT [4]) that embeds the watermark in a data structure in the application. To simplify implementation and debugging the watermarker creates a class `Watermark` that contains the code for building the mark: ⌜ `class Watermark { Watermark left, right; void createGraph() { ... } }` ⌝ A call to the method `createGraph()` is embedded into the application. Obviously, this is not stealthy. Therefore the watermarking algorithm requires that an inlining transformation and a name obfuscating transformation be run after the watermarking algorithm. This is a *postrequirement* dependency.

Pre-/postprohibition: Assume an obfuscating transformation `MergeArrays` that performs alias analysis to detect the location of two arrays to merge. This algorithm should not be run after any algorithm that makes alias analysis difficult. Collberg [6] presents such algorithms. This type of dependency is called a *preprohibition*.

Pre-/postsuggestion: Suggestions are similar to requirements in the resulting language of transformations that they allow. However, while breaking a requirement will put the program in a corrupt state or make a software watermark obvious, a suggestion is just a hint to the OE by the obfuscation author that certain transformations work well together.

In our current SANDMARK implementation each obfuscation and watermarking algorithm specifies the effects that it may have on the code. It also specifies *properties* of other algorithms that are postrequired, presuggested, etc. For example, a method splitting transformation `MethodSplit` might list `OBFUSCATE_METHOD_NAMES` as a postsuggestion, indicating to the OE that some algorithm (any one will do) that has this property should be run after `MethodSplit`. In general, to fulfill a requisite dependency **one** algorithm with the specified property must be run; to fulfill a suggestion dependency any **one** algorithm with the specified property could be run; and to fulfill a prohibition dependency **no** algorithm with a specified property should be allowed to run.

Simple obfuscators do not need to specify many dependency relationships with other obfuscators. However, when using obfuscation with software watermarking, dependencies are necessary to make sure that the obfuscations successfully camouflage the watermark without destroying the structures that it is embedded in. From a software design standpoint, the dependency framework also allows for more complex obfuscators to be created modularly and without concern for the transformations performed around it.

3   Modeling Dependencies

Our goal is to construct an OE algorithm to honor transformation dependencies and to find the "optimal" set of transformations to apply to the "optimal" set of application objects. In fact, we are interested in constructing *families* of such algorithms, to be targeted at the many and varied applications of obfuscation discussed in [5]. The most important result in this paper is the design of a model which encodes transformation dependencies, obfuscation potency and performance overhead, as well as the desired level of obfuscation and overhead of each application object. The model is based on weighted finite state automata and can be used as the basis for many on-line and off-line algorithms. Let us first consider an example with three transformations A, B, and C. A postprohibits a property that C has, A postrequires a property that only B has, and B prerequires a property that only C has:The order in which these transformations

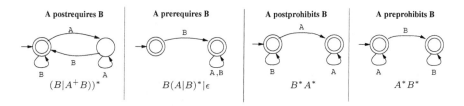

Fig. 1. An FSA for each dependency type.

can be run is CAB, $CBAB$, $CBBAB$, or, more generally, any sequence that matches the regular expression $\epsilon|C(C|B)^*(A^+B)^*$.

This observation leads us to a model where the dependencies between transformations are represented by a finite state automaton (FSA). The language accepted by this machine contains all the possible sequences of transformations that can be executed. Given this model, the design of a new OE reduces to the problem of constructing an algorithm that chooses a finite subset of the (typically) infinite set of strings generated by the FSA. The heuristics of such algorithms will make use of FSA *edge weights* representing the "goodness" of traversing each edge.

We will next describe how the FSA is built, then how edge weights are computed, and, finally, in Section 4 describe an on-line OE algorithm that makes use of the FSA model.

3.1   Building the FSA

Each type of dependency has an equivalent regular language. It suffices to consider prohibition and requirement dependencies since suggested dependencies can be modeled by modifying the FSA edge weights. This will be shown in Section 3.2.

Figure 1 shows the four FSAs that correspond to each dependency type. The figures show transitions only for the two transformations involved in the dependency; for any transformation that is not in the dependency, the transition is just a self-loop.

To build the regular language for the entire set of obfuscating transformations we take the intersection of the languages from each dependency and Σ^*. The resulting language is the set of all possible sequences in which the transformations could be applied. To model the fact that dependencies apply to properties of transformations, rather than transformations themselves, we simply replace a single transformation in Figure 1 with all of the transformations that have a particular property.

Consider the running example in Figure 2 which describes five obfuscating transformations A, B, C, D, and E with three properties p_1, p_2, and p_3. Figure 3(a) shows the models for the four dependencies in the example. Taking the intersection of the languages represented by these FSAs we get the FSA

```
class c1 {
  m1(){...}
  m2(){...}
}
class c2 {
  m(){...}
}
```

Transfor-mation	Obfuscation Level	Potency	Overhead	Prop-erties	Required Pre	Required Post	Prohibited Pre	Prohibited Post
A	Method	1.0	0.9	p_1	p_2			
B	Method	0.5	0.3	p_2, p_3		p_1		
C	Class	0.1	0.4	p_1, p_3				
D	Class	0.2	0.2	p_2			p_3	
E	App.	0.01	0.1	p_3				p_1

Fig. 2. A running example. A and B are method level obfuscators, C and D are class level obfuscators, and E applies to an entire application.

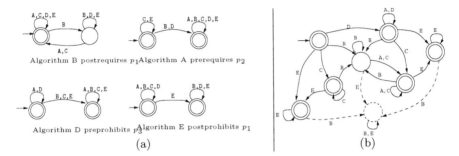

Algorithm B postrequires p_1 Algorithm A prerequires p_2

Algorithm D preprohibits p_3 Algorithm E postprohibits p_1

(a)   (b)

Fig. 3. The transformation properties from the running example in Figure 2 produces the four FSAs in (a). Taking the intersection of the generated languages produces the FSA in (b). Note that no paths exist to an accepting state from some states (dashed in (b)) so those nodes would be removed.

in Figure 3(b), which models every possible candidate sequence allowed by the dependencies.

To make full use of the finite state machine model, we must integrate the idea that transformations are run on application objects, not always the entire application. By running a transformation on one application object, possibly fulfilling prerequirements and prohibiting other transformations, the result affects only a subset of objects. In order to keep track of these object-level changes, the target of the transformation must be included with each transformation in the sequence. Thus, each symbol in our alphabet for the sequence becomes an ordered pair (*transformation, target*).

We should also note that modifications to single application objects do not just affect that object. Obfuscating a method may affect not only the class that the method is in, but the entire application. For simplicity we will assume that when a transformation is run on an object x, the effect is spread to all objects that contain x, and all objects that x contains. We will call this the *range* of an object. This is a conservative approximation on the real spread. A less coarse approximation would be advantageous but more difficult to compute.

During FSA construction the states represent sets of application objects. We will refer to the set of objects for a given state q as $s(q)$. We will refer to the set of objects that is in the range of an application object x as $r(x)$.

First we will construct the FSA for a prerequirement dependency, where a transformation T prerequires a property p. We define an FSA $(Q, \Sigma, \delta, q_0, F)$ with the following properties: Q, the set of states, is composed of the power set of the set of all application objects that are a target of T; Σ is the set of ordered pairs (T, x) where T is a transformation and x is a target application object for that transformation; The transition function δ is given in Figure 5; q_0 is the state such that $s(q_0) = \emptyset$; $F = Q$ is the set of accepting states. Figure 6 shows the partial FSA for the preprohibition of property p_3 before transformation D.

Next, we construct the FSA for a postrequirement dependency, where transformation T postrequires property p. The FSA is identical to the previous one, except for the transition function in Figure 5 and that $F = \{q_0\}$. The transition functions for FSAs for preprohibition and postprohibition dependencies are similar and shown in Figure 5.

3.2   Building the Probabilistic FSA

The FSA generates a language of strings of (*obfuscation, target*) tuples. These strings represent a series of obfuscations to run on the application. Obviously, some strings are more desirable than others in that they result in more highly obfuscated programs with lower performance penalty. To capture this, we create a probabilistic FSA by giving each edge an *edge weight*. In an edge $a \xrightarrow{(T,x),w} b$, w represents the "goodness" of applying transformation T to application object x when the OE is in state a. In Section 4 we will show how this model allows for a very simple, yet effective, on-line OE algorithm.

The tuple

$$\langle Potency(T), Degradation(T), ObfLevel(x), PerfImport(x) \rangle$$

forms the FSA edge weight $weight(T, x)$, where each element is a real number in the range $[0, 1]$. $Potency(T)$ measures the obfuscation potency of T. It is computed by running each obfuscation on a set of benchmarks and computing the change in software complexity. See Section 3.3. $Degradation(T)$ measures the performance degradation of T. This is computed by running each obfuscation on a set of benchmarks and computing the change in execution time. See Section 3.3. $ObfLevel(x)$ is the desired obfuscation level of application object x, as assigned by the user. $PerfImport(x)$ is the importance of performance of application object x, a combination of user assignment and profiling data. Our model does not specify how a particular OE will make use of the weight tuple. In our current implementation the tuple is mapped down to a single real number which represents the overall goodness of choosing a particular edge. This is explained in Section 3.3. We will next show how to estimate $Potency(T)$ and $Degradation(T)$.

3.3   Computing Edge Weights

Each obfuscating transformation T is assigned a real number (in the range $[0, 1]$) $Potency(T)$ that represents the relative potency of the transformation in comparison with the rest of the transformations known to the obfuscator. $Potency(T)$

$$\text{(a) } \Delta(P, M, T) = \frac{\sum_{m \in M} |m(P) - m(T(P))|}{|M|} \quad \text{(b) } Potency(T) = \frac{\Delta(M,T) - \Delta_{\min}(M)}{\Delta_{\max}(M) - \Delta_{\min}(M)}$$

$$\text{(c) } \Gamma(P, T) = \frac{\max(\text{time}(T(P)) - \text{time}(P), 0)}{\text{time}(P)} \quad \text{(d) } Degradation(T) = \frac{\Gamma(T) - \Gamma_{\min}}{\Gamma_{\max} - \Gamma_{\min}}$$

$$\text{(e) } Fold(w) = Potency(T) \cdot ObfLevel(x) \cdot (1 - PerfImport(x)) \cdot (1 - Degradation(T))$$

Fig. 4. Formulas for computing edge weights.

is determined by calculating a set of software engineering metrics, M, on sample programs before and after obfuscation and taking the average of the change in those metrics (see Section 4.1 for discussion on what metrics were used).

The change in a set of metrics M for a program P on a transformation T is given by Figure 4(a) where $m(P)$ is a software metric calculated on P and $T(P)$ is P obfuscated by transformation T. We get $\Delta(M, T)$ by averaging $\Delta(P, M, T)$ over all benchmark programs.

To compute the obfuscation potency for a transformation T we normalize using the highest and lowest changes in the metrics ($\Delta_{\max}(M)$ and $\Delta_{\min}(M)$) over all of the obfuscations, yielding the formula in Figure 4(b). Since we considered obfuscation as simply a change in metrics, rather than raising or lowering the metrics, we chose to calculate $\Delta(P, M, T)$ as given by Figure 4(a). Another method of selecting metrics, such that more obfuscation mapped to higher metric values would eliminate the absolute value bars from the calculation.

Each obfuscating transformation T is assigned a real number $Degradation(T)$ (in the range $[0, 1]$) that represents T's expected performance hit. $Degradation(T)$ is calculated by running every transformation T on a set of "priming" applications. These could either be a set of benchmarks such as the SpecJVM, or the application to be obfuscated itself. $\Gamma(P, T)$ is the raw performance degradation of T on program P, shown in Figure 4(c). We get $\Gamma(T)$ by averaging over all benchmark programs. To compute $Degradation(T)$ we normalize using the highest and lowest performance hits ($\Gamma_{\max}$ and $\Gamma_{\min}$), yielding the formula in Figure 4(d).

Most simple OE algorithms will want to fold the weight tuple $w = weight(x, T)$ into a single real number $Fold(w)$ to represent the goodness of choosing a particular edge. See Figure 4(e). The probability of taking an edge $a \xrightarrow{(T,x), Fold(w)} b$ is thus proportional to how potent the transformation T is and how important it is to obfuscate application object x. It is *inversely* proportional to how performance critical x is and how much T is expected decrease its performance.

4   Algorithms

Once the probabilistic FSA has been constructed, the model is used to find an effective, yet not optimal, obfuscation sequence. Our broad definition for an optimal obfuscation sequence is a sequence such that the application has maximal obfuscation, has minimal performance degradation, and is a minimal

	requirement	prohibition
pre	q', if $q \neq q'$, t has the property p, and $s(q) + r(x) = s(q')$, or q, if $t = T$ and $x \in s(q)$, or q, if t has property p and $r(x) \subseteq s(q)$, or q, if $t \neq T$ and t does not have property p	q' if t has the property p, and $s(q) + r(x) = s(q')$, or q if $t = T$ and $x \notin s(q)$, or q if t has property p and $r(x) \subseteq s(q)$, or q if $t \neq T$ and t does not have property p
post	q' if $t = T$ and $s(q) + r(x) = s(q')$, or q' if t has the property p, and $s(q) - r(x) = s(q')$, or q if $t = T$ and $r(x) \subseteq s(q)$, or q if t has property p and $r(x) \cap s(q) = \emptyset$, or q if $t \neq T$ and t does not have property p	q' if $t = T$ and $s(q) + r(x) = s(q')$ q if $t = T$ and T does not have property p and $x \in s(q)$, or q if t has property p and $r(x) \cap s(q) = \emptyset$, or q if $t \neq T$ and t does not have property p

Fig. 5. Transition functions $\delta(q, \ (t, x))$.

sequence. Here, we describe a simple on-line algorithm to determine a sequence. Given the probabilistic FSA and the *Fold* formula from Section 3.3, the on-line algorithm computes the obfuscation sequence and performs the associated obfuscating transformations.

The algorithm performs a random walk of the nodes of the FSA, starting in the start node. Each iteration selects an outgoing edge e from the current node S, performs the corresponding obfuscating transformation, and updates the edge weights to reflect the changing obfuscation level. The probability of a particular outgoing edge being chosen is proportional to its weight. As the desired obfuscation level of each application object approaches zero, the weights of the edges that represent obfuscating that application object also approach zero. Edges with a zero weight are removed from the FSA. The loop terminates when there are no available edges out of the current, accepting, state.

This algorithm is a random walk of the FSA, using the edge weights to guide traversal. While this algorithm will not yield an optimal obfuscation sequence, it will produce a sequence that obfuscates heavily with acceptable performance degradation. Furthermore, since this algorithm produces a very random obfuscation sequence, attacks against the obfuscated code are difficult. Given a list of the obfuscations available to the loop, the attacker still does not know the subsets of obfuscation that the application objects have been obfuscated with, nor the order in which the obfuscations have been applied. We can use this loop to obfuscate a fingerprinted application each time it is sold. Each copy will become entirely different, allowing us to protect against collusive attacks.

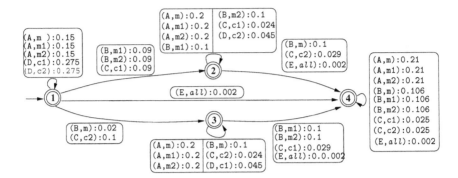

Fig. 6. The FSA that models the preprohibition of property p_3 before transformation D. Each edge is labeled with a set of tuples $(T, x) : w$ where T is the obfuscation transformation to run on application object x and w is the weight of tuple (see Section 3.2). For each node the weights of the outgoing edges sum to 1, which allows the FSA model to be used as a probabilistic FSA.

Consider again the running example from Figure 2 and the FSA model shown in Figure 6. The weights are shown as they would be computed before the first iteration of the loop. We assume that the obfuscation level of all objects is 1 and that performance importance is 0. On the first iteration we randomly choose to move from state 1 (the start state) to state 3 by running algorithm C on class c2. This will cause c2 to be obfuscated, lowering its remaining $ObfLevel(c2)$. During the next iteration any edge with c2 as its target will have a lower weight, lowering its probability to be obfuscated again. Note that moving to state 3 eliminates the possibility of ever running D on c2. This is because algorithm D preprohibits any algorithm with property p_3, such as C.

4.1   Implementation

The probabilistic FSA constructed in Section 3 provides a clean model for the dependencies between transformations. It has also allowed us to construct the simple random walk OE algorithm above. However, a straight-forward implementation of these ideas turns out to be impractical. The reason is that for sets of transformations with very few dependencies the size of the FSA grows exponentially. The solution to this problem is to lazily build and walk the FSA concurrently.

In our implementation, the metric set M used for $Potency(T)$ is computed based on a suite of standard software complexity metrics [8], including the standard ones proposed by McCabe, Halstead, Chidamber, Harrison, Munson, and Henry.

To compute $Degradation(T)$ we use a large suite of standard Java benchmarks including SPEC JVM98 (`www.specbench.org/osg/jvm98`) and the Ashes test suite (`www.sable.mcgill.ca/ashes`).

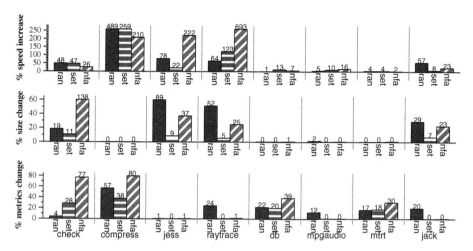

Fig. 7. Results from implemented obfuscation loops on SpecJVM.

Our current implementation supports three OEs: a simplistic set-based model (described in Section 4.2 below), the complete FSA-based model, and the lazy FSA model. All are on-line algorithms. We are currently exploring an off-line OE which uses the probabilistic FSA to compute an "optimal" obfuscation sequence ahead of time.

4.2 Evaluation

To evaluate the FSA-based OE algorithm we compare it to two simpler OE algorithms. Each algorithm was run on SpecJVM benchmarks with the desired obfuscation level for each object maximized and no user input about application hotspots. Figure 7 shows the result of running the three OEs. For each benchmark we show the change in code size, execution time, and software complexity metrics.

Random Select OE. The first OE algorithm, Random, does not split the program into obfuscation objects but instead applies obfuscating transformations to the entire program with each pass. Random applies a few heuristics to manage transformation dependencies, specifically enforcing the prerequisite, preprohibition, and postprohibition rules, but makes no effort to ensure postrequisites can be fulfilled. After determining which transformations cannot be applied to the program, a transformation is chosen at random from the remaining candidates. If the executive detects that the program has been transformed into a corrupt state, it simply halts. After each obfuscation, it computes the change in complexity metrics and halts when the desired amount of obfuscation has been applied.

The Random implementation fails to find an appropriate cost-benefit trade-off for obfuscation, notably in check, compress, and jess where the change in metrics is low in comparison to the FSA for a large trade-off in size and speed. It is important to note that the random implementation applies each obfuscation to the entire program. The results of the Random OE shows that simply running all of the obfuscations on the program randomly does not produce an acceptable amount of obfuscation; there is a need for an intelligent OE.

Set-Based OE. The second OE algorithm implements a set-based model. In this algorithm, each application object is associated with a set of obfuscation candidates, transformations that are allowed to be run on that object. In each iteration the loop uses a set of heuristics to trim the candidate set to remove algorithms that have been disqualified by running the previous obfuscation. The target application object is chosen based on the desired obfuscation level for each object and the amount of obfuscation already applied to the object. Another set of heuristics is used to extract a subset of obfuscations that can be run and in most cases will not lead to a corrupted state where required dependencies cannot be fulfilled. A candidate is then chosen at random from this subset. The set heuristics fail to detect cases such as two obfuscating transformations conflicting with each other, yielding only the empty-string as a valid obfuscation sequence. The set-based model halts when each application object reaches the desired obfuscation level.

The set-based model fails to impact the complexity metrics over the entire program, while still incurring the cost of speed and size for the attempted obfuscations. Presumably, this is due to the fact that the set-based implementation chooses the next obfuscation target in isolation to the entire application, without considering which (*transformation*, *object*) pair will yield the most obfuscation overall.

FSA-Based OE. As expected, the FSA produces a large increase in software complexity, at the cost of program size and performance. The lack of user input about hotspots is most evident in the cases of extreme performance hit, like `raytrace`. It would also be useful to re-calculate profiling data between each iteration of the obfuscation loop, with the obvious performance implications.

Overall, the numbers show that there is much to be gained over random OEs. We see that the FSA-based model had the largest average change to engineering metrics at 28.5% (compared to 19.6% and 13% for random and set) however at the cost of a larger speed penalty (50% speed increase compared to an increase for random and set of 93% and 60%). The important thing to note is that the other two models show a large downgrade to the software (random has an average size increase of 24%, very close to the FSA-based change of 27%) without affecting the metrics by the same degree as the FSA-based OE (the set based model had an average speed increase of 60% with only an average change in metrics of 13%). More analysis of individual obfuscations and their effect on speed, size, and complexity, using complexity measures to drive the direction of obfuscation, and integrating knowledge of the program designer will lead to a more intelligent OE.

The FSA-based model is superior to the other approaches. It elegantly handles the obfuscation dependencies, without the use of conservative restrictions to guarantee that the loop will not go into a corrupted state. The FSA-based model can yield several algorithms using different analyses, whereas the set-based approach is tied to the trimming algorithm and can only be adjusted in the way that the obfuscation target and candidate are chosen. In addition, modeling obfuscation sequences as weighted members of a regular language provides a straightforward solution for deriving a *family* of effective transformation sequences for use in artificial diversity.

5   Discussion and Summary

To the best of our knowledge, Collberg et al. [5] is the first description of an OE. This algorithm does not take into account restrictions on transformation ordering. Wroblewski [12] describes an OE for x86 machine code. This OE applies obfuscations in a single pass over the program using a hardcoded sequence of transformations. Lacey et al. [7] presents an algorithm which decides whether applying one optimizing transformation to a piece of code will prevent another one from being applied.

There are few theoretical results related to obfuscation. Barak et al. [2] shows that there exist programs that cannot be obfuscated. Appel [1] shows deobfuscation to be NP-easy. The proof idea is based on a simple algorithm which nondeterministically guesses the original program S and obfuscation key K. The obfuscating transformation is then run over S and K, verifying that the result is the obfuscated program. To use this algorithm to defeat our random walk obfuscation loop, K must include the seed to our random number generator. However, Appel's algorithm is only valid for obfuscating transformations that are injective; transformations such as name obfuscation or instruction reordering cannot be reversed using Appel's method.

Determining the order in which to run obfuscation and watermarking algorithms is similar to the phase ordering problem for optimizations in compilers. In the case of optimizers, the phases consist of code analyses and optimizing transformations. While most compilers hardwire the order of the optimizations, some work [11,10] has been done on automated phase selection and ordering.

The widely differing uses of software obfuscation have led us to the very general probabilistic FSA model of Section 3. The model encodes all valid obfuscation sequences as well as the goodness of any particular sequence. Two on-line OE algorithms have been implemented that makes use of this model. These algorithms compare favorably to an algorithm based on a simplistic set-based OE model. The SANDMARK framework can be downloaded from http://sandmark.cs.arizona.edu. SANDMARK consists of 130,000 lines of Java, and includes 39 obfuscation, 17 watermarking, 3 OE algorithms, and several tools for automatically and manually analyzing and attacking software protection algorithms.

References

1. A. Appel. Deobfuscation is in np.
   `www.cs.princeton.edu/~appel/papers/deobfus.pdf`.
2. B. Barak, O. Goldreich, R. Impagliazzo, S. Rudich, A. Sahai, S. Vadhan, and K. Yang. On the (im)possibility of software obfuscation. In *Crypto01*, pages 1–18, 2001. LNCS 2139.
3. C. Collberg, G. Myles, and A. Huntwork. Sandmark - a tool for software protection research. *IEEE Security and Privacy*, 1(4):40–49, 2003.
4. C. Collberg and C. Thomborson. Software watermarking: Models and dynamic embeddings. In *POPL'99*, San Antonio, TX, Jan. 1999.
5. C. Collberg, C. Thomborson, and D. Low. A taxonomy of obfuscating transformations. Technical Report 148, Department of Computer Science, University of Auckland, July 1997.
6. C. Collberg, C. Thomborson, and D. Low. Manufacturing cheap, resilient, and stealthy opaque constructs. In *POPL'98*, San Diego, CA, Jan. 1998.
7. D. Lacey and O. de Moor. Detecting disabling interference between program transformations. `citeseer.nj.nec.com/464977.html`.
8. S. Purao and V. Vaishnavi. Product metrics for object-oriented systems. *ACM Comput. Surv.*, 35(2):191–221, 2003.
9. H. P. V. Vliet. Crema — The Java obfuscator.
   `web.inter.nl.net/users/H.P.van.Vliet/crema.html`, Jan. 1996.
10. D. Whitfield and M. L. Soffa. An approach to ordering optimizing transformations. In *PPOPP'90*, pages 137–146, 1990.
11. D. Whitfield and M. L. Soffa. Automatic generation of global optimizers. In *PLDI'91*, pages 120–129, 1991.
12. G. Wroblewski. *A General Method of Program Code Obfuscation*. PhD thesis, Wroclaw University, 2002.

Author Index